THE
YOUNG
COLONIALS

THE
YOUNG
COLONIALS

A Social History
of Education in
Trinidad and Tobago
1834-1939

Carl C. Campbell

The Press University of the West Indies
Barbados • Jamaica • Trinidad and Tobago

The Press University of the West Indies
1a Aqueduct Flats Mona
Kingston 7 Jamaica W I

ISBN 976-640-011-3

00 99 98 97 96   5 4 3 2 1

CATALOGUING IN PUBLICATION DATA

Campbell, Carl C.
    The young colonials : a social history
    of education in Trinidad and Tobago,
    1834-1939 / Carl Campbell.

    p. cm.
    Includes bibliographical references and index.
    ISBN 976-640-011-3
    1. Education–Trinidad and Tobago–History.
    2. Education–Social aspects–Trinidad
    and Tobago. I. Title. II. Title:
    A social history of education in Trinidad
    and Tobago, 1834-1939.
    LC2353.T7C35 1996   370' 19 dc–20

Set in 10.5 Grand-Old-Style x27
Cover and book design by Robert Harris
This book has been printed on acid-free paper

Front cover photo inset:
    Naparima College–Flag raising ceremony at Jubilee celebration

To Dr C. V. Gocking
Trinidadian educator, historian and public servant

Contents

Acknowledgements / ix
List of Abbreviations / x

[1]   Foundations of Education in the Nineteenth Century

The first primary schools 1834-1869 / 1
The ward schools of Lord Harris 1849-1869 / 6
St Joseph's Convent, Queen's Royal College and the
  College of the Immaculate Conception 1836-1869 / 14
The evolution of the dual system 1870-1902 / 29
The financing of the dual system 1870-1902 / 41
The education of the Indians 1868-1902 / 47
The training of teachers 1836-1902 / 56
Education and social mobility 1834-1902 / 65

[2]   The Age of Marriott and Cutteridge

The imposition of agricultural education 1897-1922 / 78
The schools on the eve of reform 1902-1917 / 87
The introduction of science and progressive ideas 1916-1932 / 95
The control of the dual system 1921-1931 / 104
The integration of the Tobago schools 1889-1931 / 111
The transformation of the Government Training College 1921-1939 / 121
New perspectives on secondary education 1926-1935 / 135
The emergence of a government programme of expansion 1932-1939 / 146
The beginning of technical/vocational education 1906-1939 / 156
The growth of the educated middle class 1902-1939 / 166

[3]   The Challenge of the Teachers

The revolt of the Indians 1928-1939 / 179
The labour protest of the black teachers 1930-1939 / 191
Education and nationalist strivings in the 1930s / 202
The survival of the dual system 1930-1939 / 211
The absence of a university 1922-1939 / 215

[4]   Perspectives on Special Topics

Religious instruction and education 1834-1939 / 222
The English language and education 1834-1939 / 229
Women and education 1834-1939 / 234
Private schools and education 1834-1939 / 245
Education, the creative arts and libraries 1834-1939 / 254
The management of education 1834-1939 / 260
Society, education and educational expansion 1834-1939—
   a Summary / 266
Comparative perspectives / 283

Epilogue

The next 42 years 1939-1981 / 287

Appendixes

I   List of Island Scholars 1863-1903 / 293
II   Growth of the College Exhibitions 1872-1937 / 296
III   Winners of the Silver Medal of the Agricultural Society
         for agriculture in primary schools 1920-1937 / 298
IV   Junior Cambridge Examination results 1930-1936 / 299
V   Cambridge School Certificate Examination results
         1930-1937 / 301
VI   The Higher Class at Tranquillity 1911-1920 / 303
VII   Number of elementary schools 1834-1937 / 304
VIII   Number of public secondary schools 1836-1939 / 305
IX   Tables* / 307

Notes / 339
Select Bibliography / 366
Index / 375

---

*See Appendix IX (pp. 306-338) for Tables cited in the text. These Tables are listed on p. 306

Acknowledgements

I am naturally indebted to several persons all of whom cannot be conveniently mentioned here. As long ago as 1968 one of my students, a cerain Mr Marcelle, loaned me some rare copies of the *Teachers Herald* and the *Teachers Journal*. These are stimulating publications, further volumes of which I never encountered until 1985. The full recovery and preservation of these books in a secure repository such as the University of the West Indies Library at St Augustine would be a valuable service. Another student at St Augustine, an ex-headteacher, made a gift of a pile of dusty Annual Reports of the Director of Education which came into his possession during a long career in the classroom. At that time these publications were not as readily available as at present.

Although I did not have to rely on Dr C. V. Gocking's praiseworthy collection and republication of education documents, including the Annual Reports of the Director of Education, I wish to hail this achievement as a public service of the first order to the cultural heritage of Trinidad and Tobago. Some of these documents were in danger of permanent disappearance from the nation.

I have also benefited from interviews with a few retired teachers, of whom I may mention Mr Thornhill, Mr Hamilton Maurice and Dr C. V. Gocking. The errors are my responsibility.

I wish to acknowledge that some materials in this book have already appeared in altered form in my book *Colony and Nation: A Short History of Education in Trinidad and Tobago* (1992).

Carl Campbell
September 1995

Abbreviations

ACH	Association of Caribbean Historians
ACP	Associate of the College of Preceptors
AME	American Methodist Episcopalian
BIT	Board of Industrial Training
BOE	Board of Education
CE	Church of England
CIC	College of the Immaculate Conception
CO	Colonial Office
CM	Canadian Mission
CN	*Catholic News*
CP	Council Papers
EAP	*East Indian Patriot*
EIW	*East Indian Weekly*
ICTA	Imperial College of Tropical Agriculture
ISER	Institute of Social and Economic Research
JCH	*Journal of Caribbean History*
LCP	Licentiate of the College of Preceptors
LL	*Labour Leader*
NE	*New Era*
PAS	Proceedings of the Agricultural Society
POSG	*Port of Spain Gazette*
PNM	People's National Movement
QCS	Queen's Collegiate School
QRC	Queen's Royal College
RC	Roman Catholic
RVI	Royal Victoria Institute
SFG	*San Fernando Gazette*
SW	*Star of the West*
TG	*Trinidad Guardian*
TP	Trinidad Presbyterian
TTTU	Trinidad and Tobago Teachers' Union
TRG	*Trinidad Royal Gazette*
UWI	University of the West Indies
WIB	*West Indian Bulletin*
WG	*Weekly Guardian*

Note on currency

In the nineteenth and twentieth centuries many sums were stated in British pounds. To facilitate understanding by young readers today all such sums have been converted to Trinidad and Tobago dollars at the then prevailing rate of $1 = four shillings and two pence or conversely £1 = TT$4.80

[1]

Foundations of Education in the Nineteenth Century

The First Primary Schools 1834-1869

Slavery and the formal education of slaves were considered incompatible by the slave owners of Trinidad. As in all the British West Indian islands, the abolition of slavery in 1834, though not complete, afforded the first opportunity for a mass provision of day schools for black and coloured children. The main impulse to develop such a programme came from England, from the swell of British philanthropy, Protestant missionary zeal, and from a conscience-aroused British government. Between 1835 and 1845 an annual subsidy of £30,000, reduced gradually after 1841, was made available to build schoolhouses and to pay teachers' salaries in the British Caribbean.[1] It is not possible to calculate how much of this British subsidy reached Trinidad; the island was not in a good position to benefit maximally from the subsidy because only a handful of Protestant missionaries were at work there.

The Church of England also was badly understaffed; the vast majority of the population belonged to the Roman Catholic Church which had only a few priests. The British government was prejudiced against the Roman Catholic Church, and did not wish to give it funds to build and operate denominational schools. The two initial problems in Trinidad, therefore, were that there were too few Protestant missionaries and clergymen to cooperate with the British government and that Roman Catholic priests were not regarded as suitable recipients of the subsidy.[2] Neither of these problems existed in Jamaica or Barbados; they were limited to the Roman Catholic dominated islands of the eastern Caribbean.

From the time of emancipation, the development of education in Trinidad was bedevilled by an issue which did not arise in Barbados or Jamaica in the same form; this issue was whether public schools, primary or secondary, should be denominational and church controlled, or nondenominational (or even secular) and government controlled. This was still an issue in 1985. If the Roman Catholic Church had not existed in Trinidad, or if it had been the church of only a minority, this issue would not have arisen in so sharp a form, or it might not have arisen at all. Religious rivalries between the Roman Catholic Church and the Protestant churches, particularly the Church of England, were extremely fierce in nineteenth century Trinidad.[3] Down to the 1860s the colonial government of Trinidad, supported by the British government, displayed a consistent policy of discrimination against the Roman Catholic Church in matters of education, to the benefit of the Church of England. This was possible because under the existing Crown Colony government the Legislative Council was nominated, not elected and, therefore, not responsive to majority opinions.

The traditional doctrinal objections of the Church of England and Protestant Englishmen to Roman Catholicism from the time of the English Reformation were basic to the British and Trinidad governments' distrust of the Roman Catholic Church. But in Trinidad there was an additional difficulty of the gravest dimension: because the island had once been a Spanish possession, reinforced and energized by French immigrants from the 1770s, the great majority of its upper and middle classes were not only Roman Catholic, but also Spanish or French, especially French.[4] The labouring class, the ex-slaves, was also to a large extent culturally oriented to French or Spanish lifestyles. At emancipation, Trinidad was still a patently un-English colony after thirty-eight years as a British possession. The Roman Catholic Church was the church of the non-English people; most of its priests were French or Spanish-speaking; it was the spiritual bulwark of the non-English people; the so-called foreigners. The culture and language which predominated among the non-English people was French and the French creoles were the core of the local aristocracy. Since the capture of the island by the English in 1797 there were always Englishmen, sometimes called the 'English Party', who felt that steps should be taken to transform Trinidad into an 'English' colony like Antigua or Barbados.[5] Although some measures towards this end were taken by Governor Woodford (1813-1828), it was only after emancipation that the opportunity arose to use education as an instrument in the process of anglicizing the island.

Whereas in Jamaica or Barbados the great problem in education after emancipation was to find money to open as many schools as soon as possible, in Trinidad the difficulty was not only financial, but political and social. The British government and moreso the Trinidad government, were forced quite early to start thinking out an education policy, a framework within which schools were to be allowed to develop. The unhurried preoccupation with the need for an overall policy delayed the opening of new schools; it also delayed government support for existing schools; it was not until the late 1840s that a policy was at last decided and acted upon; this policy, which never enjoyed widespread or enthusiastic support, finally broke down within twenty years.

The social structure of Trinidad in the years immediately after emancipation was, in some ways, like other British Caribbean islands. The society was shaped like a three-tier colour and class pyramid, with the black masses at the bottom, the coloureds (people of mixed racial ancestry, mostly African and European) largely as the middle class, and the whites at the apex; but this is an oversimplification because a tiny sprinkling of blacks were in the middle class; a handful of propertied coloureds, especially those of French extraction whose families had been long freed from slavery, ranked with the white upper class;[6] some whites were in the middle class, and a considerable number of coloureds were associated with the blacks at the bottom. Lloyd Braithwaite in his insightful analysis some thirty years ago depicted a similar but somewhat more severe colour/class pyramid in the nineteenth century, in the sense that he assigned all the whites, irrespective of class, to an impenetrable caste at the top of the society.[7] The Amerindian survivors and the hundreds of migratory peons shared the bottom of the society with the black masses.[8]

All this was not too unfamiliar a social formation in the British Caribbean. What was less familiar was the extent to which differences of nationality, culture and language cut across each of the traditional colour strata in the island. The whites were Spanish, French or English, but mostly French; the coloureds were mixtures of any one of these European nationalities with blacks or other coloureds. The blacks, as slaves of European or coloured masters, had internalized a great deal of the cultural habits of their masters and hence were partly oriented to Spanish, French or English culture. Of course there were groups of blacks who, either from their recent arrival from Africa or from their greater cultural resistance (Mandingos, for example), were distinctly more African than the majority of creole blacks. The point is that conflicts arising from differences of nationality, religion and language were heaped upon class and colour divisions. Trinidad was a cosmopolitan and heterogeneous society of immigrants, few of whom or their families could claim more than thirty or fifty years' connection with the island. The complexity of the society predated the arrival of the Indians in the mid 1840s.

Left without government dictation, such a divided society would have produced Roman Catholic and Protestant denominational schools in which pupils would have been taught in French, English and, less frequently, Spanish; and the cultural values of the particular school operators would have been transmitted to their pupils without hindrance. In fact, something like this did happen, because until the late 1840s, government interference in education, was too intermittent and feeble to make a decisive impact. Between 1834 and 1838, the Roman Catholics and the Anglicans (Church of England denominationalists) went ahead and opened denominational primary schools; the Roman Catholic Church had about ten primary schools; the Church Missionary Society, a branch of the Church of England, established four schools; the Methodists had one. The Cabildo or municipal government of Port of Spain had two schools since the 1820s which were not tied to any church. The Mico Charity, a nondenominational educational organization, had five schools which were Protestant in tone. Thus, about thirty-two primary schools – leaving aside an indeterminate number of private schools run by individuals – existed during Apprenticeship (1834-1838), and about twenty-five (or 78.1 percent) were denominational.

The British government made money from the Negro Education Grant available for the building of schools and the payment of teachers in Trinidad; and the colonial government of Trinidad offered much smaller amounts between 1834 and 1846. Most of this money from both sources went to the Mico Charity which was the chosen instrument of the British government's policy of nondenominational education.[9] The Mico Charity was not a church, but a charitable body, reorganized in England specifically to assist the education of the masses in the West Indies. It decided that all its schools would be nondenominational in the sense that no specific religious creeds were taught; but there was religious instruction, and the Charity's directors and teachers were Protestants of one kind or another. Hence the nondenominationalism of the Mico Charity which the British government favoured in the particular circumstances of Trinidad was not exactly the same as the secular education which the Trinidad government supported between the late 1840s and the late 1860s. The secular schools (ward schools) excluded religious teaching from the curriculum; the Mico Charity aimed in vain at what might be regarded as a unilaterally devised 'agreed syllabus' of Christian teachings.

It was precisely because the Mico Charity taught religion that many persons refused to believe that it was really nondenominational. Some felt that it was impossible to be Christian without professing specific creeds.[10] The Mico Charity, though under suspicion, was the best instrument the British government and the Trinidad government had to hand to spearhead the establishment of nondenominational schools. In making small grants to the Church of England and Roman Catholic schools, both the British government and the Trinidad government tried to extract promises from the Roman Catholics to teach only in the English language, and for each denomination to refrain from teaching its particular faith; neither objective was really achieved. The government's attempt to influence education then was intermittent in the sense that it was only attempted when government grants were made and not many were made; it was feeble because the grants were not large enough to enable the chosen instrument, the Mico Charity, to establish a powerful range of nondenominational schools. In 1841, when the British government decided to reduce its subsidy to education, the Mico Charity schools collapsed since the Trinidad government was unwilling to find the funds to keep them in existence. Denominational schools of the Roman Catholic Church and the Church of England continued, though for the most part in straitened financial circumstances.

The policy of favouring nondenominational schools was pushed most consistently by two persons in the Legislative Council: Charles Warner, the solicitor general (later attorney general), the most outstanding anglophile on the Council, and Governor McLeod (1842-1846). But it also got support from all the other governors before the 1860s. The planters and merchants on the Legislative Council, for example, John Losh, distinguished themselves more as opponents of significant expenditure on any kind of education than as proponents of either denominational or nondenominational schools. The argument of people such as Warner and McLeod was often repeated in the island to the time of Dr Eric Williams. It was felt that denominational schools were socially divisive and financially wasteful; that they fomented religious rivalries and hardened cultural differences; promoted the spread of languages other than the English language and thus retarded the spread of English values and habits (in the case of Williams, westernized values and national habits).[11] Frankly, the great danger was felt to be the Roman Catholic denominational schools. Why not refuse government support to Roman Catholic denominational schools only? Not willing to be too blatantly discriminatory, the leaders of the 'English Party', including Warner and McLeod, had also to frown on Church of England denominational schools. In the actual distribution of the meagre funds of the colonial government, however, Church of England schools did get more money than Roman Catholic schools.

The Achilles' heel of the proponents of nondenominational schools in the nineteenth century was that these persons were not truly secularists; they were Christians urging nondenominational schools on grounds of political and social expediency; they were not able to argue that, ideally, nondenominational schools were the best type of schools, or that pedagogically such schools had an advantage over denominational schools. As men who believed that morality must be founded on religion, and that the lower classes were badly in need of religious instruction to preserve the social order, the proponents of nondenominational schools encouraged their own churches to do all in their power, outside the schoolroom or regular school hours, to teach particular religious creeds. But no church was really contented with the separation of specific religious creeds from the work of primary day schools, and the Roman Catholic Church was fundamentally opposed to it though, on grounds of expediency, its leadership did not always challenge the government's policy.[12] In the end, the government's predilection for nondenominational systems of education was thwarted by the persistent desire of both the Roman Catholic Church and the Church of England to have their own denominational schools uniting particular religious tenets with education under the same roof. If the Trinidad government could have prohibited churches from organizing schools, if it had had the funds and the political will to have an adequate number of its own schools, it might have been able to establish a permanent system of nondenominational government schools. But all this proved to be impractical because the government agreed that churches had an important role in education;

also because the government did not have either the money or the support of the social elites for its education policy, and was always inviting the cooperation of the churches, even when attempting to build a nondenominational system.

The strongest attempt ever made by government to implement its chosen policy came between 1849 and 1867. Governor Lord Harris immortalized himself in Trinidad by establishing a system of secular government schools, paid for out of local ward rates, and known as ward schools. Nothing like this existed elsewhere in the British West Indies in the mid nineteenth century. These secular schools rejected the Mico Charity type of nondenominationalism in favour of another type in which all religion was completely excluded during school hours. Before 1849, the government had asked the churches or the Mico Charity to work one type of nondenominational school; after 1849 it took a different line by itself establishing another kind. The existence of secular government schools in the end proved more controversial than the manner of financing them in the 1850s and 1860s, that is, by a local rate, and not from the general revenues. Government schools, secular or not, have continued to exist, but the Harris mode of financing them was abandoned permanently after about twenty years. At the time of the opening of the first ward schools the Protestant dominated government seemed at last to have found its feet in education: it now had its own schools; it was no longer giving financial assistance to denominational schools; its own schools would teach in the English language, bringing children of various cultural backgrounds together and teaching them English values. In short, the ward schools were intended to integrate the labouring classes on the basis of English culture. But many things went wrong.

The Ward Schools of Lord Harris 1849⁄1869

What Governor McLeod and Charles Warner had been searching for in the late 1830s and early 1840s, Lord Harris, the new governor in 1846, devised and implemented. Harris' scheme was intended to forward the general policy of anglicizing the institutions of the colony; culturally, his plan was a continuation of the lines of thought of McLeod and Warner. For instance, the new secular government schools would teach in the English language only and inculcate English values. Harris' major innovation was firstly to decide unequivocally that the government, not the churches or the Mico Charity, had to undertake the establishment and conduct of nondenominational schools; secondly, the schools were to be secular in the sense that the teachers were not to teach religion at all; thirdly, he tied the financing of the schools to local taxes (rates), collected in local districts called wards.

The ward schools were only a part of a larger reorganization of the fiscal and administrative system. Indeed, something of a political restructuring was also in the offing, but it did not materialize. To understand what Harris had in mind, it is necessary to examine together the two laws passed in 1847: the Wardens Ordinance and the Municipal Ordinance.[13] The Wardens Ordinance divided the island (excluding Port of Spain and San Fernando) into counties, districts and wards; it transferred some important responsibilities – local roads, local schools, local charity, local administration of justice – to the wards, the effective unit, not so much of local government as of local administration. A warden, at first unpaid and appointed by the governor, presided over the affairs of the ward. Elected ward auditors were put in place. The Municipal Ordinance allowed for certain developments which never took place. It provided that, when certain conditions were fulfilled by a ward, local municipal bodies of an elective nature could be formed to take over some of the functions of the warden, and to administer the local rates. The local rates were to come from direct taxes on land and houses within the ward. When the system was fully installed, it would amount to a major shift in the burden of taxation from indirect taxes on imports and exports to taxation on those who possessed property, even small houses and small farms.

Harris thought that his reorganization of the fiscal, administrative and political system would successfully address a number of problems at the same time. To those who were clamouring for representative government at the centre, that is for an elected Assembly, or at least for a partly elected Legislative Council, Harris held out the promise of the participation of elected members out in the countryside, within the wards, in municipal corporations or local councils to be formed whenever there were enough people who could make them work.[14] Harris thought that the prospect of more elections would stimulate civic consciousness. Lord Harris is most remembered by historians and students for his phrase: "a race was freed but a society has not been formed".[15] It is not often realized that the Wardens Ordinance and the Municipal Ordinance constituted Harris' greatest efforts towards the solution of the problem he posed in his famous declaration.

As an English gentleman farmer of aristocratic descent, Harris thought that to form a society in the colony, people of whatever class, race or colour must be taught that they had duties to perform, according to the position in life in which it had pleased God to put them. The first place to carry out these duties was in the districts in which they resided. This would create an attachment to their local communities; it would make workers less migratory; it would give the upper class the opportunity to offer moral, social and political leadership in their localities and the bonds of society would grow closer. Direct taxes on the land and houses of all who lived in the locality (the ward) would make a stronger impression on all than indirect taxes on imported food and merchandise. Direct taxes would stimulate the taxpayer to realize that he was making a contribution to government and he would be anxious to know how his tax dollars were being spent, and the fact that ward taxes (revenues) were to be disbursed locally would give him the chance of seeing how the money was used.[16] All this would make for greater civic consciousness. Surely schools as local institutions would be safe in the hands of a responsible citizenry.

Harris also had some practical financial difficulties to meet arising from the double-barrelled economic crisis of the late 1840s. In May 1848 he reported that the Treasury was empty. This sudden shortage of government revenues occurred within a larger long-term crisis of free trade. Harris had to make his ideas about local government part of the means to the recovery of the economy. By adjusting downwards the existing tax on exports until it was gradually abolished in 1852, and by adjusting upwards the new local rates, Harris managed to effect a major reorganization of the sources of government revenues.[17] It was less likely that the Treasury would again be empty because government revenues would no longer be so closely tied to the fluctuating fortunes of the sugar trade but would instead be more dependent than ever on land taxes.

Another problem for Lord Harris was how he could make these ward schools secular (in teaching) without breaking all educational links with the churches. The ward schools would be secular because government schools, in Harris' mind, should not impose religious creeds, and he did not think that religious morality could be taught without creeds. An agreed syllabus for religion, even if it could be achieved, would not do in his estimation. The society, especially the lower classes, Harris thought, needed a moral code based on positive religious beliefs. In 1846 Harris' way of reconciling secular ward schools with the teaching of denominational creeds was to allow the cleric whose church had the greatest support in the environs of the ward school to enter the school and give religious instruction to his coreligionists, with other pupils having the right to exclude themselves from such instruction. Harris, however, did not persist with these plans. The intense religious rivalries between Roman Catholics and Protestants appeared to have deterred him. He eventually preferred another plan which called upon the state-aided churches to develop a parallel but separate system of religious instruction for the children of the ward schools – outside the schools.[18] The government paid thousands of dollars in salaries to clerics, and large sums for Church of England and Roman Catholic buildings. If the clerics carried out their duties to teach the young – and the government expected them to – the children, would receive religious instruction in the church buildings during the same years when they were attending the ward schools for secular instruction. The government's policy, then, amounted to support for religious education generally, but for exclusively secular instruction within the ward schools. But Lord Harris and his officials, all Christian colonial administrators, placed themselves tactically in a cul-de-sac: they failed to defend the religious arrangements they made as pedagogically or morally the best. They put the policy forward as the best compromise available, thus depriving it of any real moral footing, and opening it to the winds of denominationalism.

The role of Charles Warner, the attorney general by Lord Harris's time, in the fashioning of this new scheme of education, is not documented. He was the only important adviser to the governors who had, in the previous ten years, consistently given the question of an education policy any careful attention; his opposition to the Roman Catholic Church and its priests was well known. He was totally against any policy which led to state-supported denominational schools.[19] Since the Roman Catholics were in the majority, they had a greater potential to become the operators of most of the schools in any state aided system of denominational education. The fear of this development motivated all the schemes from the 1830s to the 1860s to set up one or another type of nondenominational schools, or even secular schools. Harris put forward the entire plan as his own, but was probably influenced by Warner who was satisfied with the proposals. For Warner, the secular school proposal was a continuation by somewhat altered means of some of his own ideas about a proper government policy in education.

Harris presented his scheme to the Legislative Council twice, in April 1847 and in April 1851. In 1847 he was not ready to implement it; after the worst of the financial crisis had passed, he was better prepared in 1851, but had to change some aspects of the plan of 1847. In the 1847 proposals, a committee from each of the projected municipal councils was to manage the ward schools under the direction of the Central Board of Education. Pupils were to pay fees. In 1851 changes made to the proposals meant that wardens were to be in charge of the ward schools and that no fees were to be paid.

In 1846 Harris had spoken of two other kinds of schools, neither of which materialized in his governorship. He said he had a vision of an open system of education in which the son of the black peasant, if he had the capacity and desire, could pass through a series of schools until he arrived at the threshold of the professions. At the entrance to the professions would be a college teaching the classics as well as technical/vocational subjects, and the link between this college and the ward schools would be one or more superior district schools. The college would charge a fee, and the district schools a moderate fee. How the poor boy was to negotiate these financial obstacles was not explained specifically, but Harris might have been thinking of scholarships.[20] In 1851 the Harris scheme as presented to the Legislative Council did not include superior district schools or a college, only secular ward schools.

The major debate in the Council on Harris' education scheme came in April 1851 when he produced a simple plan. The immediate objectives were:[21]

(1)   That a committee or Board of Education be formed, the members of the Legislative Council being ex officio members, and six other members to be named by the Governor. Three members to form a Board.
[This was the first time a Board of Education was established in Trinidad.]

(2)   That an Inspector of Schools be appointed with a salary. [This was the first time such an appointment was authorized.]

(3)   That a Normal school with an able master and mistress be at once established. [This was the first time a government teacher training school was approved.]

(4)   That the wardens of the several wards be called upon to establish schools at once, in such parts of their wards as shall appear most suitable for the convenience of the population, which shall be under the direction of the Board.

(5)   That the allowance now made from the public Treasury to the several schools be withdrawn, on the establishment of the schools under the Board.

(6)   That all children be received at the schools free of expense. [This was the first time the principle of free primary education, though confined to government schools, was admitted in law.]

(7)   That no books be used in the schools without the sanction of the Board.

(8)   That the instruction given be secular – that is that no directly doctrinal teaching be given in religion. [The first time religion was explicitly taken out of school, although only out of government schools.]

(9)   The primary schools to include infant and evening schools.

(10)   Lending libraries to be attached to the schools of each ward. [A very advanced idea, not implemented, and forgotten in subsequent legislation.]

(11)   All expenses attending the schools and libraries in the ward to be met by the local rates. [The first time education was financed in this manner.]

The most important aspect of the Council debate concerned the separation of religious instruction from the formal work of the ward schools. John Losh, a planter and merchant, repeated the accusatory words which were to be hurled against Lord Harris' scheme, time and time again: it was a 'Godless' system of education.[22] Harris was even willing to see half of Wednesdays and Saturdays freed from school work to allow children to attend their various places of worship for religious instruction. No one else in the Council was interested in such a concession, though eventually such a provision appears to have been included in little known rules for the administration of the schools. Also included later in these half-forgotten rules was a provision that teachers should, through certificates from clerics, monitor the attendance of pupils for religious instruction.

Outside the Council, the response to the Harris plan was mixed, but not enthusiastic. Some seventeen years later a visiting education expert, Patrick Keenan, concluded that the scheme at first had support among Protestant laypersons.[23] The sort of person who wrote letters to the press, however, was not enthusiastic about schools to educate the lower classes. The planters had shown their hand by not even establishing estate schools after emancipation. Perhaps there were not many planters and merchants who would in the 1850s take the position that no instruction whatever should be given to the labouring classes. The prevailing attitude seemed to have been that nothing ambitious or expensive should be attempted. There were fears of losing part of the labour force if education became a lever of upward social mobility and, at the same time there was the belief that non-whites, especially blacks, were racially inferior to whites and therefore not capable of intellectual excellence. But people who held such views were not prepared to articulate them publicly. P.N. Aumaitre, an old French planter, wrote to Harris about the danger of the education plan stimulating hopes of upward social mobility. Aumaitre said he was not opposed to this for any member of the labouring classes; what he opposed was the government helping them to achieve it.[24]

The reactions of the Church of England and the Roman Catholic Church were most crucial. The Bishop of Barbados, who was in charge of the Church of England in Trinidad, did not like the scheme but would not oppose it from a predisposition to trust the governor. As long as the colonial government contin- ued, as it did between 1834 and 1846, to give most of its paltry education grants to Church of England schools, the bishop had a real interest in the continuation of state-aided denominational schools. Additionally, like every cleric he believed in religious instruction in schools as a normal part of the curriculum. Surprisingly, Dr Patrick Smith, the Roman Catholic Bishop of Olympus and from 1851 the Archbishop of Port of Spain, took broadly the same position as the head of the Church of England, but for a different reason. As the Roman Catholic Church was the victim of discrimination under the existing system of state-aided denomi- national schools, Smith had an interest in seeing a change of system and no grant at all for denominational schools actually looked like an improvement.

Smith was a conciliatory Englishman schooled in the English tradition of Roman Catholic subservience to the state. He was not the man to lead a campaign against Harris; in accepting the Harris scheme, Smith ignored the opposing views of other Roman Catholic priests, notably French priests unhappy with his administration of the diocese.[25] Smith was either ignorant of, or chose to ignore, the increasing intransigence of the papacy against Roman Catholic children attending non-Roman Catholic schools. His death in May 1852 opened the way for a more hostile and uncooperative attitude from the Roman Catholic Church to the Harris education scheme. But it took some time, and some provocation, before this attitude broke into the light of day.

In implementing the new scheme of education, Lord Harris encountered certain difficulties. The failure of elected municipal councils to materialize threw the entire local operation of the ward schools into the lap of the wardens. The first wardens were overburdened, unpaid members mostly of the planter class who, as a group, had never displayed enthusiasm for the education of the masses. If left alone, they would not, in the early 1850s, be an eager bunch of school promoters.[26] Harris did not leave them alone. Instead, he urged them to start ward schools as soon as possible and, as long as he was governor, the education aspects of the ward scheme were worked from the centre, from the Executive in Port of Spain. Harris had less power over the Municipal Councils (or Borough Councils) of San Fernando and Port of Spain than over the wardens; he had to negotiate with these urban councils. When they were reorganized in 1853, the towns of San Fernando and Port of Spain were divided into wards, but their Municipal Councils preferred to keep their schools outside the system of ward schools.[27] These towns already functioned on the principle of local rates for local purposes.

Certain education charges still had to be paid for out of general revenues, chiefly for the cost of the inspectorate and the teacher training school and Harris moved quickly to inaugurate these. Alexander Anderson, a Scotsman who knew nothing about education, became inspector of schools; a superior choice was made for the principalship of the training school which opened in July 1852 under an expatriate master, John Dixon, who was said to have worked wonders with the first trainees in a short time. A practising school, called a model school, was associated with the training school, both on Woodbrook estate, then on the outskirts of Port of Spain. Such a Model school was bound to be a cut above the ward schools, and it benefited the people of the capital. The Municipal Council of Port of Spain petulantly refused to contribute to its cost.

As soon as the Board of Education came into existence it became a centre of views not always in conformity with those of Harris. For instance, when Harris stirred the wardens to propose schools, they overreacted by suggesting so many schools that a committee of the Board demurred. This committee, under the chairmanship of Charles Warner, developed ideas deviating from the original intentions of the Wardens Ordinance. School sites, said this committee, should be chosen in relation to the population of three or four neighbouring wards; and children should attend the nearest school even if it was not sited in the ward in which their parents paid rates. Children whose parents paid lower rates in a poor ward (the wards could and did set different rates) might attend a school in a richer ward, presumably with a better school or vice versa. At best such an arrangement might be evidence that the principle of local education benefits being related to local rates was not to be worked in an inflexible manner. At worst, it might be an early indication that a school expansion programme might find the ward framework too restrictive.

By 1850, the first year in which the wards began to operate, Harris realized that some of the poorer wards could not, or would not, be willing to bear the expense of a school. He was not, however, prepared to use general revenues to assist such wards, for to him this would mean that some citizens were falling down on their ward responsibilities.[28] The outcome was that after three years there were only eleven ward schools. Then the pace picked up, and by 1855 there were 23 schools in 35 wards, the wards in 1854 having been reduced to that number, and grouped into nine ward unions. But twelve years later there were only 31 ward schools in 35 wards. In other words, in twelve years only eight new ward schools came into existence.

One of the greatest defects of the ward system, even in Harris' time, was that too many burdens were placed upon the ward rates in a situation in which a high priority was not given to education. The revenues of the wards did expand, though less so in the 1860s than in the 1850s, but most of the money was spent on other needs – hospital charges, the salaries of the wardens (after 1854), and chiefly on the annual road repairs.[29] There were large differences between wards in terms of revenues collected. In 1855 Maraval ward, with a revenue of about $1,920 in 1854, opted for a cheap infant school in preference to a ward school with a trained, more expensive teacher. On the other hand, the richer wards had not ventured into supporting more than one school each. In 1854 the introduction of ward unions presided over by paid wardens brought no relief from stagnation to the school expansion programme, judged in terms of the number of schools or the amount of funds collected in the late 1850s and the 1860s. It might have helped if the revenues of the wards in the same ward unions had been pooled, but this was not the case; each ward kept its revenues and expenditure separately. The financial responsibilities outgrew the ward revenues until only the richer wards could do anything but maintain the barest services. Eventually, in the late 1870s, the Executive in Port of Spain decided to take back gradually some of the responsibilities formerly met by the wards, including education. The Borough Council of Port of Spain, also under financial pressure, did not wait for the government to relieve it of its schools; it abruptly closed them in 1875.[30]

When the system of ward schools was attacked in the late 1850s and the 1860s, the chief indictment by residents was that the schools failed to spread religious instruction. But they were never meant to do this. The real failure, apart from their intellectual inadequacies which they shared with the denominational schools, was that they had not grown into a dynamic and expansive system. In 1858 there were 27 denominational schools; and the ward schools also numbered 27. In 1869 the number of wards schools had gone up to 31; in 1868 there were about 32 denominational schools. If the opponents of the ward schools had been faced with 80 or 100 such schools and not 31, they would have found it more difficult to push them aside. But the stagnation of the ward school system gave a more aggressive Roman Catholic archbishop and a less anti-Roman Catholic governor improved chances of toppling the Harris system.

After the departure of Lord Harris in 1854, the Board of Education failed to meet regularly or to act as the enlightened controller of the education system. Neither Charles Elliot nor Robert Keate, the two governors who succeeded him, displayed as much personal interest in the ward schools as Harris had done. Two successive inspectors of schools, Alexander Anderson and Lechmere Guppy, were left largely on their own to visit and examine the schools, and manage the system. Because of the difficulties of travelling in the countryside, and the fact that travelling expenses came out of their salaries, the inspectors, especially Anderson in his long tenure from 1851 to 1868, rarely visited the rural schools. The wardens seldom showed any interest in nonfinancial aspects of the ward schools. As Patrick Keenan insisted, the schools did suffer from lack of local supervision and local management. Teachers had too much freedom of action to teach what they wished as they liked; the comfortable judgement of Inspector Anderson in 1865 that the majority of the ward schools compared favourably with the primary schools of any country was most emphatically rejected by Keenan in 1869.

The curriculum and achievement of the ward schools left much to be desired, but Keenan's devastating critique of them should not blind us to the real condition of the existing denominational schools which he preferred on principle. If Keenan had employed the same method of judging the work of the denominational schools as he did the ward schools, the great majority of the former might have seemed worse than the ward schools. It is clear that despite local management by the clergy the denominational primary schools were nothing to boast about. The inspectors and the governors regarded them as inferior to the ward schools except on the point of religious instruction.

The curriculum of the ward schools in the 1850s and 1860s was basically the three Rs: reading, writing and arithmetic, plus some geography. Some schools also did grammar, and a handful indulged in singing. Trades, sewing, crafts or agriculture were not taught in these schools, nor in the unaided denominational schools. The existing popular culture of the black majority was completely excluded. No religious instruction was given, but the reading books in use, the Irish National School books, were highly religious.

There was a lack of serious achievement over the twelve years in the number of schools, the attendance figures or the percentage of pupils reading the various books. It was a fairly stagnant system of education. From 1862 to 1864, and in 1867 over 50 percent of the children in the ward schools were reading in the First and Second Books. If one considers the number in the Alphabet Class for the same years, one observes that about 75 percent of the children never got beyond the Second Book. Such a small percentage read the Fourth and Fifth Books that an average number of only six students in each school in 1862, 1863, 1864 and 1867 were reading the Fourth and Fifth Books. In 1862 there were six schools, and in 1863 and 1867 three, with no pupils reading in the Fourth and Fifth Books (see Appendix IX Table 1.1).

St Joseph's Convent, Queen's Royal College and the College of the Immaculate Conception 1836-1869

Between 1836 and 1869 five single-sex secondary schools were founded in Port of Spain: St Joseph's Convent (1836), St George's College (1837), the Church of

England Grammar School (1853), the Queen's Collegiate School (1859) and St Mary's College (1863). All except the Queen's Collegiate School and the Church of England Grammar School were private Roman Catholic schools. The Church of England Grammar School lasted only two years. St George's College, the least successful of the Roman Catholic institutions, was more of a private school than St Joseph's Convent or St Mary's College. It was owned at first by individual priests and then by the Roman Catholic diocese but never by a Teaching Order from abroad. Ownership of St Joseph's Convent and St Mary's College by Teaching Orders, respectively the Sisters of St Joseph de Cluny and the Holy Ghost Fathers, provided these institutions not only with outstanding management and teaching talent but also with international connections, particularly with France. Indeed, the presence of French nuns and priests from these Orders rendered St Joseph's Convent and St Mary's College rather like local branches of French metropolitan schools.

The Queen's Collegiate School, founded by the colonial government as a nondenominational college, adopted the secular principle which characterized the ward schools. This was a more truly secular institution than the ward schools since the books used for the various courses were devoid of the moralizing and religiosity of the Irish National School books. Unlike St Joseph's Convent and St Mary's College, the Queen's Collegiate School did not take boarders, the absence of religious instruction being a barrier to having boys resident on the premises. The Queen's Collegiate School, down to 1870, was the only one of the schools which enjoyed a government grant, but of the three Catholic schools, only St Mary's College sought government grants. The masters at the Queen's Collegiate School were civil servants. The principal and leading masters were deliberately recruited from graduates of Oxford and Cambridge Universities. Just as St Joseph's Convent and St Mary's College were modelled after French schools, the Queen's Collegiate School drew its inspiration from the great grammar schools of England. But there were immense difficulties in recreating the English models in Port of Spain. The graduate masters from Oxford and Cambridge Universities were without the institutional unity or corporate power of a Roman Catholic Teaching Order. Also the Queen's Collegiate School did not own the premises it occupied. This lack of its own buildings and grounds – its Achilles' heel for half a century – meant that the internal organization of the college fell far short of its metropolitan models.

The first of the secondary schools to be founded was St Joseph's Convent for girls (1836). The allegation sometimes made that it was French creole planters who invited the Sisters of St Joseph de Cluny to the island is not documented. It seems curious that persons from the French creole community should after emancipation seek to make provision for the local education of their daughters before that of their sons, but possibly it was customary to send able sons abroad for education. An alternative explanation is that the vital initiative came from clerics rather than from laymen. The key figures in the invitation to the Sisters were Abbé

Bertin, once their chaplain in Martinique, and the Roman Catholic Bishop McDonnell.[31] At that time the Sisters were working in Martinique, a French colony with which Trinidad had many family and ecclesiastical connections. Secondary education was for those who could pay for it and only the upper and the upper middle class could afford it. There is no need today for priests or nuns to be embarrassed by the social exclusiveness of their secondary schools in the nineteenth century. Whether these schools were organized under Roman Catholic or Protestant auspices, the intention was always to cater for the wealthy, which in practice meant overwhelmingly whites; the only questions were the degree of social exclusiveness to be practised, and the extent to which children of less well-off parents, white or coloured, would be admitted. Although secondary schools were not racially exclusive, it is highly doubtful that patently black students attended any of them before 1868.

Whatever sympathies the foundress of the Sisters of St Joseph de Cluny had for Africans, however racially exemplary her own work in Senegal and Guyana, it was impossible in the post-emancipation period for the Sisters to establish a secondary school for black and coloured girls or for lower class girls in Trinidad. It has been suggested by Sister Gabrielle Mason that, without pressure from the French creole community, the Sisters might have acted with less exclusiveness and that later in the century their establishments in other towns were less restricted.[32] In 1836 the Sisters, if not under French creole pressure, would have been more likely to demonstrate their open-mindedness by a primary school for non-white girls than by a secondary school for them. Indeed, Sister Mason has suggested that the eventual technique of establishing multiple schools on the same compound, one of which would be a partly free primary school for poor girls, was a conscience-saving device to offset the social compulsion to have an exclusive boarding school.[33] This is a plausible explanation, and a useful point because it is often missed that the St Joseph Convents, for example at Port of Spain, San Fernando, and St Joseph, were usually each the site of more than one school, often for pupils with differing backgrounds.[34]

The St Joseph's Convent boarding school for girls won immediate acceptance as an important educational institution. The school commenced with a modest curriculum of the three Rs, grammar, geography, history, English, French and needlework, but without any external examination. Nothing as good for the education of upper class girls had previously existed. It legitimized itself quickly by splendid public examinations and high moral standards. But it was only a school for girls, a few of whom took the veil; a school for upper class girls could not be as important as a school for upper class boys. If St Joseph's Convent gained prestige fairly early, it was the lower order prestige of a girls' school where education did not lead to professional careers, or to careers in the civil service. Good wives and mothers, and occasionally a nun, these were the only careers open to its graduates. Who was afraid of a virtuous wife or a good mother? One advantage of being a school for girls was that St Joseph's Convent was not publicly attacked by Protestants, certainly not with the bitterness which marked the later assault on St Mary's College. It survived the worst fifteen years of Protestant/Roman Catholic conflicts (1854-1870) without damage. Even Patrick Keenan, the foreign expert friendly to Roman Catholic enterprise in education, did not think of St Joseph's Convent as a serious secondary school on par with the boys' secondary schools. It was unique; it was not, in his mind, to be integrated into any public system of education.

Less is known of St George's College (1837-c.1858) than of St Joseph's Convent, and whatever is known about the former is almost uniformly unfavourable. The fullest account of the school comes from Fr Matthew Feheney, and he is in no doubt that it was a failure of management which accounted for its difficulties. It was not a question of lack of basic support from the French creoles, the principal clientele for all Roman Catholic secondary schools, but more than that, total loyalty and enthusiastic fund-raising campaigns, were needed. The College, which did not take boarders, got into debt, though not badly. For these failures, Feheney puts the ultimate blame on the islandwide rivalry between French and Irish priests, epitomized by unfriendly tussles between Abbé Bertin (pro-French) and Roman Catholic Bishop Patrick Smith (pro-Irish) for control of the college.[35] Its administration was crippled; the victory of Bishop Smith after 1842 apparently turned out to be a setback for the school. Feheney's theory is that Smith anglicized the college prematurely by sending away French priests/teachers and, presumably, by adopting more English methods and by using the English language. Smith, it is claimed, dampened the support of the French creoles who definitely wanted a French school under French priests to complement St Joseph's Convent. Feheney suggests that if the college had been supplied with full-time priest-educators in the form of a Teaching Order which could draw on its previous experience and on metropolitan connections, it would have been better managed, and would have enjoyed success.

It might be useful to consider a further aspect of the predicament of the unfortunate college: a secondary school for boys could not afford the luxury of indifference to successful public careers. It could not be satisfied with producing good husbands and fathers. It needed higher academic standards than St Joseph's Convent, leading to careers as merchants, planters, civil servants, doctors and lawyers. Attending St George's College must improve the boys' life chances. For example, Michael Maxwell Philip, a coloured student from a wealthy family and a former student of St George's College, became, after study abroad, the most outstanding lawyer in the colony. It was a question of a lack of sufficient public impact by the college. Governor Robert Keate and Charles Warner, no friends of Roman Catholic secondary education, saw no threat from St George's College as a school; but suspected that it might lose whatever English character it had because of the presence of Archbishop Spaccapietra, a foreign ultramontane priest.

Governor Keate said that he learned from Roman Catholics that academic standards there were even lower than he thought. He had even entertained the vain hope that Archbishop Spaccapietra might convert the college into a theological seminary for British born, English-speaking priests, and allow Roman Catholic parents to send their sons to a government college. Nothing of the sort happened, though it is said that Spaccapietra scoffed at St George's College; so too did Dr Louis De Verteuil, the doyen of the French creoles.[36] Spaccapietra and Dr Louis De Verteuil bent their energies towards procuring a religious Order from France to run a new college. Efforts were not directed to rescuing St George's College, but to replacing it.

In the mid 1850s, neither the Roman Catholics nor the Protestants had a satisfactory boys' secondary school. By about 1850, the Bishop of Barbados (who was also the Bishop of Trinidad) started a drive for a Protestant college. A prospectus appeared in March 1852: students not members of the Church of England would be exempt from religious instruction and a clergyman of the Church of England, recruited from England, was to be in charge. The school actually opened in May 1852 under the headship of Rev George Pix, a graduate of Oxford University. Latin, Greek, arithmetic, geography, secular and sacred history were taught. But the school never got off the ground financially; in 1854 it had only twenty students.[37] The fees were set at $72 per annum for each boy, payable in advance; those boys who wanted French and Spanish as well would have to pay an extra charge. Unfortunately, the school started in 1853 when a depression was setting in; it was hit by the serious slump of 1854 and by the cholera epidemics of 1854 and 1855. Some parents withdrew their boys. An arrangement was made with Rev Pix whereby private subscriptions would make up his salary when the fees fell short of the mark, but he resigned in 1855.

Charles Warner's explanation of the failure of the school was that it had too much of a denominational image, and therefore did not win the support of Roman Catholics. There was, in fact, a sprinkling of Roman Catholic boys attending; but a more relevant question was why did it not succeed financially as a Protestant school. Had it survived the initial economic setbacks, it might have grown into a larger school in the late 1850s when more prosperous times prevailed. But unaided by government, its permanence as a reputable secondary school was doubtful. To defray the salaries of even two or three teachers with university degrees, pay the rent (not to mention purchasing a building) would – considering the initial small numbers usually attending such schools – require fees which parents might not be able or willing to pay. In lauding the Roman Catholics for keeping St Joseph's Convent going from the 1830s without government assistance, it must not be forgotten that the Roman Catholics had one immense advantage over the Protestants: priests and nuns were not paid a living wage as teachers from the fees of students.

As we have already indicated, St Joseph's Convent was a success and St George's College a failure. Even St George's College had the merit of survival for sometime and this gave it the annual opportunity, like St Joseph's Convent, to put on a prize-giving function. Elocution was a very important matter when prize-giving day arrived at St George's College. A boy was usually chosen and obviously properly primed to deliver a long laudatory speech, suitably studded with Latin phrases, in praise of the governor in attendance. The governor would reply, without saying much of importance, and the Roman Catholic archbishop would also make a speech. At St Joseph's Convent the annual prize-giving ceremony became one of the great social events of the Christmas season, and the ladies came out in the latest fashions. The nuns still know today how to organize these school functions better than anybody else and in the mid nineteenth century, no one even pretended to rival them in this art.

With the generous assistance of the government, the Protestants solved their lack of a secondary school for boys sooner than the Roman Catholics. Governor Robert Keate and Charles Warner whose influence was at a peak during Keate's long governorship (1857-1864), established the Queen's Collegiate School in 1859. The first important moves were made in 1857. The Church of England Grammar School had collapsed and that was one reason for taking action in 1857; better yet, government revenues were rising after the depression of 1854. The entire annual cost of the college was immediately put on the budget, although it would take at least three years before the cost of staffing and the university scholarships reached the level of the annual subsidy. Keate and Warner did not, of course, propose the college as a Church of England or even a Protestant institution; they announced it was for the entire colony. That was why it had to be a first-rate college, and such a college could not survive, it was thought, without government financial support. A Protestant dominated Legislative Council unanimously approved the establishment of the college but, a few days afterwards, Archbishop Spaccapietra came out against it and began to organize a Roman Catholic campaign. Only six months after the settlement of the controversial and heated question of the payment of a government salary to Archbishop Spaccapietra, a foreigner, the dust of a religious dispute was again clogging the atmosphere of the colony.[38] The English and the French, the Church of England and the Roman Catholic Church, the governor and the archbishop, Charles Warner and the Roman Catholic planters and professionals, had once again found another bone of contention.

It is essential to understand that the Queen's Collegiate School was a projection of the policy of anglicization into the field of secondary education. Keate and Warner were hoping that boys of all European nationalities and religious beliefs would attend. In a society apparently 'irremediably disunited', said Keate, any institution which brought English and non-English youths together would be beneficial. Warner hoped that in the college:

. . . boys of all denominations will be allowed to meet and that, in the common pursuit of literature, and the common development of their faculties, they may be permitted to learn how possible it is for men to live together, striving to a common end, without dwelling on points of religious difference, and in the spirit of the most cheerful charity.[39]

But the college, without touching religion, was going to inculcate English habits and English loyalties into its students. For years Warner had been complaining that the practice of sending young French creoles to France bred in them from an early age a love of French civilization which made them misfits in the anglicized Trinidad he wished to create. Of course, at this stage, neither Warner nor Keate openly expressed a desire to discourage the French creoles from sending their children to France for education. The argument for not sending away youths to Europe at this most impressionable age was presented in a more general manner which made it applicable to all youths, English or non-English. It was not that either Keate or Warner was against a European education, especially if it meant an English education. In their view, no education in the colony could ever be quite as good as a European education, from the point of view of quality. In fact, Warner and Keate believed that the well educated man must travel to Europe, but they preferred these young men to go, especially if they were bound for France, after their character had been formed in Trinidad. As Keate said, he wished to encourage the habit of parents thinking of Europe as a place to finish the education of their children rather than a place to start it. The bonds of family affections would be strengthened if children spent their early years in the presence of their families in the colony.

It was not simply a matter that English would be the language of the government college, and that its curriculum would be like the English grammar schools. This of course was important. Warner, in a brilliant speech to the Legislative Council, envisaged that the college would teach Latin, Greek, mathematics, geography, history, modern languages and chemistry. But it was the teaching of the classics which excited his imagination. Turning his back in contempt upon the Utilitarians and their mania for schools giving what was called useful knowledge, he restated in his own terms the traditional arguments for a classical education as a training of the intellect and character:

I believe that in very early life the mind is not equal to the strain of so dry and abstract a study: that it is not safe to make the mathematics the basis of education. The object is best obtained by the simultaneous development of all the intellectual faculties, the memory, the taste, the judgement, and the power of analysis; and these results seem to me to be arrived at by the system adopted at the large schools in England. The memory is strengthened, and the taste trained and chastened by learning by heart passages of that poetry, the beauty of which has stood the test of centuries, and stirred the hearts of generation on generation. The practice, to which at Eton we gave the name of Derivations – that of tracing words from their most remote deflections up to their primal root – exercises the power of analysis. The rendering one language into another, the Greek into English, requires the exercise of the judgement, and some closeness and accuracy of thought in the selection of the happiest terms among many nearly equivalent. There is, I believe, no training equal to that of the great English schools. It was said by the Great Duke, that Waterloo was won at Eton. There, too, are won the greatest victories of English statesmanship and eloquence. It is easy to multiply testimonies in favour of this system.[40]

Warner was advertising not only the great English grammar schools, but himself, the product of one of the greatest of them, Eton. When not at their studies, said Warner, the boys at the government college might choose to keep fit by fencing. The whole paraphernalia of activity of an English grammar school could not, however, be imported into the college as it was not going to be a boarding school, but Warner and Keate intended its ethos to be a version of Eton's. The college could not in a day expect to acquire anything like the traditions and prestige of the great grammar schools of England. Perhaps it never would, but Warner hoped that, in time, it would become a matter of pride for a man to say "I too was at the Collegiate School of Trinidad". In this expectation he was fully justified by the course of events.[41]

To drive home the English character of the college, Keate and Warner intended to build bridges between it and the English universities. They did not mean the University of London, but Oxford and Cambridge Universities. The masters of the college would be graduates of these universities; and they would be well paid in order to give them the respect of Trinidad society. Warner suggested the sum of $3,360 per annum for the headmaster, and a high place in the ranks of local dignitaries. Such a man would not be subordinate to Alexander Anderson, the inspector of schools. The inspector would not be able, as Warner put it, "to stand before the principal of the Collegiate school, fresh from the triumphs of an English University . . ."[42] Warner felt unshakable pride in England's universities and Grammar schools, the traditional educational institutions of the English upper class. Every year the two leading students of the college would be given university scholarships, of the value of $720 per annum, and this would take them to Oxford or Cambridge University for three years. Keate felt that these overseas scholarships would prove so attractive an incentive that even the opponents of the college would succumb to them. The college would be the door to professional training in England. Warner drew comfort from the thought of a long succession of men trained in English universities returning to the colony to serve it, and to strengthen English habits and loyalties.

If the college was to be a cultural lever of anglicization to the detriment of French creole tradition, of foreigners and of the Roman Catholic Church, it was also intended as a social barrier against the coloured middle class, and of course against the black and coloured masses. Keate in order to give his scheme a more liberal tone told the British government:

In order too, not entirely to lose sight of Lord Harris' view in regard to children of superior intellect and industry distinguishing themselves in the existing middle and

lower schools, as I may call them, and to offer a prize and stimulate exertion in them
also as well as in the College, I propose that the government should be entrusted
with the power of nominating periodically one or more of such to the College should
instances occur, and should bear the whole expense of their education while they
remain at it.[43]

Up to 1870, the boys given free places at the college by the Board of Education
were the sons of deceased white civil servants.[44] Secondary education was a more
expensive business than primary education. In 1857, when the ward school system
was already in a financial straitjacket, Governor Keate put $14,400 on the budget
for the college. Even after deducting the anticipated fees, this grant for one college
with a projected enrolment optimistically set at fifty boys in the first year, was to
be nearly equal to the total sum which all the wards spent on primary education.
The college was a double blow to the education of the lower classes: it not only
shut them out on social grounds, but its coming considerably reduced the chances
of the government helping the wards to expand primary education. The honest
argument for Keate and Warner to have maintained was not that there were no
lower class boys who needed secondary education, but that, socially, such a step
was undesirable. The medieval notion that the occupation and status of parents
should determine the occupation and status of their children was fixed in the
minds of Keate and Warner. As Keate put it in September 1857:

> Persons of humble origin and small education have constant opportunities of
> emerging into the upper walks of life, which [sic] from the nature of the employment
> open to them the children of educated men are apt to sink to a lower level than is
> consistent with their birth. The standard of social attainment runs constant risk,
> therefore, of becoming more and more deteriorated. [45]

Keate here was grossly overestimating the social mobility of black and coloured
men of little education twenty years after emancipation if by "upper walks of life"
he meant the civil service or the independent professions. While a wealthier section
of the upper class sent their promising sons to Europe for education, a part of it
paid scant attention to the academic life of their boys. The future of many sons
was secure without a respectable level of education. They stood to inherit lands
and estates; they might become planters which generally was not thought to require
any formal studies. Some would follow their fathers into merchant houses or into
the family business. Education as a means of upward social mobility was more
important to the coloureds than to the whites, and indispensable to the blacks.

Warner, in a speech which cannot be faulted for eloquence, revealed the extent
to which ascriptive factors, especially race, colour and class, rather than education,
determined the rankings of people in the community. In presenting the proposals
for a college to the Legislative Council, he assured them that "it is of course not
desired, nor intended that the school should receive those [whose] position in
after life will be below the standard of the education which was offered."[46]

Warner can be believed when he added, a few seconds later, that in Trinidad, ". . . as in every other community, a classical education must, to the large majority be totally useless, as [it is] in no way adapted to their pursuits in after life". [47]

But why should the minority of beneficiaries exclude individuals from the lower classes? The answer is that the society would not give to the black or coloured youth with a classical education the same social status it assigned to a white youth with similar academic credentials. It is in this sense that the non-white youth, particularly the black youth with a classical education, would have a position in "after life" below the "standard of the education which is offered". Warner did not want to produce social misfits. There was, however, another way of avoiding this: and this was to change the social system.

Warner and Keate did not openly say that black or coloured students should be excluded from the college. They said that lower class children should be left out, and this took care of the blacks. With the coloureds, the problem was more complex. When defining which class should benefit from the college, Keate said with one breath that it should be the middle class, then he said it should be the upper class. Warner put it in the negative: it was not for any boy whose parents earned their living by working with their hands. The children of agricultural labourers, small farmers, petty tradesmen were out. If the son of a black primary school teacher would qualify on Warner's definition, then the proposed fee of $96 per annum would eliminate him. As it seems odd to classify the black or coloured Port of Spain shopkeeper, master tailor or teacher among the lower class, it might be said, taking Warner and Keate together, that these gentlemen intended the college for the upper and the upper middle classes.

But this would let in some coloured children. It was difficult to have a public college from which all coloureds were excluded. Neither Keate nor Warner wanted this, though they certainly did not envisage or desire a college in which coloured boys predominated. The sons of respectable coloured professional men would be acceptable. One problem for Warner and Keate was at what level to set fees which would exclude undesirables, yet give respectable people, mostly white men, the opportunity of a good education for their sons at a price they could afford. There were several white civil servants, planters and merchants too, whose social prestige was more than their cash value warranted. To keep up appearances, some of the upper class lived above their means; the slightest unfavourable turn in business would drive their backs to the wall in a fight against bankruptcy. Warner and Keate decided on $96 per annum as the fee for each boy, but where more than one boy from the same family was in attendance, the fee for each would be reduced.[48]

When Patrick Keenan visited the college in 1869 the school, after a decade, had thirteen coloured boys in a total of sixty-eight students (19.1 percent); it probably never had a higher proportion of coloureds. Where the fees had not kept out coloureds (in practice, fees had been reduced to $72 per annum), the regulation banning illegitimate children drastically reduced the number qualified for admission. Coloured people who criticized this regulation were correct in regarding it as a deliberate attempt to close the college to many coloured people in the 'middling' walks of life. Christian marriage was mostly a white upper class institution; it was certainly unfair to penalize children for their parents' lapse from what Victorian morality considered to be right. As some of the coloured boys were the illegitimate children of white fathers who belonged to the upper class, the irony of the situation might not have been missed by coloureds.

The arrangement for the college reminds us that the most consistent policy of Warner and the governors between 1834 and 1864, namely anglicization, was not to be achieved at the cost of confusing Victorian conceived class and colour lines. Warner wished all the schools aided by the government and the wards to be agents in the spread of English habits and values. But the English values and habits disseminated were to be appropriate to the class of the persons receiving them. The ward schools were to anglicize the lower classes; the Model schools and the Borough Council schools the lower middle class; and the college the upper class and the upper middle class. The college brought the education system directly in line with the social system thought desirable by Keate and Warner.

The college did not open its doors until April 1859. The delay was caused by the need to recruit two masters from England. This would have been easier if salaries had been larger or clergymen acceptable. The headmaster was being offered $3,360 per annum with a house, and the second master $2,400 and the privilege of taking private students. As the college was to be secular, no graduate of Oxford or Cambridge Universities who had gone on to take holy orders was acceptable. The jobs were for laymen. Keate thought that his friends in England could find the men he wanted but, having been disappointed in this expectation, the patronage fell to the Colonial Office. Three candidates were specifically mentioned: Edward Calvert, an MA from Cambridge; Horace Deighton, BA (Cambridge), and a Henry Caird.[49] The latter settled for the second mastership. Calvert got the job of headmaster instead of Deighton because he was strongly recommended by the headmaster of Shrewsbury Grammar School; because his qualifications and experience were superior to Deighton and because Deighton had not gone to a public school. As matters turned out, Deighton was given the headmastership after Calvert, who was anxious to get back to England because of the death of his wife and the chance of obtaining a better job there, suddenly resigned and left the island in early September 1859. Because of his short stay of only five months, it is still commonly believed that Horace Deighton, who was still the headmaster in 1870, was the first principal of the Queen's Collegiate School.[50]

Some of the initial difficulties of the college were similar to those faced by new schools of a lesser breed. Many boys were poorly grounded in primary school work, their attainments were well behind their years. Calvert himself took charge of Class I (the top class); Caird and Stuart (the latter was recruited locally) took care of the others. The curriculum consisted of Greek, Latin, French, mathematics, geography, English history and English composition. Calvert hoped to start teaching German and practical science as soon as possible. He reported that at the bottom of the school a lot of time had to be spent in teaching English, history and geography. Only Class I and Class II did Latin and, even so, only the rudiments of the subject. The teaching of French presented a special problem: inadequate supply of books. Altogether, Calvert felt that the most important thing at that stage was to organize the boys and get them accustomed to disciplined work at school and at home.

By August 1860, the number of students had reached fifty-one. Deighton, the new headmaster, kept the three-class structure, but subdivided each class into two sections. As mathematics was Deighton's strong point, he devoted considerable time to it and reported a good response from the boys. And since he knew German, this was added to the curriculum of Class I. According to his account in the *Port of Spain Gazette*, Deighton himself taught all the subjects in Class I, except French, which was taught throughout the school by Caird. No Spanish was taught, and there is no report of any extracurricular activities. Mr. Caird gave a chemistry lecture once a week, and it was hoped soon to form a class in science. Although Deighton himself was not an outstanding teacher of Latin or Greek, the school emerged along the lines of a classical school desired by Keate and Warner.[51] The boys showed proficiency in French, but this should not have surprised Deighton in a colony where French was the first language of so many people. Why German and not Spanish, even before the arrival of Deighton, should have been thought of as the next modern language after French, might appear mysterious if one does not look beyond the shores of the colony. The development of Prussia towards great power status, and the worldwide reputation of Prussian education was such that German was thought of as a more useful language for the sons of the British empire to acquire. There were many hundreds of Spanish speakers in the colony, and millions next door in Spanish America. But Spain was not one of the great nations.

The years 1862 and 1863 brought feverish activities to the college. The age of each student in relation to his achievement was beginning to look more logical. Class III, in March 1862, now consisted almost entirely of boys between eight and ten years old. They were still doing a lot of primary school work. It was however at the top of the college that the pace of the work picked up most remarkably. The explanation was that at the end of 1862, Class I would be submitted "to the ordeal of an examination conducted by gentlemen appointed from the English Universities".[52] From this point on, to 1870 and beyond, preparation for this examination dominated the whole life of the college, and stifled the development of its curriculum. Mr Stuart, the assistant master, claimed that the case of those boys who were not good enough to win university scholarships, was considered:

> . . . and all that can be said on this point is, that the utmost care has been taken to make the course of education as general and as complete as possible; the time devoted

to Greek and Latin is even somewhat less than what is usual at English public schools,
in order that English and other subjects may receive the utmost attention possible.[53]

This view, however, underestimates the extent to which the requirements of the university scholarships had already cramped the curriculum. When Oxford and Cambridge Universities reorganized their programme of studies in order to form closer linkages between themselves and the newer grammar schools of England, the Queen's Collegiate School in Trinidad became the first school in the Caribbean – indeed outside England – to participate in the Cambridge examinations. These were at two levels: the Senior for boys under eighteen years of age, and the Junior for those under sixteen years. Here began the historic connection, still existing in a modified form, between the work of the island's secondary schools and external examinations from England. In 1863, on the first entry of the college into the Cambridge examination system, J. Cadiz and H. Bowen, in that order, won the two university scholarships. They became the first Island Scholars. Cadiz went off to Cambridge University, but Bowen, still too young, received a House Scholarship, to cover his fees for another year at the college. Altogether, six boys had passed the Cambridge examination, with Cadiz almost getting a first class pass. At this time and up to 1870 the total number of students taking the Cambridge examinations in the British empire was so small, that it was possible for the examiners to grade to a fine point the performance of the best students in each subject. The exercise facilitated a comparison of the Trinidad candidates with candidates in England. This very act was a source of pride: the supporters of the college could always discover subjects in which creole boys in a colony had beaten English boys in the metropole. In 1863 Cadiz was ranked second in Greek and fourth in mathematics. It was felt by Horace Deighton, principal of the college, that if his boys were allowed to take religious knowledge as a subject – this being regarded obviously as a soft option – their overall placing would have been even higher. Each year, rivalry for the university scholarships was keenly watched, and everything was done to make the examination appear on a standing higher than any other examination.

Every year the Queen's Collegiate School recorded triumphs in the Cambridge examinations, the small number of the successful candidates detracting in no way from the pleasure of the achievement. It was almost as if forty boys, or nearly this number, and three or four masters had been gathered in a rented building to provide a setting for the glory of a few university scholarship winners. Between 1863 and 1869, eight Island Scholars went to England to study. Exactly what these early Island Scholars studied is not known except in the case of R. Gervase Bushe who did a BA degree. Bushe who later returned to the colony and became successively a master at the Queen's Collegiate School, inspector of schools and auditor general, was the only one of these early Island Scholars whose university training benefited the colony. The Island Scholars were under no obligation to return to Trinidad after completion of their studies and, since these early winners were all white boys, they could easily take up careers outside the island. It has become so much an axiom that Island Scholars invariably studied law or medicine that it should be noted that whether or not most of these early Island Scholars actually studied these disciplines cannot be confirmed. It might be that the trend towards law and medicine set in firmly from the 1870s when the sons of creole families, especially coloured creole families, began to win the Scholarships.[54] They, more than white boys, would have to come home, and would understand the importance of an independent profession.

If Oxford and Cambridge Universities were sometimes criticized in England, they enjoyed an almost boundless admiration from Englishmen in the colonies. German education was excellent; Scotland had more universities than England; but for quality, Cambridge and Oxford Universities were thought to be unsurpassed. To resident Englishmen and English creoles in Trinidad, the admission of creole boys into that "wise arena of intellectual competition, an English University",[55] through an examination which spanned the British empire, was a good thing for creoles and for the empire. The creoles would prove their worth, and stronger links between scattered parts of the empire would be forged. To excel in the metropole was to excel in the empire. When Cadiz (Island Scholar in 1863) in his first year at Cambridge won a £30 ($144) scholarship, the Queen's Collegiate School declared a half-day holiday to celebrate the feat.

From its inception, the Roman Catholic archbishop and lay leaders attacked the Queen's Collegiate School as a secular institution which separated religion from education, as an institution which cost the government too much in relation to the number of students; also as a school with a misconceived curriculum. The curriculum of the college, said Archbishop Spaccapietra, should be agricultural and commercial rather than classical. Roman Catholic boys were forbidden to attend it, but a few did.[56]

There was one ground upon which the Roman Catholics did not criticize the college: they never challenged its academic standards. Between 1863 and 1869 the academic standards of the college became one of the chief pillars of its defense. It so happened that Stuart, one of its masters, was the editor of the *Port of Spain Gazette*, a newspaper then supportive of the English interest against the French creoles and the Roman Catholic Church.

The opening of the Queen's Collegiate School in 1859 made it all the more imperative that the Roman Catholics should have a new secondary school for boys. After negotiations in Rome and France, begun by Archbishop English, with the assistance of Dr Louis De Verteuil, the Holy Ghost Fathers arrived from France in July 1863 to establish St Mary's College of the Immaculate Conception. Although the Roman Catholic leadership in the colony exerted itself much more to get St Mary's College than in the case of St George's College, it should still be remembered that an element in the emergence of St Mary's College was the particular phase of the international concerns of the Roman Catholic Church.

At this time there was a worldwide strategy by the Roman Catholic Church to counter secular schools and the general secularization of life by founding Catholic colleges wherever the political situation allowed. From 1864, Archbishop Gonin reflected this more assertive attitude of the Roman Catholic Church in education. Concurrent government endowment of St Mary's College with the Queen's Collegiate School or, alternatively, the destruction of the Queen's Collegiate School by disendowment – which Gonin himself preferred – became immediately the objective of leading Roman Catholic priests and laymen. A titanic fight was on; it was to last the rest of the century and beyond.

Between 1863 and 1869 the big advantage which St Mary's College gained over the Queen's Collegiate School was its rapid rise in student enrolment outstripping the competition and, very important, the Holy Ghost Fathers began to construct their own building. The fact that it was a boarding school increased its attractiveness and encouraged a richer extracurricular life. The pool of French creole and Roman Catholic students from which St Mary's College could draw was larger than that for the Queen's Collegiate School. In addition, lower fees and a commercial course along with the classical course meant that St Mary's College reached further down into the creole middle class than the Queen's Collegiate School. In other words, St Mary's College gave a more varied course of studies, and it eventually catered to a wider social spectrum than its rival. The French creole supporters wished to make it an exclusive school and it apparently took for the first few years only boys whose parents were married.[57] However, the urge to expand broke down the rule against illegitimate boys. The weakness of St Mary's College in negotiations with the government was that it looked more like a French secondary school teaching English awkwardly than an English secondary school teaching French tolerably badly. Its principals between 1863 and 1876 and half its staff were Frenchmen, and most of the students spoke French or Spanish at home. The advantages which the Queen's Collegiate School possessed – apart from solid government fund – were a headstart in classical studies and penetration into English universities through the Cambridge external examinations and the university scholarships (Island Scholarships). In these matters St Mary's College had to come from behind to catch up with the government college.

The agitation of the Roman Catholics obliged Governor Arthur Gordon to restructure both primary and secondary school policies. In secondary education, the Roman Catholics did get government recognition and financial assistance for St Mary's College, though at the cost of a limited but galling, academic association of subordination to the Queen's Collegiate School which was renamed the Queen's Royal College (hereafter referred to as QRC). The theory was that St Mary's College of the Immaculate Conception (hereafter referred to as CIC)[58] was an affiliated branch of QRC, hence there was still only one college in existence. For the Roman Catholics, the advantage of this compromise was government funds plus integration into the Cambridge external examination system and the university scholarship competition; for the Protestants the arrangements allowed them to keep their college much as it was before: secular, classical and at the centre of governments policy for secondary education.

The Evolution of the Dual System 1870-1902

The essence of the dual system of education was that there were two competitive types of primary schools financed concurrently by the government: government schools and public denominational schools. A key word here is concurrently, because between 1834 and 1849 the colonial government did aid denominational schools when no government schools existed; and between 1849 and 1869 it funded government schools (ward schools), but not denominational schools. During these years there was no dual system. Competition, open or submerged, was an essential characteristic of the dual system, and no predetermined proportion of government schools to denominational schools was required; only that neither sector should be competitively insignificant in comparison to the other. For instance, although the legislation (the Education Ordinance of 1870) for the dual system was first passed in 1870, it was only by courtesy that one can say that there was a dual system between 1870 and 1875; for up to 1875 only two denominational schools were within it, while there were forty-nine government schools.

Although the inauguration of the dual system is associated with the name of Governor Arthur Gordon, his legislation, as far as it concerned primary schools, did not stand the test of time. Important adjustments were subsequently made to the dual system; it evolved by degrees through conflicts and compromises. The peculiar circumstances under which it was adopted in 1870 are worthy of notice. International and local factors were both at work. The Roman Catholic Church, since the 1850s had been going through the famous nineteenth century phase in which it asserted itself against governments and secularism.[59] This led to an uncompromising assertion of the ancient doctrine of the inseparability of education and religious instruction, and the right of Roman Catholic parents to send their children only to Roman Catholic schools. The argument went beyond this; as citizens and taxpayers, the Roman Catholics had a right to government funds to support their schools. From Archbishop Gonin to Archbishop Flood these arguments were increasingly put to government. The initiation of the dual system, therefore, was the outcome of new demands by the local Roman Catholic Church leadership, especially after 1867.[60]

It might be supposed that the new demands of the Roman Catholic Church would have provoked greater resistance from the Church of England and from

Protestant Englishmen and English creoles, leading to more intense conflict between the Roman Catholic Church and the Church of England than in the immediate post-emancipation period. However, there were complications and distinctions: the struggle between the two great Christian denominations in the colony in the later nineteenth century apparently had less to do with fundamental religious issues (such as which was the established church in the colony) and more with practical details of the division of government grants within a dual system which acknowledged the principles of religious equality at the level of primary schools. This development partly switched the focus of discontent of the rival clerics and their lay supporters from religion to schools. In this sense, there was a sort of cautious reconciliation between the two denominations and the elite social forces they represented. But the strife over schools continued fiercely within the dual system. It is useful, however, not to miss the limited rapprochement which emerged; perhaps it had an economic dimension as well. According to one French creole merchant, Charles Leotaud, the international crisis of the sugar industry from the 1860s sapped the confidence of the English sugar planters, traditional supporters of the Church of England, and disposed them to a more friendly attitude towards the French creoles who were poised to recoup their fortunes through cocoa cultivation.[61]

Keenan's recommendations added to the calls for compromise. He proposed denominational schools on pedagogical grounds rather than as a right of the churches. But did the colonial government have to give in? The Protestants who formed the Education League, and who opposed Gordon's policies by organizing meetings in Port of Spain and Diego Martin, did not think that Gordon should have yielded an inch.[62] However, the protest did not endure. Considering the capacity of Crown Colony government to ignore or overcome agitation, there was nothing irresistible between 1868 and 1870 in the Roman Catholic call for reforms of government education policy. Another governor might have responded differently and kept his job. But Gordon's known sentiments not only invited calls for reforms of government policy, but predisposed him to such a reaction. Gordon was religious, though not bigoted; he was a member of the Church of England, but comfortable with Roman Catholic rituals; also, and this was important, he was a friend and protégé of William Gladstone, the Liberal prime minister of England.[63] Gladstone advocated a progressive policy in respect to predominantly white colonies. In those parts of the empire Britain would give the colonial whites more room to direct their affairs; he had no such policy for the West Indian colonies and others like them.[64] Yet Governor Gordon somehow thought that his mentor's sentiments about Canada and Australia demanded a liberal policy in Trinidad as well and this meant, *inter alia*, less domineering by the English and the Church of England over the French creoles and their church.[65] It meant less conscious anglicizing and more cooperation with the Roman Catholic and the French creoles. Let the Roman Catholic Church and the French creoles have government-supported denominational schools. Terms and conditions would be set which they would have to meet; if they complied, denominational schools would be allowed into the system along with government schools; and Gordon even wrote as though it was desirable to work towards more denominational schools and fewer government schools. But he did not behave as if he meant this transition to happen immediately. Thus while in England the dual system, which came into existence at about the same time, saw the birth of government schools to challenge the recognized government-aided denominational schools, in Trinidad the reverse was the case; the dual system meant allowing denominational schools to share the grant formerly reserved for government schools only. The metropole and Trinidad simultaneously went into a dual system from opposite directions, but under a similar banner of liberalism in education.[66]

In Gordon's dual system, the managers of denominational schools had to find one-quarter of the teachers' salaries and "other expenses". The presumption was that the government would find the remaining portion, but this was not written into the law. Nor was it clearly stated that government had any responsibility to fund denominational school buildings or school furniture. Denominational schools were left free to charge fees or waive them. To qualify for government aid, the denominational schools had to meet certain conditions, the most rigorous of which was that its teachers must be licensed by the Board of Education. After a few years, it became obvious that these financial arrangements were too imprecise, and the requirement that teachers be licensed was too onerous. The denominational school managers complained that they could not create revenues for their schools by taking up the option to charge fees because government schools were free. Between 1870 and 1875 only two denominational schools (St Thomas Roman Catholic School in Port of Spain, and a Canadian Presbyterian Mission school in San Fernando) joined the system. The dual system thus started with a considerable advantage in numbers and funds going to the government schools.

The government schools (no longer called ward schools) began to grow at a brisk pace; from 35 in 1870, to 42 in 1872, to 49 in 1875. The financing of these schools had been taken out of the straitjacket of dependence on ward rates, and tied to an education rate which brought in increased revenues in the early 1870s. Without denominational schools sharing these larger revenues, more funds for government schools became suddenly available between 1870 and 1875 than for any previous five-year period.

The first major adjustment to the dual system came in 1875. Governor Henry Irvine had two pressing problems: first, the cost of education was rising and, second, he did not think that the academic performance of the schools, as described by the inspectors' reports, justified the expenditure. In his opinion, an expansion of education could be procured more cheaply through greater government assistance to denominational schools. He also felt that a little competition for the government schools would be a good thing. Part of the solution to the financial problem was to oblige all schools to charge fees. A law was passed in 1875 requiring three pence per week for each pupil. To make it easier for denominational schools to get government aid, another law was passed in 1875 as an alternative to the Education Ordinance of 1870. This alternative law offered aid based on performance in the core subjects, provided there was a minimum average daily attendance of twenty-five pupils and 75 percent of the school fees was collected.[67] The clerical managers then paid the teachers (who no longer had to be licensed by the Board of Education) whatever they liked from the lump sum earned by the school. It was the beginning of the system of payment by results. These arrangements in 1875 were more helpful to the denominational schools than the arrangement of 1870 because teachers did not have to be licensed, and because the amount of aid was determined not solely by the Board of Education but by the capacity of the school to earn grants.

Between 1875 and 1890 a race began between government and denominational schools. Leaving aside the special schools for Indians, the denominational schools had the better of the race in the sense that they increased at a faster rate but, in absolute numbers, the government schools stayed ahead and got most of the government funds. The teachers of the denominational schools were then less qualified than those of the government schools, and earned lower bonuses under the system of payment by results. The Board of Education raised the standard for denominational schools wishing to come into the dual system. The clerical managers and heads of denominations complained that they had not been placed on a footing of equality with government schools and waged a vigorous campaign to increase their share of the grant. The Roman Catholic Church in particular, under the leadership of Archbishop Flood, boosted its efforts to have its own schools, and to oblige Roman Catholic children to attend them under pain of religious sanctions.[68] In the struggle for social influence and schools, the churches fought one another keenly, especially the Roman Catholic Church against the Church of England, and the Canadian Presbyterian Church against the Roman Catholic Church; concurrently, the churches opposed government schools. These rivalries over money for schools reached unprecedented proportions in 1889 and 1890. The Protestant churches thought they discovered in Henry Fowler, the colonial secretary, a Roman Catholic sympathizer secretly scheming to put Roman

Table 1.2: *Government and Denominational Schools 1876-1887*

Year	No. of govt. schools	No. of denom. schools
1876	47	19
1881	56	48
1887	57	45

Source: CP 44 of 1877, Report on public instruction in 1877-78; CP 26 of 1889, Report on public instruction in 1888

Catholic schools ahead at the expense of all others.[69] When Fowler was acting governor in 1889, divisive in-fighting broke out among the educators.[70] One disturbing new development was the Lumb Commission which reported in favour of denominational schools.[71] Governor William Robinson, on his return from England, decided to make another major adjustment to the dual system.

This took the form of Ordinance 17 of 1890 which might be regarded as the Magna Carta of denominational schools. J.H. Collens, principal of the government training schools and Tranquillity Boys' School, could still feel the hand of Lord Harris on the education system in 1884.[72] However, the Ordinance of 1890 marked a crucial turning point in the dual system by giving the denominational schools certain advantages which they retained for the next two generations. It put denominational schools, unequivocally for the first time since emancipation, in the mainstream of development; they became morally, socially and politically the norm. The Education Ordinance of 1875 and most of the Education Ordinance of 1870 were set aside. In respect to denominational primary schools, the government now promised to pay three-quarters of teachers' salaries and fees earned from payment by results; also three-quarters of the house rent of headteachers; and three-quarters of the rent of school buildings. Additionally, the government committed itself to making contributions towards school furniture and apparatus and, in the case of denominational schools, to pay a subsidy in lieu of school fees of those pupils exempted from it by the government. The most rigorous conditions imposed were that schools had to have a minimum average daily attendance of twenty-five pupils, and teachers had to possess certificates. However, the teachers were given five years to secure the certificates. Ordinance 17 of 1890 repeated with modifications the controversial clause of Governor Gordon's Ordinance of 1870 which stipulated that the Board of Education could lawfully discontinue a government school, if there was an adequate number of denominational schools in the district where the government school existed. Together with the increased categories of funding for denominational schools, this bias in favour of denominational schools as the preferred kind of school constituted the kernel of the churches' victory in 1890. Ordinance 17 of 1890 did, however, offer government schools a promise of protection by ruling that none was to be discontinued unless it fell below an average daily attendance of twenty-five pupils.

Almost as soon as Ordinance 17 of 1890 was passed the government realized that it had been generous to a fault to the denominational schools and that it was in danger of being unable to finance the provisions of its own law. In 1891, it immediately reduced bonuses under the system of payment by results, and raised the minimum average daily attendance necessary for aid from twenty-five to forty pupils. This did not stop the entry of new denominational schools into the dual system. A reversal of the ratio of government schools to denominational schools now took place: the number of government schools gradually fell from 65 in 1888 (the highest ever in the nineteenth century) to 57 by the end of the century, while the number of denominational schools rose dramatically from 50 in 1888 to 183 in 1900. This rapid increase was not due simply to the law of 1890 but also to the further integration of special Indian schools into the dual system and to the incorporation of Tobago with its 27 denominational schools into the colony of Trinidad and Tobago. Denominational schools began to get the lion's share of government funds for education.

The year 1890 also marked a victory for the churches in the sphere of teacher training. Provision was made to aid denominational teacher training schools at the rate of $192 per annum for each boarder, and $38 per annum for each non-boarder up to a maximum of eight students. This legislation made possible Naparima Training College, established by the Canadian Presbyterian Mission in 1894, and it underpinned the Roman Catholic and Church of England teacher training efforts in Port of Spain. The logic was that if the government funded denominational schools, it should also finance the training of denominational school teachers. This logic was extended even to juvenile reformatories.

The last adjustment to the dual system within the period 1870 to 1902 came between 1901 and 1902, and was motivated by the urge to restrain expenditure on education. School fees were abolished and henceforth, government paid the entire salary (instead of three-quarters) of teachers in denominational schools. But building and apparatus grants to existing denominational schools were reduced, and there was a total prohibition of such grants to new denominational schools. The minimum average daily attendance required to qualify for grants was raised from forty to fifty pupils. Another measure intended to restrain expenditure was the new rule that the Board of Education, not the churches, was to decide in advance if a district needed a school; if the district was not so designated, any new denominational school there would not receive government assistance even if it satisfied other requirements. These financial adjustments between 1901 and 1902 did not interfere with the essential principles of the law of 1890 nor did they stop rising expenditure on primary education.

In the evolution of the dual system, the special Indian schools organized by the Canadian Presbyterian Mission were not as closely integrated into the system as other types of denominational schools. This was particularly true between 1870 and 1890, but less so afterwards. Until 1890, these special Indian schools were not recognized by the education laws, and aid to a few of them was on an ad hoc basis within the discretion of the governor. The inspector of schools did not regard them as falling under his jurisdiction until 1890. The imposition of school fees in 1875 was rightly considered by the Canadian Presbyterian Mission as a backward step which made it impossible for special Indian schools to join the dual system. When these schools were recognized by the government in 1890, their special status was reflected in certain unique regulations: pupils whose parents were still working as indentured immigrants were exempted from school fees and teachers were required to understand both the English language and Hindi.

Interestingly, by the law of 1890, special Indian schools were not obliged to admit children of all races but by the following year they were so obliged. This change of regulations had little immediate effect, because the racial pattern of these schools was already set. Another unique condition was that special Indian schools could qualify for aid with a lower average daily attendance than other schools: thirty in 1891 and forty in 1901. Strictly speaking, not all Canadian Presbyterian Mission schools were special Indian schools. A few were really ordinary denominational schools to be conducted on terms similar to other denominational schools, but this distinction was blurred.[73]

The dual system also extended to secondary education. At this level there were some significant differences in the problems facing the system. Until the very end of the period under discussion (1870-1902), when Naparima College was brought into the dual system, only two colleges existed: the government college (QRC), and the Roman Catholic college (CIC). Whereas the rivalries at the primary school level were diffused over scores of schools all over the island, the rivalry at the secondary level was concentrated between two schools in the same town. Whereas the parents of the pupils in the primary schools were seldom, if ever, parties to the dispute in the public forums, the parents of the boys at QRC and CIC were important enough to find means of expressing their views in the press. In discussing the dual system at the secondary level, those who controlled education, as members of the Board of Education, the College Council or the Legislative Council, were talking about the education of their own children or the children of close relatives or friends. That made a difference when it came to questions of funding and academic standards at CIC and QRC.

The most obvious difference between the history of the dual system at the secondary and primary school levels between 1870 and 1902 was that while significant adjustments were made at the primary school level in favour of denominational schools, no such adjustments were made at the secondary school level. Gordon's Ordinance of 1870 was still, in 1902, the only law relating to secondary education. The fiction that CIC was a part of QRC did not prevent a fierce rivalry between them. The greatest victory of the Roman Catholic Church was to get an additional $1,200 per annum in 1895 for CIC; it was not able to get either financial equality or superiority over QRC.[74] Some significant questions were raised, mostly by CIC supporters, about the need to shift from Cambridge external examinations to those of the University of London and about the need to change the use of the university scholarships (Island Scholarships) to meet the colony's need for experts in agriculture and for engineers,[75] but no such changes were effected. The Legislative Council stoutly defended the need for a superior government college. While the high point of rivalry at the primary school level came between 1889 and 1890, the apogee of the strife between the supporters of CIC and the friends of QRC was between 1901 and 1902 when it was proposed to erect an expensive building in St Clair, a prestigious district of Port of Spain, to house QRC.[76] In retrospect, the erection of this structure marked a turning point in the relationship between the supporters of QRC and the friends of CIC. It was ridiculous to believe that after QRC moved into its expensive new building any government would close the college. Since 1863 the Roman Catholic hierarchy had pushed two strategies: destruction of QRC on the one hand or equal (if possible, superior) endowment of CIC on the other. After the new building, the only feasible strategy was equal endowment. A more mature rivalry ensued.

The fierce rivalry between CIC and QRC should not mask the genuine improvement in the standard of education at both colleges during this period. The defence of each college involved the insistence that QRC be more like CIC, and CIC be more like QRC. Generally each college preserved its identity but in respect to preparation of students for the greatest academic prize, namely the university scholarships, there was some movement towards common ground, both in terms of curriculum and achievement. CIC had to come from behind QRC since of the sixty university scholarships granted between 1870 and 1893, CIC won twenty-three scholarships and QRC thirty-seven.[77]

In the dual system, the separation of secondary education from primary education was very marked. These were two different types of education controlled by two different authorities: the Board of Education with Roman Catholics comprising 50 percent of the members was in charge of primary schools. The inspector of schools was not a member of the Board of Education until the adjustments of 1901 to 1902. The secondary schools were controlled by a College Council, chaired by the governor, and including the principals of QRC and CIC. In making other appointments to the College Council, the religious affiliation of the appointee was a capital concern for the governor. The inspector of schools, being academically less qualified than the principals of QRC and CIC, was not allowed to inspect their colleges. The Legislative Council and, ultimately, the governor and the British government were in charge of education. The relative absence of change in the arrangements for secondary education was due largely to the fact that the existing situation suited the Protestant supporters of QRC and the Legislative Council had a Protestant majority.

It is interesting to note that an area of dispute which was later to bedevil relationships between government and the churches in the dual system was almost totally absent during this period (1870-1902). The government willingly conceded the right of clerical managers to appoint and dismiss the teachers of their schools; and teachers were too disunited and subordinated to protest. As there were then no denominational Boards of Management, individual clerics as managers had vast powers over their teacher employees. There was then no legal redress against arbitrary action by clerical managers. The wardens who acted as managers of government primary schools had less power over teachers who were appointed by the governor through the Board of Education. The thin edge of the wedge of future government control of all teachers had, however, been inserted in these opening years: this took the form of certification of teachers. The training and certification of teachers remained from first to last an area in which the government, though it allowed some competition in training, insisted on its own supremacy.

The position of the inspector of schools for two-thirds of the period (1870-1902) was a difficult one. Inspector Lechmere Guppy (1868-1890) had no professional qualifications for the job, and was a secularist: that is, he would have liked to keep the churches out of education.[78] He found the constant admission of new denominational schools into the dual system distasteful. He was unable to exercise any considerable beneficial influence over the teachers. To make matters worse, the education laws did not give the inspector of schools a place on the Board of Education; he was strictly its employee. He was not the head of an Education Department which controlled the schools. Guppy thus felt free to criticize mildly the policy of the Board; the growing dominance of denominational schools made it uncomfortable for him to continue as inspector, and he resigned in 1890. His successor, Gervase Bushe, as an ex-teacher at QRC and a supporter of church involvement in education, found it easier to fall in line with the policies of the Board and the government; but he too suffered the indignity and inconvenience of not being a member of the Board.

It was obvious that dual control was a competitive system; the sources of rivalries and conflict could be quite complex. There were rivalries among the denominational schools; rivalry between particular denominational schools and particular government schools; and between denominational schools generally and government schools generally. The government was not hostile to denominational schools, though Governor Frederick Broome was sometimes equivocal. There were, however, friends of government schools, some within the government, who were hostile to denominational schools and there were sympathizers of denominational schools inside and outside the government, who were hostile to government schools. There were hundreds of middle and upper class people who saw no need for denominational schools, among whom the leading citizens were English expatriates and English creoles. Equally, there were hundreds who would have been happy to see the disappearance of every government school. The hard core of the opponents of government schools were the French creoles, all Roman Catholics. While the government succeeded in riveting the dual system onto the colony, its legitimacy, and hence permanence, as a system was far from being accepted among the elite who participated in discussions of education policy. The vast majority of lower class people were indifferent to these matters.

The case for government schools as 'open' institutions which could educate children of different religious creeds without any danger of interfering with their religious affiliation was compelling to many; the idea, first surfacing in the immediate post-emancipation era, that government schools were capable of uniting, while denominational schools divided, still had its adherents.[79] It was pungently overstated in 1910 by L.O. Innis, a well-informed black pharmacist who wrote:

> There can be no doubt that for all the young people of one district to be taught together, in one school, by a properly paid and equipped schoolmaster, must tend to foster that spirit of friendliness and unity amongst the population, which is so necessary for its advancement in social and political life, and which is at present greatly hindered, by a multiplicity of small sectarian schools carried on by incompetent teachers, at starvation wages, which only tend to accentuate the differences and keep alive the prejudices of the various sections of the community.[80]

Now that Roman Catholic primary schools all taught in English, there was no strong case for the English and their friends to project government schools as the sole bastion of English cultural values, but government schools were still believed to be more reliable purveyors of appropriate English cultural values. A parallel case is the instinctive belief of many today that contemporary government schools nurture the ideology of nationalism more securely than denominational secondary schools. In the later nineteenth century there were many who rejoicingly perceived government schools as social institutions beyond the control of Roman Catholic priests still allied to the local non-English people. It must also be recognized that in late nineteenth century Trinidad, a handful of people had firm anticlerical views, convinced that the churches, particularly Port of Spain's aggressive Roman Catholic Archbishop Flood, were making preposterous claims to direct the lives of citizens.[81] Some educated persons insisted on perceiving the Roman Catholic Church as an illiberal, obscurantist institution, unfriendly to independent thinking of the masses. A few dedicated secularists believed that the colony was priest-ridden.[82] The use of religious sanctions by the Roman Catholic hierarchy, including exclusion from the sacraments, to oblige Roman Catholic parents to send their children to Roman Catholic schools was condemned by these secularists and disliked by other churches as expressions of bigotry.[83] Very often the supporters of government primary schools were the same persons who supported QRC against the claims of CIC. Generally speaking, many of the people (Church of England clerics excluded) who wished to see the end of government primary schools also wished to destroy QRC; those who felt it was the most natural thing in the world for a government to support a government college were among the persons who thought of the closure of government primary schools as religious madness.[84]

If the supporters of government schools, stigmatized as secularists (an epithet which they did not willingly accept), placed great store by the argument that government schools had the potential to unite the population, the corresponding major argument of the denominationalists was that denominational schools were what the great majority of Christians wanted. It was the Christian majority which mattered, not the non-Christian Indians; and among the Christians, the Roman Catholics claimed to be most numerous, most prosperous, paying most of the taxes, owning most of the cocoa estates, and providing the best customers to the merchant houses of Port of Spain.[85] The implication of this point of view was that were it not for Crown Colony government, the Roman Catholics and the other denominationalists would be able to outvote the secularists. Since the word *voters* was not a part of the vocabulary of politics, the catch-phrase of the denomination-alists, especially from the start of the twentieth century, was that they were the majority of ratepayers.

On the narrower ground of the relative performance of the schools, the friends and enemies of the two types of schools developed stereotyped lines of defence and attack. The most hackneyed criticism, loud enough in the 1870s and 1880s, more muted thereafter to the level of insinuations, against denominational primary schools was that their academic standards were lower than those of government schools. Religious instruction, it was alleged, detracted from the time available for other subjects. The Roman Catholics from the 1890s led the counterattack with school statistics to prove that denominational schools pleased the inspector of schools more than government schools. But what of the tendency of government schools to have more pupils in the higher grades? Easily the two most popular arguments against government primary schools were that they failed to teach morality based on religion, and had a higher per capita recurrent cost than denominational schools. The financial argument was the one most effectively employed at the Board of Education. There was a margin of truth in all these stereotypes, although one needs to exclude the larger urban denominational schools from the suspicion of lower standards. Significantly, the churches did not spend much time trying to defend their rural schools from the charge, perhaps because they knew that the Board was much more interested in cutting the cost of education than in raising academic standards.

In the rivalry, however, the churches had certain solid advantages which they consolidated as time passed. As institutions in contact with thousands of adults and children, they had far more effective means of propaganda than the laymen opponents of denominational schools who were individuals without captive audiences or religious sanctions. The attribution of a religious and moral function to schools was widespread, hardly encountering rival philosophies about indivi-dual freedom, or any highly emotive political ideology such as nationalism. Hence a religious and moral interpretation of primary education occupied the mainstream of thought. In practice, it was always the government school sector of the dual system which seemed threatened with extinction. Leaving aside the strength of support for denominational schools, this was basically caused by the fact that it was easier to close a government school than a church school. Withdrawal of government aid would immediately close a government school; without govern-ment aid some denominational schools might still survive. Not only from the point of view of finance but also from that of authority, the government could more easily do as it would with its own schools than with denominational schools. Unfortunately for government schools, the principle that they could be discontin-ued when sufficient denominational schools became available was inserted into the laws of the dual system, thus making denominational schools morally the senior partner, although there were more government schools at the time when the principle was first enunciated in 1870. As the colony went through straitened financial circumstances in the 1880s and 1890s, government schools came under great pressure from the denominationalists; it was the British government which saved them from large-scale destruction at the end of the nineteenth century.[86]

The clerics themselves were normally the greatest friends of denominational schools. Yet the rivalry among the clerics did at least at one juncture produce a curious petition by certain Protestant churches, including the august Bishop of the Church of England, in favour of a purely government system of schools.[87] This was in 1889, at a fever point in the rivalry between the Roman Catholic Church and the other churches, in which the latter feared that they would lose their influence to an aggressive and expansive Archbishop Flood. Rather than see the rapid increase of Roman Catholic schools, and the reduction of Protestant schools, these Protestant clerics expressed a preference for a purely government system. The phenomenon was not entirely novel for in the late 1840s Roman Catholic Bishop Patrick Smith had also expressed a preference for a system of government schools to one in which Church of England schools predominated with government assistance. In the late 1920s, certain Hindu and Muslim Indian leaders in Trinidad would also express a desire for government schools in preference to the monopoly by Canadian Presbyterian Mission schools over the education of the Indians.

The history of the dual system between 1870 and 1902 might be viewed as a triumph of denominational schools over government schools. Yet the growing dependence of the churches on the government to finance their schools was, in reality, a hidden source of weakness; in the future it was to cost the churches incremental loss of control over their schools. By the end of the century, most of the denominational schools would probably have collapsed without government aid. If the churches needed government grants more than ever, they in turn strove to convince everybody that the government needed the churches' managerial skills and participation to keep down the cost of education. Having used greater government assistance to gain a position of numerical superiority for denominational schools, the churches sought – increasingly some thought – to use this position to gain even more concessions. The argument was that the churches deserved still more money from the government because they had three times the number of government schools, or educated three times as many pupils as the government schools. Such arguments and pressures created an atmosphere of instability about the dual system; but using hindsight, it seems that when the government schools were vastly outdistanced by the denominational schools in the closing decades of the nineteenth century, the dual system imperceptibly sealed itself for many generations against the destruction of either partner. Despite the fears of some clerics, the denominational schools had really entrenched themselves so firmly that their survival did not depend upon the abolition of government schools.

The Financing of the Dual System 1870-1902

It was not until the last quarter of the nineteenth century that the government was first confronted with the phenomenon of ever-increasing annual expenditure on education. In the first decade after emancipation (1838-1848) only ad hoc grants were made to schools and this was followed by the imposition of ward rates, partly to finance the government's ward schools, between 1849 and 1869. The dual system, however, led to greater expenditure on education.

The method of financing the dual system was changed during the period 1870 to 1902. Between 1870 and 1875 the ordinary ward rates were no longer required to bear the burden of financing the schools; instead a special education rate, imposed and spent at the ward level, was employed.[88] This proved financially more satisfactory than Lord Harris' method since it produced increasing revenues and government schools began to grow in number. In 1875 Governor Irvine abolished this special education rate after relieving the wards of the responsibility for poor relief and the wardens' salaries; he put the government schools back on the ordinary ward rates. But this arrangement lasted only for a short period as, by 1878, the entire cost of education was shifted to the general revenues. The year 1875 also marked the systematic imposition of school fees in all primary schools within the dual system. The changes in the financing of schools between 1875 and 1878 marked the permanent passing of the era of local rates for local schools. Henceforth, education expenditure by government was met from the general revenues (school fees excepted) unless loans were floated, but that was still to come.

The imposition of school fees was a landmark in the history of education. Hitherto primary schools had been free, except in special cases such as the Girls' Model School and the Boys' Model School in Port of Spain. Governor Irvine, who was quite friendly to the planter class, emphasized the idea (widespread among the upper class in the late nineteenth century) that government assistance to the masses in the form of free schooling or free medical facilities only turned them into dependent paupers.[89] By abolishing the special education rate, Irvine offered relief to planters and small proprietors. By imposing school fees he thought that he was increasing government's and the churches' funds for education while doing the masses a favour by requiring them to stand on their own feet. Irregular attendance, said Governor Irvine, was the main problem of the schools. He argued that parents would have a higher appreciation of education, and attendance would improve if they had to pay fees directly for the privilege.[90] Irvine was to be disappointed: the returns from school fees started promisingly and then fell off until the system virtually collapsed. Popular resistance to school fees, whether from inability or unwillingness to pay, led to its formal abolition in 1902. School fees discouraged attendance and in the end caused more problems for everybody – parents, teachers, managers and the government – than the value of the fees collected. It also became a source of contention between clerical managers and the government, between denominational schools and government schools. Within a decade most of the educators were convinced that the imposition of school fees had been a mistake. By the time a local Commission in 1895 investigated school fees and compulsory attendance, the only purpose school fees served was to keep lower class children out of four superior Port of Spain schools which charged between 50 cents and one dollar for each child per month.

While the collection of school fees brought in small revenues, the cost of education increased at a pace which soon frightened the authorities. The population of the colony grew from 109,638 in 1871 to 153,128 in 1881, and to 200,028 in 1891. The chief contributors to this expansion were Indian immigration and the migration of West Indian workers from neighbouring islands. The growth of settlements was an outstanding feature of these years; villages sprang up everywhere, mostly near crossroads and on the outskirts of estates. The Indians developed into an important sector of the population. Yet it would be true to say that they were not then perceived by the government as the ones posing a demographic challenge to the dual system. The Indians were something apart.

Inevitably, education expenditure would rise once the government accepted the challenge of providing education for an expanding school population. It wished to do this as cheaply as possible, and in fact fooled itself into believing that cheapness and efficiency could go hand in hand. Whatever the system of education, costs would increase. Whether it was a dual system or a system of solely denominational schools or solely government schools, the government would have to find more and more funds. Since the expenditure began to rise alarmingly only after a dual system was in place, the colony was never taught the lesson that any organized system of education, once the policy of educating more and more children existed, would also lead to increasing expenditure. But having said this, one might still ask how far the dual system was more costly than either an exclusively government system or an exclusively denominational one catering for the same number of students. Instead, the question was always how far the dual system was responsible for rising costs and almost everyone felt that it was a factor, although the explanation was not always the same. The dual system was inherently competitive but the competition was not over academic standards: it was for pupils, for teachers, for sites, for influence in the local community and for government grants. More schools, therefore, were established and they tended to be smaller than might have been the case in a single unified system. Consequently, the dual system tended to be costly.

A brief survey of education expenditure will establish the leading facts. Disbursements rose from $51,072 in 1875 to $160,344 in 1891, (213.9%) and to $197,376 in 1903 (23.0%). This level of expenditure was never more than, at most, 5 percent of total government expenditure, but it was thought too much by several important officials. Between 1870 and 1902, there was a major reversal of the pattern of distribution of government grants between government schools and denominational schools. In 1875, government schools received six times as much money as denominational schools but in 1891 denominational schools got slightly more than government schools. By 1903 they received two and a half times as much as government schools. Soon after the Education Ordinance of 1890, Governor Broome confessed that the provisions of this law were more generous than the colony could afford and that the government could not accurately anticipate how much money was needed each year for education.[91] Despite the increasing share of government grants, Church of England and Roman Catholic school managers, especially the latter, complained bitterly that the Ordinance of 1890 was not being fairly administered, and that government schools had a larger share of public funds than they deserved.[92] The question which cannot be answered conclusively is how much of this increasing expenditure was wasteful and needlessly brought on by the dual system. No one ever took the trouble to demonstrate by detailed estimates how an alternative system of equal educational value could cost less initially, and be prevented from costing more eventually.

Some persons blamed the government schools, others the denominational schools. The former, led by clerical managers, claimed that government school buildings cost too much, even leaving aside the additional cost hidden under other government agencies such as the Public Works Department. The government did set itself a higher standard of school design in rural areas than the churches, although in towns there was often not much difference between the architecture of government schools and that of denominational schools. But the cost of government school buildings was less often the subject of attack (in contrast to the twentieth century) than the recurrent per capita cost. That this cost was higher in government schools than in denominational schools was normally true, though in calculating their per capita cost the churches would have looked less efficient if they had included their voluntary contributions from supporters.

Government schools were also accused correctly of collecting school fees less efficiently, though few denominational schools collected as much as 50 percent of theirs. The clerics argued that if they could get their hands on the grants the government gave its schools they would make better use of them. As the Bishop of the Church of England asserted in September 1899, "we are the most efficient instructors", and "in schools administered by us, beyond all question, the most substantial economy will be effected in Elementary Education".[93] The frequent rejoinder of the supporters of government schools was that the churches opened too many small schools, often with less qualified teachers than those in government schools. It would be cheaper, it was said, to have a system of government schools only with larger schools in central locations.

The figures tell us which side of the dual system cost more money before and after 1890 when the system was adjusted to suit the churches. Before 1890 government schools got more money; after 1890 expenditure on government schools stabilized, while that on denominational schools rushed forward to new heights annually. Denominational schools came into the dual system by leaps and bounds after 1890. But were there really too many of them? Were they too small? And what was the criterion for saying that per capita expenditure in government schools was too high? What the controversies and discussions needed, and scarcely had, were some hard criteria for making judgments. There was no agreement on the question what was an acceptable per capita expenditure for any type of school: the only concern was whose per capita expenditure was higher or lower. The education authorities closely scrutinized the annual reports of the inspector of schools in order to determine this competitive point, and occasionally they resorted to examining the per capita cost in other eastern Caribbean islands; but they never declared how low such expenditure had to be to avoid the charge that money was being wasted. Slightly more progress was made in defining the criteria for a 'small' school. By 1890 it was a part of the law that no school, government or denominational, could get aid if it fell below twenty-five pupils in average daily attendance; this was quickly raised to forty pupils in 1891, and by 1902 to fifty pupils. A concession was made for special Indian schools which were eligible for aid with thirty pupils in 1891, and with forty pupils in 1902. But these minimum figures did not solve the problem, they only determined the requirements for going or staying in the dual system. The charge was that denominational schools with enrolments larger than these minimums were too small. The question of the quality of education was quite subordinate to these protracted disputes.

The push to reduce spending on education began in the second half of the 1880s and became irresistible in the 1890s, especially between 1897 and 1900. Lower export earnings from sugar in the mid 1880s posed a crisis which suggested at least a policy of holding down expenditure on education. It was decreased in 1887, but generally expanded despite the crisis. The most severe crisis of expenditure on education came in the late 1890s because Joseph Chamberlain, an imperious secretary of state for the colonies, ordered that the budget for education be held at $168,000 per annum. In the 1880s, economy in education had been largely self-imposed by the colonial government; in the 1890s it was dictated from the metropole. On Chamberlain's orders, solutions had to be found to rising cost and those advanced were not unexpected. One was simply to collect more school fees even if it meant resort to court actions. In 1892 and 1893 the Board of Education ordered the wardens to prosecute parents for school fees,[94] but this elicited protests from the Church of England and the teachers' union. It had little chance of success anyway as the sums were small and the litigation time consuming and expensive. The most optimistic assessment of what school fees were worth, even if entirely collected, did not run beyond $19,000 per annum. Assuming that 50 percent was already being collected in 1892, the government stood to gain only another $9,000 per annum by using the courts. Governor

Broome (1891-1896) was particularly keen on collecting school fees although before him, Governor Robinson had spoken of the wisdom of abolishing them and by the end of the century, Governor Jerningham was faced with the self-abolition of the system of fees.

Some proposals to reduce spending were curiously more like measures to increase it though in a controlled manner. An interesting idea was to appropriate a fixed percentage of the island's total expenditure for the purpose of education. The local Commission which investigated free and compulsory education in 1895 recommended that this be put at 7 percent of the total budget, which would mean raising existing expenditure on education which was at about 5 percent.[95] But it might have been futile to fix the percentage so low with the need for school places rising quickly; hence an additional suggestion was that a special education tax should be combined with a fixed percentage of government spending. The British government was not unwilling to consider such a tax, but the Legislative Council did not produce a proposal. Less appealing to the British government was the idea of an Education Trust which could borrow money to build schools on the strength of government contributions to it.[96] This idea emerged in 1895 and had Broome's support. It was the first time that a governor had proposed taking loans to finance education; it was too bold a step for the popular conception of education as purely an item of consumption.

Governor Jerningham brought a storm of protest from the Bishop of the Church of England and from the Roman Catholic Church by his proposal – on the recommendation of Joseph Chamberlain – not to pay the clerical managers subsidies in lieu of exempted school fees.[97] The number of exemptions had grown, but the churches had been protected from the financial implications of exempting pupils from school fees by the practice of government making grants equivalent to the amount foregone. The bishop retorted angrily that some of the denominational schools would have to close if this was done. It was done in 1902, but as part of a deal whereby the government paid the full cost of teachers' salaries.

The most hotly contested solutions were those which sought to reduce financial allocations or to trim the schools of either of the two partners in the dual system. The Roman Catholic lobby on the Board of Education and the Legislative Council, led by Dr Louis De Verteuil, aroused many opponents in 1891 and 1892 when it sought to abolish the Model schools and to use the savings to finance denominational teacher training schools.[98] A few schools, denominational and government, were occasionally closed by the Board because they fell below the minimum attendance level, but a proposal to close government or denominational schools on principle was another matter, sure to call forth strong protest from the injured parties. It was in the late 1890s, when Chamberlain ordered cuts, that the most desperate solutions, including closing schools were advanced.

The clerical managers were all sure they had the answer. In 1899 a special committee appointed by Governor Jerningham, and dominated by the clerics, launched the greatest attack on the integrity of government schools ever witnessed in the colony. The committee proposed the immediate closing of eight government schools; twenty others were to be transferred to the management of the clerics, in other words to become denominational schools (fifteen for the Roman Catholics, four for the Church of England, and one for the Canadian Presbyterian Church). This would leave twenty-four government schools "to be still maintained as such for the present".[99] All of this would save only $9,120. Governor Jerningham, a Roman Catholic, was ready to go along with these recommendations had he not been stopped by the British government. Petitions from Cedros, San Juan and Laventille against the closing of government schools in these areas had been sent to the British government; but even without these, the British government saw the unfairness of closing only government schools to the benefit of churches, especially the Roman Catholic Church. The imperial government was a Protestant government, still not at ease in making concessions to the old enemy, the Roman Catholic Church.

While the search was in progress for means to reduce expenditure on education, there were counterproposals which would certainly increase spending, or which might do so if the education authorities were not careful. Chief among the countercurrents were the proposals to abolish school fees and to introduce compulsory education. Compulsory education threatened to add a large amount, sometimes calculated at $57,600-$72,000 per year to the education budget; the abolition of school fees only looked expensive because it was so often coupled with compulsory education. The variation in the different estimates of compulsory education indicated that nobody was really sure how much it would cost, and it never looked like a practical measure. It had to wait another half-century. Primary education became free in 1902, but not compulsory.

Simultaneously with proposals to reduce expenditure on education came a plan to reorganize the structure of government grants to denominational schools. The main intention of the new package of measures discussed in the late 1890s, and implemented between 1901 and 1902, was to restrain or even reduce expenditure. But what contribution to this end was going to be made by each individual item in the new package was not made clear, and a considerable amount of fuzzy financial thinking was apparent. It took more than one exchange of letters between the colonial government and the British government before the governor could inadequately explain that the new measures would neither increase nor decrease expenditure. Whatever the Education Ordinances of 1870 and 1875 said, the practice before the Education Ordinance of 1890 was to give the churches aid for their schools in a lump sum to cover payments earned under the system of payment by results. The clerical managers would then pay their teachers whatever they liked. After the Ordinance of 1890 the government set the salaries of teachers in denominational schools and paid three-quarters of this amount. When the restructuring of aid to denominational schools was implemented between 1901 and 1902, the government paid the entire cost of teachers' salaries in denominational schools, but cut back on their grants for building and furniture. School fees were also abolished except for the two Model schools. One advantage of this reorganization was thought to be that it gave a guarantee to denominational school teachers that they would receive their entire salary at the end of the month. The British government agreed to this restructuring. Chamberlain and the British government had to give up in despair their efforts to reduce the cost of education. In fact, new financial responsibilities, such as the teaching of agriculture and the incorporation of the Tobago schools, soon thrust themselves onto the education budget.

What we have been looking at in this section, especially after the mid 1880s, constituted the first financial crisis of the dual system. It was a crisis entirely at the level of the primary schools, since spending on secondary education and teacher training institutions was relatively stable though controversial. The rise in expenditure on primary schools was indeed slowed in the 1890s and, from then onwards to World War II, the government never abandoned its efforts to keep it in check. The financial demands of the dual system became a permanent concern; no way was ever discovered to prevent expenditure from rising. The quarrels over government grants between supporters of government schools and the friends of denominational schools continued, and the arguments used to prosecute this rivalry remained largely unrevised.

The Education of the Indians 1868-1902

There was a double-barrelled population revolution in Trinidad in the second half of the nineteenth century. In 1851, after six years of Indian immigration as workers on the estates, the Indian population was 5.8 percent of the entire population; but by 1871 it was 25 percent, and by 1891 the figure was 35.1 percent of the population. This rapid increase of the Indian population constituted one aspect of the population revolution. The period 1870 to 1900 marked the establishment of an Indian community. They belonged to a non-Christian oriental culture; they were Hindus or Muslims, speaking a variety of Indian languages. They came from a mature, alien, resistant culture; they were culturally different from all other peoples in the colony, and that was the second aspect of the population revolution. By the early 1850s the Roman Catholic and Church of England authorities recognized that the christianizing and educating of this Indian population posed distinct problems. The most outstanding characteristic of the education of Indian children was the extent to which it was a special provision for a special people.

The two most powerful churches, the Roman Catholic Church and the Church of England, did almost nothing for the Indians before 1870. The government's ward schools of the 1860s did not entice more than a handful of Indian children.[100]

There was initially a genuine need to make the education of the Indians a special provision, but existing churches and schools found it difficult to switch all or part of their operations from being general to being particular. The best effort at a special provision by these agencies was the Church of England's Tacarigua Orphans' Home which came about because of a specific subgroup of Indians (namely orphans) and because funds were available from a planter, and special legislation was forthcoming. Over and above this orphanage, the only other school for Indians run by the Church of England was one in Port of Spain under Rev S.L. Richards; also three estate schools in the Naparimas (Lothians, Golconda, and Ne Plus Ultra) were vaguely connected with the Church of England.[101] The colonial government was in an even less advantageous position than these churches in respect to educating the Indians. The ward schools were deliberately organized to separate religious instruction from the teaching of other subjects. Quite apart from financial restraints on the expansion of the ward schools and their inappropriate geographical location in relation to Indian population centres, the ward schools were useless instruments for the christianizing of Indian children.

The education of the Indians between 1868 and 1902 is a fine example of the greater flexibility which new institutions have over existing ones in meeting new and different needs. Nothing is better known in the history of education in Trinidad and Tobago than the fact that the Canadian Presbyterian Mission, founded by Rev John Morton in 1868, dedicated itself to christianizing and educating the Indians. Within two generations, the Mission produced thousands of literate and semi-literate Indian workers, hundreds of Indian primary school teachers and secondary school graduates, scores of Indian catechists, plus a handful of Indian ministers of the gospel. These represented, of course, a very small minority of the Indian population, and not all of those who had benefited educationally became Christian converts. The Canadian Presbyterian Mission, it is well known, was more successful in attracting Muslim and Hindu children to its schools than in converting Muslim and Hindu adults to Christianity.[102] Yet it is not the limitations on the success of the Canadian Presbyterian Mission which are remembered today in Trinidad, but the fact that the missionaries rescued the Indian population from the neglect of the government and the inadequate attention of other churches, and provided the schools which brought literacy in English and improved chances for upward social mobility for many Indians. The record shows an enviable catalogue of 'firsts' for the Mission-trained Indians: first Indians in the lower ranks of the civil service; first Indians in politics both at the municipal level and in the Legislative Council; first Indian professionals, with or without training overseas. The gratitude of the Indians is today still profound.[103] The windfall of succour had come from a totally unexpected corner of the British empire – from the Maritime Provinces of Canada.

Before the advent of the Canadian Presbyterian Mission in 1868 Trinidad had no experience of large-scale Protestant missionary activity among the estate workers and peasants of the type which characterized some British Caribbean territories, such as Jamaica or Antigua, immediately after emancipation. Some of the strategies adopted by the Canadian Presbyterian Mission from 1868 were similar to those employed by the Methodists or Presbyterians in Jamaica a generation earlier. The same missionary enthusiasm to expand as fast as possible, to open new churches and new schools, to recruit local agents and to change the lifestyle of converts, was there in both cases. The vital difference was that whereas the Baptists or Methodists in Jamaica found one subordinate race to be christianized and educated, namely the black or coloured ex-slaves, the Canadian Presbyterian missionaries were faced with two, and chose to concentrate on one only. Rev John Morton personally made the original choice before the actual work began; the choice was not the result of trial and error; the church which he represented already had a mission in India, and all the experience of operations there would be readily available to him in Trinidad. By choosing to concentrate exclusively on the Indians, the missionaries created unique opportunities for themselves, but also placed themselves, unconsciously for the most part, before the bar of opinion on the question of how far their choice aided or hindered racial integration in a multiracial society.

The spread of Mission schools between 1868 and 1902 was characterized by certain interesting features. Although there were estate schools in the early 1860s in the Naparimas, at Lothians, Golconda and Ne Plus Ultra estates, it was the Canadian Presbyterian missionaries who first used the technique of estate schools on a large scale. The method was impossible without the cooperation of estate owners and managers, for their financial contributions were very often indispensable. The substantial financial support of planter patrons, at least until the 1880s, specifically for these schools was on an unprecedented scale for any church in the island.[104] Of no small assistance were the sympathies of nationality and religious creed between Scottish planters and managers, like John Darling, and Canadian missionaries of Scottish extraction. Part of the price of planter assistance, which was given partly from a desire to enhance stability and control over Indian workers, was a complete absence of criticism of the harsh and oppressive conditions of indentured Indian estate workers. Indeed Morton was strongly in support of the indenture system.[105]

Reversing the normal spread of welfare benefits in the colony, the Canadian Presbyterian missionaries expanded their schools from south to north, without neglecting the central areas. Wherever an Indian teacher, a group of Indian children and the funds of a planter patron could be brought together at a distance not too remote from the supervisory attention of a white missionary, there was a proper place for a school. The great majority of estate and village schools before the 1890s were in makeshift buildings of very poor quality. Small groups of Indian children could be found in several places. The ingenious truancy of children and the prolonged lack of interest of most Indian parents, especially about the education of their daughters, limited the size of schools rather than prevented them springing into existence.

A most important factor explaining the steady increase of schools as the number of missionaries grew and the Mission spread out geographically was the full freedom enjoyed to start schools, there being up to 1890 no preconditions set by the government. The fact that no Mission school, apart from one at San Fernando between 1871 and 1875, was aided by government grants, also gave the missionaries freedom to organize at will. The jealous resistance offered by Hindu and Muslim community leaders stopped short of outright violence, but was potentially the most dangerous obstacle to the success of the Mission; and unlike the other types of opposition, it entrenched itself with time. In the face of many difficulties, the Mission made remarkable progress: from one school in 1868, the number grew to 37 in 1889, to 52 in 1892 and to 60 in 1900. If the Mission deserves the credit of being the most rural of all denominational school operators, the other side of the coin was that they provided the best examples of the multiplication of small schools. But this complaint was seldom hurled against the Mission, for their small schools were not in competition with the schools of other churches.

Before the end of the nineteenth century, the Mission had superimposed two superior levels upon the primary schools. First came the theological college in 1892, followed by the training college in 1894, and Naparima College, a boys' secondary school, in about 1900. The origins of the latter are obscure, as it appears to have functioned first as a private school for the sons of missionaries, prominent Indians, and friends of the Mission in San Fernando and its environs. The role of Indian parents should be taken into account. They encouraged a reluctant Morton who had doubts and reservations about the wisdom of founding a secondary school so early. These three institutions, despite the attendance of a few non-Indian students, were designed for Indians, thus enabling the better pupils of the special Indian primary schools to continue their post-primary education in isolation from other races. Within one generation, the Mission developed these superior institutions and such swiftness was unusual by the standards of any church in the British West Indies. To begin training Indians as ministers so soon was really exceptional. The behaviour of the Presbyterian Mission signalled an extraordinary interest in education.

The establishment of three superior educational institutions and some sixty primary schools within thirty years by a Mission which scarcely had at any one time more than a handful of white missionaries raised the question of whether the Mission was not overburdened on the side of schools, and whether or not this was to the detriment of the Mission. It has sometimes been maintained that the Mission was a school system with some churches, rather than a church system with some schools. The founding missionaries clearly intended to build congregational support by the use of the schools; but although the number of pupils was small until 1902, it was always embarrassingly larger than the number of converts. Some doubts have arisen about the sincerity of Indians who accepted the missionary deal of educational opportunities in return for church membership and, as recently suggested by an Indian Presbyterian minister, that the time, energy and money spent on schools might have been better employed on the true purpose of the Mission: to create and preserve a large faithful body of Christian believers. In the opinion of the late Idris Hamid, the educational success was a pyrrhic victory, for the schools virtually destabilized the Mission.[106] Such a view remains without sufficient proof, and the presumption that greater attention to the religious needs of believers would have been rewarded with greater religious success for the Mission ignores the stout resolution of Hindu and Muslim leaders to resist the christianizing drive of the Mission more strongly than its educational efforts. Eventually even the schools themselves were completely opposed.

While the extent of commitment to schools rather than to churches could have been easily adjusted, the decision to concentrate on the Indians was more socially compelling once the first set of special Indian schools had been achieved. It was premature, in the late nineteenth century, to expect black and Indian children to be integrated successfully into the same schools. The language problem alone would have made that outcome doubtful. Even in the few ward schools which had Indian children speaking Hindi, the desired strategy was to employ Indian assistant teachers for these children. This suggests a special group, or special classes, for Indians within these schools. But there were other difficulties: mutual dislike, perhaps more between black and Indian parents than between their children; suspicion of discrimination against Indian children by black teachers; mutual failure to comprehend each others' culture. The concentration of Indians on estates and in certain villages made it easy to fill a small school with Indians only. Whoever brought schools to Caroni would have had classrooms filled mostly or entirely with Indian children. Nevertheless, the records do indicate that more non-Indian children than is usually appreciated were attending special Indian schools. For instance, on thirteen estate schools, started between 1871 and 1874, the Mission had by 1874 a total of 363 pupils, of whom 106 (or 29.2 percent) were non-Indians.[107] In the 1870s blacks and their children were still working on sugar estates.[108] How these biracial estate schools were conducted is a matter on which the records are silent; but it was not the intention of the Mission to continue with biracial schools and in San Fernando, the Mission school had only Indian children. Morton in 1891 agreed with the government stipulation to open the Mission's schools to children of all races, but in practice this rule was of little avail in most schools.[109] A problematic situation existed in which there were enough Indians in residential clusters to make a policy of special Indian schools reasonable and, at the same time, the Indians constituted a sufficiently substantial portion of the total population, one-third by 1891, to make such a policy of special Indian schools of questionable social value for the future.

If the Canadian Presbyterian Mission had not appeared on the scene, and the Roman Catholic Church and the Church of England had slowly expanded their educational efforts until they had a fair number of schools for Indians, there might have arisen a less racial pattern of post-primary schooling for Indians. For instance, the Roman Catholic Church, not being a church devoted exclusively to Indians, might have chosen to bring Indian trainee teachers from southern or central Trinidad to its teacher training facilities in Port of Spain where they would study in the company of black trainees. Or those Indian students who were thought worthy of secondary education might have been admitted to CIC. The point is this: whereas primary schools for Indians had to be sited where the Indians lived in great numbers (and would, therefore, *ipso facto* be Indian dominated schools whichever church was in charge), there was a chance for greater integration of a few Indian students at the post-primary level, had the education of the Indians been undertaken by a church which did not perceive itself as a mission specifically to the Indians. From the point of view of the Canadian Presbyterian Mission, it was perfectly logical to site Naparima College and the theological college in San Fernando and, hence, these institutions would be dominated by Indians whatever their regulations stipulated. If the Mission can be said to have encouraged Indian exclusiveness by having a tripartite range of schools below university level all in areas heavily populated by Indians, thus obviating the need for many Indians to go to schools dominated by non-Indians, this outcome followed from the original choice to be a mission dedicated exclusively to the service of the Indians, and less from any conscious advocacy of separate development of races.

An inquiry into the reasons for that choice takes us over potentially acrimonious ground. The idea undoubtedly originated with Morton himself, and he spent some time between 1868 and 1871 convincing the governor and certain government officials of its validity. As already stated, there was a reasonable residential basis for segregation, and it was culturally easier to conduct schools for one race than for two or more. Moreover, as heathens the Indians were attractive objects for missionary enterprises. Morton made remarks which indicated that there was a racial dimension to his choice; he and probably other Presbyterian missionaries recognized the Indians as Aryans, and hence felt a racial affinity between themselves and Indians who were, as Morton once put it famously, like "Anglo-Saxons toasted in the sun".[110] In their hierarchical images of the two subordinate races, Morton and Rev Grant placed Indians higher than blacks, although their stereotype of the non-Christian Indian was harsh and uncomplimentary: unprincipled, untruthful, degenerate, unfaithful, avaricious worshipper of strange Gods. These demerits did not discourage missionary attention; rather, they rendered the Indian a fit object for Christian redemption. Separate schools were still not ideologically an indispensable adjunct to the presumed racial superiority of Indians over blacks, but institutionally they suited such a theory.

The planter patron support for the special Indian schools raised the suspicion that these schools must have been ideologically satisfying to them. Assuming, however, that estate managers and owners still placed some value on the labour of such blacks as remained available, it is difficult to understand how exclusion of their children from Mission schools would have been in the economic interest of the estates. Possibly it was thought that black children not admitted would find places in neighbouring schools. The planters' approval of special Indian schools could be interpreted as a desire to drive a social wedge between Indians and blacks in the interest of planter hegemony over the divided working classes. While this view cannot be ruled out, it does seem superfluous considering the degree of separation and distrust already existing between blacks and Indians. Any theory of the origin of racial disharmony between Indians and blacks which lays all the blame on the ideological hegemony of the capitalist planters and their white missionary lackeys (for introducing the racist ideas internalized by the Indians and blacks themselves) seems, unrealistically, to exclude the cultural focus of these people and cast them in the role of social robots.[111] The persistence of cultural and racial distance between Indians and blacks should be a warning that sociological and cultural explanations are not to be eschewed in favour of historical materialism. Nor should it be too readily assumed that the colonial government gleefully latched on to the Mission policy of separate Indian schools as a means of dividing and ruling Indians and blacks. The evidence points to hesitation and reservation about this policy on the part of government and top officials between 1869 and 1871. Even after these schools were approved by government, the governors and the Board of Education tended rather to regard them as a temporary phenomenon than as permanent features of the education system. There were signs in the 1890s that the Board of Education would have liked to see a reversal of the policy of separate Indian schools but since these schools had a genuine material and cultural basis, such a reversal was difficult to effect on a large scale at that time.

It is not to be presumed, however, that the same proportion of non-Indian children attended the Mission schools at all times. The two or three estate schools in the Naparimas which existed in the 1860s before the arrival of Morton and both Indian and non-Indian children, presumably blacks.[112] So too did all the estate schools formed by Grant and Morton in the 1870s. A crude reconstruction is that there was a surprising number of non-Indian children in the 1870s, followed by a reduction in the 1880s and 1890s, then by increased numbers in the early twentieth century.[113] This imprecise curve of attendance of non-Indian children in Mission schools corresponded with three relevant phases: first, the enrolment of non-Indian children in Mission schools, especially estate schools, before a policy of exclusion was implemented;[114] then the implementation of exclusion; lastly, in the early twentieth century, some degree of breakdown of Indian residential separation, as well as the non-support by the Board of Education of the policy of special Indian schools, brought an increase in non-Indian pupils. Even in 1916 a Canadian Presbyterian missionary could confess that the minority of black children (creoles) in Caparo Mission School (20 out of a total of 120 pupils) had come there without invitation, and had not been recruited by the missionaries.[115] How much personal inconvenience and suffering was experienced by those black children and their parents who were excluded in the 1880s, or not regarded subsequently as the Canadian missionaries' 'own' children, is one of the unanswerable questions of the Canadian Presbyterian school enterprise. Where exclusion was not deliberate, Indian community pressure and black people's fears of discrimination, worked in the direction of self-exclusion. It is a mistake for Indians today to believe that the only children who suffered discrimination were Indians in schools dominated by Blacks.

The phenomenon of special schools for the Indians has led to complex social consequences. Schools for Indians taught by Indians (or by white Canadian females) using Hindi or some version of it, at least as the instrument to teach English and sometimes as the temporary working language, encouraged racial exclusiveness. But the Indians, with or without these schools, were racially endogamous and culturally resistant; the Canadian Presbyterian Mission did not introduce Indian racial exclusivism. On the other hand, the Mission and its converted Indian assistants constituted a Christian westernizing influence, spreading the use of the English language and Anglo-Saxon social customs and values. It has been alleged that Indians who accepted a measure of 'westernization' made a distinction between it and creole cultural values which they rejected.[116] Even so, the best products of the Mission schools became fitted, especially after further education, to cope with non-white peoples who themselves aspired after Christian Anglo-Saxon values.

The ability of the best educated Presbyterian Indians to enter and compete in the larger society exemplifies the integrative function of the Mission schools. Even a semi-literate Christian Indian might be relied upon to display a greater openness to the culture of other races than a Hindu or Muslim worker who had never gone to a Christian school. An Englishman wishing to hire an Indian gardener might very well prefer a Christian Indian to a Hindu or Muslim, other things being equal. In estimating the strengths of the simultaneously overlapping, but contradictory processes of racial exclusiveness and interracial openness, a possible judgment is that, while there were factors other than the schools making for racial exclusiveness (and the schools might not have been the most important of these factors), the same schools were the principal factors breaking down such exclusiveness through the spread of western cultural values, albeit among a very small sector of the Indian population and, best of all, among the tiny group of extremely successful Indian graduates. More Indians were probably fortified in their racial exclusiveness than those who were prepared culturally to attempt social integration, but if one abstracts the Canadian Presbyterian Mission completely from the scene, the racial exclusiveness of the Indians would be as solidly founded as it was in their presence. Also, without the Mission schools, it seems unrealistic to believe that as many Indians would have been able, through increased use of the existing schools, to enter the larger society as quickly as they did. While there is therefore no simple answer to the question of whether the Canadian Presbyterian Mission schools were more socially disintegrative than integrative, their role as an integrative force was the formative innovation. As an integrative force in the larger society, though, the Mission was necessarily a divisive force among Indians themselves.[117]

The missionaries seemed unaware of any social ill effects arising from their methods of evangelization or their school programme. Such an awareness came from the government. In 1890 the government had stipulated that special Indian schools, unlike other types of schools, did not necessarily have to accept children of other races. The following year, however, the government reversed its decision without explanation, and gave instructions that Mission schools should be open to children of all races. In 1895 the government terminated the free return passage of Indian immigrants. Probably the feeling was growing in the government that the Indians were, after all, in the colony to stay. In 1898, through a committee of the Board of Education, more light was thrown on the thinking of persons close to the government. The committee on which one Presbyterian Indian served, declared in favour of the integration of children, presumably of blacks and Indians, in Missions schools. Such a process, it said, was already on foot in the government schools, and it quoted a figure of 427 Indians in those institutions.[118] The Indians, said the committee, were a permanent part of the population and should not be encouraged to isolate themselves. It included a recommendation that in future only integrated schools (or, more accurately, schools with Indians and non-Indians) should be funded in new districts, unless there was a preponderance of Indian children. So far the flag of social concern waved over the thinking of the committee, but so did considerations of finance. The forty-one special Indian schools educated only 2,891 Indian children, a performance which failed to impress the cost-conscious Board of Education in a period of furious search for educational items to be reduced. Regrettably, it is not known if the Board accepted the committee's recommendation, but the expansion of the special Indian schools substantially closed at the end of the nineteenth century. The Mission seemed to have already reached most of the major clusters of Indians, though without attracting all the children who should be in school.

In a society of immigrants, racially divided and culturally fragmented even before the coming of the Indians, there were always persons who felt that a supreme function of schools was to integrate the population on the basis of the English language and English culture. The challenge of Indian immigration to anglicization made the old conflict between the 'English party' and the French creoles pale in comparison. It was only by abstracting the Indians from the society, by setting them aside mentally as a special people, that anyone could be satisfied with the pace of anglicization among the rest of the population in the later nineteenth century. Any achievement in pulling a tiny minority of educationally successful Indians towards Anglo-Saxon, western culture was a social contribution of worth. Without it, one can postulate that the Indians in 1939 would have been much further behind the rest of the population. Yet the limited social integration was achieved on a model quite different from that of the ward schools which espoused the ideal of schools open to all races.

The black and coloured ex-slaves and their children, as well as the African and West Indian creole migrants in the post-emancipation years, did not challenge the provision of schools for them by the government or the churches. Their community leaders distinguished themselves by the creation of alternative people's churches, not alternative people's schools. Not so with the Indian community. When the Canadian Presbyterian missionaries set themselves up as self-appointed benefactors, as near monopolizers of Indian education, some Hindu and Muslim priests, teachers and caste leaders offered passive resistance to their Mission rivals. Occasionally there was the threat of violence or intimidation of the missionaries, coming obviously from displaced Indian leaders who had erected their own places of worship and even, it was said, some small schools, unrecognized by the government.[119] This feeble, usually unobtrusive level of protest matured into open revolt in the late 1920s coinciding with an internal rebellion of some Indian Mission teachers, catechists and ministers against racial discrimination in the church. These expressions of dissatisfaction could only compound the problems of the white Canadian missionaries.

The Training of Teachers 1836-1902

Between emancipation and the end of the nineteenth century there was only one short period of six years (1845-1851) during which the island was entirely without a teacher training institution. This interlude occurred between the collapse of the Mico Charity training school in Port of Spain and the inauguration of the first government teacher training institution 1852 on Woodbrook estate near Port of Spain. From that point to the present, the government has always had at least one government teacher training institution and, indeed, from 1851 the government quietly claimed the right to a position of ascendancy in the field of teacher training, though not preferring a monopoly of teacher training institutions. The commencement of a dual system in 1870, and the numerical superiority of denominational schools from the 1890s did not diminish the government's resolve to be at the very centre of teacher training. When a nationalist government came to power in

1956, the training of teachers was the first area of education in which it publicly declared its intention to brook no effective competition from the churches, and it was this area in which the government most clearly succeeded in denying the churches a role in education.

As part of the provision for the education of ex-slaves immediately after emancipation, the British government helped to fund a Mico Charity training school in Port of Spain from 1836 to 1845. The same strategy was pursued in Jamaica and Antigua, and the managers of the Mico Charity in the West Indies took a regional view of their teacher training enterprise. A few teachers from other islands were brought to Jamaica, Antigua and Trinidad for training, and when the training schools in Trinidad and Jamaica were closed for lack of funds, the one in Antigua retained a regional dimension. The expertise of the Mico Charity as teacher trainers from the metropole, knowledgeable about the latest methods of infant teaching and school organization, was recognized in Trinidad in the immediate post-emancipation period; but they were not exclusively trainers of teachers.[120] The major part of their funds and energies went into the organization of their own primary schools, an activity which provided a base for their teacher training efforts, but which brought them into grievous competition with the churches, especially the Roman Catholic Church and the Church of England. Ideally the Mico Charity training school, which was coeducational, was meant to train teachers, whatever their religious affiliation, on a system which was Protestant but nondenominational in the sense that specific denominational creeds were excluded. Having identified the Mico Charity as a Protestant semi-governmental organization, Roman Catholic Church leaders became noncooperative; so too even the Bishop of the Church of England, though with him it was the failure to have control of the Charity which rankled and not its very existence.[121] The Mico Charity was the first to stand in the way of the basic desire of all the churches to have their own teacher training institution, even if they could not afford it. Opposition from the Church of England, and moreso from the Roman Catholic Church, limited the usefulness of the Mico Charity training school.

There were other difficulties, mostly related to the scarcity of suitable recruits and to the fact that everything had to start from scratch. After nine years it is doubtful if the Mico Charity training school trained more than twenty to twenty-five teachers, not all of whom stayed in teaching. The course varied from a few weeks up to two years, and there was no final examination. Teacher trainees left when their clerical sponsors wanted them, or when Thomas Bilby, the Mico Charity superintendent, felt they were ready. At the time when the Mico Charity training school was established, teacher training in England was in its infancy. The Mico Charity training school never engaged in the training of child monitors as teachers (pupil teachers), but rather adult teachers though some were still young people. It paid attention to professional training, but the general education of most trainees was too limited to be an adequate base upon which to build professional expertise, and there is no reason to believe that in those days the Mico graduate was generally an efficient teacher. He or she, however, was the best trained creole teacher in the schools from the 1830s to the early 1850s.

In analysing the training of teachers a distinction can usefully be made between their general education and their professional training. In fact, the curriculum dilemma of teacher training colleges from 1834 to the 1980s has always been to find the right balance between the competing demands of these two legitimate objectives. It is not possible to build an adequate professional training on top of a poor general education. Throughout the nineteenth century primary school teachers did not have secondary education; only a handful with it appeared in the 1890s. For the most part, the primary school education of teachers needed strengthening, and hence all efforts at teacher training in the nineteenth century, whether by informal in-service methods or in specialized pre-service institutions, were bedeviled by the temptation to concentrate on general education to the detriment of professional training. In the 1830s and 1840s the dominant pattern of teacher achievement was for very poor general education to coexist with no professional training at all, or with poor informal in-service training provided by clerics outside specialist institutions. Although the Roman Catholic Church and the Church of England were the major providers of denominational schools, they had no teacher training institutions. In fact, no church had such an institution before the 1890s. Those teachers who went to the Mico Charity training school eventually combined an inadequate professional training with a poor general education.

Two abnormal patterns in teacher training can be discerned in the immediate post-emancipation period. There was a handful of white expatriate teachers, mostly employed by the Mico Charity, whose general education was either at a superior primary school level or at a secondary school level (but without classical learning), and some of them combined this level of general education with adequate professional training. But there were also junior Mico Charity white expatriate teachers with relatively little professional training before arrival in the island who continued their education in the Mico Charity training school. In a class by himself was Thomas Bilby, the Mico Charity superintendent who was an expert. The core of white expatriate teachers attached to the Mico Charity was probably never more than eight at any one time, leaving aside nonteaching wives or husbands. Another pattern – and this was the second abnormal pattern – found only occasionally, occurred when a priest or clergyman who had high, sometimes university level general education, temporarily took to teaching schools. In this case the pattern was that of very adequately educated persons having inadequate professional training. It is a common error to believe that all clerics were by nature or theological training experienced teachers of primary schools. It was their superior social status as white professionals which led people to think that they required no further training.

The island was without any teacher training institution for six years (1845-1851). In 1845 there had been about fifty-three denominational primary day schools employing what was then the predominant pattern of one teacher for each school. If we assume that already 20 percent of these schools had teachers with some sort of training, the task of training the rest in a slowly expanding education system could be accomplished in a few years by one institution. There was at this time no insistence by the churches that their teachers must be trained by themselves, or in fact even be trained. The government, when it established its ward schools from 1849, decided to start its own training school; and this came into existence in 1852 under a qualified English expatriate teacher. A site on Woodbrook estate was chosen and a practising school, called the Boys' Model School, was associated with it from the start. The training school was a nonresidential institution for males only. Four years later, 1856, a trained female expatriate teacher, Mrs Alcock, was brought down from England to start a Girls' Model School in a different part of Port of Spain, which was meant to be the base for training female teachers. But officially the only teacher training school was the Woodbrook school for males.

The government training school produced teachers only for the government schools; as we have already argued, these ward schools did not expand rapidly between 1849 and 1869, and this meant that only a few new teachers were needed. The government training school never had more than fourteen students at any one time, and often it had fewer. More often than not it had more 'graduates' than there were vacancies in the ward schools.[122] The Woodbrook establishment had no fixed length of study and no final examination; one estimate by its second principal, Mr Sugars, was that the average stay was five months. John Dixon, the first principal, had enough applicants in 1852 to select a group with some ability; but soon afterwards, under Sugars, the standard of admission fell, and the social background of the students worried even Inspector Anderson.[123] Sugars, a hard drinker, neglected both the Boys' Model School and the teacher trainees; he was dismissed in 1861, and the school taken over by one of its former students, Louis Tronchin.

A few graduates of the Woodbrook training school became teachers of above average ability. Tronchin was solid; Samuel Proctor who taught at the San Fernando Borough Council School for twenty years was good; and J.J. Thomas achieved recognition. But these men taught themselves many things after leaving Woodbrook; and they belonged to the earlier group of students. Later groups of students often included older persons who had already unsuccessfully tried other occupations and did not have the general education to support professional training. At any rate the curriculum of the Woodbrook training school, though it included the theory of teaching and teaching practice, did not assign any special place to professional training; the employment of the trainees in the Boys' Model School was a form of cheap labour for a large, above average primary school. The trainees taught the boys for more hours than they (the trainees) were taught by the principal. Under the guise of teaching practice the Model school was provided with six or seven trainee teachers and one experienced principal. It was the sort of concentration of teaching power which only one other school – the Girls' Model School – possessed.

No other teacher was as lauded as Susan Alcock, the principal of the Girls' Model School; she remained on the job for nearly forty years, and her school was acclaimed the best primary school in the 1860s and 1870s. But Alcock's school trained very few female teachers, there being until the 1870s scarcely any posts for female teachers in the ward schools. Alcock presided over a Model school without a training school as such; Dixon (1852-1853), Sugars (1853-1861), and Tronchin (1861-c.1878) were in charge of the male teacher training school which was overshadowed by its own model school. It is of the highest importance to realize that the two model schools attracted more attention and won more praise than the teacher training schools which they allegedly existed to serve.[124] Sugars developed a "science class" at the Boys' Model School; the school found itself under strong social pressure from middle class parents in Port of Spain to give a superior type of primary school education, so too the Girls' Model School; the two schools were attended mostly by black and coloured middle class children, with a sprinkling of whites as well. Some of the prestige of these schools rubbed off thinly on the trainee teachers.

In the seventeen years between 1852 and 1869 the government training school at Woodbrook could not have produced more than fifty male teachers, and the Girls' Model School possibly as few as six female teachers. There was in fact an oversupply of trained male teachers since only the ward schools could employ them; the denominational schools, without government grants, resorted to cheaper untrained teachers, in some cases females. Of course the teachers who had been trained at Woodbrook were mostly unsatisfactory. Inspector Anderson realized that their stay there was too short, but he usually praised the trainees once they became ward school teachers. Anderson was sympathetic to the difficulties they faced on the job, and he did not really expect the education of the working class to make rapid strides. To him dedication and discipline, plus a little teaching ability were more important than academic soundness. If the teachers were inadequately prepared they were still good enough for the ward schools. Keenan, the expert from abroad, on investigating the education system in 1869, was horrified by what he saw at Woodbrook: a handful of pretentious adult dropouts from other jobs, with weak general education, aspiring to become teachers in a hurry.[125] No religious instruction was given at the school, as was the policy and this would have made it an inappropriate training institution to a deeply Roman Catholic advisor such as Keenan. He recommended strongly that the training school be closed.

As emphasized earlier, the inauguration of the dual system in 1870 was a major turning point in the history of education in Trinidad. In the last thirty years of the nineteenth century the entire system of education became more organized and more formalized than at any time previously. The dual system established specific criteria for government assistance; the system of payment by results demanded frequent examinations, not just inspections. In the area of teacher training, major changes accompanied the commencement of the dual system. Governor Gordon took some of Keenan's advice and rejected others; the government training school was not abolished,[126] but it was removed from the centre of the government's teacher training programme.

Any student of the history of education in Trinidad and Tobago might well be wondering by now why the famous or infamous pupil teacher system has not yet been mentioned. The origin of pupil teachers goes back to the earliest post-emancipation schools; at that time the more popular nomenclature was monitor. A monitor was a senior pupil, officially unpaid, who assisted the teacher usually with the junior children. In return, teachers were supposed to give them some extra tuition; in time some monitors became teachers and might even get to a training school. Before 1870, however, monitors were not officially recognized by the government, even in the ward schools; this is what Keenan meant when he said that monitors were conspicuous by their absence in government and denominational schools. There was no systematic programme for their training or induction into the teaching force. Keenan astonished everybody by proposing that these lowly young servitors of the education system be converted into the building blocks of the trained teaching service, without the benefit of a training school.[127] His theory was that every good primary school could train a few monitors by an organized course of instruction over a five-year apprenticeship period, from age twelve to age seventeen. The urban school with superior headteachers would be ideal; such headteachers might even with justification, be given a bonus for training monitors, who were eventually employed as teachers. In addition Keenan recommended introducing the Teachers' Certificate to be obtained by examination which monitors, or indeed any young person of good character, should be allowed to sit. Neither the training of monitors nor the setting of a certificate examination, thought Keenan, required a specialist training institution.

Keenan was right and he was wrong; he was wrong to recommend the abolition of a specialist teacher training school. The tide of opinion in the metropole had turned in favour of such specialist institutions.[128] If the training institution in Trinidad had been under the control of a church, Keenan probably would not have recommended its closure, but he was fundamentally opposed to government schools of all types. Keenan was right most of all in perceiving that the training of teachers required a recognized standard formalized through examination, something which it never had previously. He was also right in recognizing the monitors as the natural reservoirs of talent from which teachers should be drawn; and he was the first to suggest a possible involvement of secondary schools in teacher preparation. Keenan suggested that for a small bonus QRC and CIC might prepare some of their students to sit the Teachers' Certificate Examination. The social composition of the QRC and CIC student population does not suggest that this was feasible in 1869, but Keenan's idea took him to the outskirts of the bursar system of teacher training which developed in the 1920s.

Governor Gordon decided not only to institute a Teachers' Certificate Examination, but to oblige all teachers, even those who had already gone through Woodbrook, to take this examination and secure certificates as the indispensable requirement for appointment as a qualified teacher.[129] This Teachers' Certificate Examination, set and marked locally, immediately became the centre of the government's teacher training programme. It enabled a much larger number of persons to qualify as teachers; at once more persons applied to take it than could be accommodated in the government training school; by the end of the century nearly ninety candidates could be relied upon each year to sit this examination. At the same time the government training school underwent no significant expansion in the last thirty years of the nineteenth century; in 1902 it was still catering for fewer than twenty students.

Of course the Teachers' Certificate Examination could be taken by the students at the government training school, and in fact they could be relied upon to pass it. But it was not necessary to attend the school to take this examination. At that time, the government training school did not have its own diploma examination. Had the government school been reorganized to offer highly professional skills not available elsewhere, it would have secured the premier place in the training system; but teachers who had never attended it felt no sense of loss. The clear distinction which was made from the 1920s between a certified but untrained teacher and a trained certified teacher did not exist in the later nineteenth century. One of the three most important developments at the government training school in the last thirty years of the nineteenth century was its relocation to the Tranquillity Estate, which had space for the Boys' Model School and the Girls' Model School. The latter became a fully fledged teacher training school for females, but under a female principal independent of the principal of the male training school. The second major development was the conversion of the government training school at Tranquillity into a partially residential school, the boarders being mostly monitors from the rural districts.[130] Thirdly, the government training school began to draw its recruits primarily from senior monitors, whose nomenclature in the system changed to 'pupil teachers'.

The link between the government training school and the pupil teachers was dependent upon their systematic preparation in selected primary schools. Rules for the examination and pay of pupil teachers first appeared in the Code of 1876; these became quite elaborate in the Code of 1890. Ideally a pupil teacher should start at the age of fourteen, after passing Standard IV of the primary school syllabus; in the following four years there were graded annual examinations to be passed in reading, writing, arithmetic and grammar, each success bringing a minuscule increase in allowance. Failure to pass an examination – there were no examinations in practice teaching – after two attempts resulted in dismissal. After the fourth year, at about age eighteen, the pupil teacher graduated into the lowest rank – class IV – of the teaching service. To proceed further he or she now had to pass the Teachers' Certificate Examination outside or inside the government training school. The inspector of schools favoured admitting rural pupil teachers into the government training school because they were said to be the only ones willing to teach in the rural areas.

One of the criticisms usually made against the pupil teacher system was that a girl or boy of fourteen years hardly knew whether she or he wished to undertake teaching as a career. But for a poor boy or girl who had failed to get a College Exhibition, and had no means of getting to a secondary school, this systematization of pupil teacher examination was a precious ladder to be slowly climbed. It was eagerly seized upon by ambitious parents as a means of keeping studious children in school, getting free extra lessons from headteachers; within a generation the number of pupil teachers grew from a handful to four hundred at the end of the century. By the 1890s pupil teachers constituted 50 percent of the total teaching force in primary schools. This situation reflected not only the expansion of the number of schools, but the mutual popularity of the pupil teacher system to parents and the government. Its cheapness was no inconsiderable attraction to the government.

For the average youth the road from a humble pupil teacher to a first class teacher was long, and strewn with many examinations. Teachers could be summoned by the inspector of schools to take examinations against their will. Perhaps no other "professional" had to take as many examinations, or to suffer as frequent relocations, as the teacher who came up the ranks through the pupil teacher system. A substantial number of the pupil teachers, usually over 70 percent did pass the pupil teachers' examinations each year; but when they got to the Teachers' Certificate Examination the road was blocked by the relatively low rate of passes, seldom over 40 percent, for even the aspirant to a third class certificate. Having passed the third class certificate the teacher had to serve one or two years probation as an assistant teacher, and then attempt the second class certificate. If successful, another period of probation followed, but a first class certificate examination was mercifully waived; in lieu, it required seven years of satisfactory service after obtaining a second class certificate. Some teachers spent fifteen years studying and waiting to reach the top. But life as a first class headteacher was not a financial bed of roses: a maximum of £100 ($480) was the lot of a very senior male class I teacher; and females received less.

Yet there was no shortage of candidates for training as teachers in the last thirty years of the nineteenth century. Competition for jobs was quite keen. Although the number of schools in the dual system increased significantly, especially after 1890, the available posts as assistant teachers and headteachers lagged behind the number of applicants. Temporary reduction of the demand for headteachers in 1881 forced graduates of the government training school to remain a third year in training, or to become assistant teachers. It was not unusual for a teacher, after qualifying for a higher post, to wait years to be placed; thus a few persons who qualified as assistant teachers could be found any year working as senior pupil teachers. The teaching service was then, as always, riddled with grievances, but clerical managers, the inspector of schools and the Board of Education kept teachers strictly under control.

It remains to mention the advent of denominational training schools in the 1890s. The government got itself into a tangle over these schools. The adjustment of the dual system in 1890 allowed for denominational training institutions to be aided by the government. Having passed this law, however, the government then tried, inconsistently and unsuccessfully, to prevent such establishments, in the hope that the Roman Catholic Church and the Church of England would patronize the government training school or, at most, erect only denominational hostels for their own students. The Roman Catholic Church started two residential teacher training schools in Port of Spain (the Roman Catholic Female Training School and the Roman Catholic Male Training School), and the Canadian Presbyterian Mission commenced Naparima Training College, also residential, in 1894.[131] The Church of England chose the option of using the government training school in combination with its own hostel. The ideal of teacher trainees residing within their training institutions was highly cherished by the churches. The Roman Catholic and Presbyterian training schools each had fewer students than the government training school, which itself had fewer than twenty students. Hence three small training schools existed where one would have sufficed.

The training of Indian teachers was undertaken almost exclusively by the Canadian Presbyterian Mission starting with a thoughtful in-service programme in the 1870s and 1880s run by the missionaries themselves, and then graduating to a training school. The first Indian teacher was Charles Soodeen who, having arrived as an illiterate twelve-year-old boy in 1861, served out his indentureship by 1870 and joined the Presbyterian education team about the same year.[132] Soodeen was recognized to be good material and was trained. In the 1870s and 1880s the in-service programme teachers, who were often catechists as well, were brought in on Saturdays from outlying areas to a central point for instruction; in 1885 and 1886 a single missionary, Rev J.W. MacLeod, was allocated the sole task of training these teachers. In 1871 Inspector Guppy recorded that a few Indians were taken to the government training school but, unfortunately, he gave no further information about their fate. Indians intending to teach in special Indian schools had to know Hindi, and by 1902 the Teachers' Certificate Examination had a compulsory Hindi paper for these students. Anticipating that Indian teacher trainees would perform less well than non-Indians in the Teachers' Certificate Examination, the government created for them a special fifth class certificate.

It is clear that towards the end of the nineteenth century most of the teachers without certificates had been weeded out, except for the large phalanx of pupil teachers. However, the class of certificates held reflected a less satisfactory situation: 68 percent of all headteachers had only third or fourth class certificates; 85 percent of the assistant teachers had third class certificates or lower qualifications.[133] The theory or practice of teaching had not been given any special place in the training of these teachers in or outside the training schools. The general education of the teachers had benefited more than their teaching skills.

Education and Social Mobility 1834-1902

Before emancipation the core of the middle class consisted of scores of wealthy and respectable free coloureds whose economic base was in the ownership of plantations, urban houses and, to a lesser extent, merchant businesses. Although most of these coloured families were of French extraction, some had English or Spanish blood. Their status as a middle class had not come about as a result of personal achievement in education but from their participation in the development of the plantation system.[134] Indeed, before 1838 no social group owed its standing to its education: race and wealth were the predominant determinants of class.

While these factors continued to be significant after emancipation, a new element of incalculable importance entered the scene. The establishment of schools for the masses, however inadequately, brought into existence a new mechanism of upward social mobility, mostly within existing class lines, but potentially across class lines as well. Even if nothing but inefficient primary school had been started after 1838, such schools constituted a base from which a few ambitious blacks and coloureds, by private study, would have advanced socially. In fact primary school teaching became such a new upwardly mobile career even before training for teachers became general. These poorly educated black and coloured teachers of the 1830s and 1840s were the vanguard of a new middle class who, unlike the pre-emancipation free coloureds and their descendants, owed their social position to personal achievement in education. They were self-made people.

For black and coloured children of the ex-slaves the road out of the cane fields and the domestic servants' quarters passed through the primary schoolhouse. Those who had access to land for small farming, or those who became skilled craftsmen in the towns had indeed found ways of improving their economic base and their social standing. But for every black or coloured who could become a successful farmer or a comfortable artisan there were a thousand who had no land or capital or any great desire to exchange forced manual labour for paid manual labour. As Bridget Brereton has argued, white-collar occupations became the hallmark of the black and coloured middle class of the later nineteenth century.[135]

To achieve these occupations the children of the ex-slaves had to go beyond primary schooling to post-primary education locally or abroad. For this reason, any discussion of upward mobility though education has to be a discussion of post-primary schools and colleges; in other words, essentially of secondary and university education.

It took time, naturally, for some descendants of the ex-slaves to become the beneficiaries, even to a limited extent, of such secondary level education and opportunities as existed on the island. For at least the first thirty years after emancipation it was the children of the older French free coloured families, and of course the whites, and not the children of the ex-slaves, who were able to capitalize on the two or three institutions of secondary education. The black and coloured children of the ex-slaves, in the denominational or government primary schools of the 1830s to 1860s, were still just proving that they could be educated. Significant also was the fact that in the first thirty years after emancipation it was the descendants of the free coloured families, not the descendants of the ex-slaves, who provided the few spokesmen for the non-white middle class interest. Not until the later nineteenth century did a few black and coloured descendants of the ex-slaves receive enough education to achieve middle class status, thus enabling them to begin taking leadership roles. When this happened it significantly changed the character of public opinion.

It is not without reason that a liberal press (for example *New Era* or *San Fernando Gazette*) edited by coloureds arose in the later nineteenth century and not in the 1830s; nor is it without reason that black and even coloured promoters of black race consciousness were more in evidence from the 1860s than in the 1840s.[136] It took some time for discerning people to realize that although the economy and politics of the colony were still controlled by whites, the social contours of the society were changing under the impact of black and coloured teachers, medical practitioners, lawyers, solicitors, surveyors, pharmacists, journalists, minor civil servants and clerks. A new non-white middle class was insistent that it should be seen and heard.

The first schools after emancipation to offer education above the primary school level to ex-slaves or their children were the teacher training schools: first, the Mico Charity training school established in 1836 but closed soon after, and, more particularly, the government training school at Woodbrook. Associated with the training of teachers were two practising schools, the Boys' Model School and the Girls' Model School. These latter institutions, later removed and renamed Tranquillity Boys' School and Tranquillity Girls' School, stood at the centre of the primary school system for nearly a century, and their importance cannot be overstated. Because they were the practising schools they were allowed to set themselves a more advanced curriculum than the ordinary primary schools; this was more true of the Boys' Model School than the Girls' Model School. The Girls' Model School always had a white expatriate headmistress, and the Boys' Model

School had two successive white expatriate principals (1852-1861), before reputable coloured principals took over. Under pressure from the middle class of Port of Spain for cheap secondary education these schools became very superior primary schools, as yet not quite 'intermediate' schools, in the nineteenth century; in the highest forms students could be asked to do work similar to that in the lower forms of St Joseph's Convent or St George's College, without the classics.

The Boys' Model School and the Girls' Model School even attracted a few white children who sat in the same classes with blacks and coloureds whose parents were capable of paying the fee of one dollar per week. Within ten years of its establishment the Boys' Model School could boast that some of its former pupils had become planters, managers, estate overseers and clerks, and others had gone overseas for university education.[137] We can be quite certain that it was white or coloured students rather than black students who had embarked on these careers. About twenty-five years after its foundation Louis Tronchin, its first non-white principal, on the occasion of his retirement, proudly proclaimed the school to be one of the most important educational institutions in the West Indies.[138] No such importance or achievement was credited to the Girls' Model School, one obvious reason being that women were expected to be only good wives and mothers. The Model schools, however, offered some black and coloured children, boys more than girls, the chance to improve their social status through an education superior to that of the ordinary primary schools. To a lesser extent, the schools of the Port of Spain Borough Council, and the San Fernando Borough Councils also provided a better base for social advance than the rural primary schools.[139] The same point can be made about a handful of above average Port of Spain primary schools run by the Roman Catholic Church, the Church of England and the Methodist Church.

Although, ironically, the model schools overshadowed the training schools whose students helped to teach them, the government training school for men was not to be underrated as a lever of upward social mobility, most obviously within the non-white community. The fact that Keenan scoffed at it does not mean that this institution was without social merit. Significantly, Keenan observed that the teacher trainees were pretentious, reflecting perhaps their appreciation of their own worth in the teaching hierarchy.[140] It was not a good teacher training school, but it was all the island had between the 1850s and the 1880s. Its graduates established themselves as headteachers of many primary schools; they were the best examples of successful products of the primary school system for black and coloured working class people to emulate. They were self-made men on meagre salaries. Their efficiency as teachers might be doubtful in several instances, but they held key positions among the descendants of the slaves in rural communities. To these persons teaching offered an improved lifestyle compared to the option of hard manual labour which was the usual fate of others of their own social origin.

Unlike the early decades of the twentieth century no one thought seriously that secondary education was necessary for primary school teachers, hence the nineteenth century graduates of the government training school were without the prestige which flowed magically from attendance at St Joseph's Convent, or later CIC or QRC. It must be distinctly understood that graduates of secondary schools up to the 1870s belonged, by birth or association, to a different class from the primary school teachers, trained or untrained. So enormous was the prestige of secondary education to which the children of the ex-slaves had no access before the last quarter of the nineteenth century that no secondary school graduate would condescend to teach in a primary school unless forced by dire necessity. Something like this began to happen in 1880 when two or three College Exhibitioners, having spent three years at QRC, resorted to teaching in primary schools. Presumably these boys had not done well at the college.

Perhaps the best known black school teacher, scholar and man of letters in nineteenth century Trinidad was J.J. Thomas, author of *Creole Grammar* and *Froudacity*. Thomas is today best remembered for his study of the French derived Creole, spoken by the Trinidad masses, and for his race consciousness and race pride as a black man. He was talented and his intellectual achievements were exceptional. However, here we are concerned with how the son, possibly of an ex-slave, could rise to middle class status through education. Born about 1840, Thomas went to an ordinary primary school, then on to the government training school where he distinguished himself, and then to various teaching posts. Thomas also gained distinction by self-education, for he gave himself more than a secondary education without having gone to a college or a university. Several other teachers took to private study, though with less conspicuous results. Thomas became secretary to the Board of Education and the College Council, and after the retirement of Inspector Anderson in 1869 he was thought of by some blacks and coloureds as a worthy successor to Anderson.[141] The point is that black and coloured teachers, especially the headteachers, were among the most ambitious and enterprising of the descendants of slaves. Their business was education, and the acquisition of European culture through reading and study. Real promotion for these men meant leaving the teaching service, possibly for a job in the junior ranks of the civil service, which was the white-collar job to which literate and ambitious black and coloured men aspired. A civil service job was the first major turning point in the life of J.J. Thomas.

Thomas was born too early for the Queen's Collegiate School which opened in 1859. But even if he was not too old he would not have been able to afford the fees. As shown previously, the advent of this college, later to become the famous QRC, marked a new chapter in the history of education in Trinidad. In 1863 the Roman Catholic Church leaders started CIC, thus inaugurating years of rivalry, not altogether sterile, between CIC and QRC. These two colleges were not racially exclusive, but they were attended mostly by the white upper class boys, French or English, and by the sons of the older and respectable coloured families. Because apartheid did not exist in the colony, it proved impossible, in the long run, to keep out black children, however undesirable an addition to the secondary school population they were thought to be by illiberal white and coloured people.[142]

With the advent of the Queen's Collegiate School in 1859 the range of schools supported by public funds was brought in line with the social assumptions of a class and colour conscious community. The denominational schools unassisted by government and the ward schools were intended for the labouring class who were to remain labourers. Most of them were black; some coloureds. The Borough Council schools in San Fernando and Port of Spain, and the Model schools, were expected to be above the standard of the ward schools and rural denominational schools because they provided partly for the middle class, largely coloureds, but with some blacks and some whites. There is evidence of social class tension in the above average urban schools, because of the greater range of class and colour among the pupils. In the Port of Spain Borough Council School in 1857 there were the boys who wore shoes and the boys who did not. There were early difficulties at the Boys' Model School in 1852 which led to suggestions that the students should be separated along class lines, but this was apparently not done although some boys left the school in 1859 to attend Queen's Collegiate School. Queen's Collegiate School maintained the distinctions which appeared threatened at the Boys' Model School. It prevented the "toe of the peasant coming too near the heel of the courtier as to gall his kibe".[143] The Queen's Collegiate School gave a classical education to the upper and upper middle class boys, and nothing the Boys' Model School offered could compare with the glory of an education along the lines of an English grammar school.

The resistance to the education of non-whites by the whites mainly took the form of not wanting education to be a lever of upward social mobility. Inspector Anderson explicitly denied any intention to promote pupils above their "station in life";[144] he defined the purpose of the ward schools as giving the common people an education in the elements of learning to make them "industrious, contented and happy".[145] The Roman Catholic Archbishop of Port of Spain, in his Lenten pastoral letter of 1883, unequivocally expounded the doctrine that the class structure of the colony was God-given, and that the aspirations of lower class children in primary schools for social mobility was unchristian.[146] However, at least there were no sustained attempts in the nineteenth century to turn the schools into instruments to habituate children to the routine of agricultural toil under the euphemism, as in Jamaica, of industrial education. There were not more than three estate schools before the Indians arrived. The presence of Indian immigrant labourers rendered it unnecessary for the planter class to attempt to control the curriculum in the interest of the preservation of the plantation labour force.

Colour and class played some part in the reaction of the ex-slaves and their children to educational opportunities. Black and Indian estate workers gave the ward and denominational schools least support; Inspector Anderson estimated that most of the pupils in the rural ward schools were children of peasant farmers.[147] But the social demography of the colony was also a factor because in rural areas where the population was scattered, and peasant farmers lived near subsistence level, free from the competitive pressures of towns, ports or productive estates, attendance at school was very poor. Of course the middle class coloureds and whites in Port of Spain and San Fernando ensured that attendance at schools in these towns, especially the model schools was unsurpassed in the colony. Schools had more meaning for aspiring urban parents and children. This was well illustrated by the new opportunities in the later nineteenth century in secondary education which was an urban phenomenon.

The single most important mechanism for the penetration of QRC and CIC by black and coloured boys was the system of scholarships called the College Exhibition which started in 1872. The College Exhibition (the coveted forerunner of the nerve-racking Common Entrance Examination of today) took only a handful of bright boys, about four per annum, first to QRC and then to CIC as well.[148] This was a development of the greatest social importance because it was not long before a few of these boys began winning the university scholarships (Island Scholarships) which took winners abroad to study for professional careers, usually in law or medicine. The idea of bright black and coloured boys from the primary schools moving on to secondary schools through assistance from the government appears to have been at the back of the mind of Governor Lord Harris in the early 1850s. However when the Queen's Collegiate School was opened in 1859, the governors up to 1871 only nominated to free places the sons of deceased senior civil servants and clergymen of the Church of England. All these boys were white and did not have to face a competitive examination for entry.

The idea of free places for bright boys was revived by Governor Gordon as part of the reorganization of QRC to which CIC was affiliated. The number mentioned was two per year but, by the following year, when Governor Longden moved to implement the idea, the figure had climbed surprisingly to six per annum, provided that no more than twenty-four such exhibitioners were at any time in the college (QRC). To allow six exhibitioners per year in 1872 was perhaps not ungenerous to start the programme but, unfortunately, it never worked in this manner. The original quota was soon seen to be dangerously high for by 1875 the limit of twenty-four exhibitioners would be reached; at that point the college exhibitioners would have been about 40 percent of QRC's enrolment. Governor Irvine, Inspector Guppy and the Board of Education reduced the number to three per annum, raised the standard and lowered the age limit.[149] In other words, winning was made more difficult. By 1878 a pattern of winners which was to last a long time was emerging. The leading schools which won were in Port of Spain, and the winners were mostly black or coloured boys, not Indians, especially from the fee-paying, extraordinarily well staffed Boys' Model School (see Table 1.3). The parents of boys from the Boys' Model School and from St Thomas Roman Catholic School might have been mostly lower middle class; but this did not mean that they, much less the lower class parents of the later winners from rural primary schools, were financially able to clothe or feed their sons at QRC.

Between 1872 and 1903 there were four university scholarships to be won annually. These glittering awards, the 'educational blue ribbon of the island',[150] taking winners overseas to an English university were based on the Cambridge School Certificate examinations. Most of the winners studied law or medicine (see Table 1.4). All the Island Scholars prior to 1872 were white youths. It would obviously be a social innovation of consequence if non-white students in QRC started winning these university scholarships; and the College Exhibitioners, the 'free place boys' were the ones most likely to threaten the hold of white boys on these scholarships. The principal of QRC, William Miles (1872-1894) took a prejudiced view of 'free place boys'; he felt that they lowered the tone of the college.

Miles and the white supporters of QRC were indeed faced with a difficult situation; since QRC's enrolment was small, the advent of even a handful of black and coloured 'free place boys' threatened to change the composition of the student body. Miles allegedly chose to make progress difficult for these exhibitioners.[151] There were reports that bright boys did not advance beyond Form III (Junior Cambridge examination form), and that it was difficult for them to get into Miles' own class which was the only one from which the university scholarships could be attempted. Discrimination probably contributed to low performance by some exhibitioners. Nevertheless, the historic and all-important link between College Exhibitioners and university scholarship winners began while Miles was at the college. By the 1880s about four exhibitioners, including Stephen Laurence (coloured, 1883), and C. P. David (black, 1885) had won university scholarships.[152] Among the winners in the 1890s was Arthur McShine, a black boy who went to QRC by way of an Exhibition from the Eastern Government School in Port of Spain. Such achievements encouraged J.H. Collens, principal of the government training school and of Tranquillity Boys's School, to gloat that:

> the advantages offered to boys by our educational system are hardly surpassed in the world . . . It may indeed be said that the highest positions in the British empire to which mental acquirements are a passport are open to the poorest boy in Trinidad by the educational advantage at his command.[153]

In 1890 the College Exhibitions were discontinued when, in the heated religious discussions surrounding the Education Ordinance of 1890, the provisions supporting them were omitted. From this point of view, the death of the Exhibitions seemed more accidental than premeditated; however, the discussions about their resurrection suggest that perhaps murder had been silently committed.[154] They revealed that apart from Miles there were other important enemies of the Exhibitions (for example, the French creole legislators, Eugene Lange and John Bell-Smythe). A motion in the Legislative Council in January 1893 to block funds ($720) for the College Exhibitions was defeated, but it elicited this response from the French creole editor of the *Port of Spain Gazette*:

... to make the upper and middle classes pay for the higher education of the children of the poorer class is to make them pay three times for education – first for the higher education of their own children, secondly for the elementary education of the children of the poor, and thirdly for the higher education also of the poor,

The social disadvantage it would have would be to artificially foster ambitions for which the natural walk of life would provide no place except in the case of real geniuses. Every boy in the colony cannot be a clerk, a lawyer or a doctor, nor can every girl be a schoolmistress or fashionable dressmaker.

Educated or non-educated, the people of the colony must split up into the various classes marked out for them by their means or the means of their parents, and the place they can find in the race of life.

It is therefore right that the line should be drawn in the matter of free education at elementary level.[155]

The editor of the *Catholic News* offered a similar sentiment in July 1901 when, opposing a new building for QRC, he propounded the view that: ". . . the bottom has been touched in the social strata of the colony whence College students are recruited and . . . no brand new college will add to the number of such students".[156] However, the College Exhibitions under attack in 1893 had friends. The coloured lawyer Vincent Brown refuted the allegations of Lange and Bell-Smythe that the free place boys contaminated those boys whose parents could pay for their education. A petition signed by eight hundred residents of Port of Spain, headed by some merchants, offered support to the College Exhibition.[157] The anti-College Exhibition lobby was defeated; in fact, the Exhibition was restored in 1893 to a higher level of eight students per annum, but was quickly reduced in 1894 to four each year.

Independently of the College Exhibition, CIC organized, from 1867 to about 1913, its own exhibitions open only to pupils of Roman Catholic primary schools.[158] The award of exhibitions independent of government was a trend followed by new secondary schools, private or public, in the early twentieth century. Eventually non-government exhibitions to secondary schools outnumbered the government exhibitions, thus opening up a new era in educational opportunities for black and coloured children. The College Exhibition system grew from an uncertain indulgence to an expected privilege by the start of the twentieth century, and finally to a political right in the 1930s.[159] In turn these exhibitions encouraged a partly healthy competition among the headteachers of the leading primary schools for the fame of producing exhibitioners, especially College Exhibitioners. It might not be an overstatement to say that the headteachers who prepared a few winners of College Exhibitions generated more public acclaim than their happy protégés.

Concurrently with the increased penetration of the secondary schools for boys in the last quarter of the nineteenth century was the opening up of new opportunities for advancement of non-whites in the junior ranks of the civil service and in the field of law. A most important development was the arrangement whereby locals could study to become solicitors without leaving the island or going to a university. From the late 1820s, when the first coloured youths began to assume clerkships in the judicial departments, a supreme career objective of ambitious non-whites was to become lawyers which, like the study of medicine, gave independence, privilege and an adequate income. At a time when there were only ten solicitors in practice Ordinance no. 7 of 1871 permitted locals to be articled in Trinidad, and after passing the examinations of the Incorporated Law Society of London to practice as solicitors.[160] Although they could not become barristers without expensive study abroad, the black and coloured youths who succeeded in becoming solicitors had raised their social standing enormously. Some of them had already gone through CIC and QRC as exhibitioners, but without winning university scholarships; others had gone to secondary schools at their parents' expense. French creole youths, for example F. J. Maingot and J. D. Sellier whose families already had status, after attending CIC grasped the opportunities of studying locally to become solicitors, articling themselves to French creole solicitors.[161] The opportunity to qualify locally greatly altered the racial composition of the profession, breaching the walls of white occupational privilege in one of the traditional high status fields. It could not be allowed to continue. In 1894, when there were thirty-eight solicitors and eighteen articled clerks, a group of lawyers, solicitors, and merchants successfully petitioned the government to restrict the admission of new locally trained solicitors.[162] The public objection was, of course, not related to race but to the alleged overcrowding in the profession, and the low standard of education and training of the locally trained solicitors. A new law in 1894 made it necessary to study in England to become a solicitor.

There was a Trinidadian youth of Chinese extraction whose academic career in the late nineteenth century was the foundation for a remarkable life in China. Eugene Chen, born in 1875 of Chinese shopkeeping parents, went to CIC where he failed to win a university scholarship, despite herculean efforts. He took the opportunity of studying locally to be a solicitor by being the articled clerk of E. Marese-Smith. He had a longing for education in England which led him to study the tenth edition of the *Encyclopedia Britannica* at night in the hope of winning a certain overseas scholarship based on its contents. Chen's nocturnal labours were not unlike those of scores of other ambitious young men who studied one thing or another outside the school system, often with the help of correspondence courses. Chen became a solicitor and had a practice in San Fernando, but sometime in 1911 he suddenly disappeared from the island. He was always interested in politics. Trinidadians were astonished to hear later that he had made his way to China and had taken part in the Chinese revolution, rising to the rank of foreign minister of the Republic of China.[163]

A very narrow channel to improved social status was opened with the advent of competitive examinations for the civil service. One of the first blacks to benefit was J.J. Thomas who topped the examination in its first year and was subsequently employed in the junior ranks of the civil service. He later became the most senior black civil servant in Trinidad. But there were obstacles: passing the examination did not give a right to employment, though failing it was a bar. Competitive examinations for entry into the civil service soon looked like such a dangerous experiment that they were suspended.[164] The whites who monopolized the senior civil service posts preferred the governor to have absolute discretion in appointments, unhindered by blacks and coloureds waving certificates.

In the last quarter of the nineteenth century competition in education, waged through examinations, reached proportions hitherto unknown in the island. There are two ways in which we can explain this, and these ways are not mutually exclusive. One can simply say that Trinidad followed the English metropolitan model, and moved from non-competition to competition in the nineteenth century. Additionally there was a local dynamic at work determining the colony's willingness to follow the metropolitan model. In the first generation after emancipation, competition in education was substantially absent from all the schools largely because the social system was relatively unresponsive to intellectual achievement. This indifference was a legacy of slavery and the plantation system where muscle power was more important than ideas, and business success more vital than formal education. It has been argued recently that a new plantation system established itself in the later nineteenth century.[165] Some whites were not convinced that substantially more education was needed to run post-emancipation Trinidad than a slave plantation society. Nevertheless, educational opportunity grew after emancipation until it had to be systematized by competitive examinations. Concurrently with competitive College Exhibitions, primary schools were put on a system of payment by results. Teachers competed to improve result-fees; pupils had to pass examinations to move to higher grades; as for the pupil teachers, they faced a long series of examinations; uncertified teachers were obliged to present themselves for examinations, and indeed even for the certified teachers there were higher certificates to be obtained. In other words, the clearest path to upward social mobility for non-whites was to study and to pass examinations which were very competitive. While this seems normal today, it was a new phenomenon for the sons and daughters of slaves, of poor free coloureds and free blacks.

The supreme examination in the nineteenth century was for the Cambridge School Certificate. It derived its importance from being an external examination set by a prestigious academic authority in the metropole. It set a definite standard for secondary schools. It was also the examination on which the university scholarships were based; only the senior students at QRC and CIC could take it until Naparima College joined the select club in 1909 (see Table 1.5). For many years it was thought too strenuous, or otherwise inappropriate, for girls at

St Joseph's Convent, and private candidates were not yet allowed. It took some time before even CIC or QRC mastered the curriculum. It might be surprising to learn that between 1870 and 1893 as few as 13.3 percent of the Island Scholars (winners of university scholarships) achieved first class certificates. But there was a great improvement at the turn of the century: between 1894 and 1903 as many as 60 percent of the winners got first class certificates.[166] The rise in the level of mastery of the Cambridge examinations, as well as the greater social acceptability of black and coloured exhibitioners in the colleges, created the conditions for the triumph of intelligence and industry at QRC and CIC. By the early twentieth century, before World War I, the College Exhibitioners, black and coloured, had come completely into an inheritance of university scholarships which led to overseas training in the professions.[167]

Of course it should not be forgotten that only a minority of black and coloured working class youths managed to raise themselves through education to middle-class status. Many simply improved their standing within the labouring class. Most of those who attended primary school fell back into the ranks of the illiterate or semi-literate working classes, despite the fears of illiberal whites that primary school education would render them unfit for agricultural labour. Many of the better graduates of the primary schools did study for pupil teacher examinations, and a few went to teacher training schools. There were a number of youths who received secondary education in England or Europe and returned to the colony. The route to the United States of America to work one's way through college existed, but these students did not return.[168] By a process of gradual accumulation one could find by the end of the nineteenth century, among the blacks and coloureds, about three hundred trained teachers, the most numerous of the educated non-white middle class; scores of clerks, tens of minor civil servants, pharmacists, surveyors and solicitors, a handful of lawyers and doctors, and a few newspaper editors. Other occupations were represented, but an exhaustive list is not intended. Men outnumbered women, despite the authorities' preference for less expensive female assistant teachers. At least we know of one fearless coloured female, Emilie Marese Paul, who must be reckoned among the intelligentsia of San Fernando.[169]

Some examples of individuals who benefited from the schools will make the point. It would be an error to believe that whites were unrepresented in the race for academic honours. If they tend to be undermentioned it is because some were secure in their social position without the need for success in academic competition. R. S. A. Aucher Warner, born the son of Charles Warner in 1859, would most likely have had university education even if he had not won an Island Scholarship from QRC in 1876. He studied law at Oxford University, and later became attorney general in Trinidad and Tobago, a post once occupied by his father. The same point, perhaps with less certainty, could be made about the three sons of Rev John Morton, who all won university scholarships from QRC in 1887, 1890 and 1892. The point about upward mobility through education has to be made with greater force for non-whites. Two great examples were Henry Alcazar and Stephen Laurence, both coloureds who had won university scholarships respectively in 1877 and 1883. Alcazar had a brilliant career as a lawyer, being with the French creole Edgar Agostini the earliest Queen's Counsel (QC) in the island. Alcazar was appointed to the Legislative Council. Laurence became a medical practitioner and indefatigable member of many boards and a staunch supporter of government schools. Alcazar was born four years earlier (1860) than Emanuel Lazare (also known as Mzumbo Lazare) who became a black solicitor and Legislative Council member. As a boy Lazare went to two of the leading Port of Spain schools, the Boys' Model School and St Thomas Roman Catholic School, as well as either QRC or CIC. He became articled to the French creole solicitor, Andre Maingot. Lazare became the first person to pass the local examinations of the Incorporated Law Society of England without going abroad. He later became a barrister. He was a great supporter of the volunteer militia and as a senior militia officer went as part of Trinidad's delegation to the Golden Jubilee of Queen Victoria in 1897. He reportedly caught the eye of the Queen and dined with royalty, some of whom took a liking to him. Lazare was from many accounts a colourful and popular personality.[170]

Because the Indians were late in getting even primary education, the rise of an Indian middle class through education lagged behind that of the blacks and coloureds, although the Canadian Presbyterian Mission was remarkably swift in starting a secondary school. For instance, the Indians missed the opportunity, because of lack of secondary education, to become solicitors by local study in the last third of the nineteenth century, as blacks, coloureds and French creoles were doing. In 1919 there was only one Indian solicitor at a time when Indians already had a long tradition of purchasing Crown lands. In the later nineteenth century the ownership of land, not education, was the primary mechanism for social and economic advancement by the Indians. At the end of the nineteenth century Naparima College ran a very poor third behind CIC and QRC. But a fruitful link between it and the Presbyterian Mission's theological college unobtrusively gave a few Indians greater opportunities than in the case of members of other churches to study locally for the priesthood. Failing to enter adequately into the education stream which led from primary schools to the College Exhibitions, to QRC and CIC, and perhaps university scholarships, the Indians were fortunate to find in the white leadership of the Canadian Presbyterian Church clerics who had contacts with Canadian colleges and universities, and this later opened a peculiar side door for the better products of the Mission in a less well-known part of the British empire.

As Bridget Brereton has clearly seen, the black and coloured educated middle class of the late nineteenth century paraded their education and culture because it was the only thing they had to boast about. Some of them gave lectures, slide demonstrations (lantern demonstrations); a few became amateur naturalists proud of their small collections of stones or insects. One such was Hubert Alphonso Nurse, a well-read local naturalist and teacher.[171] We might begin to see in the later nineteenth century the early foundations of the literary and debating societies which blossomed into a craze in the early twentieth century. The lowly paid teacher, bossed by a white inspector of schools, and sometimes harassed by white clerical managers, was the base of the new unrecognized intelligentsia in the colony. The black and coloured middle class – followed by the Indians – had begun the long march to overtake the French creoles and resident Englishmen as the intellectual leaders of Trinidad and Tobago. They had, of course, neither economic power nor political influence to match the revolution in educational achievement which was in progress.

[2]

The Age of Marriott and Cutteridge

The Imposition of Agricultural Education 1897-1922

The origins of the drive to have agricultural education lay primarily in the disaster suffered by Trinidad's sugar industry, indeed by the British West Indian sugar industry, in the mid 1880s and 1890s, and also in the energetic pursuit of imperial development by the secretary of state for the colonies, Joseph Chamberlain (1895-1903). Competition with European beet sugar revealed the inefficiency of British Caribbean cane sugar production.[1] Recovery necessitated metropolitan protection and subsidies but, additionally, planters in Trinidad (as in many of the other islands) became more convinced that agricultural education was needed locally. This did not mean that planters understood precisely how school gardening in primary schools would help the sugar industry; rather, it was a common-sensical assumption that agricultural education in general could not fail to improve the situation. For the entire nineteenth century agricultural education was absent from the schools except in one or two Canadian Presbyterian Mission schools from about the mid 1880s and, of course, in orphanages and reformatories.

Restructuring the curriculum of the primary schools came before changes in CIC or QRC. The introduction of agriculture into primary schools was preceded by the establishment of three important institutions which fostered it: the Agricultural Society of Trinidad (1894); the Department of Agriculture (1908) and the Imperial Department of Agriculture (1898). The latter came into existence on the recommendation of the West Indian Royal Commission (the Norman Commission) of 1897 which insisted on the urgent need to spread agricultural education in the West Indies. This Commission proposed a special imperial agency located in the West Indies, but funded entirely by the British government, to promote agricultural research and education. Chamberlain approved a budget of about $84,000 per annum and in 1898 the Imperial Department of Agriculture came to life in Barbados under the leadership of Daniel Morris, formerly assistant director of Kew Gardens, England.[2] As is well known, Chamberlain was one of the leaders of the 'new imperialists' in England. His concern was for improving the agricultural resources of the empire, including the growth of export crops by peasant production. The establishment of the Imperial Department of Agriculture was an extraordinary and unprecedented development, which had important consequences for agricultural research and education in the British West Indies. For the first time, the British government implanted an aid organization within the West Indies to operate on a regional level.

It was the Imperial Department of Agriculture which was most directly responsible for the introduction of agriculture into the primary school curriculum. Half a century earlier, in 1847, the British government had sent information to West Indian colonies about agricultural education, but had not made the teaching of agriculture an imperial policy. The immense difference between 1847 and 1898 was that Chamberlain insisted on the teaching of agriculture in primary schools as a matter of official policy in the West Indies.[3] The Imperial Department of Agriculture, as the local arm of the British government in these matters, offered free advice; the planters and the governors welcomed this new departure. It would not be accurate simply to say that agricultural education was imposed on the colony by the British government; this would imply that the colonial government was an indifferent or protesting bystander. On the contrary, the planters and the governors were thinking along the same lines. If, however, the decision is looked at from the point of view of the parents of black, coloured and Indian children who had at least reservations about agricultural education, if not open hostility to it, then there was an element of unpleasant imperial imposition, without any attempt to improve the social conditions of rural life.

Unable to make headway on the proposal to reserve one of the university scholarships for agriculture, the governors found among the chief educators a more substantial area of agreement on agricultural education in primary schools. A committee established by Governor Robinson, consisting of Dr Louis de Verteuil, the ubiquitous leader of the French creoles; Gervase Bushe, inspector of schools; J. Hart, head of the botanical gardens; and Professor Carmody, who was in charge of the government chemical laboratories, agreed in 1892 that there was a need to include agriculture in schools, and that the first place to start was the training of teachers. The only area of disagreement, then and for some time in the future, among these bureaucrats and the planters, was over the extent of the practical component in agricultural education. In effect, this disagreement concerned the balance between theoretical teaching in the classroom and the practical work in the school gardens. When the Imperial Department of Agriculture began to function from Barbados in 1898, it found that it had in the government of Trinidad, in the Trinidad Agricultural Society and in Carmody, Hart and Bushe, eager collaborators in agricultural education.

Agricultural education in the primary schools began in a logical manner, with holiday crash courses, usually of three weeks duration, to batches of selected headteachers and a few teacher trainees from the government training school. The chief instructors were Carmody and Hart, and between August 1899 and August 1901, some 140 teachers and 17 teacher trainees took the courses, not to mention 17 teachers in Tobago.[4] There was nothing to stop the introduction of agriculture as soon as the teachers were ready. A paper on agriculture was made compulsory for male candidates sitting the Teachers' Certificate Examination. No previous innovation spread in the primary schools with such rapidity. By 1913 school gardens existed in 213 schools out of a total of 265 schools (80.3 percent). It is of interest to note that this proliferation of school gardens in the early twentieth century was widespread throughout the British Caribbean; and that before Trinidad got the Imperial College of Tropical Agriculture it was behind Jamaica in the rush to emphasize agricultural education. Perhaps nowhere else in the tropical world was agricultural education as much in the forefront of government policy in the early twentieth century as in the British Caribbean.

In Trinidad there was some initial resistance to school gardens by some parents, no doubt from the reluctance to have their children do manual labour. Assistant Inspector of Schools William Robinson sadly reported a case where parents of children at the Canadian Presbyterian Mission school at Roussilac had flatly refused to cooperate.[5] These might not have all been Indian parents as at this time minorities of black children could be found in some rural Canadian Presbyterian Mission schools. Robinson felt that the remedy in this and other such cases was to encourage the parents to come to the school to observe the results for themselves. This resistance from some Indian parents is intriguing for two reasons. As an agricultural working class with a love for the land and farming, it might have been expected that rural Indian parents would react favourably to school gardens. But this was to assume that such persons thought that school gardens could teach their children anything not already known from peasant cultivation. The second consideration is that Canadian Presbyterian missionaries, more than any other clerics, seemed comfortable with the notion that primary schools were appropriate places for practical work in agriculture or in crafts. Perhaps at least one of their schools had a school garden before school gardens became general policy.[6] The Canadian Presbyterian missionaries had no memory of West Indian plantation slavery; instead they had good relations with owners and managers of sugar estates. They were untroubled by misgivings about the association of agricultural labour with slavery.

How much resistance there was to school gardens across the colony is not clear. In 1914 Hubert Alphonso Nurse, senior agricultural inspector of the Department of Agriculture, reported continuing parental dislike of school gardens especially of work with the hoe, the traditional field implement of slaves.[7] Nurse was a self-taught black intellectual who might be relied on to sense such misgivings among the working classes. An interesting observation by him was that because schools often lacked their own tools, many children had to carry cutlasses, forks and hoes from home to school, much to the chagrin of parents. Children were expected to carry books to schools, not agricultural implements. It is probable that opposition to school gardens, including resistance from some teachers, even senior headteachers, Indian and non-Indian, was underreported. Nor do we know whether it was black parents more than Indian parents who disliked school gardens. In the 1920s some members of the planter interest felt that there was then less resistance than at the start of the programme. The feeling was that parents were overcoming their dislike of school gardens. Clearly something of extraordinary importance was thought to have been achieved: hundreds of children, more boys than girls, were actually at work in school gardens, preparing themselves, it was thought, for their life's work. School gardens became, in the first two decades of the twentieth century, as much an article of faith among educators as technical/vocational education is today.

The question of introducing agricultural education at a higher level of the education ladder proved problematic. The disagreement was over the strength of the demand in the colony for employees trained in scientific agriculture; also over the level of scientific agricultural education such persons should be trained to possess, and whether or not all this could be accomplished by utilizing existing institutions or, if necessary, by a new institution such as a college.[8] Social questions also plagued agricultural education above the level of primary schools. The provision of agricultural education had to be fitted into the social system. Where would black or coloured young men find employment after they had a scientific training in agriculture at a post-primary level? There were two obvious types of openings: on the estates and in the Department of Agriculture. The superior jobs in the latter were out of the reach of non-whites and only somewhat less so on the estates. There were inferior slots as overseers or headmen on the estates, experimental stations and government farms; but these jobs were often in the gift of white relatives or white government officers.[9] If non-white youths were overtrained they would aspire to these jobs, or to jobs higher than these. Education in a college, worse if residential, would develop the aspirations (or, as upper class persons would say, 'pretensions') of the young men. And then there was the unsolved question of the extent of the demand for scientifically trained professional agriculturalists. Such a question did not arise in the case of primary school pupils who, without subverting the social system, could all become estate workers and peasant farmers. A college might result in an oversupply of trained personnel, some of whom would be non-whites. Some of the planters and top civil servants in the Department of Agriculture thought that the solution was to train only a handful of carefully selected persons in existing institutions in such a manner that their ambitions would not run ahead of their social positions.

By 1909 the Imperial Department of Agriculture had hit upon a scheme of training youths above primary school level which seemed socially safe. As this agency operated on a regional level, this solution was available to all the islands. Selected youths were to be apprenticed to the experimental stations and government farms, after which they would face an examination. It was to be a work-study programme. They would do all the ordinary manual work of these stations and farms, while getting a few lectures on a wide variety of subjects connected with agriculture. The right youths might even be given an allowance, a sort of scholarship. They would – and this was important – live at home, close to the conditions in which they would eventually work as headmen or overseers. A proposal that they might be given temporary employment for one year in the lower ranks of the Department of Agriculture elicited the rejoinder from a planter that if this was done, they would hang on to the civil service for the rest of their lives.[10] This scheme, called the cadet system (also the agricultural pupil system), was tried in Trinidad as well as in some eastern Caribbean islands, but it is not known with what success.

Agricultural education in the primary schools was to produce droves of labourers and small farmers; the cadet system, a small number of headmen and junior overseers. What about senior overseers, managers and planters themselves already on the job? These men could not spare the time for school, but if they could find time to study, they could take a course of readings which the Imperial Department of Agriculture developed specifically for them. The plan seemed unrealistic. But it would produce a still socially higher level of skilled agriculturalists, some of whom would be white owners of estates and their relatives.

There was one other type of scientifically trained persons whom the island needed: the specialists, the persons trained more like scientists than farmers, for example the entomologists, and the mycologists, the research oriented professionals who might discover a remedy for tropical plant diseases or pests. Although the arguments about the uniqueness of tropical agriculture as opposed to temperate zone agriculture carried the greatest weight at this level, it mattered as well in respect to all levels of farming. Tropical agriculture could best be scientifically investigated in the tropics. Here at last was a branch of higher education where the colony, not the metropole, was the inescapable and preferred location for its pursuit. Recognizing the greater flexibility which new institutions have over old ones in meeting new needs, a few members of the planter interest spoke in favour of a superior college in Trinidad to meet the needs of specialist agricultural research.[11]

Trinidad already had two well known colleges, CIC and QRC. The question arose whether any of the needs for trained personnel above the cadet level could be met by these colleges. Scientific agriculture required the teaching of science, especially chemistry. QRC and CIC were set in their ways as grammar schools, especially QRC. Neither had a full-time science master. From about 1905 a scheme was worked out whereby the boys from Forms III to VI from these two colleges went over to Professor Carmody at the government laboratories for, at most, two hours each week.[12] But the boys at the colleges took agriculture as an examination subject only, showing no interest in it as a career. As William Burslem, the principal of QRC was to say in 1914, agriculture was taught there without any advantage to agriculture.[13] The same might be said of CIC.

The question of a superior specialist college of agriculture at first split the Agricultural Society and the Department of Agriculture. Professor Carmody, the first head of the Department of Agriculture, was stoutly opposed; William Freeman, his assistant, was more accommodating. These civil servants carried their attitudes over to the Agricultural Society; in that Society, there were planters for and against it. Carmody argued that a specialist college was premature; it would be too costly, and the graduates would be "too little educated for their opinions to carry any weight with estate owners or managers, and too dignified to become the intelligent labourer or peasant proprietor who is the backbone of agriculture".[14] Part of the problem behind the division of opinion was that different people had varying conceptions of what such a college was to do; and how many graduates it was to turn out. The arguments for such a college were more insistently put by A. Fredholm, A. Stollmeyer and Norman Lamont, the latter of whom distinguished himself by a long consistent campaign for a college, both in Trinidad and in London.[15] Lamont argued that agricultural education had begun at the wrong end: they should educate the 'generals' of agriculture – the proprietors, instructors, managers, teachers, experts – before they turned to the 'privates'[16] (namely primary school teachers and pupils). Only a superior specialist college could accomplish this. Lamont carried his campaign for the education of professional agriculturists to the chief education administrators, and helped to convince them that the colony's university scholarship system should be reorganized to create an Agricultural Scholarship. This was started in 1919.

With the headquarters in Barbados, the Imperial Department of Agriculture was placed in an awkward position by the development of the movement for a superior specialist college of agriculture in Trinidad. The most logical thing would have been to develop such a college in Barbados on the base of the Imperial Department.[17] The fact that this did not happen, but rather that the Imperial Department was dismantled and its staff absorbed into a college which was located in Trinidad, is an indication of the astonishingly successful campaign of the pro-college lobby in Trinidad.

In 1913 the Trinidad Agricultural Society managed to sink its differences and reservations about the college, and agreed to promote it; a standing committee on which Norman Lamont was a key figure was established. Lamont, from his residence and experience in the metropole, was able to encourage the Agricultural Society to pitch the campaign for a college at an imperial level; it was not simply to be a college for Trinidad, not even for the West Indies, but for the British empire. This line of promotion was crucial to the success of the entire enterprise.

Once the college was perceived as a prospective imperial institution serving the large metropolitan manufacturing interests and companies, such as the Imperial Cotton Growers, or training Englishmen for service in tropical Africa; once it appeared practicable as an instrument to exploit the tropical empire for the benefit of metropolitan interests, then it acquired a rationale stronger than anything upon which the Imperial Department of Agriculture rested.

While it is true that sentiments in favour of imperial unity and imperial development were running high among the 'new' imperialists in England, and that several advanced imperial institutions of learning were established from the 1890s to the 1930s,[18] the role of the Trinidad planters must not be underestimated, and that of Lord Milner, then secretary of state for the colonies, overestimated. The support of Milner, inheritor of Joseph Chamberlain's mantle of 'constructive' imperialism, was indeed crucial, but it was the Trinidad planters who gained the attention of Milner.[19] Lloyd Braithwaite's explanation of the birth of the Imperial College of Agriculture, previously the most elaborate, fails to integrate the propaganda of the Trinidad planters with Milner's subsequent recommendations in favour of a specialist college of this kind. That the Trinidad planters should have been able to transcend the horizons of their island and leap upon the imperial stage, with the audacity which caught the other islands off balance, was partly a tribute to the transformation of the structure of sugar operations which had been taking place since at least the 1870s.[20] Most of the sugar estates were owned by absentees in England and the Colonial Company based in England was the leading corporate owner. These absentee owners wielded enormous influence in British government circles. The leading planters in Trinidad, by being integrated into this structure of absentee ownership, shared in the international corporate influence of the sugar industry.

World War I postponed the resolution of the question: the British government had said at the end of 1913 that it could not see where the money would come from. The war therefore worked in favour of the pro-college lobby by heightening England's consciousness of her empire, by revealing the backwardness of British science, and by creating a world sugar market which by 1919 and 1920 ushered in a return to sugar prosperity in Trinidad. The final victory occurred in this temporarily auspicious postwar sugar market: a decisive push by the Agricultural Society which was strongly supported by Governor John Chancellor induced the British government to set up a Tropical Agricultural College Committee, which quickly reported in favour of such a college. The claims of Trinidad as the location of the college, in the face of a late challenge from Jamaica, was that it had superior sea communications with the rest of the eastern Caribbean: Barbados had already been beaten by the apparently unanswerable argument that Trinidad had a greater variety of soils and agricultural production.[21]

The British government's decision to allow a specialist agricultural college in Trinidad was quickly acted upon, partly from fear that at the eleventh hour Jamaica might snatch it from Trinidad's grasp. Rapid implementation was possible from the fact that the college was partly the Imperial Department of Agriculture reassembled in a new guise, and with a somewhat new purpose, in Trinidad. Imperial commissioner of agriculture, Dr Francis Watts, became principal of the new West Indian Agricultural College; some of the professors of the Imperial Department of Agriculture were transferred to the college so that immediately, and to the delight of visitors, it had a fine library stretching the entire length of the building. Watts knew what he was doing: the Trinidad Legislative Council speedily imposed a produce tax on sugar, cocoa, and coconuts to provide the colony's financial contributions; the government gave eighty-four acres of the St Augustine Government Farm; and in two years from authorization the college opened its doors. This was in October 1922; it had fifteen students from England and the West Indies.[22] It was the first intercolonial enterprise in education. Two years later its name was changed to the Imperial College of Tropical Agriculture (hereafter ICTA), on metropolitan advice, with the hope of attracting wider funding.[23]

By the time the ICTA – the college to educate the 'generals' of agriculture – had opened, the agricultural education of the 'privates' had been deemed a failure by an important team of investigators. At first there were favourable reports, bordering on euphoria, of the teaching of agriculture in the primary schools; the favourable reports began to be mixed with warnings and finally, towards 1914, the inspector of schools and his assistant inspectors became more critical of what was happening. Then an Education Commission of 1914/1916 which took evidence about the general state of education was flatly condemnatory in its report filed in 1916. What had gone wrong? First of all, it is important to stress that at least the school garden side of agriculture was quite different from any other type of work being done in the schools, with the exception of needlework by the girls which the male inspectors cheerfully confessed their inability to judge. A school garden was something which could be plainly seen; its condition could be more readily assessed than that of any 'bookish' subject; the result of the gardening was visible and even edible. The enterprise was new and therefore attracted attention and invited judgement. Had it been a new scholarly pursuit such as hygiene, it might have escaped condemnation for lack of sufficient opportunities of judging it. Had it been a subject not so apparently relevant to economic development, not so dear to the hope of economic betterment, fewer important people, apart from those directly involved in education, would even have noticed that anything had gone wrong. After all, nothing was well taught in the average primary school, especially in the rural areas. But the administrators of education and the other persons who criticized the lack of achievement in the school gardens had already become accustomed to low standards in reading, writing, arithmetic, English and geography.

It was school gardens rather than nature study which came in for condemnation. The Education Commission of 1914/1916 arrived at the firm conclusion that under the system of payment by results the bonus for school gardens was too generous, and that headteachers had found that for very little work in the school gardens they could get additional salary.[24] The bonus was not related to the size of the school garden or the number of boys who worked in it, but to the number of students who were in attendance during the year. Hence, a headteacher of a large urban school with a small school garden could earn a higher bonus than his counterpart in a small rural school with a large school garden. Enthusiasm for agriculture waned after headteachers whose school performed well in agriculture had received their promotion from third class to second class headteachers. The agricultural inspectors (black men) were declared, somewhat unfairly, to be very lax; they applied too low standards with the excuse that high standards would have resulted in few gardens passing the test. All the white inspectors of schools were doing the same thing regularly in respect to the core subjects. The agricultural inspectors paid few visits, claiming rightly that their travelling allowance was insufficient. When they did visit they inspected the garden, which the headteacher had spruced up for the occasion, rather than examine the pupils.[25] The outcome was that after a tour of inspection the commissioners found few school gardens in a commendable state. From this it was readily inferred that few pupils could have learned many things about agriculture as a science.

There remains a strong suspicion that the Education Commission had overreacted to the poor conditions of school gardens. The British government seemed only to have expected school gardens to introduce children to the principles of agriculture. The senior agricultural inspector thought that the main idea was to develop the pupils' powers of observation. In 1914, Watts warned against unrealistic expectations of the programme and advised that only elementary familiarity with the most striking facts about animals and plant life, together with practical operations like the sowing of seeds and propagation by cuttings, could be reasonably hoped for.[26] There was no agreement on the objectives of teaching agriculture. The organization of annual agricultural shows from 1902, with prizes for the best exhibits, indicated that the administrators of education, the Agricultural Society and the planters wanted more than basic knowledge: they wanted to have on exhibition the superior produce (a bigger yam, for example) of improved farming in the school gardens. The Education Commission of 1914/1916 recommended the cessation of bonuses for agricultural education and of the practice of promoting headteachers for successful school gardens. While excusing urban schools from school gardens, it sought to raise the standards to which school gardens in rural schools should aspire. However, the question of objectives was not really addressed. Subsequently the schools of the Canadian Presbyterian Mission established a clear ascendancy in school gardening (see Appendix III).

If the standard of agricultural education was called into question at the primary school level, it was the small size of the student body and the uncertainty of the arrangements for funding, as well as the method of articulating QRC and CIC to

ICTA, which posed the main problems in the early years. In hindsight we can see that ICTA opened at the start of a period of expansion, not in agriculture but in oil production.[27] There had been a suggestion by the Tropical Agricultural College Committee of England that ICTA should also serve the oil industry, but such a link would have been most difficult and the planters were not keen.[28] The suggested professorial chair in geology was not funded, and the new and distant oil industry at Point Fortin, Brighton, Guapo and Fyzabad saw no use for ICTA. Drillers and cheap labour, not engineers or scientific researchers, were then what the oil industry thought it most needed. The oil companies had their own geologists. A most remarkable event was that two years after ICTA opened its doors, the Agricultural Scholarship (1919-1924) was abolished in favour of the Science Scholarship.[29] But the Science Scholarship was not linked in the mind of educators with the oil industry, but with the study of medicine.

The Schools on the Eve of Reform 1902-1917

In the first decade and a half of the twentieth century, the schools were on the eve of several major reforms which commenced about 1918 and continued into the 1920s. However, this did not mean an absence of important changes between 1902 and 1917: the introduction of agricultural education and the drive for a specialist agricultural college were the most vital new developments at this time. Outside the schools, as we shall see later, interesting new moves to upgrade the skills of tradesmen were afoot. Nevertheless, the years between 1902 and 1917 constituted a period in which the problems of the dual system, which had been instituted in 1870 and consolidated in 1890, continued to accumulate without reform. The clerical school managers and the government conceived the problems of the primary schools predominantly in religious or financial terms, and hardly in pedagogical terms. Between 1914 and 1916 a local Commission investigated the system of education, with an eye to saving money. Its recommendations formed part of the basis for reforms after World War I.

There were several problems facing the primary schools, government as well as denominational, between 1900 and 1917. Let us take first the problem of an inadequate provision of school places. There are no reliable figures of the size of the school-age population between 1900 and 1917. In 1902 the inspector of schools, Gervase Bushe, guessed that "the total number of children of schoolable age is over 50,000, on the usual assumption that this class of children comprises about one-fifth of the total population".[30] At that time the total population was about 258,000 persons, of whom about 86,000 (33.3%) were Indians. In 1902 there were 237 schools with about 33,872 pupils enrolled, and an average attendance of about 19,562 (57.7%). If Bushe's figure is taken seriously, it would mean that there were no school places for approximately 33 percent of the school-age population. But it is possible that Inspector Bushe underestimated the actual size of the school-age population, since he did not have a precise definition of the age group to be so regarded. If one uses Bushe's guide of one-fifth of the population, then in 1911 there were about 66,000 children attending school. In 1911 there were 263 schools with an enrolment of about 47,719 children, and an average daily attendance of 27,083 children. This would mean that, at that time, there were no places for about 29 percent of the school-age population – an insignificant improvement on the position in 1901. The most consistent policy towards education was economy. The government held down spending on primary schools to a fairly steady average of 6.5 percent of the colony's total expenditure between 1900 and 1914.

One strong argument used by opponents of increased government financing of primary education was that inadequate use was made of the existing schools. Irregular attendance was a chronic problem, not automatically remedied by the abolition of school fees. While enrolment did increase steadily from 33,872 (1901-1902) to 47,719 in 1911, the average daily attendance did not improve in this period and rarely rose above 57 percent. The official explanation placed the blame mostly on children and parents. Many parents just did not care enough about education for their children. Of course, additionally, the government was to be blamed for bad roads in the rural areas which inhibited attendance on rainy days; also the government and rural employers must share some of the blame for low wages which obliged peasants and estate workers to supplement their earnings with those of their children. Since schools were understaffed and badly constructed or housed in inadequate premises, if all the children on the rolls were to appear on the same day many schools would have found it impossible to seat them. Also of great importance in discouraging regular attendance, especially in rural districts, was the low standard of achievement of some schools, the dysfunctionality of some aspects of their curriculum, and the failure of a modicum of literacy to ensure better jobs or upward social mobility for any but a handful who kept on studying.

Among the Indian population a particular problem, arising partly from their own ancestral culture, was a persistent unwillingness to send their daughters to school; it was said that a few Indian "advanced thinkers" around Princes Town were totally opposed to the education of girls.[31] The practice of child marriage also militated against the education of Indian girls. Indian parents were urged by Canadian Presbyterian missionaries to send them, but not much progress was made until later in the twentieth century. In the face of all these difficulties and obstacles to regular school attendance, the government turned its back on a compulsory education law. This had been recommended in 1895, but the financial implications made the law too serious for the government to accept. Education could not be compulsory unless adequate school places existed.

A most important problem for primary education at the start of the twentieth century was curriculum direction. The main subjects of the ordinary primary school were reading, writing, arithmetic, English grammar, and geography. These subjects, on closer examination, had more branches: reading included dictation (spelling and writing) and even composition; English was basically grammar plus recitation of poetry. A few schools did some singing and history; many did needlework; but the foundation of the curriculum involved the three Rs. This had been the basis since the start of primary schools in the immediate post-emancipation period, with the difference that the further back into the nineteenth century one went, the smaller was the core, consisting sometimes of only reading and writing or even reading alone. The core subjects were always 'bookish'; that is, they were studied from books. In the later nineteenth century one occasionally finds criticisms that these basic subjects did not meet the educational needs of the children of peasants or landless agricultural workers or tradesmen in the towns. The metropolitan models of primary school education were English or Irish, and these were also 'bookish'. The churches, which were early in the field as school providers, were not organized to teach practical subjects leading to skills as tradesmen or agriculturalists. The government's ward schools of the nineteenth century were also not geared to practical subjects; at any rate, everyone who was friendly to education agreed that basic literacy and character training (with or without religious instruction in the schoolroom) were the top priority for primary schools.

It is worthwhile to note that about the same time that agriculture was introduced, other attempts were being made to enrich the curriculum. For instance, hygiene was introduced into many of the primary schools. Only the rudiments were taught in the upper standards, with much emphasis on practical problems such as how mosquitoes bred, and the danger of drinking contaminated water. Nobody pronounced this new subject a failure, and therefore there was no special problem involved in the introduction of hygiene which, unlike school gardening, was a 'bookish' subject. A beginning was also made, as will be seen later, in the systematic training of tradesmen, but outside the primary schools.

The primary schools worked by a system of payment by results which, though adopted from England, had distinctive local features. The salary of the headteacher depended on the class of his or her certificate, the size of the particular school, and the bonus attached to the particular subjects. Actually the payment depended not only on the number of children who passed, but on the number presented for examination in the various subjects and only children who attended one hundred times for the year could be presented. This system put a premium on the size of the school, hence the temptation – to which several headteachers succumbed – of dishonestly inflating the attendance registers. The assistant inspectors visited, inspected and examined the pupils, but it was examinations which really mattered. The examinations took two forms: hurried oral examinations, especially for the lower standards (grades); and written examinations on cards or paper of the upper standards in the three Rs and geography. This work was taken away by the inspector to be marked at his leisure. The outcome determined the 'result-fees' under the system of bonuses. The overwhelming impression is that the Education Department did not have enough inspectors to examine the pupils thoroughly, or even to administer strictly the bonus system. For example, the level of bonuses for headteachers ought to have been reduced when attendance fell, but this was hardly ever done. Hence on the admission of the inspectorate itself, every year the government paid out more in bonuses than it should.[32] It was a cumbrous system creating a lot of paperwork and formalism in the administration of education, without any guarantee of improved education.

The lack of achievement in the core subjects of the primary schools was quite serious. The majority of children were in the lower grades, for example Standards I-IV, with the great majority of pupils in Standards I, II and III (see Table 2.1). In 1901-1902 about 77.5 percent of pupils in government primary schools were in the first three grades, but by 1911-1912 the situation had improved somewhat, decreasing to about 69 percent in the first three standards (see Table 2.2) The pattern was basically the same in the denominational schools, the percentage in the first three standards being greater (80.9 percent) than that of the government schools. Standard III was about the highest standard reached by the majority of pupils. If one can guess sensibly that most of the pupils who reached this level could master no more than 50 percent of the work, the real achievement of the majority of school leavers becomes clearer.

However, in making such a generalization one must keep in mind that more often than not a school was judged on the basis of the achievement of a few top pupils than by the shortcomings of the scores of average and below average pupils. There were larger urban schools in Port of Spain which had a higher percentage of pupils in the upper grades (Standards IV-VII, the last of which, namely Standard VII, being rare). The Roman Catholic Park Street (St Thomas) School, the Roman Catholic Nelson Street Boys' School, and the Church of England Richmond Street School were among these schools. In a special category were the government's Tranquillity Boys' School and Tranquillity Girls' School (formerly the Model schools). It was these better urban schools which provided many of the winners of the four College Exhibitions to QRC and CIC.

If one were to use the achievements of the top pupils of the best Port of Spain schools to judge the performance of all the schools, one would arrive at a false picture of the general state of primary education. One really has to study the reports of the assistant inspectors in order to get a true picture. It is also necessary to contrast the statistical parts of the reports with the text. The level of criticism in the body of the report and the percentage of passes in the statistical parts were too high if taken in relation to the critical dissatisfaction with the performance of the pupils. The high percentages of passes (see Table 2.3) did not necessarily indicate that many pupils received high marks, just that they passed. As in England, the assistant inspector passed pupils who could read even if they did not understand what they were reading.[33]

In the period 1902 to 1916 the dual system remained substantially unchanged: government primary schools fell from fifty-six in 1901 to fifty in 1904, and then rose slightly to fifty-four by 1914. The cost of education rose, but not steeply. There was no new financial crisis over the dual system; the churches found it difficult to start schools without building grants or furniture/apparatus subsidies from the government. Indeed the churches, towards the end of World War I, were coming to the end of a period of school building which stretched back to the second half of the 1870s. Still the quarrel between supporters of government schools and the friends of denominational schools continued relentlessly, not to mention rivalries among the denominational schools.[34] The Education Commission of 1914/1916 suggested that some schools should be amalgamated, but recognized that this was a difficult policy to implement in the teeth of denominational rivalries. If a denomination lost a school in one district, it should, if possible, be compensated by being allowed to open another school elsewhere – so recommended the Education Commission. The primacy of denominational schools over government schools was to be maintained by allotting to the latter the unenviable task of pioneering education in remote areas with small school populations. Populous districts were to be reserved for denominational schools. "Any system of Education", said the Commission, "which does not recognize the divergent views in religion so strongly held in the community, must prove unsatisfactory".[35] Parents should be enabled to send their children to a school controlled by the clergy of the denomination to which they themselves belonged.

In the field of teacher training a problem was the persistently high proportion of pupil teachers in the schools. Another problem was that the training of teachers in the dual system remained splintered among too many small training schools. There were five such schools; a government male training school, and a government female training school on the same premises at Tranquillity; the Roman Catholic Male Training School at Nelson Street, Port of Spain; the Roman Catholic Female Training School, and the Canadian Presbyterian Mission training school (Naparima Training College) at San Fernando. In 1908 these five training schools had a total of forty-two trainees, and fifty-two in 1912 (see Table 2.4) These students all studied for the Teachers' Certificate, but without adequate teaching staff to assist them.[36] The Teachers' Certificate Examination consisted of many subjects, but each training school virtually had one teacher, the principal.[37] The ideal of one training school for males and one for females, even government owned, was unattainable in view of denominational rivalry. It seems worthwhile to point out that since the government aided teacher training by the churches mostly through a fixed per capita grant, the government would save nothing by amalgamating the training schools unless the terms of aid were renegotiated. The churches stood to make savings through an amalgamation, but each felt that it had something particular to impart to its own teacher trainees.

The Education Commission of 1914/1916 thought it had a solution which would both raise the standard of teacher education and close all the male teacher training schools: instead of subsidizing their preparation in denominational training schools, the government should send 'ex-pupil teachers' to QRC, CIC and Naparima College on bursaries to study for Junior Cambridge and the Cambridge School Certificates, while at the same time doing teaching practice with a skilled primary school headteacher, as well as agriculture at the botanical gardens, and school management with the inspector of schools. In this way primary school teachers would acquire a prestigious secondary education. No religious difficulties were foreseen as the Roman Catholics would go to CIC, Presbyterians (or Indians) to Naparima College and the rest to QRC. In a later chapter it will be seen what became of this idea.

There was a great need to increase the number of scholarships enabling bright boys to gain free places at the recognized secondary schools. From 1893 the College Exhibition system began to assume the status of an expected privilege, not to be reduced. This meant that each year all four were usually made. An important means to the regularization of the system of College Exhibitions was the accession of CIC to it, at first on a senseless arrangement which obliged an equal division of exhibitioners between it and QRC. This at least had one beneficial effect for the Exhibitioners: it raised the acceptability of these 'free place' boys in both colleges. Henceforth, academic brilliance triumphed over race and class prejudice.

There was no concern for equality of educational opportunity. Boys from Tobago and from remote rural areas of Trinidad had little or no chance of winning a College Exhibition unless they resided and studied in Port of Spain. The Indians' poor grasp of the English language kept them, as a group, out of the race for College Exhibitions and university scholarships (Island Scholarships) although some rural Canadian Presbyterian Mission schools were rated as good schools.[38] There were exceptions to the rule. The first Indian to win a university scholarship was F.E.M. Hosein from QRC in 1901, but it is not known if he had gone there on a College Exhibition. Rawle Ramkessoon, an Indian, won a College Exhibition to QRC, possibly about 1910. He passed the Cambridge Higher School Certificate Examination three times in an unsuccessful attempt to win a university scholarship.

In 1900 QRC had 88 students and CIC had 213. QRC experienced rapid expansion up to 1913 (209 students), and then suffered a falling away of students just before and during World War I. CIC on the other hand experienced near stagnation in the size of its student body between 1900 and 1911, followed by a rise from 1912 through to the end of World War I. In 1916 QRC had 135 students; CIC had 267; St Joseph's Convent (Port of Spain) had 210 girls (most of whom were not secondary level students); and Naparima College had 87 boys.

Naparima College had nearly doubled its enrolment between 1902 and 1916. Together the four recognized secondary schools had in 1916 about 700 students (see Table 2.5); the primary schools had about 50,000 enrolled. The greatest need, therefore, in secondary education was to find more places.

Despite the rising academic standards at the recognized secondary schools, there were serious problems. From about 1889 the French creole editor of the *Port of Spain Gazette*, the principal of CIC and its friends, put forward a reform programme for CIC and QRC which placed less emphasis on the classics to the benefit of commercial subjects; based the university scholarships on the London University Matriculation Examination instead of the Cambridge School Certificate; and reserved two of the four university scholarships for professional studies overseas in agriculture and engineering.[39] William Miles, the principal of QRC (1872-1894), stoutly resisted these proposals, being less hostile to the introduction of commercial studies than to the shift from Cambridge.[40] The College Council, which governed secondary education, was split on this programme, with a small majority being in favour. Governor Robinson, and moreso Governor Broome were favourably disposed; so too was the British government, although it felt that these were local matters to be decided by the colonial government. Each proposal had serious merit, but put together as a programme and emanating from the opponents of QRC, in an atmosphere of intense rivalry between QRC and CIC and their respective principals, it was difficult for Miles, a stubborn classicist, to believe that some injury to QRC was not intended. Reforms which were desirable on pedagogical grounds were inextricably bound up with religious rivalries and social conflicts; such reforms were quickly associated with either Roman Catholics or Protestants; French creoles or Englishmen. Governor Broome suspected that the reform programme, narrowly passed by the College Council, might be defeated in the Legislative Council; he did not put it forward there. Miles' death in 1894 brought a less stubborn principal, William Burslem, to the helm of QRC.

Burslem and Fr Crehan, principal of CIC, realized the narrowness of the classical curriculum and the need to liberate the work of the colleges from the straitjacket of the Cambridge examinations. The CIC authorities had always been critical of QRC's curriculum. Whereas in the 1880s and 1890s this critical attitude arose as part of the rivalry between the two colleges, by the early twentieth century CIC had joined QRC in the same curriculum without losing its broader base in the commercial subjects. In neither college did science count for much; the feeble agricultural chemistry courses mounted for them at the government laboratories failed miserably. The principals of QRC and CIC were more apt to laud their achievements than to be self-critical, but self-criticism was growing, reaching a stage at the time of World War I when the principals openly confessed that their curriculum needed reforms. Burslem suggested that boys aiming at one of the professions should be educated on the existing classical curriculum; those going into business should receive a thorough training in English and modern languages;

those heading for agriculture should be trained in science.[41] Fr Crehan of CIC
would have agreed with this except that he was keen on commercial subjects for
boys entering business. Of course part of the problem of curriculum planning was
that many boys did not know what career path to take or could not keep to the
chosen career path. For instance, Ray Dieffenthaller entered CIC in 1913, at twelve
years of age, on a CIC exhibition. Winners of any kind of exhibition to CIC or
QRC fancied that they had a chance to win an Island Scholarship, and would
want to follow the classical curriculum. This was the path Dieffenthaller took. But
after only four years of these studies, including Latin and Greek, family misfortunes
forced him to join the labour force in 1917 and thereafter his life was entirely
devoted to business.[42]

If the principals of CIC and QRC were asked in the first decade of the twentieth
century to name their greatest nonacademic problem, they would most likely have
pointed to grievances over subsidies from the government and mutual rivalries for
bright boys.[43] The dissatisfaction of CIC with its level of government subsidy went
back to the commencement of the dual system in 1870. The struggle between these
two colleges was, after 1902, no longer for existence itself for each was now safe
within the dual system. Fr Crehan's case in 1916 was not that QRC should get
less money, but that CIC should get more (see Table 2.6). He also wanted
government assistance to build a science laboratory. The attitude of Burslem was
that government should pay capitation grants to CIC only for Roman Catholic
fee-paying boys. If it subsidized the boys not paying fees or those paying half the
fees whom the principal himself had chosen as CIC exhibitioners, then free
secondary education, at the cost or partly at the cost of government, was wrongly
in the gift of a private person, i.e. the principal of CIC. Burslem was troubled by
the ability of CIC to give its own exhibitions while QRC had to rely solely on the
College Exhibitioners who chose to attend it. Between 1913 and 1914 CIC won
five of the six university scholarships, and in each case, the winner was the holder
of a CIC exhibition offered to students from Roman Catholic primary schools.
Some of the five winners were not even Roman Catholics.

As the education system grew in the later nineteenth century, the management
of the system became more complex and demanded more expertise. Inspector
Lechmere Guppy (1870-1890) had been rightly accused of being a novice in
education, though an intelligent man with serious interest in natural history; his
critics, some non-white, felt that he would be unable to teach a class properly, if
anyone ventured to assign one to him.[44] Guppy was given assistant inspectors who
were white (or nearly white) clerks from other sections of the civil service, persons
mostly without teaching experience.[45] The system of payment by results enabled
these inspectors to escape the role of advising teachers about teaching, since it
called more for an examination of the pupils than an inspection of the schools.
The appointment of Gervase Bushe in 1890, an ex-QRC master, inaugurated the
era of inspectors knowledgeable about education; Bushe was followed by J.H.

Collens, the principal of the government training school, and then by H. Hancock, another ex-QRC master. The appointment of Collens opened a route to the top of the education hierarchy – from the principalship of the government training school to director of education – which was to endure from Capt Cutteridge in 1921 to the advent of the PNM government in 1956. However, the assistant inspectors between 1900 and 1916, with one exception white males like the inspector of schools himself, were untrained persons who could not get a job at a teacher training school. The Education Commission of 1914/1916 recommended that only university graduates, or persons possessing special educational qualifications should be appointed assistant inspectors. No university graduate was available and the desire to raise the standard of the assistant inspectors unintentionally soon led to the policy of elevating the most experienced of the headteachers (who were non-whites) to temporary assistant inspectorships. Since at least the time of J.J. Thomas in the 1870s, some non-white persons realized that the body of experienced senior headteachers was, actually or potentially, the most logical place to look for administrators of the school system.

Naturally the assistant inspectors were not allowed to inspect a secondary school; the same applied to the inspector of schools except Bushe and Hancock who had been masters of QRC. The administration of the secondary schools remained separate from that of the primary schools. Since 1895 there had been proposals to unify the two administrations; this was mooted again by the Education Commission of 1914/16, but it was not possible to do it without upgrading the post of inspector of schools to attract an appointee who would be respected by the principals of CIC and QRC. Hence the recommendation of the Education Department that the inspector of schools should be redesignated director of education; he should be the head of the Education Department, with a right to chair the Board of Education supervising both secondary and primary schools. The idea also emerged that the director of education was worthy of a seat on the Legislative Council.

The Introduction of Science and Progressive Ideas 1916-1932

The Education Commission of 1914/16 set the stage for changes which began the modernization of Trinidad and Tobago's schools. A law was passed in 1918 which signalled some of the coming developments in secondary education, teacher training and the administration of education; but not much action was taken until after World War I. In a word, the outstanding innovation in secondary education in the 1920s was the introduction of science teaching on a systematic basis, leading to the virtual elimination of Greek and to a significant reduction of the focus on Latin. Consequently, the subjects on which the university scholarships (Island

Scholarships) were based were regrouped in such a way that one university scholarship was based essentially on the science subjects, and the other on the revised arts curriculum. It is important to note that the secondary education to be modernized was expanding faster in the 1920s than at any time previously.

In 1916 there were four recognized secondary schools (QRC, CIC, Naparima College, and St Joseph's Convent, Port of Spain); by 1926 there were three more, viz. Bishop's High School in Port of Spain (1924), Naparima Girls' High School (1925), and Bishop's High School in Tobago (1925). As shown earlier, a very meagre base for science teaching (classes in chemistry at the laboratories of the government chemist) existed for some QRC and CIC students from 1905; in the first two decades of the twentieth century powerful campaigns for scientific agriculture and a specialist agricultural college underlined the indispensable need for a science programme in the secondary schools; then came World War I. This war convinced England that she was behind Germany in science, and more science was programmed for England's secondary schools after the war. The Education Commission of 1914/16 felt all these influences keenly and recommended a proper programme of agricultural science in the secondary schools. Certainly the decision to reserve one of the university scholarships from 1919 for the study of agriculture provided an incentive to the development of science teaching.[46]

CIC first set off in the direction of science teaching, thanks to the greater flexibility which a non-government school usually has over a government institution, and thanks also to private donations. QRC had to await government funds for science teachers and laboratory facilities. At CIC a chemistry laboratory was in place from 1916; followed by a botany laboratory from 1919, and then a laboratory for zoology and physics from 1921. By 1923 the principal, Fr English, could report that with the introduction of physiology, hygiene and drawing classes, the science programme was complete. QRC under the principalship of Alfred Low, went in the same direction, though much more slowly, with the result that it could not compete successfully for the Agricultural Scholarship (university scholarship) while it lasted (1919-1924);[47] and when the Agricultural Scholarship was converted into the Science Scholarship, QRC won it only once (C. B. Franklin in 1925) in the later 1920s. On the other hand QRC continued to excel in winning the other university scholarship which was based on what was called modern studies, and for which the competition was tougher.[48]

The newly recognized secondary schools talked about following CIC and QRC into science teaching, but they had neither the resources nor the incentive of likely Island Scholars. From 1922 Naparima College said it was thinking of science teaching, but it did not include it during the 1920s; neither did Naparima Girls' High School and Bishop's High School (Tobago). Bishop's High School (Port of Spain), a girls' school otherwise known as Bishop Anstey High School, contented itself with a little botany as early as 1925. St Joseph's Convent, in many ways midway between the two premier boys' colleges and the newer girls' schools, started with botany in 1920, then added hygiene and physiology in all forms, and by 1923 included elementary chemistry and physics in the upper school. Although there was a science laboratory from 1921 for physiology, hygiene and botany, the school refused to follow QRC and CIC fully into the unladylike subjects of chemistry and physics.

There was no real opposition to the introduction of science into QRC and CIC, although there was a fair amount of disagreement among members of the Board of Education about the wisdom of having an Agricultural Scholarship. By extension, some doubts were also cast upon its successor, the Science Scholarship. But this was a quarrel about university scholarships, about their number, and the careers to be followed by the winners of science based scholarships. It was not a quarrel about the introduction of science.[49] An area more fraught with potential disagreement concerned certain fairly new notions about secondary education which were being aired by Director of Education Frederick Marriott. He promoted the idea that secondary schools should be more flexible, to the point of admitting the possibility of very different types of secondary education: technical secondary schools, classical secondary schools, and something called modern secondary schools. But this potential area of disagreement did not mature into conflict in the 1920s; the newly recognized girls' schools and the coeducational Bishop's High School (Tobago) set out in the same direction as QRC, CIC and St Joseph's Convent.

If the modernization of the secondary schools and their curriculum did not stir conflict, the same cannot be said about the effort to modernize the course of study in the primary schools.[50] Whereas the insertion of a modicum of science into CIC and QRC left their curriculum still dominated by a reduced classical programme, what happened in the primary schools in the 1920s was more like revolution: a curriculum revolution involving innovations in the core subjects.[51] Whereas the reforms in QRC and CIC were largely self-imposed in the sense that the principals thought them out and carried them through to their satisfaction, the changes in the primary schools were imposed from outside by white expatriate directors of education upon classroom teachers, pupils and parents. Whereas nothing could be more impersonal than the science taught in QRC and CIC, there was something emotional about the curriculum revolution in the primary schools. The science teaching at CIC and QRC addressed itself to things: the revolution in the primary schools touched peoples and cultures.

The essence of modernization in the primary schools was not the introduction of new subjects, although drawing and handwork (later called handicraft or crafts) were introduced, but a new attitude to children and to teaching, and new textbooks for old subjects. As in the case of science in secondary schools what was now thought to be right and modern for primary schools was inspired by developments overseas. The intellectual base of the new philosophy of education consisted of the new psychology (sometimes not so new) coming into vogue in England and elsewhere. The child was a living personality, with instincts to be developed. Education should be designed for the child, not for the teacher. The motto was 'Children first'.[52] All action was ultimately mental action, thus the brain could be improved by the use of the hands. The new psychology indicated the need for more individual attention to children; for systems of teaching which allowed for a varying pace of learning; for self-expression, freedom and even independence for children.[53] It called for reality in school work, for a closer relationship between school work and the environment. It proclaimed that children learned from the known to the unknown. In one way or another these ideas belonged to the progressive education movement.

In the 1920s this new philosophy became current in Trinidad because after 1919 the post of inspector of schools was upgraded to director of education, and all directors of education were required to be graduates of English universities with special qualifications in education. This tended to favour Englishmen recruited directly from England or from service in another part of the empire. H. Hancock, ex-QRC master and inspector of schools became the first director of education, but retired shortly after the new law of 1918 and the Code of 1921 had been put in place. It was left to his successors to carry out the revolution for which he had prepared the way. By the early 1930s many teachers, looking back on Hancock's era, expressed admiration for him as "a good type of Englishman",[54] who understood and sympathized with their aspirations. The colony, after Hancock, had successively three directors of education, George Mackay (1922-1925), Frederick Marriott (1926-1934), and Captain J. Cutteridge (1934-1942); Mackay and Cutteridge were recruited from overseas. Marriott had taught at QRC and had worked in the Immigration Department of the colony and, in this sense, was something of a local figure. Mackay, Marriott and Cutteridge were knowledgeable about trends in England and elsewhere, and Cutteridge had the unique experience of having taught in a variety of schools in England, including technical schools and teacher training schools. When these directors spoke of modernizing primary education they meant the introduction of some of the ideas of the Progressives in England; but they never went as far as those idiosyncratic English intellectuals and self-employed English school masters who gave bizarre expression to advanced thinking in education.[55]

The three directors concluded that a new orientation had to be given to teacher training and primary education, and that new textbooks had to be introduced. Cutteridge was particularly associated with both innovations, because even as assistant director under Mackay and Marriott, he was in charge of teacher training, and he himself undertook single-handedly to write new textbooks for reading, arithmetic and geography. Starting at the government training school at Tranquillity, and then developing a series of in-service courses, Cutteridge taught the teachers the value of handwork (crafts). This was said to be both a method and a subject. As the latter, it covered anything from paper cutting to school gardening.

As a method, Cutteridge claimed that it was educational, not vocational: the stock phrase was using the hands and the eyes to develop the brain.[56] Cutteridge emphasized the need for reality in teaching. For instance, he began to take teachers on educational excursions to aid the study of geography. He set the teachers to work making charts, maps and diagrams for the walls of their schools. Caroni Canadian Presbyterian Mission School under Cyril Guyadeen (or Gayadeen) quickly became Cutteridge's showpiece in rural Trinidad.[57] In the teaching of reading Cutteridge emphasized phonetics: the importance of teaching the sounds of the letters of the alphabet, rather than the letters themselves. Who could object to any of this? But Cutteridge found himself in trouble when he began to write new textbooks.

Between 1927 and 1931 Cutteridge published five reading books (*Nelson's West Indian Reader*, 5 vols), seven arithmetic books (*Nelson's West Indian Arithmetic*, 7 vols), and one geography book (*Nelson's Geography of the West Indies and Adjacent Lands*). The classroom teachers were not consulted, and as soon as the books came off the press they were introduced fully into the schools. If Cutteridge had done this in 1850 or 1880 he would have met no opposition, but it was his misfortune that his long regime in Trinidad (1921-1942) coincided with the rise of middle class spokesmen for the working classes who, through the press of the labour movement, for the first time claimed the right of helping to shape education policy. This development was in keeping with major political changes and pressures in the colony, with demands for representative government leading in 1925 to the inclusion of a handful of elected members in the Legislative Council. But worse yet for Cutteridge, some of these spokesmen for the working classes subscribed to Garveyism, a new and more radical variant of black consciousness which swept sections of the lower middle class and working classes in the 1920s, feeding on the unsatisfactory conditions of the post–World War I era.[58] As advocates of black consciousness, led by Howard Bishop, general secretary of the Trinidad Working Men's Association, Garveyite writers in the *Labour Leader* and *The People* were infuriated by the inclusion of African and Afro-Trinidadian folk tales in Cutteridge's reading books. For example, a writer in the *Labour Leader* in October 1928 objected to the "heaps of Nancy stories",[59] stigmatizing them as remnants of superstition, no better mental food for children than the husks which swine ate. Another writer in September 1928 accused Cutteridge of insulting the entire Negro race with his "Nancy Story" books; and informed him that the Negro race were builders of civilization on the banks of the Nile while his ancestors were living in caves and trees like monkeys and running naked in the woods.[60] The critics demanded the return of the old reading books, wondering how Cutteridge, a man who had no university degree, and who was not known as an education expert in England, could introduce books "teaching little children that monkeys can wash their livers, and hang them out to dry".[61] As if to confirm the Garveyite suspicions that Cutteridge was a racist, his *Reader* Book I had a lesson which subsequently had to be revised after protests. It seems that certain drawings accompanying the lessons made the black people look somewhat like gorillas.[62]

Other aspects of the Cutteridge innovations were criticized. The need to change reading books frequently as pupils moved from one standard to another meant more money for school books. There had been, it was said nostalgically by one critic thinking of the pre-Cutteridge era, "books which took you in and carried you out of school . . ." [63] Cutteridge's *Arithmetics* were said to contain certain inaccuracies, his geography book was once said to be full of useless details, but it was the *Readers* which attracted the harshest criticisms, and it was the folklore stories which drew most fire. By including a great deal of local material Cutteridge was suspected of wishing to cut off black children from the wider world of knowledge. Cutteridge's de-emphasis of grammar was said to be disastrous for poor black children struggling to learn the English language. The most important charge against the Cutteridge regime, which subsumed all others, was that of a conspiracy to lower the standard of education in the primary schools, and thus halt the progress of the masses. The proof, said the critics, were the complaints that pupils in Standard VII could not read as well as Standard IV pupils could in the early twentieth century.

In November 1931 a critic of Cutteridge confidently predicted that "the evil [of the *Readers*] is so apparent that posterity will be able to prove it abundantly".[64] But let us take for example the much discussed folk-tales. A content analysis of the *Readers* shows a sharp fall in the percentage of folk tales as the series progressed from lower books to higher books; 22.5 percent in Book I; 15.1 percent in Book II; 9.7 percent in Book III; 2.4 percent in Book IV; 2.3 percent in Book V. How far this was a result of the early attack on Book I is not clear. The fact is that only Book I had a high folk tale profile. The outstanding characteristic of the *Readers* was the local nature of nearly half of all the lessons, excluding poetry.[65] Still, it would not be true to say that Cutteridge did not compile lessons on people and things outside Trinidad and the West Indies. Foreign lessons of all types, excluding poetry, were a substantial part of all the books except Book II. On the whole, the *Readers* now seem hardly offensive in their contents. What they left out was the real problem: they omitted lessons on blacks and coloureds as people. These appeared incidentally and briefly in lessons about crops, and they always appeared as labourers. There were no lessons about the descendants of the ex-slaves as people of worth.

Cutteridge's *Arithmetics*, which escaped with little criticism, were class and culture-bound productions with few exceptions. Cutteridge set sums involving yams and plantains; cutlasses and hoes; chicken houses and one-room houses. He insensitively called on teachers and pupils to make calculations of items reminiscent of slavery or of aspects of working class culture of which they could hardly be proud. The cultural direction of his *Arithmetics* was agricultural, just as his *Readers* had a rural bias.[66] Significantly absent or rare in his *Arithmetics* were items associated with the upper class: motorcar, jacket and tie, bowler hat, tea and sandwich. In other words, Cutteridge in his *Arithmetics* was more prone to ask pupils to add two and two oxcarts than two and two motorcars. The *Arithmetics* were not only local, but specific to working class culture. This was what Cutteridge called going from the known to the unknown; in other words, reality. It was almost as if the pupils did not have to learn to calculate items associated with the social class to which they would not belong.

Although the labour press criticism of Cutteridge's books abated in the 1930s, he was disliked by many people, including some teachers, for many years to come. Of course, Cutteridge defended his work, and he had some supporters. One of his lines of defence was to part company with those who felt that what was good for their parents was good for their children. His trusted elaboration of the point was that forty years previously people of Trinidad fought malaria with bush tea, not with quinine, and travelled from Port of Spain to San Juan in a horse and buggy, not a motorcar. His coup de grâce was his contention that nobody untrained in his teaching methods, not even a parent, could accurately judge the progress of children taught according to his methods.[67] Cutteridge took the opportunity at a Parents Day function at San Fernando Canadian Mission School in March 1932 to elaborate on his methods. He pictured the teacher of the past as a stern, elderly, bespectacled man with a rod in his hand. He kept pupils quiet and made them read from a book. He sought to develop the intelligence of his pupils by improving their memory. Under Cutteridge's new methods, the emphasis was on the activity of the children; the book was just an aid. The modern idea was to make the children think and become self-reliant. Instead of teaching the child to spell hippopotamus and rhinoceros, the new thing was to ask him to spell cocoa, plantains and cassava, all things within his environment. In geography children were now to study the conditions of coconut and cocoa cultivation, not wheat growing. Some critics moped that the lessons in Books II and III of the *Readers* were too hard because of words like coconut, centipede, cassava, pumpkin and pawpaw, but he maintained that these things were familiar to the children and that they enjoyed reading about them. In arithmetic, Cutteridge ruled out clock sums, train sums, sums about mixtures, discount and compound fractions, and brought in a wide range of everyday calculations covering real problems. In reading, infants were to be made to learn phonetically, by the sounds of letters. For example, the infant looks at the picture of a bat, and makes the sound 'b'; at an apple and says 'a'; at a top and says 't'. By combining these sounds the infant learns to pronounce 'bat'. This helps the infant, Cutteridge declared, to read with comprehension. Cutteridge said that psychology had revealed many new insights into the process of learning, and that the innovations were not fads, but based on sound scientific principles.[68]

It would be of incalculable advantage in the assessment of the Cutteridge regime if we really knew what most of the teachers thought. In 1928 Cutteridge and

Marriott attempted to show the public that their innovations had the support of the teachers. A questionnaire was sent to all headteachers, requesting them to say which lessons made the strongest appeal to the pupils, and which lessons they as teachers objected to, apart from the particular one in Book I; and finally, teachers were asked if they wished to revert to the old Readers. The reporting of the results of this survey is confused: 282 headteachers were reported to have said "Yes", and one said "No", but to what question or questions is not known. The result was said to be an overwhelming victory for Cutteridge, but his opponents were at pains to point out that the teachers were not free to give their real opinions.[69] Each headteacher had to sign his name and that of his school on the questionnaire: how many headteachers would dare tell Cutteridge that they disliked his books?

It must be noted that although Indian nationalism was growing concurrently with black race consciousness, Cutteridge's *Readers* were not attacked by Indians or by the Canadian Presbyterian missionaries who often spoke in their name. There were only three lessons in the *Readers* about Indians, and Cutteridge treated them respectfully. Cutteridge's *Readers* were also put in the schools for Indians. The culture of the Indian, though seriously altered from that of ancestral India, was too satisfied with its own values, too comfortably immune to feel threatened or hurt by the *Readers*. Indian culture could only be hurt by an outright attack, and such an attack was perceived to be coming not from Cutteridge or Marriott, but from the christianizing mission of the Canadian Presbyterians who were obstacles to the establishment of Hindu and Muslim denominational schools. The spokesmen for the people of African descent, trying to establish their cultural identity, were the ones who felt threatened implicitly by the *Readers*; the Indians were mainly anxious to preserve their traditional culture by removing obstacles to its expression.

It is not difficult to concede that Marriott and Cutteridge did modernize some aspects of education in the primary schools. They managed to raise the standard of teacher training, although there was a great deal of confusion over the bursar system of teacher training. Whether by the bursar system or by the system which succeeded it, Marriott and Cutteridge based teacher training on secondary education, and that was one source of its improvement. Also schools had more and better apparatus; there were more school shows, more seminars, more activity than ever before. School excursions had become popular. The idea that the content of the curriculum of primary education should reflect the local environment was firmly implanted. There were, however, legitimate considerations about which Cutteridge seemed unconcerned.

First of all, the charge that performance in reading had fallen was more than idle anti-Cutteridge propaganda. Any revolution in an important aspect of education is likely to bring some less acceptable results, if only in the short run. Fr L. M. Loughlin, a white Roman Catholic priest and manager of several Roman Catholic schools, was no supporter of black consciousness, but he came to the conclusion that standards had fallen and said so publicly to an assembly of teachers.[70] Still, it is not possible to blame this simply on the Cutteridge *Readers*, and his opponents conveniently forgot the mechanical reading of the previous school books. The critics were not interested in whether or not many pupils were more self-reliant, more thoughtful, more imaginative or happier because of Cutteridge's innovations. Perhaps pupils had made gains in these areas at the expense of basic reading skills. If so, Cutteridge was wrong to ignore the complaints.

Black and coloured people in Trinidad and Tobago were obliged by circumstances to think of formal education not simply as cultural enrichment, but as the indispensable vehicle of upward social mobility. The schools could not leave the task of teaching fundamentals, especially grammar, to the homes of lower class children. What a boy needed to pass examinations, to get a College Exhibition, even after Cutteridge had unilaterally altered the examination in the direction of an intelligence test, was mastery of the three Rs. What a boy needed to compete with white boys in a world dominated by whites was knowledge of the white man's world. This was why the very concentration on local material in the *Readers* – though not itself the overt object of the critics – was sensed to be full of risks for blacks and coloureds. The reading books in the schools in the pre-Cutteridge era, for example the *Royal Readers*, had almost always taken the minds of boys outside Trinidad to the white man's world in distant places. As one critic declared: "Any system of education which confines children mainly to possessing a parochial outlook in life is preposterous and wicked."[71]

Of course it is now clear that the anti-Cutteridge campaign reflected the confusion and contradictions of a race and class conscious colonial society. Garveyite advocates of black pride were, after all, objecting to bringing elements of the popular culture of the black majority into the schools. Many black people preferred English school books to books dealing with local topics. Middle class defenders of the working classes had themselves internalized a great deal of the values of the colonial English. There were, however, a few teachers, including DeWilton Rogers, who advocated the introduction of some aspects of black culture into the schools. The contention of these avant-garde black teachers was that:

> . . . children would not be the losers if the teacher when teaching of the great men of Europe and America, brings to their notice the Negroes who have distinguished themselves along similar lines. When expounding the poems which treat of blue eyes, flaxen curls and snow-white breasts, he leads them to see beauty in raven's plume, pearly teeth and jetty skin too; when posting up in his school the portraits of men who have become famous through their literary contributions, scientific discoveries, social organizations or even human slaughter, he neglects not the ebony sons and daughters of Africa.[72]

The lives of great black men was one thing; pride in African or Afro-creole culture of the black masses of Trinidad and Tobago another. There must have been a majority of teachers who as part of the black and coloured middle class were oriented by education and aspiration towards European culture. However pedagogically sound the policy of locally oriented textbooks appears today, it was culturally shocking in the 1920s and politically suspect. It remained so until, through their access to political power, non-white peoples had more control over the system of education and began to turn it to nationalistic ends.

The Control of the Dual System 1921-1931

Control of the dual system passed successively from the Board of Education, dominated by the churches in the later nineteenth century and the very early twentieth century, to the directors of education in the 1920s and 1930s; and finally to the Cabinet and prime minister in the 1960s. In the 1940s and 1950s elected politicians as members of the Legislative Council came to have influence over the dual system, without taking responsibility completely out of the hands of the directors. Shifts in power over the dual system were not effected without resentment and even resistance; the directors challenged the Board of Education and were resented and resisted; the elected politicians challenged the directors and were resented. Put another way, the churches and their representatives (the Board of Education) were challenged by civil service professionals (the directors of education), who were subsequently challenged by elected representatives (politicians) of the people. The civil servants and elected politicians were different facets of government; essentially the churches and their representatives were challenged by government, notably from the 1920s. Unless this long drawn out process is understood, it will appear – mistakenly – that the nationalist attack on the churches' power in the dual system from the mid 1950s was sudden and without precedent; the fact that there was still much to attack in the 1950s was a tribute to the resilience of the churches.

Inspector Guppy was never on the Board of Education; his successor, Bushe was only appointed in 1902. The Board of Education continued to administer the primary schools until 1917; the College Council administered the secondary schools separately until the same year. Then changes began to occur; a law in 1918 united the College Council with the Board of Education; it also confined the Board of Education to a consultative and deliberative role, leaving the administrative or executive functions to a director of education who became chairman of the Board.[73] This shift had neither been recommended nor approved by the Board of Education; the legislation was the doing of Governor Chancellor, Inspector Hancock and the Legislative Council. The Roman Catholic archbishop predicted, disapprovingly, that the director would be "a petty tyrant with an advisory Board of thirteen".[74] The change in itself might not have meant much if it had not been followed by two other developments: first the successive appointment of three professional directors of education, Mackay, Marriott and Cutteridge; and the inclusion of the director of education on the Legislative Council as a head of department from 1925. After 1918 the Board of Education came to occupy a less overpowering place in the decision-making system.

It must not be thought that everything the directors did was designed to undercut deliberately or consistently the Board of Education or led to conflict with it. To a certain extent the directors were simply doing their job in taking charge of the Department of Education, of the schools, of the teachers, of Tobago: they were assuming leadership in policy making which their position demanded. For instance, if there was legislation to be introduced into the Legislative Council, it would be the director who would pilot it; it so happened that the 1920s was not a decade for important legislation in education; there were adjustments in the regulations for the university scholarships, in teacher training, and in teacher salaries, but not until October 1930 was an important law introduced. However, it was the director who provided the government with the answers to the questions about education which the elected members asked in the Legislative Council.

The incorporation of pedagogical questions into the discussions about education also gave the directors an advantage over the members of the Board of Education. The Board of Education was more knowledgeable about secondary education than primary education; this was because the principals of QRC and CIC were always on it, and because the doctors and lawyers who were board members had attended QRC or CIC. Additionally, those on the Board might have had some of their own children or at least near relatives in the secondary schools, but hardly ever in the ordinary primary schools. Once the directors imported new methods and textbooks into the primary schools this entire area of management was left completely to their better judgement. The changes in the curriculum of the primary schools and even that of the government teacher training school were not discussed by the Board of Education except for some books in the case of the latter institution. It was the director of education, not the Board of Education or the Legislative Council, who attempted to modernize the primary schools and the government teacher training school.

It was not until the late 1920s that Director Marriott began to give Tobago his personal attention. One of the assistant inspectors did visit Tobago in the early twentieth century, perhaps once a year, to inspect and examine the schools; but neither Inspector Bushe, Inspector Hancock, nor Director Mackay went to Tobago. As we shall see later, when Director Marriott and Governor Hollis descended on Tobago in 1930 it was an event in the sister island. Thereafter came a resident assistant inspector and other visits by Director Cutteridge. The closer supervision of Tobago in the 1930s was a belated outgrowth of the professionalization of the directorship of education, and also of the vigorous representation of Tobago's interest by its elected representatives.

The Board of Education did not offer any objection to the directors taking charge of the correspondence with the schools, or of the clerks in the Education Department, or of the curriculum of the primary schools, or even of Tobago. But there were problems when the directors tried to take charge of the Board itself. The principals of CIC had a tradition of outspoken leadership on the Board of Education, as the highest Roman Catholic authority on the Board and on education questions which touched the doctrines of that church, the lay Roman Catholics on the Board followed his leadership. As a cleric, he normally followed the line of thought of the Archbishop of Port of Spain. The Roman Catholics on the Board of Education were always a tighter lobby than the Protestants who were split among representatives of the Presbyterians, Methodists and Anglicans. The rule, which for the last thirty years of the nineteenth century, allowed the Roman Catholics 50 percent of the membership of the Board gave them a great advantage during the periods when the Board of Education was in charge of the administration of the dual system. On the Education Commission of 1914/16, the principal of CIC had been unfriendly to the idea that the director of education should be the chairman of the Board of Education.[75]

The director of education did become the chairman of the Board of Education; and a capable chairman who is also the head of a department and more knowledgeable about education than most Board members can seldom be prevented from having a tactical advantage at the Board. When the director could find an ally in the governor, his ability to outmanoeuvre the Board was greater but there were always limits to what he could do safely. Before the advent of the directors, education regulations were made by the Board of Education, with the help of the inspector of schools, then sent to the governor in Executive Council which could either approve or disapprove them; if they were not disallowed within a certain period, they would automatically be regarded as allowed. If there were any aspects of the regulations which required legislation, then the governor or colonial secretary would take the matter to the Legislative Council. After the introduction of directors this line of procedure was not changed except that the directors made the regulations with the help of the Board of Education. But a few members complained that they were unaware of certain new regulations; or, as in the case of the Code of 1921, that an entire set of regulations were hastily devised by Hancock and Governor Chancellor without the Board having the chance of scrutinizing them carefully. Governor Chancellor had set up a committee to settle the details of the Code of 1921, but most of the work was done by Hancock. The editor of the *Catholic News* later explained that Chancellor had not taken the Board of Education into his confidence on certain parts of the Code of 1921.[76] In a small colony it was not a matter that members of the Board of Education did not know what the governor was doing; it was failure, out of respect for his authority, to challenge him when he was doing it. Chancellor departed the island shortly after the Code of 1921 was made.

The director of education was a senior civil servant appointed by the British government, an expatriate expert and not a local employee of the Board of Education, as was the case with the inspectors of schools. To this extent he assumed some of the respect afforded to close advisers of the governor. The directors might choose to raise an issue with the governor before bringing the matter to the attention of the Board of Education.[77] The Board disapproved of this. It was because the director was adviser to the governor and chairman of the Board that Capt Cutteridge's lack of a university degree seemed at first so subversive of the social relations of the civil service, and of the relationship between the directorship and the Board of Education. Before Cutteridge had achieved enough on the job to partially reverse the initial unfavourable reaction to his lack of a university degree, the death of Director Mackay plunged him into the position of acting director and acting chairman of the Board of Education. This was for a year, between May 1925 and April 1926. It so happened that at that time the Roman Catholic members of the Board, led by Fr English, had begun a stubborn refusal to cooperate with the government policy for the training of teachers. The redoubtable Fr English, in the heat of debate, called into question Cutteridge's qualifications as a non-university graduate to be chairman of an august body of university trained principals, lawyers and doctors.[78] It was a very embarrassing moment for the Captain and the incident gave comfort to his enemies. Fr English later apologized, but the damage was already done. When Cutteridge became director in 1934 his personal stature was much higher than in 1925; he was by then a MBE (Member of the Order of the British Empire); no Board of Education could challenge his legitimacy then.

A most important consequence of the appointment of professional directors of education was that with or without the approval of the governor or the Legislative Council, they were disposed to place upon the government a greater responsibility for education than anyone previously ascribed to it. To a certain extent this was simply an assertion of their personal desire for more power and influence; but as changes in the constitution, especially the inclusion of elected representatives from 1925, gave government a greater legitimacy, its agents, even if themselves not elected, transmitted this sense of legitimacy into a claim for a larger share in policy making against persons (for example the clerics) who formed no part of the government.

In August 1927 Director Marriott put a magnificent question to the Board of Education: who was assisting whom in education? Was it the government assisting the churches, or the churches assisting the government? The churches had an obvious answer to such a question; it was the government which was assisting the churches. The Bishop of the Church of England had clearly stated in 1898 that education was the business of the churches; and that it was the duty of the churches to teach the government that central fact. On this account government was the junior partner in the division of responsibility. This was also the view of the Roman Catholic Church authorities. Undoubtedly the professional directors of education wished to turn this around by incremental changes without any open fight with the churches; they wished it understood that it was the government's responsibility to provide education, and that it was the churches who were the junior partners. The facts of the case were partly opposed to such an interpretation: the churches had by far most of the schools, primary and secondary; and also most of the pupils; but the government – and this was its trump card – had by far most of the money available for education. The directors were not secularists or against denominational education: they were for a larger measure of government control over, and responsibility for, education; but this could only be accomplished at the expense of the churches' role and responsibility in education.

The directors did not try to increase the number of government schools at the expense of denominational schools. The dual system was still regulated fundamentally by the Ordinance of 1890 and the Ordinances of 1901 and 1902 which had a built-in bias in favour of new denominational schools.[79] The number of government schools actually decreased slightly in the 1920s; but on the other hand the number of denominational schools did not increase though the churches which were able to command private funds did improve the capacity of their existing schools to accommodate more children (see Table 2.7). The slower expansion in terms of new school buildings was partly the result of the stringent administration of the system. Clerics wanting to get aid for new schools had to complete forms declaring the distance from the nearest school, the size of the classroom and the state of the toilet facilities. At schools where attendance dropped below required levels for the number of teachers on staff, the managers found the directors ready to cut off the salary of the teacher or teachers deemed unnecessary.[80]

The official policy of the directors was economy, and the most desired way of accomplishing it was by the amalgamation of schools. The Board of Education was in favour of more expenditure on schools; it was the government which disapproved of increased expenditure. A serious policy of amalgamation could not be attempted because the Board resisted such proposals, no church wanting to lose a school if it could at all be avoided; and by convention a church which lost a school had moral claims to be allowed to erect a new school in another area where it was required. In a colony which needed more schools absolutely, amalgamation of three existing schools into one large school might, in the short run, save two headteachers' salaries in exchange for the greater immediate capital expense of a new building or extension and the future expense of other denominational schools allowed in compensation for the closed schools. It is not very clear that any long-term savings were made by amalgamation; if there were some savings, they were quickly wiped out by gradually rising expenditure in education (see Table 2.8). As the existing schools were better attended in the 1920s the issue of overcrowding surfaced, especially in some Port of Spain schools. Hence some confusion in objectives arose when amalgamation and overcrowding had to be considered simultaneously. The point, though, is that it was Director Marriott who assumed the responsibility of solving these problems.

There were quarrels about the relative claims of government schools and denominational schools in the dual system in the 1920s. The economic stringency of the 1920s exacerbated these quarrels; also the controversy over the training of teachers, that is over the bursar system (which will be discussed later), also gave rise to angry feelings. But there was a difference between the situation in the 1920s and that in the late nineteenth century. The quarrels, except in relation to the bursar system, were not really centered in the Board of Education or in the Legislative Council, but in the newspapers reflecting splits in the opinions of churches and the public.[81] The directors recognized the importance of denominational schools; they accepted the arguments that such schools if controlled could save government money. There were some fears that the talk about amalgamation of schools might mask a desire to substitute government schools for denominational schools and, as we shall see later, there was a misunderstanding about the extent to which the government intended to go in introducing government schools in Tobago, which had no such schools. On the whole there was understanding in the Board of Education that the government needed the churches and the churches needed the government. The dual system itself was not at stake, only the issue of who was to control it.

When the Board of Education was in control of the dual system there was a natural alliance between it and the clerical managers or warden/managers of government schools against the teachers. The inspector of schools as an agent of the Board of Education behaved accordingly. This axis was disturbed by the advent of the professional directors and the Trinidad and Tobago Teachers' Union (TTTU) in 1919. The director now dealt with the managers; he needed their assistance in controlling the teachers, but he also realized that there were ways in which he could use the demands of the teachers to further his control of the managers. The best example of this was the issue of security of tenure: this question of the appointment, promotion, transfer and dismissal of teachers became the weather-vane of the dual system in the twentieth century, although it had not been an issue in the nineteenth century. Identifying who was in control of the teachers (or which way the battle for control of the teachers was going) revealed who was in charge or who was gaining power in the dual system. Many teachers in denominational schools disliked the regulations which gave individual managers the right to appoint and dismiss them. They imagined that they would find greater security in the directors or in denominational Boards of Management.[82] Denominational Boards of Management were devised and incorporated into the dual system in response to the needs of the TTTU. Until 1925 these Boards had no legal existence – a source of dissatisfaction to the TTTU.[83] These Boards, according to a statement by Acting Director Cutteridge in September 1925, were not to require that teachers do any work not connected with their duties as educators.[84] The churches were at first unhappy at having to form boards of management.[85] Some individual clerical managers had got themselves or their parishes (not so much their denomination) into debt to construct schools and therefore regarded the schools they managed as their personal responsibility. The churches developed ways of keeping the individual managers at the centre despite requirements to organize boards of management; but there were gains in the new arrangements for the directors. It was undoubtedly easier to conduct business with a denominational Board of Management representing a number of schools than with many individual managers of schools of the same denomination. It facilitated control by the director.

When Director Marriott finally decided in 1930 that it was time to have a new law to replace the Ordinances of 1890, 1901, 1902 and 1918, he introduced certain features which angered the churches. The institution of boards of management was unwelcome. Bishop Anstey of the Church of England felt he did not have the resources to run one board of management for all Church of England schools.[86] The requirement that boards of management give an account of government grants elicited a surprising resistance, especially from the Roman Catholics.[87] The Catholic Social Guild was mobilized to fight it. It was also noticed that whereas the Ordinance of 1918 gave the Board of Education power to make regulations, the Ordinance of 1930 conferred this on the governor in Council (Executive Council). Marriott explained that the Ordinance of 1918 had inconsistently given the Board of Education an advisory role, and at the same time power to make regulations. The regulations respecting university scholarships, according to the proposed Ordinance of 1930, were also to be made by the governor in Executive Council, and not by the Board of Education. Above all, Marriott had gingerly proposed a stronger role for the director in the appointment and dismissal of teachers in denominational schools. From September 1925 Acting Director Cutteridge had introduced into the Board of Education the idea that the director should approve all appointments before they became effective; but the full implication of this was lost in the dispute over the training of teachers. In the proposed Ordinance of 1930 teachers were still to be appointed and dismissed by the denominational Board of Management, but subject to the director of education.[88] Here was the thin edge of the director's wedge under a very sensitive plank of the dual system. It prompted Bishop Anstey to declare in a spirit of defiance that the government might, if it liked, appoint teachers of denominational schools, but those teachers would have to teach outside the school buildings which had been erected at the expense of the Anglican parish.[89] The proposed Ordinance of 1930 was bombarded with so many amendments that Marriott realized that his efforts to give legal backing to the stronger leadership role he wished to assume in the dual system were premature.

In 1930 the British government at the insistence of Arthur Mayhew, secretary to the Advisory Committee on Education, decided to conduct an on-the-spot investigation of education in Barbados and the eastern Caribbean. Trinidad was eventually included. As the impetus for this investigation came rather suddenly and from outside the colony, reflecting new concerns by the British government for education in the tropical empire,[90] it aroused suspicion in Trinidad. The Board of Education had not asked for an Education Commission; neither had the governor nor the Legislative Council; the churches, nor the director. But Director Marriott and his deputy Cutteridge welcomed it. The suspicion was that such a Commission, which Marriott was asked to join, would recommend something unfavourable to the role of the churches or even to the non-white people.[91]

The Integration of the Tobago Schools 1889-1931

On the eve of the union between Tobago and Trinidad in 1889, the schools in Tobago were suffering as a result of the disastrous collapse of the sugar plantation economy in the 1880s. The Tobago government's subsidy for schools, all denominational, which stood at $3,840 in 1883, went down to $2,400 in 1889; a small secondary school had gone out of existence. The highest paid teacher was getting no more than $115 per annum. The government could not afford to inspect the schools regularly; and the chief occupation of the Board of Education was to argue over the division of the government subsidy among the Anglican, Methodist, Moravian and Roman Catholic schools. Change was particularly difficult to bring about because the Board of Education was composed of the very clerics who managed the schools. The members of the Board of Education literally issued instructions to themselves.

The union of Tobago and Trinidad was undertaken in stages. Tobago enjoyed a semi-separate existence between 1889 and 1898 during which it had its own commissioner, appointed by the governor of Trinidad, and its own Financial Board to control its finances. It also had its own Board of Education. The union with Trinidad in 1898 brought these privileges to an end. Henceforth there was one governor, one Legislative Council, and one Board of Education, all located in Port of Spain. It must not be assumed that in the 1890s this total incorporation was anticipated by all Tobagonians, and the attitude of some of its leading citizens reflected pride in the island's past separate identity and great scepticism about the union. The view of some Trinidadians that the union saved Tobago from total disaster was not always shared by Tobagonians, some of whom by 1893 claimed that the island was recovering on its own when amalgamation of the two islands was imposed by the British government.[92]

Tobago was allowed to have its own Board of Education chaired by the commissioner between 1889 and 1898 because it had one previously, and because the Anglican, Methodist and Moravian churches in Tobago petitioned Governor Robinson to save them from falling under the jurisdiction of the Board of Education in Trinidad which was dominated by Roman Catholics. Robinson agreed, but imposed inspection from Trinidad upon the Tobago schools. This was not carried out regularly because Tobago had to pay for the inspection and because the education administrators of Trinidad were not overanxious to take on the responsibility of administering the Tobago schools. In 1892, 1895 and 1896 Assistant Inspectors Charles Hobson and William Robinson were sent to Tobago to examine the schools and to advise the Tobago administration.

Naturally the reports were not flattering. Judged from the standard of Trinidad's schools, the Tobago schools needed more and better trained teachers, improved organization and a larger subsidy from government. There were no female teachers, no pupil teachers taking examinations; far too few of the headteachers, in fact only six out of twenty had certificates and none of these were obtained in Tobago. Fourteen of the twenty teachers were creole Tobagonians and only two of the fourteen had managed to obtain certificates, both from the Mico Charity Teacher Training School in Antigua. Most of the schoolhouses, especially those of the Church of England, were dilapidated. The Moravians had the best buildings. The two top schools were conducted by the Moravians, but ironically these two headteachers were among those without certificates. Assistant Inspector Hobson felt that it would have been better to amalgamate a few of the schools. Mistakenly he thought that because all the schools then getting government aid were Protestant, a policy of amalgamation could be carried out without rancour.[93]

The Board of Education of Tobago was unable to move the Tobago schools appreciably in the direction desired by Hobson. It lacked the funds and the will; but the reports by an outside 'expert' (Hobson) were used by the teachers in Tobago to lobby for more pay, and by some clerical managers to get more funds for their schools at the expense of rival schools which had received unfavourable reports. Not anticipating that Tobago would be fully amalgamated with Trinidad, the Board of Education rejected some of Hobson's advice; it also indicated a preference to modify rather than adopt entirely the Education Code of Trinidad in order to meet Tobago's needs. As far as Hobson was concerned, it was always a matter of Tobago adjusting to the Code of Trinidad.

The amalgamation of Tobago with Trinidad in 1898 was not without problems in the field of education. Tobago became a ward of the unitary colony of Trinidad and Tobago at a time when a tight money policy in education was in effect in Trinidad, and on the eve of the introduction of agriculture into the work of the primary schools. Tobago went readily into the era of school gardens, but since its teachers had a lower pay structure than Trinidad (but a lower cost of living), the teachers there either had to be given a sizeable increase of salary immediately, or a lower salary scale had to be devised for the Tobago teachers. The latter course was temporarily adopted, but there were compensations. In 1895 the Tobago administration had put $3,024 into the schools; by 1900 the Trinidad and Tobago government made $4,665 available for Tobago and in 1904 a total of $11,606 (see Table 2.9). The Tobago schools had benefited immediately from the union whatever doubts about its overall financial effects might have been entertained by Tobago planters and merchants.

The history of the relationship between Tobago and Trinidad from 1889 to the present has been overshadowed by tensions arising from the fact that Tobago is a separate island; and from the denial of this fact, partially or fully, by those who saw no difference between Tobago and any other remote part of the unitary colony of Trinidad and Tobago. These tensions could not be redressed by steamboat communication between the two islands even if there was a satisfactory service, which was hardly ever the case. Leaving aside the inconclusive evidence about the extent to which Tobago was a 'paradise' for peasants rather than a depressed agricultural economy dependent on Trinidad, the frequent characterization of Tobagonians as hardworking, kind, respectful, neighbourly, predominantly black creole owners of their own small parcels of land, held good for all the years between 1889 and 1931.[94] In education Tobago had twenty-seven schools in 1889, twenty-three in 1891; and forty years later it had only thirteen more. The population increased by 6,607 (26%) between 1901 and 1931. There were, however, sufficient school places both in 1891 and in 1931. Enrolment had doubled between the inauguration of the union with Trinidad and 1933. Every village had a school less than a mile away.[95] As Archdeacon H. R. Davies once wrote of Tobago: "The Church and the elementary school was [sic] the central social theme, with a good funeral or wedding for a highlight."[96]

Tobago's problems in education, as in several other matters, could appear differently depending on whether one saw the island as a separate entity or as a an integrated ward of Trinidad and Tobago. Those who took the integrationist approach tended to downplay problems, and it is this view which dominated the historical records between 1898 and 1925. Reading the reports of the inspector of schools (or director of education) and his assistants in the early twentieth century, one would not get the idea that there were any special problems in education in Tobago. In the narrative sections of these reports, no separation was made between Trinidadian and Tobagonian schools; and in the statistical sections, where such a distinction was made, the Tobago schools appeared just as good or as bad as the rural schools in mainland Trinidad, except on the point of attendance where they were considerably superior. From the integrationist point of view Tobago schools were like the schools of remote rural areas of Trinidad and, as such, no alarms were to be raised if they were not as good as the Port of Spain schools.

There has always been a separatist point of view, held almost exclusively by Tobagonians, but not always well articulated. Seen in this way, the education system of Tobago did not fit easily into that of Trinidad. First of all there was no dual system in Tobago as in Trinidad. All the schools were denominational. Even among the churches, relative strength judged from the number of schools was inverted: the Roman Catholics, such a major force in Trinidad, were weaker in Tobago, and the Methodists and Moravians were the main educators in Tobago but of little account in Trinidad. Of course there were no Indians, and no Canadian Presbyterian Mission schools.[97] There were no primary schools attempting a secondary school syllabus; no Model schools; no teacher training school; no secondary school until 1925. In other words Tobago was entirely without that upper level of higher schools which existed in Trinidad. And who could miss the fact that there were no Tobago winners of the College Exhibitions and no Tobago Island Scholars?[98] Seen in these ways, Tobago not only had a different system of education but an inferior one. If Tobago had, as was shown in the census of 1911, a lower rate of illiteracy than Trinidad (largely because of better school attendance), that was hardly a compensation.

As will be seen later, the first decade of the twentieth century marked the beginning of technical/vocational education by the Board of Industrial Training. Tradesmen in Tobago were just as eager as those in Trinidad to obtain Board certificates, whether by recommendation or by examination. Boys were ready to learn trades,[99] but there were no firms or government departments in Tobago which could train apprentices and when the Board of Industrial Training started evening classes in Port of Spain, it could not see its way to organize any in Scarborough. In fact, it was not until 1957 that the classes of the Board were extended to Tobago. Here was another area – technical/vocational education – in which Trinidad had an advantage over Tobago. In 1909 the governor instructed that one of the two trade bursaries awarded by the Board of Industrial Training each year should be reserved for Tobago candidates; and in the following year, Gabriel Alleyne became the first Tobago bursar, and apparently the last in this period.[100] The concession to Tobago turned out to be only for one occasion. Although Alleyne chose to train as a carpenter, wisely avoiding the competitive engineering trades, it proved impossible to arrange for his apprenticeship in Tobago beyond the second year. Like so many other bright boys, Alleyne finished his training in Trinidad.

Some new developments in the 1920s brought the unarticulated grievances associated with the separatist view into sharper focus. The contented indifference of the integrationist posture came under review. The introduction of elected representatives into the Legislative Council was a major turning point in the history of the relationship between Trinidad and its offshore sister island. In 1925 a black pharmacist, James Biggart, with a reputation as a radical reformer, became the elected representative of Tobago.[101] As spokesman for Tobago, Biggart boldly began to ask in effect that special consideration be given to Tobago in matters of education. He requested more money and was told that Tobago got more funds for education than many a Leeward or Windward island except Barbados or Grenada.[102] Biggart asked that two College Exhibitions be set aside for Tobago tenable at Bishop's High School, and was told by Director Marriott that this would lower the standard of the examinations as Tobago candidates could not even pass, much more reach to exhibition level.[103] Biggart then asked for a special Tobago representative on the Board of Education. The government's reply was that the director of education could best represent Tobago, and he was already on it. Biggart also wished for a resident inspector for Tobago. At first he was told that such an officer would lose touch with developments in modern methods of education in Trinidad, and would therefore not be able to bring the gospel of modernization to Tobago. Steamboat communication between Tobago and Trinidad was unreliable, and visiting Inspector George Von Weiller once had to examine five hundred Tobago pupils in a single day in order to catch the returning steamer to Port of Spain. The authorities eventually relented and Tobago got a resident inspector. This was the first serious breach in the integrationist position that Tobago was not a special case; that it could not be given by the government any privileges not afforded other wards.

The other development of the 1920s was that the integrationists, meaning here the education authorities in Port of Spain, became aware of the widening gap between the primary schools of Trinidad and those of Tobago. As was to be expected the modernization of the curriculum of primary schools was first implemented in Trinidad, and more quickly in government schools than in denominational schools. Tobago, for easily understandable reasons, was left behind. Director Marriott and his deputy Cutteridge were not on the spot, there was no government teacher training school there to lead the way, and no teaching bursars bringing their secondary school education into the primary schools. It should have been easy enough to get Cutteridge's *Readers* into the Tobago schools; but modernization of the curriculum required newly trained teachers committed to new methods. There was at first no resident inspector to mount in-service courses.

The realization that Tobago had been left behind in the modernization of the curriculum of the primary schools grew after 1927; and Biggart must be credited partly with the creation of the atmosphere which led the education authorities to admit openly that all was not well with the Tobago schools. But unfortunately for everybody, the education authorities, when they were aroused, overreacted and gave offence to the clerical conductors of schools in Tobago, ironically even to Biggart himself. Their condemnation of standards in Tobago was severe, and their threats of reforms too radical for the clerics. This led to what might be called the Tobago school 'controversy' of 1930. Governor Hollis went over to Tobago in July 1930 and, departing from the tradition of laudatory speeches at school functions, told a Tobagonian audience at Scarborough Anglican School that their school buildings were substandard, their teachers poorly qualified, and that anyway they had too many small schools wasting the government's money.[104] Director Marriott who accompanied Hollis said or implied that Tobagonians lacked 'brains', and this of course deeply offended Biggart and others.[105] Apparently it had been several years since a governor had visited Tobago: such a visit with accompanying officials elicited feelings both of welcome and suspicion. Biggart's rebuke of Marriott in the Legislative Council later in the year led him to pronounce sentiments which could have emanated from a Tobago nationalist of the 1980s:

> If a history of Tobago were written all these things would be made clear to people, and they would be able to realize that we [Tobagonians] are not the nonentity as some people seem to imagine, and that the children have brains. We have been tutored in representative institutions; we had what Trinidad did not have.[106]

The remedy of Governor Hollis and Director Marriott, which was pronounced as a threat, was that some of the denominational schools in Tobago would be amalgamated and government schools established to set higher standards. The Methodists and Anglicans, as major school providers in Tobago, defended their denominational interest with almost as much spirit as the Roman Catholics habitually did theirs in Trinidad.[107] The Moravians expressed willingness to give up their schools in Tobago if the government wanted them, but the other churches would not hear of it. In the second half of 1930 there was a considerable stir in Tobago over the question of government schools versus denominational schools and out of this ferment the Tobago Teachers' Union came to life.[108] It is impossible to tell how the majority of the people in Tobago felt about government schools versus denominational schools; but denominational schools had too long a tradition not to have strong grass-roots support.[109] At the same time, there were teachers who wished to have government schools, hoping for greater job security as government school teachers; there were others who did not like the talk about amalgamating denominational schools, fearing that some teachers would lose their jobs.

Marriott realized that the reaction against the government was stronger than was justified by what the government planned on doing. The education authorities really intended two new lines of action in Tobago: first, to establish one government school at Mason Hall as a superior institution, a sort of pacesetter for education; and second, through a resident inspector and visits by Cutteridge to spread new methods of teaching. There was no significant opposition in Tobago to the spread of the Cutteridge revolution there and it became increasingly apparent, both by the restricted plan for only one government school and by the dilatoriness of government in executing this plan, that the traditional ascendancy of denominational education in Tobago was not going to be overturned. In fact, Marriott assured Tobagonians – as well as anxious denominationalists in Trinidad – that it was only because religious loyalties were so divided at Mason Hall as to render a large denominational school impossible that he planned to erect one large government school.[110] The only people really threatened were the clerical managers and, moreso, all but one of the headteachers of two or three schools to be amalgamated at Mason Hall to make way for the government school there. As for the proposed government school, it obviously had to be very good to justify its existence. All sorts of expectations were voiced: it should be like the Tranquillity Boys' and Tranquillity Girls' schools in Port of Spain (the former Model schools); it should train teachers like the government training school in Port of Spain; it should have a headteacher with a university degree; it should have superior apparatus. Established in 1939 under Ben Sealey, its first headteacher recruited from Tranquillity Boys' School, the government school at Mason Hall made a remarkable initial impact which is still remembered today with respect in the sister island.

It was easier to dispatch a resident inspector to Tobago than to establish a superior government school. E.B. Grovesnor as resident inspector began to do what was expected of him: conduct in-service courses for teachers, none of whom, up to 1929, had the chance of studying at the government training school in Port of Spain. Grovesnor was succeeded by Rawle Ramkessoon who inaugurated 'Education Week', something which Trinidad did not yet celebrate.[111] Cutteridge himself, the master of methods, appeared on the scene and spread the message of the importance of crafts in schools. Tobago teachers responded well, coming from their districts to listen to the teacher-director and his assistants. As in Trinidad, it was only a matter of time before a teacher in Tobago distinguished himself by mastering what Cutteridge was propounding. This happened firstly with Lionel Mitchell, headteacher of Scarborough Anglican school, who became the local Tobago expert on crafts in schools.[112]

The clerical managers and teachers of Tobago were sometimes embarrassed by the failure of the Tobago schools to produce College Exhibition winners to QRC and CIC. Tobago seemed devoid, in these times, of young education heroes. However, the view that this was proof of lower education standards in Tobago than in Trinidad was vigorously refuted by L.E. Edwards, headteacher of Upper Scarborough Anglican School.[113] It must also be remembered that talent, sometimes young talent, was constantly being drained from Tobago to Trinidad. One really cannot be sure that a few of the bright boys in the Trinidad primary and secondary schools were not Tobago born: it was said that some of the headteachers of Trinidad originated in Tobago, and there was one successful teacher in particular, Charles Smith, who was said to have been born and bred in Tobago, but who gave his talent to the Richmond Street and Chacon Street Anglican schools in Port of Spain.[114]

With or without a resident inspector, before and after Cutteridge extended his influence to the island, Tobago continued to disappoint in the College Exhibition examination. Nor did Tobago schools win the Handicraft Exhibition, the Board of Education's counterpoint to the trade bursaries of the Board of Industrial Training. But there was relief in sight: in 1925 Tobago got its first secondary school. Bishop's High School was largely the result of the creative energies of Bishop Anstey of the Church of England, the quiet on-the-spot management of Archdeacon H.R. Davies who spent a lifetime in Tobago, and the political ambitions of James Biggart. In the contemporary folklore of Tobago, Biggart, as a factor in the establishment of the school, runs a poor third, if remembered, behind the majestic figure of the philanthropic Anstey and the patient dedication of Davies. It would, however, be an oversimplification and a denial of the felt need for a superior institution to turn Anstey into the sudden and sole originator of the idea of a secondary school in the island. His boldness in executing the work (or in ordering Davies to execute it) swept away objections: this, after all, was unmistakably going to be a secondary school for black boys and girls, the children of peasants.[115] Anstey even managed to win some support from the Tobago planters after their initial astonishment and show of disapproval.[116] Perhaps the advance of cocoa cultivation between 1923 and 1925 – unwittingly on the edge of the cocoa price collapse – had cocoa planters in a receptive frame of mind. The school was first housed in a cottage donated by an English lady, and miraculously Anstey found a young black Barbadian, twenty-two years old, with an external degree from Durham University, won at Codrington College in Barbados. This was Rawle Jordan; he took a small salary and gave an immense service. There was no other black principal of a denominational secondary school in the colony, and in 1925 this astounding appointment could have been made in no other part of Trinidad and Tobago.

The campaign for the 1925 elections in Tobago reminds us that the foundation of Bishop's High School was not simply an affair of churchmen entirely removed from politics. In the elections both candidates pledged to work for a secondary school in Tobago. Biggart wrote in his manifesto:

> . . . as matters stand educationally only the rich and well-to-do people of Tobago are able to give their children a good education. This is so because the centre of education is so far removed from us, to say nothing of the cost by virtue of the situation. My aim is to bring to the notice of the Govt. the necessity of a school of Higher Education where the boys and girls of our Island will receive a good foundation, which is so necessary to meet the requirements of modern civilization. My object is to request that such a school be placed within the reach of the poor man's pocket, and bring to his door educated benefits, which are now only open to those who are able to send their children to Port-of-Spain and other centres.[117]

Biggart and Anstey began to lobby for a government grant and affiliation to QRC (that is recognition as a public secondary school) even before the school was started, using the not infrequent clerical strategy of suggesting that if the government did not aid a denominational college, it might have to establish one of its own at a greater expense. Between 1921 and 1924 Bishop Anstey had to struggle to convince the Board of Education to affiliate and aid his other new secondary school, also called Bishop's High School but located in Port of Spain. To approach the Board of Education in 1926 with another application for affiliation and government aid was viewed by the Roman Catholic board members as disrespectfully overambitious, especially as the school in Tobago was only opened in September 1925, and had not yet demonstrated efficiency or viability as a secondary school. In the 1920s the secondary school level of the dual system was again in the process of expansion, in terms of new schools, and the rules to control government grants to new schools became suddenly as important as those for primary schools. The question of the affiliation of Bishop's High School, Tobago, became a public issue debated in the press.[118] Inevitably Roman Catholics and Protestants were in opposition. The editor of the *Port of Spain Gazette*, suspected of religious bigotry in his opposition to Bishop Anstey's proposal, argued that it might have been just and more economical for the Church of England to establish scholarships for Tobago students to secondary schools in Trinidad. The editor's line of thinking ignored the sentiment that Tobago was a special case; it was insensitive to Tobagonians' self-perception as islanders; and Biggart was conscious that he was speaking for the people of an island, not the residents of a ward such as Tacarigua or North Naparima. Biggart's allegations that the editor and others wished to keep Tobago in 'darkness' carried more sinister political weight than any similar complaint from another ward. It was not the moral force of Tobago's position as a special case as much as the prestige of Bishop Anstey, the enthusiastic educator, which won Bishop's High School in remote Tobago a place in the dual system in 1926. But even so, the Roman Catholic members of the Board of Education and the Rev H. Morton of the Canadian Presbyterian Church surrendered only in return for a promise by the acting director of education that he would urge the government to revise upwards the grants to the older secondary schools of Trinidad.[119]

As the only secondary school in Tobago, Bishop's High School had to respond to many different needs simultaneously. It had to be for boys and girls; in fact it was the first coeducational secondary school to be recognized and aided by government. It had necessarily to develop along the path of the older secondary schools to fulfil the strong aspirations of Tobago parents for Cambridge Certificates for their children; it had to do at least Latin to be recognized as a genuine secondary school; but it was totally unprepared to join in the new trend to science teaching. There was, additionally, another kind of pressure upon Bishop's High School. Tobago, everybody sermonized, was an agricultural colony; everybody agreed its greatest asset was the land. It had no manufacturing enterprises. One of the early benefactors of the school was Kenneth Reid, a leading Tobago plantation owner; he and others were anxious that agriculture should be added to the curriculum and that the students should have practical experience in it.[120] From early in the life of the school agriculture, as well as domestic science and carpentry, were added to the curriculum;[121] but these subjects were not given the importance accorded to traditional Cambridge examination subjects, even after papers in agriculture were later sat in these examinations. It became immediately clear that the quality of Bishop's High School would be judged by the annual tally of passes in the traditional subjects of the Cambridge examinations, the single most important influence upon secondary education in Trinidad and Tobago.

Bishop's High School, Tobago, remained the smallest of the new secondary schools in the late 1920s and early 1930s. It proved wrong those sceptics who doubted that it could ever increase beyond the forty-four students enrolled in 1928; but after a decade it still had not demonstrated beyond doubt the error of the critics who claimed that the clientele for secondary education in Tobago was very limited. As time passed the clientele expanded through the ambition of black small farmers fortunate enough to have cocoa on their land. The farmers with twenty-five acres or more were men of substance who sent their children from remote districts to board near the sole secondary school, Bishop's High School. Its great social importance was in being a school with a student body almost totally black, a unique phenomenon in the unitary colony of Trinidad and Tobago. In time it raised up a black middle class in Tobago. Eric Roach, a Tobagonian student of Bishop's in the very early 1930s, wrote passionately some forty-four years later that: "Bishop's High School elevated the sons and daughters of the peasant proprietors first into clerkships, later into the universities and professions, and thrust the island's strong peasant conscience and integrity into the Trinidad administration."[122]

The tension between the classical and nonclassical aspects of the curriculum remained, and the school escaped the doubtful honour of being fully the new type of secondary school, the secondary modern school, which some of the education authorities in Port of Spain desired, without being a distinguished performer on the older model of the classical school.

It would be wrong to understate the influence of Bishop's High School on the schools of Tobago itself. The college, in its early years, did produce one or two very outstanding students, like the girl who passed Junior Cambridge at the age of twelve years, and Senior Cambridge at fourteen-and-a-half years old.[123] This feat and the name of the girl were still remembered in 1986 by the former principal, Rawle Jordan, then eighty-three years old. Had she been a boy this student's name might not have disappeared from the written records as quickly as it did. Such students served as models to be emulated by the pupils in the Tobago primary schools. A reassuring development in the short run was the increase of privately funded scholarships from Tobago's primary schools to Tobago's own secondary school. Failing to compete successfully in the College Exhibition examination of Trinidad and Tobago, Tobago created its own exhibition system and even hinted at organizing its own university scholarships.[124]

The Transformation of the Government Training College 1921-1939

The attempts to modernize the curriculum of the primary schools from the 1920s had a parallel in the remodelling of teacher training; and the increasing control of the directors of education (Mackay, Marriott, Cutteridge) over the dual system expressed itself forcibly in the evolution of a higher standard of teacher training, particularly in a reformed Government Training College. The starting point of these reforms was the recommendation of the Education Commission of 1914/16 that all the teacher training colleges for males (the government training school, the Roman Catholic Male Training School, and Naparima Training College) should be closed, and a new system of training teachers be implemented whereby youths were selected for secondary education, sent to either QRC, CIC or Naparima College, according to their denominational affiliation, and then given professional and agricultural training by the director of education, the Department of Agriculture and selected headteachers. These youths were to be given government bursaries and the system came to be known as the bursar system. England had adopted something like it from 1907, the rationale being the need to upgrade the general education of primary schools teachers. Nothing was said about the training of female teachers; presumably the female section of the government training school (based at Tranquillity Girls' school), and the Roman Catholic Female Training School were to continue. The two important things to remember about the proposals were the upgrading of the general education of trainee teachers by exposing them to secondary education, intending to go no further in the short run than Junior Cambridge level, and the closing of the existing training schools for male teachers.

It was impractical to effect such closures. The government training school had been in continuous existence for sixty-four years; and the two denominational male training schools for about twenty-one years each. Even if the government withheld subsidies from the latter two, it would not necessarily close them. In 1869 the government protected its training school from Keenan's recommendation to close it, and it chose to defend it again during World War I. The government, however, favoured the policy of converting the denominational training schools into denominational *hostels*, that is student residences, while retaining the government training school.[125] At the same time, it agreed to the proposal to have bursars; hence it put the bursar system on top of the reformed network of a government training school and denominational hostels. What followed was a very controversial system of teacher training which lasted between 1921 and 1927. The programme was attacked by the Roman Catholic Church from 1925 and began to break down from that time. Although it was reformed from 1927, elements of the old system lasted until about 1931. The misunderstandings between government and the churches over the bursar system of the 1920s resulted in the greatest tangle in the history of teacher training in the colony.

The story of the remodelling of teacher training has to be recounted on three levels: there was the rise and fall of the bursar system; then the attempts to develop a central training college in Trinidad to serve the eastern Caribbean and Guyana; and lastly the genuine rise in the standard of teacher education at the government training school and the denominational training colleges. These three levels interpenetrated; it was partly due to attempts to have a central training college to serve students of different religious affiliation from other islands that denominational hostels were combined with the bursar system; it was also because the standard of education at the training schools, especially the government training school, had risen that Trinidad retained the edge as the site of a proposed central training college. In this interpenetration, the most enduring fact was the unprecedented rise of a larger Government Training College to an outstanding position in the education system. It was in the later 1920s, and moreso in the 1930s, that the Government Training College first became a tertiary institution.

According to Roman Catholic sources, in 1915 and 1916 Inspector Hancock wanted to combine the bursar system with denominational teacher training schools, but was overruled by Governor Chancellor who, together with unnamed advisers, neglected to consult the Board of Education on all the details of the Code of 1921. In this Code the denominational training schools were downgraded to denominational hostels, leaving the government training school as the sole institution to carry on teacher training. The bursars, the government planned, were to do their professional training in the government training school after leaving secondary school. Those who wished to reside in denominational hostels in order to receive religious instruction could do so and the government would aid these hostels. The churches, especially the Roman Catholic Church, claimed not to have known until 1925 that the Code of 1921 passed by the Legislative Council in May 1921 required them to convert their training schools into hostels. The Church of England did not possess its own training school, but was also uncertain about the plans of the government; the Canadian Presbyterian Church was not sure where Naparima Teachers' College stood in the new system. Part of the explanation for the general uncertainty was that the government allowed the denominational training schools to continue as such, despite the Code of 1921, because until the first batch of bursars (the 1921/25 batch) was ready to do the professional part of their training, there was no need to change the pre-1921 system of teacher education. Between 1921 and 1925, therefore, the Roman Catholic and Canadian Presbyterian denominational training schools for males and females continued to train their own teachers, and to get government aid as training schools, while the government Code of 1921 said that they were *hostels* only. Of course since these training schools were also residential they did operate as hostels.

In 1921 the British government sponsored a West Indian education conference in Port of Spain. Since the 1890s several West Indian conferences on different matters had been organized by the British government which was thinking of bringing the islands into some sort of federation. The most important item on the agenda was a proposal to develop a central training college to serve the eastern Caribbean. At the conference it was clear from the start that the main rivals for the site were Trinidad and Barbados.[126] If it could be said that Trinidad was malarious, it could also be maintained that Barbados was a Protestant colony which would have difficulties in providing the religious instruction required by the trainee teachers from Roman Catholic St Lucia or Grenada. Trinidad had the greater diversity of clerics and churches; in this connection the device of having denominational hostels which could accommodate coreligionists from other islands was an important strategy of the Trinidad delegates in improving the island's chances of getting the site. Even Fr Lacy, the principal of CIC, acted like a statesman and pledged Roman Catholic cooperation, perhaps unwisely, in working out a system of denominational hostels. Since Trinidad virtually had ICTA already where agricultural training could be offered to the teacher trainees from other islands, Barbados could only come second in the race for the site.

On the assumption that bursars would teach in the schools of the church to which each belonged, fourteen bursars were chosen in 1921 in such a manner that each of the major denominations got an allocation related to the number of pupils in its schools.[127] The candidates for bursaries had to compete for their valuable scholarships by taking an examination set by the government; but the involvement of the churches in the approval of their moral character and in having a certain number earmarked for their schools created a vital clerical interest in the academic career of these youths. Everything went smoothly until 1925 when the first batch of bursars, having succeeded in their Junior Cambridge examinations, was ready to go to the next stage, professional training. Among them was Harry Joseph, perhaps the best known from his subsequent teaching career.[128] Since it was uncommon for secondary school graduates to become primary school teachers, these youths occupied a privileged position. Some of them came from the superior schools in Port of Spain, for instance Tranquillity Boys' School, the same school which produced several College Exhibitioners. To re-enforce this privileged position, after professional training, they were to constitute a special category as trained certified teachers. They were to be better paid; they were to become the shock troops of the modern methods which the professional directors of education were trying to introduce into the schools. The government felt that only the reformed government training school would be good enough to train these young men and women.[129] The Roman Catholic Church authorities astonished the government by suddenly declaring that it was hearing for the first time that all these youths, including the Roman Catholic ones, were to go to the government training school. It only struck them then, they said, that their role was simply to board these youths in their hostels, not to teach them.

It is not clear what the government wanted the churches to do with the non-bursars already in the denominational teacher training schools; perhaps they were to be phased out gradually. The Church of England had nothing to lose immediately, but in the long run it would lose the right to have its own denominational training school. Even if the Roman Catholic Church was preparing to go along with the plans of the government, the Canadian Presbyterian Church in San Fernando had a special problem; since they were thirty-five miles from the government training school in Port of Spain, they could not send their bursars there for classes while boarding them in San Fernando. Additionally, the Canadian Presbyterian Church leadership was not convinced that Indian trainee teachers would mix socially with non-Indians in a government institution; they pleaded a special need to expose their trainee teachers to practical agriculture and a rural environment such as was not possible in Port of Spain. The government and the Canadian Presbyterian Church met these difficulties by what appeared to be an ingenious device: Naparima Training College was declared to be a branch of the government training school, subject to the latter's supervision. The principal of the government training school was to visit and bring Naparima Training College in line with the government training school.[130] The Roman Catholic Church authorities felt that the Canadian Presbyterian Church had deserted the defence of denominational training schools while arranging to keep Naparima Training College intact. The Roman Catholic authorities were irreconcilably in favour of denominational training schools: they wished their bursars to attend their training college to be taught, not just lodged. They sent a petition to the British government in 1926.[131]

Led by Fr English, principal of CIC and a member of the Board of Education, the Roman Catholic authorities thought that their case was strengthened when Cutteridge revealed the new curriculum of the government training school. In pedagogy the bursars were to study Dewey, Rousseau, Luther, Spencer and Montagne. These were declared by the Roman Catholics to be atheists, agnostics and freethinkers.[132] Acting Director Cutteridge immediately offered to modify this part of the curriculum, but he would not back down from the requirement that the churches run hostels, not schools. The crisis continued into 1926 when Marriott became Director of Education. In the meantime the bursar system was in chaos; some of the Roman Catholic bursars, threatened with a ban from employment in Roman Catholic schools, did not enrol in the government training school.[133] Bishop Anstey of the Church of England would obviously wish to have the option of a training school if the Roman Catholics were allowed to have one. Other batches of bursars were due to emerge from secondary schools in 1926 and 1927. In the struggle to control the bursars who came out of the secondary schools in 1925, 1926 and 1927, it was not clear how many of the Roman Catholic ones actually went for professional training to the government training school. The bursars were treated too much like pawns belonging either to the government or the churches, instead of independent young persons free to make their own choices.[134] A key to the dilemma of training teachers was the assumption by the authorities that trainee teachers should ideally be in residence. There were persons, including the Port of Spain parents of some bursars, who rejected the supposed superiority of residence in a hostel: turning the pro-hostel argument on its head, they declared that vices could also be learned in hostels. The parents' arguments often reflected a financial need to augment their household budgets with the government's allowance for each bursar not living in a hostel. Those bursars who whispered their dislike for hostel life were in Marriott's thinking not fit to be teachers.

Marriott's solution as soon as he assumed charge of education was to scrap the bursar system and to give the churches the right to have a denominational training school or a hostel affiliated to the government training school. The government would aid either a denominational training school or a hostel, or a denominational training school combined with a hostel. His explanation was that it was wrong to take persons as young as fourteen or sixteen years old and turn them into teachers before they really knew what they wanted to do; for social peace, it was better to give in to the Roman Catholic authorities' desire for their own denominational training school. The theory behind the bursar system, however absurd and unjust it might sound, was that the bursars were the only trained teachers in the colony; all others, even experienced headteachers holding certificates from previous training institutions were technically untrained.[135]

The bursars were to elevate the government training school, and the school was to elevate them. They would receive a diploma which could not be obtained without attending at the government training school. By abolishing the bursar system, Marriott went back to the pre-1921 system of allowing denominational training schools; but he went forward academically by retaining the new connection between secondary education and the training of teachers. Because the number of holders of Cambridge Certificates was increasing, and some were taking these examinations as private candidates, Marriott estimated that without paying directly (through bursaries) for the secondary education of a few teachers, the government could invite secondary school graduates to offer themselves for training. He felt that the secondary schools were then producing more Junior Cambridge and Cambridge School Certificate holders than could find employment in traditional areas. He envisaged training more teachers annually with voluntary candidates than by using the bursar system; and it would, he thought, be cheaper since the government did not have to pay directly for their secondary education.[136] One can only assume that Marriott took into his calculations the greater cost of subsidizing denominational training schools rather than hostels. The Roman Catholics and the Canadian Presbyterians continued their male and female training schools, and the Church of England started a male hostel about 1926 and added a female one later. The trainees from the Church of England continued to study at the government training school.

Marriott also revealed that some teachers were resentful of the bursars. Some bursars, for example Eric Kirton, Samuel Thornhill, Oswald Stroud, Harry Joseph, J. Hamilton Holder, W.J. Alexander, and Gabriel Wong, later studied successfully (mostly in the 1940s) for external degrees of the University of London. In the 1920s they were seen by rival teachers as a youthful elite creating more divisive categories among teachers. In accommodating them the Code of 1921 had created three categories of teachers: the trained certified teachers of whom the bursars would be the first; certified teachers meaning all those who already had Teachers' Certificates; and uncertified teachers, including the army of pupil teachers. Headteachers with ten years experience or more, with even a first class certificate, found that they were now classified below youths (successful bursars) in their twenties whose only teaching experience was that which they had gathered during teaching practice. The foundation of the bursars was their possession of prestigious secondary education and attendance at the government training schools. The bursars were upstarts, and placing them in jobs required tact.

The debate in the Legislative Council on Marriott's proposals was lively. It turned not on the abolition of the bursar system, but on the issue of denominational training schools versus a monopoly of teacher training for a government training school. Captain Arthur Cipriani and C. Henry Pierre, elected members, supported the principle of denominational training schools; the other four elected members, Sarran Teelucksingh, A.V. Stollmeyer, J. Biggart and Dr McShine voted with L.A.P. O'Reilly, the leader of those lobbying against denominational training schools. O'Reilly was no friend of priestly opinions; he maintained that the principle of denominational training schools was wrong; taxpayers were asked to pay for four or five training schools to train a handful of teachers. A.B. Carr, a nominated member, and surprisingly the director of agriculture as well, voted with O'Reilly who was defeated seven to fifteen.[137] Marriott agreed that ideally it would be superior to have one central training college (which of course would have to be a government institution), but stated that the Board of Education was unanimously in favour of denominational training schools. He argued additionally that if, for instance, Naparima Training College was closed, the government would have to open a training school in southern Trinidad. No other West Indian island had only one training school as a matter of government policy.

Marriott and Cutteridge's critics who had a Garveyite perspective thought they saw another conspiracy to stop the rise of the black man.[138] The Trinidad and Tobago Teachers Union (TTTU) was unhappy with the decision to terminate the bursar system and asked the Marriott/Mayhew Commission of 1931/32 to recommence it.[139] After all, the ending of the bursar system was a curtailment of direct government support for the secondary education of black and coloured youths, over and above the College Exhibitioners. By 1927 there were twenty-seven bursars in the secondary schools; some were trying to persuade the authorities to allow them to stay on to do the Cambridge School Certificate.[140] Marriott and the Board of Education refused: if that were allowed, they would want to go on to Higher School Certificate and even to aspire to university scholarships. They would be lost to teaching.

It cannot be overemphasized that the social importance of the bursar system was that it included free secondary education; bright youths who were facing the end of their formal schooling at about fourteen years of age suddenly had opened before them a narrow channel of upward social mobility. Samuel Thornhill, one of the early bursars, was about to leave school when his chance came with the bursar system. Harry Joseph, who became principal of Mausica Teachers' College in 1963, left from a lowly monitorship at Piccadilly Anglican School in 1922 to enter QRC as a bursar. Success in the Junior Cambridge Examination in 1925 was a turning point in his career; as Charles Warner had hoped sixty-eight years previously at the founding of QRC (but with his mind on white boys) the black Harry Joseph in 1925 could have declared with pride, "I too was at the Collegiate School [QRC] of Trinidad".[141] Of less importance to the bursars was the pedagogic advantage of attendance at a teacher training school. It was the secondary education that mattered. Hence the abolition of the bursar system without any immediate compensation in terms of increasing the College Exhibitions was for the Garveyite editor of the *Labour Leader* a crime against the social aspirations of the people. The non-Garveyite editor of the *Teachers' Herald* also condemned its abolition, and not surprisingly the demise of the bursaries was in the long run romanticized into a kind of 'paradise lost' of primary school teachers; the enlightened gift of the popular Hancock, snatched away by lesser men.[142]

Having settled the dispute over denominational training schools or hostels, Marriott concentrated on continuing the reform of the government training school which Cutteridge had begun in 1921. At the Education Conference of 1921, Cutteridge had warned that the teachers needed a "liberal education". This meant raising the standard of general education, but more importantly they needed "some technical preparation" for their specialist function of teachers. The teachers must make a study of "various teaching devices, such as the art of questioning, the mode of dealing with answers given . . ."; he or she must have the power "to describe clearly, to narrate vividly or to tell a story well . . ." The teacher should have "some acquaintance with the simple laws of logic" to prevent students from drawing faulty conclusions; the teacher must learn the art of teaching not from books but from observation and studying a course of lessons given by a trained teacher, and by actual practice in the classroom. Teaching practice should be sufficiently prolonged and continuous for the teacher trainee to make a detailed observation of the same set of pupils. The teacher needed to study psychology. Cutteridge repeated the witty quotation: ". . . not so long ago it was considered that when the master taught

John Latin, it was enough for him to know Latin, now it is agreed that it is equally important that he should know John . . ."[143]

As principal of the government training school from 1921 to 1923, Cutteridge widened the curriculum to include drawing and crafts, and he insisted on each trainee giving, in front of his colleagues, a complete 'criticism' lesson once a week. Cutteridge, himself a trained teacher with special qualifications and experience in pedagogy, began a trend which became the hallmark of the Government Training College in the late 1920s and 1930s; the principal must have specialist training in the principles of teaching. The principals after Cutteridge were A. Wilson Campbell (1924-1926) and Captain William Daniel (1927-1937). The former was a Scotsman with two degrees, and special training in pedagogy; Daniel was an Englishman with a BA and with special training in pedagogy. The intention in the early 1920s was to lift the general education of the students by yoking it to secondary education, and to prepare them for teaching by exposure to teaching methods taught by specialist expatriate teachers. A subsequent development of the greatest importance from about 1927 was the employment of specialist instructors in certain subject areas. By 1927 Muriel Coke-Johnson was the specialist instructress in infant school methods and crafts; she was soon succeeded by Miss Boxhill working part-time; then in 1930 came Ernest Davies, a specialist instructor in drawing and crafts. Every effort was made to encourage practical subjects, such as woodwork, needlework, crafts (straw work) and cookery, but not practical agriculture.

Since the commencement of teacher training at Woodbrook in 1852, the institution has consistently been referred to in this study as the 'government training school'. To capture the total effect of the upgrading of this institution from the late 1920s and the early 1930s, it seems appropriate to accord it from this era the title of the 'Government Training College'. Between 1930 and 1933 the Government Training College acquired a staff of four expatriate specialist teachers with good salaries, which raised it to the level of a college superior to the denominational training schools in teaching power, but less distinguished than QRC or CIC in the sense that the staff, for the most part, did not possess university degrees and were not masters of the prestigious classics. More students attended the Government Training College in the late 1920s and the 1930s than before World War I, or indeed at any time since its foundation. The government spent more money on its training college in the 1930s than in the 1920s (see Table 2.10), and the institution became central to the certification of teachers. Since the basic entry level was the Junior Cambridge Certificate, it might be inferred that the level of work in the academic subjects at the College was somewhat below the Cambridge School Certificate. The level of work in the two-year course is largely unknown, but in the 1940s it appeared lower than the Cambridge School Certificate. The Maurice Report of 1959 also suggested that entrants with the Cambridge School Certificate found some parts of the curriculum (algebra and geometry) no more difficult than third or fourth form work in secondary schools. Nevertheless the new standards reached in the Government Training College from the 1920s were very clearly higher than anything which existed previously.

A most important development was the recruitment of two black assistant instructors, George Byam and J. Hamilton Maurice – the latter of whom had a BA external degree – to help with general education. From 1927 also the government had ended the independent position of the headmistress of Tranquillity Girls' School which was on the same premises as the Government Training College: the training of female teachers henceforth was integrated into the government college, with Constance Fraser, headmistress of Tranquillity Girls' school, becoming, not without protest, its vice-principal. The Government Training College thus became coeducational. In 1934 the whole establishment, minus the Tranquillity Boys' School and the Tranquillity Girls' School, was moved from Tranquillity to a larger, renovated building on St Vincent Street.

The figures for the number of students in the Government Training College in the 1920s and 1930s are not always consistent, reflecting the confusion over the aborted bursar system, and the subsequent subterfuge regarding Naparima Training College as a part of the Government Training College. (See the slight discrepancies between the totals in Tables 2.11 and 2.12.) From early 1931 the students from the Roman Catholic Male Training School joined the classes of the Government Training College, their school having been closed after the death of its principal. Between 1927 and 1932, 143 trained teachers graduated from the Government Training College. By mid 1930s the training schools together were turning out about 35 teachers each year. Naparima Training College in this period would normally have less than 25 males and 15 females in training; the Roman Catholic Female Training School rarely had more than 10 trainees. The Roman Catholic and Presbyterian training schools did not grow as fast as the Government Training College, nor did they have the same emphasis on specialist teachers. A. J. Cooze, and his wife arrived in 1928 to be principal of the Roman Catholic Male Training School, but he died two years afterwards. Domestic science started at the Roman Catholic Female Training School in 1932. J.S. Sammy, a Trinidadian Indian teacher, did more than his share of work at Naparima Training College, and the college had R. Asbell, BSc, as a specialist domestic science mistress (1932). Naparima Training College, the only rural training school, took domestic science and crafts very seriously, utilizing the traditions and skills of older generations of Indian craftsmen born in India. Additionally, Naparima Training College could call on the part-time services of Cyril Guyadeen, an expert in infant school methods. The denominational training schools managed to raise their standards of teacher training in response to the higher standards demanded in the Teachers' Certificate Examination. Each denominational training school had its own examinations in professional subjects, and it is not known how far they were able to simulate the work done at the Government Training College. Both Naparima

Training College and the Roman Catholic Female Training School believed that without all the new 'fancy' emphasis on pedagogy they could produce teachers just as academically qualified as those at the Government Training College, and better motivated since they had received religious training.

Captain Daniel, the principal of the Government Training College, provided a good description of its internal organization in 1933: it had a three-year course, a two-year course and a one-year course; entry depended on the possession of the Junior Cambridge Certificate, the Cambridge School Certificate or the Higher School Certificate respectively. Experienced certified teachers who had no Higher School Certificate were allowed to do the one-year course which consisted partly of the third-year work of the three-year course. In the three-year course, the first year was devoted to general education; in the second year the trainees started studying psychology and pedagogy while attending demonstration lessons and doing teaching practice; they also did the history of education in Trinidad and Tobago as well as Europe.[144] They had at the same time to keep up their general education. The third year was devoted exclusively to professional subjects; the students were sent to different types of schools, urban and rural, for practice and observation. In the one-year course it appeared that trainees were allowed considerable freedom of activity. In the 1930s if a trainee was good enough to get past the first year examination (in the three-year course), he or she would almost certainly acquire the coveted diploma. Pass rates of 100 percent or nearly 100 percent in the final diploma examination plus a plethora of distinctions led to a few raised eyebrows among the sceptics. The students were a select group, and the publication of lists of distinctions in the newspapers might have been a powerful incentive to excel in a colonial society.

The categories of persons admitted to the Government Training College were in the order in which the directors gave them preference: first, young graduates of the secondary schools without teaching experience; experienced certified adult teachers taken off the job temporarily; pupil teachers who had already passed the preliminary examinations (Parts I and II) of the Teachers' Certificate Examination. There was another category of trainees which showed the growing prestige of the College, namely unofficial fee-paying students with secondary education who were not necessarily committed to teaching. There was a teaching service of nearly two thousand teachers (including pupil teachers) in the mid 1930s, many of whom were undereducated or untrained, or certified but untrained, and getting into the Government Training College was extremely difficult. Tobago teachers did not get there. There were disappointed hopes that the long-awaited government school at Mason Hall in Tobago might also do some teacher training. The in-service training efforts of the inspector resident in Tobago was the main channel to upgrade the teachers there.

Competition for entry into the Government Training College inevitably led to bitter accusations of favouritism or arbitrariness.[145] Cutteridge seems to have paid little attention to seniority in his admission policy. He apparently converted the absence of teaching experience, especially when combined with youth and secondary education, into a virtue, much to the chagrin of assistant teachers on the job for five or ten years, or youthful pupil teachers without a Cambridge certificate.[146] Hence youths who did not necessarily like teaching were allegedly catapulted into the Government Training College because they had Junior Cambridge or Cambridge School Certificates. It was not until the 1970s that the government's capacity to train teachers outstripped the demand for admission into government training institutions. Admission to the Government Training College in the 1930s, and indeed until the 1960s, was an enormous privilege, a turning point in the careers of hundreds of young people.

It must not be forgotten that the Teachers' Certificate Examination which started in the 1870s, continued to offer an opportunity for persons who could not get to any of the training colleges to acquire the basic teaching qualifications. It became largely, but not entirely, an examination external to the training colleges. However, the Code of 1935 made attendance at a training college obligatory for those who wished to gain the full Teachers' Certificate. The number of candidates for the Teachers' Certificate shot up from 53 in 1922 to 126 in 1927 (including persons in training colleges), but remained fairly stable, or fell back in the 1930s, to rise slightly to 146 in 1937 (including persons taking the full Certificate). The pass rate was significantly lower than in the later nineteenth century, seldom rising above 35 percent. The directors of education had raised the standard of all the examinations. There was also a low pass rate for pupil teachers' examinations as well as in Preliminary Part I and Part II of the Teachers' Certificate Examinations. Pupil teachers' pass rate, which ran regularly over 80 percent in the 1890s was down to an average of 38 percent in the 1920s and 50 percent in the 1930s. The directors were in the fortunate position of the demand for teacher qualifications exceeding the available vacancies.

The pupil teachers were like hundreds of captured crabs struggling to climb over the top of the barrel into the relative freedom of an assistant teachership.[147] Mixed in with them, on a pittance, were monitors who were unofficially unpaid but often received a few dollars from busy headteachers.[148] The avalanche of pupil teachers and monitors was evidence that teaching was the main avenue to upward social mobility for youths who failed to get one of the few free places in secondary schools.[149] Anxious parents wanted their bright children to take these examinations if only as a sort of school leaving certificate.[150] The lowest and highest number of pupil teachers and monitors taking examinations any year in the 1920s were 564 and 871; in the 1930s, the corresponding figures were 729 and 981. This meant that in the 1920s and 1930s anything from 38 percent to 48 percent of the entire teaching force consisted of pupil teachers and monitors (see Table 2.13). Marriott and Cutteridge had ambivalent attitudes towards pupil teachers. (The monitors were ignored officially although they were allowed to take the Pupil

Teachers' Examinations.) The pupil teachers had to be utilized, two pupil teachers counting as the equivalent of one assistant teacher; but they could not be relied upon as effective practitioners of the new methods which the directors desired. Worse yet, the tendency to use pupil teachers in the infant classes made nonsense of the new infant methods the Government Training College tried to inculcate. An indication of the suspicion of pupil teachers was that the Tranquillity Boys' School and the Tranquillity Girls' School, the most renowned primary schools, never employed them, and they were more common in rural schools than in the major urban schools. Yet there was talent among the pupil teachers, and certainly a tremendous amount of dedication to teaching. So many teachers came up via the route of pupil teachers that it cannot be considered as the path of laggards; it was the normal route. Several pupil teachers who escaped as adults into the ranks of certified teachers or trained certified teachers ranked, in folk tradition, among the best teachers of primary schools.

In the 1920s and 1930s the directors imposed additional demands on primary school teachers. The new methods led to more work. Teachers were expected to be sympathetic to children, enthusiastic, self-sacrificing. The model of a teacher was still a missionary, a priest or a clergyman. Any moral failing would lead to speedy dismissal from the Government Training College; improper behaviour after graduation could lead to serious penalties. Yet teachers who sometimes had more than secondary education were treated as the social inferiors of civil servants who had only secondary education. This prejudice was explained by a theory which relied heavily upon the distinction between a select group and an omnibus group. A government committee in 1934, including Cutteridge, denied any comparison between the salaries of assistant teachers and junior civil servants:

> Entrants into the Public Service have qualified at their parents' expense in Secondary Schools where they have reached the standard of at least the School Certificate, and during that period they have not been wage-earners. Only a few of the applicants are accepted and these are carefully selected. Government service therefore represents the employment most desired but attainable only by the very best. On the other hand teachers are trained for three years at government expense, and during that period their accommodation and board are provided for them, as well as grants for pocket money and books. The average cost to government of training a teacher is £250. Teachers who qualify by passing the external examinations [Teachers' Certificate Examinations] have been wage-earners since the age of 14, and their education had been entirely free.[151]

Here a distinction was being made between those whose parents could afford secondary education, and those whose parents did not pay for their post-primary qualification. Training for teaching was in fact the first skill giving access to social mobility which was 'free' in the sense that it was paid for by the government. In making the distinction it seems that the government committee was euphemistically drawing a subtle social difference between people of lower class or lower middle class background and people of middle class origin.

If a professional is defined as someone who delivers a desirable public good, someone who has been specifically trained to do it and spends most of his or her working hours doing it, then the certified teachers and the trained certified teachers were professionals. Fortunately the leaders of the TTTU had a proper opinion of such teachers as professionals who deserved more from the government, and from 1925 they found sympathizers among the elected members of the Legislative Council who had a higher opinion of teachers' services than the government or director of education. In an age of open racial prejudice there was no doubt that the teachers suffered from being a body of non-white persons. More females were coming into the teaching service despite discrimination against them; and their entry became an additional burden on the struggle of male teachers to reach a recognized professional status.

It would be reasonable to believe that the better educated, better trained sections of the teaching force in the 1920s and 1930s were able to move the education system at least slightly out of the formalism and mechanical learning of the late nineteenth and early twentieth centuries. On some accounts the process of learning was pleasantly different in the 1920s and 1930s from previous years. But we have to be careful not to underestimate the resistance of educational systems to change, leading to a slow and unreliable rate of diffusion of innovation.[152] It remains a moot point how much the directors, with their new methods, new curriculum, more difficult examinations and better organized training schools, were able to change the average primary school in rural Trinidad and Tobago in twenty years. The inability to reach a decisive conclusion on this issue constitutes the most disappointing aspect of the study of the history of education in the first half of the twentieth century. The reorganized Government Training College itself and its youthful graduates came under strong criticism from some senior teachers who apparently had not attended it, or had attended it before the regime of Marriott and Cutteridge. The staff was sometimes said to be below the level required for a reputable teachers' college; another criticism was that white expatriate staff were suspected of treating with indignity the insecure black junior staff members.[153] The discipline was thought to be too severe, evincing a desire to "crush any little show of spirit or independence in [students]" who were in "fear of losing their places for some trifling offence".[154] The radical criticism of the Government Training College was that it was a colonial institution in which the white management, especially Principal Daniel, lacked sympathy for and understanding of the non-white students and staff.[155] And the graduates of the Government Training College? To understand the criticism of senior teachers, one needs to separate the young graduates who did the three-year course, or even the two-year course, from the more mature students who did the one-year course. The latter group did not always feel that they had learnt much after a year of study; the criticism was not really aimed at these more mature graduates. The younger students of the full three-year course had come away, senior teachers were convinced, with more 'style' in teaching than depth of knowledge, with little commitment to teaching and a lot of disrespect for older teachers.[156]

A number of factors must be kept in mind in attempting to come to grips with the validity or invalidity of these strictures of the staff and students of the Government Training College. Once the internal operations of the expanded Government Training College were formalized in the 1920s and 1930s, the social relations of racial subordination of blacks as junior staff or students to whites would become more obvious, especially in an age of growing political resentment of Crown Colony government. Concurrently, there was racial prejudice and snobbishness at the Imperial College of Tropical Agriculture (ICTA), itself undergoing a process of formalization; this had also been the case at QRC under Principal Miles in its early years in the 1870s. Opinions have usually differed on the relative responsibility of teacher training colleges for the improvement of general education or the advancement of the professional skills of teachers. Obviously the Government Training College in the age of Marriott and Cutteridge was expected to do both well. The bursars were impressive because of their general education, but lacked teaching skills on graduation; the young graduates of the post-bursar era, possibly because they were a less select group than the bursars and might have obtained their Junior Cambridge Certificates without going to QRC, CIC or Naparima College, were felt to have less general education, but rather more teaching skills, even if these skills were suspect. As a writer put it in December 1931:

> The young men and women bursar teachers have a wider outlook, they seem more cultured, and they only need encouragement to enable them to make good. The prejudice of college masters or principals and the jealousy of small minded head and assistant teachers, because they [the bursars] had a better education, and began at a higher minimum pay, had much to do with the charges which obtain today. Mr Marriott's substitution gives a teacher, perhaps with better methods, but with an inferior education, one which will not command the respect of an educated man. It is therefore a retrograde step . . .[157]

These alleged competencies or incompetencies were all value judgements without any systematic assessments. There was also the irritant of intergenerational conflict and competition, of one generation of senior teachers passing unfavourable judgement on another generation of younger teachers; by the mid 1930s the bursars of the mid 1920s were among the elite of the senior teachers. Behind the senior teachers of the mid 1930s were even older teachers, or ex-teachers like Alexander Brown, courageous editor of the *Teachers Herald*, who remembered the conditions of training of the late nineteenth century and the very early twentieth century. Some of these persons distrusted the new methods and hankered after the old ways and the old textbooks. Brown went to the government training school in the mid 1890s; he cast doubts on the graduates of the mid 1930s in these words:

Twenty to forty years ago in local training schools one man sat with his 14 to 18 students in a room working continuously all day, and he produced the stalwarts of past years and even of today. The products of these modern improvements are smarter dressed young men and women, glibber speakers, and more adept demonstrators, but they do not seem as sound, as hard-working and as conscientious as those students of the past.[158]

Incidentally, it is the same sort of judgement which many persons now make of the teaching force of Trinidad and Tobago. They are said to be unlike the stalwarts of the 1920s and the 1930s. Nor were the teachers of the 1920s and 1930s, according to the critic above, like the stalwarts of the 1890s. Teachers as a body are peculiarly susceptible to public criticism and to differential deprecatory assessments of colleagues. It seems indisputable to us from this distance in time that the Government Training College of the 1920s and 1930s was a superior institution to any teacher training institution which existed previously; that it had been transformed into a reputable, socially attractive educational institution for the first time in its long history. This new status, however, does not preclude the criticism that it was not as good as it should have been.

New Perspectives on Secondary Education 1926-1935

The model of secondary education adopted by QRC and CIC was the grammar school type of secondary school, so well known in England and western Europe. Essentially it required the teaching of classical languages (Latin and Greek), modern foreign languages (Spanish and French in the case of Trinidad), and mathematics. In practice CIC developed a more varied curriculum than QRC since it included commercial subjects; but the grammar school curriculum took pride of place also at CIC; it was upon performance in the grammar school subjects that the reputation of CIC, like that of QRC, rested. The full grammar school curriculum was thought to be too strenuous for girls, who at any rate were not being prepared for the professions; hence St Joseph's Convent had a watered down version of it, supplemented by music and art. Naparima College aspired to the full grammar school curriculum.

The grand rationale for the secondary education of boys in Trinidad in the nineteenth century was a preparation for entry into the professions, especially law and medicine. As such it was essentially an education for a tiny minority. Since secondary school was ideally a preparation for university, it was essential to coordinate the work of the secondary schools with the entrance requirements of the universities of England. There were lesser occupations, such as solicitor, surveyor, clerk in the civil service, which did not require university training, but which could benefit from a secondary school course. Women were not being prepared for these fields and, as a result, their secondary education, where it existed, was not as rigidly tied to the grammar school curriculum as the secondary education of boys. Girls at St Joseph's Convent were being groomed to be good wives and mothers, at best educated companions of professional husbands and sons. However, the nineteenth century rationale for secondary education was broadened from the 1920s with the admission by the education authorities that secondary education was a suitable base for teaching in primary schools. From the 1920s secondary education was also seen as desirable for girls who wished to become first-class secretaries to urban business firms. Hence there was a sort of educational inflation from the 1920s which involved key agencies requiring secondary school qualifications for jobs previously done by people with less training. The overproduction of Cambridge Certificate holders by the recognized secondary schools and by new private schools forced up the ideal qualifications for primary school teaching and secretarial work; and these new requirements in turn demanded the greater availability of secondary education. The secondary education of girls benefited tremendously from this inflation in qualifications. It was not long before the directors posed the eternally complex question: if secondary education was going to be available to hundreds in the early twentieth century, and not a few scores as in the nineteenth century, could it or should it retain its original shape and meaning?

The grammar school model of secondary education meant that it was completely different from primary education; most of the students who went to recognized secondary schools, with the exception of Naparima College, had not gone to the ordinary primary schools, but to private primary schools, or to the preparatory departments of the recognized secondary schools.[159] Criticism of QRC's grammar school focus began almost as soon as the college commenced. At first it came from the friends of the rival CIC, and was dismissed as malicious propaganda, but by World War I both CIC and QRC merited the same criticism. The principals of both colleges, until the 1920s the foremost authorities on education in the colony, recognized the need for reform, but neither would initiate it unilaterally for fear of losing prestige or standing in the fierce annual competition for university scholarships and medals. Indeed as long as only a handful of candidates each year took the Cambridge School Certificate, it was difficult to argue convincingly that new perspectives were urgently needed for secondary education. But the situation was significantly altered in the first two decades of the twentieth century, not only by the growth of the student population of Naparima College, QRC and CIC, but by new secondary schools which adopted, as nearly as possible, the grammar school model of the leaders: Naparima Girls' High School (eventually for Indians mostly); Bishop Anstey High School (in Port of Spain), and Bishop's High School in Tobago (the latter overwhelmingly for blacks). These newer schools could not aspire to win university scholarships or medals, but they took success in the Cambridge School Certificate, or at least the Junior Cambridge, as the grand criterion of progress; and they too wanted good passes in the core subjects of the grammar school curriculum.

All the secondary schools so far mentioned became recognized secondary schools, that is they were aided by the government and, up to a point, subjected to government supervision. It is important to realize, however, that the provision of secondary education from the early twentieth century ceased to be the preserve of the churches and the government. This happened through the development of private candidates sitting the Cambridge examinations, and the emergence of a new type of private secondary school. Whereas private secondary education always existed for the upper class, it was only from the early twentieth century that affordable private secondary schools started for black and coloured youths. These schools were run by lay owners or managers who considered them a form of business. Simultaneously, private commercial schools appeared; these and the new, less expensive private secondary schools began to send up students for at least the Junior Cambridge examinations. Also more private candidates came forward for both the Junior Cambridge and the Cambridge School Certificate examinations (see Table 2.14 and Table 2.15). In 1920 private students (private school candidates plus private candidates not in any school) comprised 38.9 percent of the total Junior Cambridge candidates; in 1929 the figure was 38.1 percent; for the School Certificate the percentage of private students was 15.5 percent in 1923 and 23.5 percent in 1929. No private candidate or private school candidate as yet dared the Oxford and Cambridge Higher School Certificate, but more persons were getting some sort of secondary education and receiving those precious Cambridge certificates.

Even within the schools supervised by the government in the dual system, the social demand for secondary education exerted pressure in the direction of more candidates for Cambridge examinations. For instance, the whole development of what were called intermediate schools in the early twentieth century was a reaction to the social demand of lower middle class urban families for access to the secondary education they could not afford at QRC, CIC or St Joseph's Convent.[160] The earliest of these intermediate schools grew up unofficially, at first at the Tranquillity Girls' School where a teacher formed something called the 'Higher Class'. By 1918 the Higher Class at Tranquillity Girls' School was getting results in Junior Cambridge not very inferior to those at Naparima College.

Some new perspectives in education, which emerged strongly in the decade between 1926 and 1935 were associated with Marriott and Cutteridge, the former in particular. These ideas formed a part of the directors' plans to modernize education, the difference being that whereas science teaching was actually introduced into CIC and QRC, and the curriculum drastically altered in the primary schools, the ideas we are about to discuss were not actually implemented at this time, nor indeed for many years to come. However, they formed a seminal stock of principles for the evolution of government thinking for at least twenty-five years after 1935.

The essence of these ideas was that more than one type of secondary education could exist; that secondary schools could not only be of the grammar school type, but could also be technical and vocational. This might be obvious today, though not always socially acceptable; in the 1920s and 1930s it was a radical idea, perhaps more extreme than the localization of the contents of primary school reading books. Intimately associated with the idea of a plurality of types of secondary education was the conviction that a systematic break in the school life of children should occur about age twelve; that primary schools should cater for children six to twelve years old; students twelve to eighteen years old should attend secondary schools of one type or another. Marriott and Cutteridge talked about these age groupings as though their ideas were original; but it was clear that, as with other aspects of modernization, they were drawing directly on contemporary ideas of English education experts.[161] The idea of secondary modern schools was borrowed from an important English document. In the Hadow Report of 1926, it was argued that:

> All normal children should go forward to some form of post-primary education. It is desirable, having regard to the country [England] as a whole, that many more children should pass to 'secondary' schools, in the current sense of the term. But it is necessary that the post-primary stage of education should also include other types of post-primary schools, in which the curricula will vary according to the age up to which the majority of pupils remain at school, and the different interests and abilities of the children.[162]

But Marriott and Cutteridge could find in the education system of Trinidad and Tobago enough justification to make it unnecessary to call upon English examples. The existence of the College Exhibitions, which were fought for by eleven and twelve year-olds (and sometimes younger children as well), indicated that for many years previously the education authorities had recognized the wisdom of making the transition to secondary school at about age twelve. Without introducing the psychological arguments of the Hadow Report, Marriott made a case for a systematic break in the education system at age twelve, in virtue of the fact that most children left the primary schools at about this age, when some were in Standard III.[163] He suggested that part of the explanation for the exodus from primary schools was that the existing primary school syllabus was unappealing for children above twelve years of age. If the education of older children was to be continued, it had to be done either by creating in the same primary schools a new syllabus for them, or by physically transferring them to other schools which used the new syllabus. It was the latter alternative, the so-called secondary modern school (sometimes referred to as central schools), which proved the more attractive to Marriott.

The other part of the justification for change which Marriott and Cutteridge employed was the need for technical/vocational education. This need was so well admitted by respectable people that Marriott and Cutteridge did not have to convince such persons of its importance. There was disagreement, however, about the level of the education system at which it should be offered, about the age groups which were the most appropriate recipients and, most of all, whether or not this type of education could be regarded as secondary at all. If asked why the education of most children above the age of twelve had to be technical/vocational instead of classical (the grammar school type, pure or modified by science teaching), Marriott and Cutteridge would have answered that the grammar school type of education was best suited for children who were going to be professionals, and that technical/vocational education suited the great majority who were going to other occupations. The professions, except agriculture, in Marriott's view were over-crowded.[164] It seemed a better idea to prepare youths with some skills to earn a living in agriculture or the trades.

Before proceeding further, it might be useful to review briefly the scope and types of practical education provided at that time. From the late nineteenth century, girls did sewing in primary schools. The most recent type of practical work in primary schools was agriculture in school gardens attached to these schools. The orphanages and reformatories operated the primary schools which were most fully vocational. They did agriculture with a view to feeding themselves; they also did trades training. Apart from two urban Church of England primary schools there was no trades training within other primary schools.[165] Light craft work (called handwork) had been introduced in the 1920s, but not trades. The strongest thrust in the field of trades training occurred outside the primary schools. The Board of Industrial Training held evening classes at the Royal Victoria Institute for artisans and apprentices, and it also supervised the apprenticeship of youths to certain firms. All the feeble efforts at practical work in schools had developed as adjuncts or extensions of the primary schools; secondary education for boys was based completely on 'book' work. Bishop's High School in Tobago was partially an exception.

One of Marriott's problems was how to shift the concept of vocational education to the secondary level of the education ladder. It involved persuading the colony that there were varied types of secondary education. It involved making the deliberate distinction that although the primary schools could include practical work of all kinds, they should not be technical or vocational. Indeed Marriott and Cutteridge had introduced light crafts (and also drawing) into the primary schools; but this they maintained was to provide a general training of the hand and eye with a view to developing the brain.[166] It was not, and should not be, technical or vocational. This point brought Marriott and Cutteridge into disagreement with the Agricultural Society, which in the late 1920s became convinced that the time was ripe for renewed enthusiasm for properly organized school gardens in primary schools – with vocational intentions.[167] Parents, it was said, were now more receptive than at the time school gardens were first introduced. But ironically Marriott and Cutteridge, whom the Garveyite wing of the labour movement suspected of wanting to hold back black people's education, did not advocate one of the traditional means of doing this: practical work in primary schools with direct vocational intentions.[168] Marriott thought school gardens had failed.

To convince people that technical/vocational education could be secondary education, Marriott and Cutteridge, especially the former, had to attack the entrenched conception of secondary education, and they had to lance it at its heart: the Cambridge examinations. The assault was understandably not on the standard of the Cambridge examinations, but upon their hold on the public's imagination; on the complete identification of secondary education with them, and on the manner in which they still restrained the secondary school curriculum in a straitjacket even after the introduction of science teaching. If one was not studying for Cambridge examinations, the perception was that one was not undergoing secondary education. There were also persons who went further than this: without Latin and Greek, or at least Latin, one was not getting secondary education.[169] The way forward to the new type of secondary education, according to Marriott and Cutteridge, involved dropping one of the modern foreign languages (French or Spanish) and both Latin and Greek in order to take up practical subjects. The directors declared that they wished to train character and develop the man, the citizen. There were no Cambridge examinations for this. Starting from the desire to diminish the prestige of the Cambridge examinations, and perhaps not unmindful of some of the anti-examination rhetoric of some English educators, Marriott and Cutteridge began to propound the unthinkable heresy that examinations in general might have little or no educational value. But there were apparent contradictions in their approach: while detracting from the Cambridge examinations, they were attempting to make the Cambridge School Certificate the ideal qualification for entry into the reorganized Government Training College.

The attack on the Cambridge examinations appeared to receive some justification from the uncertainty over whether the colony could provide the kinds of jobs expected by all the youths acquiring these certificates. Unemployment, often only temporary, among secondary school graduates had already emerged. The civil service had a long waiting list of applicants.[170] The director of education was alarmed at the rate of production for holders of Cambridge certificates in the 1920s. For example, in 1925 there were 127 successful candidates in the Junior Cambridge Examination, 65 successful candidates in the School Certificate Examination and 20 successful candidates in the Higher School Certificate Examination (see Tables 2.16, 2.17, 2.18). It was tempting to assume that if these boys and girls had done technical/vocational courses they would somehow have found a job or been able to employ themselves. QRC and CIC boys were asked to look to fields other than the civil service and clerkships in Port of Spain firms, such as vacancies in the oil industry. Governor Hollis, who delighted in plain speaking to school audiences, called for a back-to-the-land movement among the youths.[171] The island was said to be overstocked with lawyers and doctors. A few persons opined that the West Indies had adopted the wrong model of education all along: instead of the British 'academic' model they needed the Tuskegee model of vocational training in the USA.

Yet agreement was not reached about the way to increase the component of technical/vocational education within the schools. Some members of the upper class wished to see an increased input of vocational education at the primary school level, which they thought would be the cheapest and surest way of stemming the tide of would-be white-collar workers. On this account all primary education should be vocational. Then there was the curious fact that some merchants and planters who normally favoured technical/vocational education had reservations which betrayed a fear that too much of even this type of education might pose some social danger. Marriott asked the Chamber of Commerce if it foresaw any need for female graduates from the commercial classes of the Royal Victoria Institute. The Chamber demurred, saying that its members preferred to select their own trainees and improve them on the job. This left a big loophole for racial discrimination: the members of the Chamber of Commerce were mostly white; the female graduates of the Royal Victoria Institute's commercial classes were black and coloured. Young ladies of the right colour and social background who graduated from St Joseph's Convent, or from Bishop Anstey High School, and who combined commercial skills with secondary education – with or without Cambridge certificates – were in demand by commercial firms in the capital. It was in the 1930s that women began to seek jobs in fields hitherto 'monopolized by men, especially secretarial positions in business firms. Race and colour discrimination was a disincentive for non-white girls in this type of employment. Something also happened which Cutteridge himself found puzzling: Marriott, in his commendable attempt to ascertain what types of graduates the economy needed, found out that planters were saying that what was needed was education in trades; and merchants were saying that what was lacking was education in agriculture.[172] Some answers to this riddle surfaced from the discussion which Marriott and Cutteridge stirred: no white group wanted a great number of qualified non-whites aiming for jobs in its sector on the basis of certificates. Neither farm schools nor trades schools beyond the primary school level were really welcome if they encouraged competition from non-whites for jobs held by whites.

Some of the non-whites had taken to education with such zest that any type of examination, local or external, which they were called upon to take, would be passed in increasing numbers once it was clear that these were the routes to upward social mobility. The stage had been reached where an expanding education system at the post-primary level, however it was oriented, had the potential of putting out more graduates than there were suitable jobs available.[173] This was so not only because of the actual size of the civil service and the private commercial sector, but because the upper class found it unacceptable that all jobs should be open to talent. A black youth who graduated from a secondary school after doing several courses in agriculture, who could not employ himself because he had no land – what job in agriculture awaited him? Surely a white or coloured estate owner or manager would prefer his own relatives or friends' relatives as junior estate employees. This is not to say that no openings would ever be found, but that the way forward was not usually clear. These observations do not hold as truly for the youth who, from his technical/vocational training became a skilled workman: he had a good chance of being self-employed; but still one must note that industrial firms were few and small, and riddled with racial discrimination. The point is that we are not looking at a society or economy which could easily place all or most of the graduates who might emerge from technical/vocational schools, if these could have been started. It is the economy, not the education system which creates jobs; and it is the social system which determines the distribution of employment.

After World War I the political consciousness of Trinidad and Tobago outgrew the methods of decision making in education. The decision makers were the director of education, the principals of QRC and CIC, and the Board of Education. These authorities were distrusted in varying degrees by spokesmen for the black working classes who were organizing labour unions and protests. These working class spokesmen did not judge education policies solely or primarily on educational criteria, but from a political point of view. If the right education policy was put forward by the wrong people, it was wrong. Severe criticism of education policy from the centre and left of centre was endemic from the 1920s. Marriott and Cutteridge probably felt that they were only advising what was being advocated in enlightened circles in the metropole; they made speeches at school functions indicating that they were in favour of an expansion of secondary education; but they were perceived mostly as persons who wished to take away, rather than to enlarge opportunities for the non-white population.[174] England had problems of class, but not a serious race problem. Trinidad and Tobago had both, and they were just below the surface of the discussions on education. White directors were telling non-white parents not to overestimate Cambridge examinations which white officials and professionals took seriously for their own children; whites were telling non-white youths to look to areas of employment other than the civil service when whites were holding on to well-paid civil service posts by all means available. As long as white-collar jobs were the best paid and most prestigious positions in the society, it was useless advising people that they should prefer to study agriculture and trades. The directors were mistaken in their belief that they could manipulate the job market by shifting the curriculum of schools.

In 1922 the Cambridge examinations for the lower forms of secondary schools were discontinued by the Cambridge Syndicate. This met with the approval of the director and the principal of QRC, but not the principal of St Joseph's Convent.

Then in the later 1920s came the director's attack on the Cambridge examinations (Junior Cambridge and School Certificate) for older students. From 1936 the government withdrew its subsidy of fees for taking the Junior Cambridge, thus discouraging students from sitting it. The action of the government amounted to a withdrawal of recognition of the Junior Cambridge; students became wary of taking it. Those who distrusted the directors thought they saw another conspiracy to remove the lower rungs of the Cambridge examination ladder which were the only ones which many non-whites ever scaled. The directors talked about the desirability of locally set examinations to introduce flexibility into the work of the secondary schools; but they did not produce draft plans. They said the new girls' secondary schools (Bishop Anstey High School and Naparima Girls' High School) should not feel bound to follow the same Cambridge syllabus at QRC and CIC. Marriott and Cutteridge were not enthusiastic about women entering the same professions as men. But criticism of the Cambridge examinations was no substitute for these examinations; in fact, the society was unwilling to accept any local substitute for external examinations and the Cambridge certificates were not the only ones which were cherished.

The principals of the leading secondary schools measured their scholars' performance by Cambridge criteria. Although they did not support the attack on these examinations, they probably had some reservations about them because there was, and will always be, a commonsensical truth that examinations are not everything in education. The principal of Bishop Anstey High School, Miss A. M. Stephens, said as much; and Bishop Anstey put it beautifully by declaring that a school with good examination results was not necessarily a good school, but a school with bad examination results had to be a bad school.[175] He suggested indirectly that Marriott and Cutteridge did not have a better test than the Cambridge examinations. The principals of CIC and QRC, locked in permanent rivalry for medals, honours, distinctions and university scholarships based on the Cambridge examinations, kept their reservations locked in their hearts and their annual prize-giving speeches evinced overwhelming faith in the Cambridge examinations.

When Marriott and Cutteridge, either from honesty or foolhardiness, declared their dislike for basing entry into the civil service on the Cambridge examinations, their opponents felt satisfied that they were unmasking themselves openly as the enemies of the aspiration of the non-white peoples.[176] As T.M. Kelshall, a coloured lawyer, once remarked publicly, at a school function where Governor Hollis was present and Director Marriott had just delivered another attack on the veneration of Cambridge certificates and civil service posts: when the youths at Naparima College looked at persons in the civil service, not excluding Marriott, they could not help being struck by the appearance of prosperity.[177]

As Marriott said on another occasion, schools could not educate people; he knew of many who had no Cambridge certificates, but were better than those who had them.[178] Although this was quite possibly true, it was a very suspect doctrine to non-whites who had acquired Cambridge certificates against all odds. For Indians, blacks and coloureds the civil service was the great desideratum for all educated non-professionals. Trade union spokesmen, especially Captian Cipriani, were anxious to have the government bring back competitive examinations for entry into the civil service; these had been dropped since the later nineteenth century. The government, viewing the civil service as a highly selected cadre of administrators, preferred to choose candidates on personal merits as determined by the governor and the colonial secretary. The argument was that there was no reason to assume that competitive examinations would unearth candidates of higher moral or educational qualifications.[179]

In 1931 the British government set up a Commission to probe education in Trinidad and other eastern Caribbean islands. Marriott had the distinction of being selected to share the work of this Commission with Arthur Mayhew, chief adviser to the British government on education in the colonies. One of the key recommendations of this Commission was for a new type of secondary school:

> A new additional type of school in needed providing courses of instruction that are practical in the broadest sense, not merely vocational or utilitarian, but with a cultural bias of general education, directed essentially to the stimulation of interest in the pupils' social and industrial environment, and calculated to create a taste and aptitude for industrial, agricultural, or commercial pursuits, or for social service in primary schools and elsewhere, rather than for the 'learned' professions and sedentary or clerical posts in Government service. We propose to call this new type of secondary school the 'Modern School' . . .[180]

The Marriott/Mayhew Report recommended that some children in the age group twelve to fifteen years old, be transferred from the primary schools into the secondary schools. A new corridor for students from primary to secondary modern schools was to be opened via a test, the successful ones – to a limit to be set by the government – could be allowed free education up to the junior course of the secondary modern school (age group twelve to fifteen years). The senior course (age group sixteen to eighteen years) had to be paid for by the students who had succeeded in the junior course, although scholarships were also envisaged. This scheme was an early variant of the present two-tier system of government secondary schools (junior secondary and senior comprehensive schools), with the difference that the two courses were in one school, and not in two separate schools. The Marriott/Mayhew Report did not call urgently for an expansion of education by the immediate construction of these secondary modern schools, but it hoped that once government and churches had the resources they would move in this direction.

Education in the secondary modern schools, according to Marriott and Mayhew, was to be agricultural, technical and commercial, but without being directly vocational. That is, students were not to be trained directly as farmers, artisans or secretaries, but the studies (pre-vocational) would give them both practical and theoretical experience to undertake these occupations. The junior course students were to study up to a level equivalent to the Junior Cambridge examinations (to be abolished); in the senior course students were to study up to a level equivalent to Cambridge School Certificate. Successful students were to be awarded either local certificates (the junior course) or a special local certificate from the Cambridge Syndicate (the senior course). English language and literature were to be key courses, being the 'cultural' subjects *par excellence*, which would save the curriculum from being too narrowly associated with skills rather than the cultivation of taste. Geography and history were to be taught as by-products of English language and literature. Elementary science was to be the base of the skills taught. Girls in the junior courses would have to do domestic science, but those in the senior courses were also to be given commercial courses, shorthand and typing.

When the Marriott/Mayhew Report became public in the colony, the proposal for the secondary modern school was not immediately the most controversial suggestion. What sparked angry reaction were recommendations that the school life of children in primary schools should start at age six and end at age twelve. The existing practice was to send children much earlier, sometimes at three or four years old. Since the Report did not propose free infant schools, it looked as though the two English experts wished to clip off two or three years of schooling without any compensation. In some circles, it was thought to be another malicious plan to restrict the advance of the non-white peoples. The TTTU protested the age restriction; petitions were signed in Tobago as well as in Trinidad against it. A compromise was devised: in the districts where compulsory education was to be enforced, the age range could be six to twelve years; otherwise it would be five to fourteen years.

But how were secondary modern schools to be brought into existence? The Trinidad government accepted the Marriott/Mayhew Report for the most part, and by 1936 the Education Code made allowance for the two types of secondary schools. Cutteridge became director of education in 1934 and his policy was that if more money was to be spent on education, it should be at the bottom of the system, on compulsory primary education, on primary school buildings, school medical service and school meals. As in England, there was no government money to build secondary modern schools in the 1930s. When more funds were available in the colony in the 1940s, the government preferred to assist the churches to erect denominational secondary schools, and the churches were not interested in converting their grammar schools or even their intermediate schools into secondary modern schools. Additionally, these were socially suspect as inferior secondary schools for lower class children.[181] Hence the proposal of Marriott and Mayhew remained a dead letter in practice, although it retained its vitality as the most plausible policy to be implemented whenever the government was ready; and clearly only the government could lead the colony into the new era of secondary modern schools.

The only part of the new idea which was immediately implemented was the extension of domestic science classes for girls and craft classes (woodwork) for boys within, or in association with, primary schools. During and after World War II, the directors also attempted to reorganize some primary schools by encouraging headteachers to divide them into two sections at about the eleven-plus age group. But domestic science and woodwork classes were more prominent changes. As Errol Furlonge saw, for the next generation these vocational endeavours in primary schools (domestic science centres) became almost a substitute for the secondary modern school itself.[182] Eventually the first secondary modern schools were erected in the early 1960s by the nationalist government of Dr Eric Williams. The right policy became more socially acceptable – but not completely – when done by the right people.

The Emergence of a Government Programme of Expansion in Education 1932-1939

The Marriott/Mayhew Report concluded definitely that the system of education in Trinidad and Tobago was in advance of that in the Leeward and Windward Islands, and even in Barbados in some respects. If Marriott alone had said this, he might have been suspected of prejudice in favour of Trinidad and Tobago; but Arthur Mayhew, an eminent authority, was alleged to have said that Trinidad's schools were 50 percent better than he expected.[183] Trinidad had a professional director and assistant director of education; there were secondary schools for boys and girls; science had been introduced in some secondary schools and the content of the curriculum of primary schools had been reformed in the direction of local subject matters; and very important, it had improved professional training in the Government Training College which had specialist teachers on its staff. The British government was at this time actively promoting movements towards a West Indian federation; and as the island with the most developed education system in the eastern Caribbean Trinidad was seen by Marriott and Mayhew as the centre for the training of teachers in that region, and generally as a focal point from which schools in other islands could be supervised. What was needed in Trinidad was expansion on the solid base already in place. Since all the islands, Trinidad included, had limited financial resources, especially in the international economic downturn of the early 1930s, the Marriott/Mayhew Report emphasized the need for each island to formulate a well considered programme of expansion. This advice was the main origin of a definite plan for developing education by the Trinidad government in the 1930s.

At the core of the programme of expansion which the Marriott/Mayhew Report recommended for Trinidad was the proposed central training college for one hundred trainee teachers at a recurrent cost of about $17,640 for staff salaries. Since about a half of this sum was already being spent on staff at the existing Government Training College, the extra funds needed totalled about $9,000, minus the fees of the students from the other islands.[184] The great hurdle would be the capital cost of the new building which was unspecified. The government was also advised to build two secondary modern schools (one in Port of Spain and the other in Sangre Grande or Princes Town) rather than two junior technical schools. The hope was expressed that the Roman Catholic Church and the Church of England would convert St Benedict's College at San Fernando and Bishop's High School, Tobago, into secondary modern schools. Even the domestic science classes which the Canadian Presbyterian Church held at St Augustine might be encouraged to grow into a secondary modern school.

With respect to primary schools, the Marriott/Mayhew Report did not recommend compulsory education, which it thought too costly. It recommended the amalgamation of schools, in the case of two church schools of different denominations, under a joint Board of Management. No school should be given government aid if it was less than three miles from another school, unless it had at least two hundred or more children in attendance. Districts where the existing number of schools could be reduced were: Arouca, New Grant, Indian Walk, Ste Madeleine, Mayaro, and Mason Hall, Delaford, and Roxborough in Tobago. The dual system was not to be abolished, but widened by the admission of non-Christian denominational schools (Hindu and Muslim schools), provided they were not competing with other schools. The government was to put more money into denominational schools by way of building and equipment grants. Many denominational schools had deteriorated, and were without equipment because the churches had insufficient funds. Since 1902 the government had not financed new denominational school buildings or apparatus and equipment for denominational schools built after that year.

The formulation of a programme of development by the Trinidad government along the lines of the Marriott/Mayhew Report was facilitated by the fact that one of the authors (Marriott) was also director of education. Assistant director Cutteridge was in tune with Marriott's ideas, and succeeded him in 1934. Since the Marriott/Mayhew Report was commissioned by the British government, as a Crown Colony, Trinidad and Tobago had to take its recommendations seriously. The idea that an education plan was necessary is a notable innovation: this was the first time that the government attempted to execute a plan consistently over a number of years. It should be remarked at once that this was not an integrated plan, only a statement of priorities. Such a limited attempt at planning was consonant with notions of social and economic development which, in the 1930s, were beginning to inform the policies of the Trinidad and Tobago government, and in fact other West Indian governments. The government had gone beyond the mere execution of public works to the active promotion of minor manufacturing establishments and an Agricultural Credit Bank. The colony did not escape the grave economic depression of the western world in the early 1930s and this encouraged the government to take planning (not yet a science) more seriously. The education planning of the early and mid 1930s was part of a complex of reactions by government which presaged the era of development plans just before and after World War II.

The first attempt at planning in education came exactly when the government felt it had no extra funds to spend. Trinidad's particular predicament within the western world's depression was that greater production of oil, sugar and cocoa earned less foreign exchange or, at most, the same amount. Prices had slumped; the revenues of the country, dependent mostly on export and import duties, fell. The imperial power, itself in troubled waters, offered preferential rates for sugar; but the most effective and most immediately available strategy was simply to reduce expenditure, or at least to hold it down to the existing levels. In comparison to some of the other British islands, Trinidad and Tobago's economy had in the oil industry, which was earning an increasingly higher percentage of the total foreign exchange, an anchor in the later 1930s which prevented disaster to the government's financial position without avoiding an economic crunch.[185] While hardships piled up on the unemployed and underemployed and on the lower wage section of the population, the Trinidad and Tobago government seemed to have weathered the fiscal storms of the 1930s rather well. Expenditure on education was not cut back: in fact it grew by about 18.8 percent between 1931 and 1936. Most of this increased spending, however, was not to finance an expansion programme, but to meet recurrent costs: increasing teachers' salaries, renewed equipment and apparatus grants for primary schools and more capitation grants for secondary schools. Only a minor part of the expansion programme involving new structures had been attempted by 1936.

In considering the education expansion programme, it is convenient to separate the period 1932 to 1936 from the period 1937 to 1939. Development in terms of new school buildings was not much in evidence between 1932 and 1936. There was no money for it. The extension of QRC buildings was postponed until 1935 when the college got an annex and two more masters;[186] a programme for two junior technical schools was postponed indefinitely; so too was the proposed central training college, though a start was made by removing the Government Training College from Tranquillity to the newly acquired Portuguese Club building on St Vincent Street. The total number of primary schools crept from 254 in 1932 to 256 in 1936, but in the process a few schools were closed and others opened. New expenditure was incurred by the commencement of six centres for domestic science in Port of Spain and San Fernando, and two centres for craft for boys in Port of Spain. Since these centres were not entirely new or substantial structures, but attachments to existing schools, their cost was not great. The recurrent spending was greater, and was financed from revenues.

In 1934 Governor Hollis appointed a committee to ascertain how far a development plan could be carried out in a tight money situation. This committee recommended over a five-year period $103,464 worth of new recurrent expenditure and $479,280 worth of capital expenditure on buildings. The high point of this programme was to be the construction of a secondary modern school after the fashion of the Marriott/Mayhew Report ($26,784); the extension of the QRC building ($76,080); the erection of the central training college ($144,000); and the construction of new government primary schools in central areas (also called central schools) to replace small schools ($259,200). Aid to denominational school buildings was also to come from the latter sum. By far the most important recommendation of this committee, however, was that a loan to finance the programme should be raised.[187] Loans were being raised for other purposes, but the suggestion to raise a loan for education (which would be a part of a larger loan for other purposes including health) was a major new development. It was almost unthinkable in the age of school fees; it was improbable even in the 1920s. The proposal for a loan signalled the arrival of the conception of education as a development cost, though what was to be developed was perceived more as physical facilities than as human resources.

Early in 1935 the Legislative Council authorized a loan of $1.4 million, $240,000 (17.1%) of which was reserved for education. This released the government from the burden of trying to finance an education expansion programme from its revenues in a period of depression; the results were apparent from 1937. The years between 1937 and 1939 saw more active school building than the period 1932 to 1936; among the major achievements was the building at last of the government primary school at Mason Hall in Tobago, as well as a government primary school at San Fernando which enabled compulsory education to be declared in that town.[188] The churches were now treated more generously, a major new policy being to give up to 50 percent assistance with a new school building and with extensions or repairs of existing buildings. The government was also able to proceed fully with its plan to resume apparatus grants to denominational schools; seventy-three such schools built since 1902 had never received any such assistance. It must not be thought, however, that the loan funds were distributed lavishly or quickly, for the building of government schools, even on the new open-air model, took usually more than one year between site identification and completion. The churches still had difficulty in finding their share of building costs, one reason being their insistence that the funds be raised by the parishes affected and not provided from a central church fund. It is understandable, then, that World War II began in September 1939 with the greater part of the loan funds still unspent.

QRC got a new wing for science laboratories; CIC laboratories also received funds for an extension; so too did Bishop's High School, Tobago, which moved to a new site. This school was said to be converted into a secondary modern school. No progress was made, however, with what had been perhaps the bravest new proposal in the expansion programme, namely the construction of a central training college to serve the eastern Caribbean. The government had accepted the responsibility of finding the capital sum for this building, but the cost proved too high, and it was not urgently required by the Trinidad and Tobago education system.[189] As might be expected, delays and hesitancy on the part of the other islands in committing themselves to the project worked as a disincentive. Even after the Carnegie Corporation of the USA offered $288,000 towards the cost of the building, the project floundered.

The government expansion programme in education of 1932-1939 revealed some interesting new lines of thought. It was recognized that the government tended to build schools too expensively, and a new design for a school building was developed: the open-air type with tapia and cement wall on two sides only, and 'expanded metal work' walls and ten-feet wide concrete veranda on the other two sides. This was said to combine cheapness with suitability to the tropics. The new government schools in the mid 1930s were constructed on this architectural model. Wherever possible, domestic science centres for girls and craft centres providing mostly carpentry for boys, were attached to schools, as cheaply as possible, in central locations to serve a number of schools. The idea was to extend the practical bias of education which had commenced at the beginning of the century with school gardens within the schools and trades training outside them. The domestic science and craft centres led the government into the new idea of providing a school bus service, not from home to school, but from school to the centres. Another new idea born at this time was the need for government to supply textbooks, clothes and a meal for needy children who were being obliged to attend schools in the compulsory attendance areas of Port of Spain and San Fernando. With the school medical service already in place from the 1920s, the government in the 1930s was slowly and feebly expanding its conception of responsibility for the welfare of children beyond the provision of buildings and teachers. It was still a long way from the millions of dollars spent annually on these services from the mid 1970s.

It was the proud boast of Governor Hollis and the director that enrolment and attendance grew in Trinidad in the 1930s even while the school building programme lagged behind needs. In 1932 enrolment and attendance were up respectively by 11.3 percent and 24.4 percent on the 1927 figures with only two more schools than in 1927; and by 1937 enrolment and attendance were up by 8.1 percent and 8.3 percent respectively on the 1932 figures with only three more schools than in 1932 (see Table 2.19). Compulsory attendance in Port of Spain had little impact on these figures; and Tobago without it had a better attendance record than Trinidad (see Table 2.20). The economic depression had no negative effect on total enrolment in primary schools in Trinidad; but in the secondary schools, there were signs of falling enrolment due to unfavourable economic times. The number of students attending QRC, CIC, St Joseph's Convent, Bishop Anstey High School, and Bishop's High School (Tobago) fell between 1933 and 1935; but not so at the Indian dominated schools of Naparima College and Naparima Girls' High School. Enrolment began to recover from 1936, except at St Joseph's Convent, ending on a strong note just before World War II. But about 50 percent of the increase between 1930 and 1938 came from two new schools, St Benedict College and St Joseph's High School, which had come into the dual system only in 1936. In 1938 a total of 2,259 students attended nine recognized secondary schools for girls and boys (see Table 2.21). This represented about 2.9 percent of all the children attending primary and secondary schools in the dual system.

From the 1920s the directors and assistant inspectors had switched emphasis from examining to inspecting schools – according them an efficiency grade in five categories ranging from very good to unsatisfactory. Inspectors were apparently using different criteria, after the 1920s, than those in the era of payment by results (1870-1921). The teachers' methods, the order and discipline of the schools, and the cleanliness of their physical environment were now more important than how well the pupils answered. On the basis of these new criteria, Marriott and Cutteridge were satisfied with the schools' overall achievement in the 1930s. For instance in 1934, 42.4 percent, 54.1 percent and 3.4 percent of the schools in Trinidad and Tobago were rated respectively very good, good and fair. Looking at the period 1934-1937 there was some falling off in the percentage of schools rated as very good, and a rise in those rated as only fair, but this was not enough to make the directors feel anything but satisfaction with the general situation in the schools. It might be of interest to note that between 1934 and 1937, when the fullest figures were available, government schools had a higher percentage of schools rated very good than any group of church schools; and among denominations, the Canadian Presbyterian Mission schools had the highest percentage of the very good schools, a remarkable situation in view of their low performance (on different criteria) at the end of the nineteenth century.

There were however some considerations which reflected unfavourably on the state of education in the colony. The schools were divided into an infant section and seven standards. A most important fact to keep in mind is that a significant percentage of pupils was in the infant division and the first three standards (I-III) above the infant division. Taking Port of Spain only in 1937, a compulsory education area, 39 percent of the pupils were in the infant section, and 34 percent in the first three standards above the infant division. Altogether 73 percent of the pupils were in Standard III and below. In the entire colony 45.5 percent of pupils were in the infant section and 76 percent in Standard III and below. In some areas of the colony pupils were not admitted to school until they were six years old; partly because of irregular attendance, the infant section of schools housed many pupils who were not physically infant. Boys and girls of ten or eleven years of age were in infant classes, while younger children were in higher standards. It was the work of Director Hogben in the mid 1940s to introduce age grouping on an experimental basis, not without some dissentient voices. In the age of Marriott and Cutteridge, senior pupils in the higher standards appeared to be underrepresented in the schools.

An analysis of the performance of the secondary schools in the 1930s has to be confined between 1930 and 1937 when the figures were fullest. At this time the recognized secondary schools were QRC, CIC, St Joseph's Convent, Bishop Anstey High School, Naparima College, Bishop's High School (Tobago), Naparima Girls' High School, and from 1936 St Benedict College (in San Fernando) and St Joseph's Convent (in St Joseph). In estimating their relative academic performance it is impossible to use any other measure but the Cambridge examinations. QRC can be usefully compared to CIC only as in the 1920s. Whereas in the 1920s QRC was more efficient than CIC in passing students at all three levels – (Junior Cambridge, Cambridge School Certificate and Oxford and Cambridge Higher School Certificate) – in the 1930s it lost this advantage in respect to the Higher School Certificate (see Table 2.22), but not in respect to Junior Cambridge and Cambridge School Certificate (Tables 2.23 and 2.24). The university scholarships were shared almost equally between CIC and QRC.

Naparima College's pass rate in Junior Cambridge and Cambridge School Certificate was about the same as CIC's, but the number of students sent up was considerably smaller. Since Naparima College did not send up students for the Higher School Certificate until 1935 and did not win any university scholarships, and since its pass rate was not as good as QRC's, it was a long third behind QRC and CIC in academic performance. Its pass rate was not as good as Bishop Anstey High School, though the latter sent up on average fewer students than Naparima College. Bishop Anstey did better than St Joseph's Convent in terms of the pass rate at the Junior Cambridge level, but the latter turned the tables on it at the level of the Cambridge School Certificate (see Appendix IV and Appendix V). Of course St Joseph's Convent did send up a handful of girls for the Higher School Certificate. It also remained the largest girls' school sending up the most candidates.

In terms of number of candidates, Naparima Girls' High School was similar to Bishop's High School in Tobago. But it had a better pass rate than Bishop's High School (Tobago) which must rank at that time as the weakest performer of these schools that had been recognized by the government in the 1920s (see Appendix IV and Appendix V). Perhaps this was one reason for its selection as the institution most ripe for conversion to a secondary modern school. The two newest affiliated schools, St Benedict College and St Joseph's Convent (St Joseph), were too new to be compared with others, but they made a fair start in the Cambridge examinations. All these secondary schools were sources of pride.

The directors, the colonial secretary and the treasurer were chiefly responsible for the expansion programme in education. From 1925 a handful of elected representatives had been added to the Legislative Council; and very soon they began to criticize the government's policy in education by the constitutionally permissible method of asking questions in the Legislative Council. As resentment against Crown Colony government grew in the later 1920s and the 1930s the elected members, and even nominated members like L.A.P. O'Reilly, claimed on behalf of the people a share in the shaping of education policies. This tendency, together with constitutional changes after 1942, eventually brought the elected members within the Legislative Council into the controlling centre of the education system. The elected members had no objection to the details of the expansion programme in education in the 1930s, but they wanted, as might be expected, more done more quickly. They were particularly critical of the delay in the implementation of the Compulsory Education Ordinance of 1921, and then of the feebleness with which it was done in 1935; and they were sensitive about the opportunities in secondary education for non-white children. The question of an increase in the university scholarships provided an opportunity to study some of the new political pressures brought on the education system and its administrators in the 1930s.

C. Henry Pierre, an elected member, presented a motion in the Legislative Council in 1936 requesting an increase in the number of university scholarships. He was acting in support of a petition to the governor by members of some friendly societies. Pierre claimed a discussion of the issue in the press supported an increase. A Citizens' Committee had been formed by men whom Pierre regarded as respectable members of friendly societies, serious, solid citizens. It was this committee which drew up the petition, led by its Chairman George Chambers, president of the Trinidad and Tobago Friendly Societies Union. Also, a Parents' Union had arisen including some of the Port of Spain intelligentsia; one of its objects was to promote the higher education of youths. Pierre argued that the growth of population and revenues warranted an increase, but he was not suggesting new expenditure at the expense of primary education. Additional revenues had become available beyond the dreams of the government. A sinister interpretation could be given, he claimed, to the reduction of the university scholarships from four to three (1902) and from three to two (1919). He rejected the notion that university scholarships only overcrowded the medical and legal professions. Even if these professions were overrepresented, such a situation was not unique to Trinidad and Tobago. At any rate, it was the fault of the government that young men could not see any alternative to law and medicine. The government failed to encourage them to qualify for technical jobs in the civil service. Recently there were such jobs, said Pierre, and no locals to fill them. Government should set up an advisory board to channel youths into training in areas where a need was foreseen, and government should select from candidates of university scholarship standard such youths as were willing to undergo training. There was a need, said Pierre, for teachers and inspectors of schools with overseas training. Even if some of these men did not return to the island, a gifted Trinidadian youth, well educated, would be a contribution to the world. The university scholarships were to benefit the individual as well as the island. He deplored the failure of the Marriott/Mayhew Report to recommend an increase in the university scholarships, and was angry that one of the authors wished to reduce the two scholarships to one. Pierre warned that this might be viewed as class oppression. He alleged that with the decline of cocoa, some parents who in the past had sacrificed their lands to send their children abroad for education could no longer find the resources. The question of the university scholarships was of no interest to the British government, but a domestic issue concerning the people, and the colony had the money. Pierre moved for a committee to advise the government on the matter.[190] This was seconded by Dr McShine, a nominated member. T.M. Kelshall, then an elected member, was supportive, arguing that he did not view the question in relation to the services rendered by the winners to the island. The university scholarships, in his view, existed primarily to serve the interest of culture. Winners who served outside Trinidad would be ambassadors of goodwill to break down racial prejudice in a shrinking world. Kelshall reminded the Legislative Council of Bernard Acham, former foreign minister of China, a Trinidad boy (then named Eugene Chen) who had risen to prominence on the international scene, with his picture drawn in *Punch* by Bernard Partridge.

Captain Daniel, who was acting director in the absence of Cutteridge, admitted he had seen the petition but said he regarded petitions as suspicious documents. Many of the signatures seemed to him to be in the same handwriting; apart from names of persons from Port of Spain, he claimed not to recognize signatures from residents of towns, for example San Fernando, Arima, Sangre Grande or from Tobago. However strong the demand for an increase in the university scholarships, he thought it inexpedient to comply at that time. His view was that the reduction of the scholarships to two had improved the standard of work. Daniel said that over the previous ten years about thirty students each year sat the scholarship examination, and about fifteen qualified on average for the Modern Studies Scholarship, and about nine for the Science Scholarship. The winner, the first and second runners up for the Modern Studies Scholarship (also called Open Scholarship) over the previous ten years got (presumably on average) about 71 percent, 66 percent and 65 percent respectively of the total marks; in the Science Scholarship, the corresponding figures were 59 percent, 52 percent and 45 percent. His contention was that the marks of second place boys were not good enough for university scholarships. In England the competition was greater and the value of the scholarships less. To give extra university scholarships would be to lower the standard. The clamour for increased university scholarships was not general, concluded Daniel, but raised by interested parties whose children or relatives would otherwise not get scholarships. Friendly societies were not education authorities. He would rather hear the views of the principals of recognized secondary schools. He wished to see a minimum mark established; if in a given year no boys reached it, no university scholarships would be given; if in another year two or three boys attained it, then as many scholarships would be given. Daniel was pellucidly clear that the university scholarships did not exist to train professionals to fill civil service posts which expatriates traditionally occupied, or which might be left vacant for lack of interested expatriates. It was such demonstrations of a lack of sympathy for the aspirations of the non-white people which made some of their thoughtful spokesmen suspect Daniel of racial prejudice at the Government Training College, or distrust his books on West Indian history. Daniel also added that he and Cutteridge wished to use any additional funds available at the bottom of the education system: on compulsory education, school buildings, school medical service, school meals and crèches for preschool children.[191]

One of the best speeches in the Legislative Council in opposition to Daniel came from the eloquent L.A.P. O'Reilly, not an elected member, but no friend of white expatriate officials. He instructed Daniel:

> You are dealing with a subject which touches this community at a vital point. You are not to look only to what the educational authorities tell you. You are dealing with the needs and the aspirations of the people, something entirely different. And you can take it from me, sir, that whatever decisions Government may arrive at in the end, if the demand is strong enough they are bound to get whatever they want. You cannot stifle the nascent aspirations of the community. Government would be wise in this instance to follow and not lead. [192]

A committee was established by the government. It consisted of Errol dos Santos (treasurer), Cutteridge, five nominated unofficials (McShine, O'Reilly, Fred Grant, S.W. Fitt, A.B. Carr), and four elected members (Isaac Hope, T.M. Kelshall, A. Maillard, and T. Roodal). This was a large committee, reflecting perhaps the social importance of the matter. By the time it reported in 1937, Pierre was dead. It listened to evidence from the Citizens' Committee, the Parents' Union of Trinidad and Tobago, and the Old Boys' Association of QRC and CIC. Its terms of reference covered not only the question of the increase in university scholarships, but the method of awarding them. The Government's Committee recommended that the scholarships be increased from two to three per year, one each being awarded to the top performer in each of three groups (maths, modern studies, and science). It did not agree that a minimum standard should be set without which no awards would be made. Nor did it agree on a special university scholarship for girls. However, by including religious knowledge on the list of subsidiary subjects, the committee made it easier for a candidate from a girls' school to win the scholarship. Winners were left free to choose their professions, except that in any year, once due notice was given, the governor might rule that one scholarship was for study in a specific area. The emoluments of the scholarships were increased to make it possible for winners after all fees were paid, to live without undue hardship or excessive comfort. Altogether the extra expenditure would be about $8,890. Hence a financial increase of substance was proposed, but not a substantial increase in the number of scholarships. The committee rejected the idea of minor scholarships to support study locally, presumably at ICTA; and it did not interfere with the method of selecting scholarship winners for ICTA. What it recommended was that the government should look sympathetically on the absorption of the better, but unsuccessful, university scholarship candidates, into the civil service.[193] It also recommended that Island Scholars after qualifying in their professions should get preference for posts in the civil service. As might be expected in the circumstances, the report was a compromise. It leaned towards the view of Daniel and Cutteridge in terms of the number of university scholarships, but Pierre's views that the civil service needed professionals trained through the university scholarships found fertile ground.

The government agreed to increase the university scholarships to three per annum. It also offered a guarantee of employment in the civil service to the two Island Scholars in 1936 (Ellis Clarke and G. Wattley) if they studied civil and electrical engineering.[194] Both scholars declined the offer and Clarke chose law and Wattley medicine.

The Beginning of Technical/Vocational Education 1906-1939

Technical/vocational education as used here means the education and training of tradesmen, it does not include needlework or agricultural education. Commercial education was included only incidentally, in the sense that the Board of Industrial Training (hereafter BIT) – the main agency responsible for technical/vocational training – took over the property and activities of the Royal Victoria Institute from 1931 and one of the activities of the latter was commercial education. In the early twentieth century, a major characteristic of technical/vocational education in Trinidad and Tobago was its marginality. This arose from the lack of institutional links between the established controllers of primary and secondary education on the one hand, namely the Board of Education, the College Council, and the inspector of schools (director of education after 1921) and on the other hand, the providers of trades training. The BIT was specifically established to take responsibility for the training of tradesmen: it was a new and separate agency for a new type of education. As in the British model, the training of tradesmen was done outside the formal structure of the education system. The recruits for trades training came from the primary schools, but trades training was neither primary school education nor secondary education as it was then understood. It was a peculiar type of training, itself without much prestige, undertaken by a board of government officials and representatives of employers in the private sector who together fashioned rules for the on-the-job training and evening trade classes of apprentices. The quarrels of the clerics were completely absent from the operations of the BIT; so too was competition between French creoles and English creoles. The BIT kept a public profile relatively lower than the Board of Education, but not as low as its modern counterpart – the National Training Board.

The thrust towards teaching agriculture in the primary schools at the very start of the twentieth century was strongly supported by the British government, and found immediate favour with the upper class and with government officials. The simultaneous plunge into trades training originated, not from the British government, but from Governor Maloney who asked his officials in 1903 what was wrong with tradesmen in the colony, knowing full well that the answer would be low standards of workmanship arising partly from lack of organized apprentice training.[195] Why Governor Maloney should have struck out in this direction at this particular time is not clear beyond a general feeling at that time that too many primary school leavers expected white-collar jobs, and hence a more practical bias was needed. In the later nineteenth and early twentieth centuries new technologies were introduced into the island in consequence of developments in the sugar industry, in railway travel, telegraphic communications and street lighting. The expansion of the population and the prosperity brought by the cocoa boom encouraged the construction of new houses. These developments underlined the need for more tradesmen. Skilled artisans came from Barbados and the eastern Caribbean and found work. Also the very initiation of organized agricultural education in the primary schools might have highlighted the logic of improving trades training.

It was not argued that technical/vocational education was a strategy for economic development. The rationale was to give a practical bent to education for the masses, to increase the number of skilled tradesmen, and to raise the standard of workmanship for the benefit primarily of the public served by them. Among the persons best able to afford these services would be the upper class whites and the coloured middle class. The BIT did not justify trades training as a method of increasing the earning power of artisans, although it seems obvious that this would happen in most cases. Nor did the BIT seem concerned with creating employment. The point is that the BIT was thinking of benefits to the public rather than to the artisans, decidedly the opposite way to which the Board of Education thought of the professional education of Island Scholars. The training was not aimed at the technical level. Though from the point of view of administration, the thrust into agricultural education and into trades training was separate, they came on stream together in the early decades of the twentieth century and they signified a determination by the government, by officials and the upper class to impose a strong practical bias on the education of the masses. This was also the direction of a good deal of thinking in the USA about the education of blacks in that country. If there were differences of opinion over the vocational or pre-vocational purpose of school gardens, there was no misunderstanding the direct vocational intention of trades training. Had trades training under the BIT been investigated by a committee in 1914 or 1916 (as school gardens were), the investigators would possibly have decided that it too, like school gardens, was a failure: no kind of education below that of secondary education in the recognized colleges could stand the glare of public inquiry.

The operation of the BIT between 1906 and 1939 developed in four phases. The first (1906-1911) was the few years before the start of organized evening classes or night classes; the second phase (1911-1920) occurred between the start of these classes and the destruction of the Royal Victoria Institute (hereafter the RVI) by fire in 1920; the third phase covers the years 1920 to 1926, between the fire and the resumption of classes at a new venue; and the fourth period, from 1926 to 1939, was when classes returned to the rebuilt quarters in the RVI. Throughout these years a constant feature was the organization of on-the-job training of young apprentices in a variety of trades; except for the years between 1920 and 1922, another constant was the provision of evening classes at either the RVI or at Tranquillity Boys' School. The Junior Technical School, started in San Fernando in 1943, usually is regarded as the first technical school in the colony; but there is a sense in which the BIT was running a part-time evening technical school from the early twentieth century, albeit mostly for apprentices, on sites designed for other purposes. The BIT itself, however, never thought it was operating a technical school, only technical training.

The legislation of 1906 which brought the BIT into existence authorized it to oversee apprentices and to register artisans, but not to provide classes. The BIT made a false start by registering thousands of artisans without any examination. All that was needed were recommendations from three reputable artisans in the same trade. Thousands of artisans all over the colony, including Tobago, rushed forward between 1907 and 1908 to get the BIT's certificate of registration for a small fee.[196] Supervision of apprentice on-the-job training and the registration of adult artisans without examination were the earliest activities of the BIT; then came the decision to insist on the examination of artisans, without which standards of workmanship would not be improved. At first the BIT chose to examine individual artisans in the theory and practice of their craft by specially appointed examiners.[197] Naturally, requests for such examinations were not as frequent as the earlier applications for registration without examination. Still, the fair number of requests attests to an early recognition by the colony's artisans that a new regulatory agency of some influence had appeared in their midst. From examination of individual artisans, it was a short step to the organization of evening classes for both artisans and apprentices. This started on a small scale about 1908 with drawing, English and arithmetic, and became well established from 1911 when, through the generosity of Port of Spain businessman and philanthropist Bruce Stephens, a building to the rear of the RVI, called the Arts and Crafts Hall, was erected specially to house the classes of the BIT.[198]

The RVI was an institution whose history became closely interwoven with that of the BIT from 1908 to 1976. Opened in 1892 to mark the Jubilee of Queen Victoria, and extended in 1901 and 1911 the RVI (up to 1913 called the Victoria Institute) boasted an impressive building in a prestigious part of the town, near to the Queen's Park Savannah. Originally the RVI was intended to be a public museum and cultural centre, but these intentions became secondary to two apparently contradictory extensions of activity. It was used for the upper classes' recreational activities (tennis courts and billiards room), and for lesser mortals it started to function as a sort of polytechnic with fee-paying classes in dressmaking and commercial studies (shorthand, bookkeeping, typing, Spanish).[199] Its greatest long-term asset was its building, used for all kinds of cultural activities. The BIT rented space there for its classes; it was an important decision for the future relationship of BIT and RVI when the philanthropy of Bruce Stephens in 1911 gave the BIT an extraordinary position on the premises of the RVI. Coming first like a lodger inside the household of the RVI, the BIT outgrew the RVI until it seemed the most logical thing to entrust the lodger (BIT) with all the property and the responsibilities of the householder (the RVI).

The obligation to provide classes for apprentices, which had a legal basis from 1911, was always taken with great seriousness by the BIT and remained, until the Eric Williams era, one of its continuing commitments though the actual provision of the classes passed to other hands. By recruiting part-time instructors from government departments and private industry in Port of Spain, the BIT managed in 1911 to put together classes in practical workshop drawing, practical workshop arithmetic; building construction (carpentry, masonry); bookbinding and typography; tailoring; launch and boat building; and farriery (the latter by practical demonstrations and lectures in certain localities). The classes were both for adult artisans and young apprentices; the type of classes put on was determined by the demand and the availability of instructors. Although the classes in farriery came about at the request of the governor and reflected the dissatisfaction of the upper class with the standard of horseshoeing in the colony, the BIT otherwise seemed to have attempted what appeared most feasible in the light of social demand and teaching resources rather than acting from a plan to steer technical/vocational education towards specific occupations. The engineering trades available (fitters and turners) soon became the prestige trades; opportunities to apprentice boys were strictly limited in these fields. It must not be forgotten that for the entire period between 1906 and 1939, the apprenticeship programme was substantially confined to Port of Spain, and that the oil and sugar companies in southern Trinidad were not yet involved. In Port of Spain the engineering firms had suitable workshops for training purposes: the Government Railways, the Floating Dock and the East End Foundry were the outstanding examples. The number of the apprentices grew rather slowly, and most took up the building and printing trades. It was not until the classes and apprenticeship programme of the BIT were extended to southern Trinidad after 1939 that the pattern of apprenticeship was drastically reversed to the benefit of the engineering trades, particularly electricians, motor mechanics, and welders, and to the detriment, up to the present, of the building trades.

The destruction of the RVI in 1920 by fire, though the Arts and Crafts Hall was spared, brought the evening classes of the BIT to an end for two years. World War I, followed by the fire, had caused a drastic reduction of the number of apprentices (see Table 2.25) and employers generally did not take on new apprentices; also part-time instructors for the engineering classes became more difficult to find. A most important link with the City and Guilds Institute of London was forged on the eve of the war. Prior to this, the BIT had conducted its own local examinations; henceforth it submitted to external examinations of both artisans and apprentices. The BIT's association of technical/vocational education with the City and Guilds Institute of London lasted from 1918 to 1965. This was the counterpart in technical/vocational education to the role of the Cambridge Syndicate in the examination of secondary school students. But City and Guilds, the largest technical examination body in Britain, proved to be more flexible than the Cambridge Syndicate. Indeed, City and Guilds seemed to possess, or could make up on request, examinations to suit any trade at any level, always with a business sense of the examination fees to be collected. Eventually the number of different City and Guilds examination papers at various levels, available in the colony, threatened to get beyond the management capability of the BIT secretariat and of the various regional superintendents of classes. The City and Guilds Institute of London shaped the teaching of technical/vocational classes for half a century apparently without putting them in a curriculum straitjacket.

The work of the BIT fell on harder times after World War I. Without classes the BIT partially lost contact with its apprentices. There were at this time no trade school inspectors to make on-the-spot checks on employers and apprentices; there were then, and perhaps always, more unregistered apprentices than registered ones, and the high cost of living as well as labour disputes in the early 1920s took a toll on both the number of apprentices and the discipline of those who stayed on. By 1924 the BIT had only forty-eight registered apprentices, whereas in 1910 it had sixty-eight. The BIT 1922 enquiry into the responsiveness of youths to apprenticeships produced inconclusive results. Many boys left school too early to have the educational base for proper apprentice training. The high cost of living after World War I forced some to seek full-time jobs immediately after leaving school. An interesting social factor was the existence of unfavourable public reactions to words like 'apprenticeship' and 'indentures', important words in the vocabulary of technical/vocational education. These words were unpleasantly associated with black slavery and Indian indentureship. But apart from these factors, apprenticeships which ranged from three to five years, coupled with attendance at evening classes, called for the greatest discipline and strength of purpose from youths at an age of adolescent rebelliousness. It has always been characteristic of apprenticeship programmes and evening technical classes to have a high rate of dropouts; a regular feature of almost all BIT meetings was the cancellation of apprenticeship indentures. But others enlisted.

It is not possible to calculate for any period how many apprentices completed their apprenticeships and passed the City and Guilds examinations. Completion of apprenticeship, however, appeared to be more frequent than success in the City and Guilds examinations; in order to get certificates attesting to the completion of apprenticeships, boys were obliged to attend classes, but not to pass their City and Guilds examinations. Success in the examinations was really an additional qualification. Clearly though, the work of the BIT became more successfully organized and better established in the later 1920s. In 1922 classes were resumed at a new venue, Tranquillity Boys' School, under the eagle eye of Cutteridge who was not a teacher in the programme but the principal of the government training school at Tranquillity.

Both the number of apprentices and the number of evening students grew in the later 1920s. By 1926 the classes were back again at the RVI on terms which began to change appreciably the relations between the BIT and the RVI. Another of the Stephens, this time J.W. Stephens, donated $2,000 to the rebuilding of the Queen Victoria Memorial Wing of the RVI on condition that it be used for technical classes, and that the BIT and RVI come to some long-term agreement to secure permanently the existence of these classes at the RVI. A joint board of the BIT and the RVI emerged to supervise the classes. BIT had a clearer sense of purpose than the RVI; for it was providing skills recognizably needed in the community. On the other hand, RVI as an institution suffered from a lack of public support and confidence in the later 1920s. Only its commercial and dressmaking classes had any sustained level of public support. The RVI leadership began to consider institutional amalgamation with the BIT, but when the details were worked out in 1931 what took place was more a complete takeover than a merger on equal terms.[200] From 1931 the BIT had to carry on the objects of the RVI, and from about 1922 it had to manage the Institute for the Blind. Teaching basketry to the blind was not inconsistent with the technical/vocational aim of the BIT, but the commercial and dressmaking classes inherited from the RVI, especially the commercial classes, proved a source of embarrassment to the BIT and were tolerated rather than promoted.

By assuming responsibility for the Institute for the Blind and RVI's commercial and dressmaking classes girls and women as students were brought under the care of the BIT. With regard to girls as possible apprentices and students of technical classes, however, the BIT failed to find a satisfactory policy. It was not until 1975 that the apprenticeship law recognized girls as legal apprentices. The law was not the problem, though. There was a genuine difficulty in finding employers who wanted to have girls as apprentices and secondly, there were fears on the part of the male dominated BIT that opportunities for boys would be reduced if girls were admitted. There were a few girls working as printers and furniture polishers, but without formal apprenticeships.[201] The Board of Education unwittingly placed the BIT in an awkward position from about 1926 by providing one Handicraft Exhibition (scholarship) each year for which girls were eligible. The winner would have to be placed by the BIT as an apprentice. Thereafter a girl was occasionally found worthy of an award. One might imagine that some of the numerous Port of Spain dressmakers would at least be able to meet the BIT criteria as employers of apprentices. In 1929 the female Handicraft Exhibitioner (Carmen Cockburn) was apprenticed to a dressmaker, but other such possibilities failed to materialize.[202] All this did not mean of course that many girls from the primary schools were not becoming dressmakers (see Table 2.26); only that they were unofficial, unregistered apprentices. Photography was added to the list of trades in 1926, apparently with a view to it being taken up by girls. Satisfactory openings for girls were never found, and the Handicraft Exhibition for girls was abolished in 1935.

From 1907 the BIT started to give annually two, sometimes three, trade bursaries to bright boys, fourteen to seventeen years old, who topped the special examinations. The level of the examination was Standard VII of the primary schools; very few boys reached this standard. The potential bursars came from the same pool of promising primary school pupils from which pupil teachers were recruited. As teaching was a more dignified occupation than trades, it is not surprising that very few pupils came forward initially to take the BIT's trade bursary examinations, or the Handicraft Exhibition examination set by the BIT on behalf of the Board of Education. Winners of these bursaries sometimes changed their minds when other prospects suddenly opened up; eventually dissatisfaction by employers with the attitude of bursars reached a pitch, causing the BIT to terminate the trade bursaries. It was not the academic capacity of these boys which caused problems, but their attitude to trades: in some cases they would rather be doing something else and, as a section of the top performers of the primary schools, they felt they were entitled to a chance at secondary education or a white-collar job. But it took several years before the crisis with the trade bursars matured in the 1930s; in the first three decades of the twentieth century the trade bursars were the cream of the apprentices, always wanting to get into engineering rather than the building trades. It is obvious that a trade bursary was not as great a lever of upward social mobility as an exhibition to QRC or CIC; but it can be guessed that some of the trade bursars, after successful completion of apprenticeships and perhaps even of City and Guilds examinations, did manage to put themselves in an economic and social bracket from which their children would be more certain to attend secondary schools.

If one leaves aside the possibility that there were Indian boys with non-Indian names in the various lists of apprentices, then one must conclude emphatically that very few Indians were apprentices or students of the evening classes of the BIT between 1907 and 1939. Trades training before the era when the BIT moved operations to southern Trinidad was almost completely for black and coloured youths of working class parentage. Yet there were notable exceptions: two of the earliest winners (1908 and 1909) of trade bursaries were Indian boys from southern Trinidad, one of whom (Monassam) was apprenticed at Usine St Madeleine, without benefit of classes in Port of Spain. The second Indian boy (Dudley Beharry) lost his bursary when he became ill.

An attempt to explain the pronounced absence of Indians might start with geography. Until 1939 the work of the BIT was confined substantially to Port of Spain; but surely there must have been Indian boys in Port of Spain itself, and along the east-west corridor to Tunapuna. Other explanations seem necessary; perhaps the later start of Indian primary schools meant that in the very early twentieth century only a handful of Indian boys in northern Trinidad got into the higher standards. Perhaps private employers, heads of government departments, and non-Indian foremen in the sugar industry discriminated against Indian boys by perceiving them solely as potential agricultural or casual labourers rather than as potential tradesmen.[203] It should be remembered that it was the responsibility of the individual boy or his parents, not that of the BIT, to find an employer, and one had to be found before the BIT could enter into an apprenticeship agreement. Hence, in the early twentieth century, the question of Indian parents' readiness to apprentice their sons to trades was also a factor. Perhaps Indian parents perceived themselves as an agricultural people and, even in Port of Spain, were slow to encourage their sons to be tradesmen. By the 1940s the gap between the educational standard of Indian and non-Indian boys narrowed, and this could explain why more Indian apprentices were then available. Of course, by then the availability of classes and of apprenticeship openings in southern Trinidad also sealed the issue of Indian participation in technical/vocational education.

In the 1930s there were a number of important developments in technical/vocational education. The BIT undertook a new thrust in 1936 when it started continuation classes in Port of Spain. Basically the idea here was to offer boys classes in arithmetic, English and drawing at a level equivalent to the upper standards of primary schools, in order to improve their chances of success when they entered technical classes.[204] This became an important long-term component of the operations of the BIT. The Uriah Butler riots in June 1937 also brought technical/vocational education, like so many other things, to a new turning point. The Forster Commission of Inquiry in late 1937 advised the implementation of the Marriott/Mayhew model of secondary modern school, and also the desirability of schools keeping in touch with industry. When the Moyne Commission took evidence in early 1939 there was a rash of proposals for trade schools and farm schools. As in 1970 after the Black Power disturbances, more technical/vocational training was widely seen as part of the answer to unemployment, unemployability and perhaps indiscipline among the youths. Crown Colony government had no difficulty in taking seriously the recommendations of official commissioners sent by the British government. Obviously a chance for some new thrust in technical/vocational education opened up in 1938 and 1939, giving rise to the question of who was to direct it, the director and the Education Department or the BIT.[205]

Technical/vocational education grew up separately from the administration of primary education and the secondary schools. Individuals from the Department of Education, for example Cutteridge, sometimes served on the BIT, but the latter had been left alone as sole arbiters of technical/vocational education for the first thirty years of the twentieth century. In the late 1920s and early 1930s the government through Marriott and Cutteridge began to develop its own ideas about technical/vocational education in formal education institutions. Cutteridge assured the BIT in 1931 that there would be no clash between the interest of the BIT and the junior technical schools the government had in mind to erect;[206] but there was still the question of which institution was the superior authority in technical/vocational education and, once this was posed, the director quickly won the argument. In 1938 Cutteridge, then director and no longer on the BIT, successfully argued that by law the director of education had supreme advisory power over all types of education, and that the BIT could only function in an executive capacity.[207] This was the beginning of the BIT's subordination to the Education Department and to the director, reproduced later in the current integration of the National Training Board within the Ministry of Education.

Taking the initiative, in September 1938 Cutteridge sent a questionnaire to selected employers representing a variety of trades. Of the six replies seen (most have not survived) five firms said yes to the question whether a full-time technical school was needed, and five returned an emphatic no to the inquiry whether a trade school was required.[208] All firms were suspicious of any proposal to prepare boys in primary schools for technical education before they became apprentices. The feeling was that the employers had to correct too many bad work habits already learnt, so it was better to send the boys in a state of ignorance of technical/vocational training to begin apprenticeships. The strange refusal to countenance trade schools possibly arose from a feeling that such schools might become a substitute for on-the-job training. If there is anything which employers are perennially certain of, it is that their on-the-job training produces a workman more suited to their purpose than formal technical/vocational education in schools. The positive approval of a full-time technical school with a higher admission age than a trade school was perhaps a sign that employers were feeling the need for some superior tradesmen. In February 1939, Cutteridge and a special committee of the Board of Education decided that trade schools might flood the labour market with semi-skilled tradesmen and that the time was not right for a full-time technical school. They felt that the BIT was doing the right thing in technical/vocational training, and that its work, with a larger budget, should be allowed to extend to southern Trinidad to take in the oil and sugar industries.[209] One gets the distinct impression that the Board of Education was then competent to undertake the management of either trade schools, technical schools or farm schools. Having asserted a role in technical/vocational education, the Education Department left the BIT to undertake its projected expansion to southern Trinidad.

The oil industry as a possible factor in the education system of the country dates from the end of World War I, almost from the birth of the industry itself. In recommending the establishment of a specialist agricultural college, the Tropical Agricultural Committee advised that a branch of the college be devoted to oil technology using, presumably on a part-time basis, the engineers directly involved in the recovery of oil. This was not a well thought-out suggestion and the British government disliked it; the oil industry turned its back completely on what happened at ICTA although the local planners of ICTA suggested the establishment of a professorship in geology if the oil industry wished to participate.

The centre of the oil industry in the 1920s was in the bushes far south of ICTA (for instance, at Tabaquite, Forest Reserve, Point Fortin, Brighton and Guapo), and the operations of the BIT were in Port of Spain. It was an enclave industry of white engineers and black labourers, which soon realized its own needs for a few trained local engineers and especially for drillers and so it created its own training opportunities separate from the colony's education system.[210] It did so on terms strictly consistent with the unwritten law of the white monopoly of any job above the rank of labourer. Few of the local white youths of CIC or QRC, because of the poverty of science teaching before the mid 1920s, could have been oriented to careers as engineers; but the talent was there at QRC and CIC to study anything from scratch if scholarships were provided. Ralph Cambridge, principal of QRC, in his speech at prize-giving in April 1928, called the attention of graduates to new openings in the oil industry in semiscientific work in field laboratories,[211] and a few trade bursars got jobs as fitters in the oilfields in 1926.[212]

It appears that the oil industry began to organize its own apprenticeship training classes in the 1930s, a period of rapid rise in petroleum production and export earnings. Although these classes were quite separate from the work of the BIT or the director of education, it became clear that the way forward for technical/vocational education was to link up the work of the BIT with the apprentice training of the oil industry and, at a higher level, to offer locals the chance of using the university scholarships (Island Scholarships) to study engineering. In March 1938 A. C. Rienzi boldly suggested to the Legislative Council that the three university scholarships for the following ten years should be reserved for the study of petroleum engineering, engineering and agriculture, and that the winners should be bonded to return to serve the colony.[213] This rather drastic advice was not heeded, although, as indicated earlier, in the previous year the government had begun unsuccessfully to steer Island Scholars towards the study of engineering, even dangling before them guarantees of employment in the civil service. In 1939 the BIT extended its classes to San Fernando where it made fruitful contact with the oil industry. Out of these efforts grew the San Fernando Junior Technical College.

The Growth of the Educated Middle Class 1902–1939

In the early twentieth century the social processes which assisted some black and coloured people to rise to middle class status through education underwent expansion and consolidation; the Indians, whose advance by similar routes had been retarded in the late nineteenth century, in some cases experienced an accelerated pace of upward social mobility. Indian professionals outside the teaching service, especially medical practitioners, began to appear in significant numbers. It was an axiom that almost all the educated middle class Indians of this era were products of the Canadian Presbyterian Mission schools. The routes were from Canadian Presbyterian Mission primary schools to Naparima College, to Naparima Training College, then study abroad; or the route could be extended by the addition of study at the Presbyterian theological college (St Andrew Theological College). Very often, somewhere along the route, the Indian youth paused to teach for a few years. Occasionally one finds the Indian youth who had used yet another route which took him, after primary school or even after Naparima College, to QRC or CIC in Port of Spain.[214]

Without Naparima College the accelerated accession of Indians to the educated middle class would not have happened. However, several Indians went beyond Naparima College to universities abroad, and this would not have been possible unless their parents had established themselves economically to generate the necessary funds to pay for higher education. Hence behind the complex of Canadian Presbyterian Mission schools, of which Naparima College was the key, lay the success stories of several Indian families in the chosen field of business enterprise. An outstanding example was David Bunsee, wealthy Indian merchant of Penal and Debe. He was born in poverty at Bon Accord; he left school at age ten, but in 1924 his eldest son was at QRC.[215] There were Indian merchants and shopkeepers who came up from indentureship by the hard route of self-help, who were then capable of paying for a medical course in England.[216]

There were Indian headteachers of ten or fifteen years standing who sometimes had several farm lots or even cocoa estates who were willing to make sacrifices for their promising sons. A medical education was a considerable investment. One knowledgeable estimate was that in the mid 1920s it cost $4,800 to $7,200 to complete a medical course in England.[217] Of course the sons of those Indians who had been among the earliest beneficiaries of the schools of the Canadian Presbyterian Mission were in a good position to try for the professions. For example, Clarence E. Soodeen, the son of Charles Clarence Soodeen, left to study medicine in Edinburgh in 1921; by 1930 he was practicing medicine in Trinidad.[218] His father was one of the first Indian converts of the Canadian Presbyterian Mission, a man who rose to be a successful cocoa farmer, merchant and member of the Board of Education. Frank Ragbir, son of Leo Ragbir, a long-serving headteacher of Elswick Canadian Presbyterian Mission School at Tableland, not only went to QRC, but was sent by his father to study medicine.[219] If one is left to wonder how Indian and black headteachers financed professional studies abroad without university scholarships,[220] one need not be surprised in the case of Sankerali Brothers, local contractors for the Public Works Department, who were able to pay for the medical education in Ireland of E.T. Sankerali.[221] Gookool, a wealthy cocoa contractor in Diego Martin, had a son who studied medicine in Scotland in the early 1920s. Indeed, it is clear that the medical profession was particularly favoured by Indian parents of means. They at first did not appear to place great store by the study of law, unlike ambitious black and coloured parents, and an apparently extraordinary respect for a medical career has characterized the Indian community to this day.

The notion that Indians had a uniquely shrewd economic interpretation of schooling which led them to calculate the cost of education carefully against the economic returns has been urged by Kazim Bacchus, in relation to the Indians of Guyana.[222] According to this theory, Indian parents, as a matter of strategy, withdrew unpromising children from school to make way for greater concentration on a particular son who demonstrated an ability to succeed. The intention was to promote the higher education of this bright son up to the professional level where the investment in education would bring the highest economic returns, and this could best be achieved by a medical education. The theory has the merit of appearing to explain low Indian attendance patterns in the schools of Guyana in the late nineteenth and early twentieth centuries, without a pejorative evaluation of their cultural heritage from India. They did not carelessly undervalue education, but in fact placed an appropriate economic value on it as a form of investment. The theory is compatible with a widely held view of Indians as shrewd business people who looked to economic prosperity as the means of upliftment. It also conforms to the notion of Indian family solidarity: the favoured son given professional education not only benefits initially at the expense of other children, but is expected after graduation to help other family members. If all this was true of Indians in Guyana, it might well apply to Indians in Trinidad because of the similarities of indentured immigration and settlement in both colonies. Two difficulties, however, are the weakness of the empirical evidence for the theory, and the danger of believing that blacks and coloureds did not also appreciate higher education, especially education in medicine, as forms of investment.

The first Indian lawyer was George Fitzpatrick who also became the first Indian member of the Legislative Council. Fitzpatrick was born in Trinidad in 1875, and was a pupil of Rev Kenneth Grant, the second Canadian Presbyterian missionary at San Fernando. Fitzpatrick took to business, and was able to finance his study of law in England where he was called to the bar in 1909.[223] Fitzpatrick's death in 1920 left the way clear in the Indian communities for another legal star. The brightest Indian talent in the legal field in the 1920s was F.E.M. Hosein. Hosein had won a university scholarship from QRC in 1901, the first Indian to accomplish this feat. He ranked high in the coterie of educated Indians of professional status being unsurpassed in Port of Spain.[224] Hosein was strongly opposed to the dilution of the Indian cultural heritage.[225] The Indian doctors, lawyers and teachers shared the leadership of Indian communities with pundits and *moulvis*, religious leaders who had sometimes little or no western education but who might be knowledgeable about the religions and literature of India. Then there were the businessmen and landowners whose wealth had moved them into the middle class after perhaps only an incomplete primary school education; and increasingly, after 1925, there were the part-time politicians who might overlap with any of the above occupations except the teachers.

The leadership of the Indian communities seemed very varied; but it was obvious that a hierarchy of educated Indians at various levels, from medical practitioners to sanitary inspectors and primary school teachers, was rising in numbers significant enough to give the Indian communities the intellectual means of asserting new claims against the rest of the society which too often treated them as less than equals. In 1931 Sarran Teelucksingh, elected member of the Legislative Council for Caroni, looking back over the previous decade, felt that a stream of Indian youths with Cambridge certificates had arisen;[226] they were knocking in vain at the doors of the civil service. A few Indian girls had fortunately been taken into the hospitals to be trained as nurses.[227]

As in the later nineteenth century the teachers were the most numerous sector of the small educated middle class. As one teacher put it in 1935: "Elementary teachers are generally the most enlightened of the poor, in fact they bridge the gulf between the better off and the poor, and in a way pioneer in the upward march which is always in progress towards better things, or rather rising in the world."[228] Teachers were in an excellent position to promote, by encouragement and extra tuition, the academic success of their own children and those of relatives. A handful of Port of Spain teachers enjoyed a considerable local reputation as tutors of College Exhibition winners. In 1918 there were 596 teachers with certificates, of whom 217 (36.4%) were women. These were all non-white except for a few nuns and English women. In the same year the island possessed 59 lawyers, 76 solicitors, and 94 registered medical practitioners, 25 of whom were no longer resident on the island. Of dentists there were 41, of whom 19 were nonresident.[229] Apparently only a small but probably significant percentage of these professionals were non-whites. But it was different with the 99 pharmacists (druggists) and 254 midwives; these were almost all non-whites, the pharmacists being described interestingly by one of them in 1931 as sons of "middle class working men"[230] which must be taken to mean lower middle class people.

In the early twentieth century Indian, black and coloured teachers asserted their rights as teachers to participate in the shaping of education policy, and generally in the creation of public opinion. The TTTU, formed in 1919, acted mostly as a pressure group seeking to improve teachers' pay and working conditions, particularly teachers' pensions.[231] But in the 1920s there was a widening of interest and teachers were more willing to express their views on aspects of education, although without directly contesting those of the directors (McKay, Marriott and Cutteridge). At the annual conferences of the TTTU teachers began to say what should be done in education. It might even be suggested that Marriott and Cutteridge unwittingly prepared the teachers to be their eventual challengers. Their reforms aimed to upgrade the teachers and to activate them into becoming key agents in the modernization of the curriculum. Some of the teachers slowly developed an image of themselves as experts in primary education, or at least as voices which should be heard. This growing confidence led to the view that teachers should be promoted to the ranks of the inspectorate. In the early 1920s an aspiration of the TTTU was to have a classroom teacher on the Board of Education.[232] J. Hamilton Maurice, as a young 'independent teacher', wrote to the press a brief but forthright letter which could not have emanated from the TTTU at this stage. Maurice indignantly protested against the Island Scholar syndrome which brought Dr Prada, Dr Masson and Dr Laurence (all former Island Scholars) onto the Board of Education, instead of classroom teachers.[233] How much did these medical gentlemen know about primary schools? Eventually, in 1932 the government did put a teacher on the Board, and the TTTU was consulted more on education policies in the 1930s. But in the 1920s the TTTU felt more confident in speaking about pay, pensions and security of tenure than about policies in education. It was anxious not to enter into politics. As will be soon seen, the TTTU did not assume the mantle of overt opposition to the directors until Cutteridge proposed the Code of 1935, and more important until the labour unrest of the masses had created new conditions for protest.

From the 1920s, some individual teachers came forward as makers of public opinion, even political opinion, at a level which would have been unwise for the

TTTU. This was done through respectable organizations called literary and debating associations which proliferated after World War I. The primary school headteachers were the lifeblood of these associations. The emergence of scores of literary and debating societies has so far not been studied in the social history of the colony. They were the accumulated intellectual outcome of two or three generations of primary schools since emancipation. They grew not from the recognized secondary schools, but from rural and urban primary schools; and they signalled the continuing urge of the non-white peoples, especially Indians and blacks, to bid for the intellectual leadership of the colony. These organizations were also a warning to the colonial rulers of dissatisfaction with Crown Colony government and its assumption of the racial inferiority of the masses.

It is not widely recognized how significant a contribution to the confidence of the Indian community was made by literary and debating associations. This sharpening of the consciousness was taking place in black and coloured communities at the same time by the same means. A list of Indian debating clubs reads like a record of the major concentrations of Indians in the colony: they could be found in Couva, Chaguanas, Sangre Grande, San Fernando, Princes Town, Cedros, Tunapuna, St Joseph and elsewhere in smaller settlements. From 1923 these clubs were grouped together in the East Indian Literary League, whose gatherings were described as assemblages of future Indian leaders. The literary and debating societies of the 1920s were an important forum for increasing political awareness expressed in ways compatible with the Education Code. They debated a wide range of topics, some of which could not have been seriously explored without an expansion of political consciousness about local conditions. Indian teachers, especially headteachers, participated fully in the leadership of these societies, which in some places like Sangre Grande brought Indians and blacks together for discussion. Some of the topics discussed were "Should Indian immigration be abolished?" (East Indian Literary Debating Club of St James); "Is representative government beneficial to Trinidad?" (Chaguanas Literary and Debating Club, October 1924); "The time has arrived for Princes Town to be granted municipal rights" (St Andrew Literary and Debating Association, August 1924); and "Should East Indians in Trinidad adopt western habits and customs?" (Trinidad East Indian Literary League, July 1924); and an interesting debate, both because of the theme and because it took place between Indians and black creoles, had the following moot: "Is western civilization a failure?" (San Fernando Literary and Debating Society vs. Southern East Indian Debating Association, July 1925). Significantly the Indians Krishna Deonarine (the future Adrian Cola Rienzi) – a stalwart of friendly societies and debating clubs – and Harold Mahabir argued for the affirmative, and the blacks (Cyril Burkett and Oscar Nurse) for the negative.[234] There were non-Indian judges and one Indian judge: the blacks won.

The thesis that these societies were a sort of training ground for politically conscious individuals is strengthened by looking at the career of Krishna

Deonarine who came to notice from the mid 1920s in southern Trinidad as a very youthful debater and administrator of the Southern East Indian Literary and Debating Association. He was also on the Executive of the Southern East Indian Friendly Society. Deonarine was congratulated in January 1924 by Harold Mahabir, chairman of the Southern East Indian Literary and Debating Society, for the "remarkable way in which he flew into prominence as a Secretary and a debater from the ranks of Floor members".[235] Prominent Indians like Presbyterian minister Rev C.D. Lalla, A. Bharat Gobin, a Chaguanas merchant, Jules Mahabir and Dr Frank Mahabir, a lawyer and doctor respectively, and F.E.M. Hosein, gladly accepted the honour of being patrons of these Indian associations.

Indian debating associations and friendly societies were only a part of a larger awakening of the Indian community in the 1920s. This awareness took many forms, chief of which was interest in ancestral India, its languages and culture, and an insistence on the need to preserve Indian culture locally by teaching Hindi and Urdu, and by the preservation of Islam and Hinduism against the inroads of Christianity. The movement emphasized differences between Christianity and non-Christian religions rather than those between Hinduism and Islam, and was preeminently the work of educated middle class Indians. To a large extent, it involved a rebellion against the leadership and influence of the Canadian Presbyterian missionaries. The incipient Indian nationalism of the 1920s emerged side by side with black consciousness characterized by Garveyism, but the two ideologies were as yet more parallel than conflicting, and there was significant cooperation between black and Indian middle class trade union leaders to the benefit of working class solidarity expressed at the level of labour politics. It would be a mistake, however, to believe that the rising community power which education gave to the non-white peoples was exercised at the level of social institutions in racial unity: racial separation was in fact a pronounced feature of the heterogeneous population. The education system, as in the nineteenth century, still reflected the social divisions of the colony. The new secondary schools of the 1920s did not interfere with the established alignment of Naparima College with Indians, of CIC and St Joseph's Convent with the French creoles, and of QRC with the sons of English officials and businessmen and middle class blacks and coloureds. Indeed, the new secondary schools accentuated these divisions; Naparima Girls' High School fell into the orbit of the Indians eventually; Bishop Anstey High School came to life as the female counterpart of QRC, and Bishop's High School in Tobago was almost entirely black.

In the first forty years of the twentieth century the number of medical practitioners, solicitors, lawyers, teachers, surveyors, pharmacists and minor civil servants increased as the population grew, and the demand for complex services became greater in the towns. The black and coloured people were now irresistibly on their way, followed by Indians, to an ever increasing penetration of the professions. Not even the most liberal white person of 1875 could have imagined the transformation of the racial composition of the professions which took place by 1935. Any listing of prominent non-white professional Trinidadians in the 1920s and 1930s would include Gaston Johnson, T.M. Kelshall, L.C. Hannays, F.E.M. Hosein, H.O.B. Wooding, Jules Mahabir, C. Henry Pierre, Henry Alcazar (lawyers); Dr A. McShine, Dr S. Laurence, Dr Frank Mahabir (doctors); Rev C.D. Lalla, Rev J.D. Ramkessoon and Rev Ragbir (Christian ministers). Among the professionals C. Henry Pierre was often used as an example of what hard work and self-help could achieve. It was a matter of pride for Pierre, a man of mixed African and Indian ancestry, to repeat that he never went to college. After Arima Government Primary School, he worked his way to law school in England from earnings as a cocoa estate overseer.[236] Obviously he must have engaged in private study. When elections were held in 1925 Pierre was the first to be declared elected. He was able to finance the medical education of his son Dr J. Henry Pierre who returned to the island in 1931, and later became the most famous surgeon in the island.

Among the teachers who occupied a lower rank from the gentlemen named above was the coloured Joseph A. Desouze, the dean of teachers, with some fifty years of service, mostly at St Thomas Roman Catholic School in Port of Spain. He was the author of *Little Folks Trinidad*; and was cheerfully adopted by the educational establishment as a sort of 'honorary' white teacher.[237] Desouze took a curious route from business to teaching and reached maximum social recognition as a teacher.[238] But for the teaching service generally, the way up the ladder of promotion led out of teaching into at least the junior ranks of the civil service. The teachers who were considered very successful were those who broke, even temporarily, into the Education Department's hierarchy as assistant inspectors; for example Sydney Smith, Nelson Comma, E.B. Grosvenor, Cyril Guyadeen, A.J. Mohammed, and V.R. Vidale (see Table 2.27). Guyadeen had letters behind his name signifying special knowledge of modern methods of infant teaching; and Rawle Ramkessoon, who was not a primary school teacher, came into the inspectorate with a University of London external degree, wisely followed by training in England for the LCP (Licentiate of the College of Preceptors). These headteachers had to be drafted into the inspectorate because the emphasis had shifted from examining pupils to giving advice and leadership to teachers. The white or near-white assistant inspectors of the late nineteenth and early twentieth centuries were out of their depth because they had not been teachers. The significance of these promotions was not missed. Headteachers were not civil servants, but assistant inspectors were, and the latter had bigger salaries.[239]

Nelson Comma was the first black teacher to receive a permanent appointment to the inspectorate. Sydney Smith, Comma's predecessor in the inspectorate, had actually retired from teaching when made assistant inspector. Comma was the first teacher in service to move into the inspectorate. At a function in his honour he was hailed as one of the most successful headteachers with thirty years' experience in teaching. His fame rested largely on the College Exhibition winners he had coached at Mouton Hall Methodist Primary School in Port of Spain. This school had a remarkable run of success in the College Exhibition examination just before and during World War I, beating the favoured Tranquillity Boys' School into second place (see Table 2.28).[240] One of Comma's prize pupils, it was well known, had been H.O.B. Wooding. Successful professionals then normally credited their headteachers with greater influence on their careers than today.

These ex-headteachers turned assistant inspectors at least stayed in education, but there were those who left for the junior civil service. Not to be discounted were those teachers, often Indians, who became sanitary inspectors and who got there by quiet study and success in locally sat examinations set by an English examination authority.[241] The job of sanitary inspector had a low profile, but when combined with certification from an external examining body, it was a more desirable and remunerative post than that of a rural headteacher. There was an amazing number of occupations for which Trinidadians could get external qualifications by self-instruction without leaving the island.

In the 1920s and 1930s black and coloured men and women came to maturity in an age when black consciousness was awakened, and intellectuals who never achieved fame felt the urge to express themselves in literary composition. An interesting Tobagonian was Levi A. Darlington who went to an early grave in 1938. He was born too early to take advantage of Bishop's High School in Tobago; he became a teacher for the Seventh-Day Adventist Mission at the age of sixteen. About the same time, a handful of other black Tobago youths were converted to the Seventh-Day Adventist Church, drafted into formal or informal institutions, and given a start on the road to upward social mobility as full ministers, some later reappearing in leadership roles at the Maracas Valley Seventh-Day Adventist schools in Trinidad. In the case of Darlington his parents recognized he was a studious youth and began to prepare him for the ministry. Such private instruction was not extraordinary in Tobago before the age of Bishop's High School. His studies took him to Trinidad where he came into contact with Rev W.A. Mayhew of the American Methodist Episcopalian Church. Darlington became one of Mayhew's students, possibly at Gaines Normal School (a private institution); he also did missionary work and was ordained. Although he was appointed a pastor at San Juan, the ministry was not his true vocation. He was a lover of literature, but could not gain his living this way. Darlington left the ministry and became a sanitary contractor to the Education Department. In the meantime he formed a literary club, promoted lectures, debates, literary evenings, wrote letters to the press, wrote poems, founded a 'Thespian Club'. He produced a collection of poems called *Calliope* in 1938.[242] Darlington was a race conscious black man. He was, as one writer put it, a West Indian variant of the type of English literary gentleman who frequented coffee houses in the eighteenth century.

A notable development in education in the early twentieth century was the emergence of a new type of private secondary school, and the opening up of the Cambridge examinations to private candidates. Whereas private secondary schools had always existed for the upper class, it was only from the early twentieth century that affordable private schools started for black and coloured youths. In 1905 Pamphylian High School was started by Patrick Alexis, once called the 'father' of affordable private secondary education.[243] In 1907 Iere Central High School was founded by J.D. Regis; and in 1910 it was the turn of David Bichlow, an ex-CIC student, to establish Sangre Grande High School.[244] The number of these private secondary schools continued to increase in the 1920s and 1930s, not only in Port of Spain, but in other towns. The Haig High School was among the better known ones in the 1920s. These schools, like the newly recognized denominational secondary schools of the 1920s, charged lower fees than the older, well-established secondary schools. The expansion of secondary education in the 1920s depended on its increased availability at a lower cost. All these new private secondary schools felt strong enough to try their hand at least at the Junior Cambridge Examination; even some private commercial schools now sent up a few students as Junior Cambridge candidates. More private candidates also came forward for the Cambridge School Certificate Examination.

In 1920 private students (private school candidates plus private candidates not in any school) comprised 38.6 percent of the Junior Cambridge candidates; in 1929 the figure was 35.6 percent. For the Cambridge Schools Certificate the corresponding figures were 15.5 percent in 1923 and 23.2 percent in 1929. No private candidate or private school as yet dared to attempt the Higher School Certificate Examination. But more people were getting some sort of secondary education and collecting those precious Cambridge certificates. As we have already seen, part of the response of Marriott and Cutteridge to this growing number of non-whites with Cambridge certificates was to downplay their importance, especially for entry into the civil service. The expansion of secondary education was a potential threat to the racial composition and class association of the junior civil service.

Another development which indicated the pressure for more secondary education, this time for girls, was the establishment of the Higher Class at Tranquillity Girls' School (the former Girls' Model School). One of the senior teachers (Gladys Bushe), without prior permission from the Board of Education, decided to prepare a number of the older girls for the Cambridge preliminary examinations, the Junior Cambridge and School Certificate examinations – for a fee.[245] One of its earliest students was Audrey Jeffers, of black well-to-do parents, who transferred from Tranquillity Girls' School to the Higher Class.[246] When the Higher Class had grown to 48 students in 1920, permission was given to move into the Princes Building vacated by QRC. By 1918 the Higher Class at Tranquillity Girls' School was getting results in Junior Cambridge not very inferior to those at Naparima College, and in the Cambridge School Certificate results were better than at

Naparima College (see Appendix 6). One of the better known graduates of the Higher Class was Umilta McShine, daughter of Dr Arthur McShine. She passed Cambridge School Certificate with six credits, and returned from study overseas in 1936 to be Headmistress of Tranquillity Girls' School.[247] The Higher Class came to an end partly because Tranquillity Girls' School became an intermediate school in 1922,[248] which meant that it could officially send up candidates for the Cambridge examinations. Shortly afterwards Bishop Anstey High School was founded, and it could be said that this school was the spiritual successor to what Roman Catholic leaders regarded as the 'illegal' Higher Class. At Bishop Anstey High School girls of the same Protestant middle class families were the favoured clientele.

The development of the Higher Class at Tranquillity Girls' School mostly for Protestant girls served to spur on St Joseph's Convent, the pioneer in girls' secondary education, to seek recognition and financial assistance from government (1911), thus accelerating the transition from being a 'French' school to an English school. A decade previously, Naparima College had also sought recognition and aid but, up to 1916 at least its work could more fairly be compared to that of St Joseph's Convent than to QRC or CIC.

The most significant development at CIC and QRC in the early twentieth century was the remarkable rise in the level of achievement, judged by the standard of the Cambridge examination results. After 1910 it was rare for any student who did not get first class honours to win a university scholarship. Taking the CIC and QRC students together between 1910 and 1916 there were approximately ten to twelve boys each year who did very good work in an examination of the highest type for secondary schools in the empire. Two famous headmasters, William Burslem of QRC (1894-1919) and Fr Crehan of CIC (1910-1920), were most credited with the rise in academic standards, practising something called the 'intensive' method. It referred to the meticulous preparation of students for the Cambridge examinations; in the case of candidates for the university scholarships, it involved the repetition of the same work, or the same kind of work, in the search for accuracy. QRC and CIC had an equal share of university scholarships (Island Scholarships) between 1904 and 1919, and again in the 1920s when the scholarships were reduced from three to two annually.[249] This reduction of the annual quota of university scholarships, plus the increase of the College Exhibitions to eight per year, made certain that the great majority of Island Scholars had previously won College Exhibitions. The university scholarships continued to be a most important lever of upward social mobility, a dazzling prize fiercely contested.

Although it is clear that black and coloured boys climbed up through this route, it must not be overlooked that a few French creole boys, from well-established families, in the early twentieth century as in the late nineteenth century, continued to win university scholarships at CIC, especially from the science-based subjects. Before the teaching of science was established at QRC and CIC – and indeed afterwards – some Island Scholars, educated in arts subjects, amazed everyone by distinguishing themselves abroad in medicine, without ever having studied science in Trinidad.[250] The scholarships, especially when won by father and son, or by two other near relatives, had enormous impact on the destiny of entire families, even those already possessing professional members. Some notable 'double' winners from the same family were Dr A. McShine (1896) and his son Louis H. McShine (1932); Dr Stephen Laurence (1883), and his son Noel Laurence (1917); also Dr K.O. Laurence, Stephen's grandson. Other interesting winners were H.O.B. Wooding (1923), Patrick Solomon (1928), and Eric Williams (1931).

The Cambridge examinations, particularly the Junior Cambridge and the Higher School Certificate examinations, after the latter was introduced in 1917, continued to dominate all education in Trinidad and Tobago. The special significance of the Junior Cambridge examinations was that it was a turning point in the secondary school career of most girls and boys, and a crucial stage organizationally in the life of the older secondary schools. It was at this juncture that most boys, including the College Exhibitioners, were judged worthy of further secondary education. House Scholarships were based on this examination. Teaching bursars in the 1920s also left after Junior Cambridge. Some students from private schools like Pamphylian High School made the transition to the prestigious secondary schools after success in this examination. Ambitious Indian boys from Naparima College might enter QRC after passing the Junior Cambridge Examination. And of course at QRC and CIC the highly prized Jerningham Silver Medal was first based on the Junior Cambridge, and, after 1936, on the Cambridge School Certificate Examination. It was at the Junior Cambridge examinations up to 1936 that probable winners of the university scholarships could be first discerned clearly. Before 1936 the Cambridge School Certificate Examination, though it was a higher examination than the Junior Cambridge Examination, was, at QRC and CIC at least, less recognized in the academic march forward to a university scholarship. But leaving the premier secondary schools aside, the wider social importance of the Junior Cambridge Examination was that it was the terminal Cambridge examination for most students in secondary schools.

The College Exhibition examination continued to select a few bright pupils for free secondary education. Between 1902 and 1916 the number awarded was four per year, doubling to eight per year between 1917 and 1934. Thereafter, to the end of the 1930s, it was increased by small annual increments.[251] In the 1920s Captain Cutteridge was held responsible for converting the College Exhibition examination into a brain-racking exercise in which few candidates could succeed without intensive private lessons. But the examination was already difficult, if we are to believe a good description of it in the *Port of Spain Gazette* of the November 29, 1914. The reporter wrote:

> Not many people realize what it means for a little boy to sit for the Exhibitioners'
> Examinations with some reasonable hope of success. In Geography he must be

familiar with all the more important facts about the British empire, and should be able to draw from memory a map of any one of the larger possessions, Trinidad and Gt. Britain. In Grammar, besides being able to answer questions on the definitions and rules, his chance will be extremely poor if he cannot also with ease, negotiate the analysis of complete sentences and parshing [sic]. In Arithmetic he must be ready to cope with anything from a mammoth, tedious Addition to test his accuracy right up to a intricate problem in Percentages to measure his reasoning ability. He must write a passage of moderate difficulty from dictation and punctuate it himself. For Composition he is generally required to reproduce in his own words a short story read twice by the examiner; and sometimes the task is a letter on a given subject. Then comes General Knowledge, and as the names implies, he must have a general acquaintance with everything to pass in this subject. In Dictation and Arithmetic, the candidate must secure 60 per cent, and in each of the other four subjects 50 per cent of the marks obtainable to get mentioned on the pass list. But to get within the 'Box' as the first four places are called, is another question. Of late years the competition has got so keen, that a boy can scarcely win an Exhibition with anything less than 85 per cent everywhere, and teachers who know the ropes feel safe only when their boys can be depended on to keep near 90 per cent all the time. The examination is a contest in which only boys of exceptional ability can finish at the top.

The fiction was that the examination was based on the work of Standard V of the primary schools; but only boys under twelve years old who had reached Standard VI had a chance of winning. Still, the number of aspirants grew so large that Marriott and Cutteridge sought to discourage teachers from sending up too many pupils by exposing publicly the margin of their failure. But the teachers were under pressure from parents to send up their children. The new secondary schools of the 1920s granted a few scholarships on their own. Desperate parents sometimes entered children for all available scholarships to secondary schools. A notable development from the later 1920s was the increase of female candidates. In 1926 two girls (Valeria Batson and Marjorie Guy) created history by winning College Exhibitions for the first time; and in 1929 a girl (Bernice Grant) shocked many and delighted a few in Port of Spain by topping the list of College exhibitioners for the first time.[252] There were in the 1920s more colleges which female exhibitioners could attend, but as none competed for the university scholarships it was impossible for a girl to take the same route as boys to professional studies abroad. Nevertheless a female College Exhibitioner who came away from secondary school, especially from St Joseph's Convent or Bishop Anstey High School, with a Cambridge School Certificate was an extraordinary young woman in the late 1920s and the 1930s.

Some mention should be made of another type of exhibition which was offered by government in the 1920s. Supplementing the trade bursaries offered by the Board of Industrial Training, the government provided funds for three Handicraft Exhibitions per year, two for boys and one for a girl. The candidates had to be older (fourteen to sixteen) than the College Exhibitioners, and the prize was a period of training to be a skilled craftsman. It was not until 1926 that a girl (Elsie Padmore) satisfied the Board of Industrial Training and, as already suggested, this inclusion of females created problems of apprenticeship which were never solved. The chief problem was where to apprentice female winners.

Although the directors, especially Cutteridge, wished to encourage the acquisition of practical skills, they failed to laud and honour the winners of Handicraft Exhibitions, and middle class parents paid comparatively little attention to these awards. But it would be a mistake to believe that Handicraft Exhibitioners who successfully completed their training had not secured a lever of social advancement. Perhaps this was the reason why some pupil teachers took the Handicraft examinations.[253] The achievement of winners of Handicraft Exhibitions was deemed unspectacular; their schools held no functions in their honour. But a skilled craftsman would enjoy a higher standard of living than an unskilled labourer or a landless estate worker. Their children would probably be among the College Exhibition hopefuls of the next generation. Part of the lack of respect for Handicraft Exhibitions sprang from the fact that they did not lead to a secondary school career, but only to further training. The financial and social rewards of trades training were less certain and more moderate than those of a secondary school graduate.

[3]

The Challenge of the Teachers

The Revolt of the Indians 1928-1939

The last thirty decades of the nineteenth century have been correctly characterized by Gerad Tikasingh as a period in which the Indians established themselves as permanent communities of estate workers, villagers and small peasant settlers. By the early twentieth century the Indians consolidated their position and became wealthier, better educated, more confident and ready to assert their rights. There were now more Trinidad born Indians than immigrants. There was nothing unique about this transposition of poor, diffident, foreign born immigrants into wealthier, more assertive groups dominated demographically by persons born in the country of adoption. This has happened to immigrant groups in other countries, for example the West Indians in England. Although Indian immigration continued until 1917, the proportion of Trinidad born Indians increased from 44 percent in 1901 to 69 percent in 1921.[1] The rate of natural increase had outpaced both the number of arrivals of new indentured immigrants from India and the mortality rate. Even if many Indians had not acquired a share in the most valuable asset of the colony – land – the increasing proportion of locally born Indians would have transformed their self-image, giving them a higher sense of their rights against other sectors of the population. Although many Indians made important social and economic progress, the masses remained in dire poverty. Their significant increase in land ownership in the late 1800s and early 1900s provided them with a share in the cocoa prosperity, and established them as the leading producers of food for local consumption.[2] Many turned to commercial occupations off the land, of which shopkeeping was perhaps the most remunerative.

It is not unusual for a group to project an image of itself consonant with the social and political demands it makes. The French creoles had a legend, at least half-true, about their saving Trinidad from economic ruin at least twice, at the end of the eighteenth century and again at the close of the nineteenth century. The English officials and English creoles should, it was felt, respect the achievements of the French creoles, the true Trinidadians. The stage of development of the Indians in the early twentieth century, as well as their self-image, was not unlike those of the free coloureds one century earlier. The first generation of free coloured immigrants at the end of the eighteenth century was largely made up of foreigners without major plantations, and they did not claim equal civil rights with the whites. The second generation, however, was less dominated by foreign born immigrants and was a wealthier group, more firmly based on the land, more confident of their right to ask for equal treatment. The free coloureds in the 1820s perceived themselves to be a wealthy, taxpaying sector of the society, numerically significant in the total population, peaceful and loyal subjects posing no danger to the social fabric.[3] The Indian leaders of the early twentieth century projected an almost identical self-image. The free coloureds, however, wanted full integration into the government and society, not having any particularistic culture to protect and nurture; the Indians wanted only enough integration to protect their separate identity.

A small section of the urban free coloureds in the mid 1820s rebelled against the Roman Catholic Church, not on doctrinal grounds, but because it failed to help them in the movement for civil equality.[4] Many people from the Indian community rebelled against the Christian churches and particularly the Canadian Presbyterian Mission, also because they failed to assist with the realization of Indian objectives. The alternative church which the free coloureds established was just another Roman Catholic chapel under free coloured management; the alternative to Christianity for the Indians was the intensification of their own religions: Hinduism and Islam. No reconciliation was sought, or seemed possible, between Christianity and Hinduism or Islam; if Hinduism and Islam were allowed to strengthen themselves it would be the end of the dream of christianizing all the Indians.

It has just been suggested that the Indians went from a period of establishment in the later nineteenth century to one of consolidation, and that important socioeconomic, psychological and demographic changes accompanied their march to citizenship. It appears that in the period of establishment and for part of the period of consolidation, perhaps up to about 1930, the Indians created new political, social, economic and intellectual organizations, for example, the East Indian National Association, the East Indian National Congress, friendly societies, and numerous literary and debating societies, but generally without new religious organizations. Of course individual pundits and moulvis existed, even flourished, and the Islamic Guardian Association was founded in 1906; but the point is that the new pre-1930 organizations were not generally religious, and so they could be Hindu/Muslim in orientation, instead of being Hindu or Muslim.

In the early 1930s things changed. The incorporation of the Tackveeyatul Islamic Association of Trinidad (1932), the Sanatan Dharma Board of Control (1932); the Sanatan Dharma Association of Trinidad (1932); the Kabir Panth Association (1932); the Anjuman Sunnat-ul-Jammat Association of Trinidad (1935) marked the advent of more overtly religious bodies, at a time when the East Indian National Association and the East Indian National Congress were in decline, and literary and debating societies had lost some of their glamour. These new religious institutions of the 1930s were the fruition of earlier missionary activities, and they ushered in an era of heightened splits and factionalism within Hindu and Muslim communities. It became increasingly difficult to maintain the Hindu/Muslim front from the previous years and this eventually broke down or became recessive.

The revolt of the Indians as it affected education began about 1928 to 1930, just before new Hindu and Muslim religious organizations emerged. The revolt in education was clearly a part of a larger awakening of Indian race and religious consciousness, but it first expressed itself socially and institutionally through the Hindu/Muslim front; there were protests against the Canadian Presbyterian Church, and there followed the establishment of a Hindu/Muslim primary school at Chaguanas. Almost as soon as the Hindu/Muslim school was founded, it had to stand against the new tide of religious institutional fervour for Hinduism and Islam; and hence it did not, and could not, provide the religious model for future Indian schools. No more Hindu/Muslim schools emerged.

A missionary church often trains 'native' agents below the level of ordained ministers to assist the white missionaries, and the Canadian Presbyterian Church had a distinguished record in training Indian teachers, catechists, 'Bible women', and a smaller core of ministers of the gospel. The early ordination of Indian ministers had important consequences for the Mission. Between its inception and the revolt of the Indians the theological college had three graduations, in 1896, 1915 and 1929; but it is doubtful if at any time before 1928 more than five Indian ministers were employed simultaneously in the Mission. The pace of the training of Indian ministers was a factor in the gestation of the internal rebellion in the Mission; the Indian ministers were trained quickly, before the individual white missionary was prepared to yield equal status to them. Size was another factor in the crisis: if there was only a handful of Indian ministers, the number of white missionaries was only slightly greater; the size of the congregations was sufficiently small, especially the communicants, for the influence of an individual Indian minister to reach far down into the ranks; and finally there was the factor of race. In the Canadian Presbyterian Church, Indians and whites faced one another without a significant intermediary group to diffuse the confrontations. Every other major Christian denomination in the island had a more varied racial composition. Of course, white priests and clergymen were at the top of the Roman Catholic Church and the Church of England; but the varied racial structure of their congregations, their stronger traditional ecclesiastical hierarchy and the near absence of non-white clerics, prevented rising black race-consciousness from being used internally as a weapon against the leaders of these churches. The Indian agents could not escape the winds of ethnic pride sweeping through the ranks of their Hindu or Muslim brothers. A numerically small Mission, devoted exclusively to one race, spawned some of its own challengers with a rapidity which surprised the white missionary controllers.

An early indicator of the internal problem was a letter of protest in 1900 from Egbert M. Madoo, a Presbyterian layman, against the passing over of Rev Paul Bukhan and Rev Lal Behari (one of the two earliest Indian catechists) in favour of Rev Harvey Morton.[5] At issue was a post once occupied by the founder of the Mission, John Morton, Harvey's father. It was almost impossible for white missionaries of the early twentieth century to afford equal status to Indian ministers; the social and racial assumptions of the society did not allow it. It would be an error to believe that the Christian charity of the Indian ministers overcame resentment; Rev Charles Ragbir resigned from the Mission early, though it cannot be certain that he found any greater comfort in the Church of England. In the 1920s Harvey Morton was disliked by the Indian ministers because he was believed to be a source of prejudice and discrimination.

The case of the teacher/catechists was somewhat different: the traditions of teaching, as well as the Education Code, enjoined subordination to managers, boards of management and inspectors. It was in association with, and in sympathy for, the Indian ministers that some of the Indian teacher/catechists shared in the dissatisfaction within the Mission. When the storm broke fully, in the form of petitions in 1928, the teacher/catechists did not have a separate platform. The Indian ministers did not articulate the grievances of the teachers, but from other sources we know that the teachers harboured some. The ministers wanted a larger share in the government of the church; they wished to be appointed managers of schools.[6] The self-image of the Indian ministers and teacher/catechists was not unlike that of the Hindu and Muslim leaders outside the church. They thought of themselves as the backbone of the church; just as Indians in the wider society felt that Trinidad would have collapsed economically without them, so the Indian ministers and teacher/catechists were convinced that the Mission would vanish without their support. They had a higher appreciation than the white missionaries of the amount of financial contributions the Indians made to the Mission.

It is of interest that no major demand by the Indian teacher/catechists for reforms in their terms of employment has been discovered. They should at least have been interested in closing the salary gap between themselves and their white Canadian Mission counterparts. It is part of the oral traditions of the country that Canadian missionaries unfairly heaped upon their teachers extracurricular duties seemingly beyond those demanded by other churches. All teachers were essentially catechists and Sunday school teachers: they were expected to come out in full force to church services; to contribute, it was alleged, more of their salaries to missionary causes than they wished.[7] Only the very faithful could hope to gain places in Naparima Training College, or promotion to headteacherships. Sabbath-breaking, addiction to drink or suspicion of immorality were met with speedy punishment.[8] The charges hardly seem unique to the Canadian Presbyterian Church: all denominational school teachers had managers who thought along the same lines.[9] It might be an error to believe that denominational school teachers, specifically the Mission teachers, did not accept the clerical view of teachers as essentially religious agents.[10] Of course government school teachers who worked in government schools most of their lives and were not pressured to become Sunday school teachers were among the first to develop a secular image of the teacher. To them it appeared that denominational school teachers were victims of their clerical managers against whom they dared not complain.[11]

The internal threat to the Mission was partly met by a seemingly significant concession: Rev C. D. Lalla, a leading critic of discrimination in the Mission, was made moderator of the Church in 1924; also in 1931 a local presbytery, headed by Lalla, was established to assume some of the work of the Mission Council on which Indian ministers were not allowed to sit. This concession, however, did not bring any lasting satisfaction, as it was soon realized by the Indian ministers and teacher/catechists that power rested with the Mission Council. The final resolution of this conflict was the taking over of the Church by the Indian ministers, an objective so consonant with the long-term official mission policy in Canada that its realization in the late 1960s and 1970s seemed not a defeat for the Church but a triumph. Not so with the earlier challenge of the Indians from outside the Presbyterian Church.

There is perhaps no other part of Trinidad more instinctively associated with Indians than Caroni. Caroni is as Indian in the popular imagination of the country as Laventille is black. There was talk about the desirability of Hindu/Muslim schools generally among Hindu and Muslim leaders in the 1920s.[12] The Hindu and Muslim residents of Picton village protested vigorously against government's plan to transfer its school there to the Canadian Presbyterian Mission.[13] But it was at Chaguanas in County Caroni that a Hindu/Muslim school first came into existence as an alternative to the Canadian Presbyterian Mission school. Chaguanas was one of the most important centres of Hindu and Muslim religious activities in the 1930s. The Tackveeyatul Islamic Association was founded at Chaguanas, and the breakaway movement which culminated in the rival Anjuman Sunnat-ul-Jammat Association was also centred there. The immediate origins of the Hindu/Muslim school movement in Chaguanas are obscure, but it seems to have come from lower down the hierarchy of local Chaguanas leaders, not at the top; it did not originate with successful businessmen like A. Bharat Gobin or Sarran Teelucksingh. (One person mentioned among the originators was Nazar Hosein.) The development of the movement was apparently spurred on by a speech made by a Mission agent, Rev J. Netram, a Christian Indian 'counter missionary' from India. Netram was alleged to have made insulting remarks about Hinduism. Another possible factor was also rivalries and jealousies involving Indian Presbyterian headteachers who had won seats on the Local Road Board in Chaguanas. Chaguanas quickly became the storm centre of the Hindu/Muslim attack on the education policy and institutions of the Mission. This gave rise to the Hindu/Muslim school, the most controversial primary school in the century after emancipation, and certainly the first Indian controlled school which taught the full curriculum of a primary school.

The first protest action of the Hindu/Muslim group in Chaguanas was to withdraw their children, about 102 in number, from the Canadian Presbyterian school there. Since there were no places for them in the government school at Chaguanas, the Hindu/Muslim group called for the extension of the government school, and generally for government schools to replace those of the Mission. At a 'monster' meeting in Teelucksingh's Electric Theatre in Chaguanas in October 1929, a programme of demands was drawn up. The government was to be asked to introduce Hindi and Urdu as additional subjects in schools attended by Indian children as well as the textbooks of the 'vernacular schools' in India; the clauses of the Education Code relating to exemption from religious instruction were to be enforced; presumably the protesters wished for strict observance of the conscience clause. Hindu priests and Muslim moulvis were to be allowed to enter schools to give religious instruction; Hindu and Muslim teachers were to be admitted to denominational training colleges, and were not to be prevented from becoming headteachers in Christian schools. The meeting also wanted an Indian representative restored to the Board of Education. Most difficult of all, the meeting called on the government to abolish the denominational system of education gradually.[14] A Hindu/Muslim deputation was sent to the governor; among its members were Haji Rukmudeen, Mohammed Hosein, Mohammed Ibrahim, H. Gokool, T.R. Mahabirsingh, Rampaul Maharaj, Jairam Gosine, Mohamed Azir and C.B. Mathura. The strongest support came from Penal where a Hindu/Muslim mass meeting at which Timothy Roodal and Adrian Cola Rienzi spoke, passed resolutions similar to those at the Chaguanas meeting.[15]

With the help of local donors, the Indians at Chaguanas acquired a spacious shed to serve temporarily as a Hindu/Muslim school; ironically a Mission educated Indian, Sam Supersad, became headteacher. A Hindu/Muslim hall was constructed as a meeting place. The government school was apparently extended, but the Hindu/Muslim school continued; so did the Mission school. Some very instructive points were made in articles in the *East Indian Weekly* in late 1929 and in 1930 about the Chaguanas imbroglio. Not every Indian at Chaguanas was angry with the missionaries; there were supporters of the Mission; also voices of moderation. Negotiations were said to be necessary, not unilateral action; it was also suggested that the missionaries might have been willing to reform certain aspects of their policy.[16] The Mission schools, said another writer, were as Indian as schools could be in a western country. Where would the Indians have been without the Mission, and who would employ the hundreds of Indian teachers and pupil teachers if it left the island?[17] C.B. Mathura, the editor of the *East Indian Weekly* was sympathetic to the Mission, recalling affectionately the names of John Morton and Kenneth Grant as benefactors to the race.[18] The need for gratitude was acknowledged by other writers. The Indians were said to have gained more than they had lost from the presence of the Mission, with its slow rate of Christian conversion and high ratio of primary school pupils to Christian converts. One writer identified the real enemy, not as the white missionaries, but their Indian assistants who tried to convert children.[19] The absurdity of calling for the abolition of the denominational system of education, when the Hindus and Muslims really wanted to join it, was pointed out in a letter to the press. Another correspondent observed that it was unrealistic to expect a better deal for Indian children in government schools at a time when these were mainly staffed by black headteachers.[20] Apparently there were also Indians who felt that child labour and compulsory education were more important issues than the threat to Indian religions and culture posed by the Canadian Presbyterian Church.[21]

One of the most complex of the Hindu/Muslim demands was the teaching of Hindi and Urdu in the schools. This request was sometimes posed as though the English language was not to be used as well; sometimes it was clear that the intention was to have Hindi and Urdu as ancillary languages. One Indian language was difficult enough to introduce; two was quite unrealistic. Indeed only the requirements of the Hindu/Muslim front kept Urdu in the proposal. The issue was essentially about the inclusion of Hindi, the language of the Hindu majority. But there were contradictions in the position of the Hindu/Muslim leaders. It was a matter of dispute how many persons wanted their children to learn Hindi, or to learn it at the expense of the English language. Some critics pointed out that Hindi was not the language used in the homes of Trinidad born Indians, but Creole or English, or a mixture of Hindi and English.[22] English was clearly the prestige language in the society; those in the Hindu/Muslim front who could speak English well had an advantage.[23] Indian leaders who wanted more Indians in the civil service and more Hindi in the schools were going, up to a point, in two different directions at the same time. Yet it seemed to some Indian leaders that their culture and religions could not be safeguarded without the spread of Hindi.

Had he not proceeded carefully, Director Marriott could have been caught in the crossfire between the Hindu/Muslim group and the Mission. The Roman Catholic newspaper, the *Catholic News*, carried an editorial which might very well have reflected the sentiments of the Church of England as well: Trinidad and Tobago was declared to be a Christian country and the government should at best tolerate non-Christian religions, not encourage them by subsidies.[24] The Hindu/Muslim group had quickly shifted its position from the abolition of the denominational school system to its own admission to it on equal terms with the Christian churches. Marriott, who had served in the Indian Immigration Department and therefore had some experience in dealing with complaints from Indians, thought he had a solution: in his proposed new Education Ordinance of 1930 he was careful not to mention the word 'Christian'. The government was prepared to consider aid to schools which were under a 'head' of denomination. This formula brought to the agenda an old and very difficult question: did the Muslims or Hindus have a 'head' of denomination in the island? The East Indian National Association and the East Indian National Congress were political bodies, so the government was not going to give school grants to them.

The organizational problems of the Indian communities were considerable. When C.D. Lalla was the sole Indian nominee on the Legislative Council, he automatically became, in the eyes of the government, the representative of the Indians; but he was not their religious leader. When the Indians in the late 1920s had three elected Legislative Council members (Teelucksingh, Roodal and Hosein) it was impossible to use membership of the Legislative Council as the easy determinant of the political leader. As far as the government was concerned, the difficulty of defining the political leadership was not as serious as settling the religious leadership. Crown Colony government in fact only officially recognized religious leaders; they could assist in the distribution of benefits to the society; they were needed as official marriage officers, as managers of schools, as responsible recipients of government subsidies for religion. One of the problems of framing an acceptable Indian Marriage Ordinance was that the Hindu pundits refused to accept the necessity of being licensed by the government; and no pundit was himself sufficiently the undisputed leader to license the other pundits. Each pundit was equal to any other pundit. The religious leadership of the Muslim community presented fewer difficulties; but the government appeared to want, for purposes of education, a single person as leader of the Hindus and Muslims. The Hindu/Muslim front made no allowance for such a leader.

Marriott placed the question of non-Christian denominational schools and the teaching of Hindi on the agenda of the Marriott/Mayhew Commission. At a meeting in Chaguanas a Hindu/Muslim delegation was appointed to meet the Commission. It was led by Sarran Teelucksing, and included Shorab Khan, and Sam Supersad, respectively the secretary and teacher of the Hindu/Muslim school at Chaguanas; also J.H. Dube, J.A. Jamadar, Shaffie Mohammed, Mohammed Hosein, Moulvi Ameer Ali, Popo Roopnarine and Aknath Maharaj. However, by the time the Indians met the Marriott/Mayhew Commission the fissiparous pressures created by the new Hindu and Muslim religious organizations of the early 1930s had cracked the Hindu/Muslim front. Delegates from four separate organizations actually met the Commission in secret session: Pundit Ramnarine Permanand, representing the Southern Dharma Association; Shorab Khan, secretary of the Management Committee of the Hindu/Muslim school;

S. Lutchman, secretary of the East Indian Education Committee and M.H. Khan, secretary of the Tackveeyatul Islamic Association of Trinidad. Evidence was also heard in secret from the Board of Management of the Canadian Presbyterian Church. The latter provided a defence of Mission policy. It was not true, it said, that the Mission did not employ non-Christian teachers; it had Hindu and Muslim pupil teachers and assistant teachers, but it could not employ non-Christian headteachers. The Christian tone of the school depended heavily on the headteacher; it would be a subversion of the Mission's entire purpose to have Hindu and Muslim headteachers. The spokesmen for the Mission said it was not unwilling to admit non-Christian trainees into Naparima Training College, but they would have to pay fees; they could not be on the quota of students subsidized by the government. The spokesmen also insisted that the Mission worked the conscience clause, which protected non-Christian children whose parents objected to Christianity. Additionally, they said that the Mission was willing to have Hindu pundits (no mention of the Muslims) selected from the community to enter Mission schools to give religious instruction. It would appear that this concession would be afforded only to Hindu pundits resident in the community to which the particular Mission school belonged.[25] The total impression the Mission spokesmen attempted to convey was that it was not forcing any Indians to become Christians.

The most vigorous defence was on the question of Hindi. Here the Mission spokesmen were in the commanding position of being able to represent it as pioneers; it was they who had introduced Hindi into the schools. They had allowed the Indians to recommend their own Hindi books. But the Mission spokesmen issued a warning: the curriculum of the schools was already overcrowded; Hindi should not be made compulsory; Hindi was not the language spoken in Indian homes ordinarily, and many Indian parents did not want it for their children.[26] The Mission spokesmen made no mention of Urdu or of the Muslim minority. Nor did they seem to understand the difference between teaching Hindi as an instrument to facilitate the spread of Christianity and the English language, and the demand for Hindi as a cultural tool to preserve Indian customs and religions and to strengthen group solidarity. Or if they understood, they could not accept these objectives as legitimate.

The Mission spokesmen before the Marriott/Mayhew Commission disclaimed responsibility for the alleged decline of Indian traditions and culture. They denied that Christian Indians constituted a separate group inside the Indian communities, or that they had lost touch with non-Christian Indians. In fact, said the Mission spokesmen, there was a time when Christian Indians (meaning perhaps persons like Lalla) took the lead in arousing Indian nationalistic sentiments. In other words, the Mission spokesmen did not see Christian Indians as a divisive force. This was certainly an unrealistic view, underplaying conflict between Presbyterian Indians and Muslims or Hindus and, indeed, friction within Indian families.

There was no incompatibility, contended the Mission spokesmen, between being a Christian and being an Indian. They said they would not oppose non-Christian schools in areas where Indians still lacked schools, nor would they oppose government aid to such schools; but the establishment of non-Christian schools in districts already adequately supplied with schools should not be allowed.[27] Chaguanas fell into this category.

The Marriott/Mayhew Commission felt that the Indians had an undeniable claim to their own denominational schools. They represented 38.8 percent of the population by the 1931 census; they were 43 percent illiterate in English. What they needed to do, as a prerequisite for government aid, was to organize themselves on a model recognizably similar to the Boards of Management of the Christian churches. The Commission with less gusto and clarity recommended that the government accept "an Indian language" as an alternative in primary schools. It did not recommend legislation to authorize pundits and moulvis to enter Christian schools, although it had heard that such arrangements existed. Possibly this was so only in Chaguanas, and only between the Mission and the Hindus. If the Marriott/Mayhew Commission had recommended a right of entry it might have spread the conflict to other Christian denominations, some of which had Indian children in their schools.

The Education legislation which followed the Marriott/Mayhew Report, namely the Education Ordinance of 1933 and the Code of 1935, continued to speak of Boards of Management as the indispensable link between the schools and the government. These Boards were religious organizations of people of the same faith. The first challenge to the Indians was to structure themselves along these lines, which meant not a Hindu/Muslim political body or even a Hindu/Muslim religious body, but separate Hindu and Muslim religious bodies. This need was partly anticipated, for the dominant new trend of the 1930s, despite the formation of an inoperative Hindu/Muslim organization called the Indian Educational Association, despite the Hindu/Muslim front at Chaguanas (and even Hindu/Muslim cooperation over a wider field up to the late 1940s) was towards the incorporation of separate Hindu and Muslim religious organizations dedicated to the establishment of their own schools. But the Hindu/Muslim school at Chaguanas lived on precariously for a few years, apparently up to the end of 1936.

Yet the newly incorporated Hindu and Muslim religious groups of the 1930s did not get aid from government for a range of denominational schools. It is not clear if they all asked, or if they asked insistently, for such aid. The fact that Hindus and Muslims or the Hindu/Muslim front indicated a strong desire for their own schools was not quite the same thing as having the resources to finance their part of the cost of new schools. In the early 1930s the government felt that it could not finance school expansion because of the depression, although it did adopt a programme of expansion to await better financial times. When a loan was negotiated in 1935, very little of it was spent on new primary school buildings.[28] Then came World War II. It is known that Moulvi Ameer Ali, president of the Indian Educational Association (Hindu/Muslim) and the Tackveeyatul Islamic Association (Muslim), asked Governor Hubert Rance for aid for Indian denominational schools and was refused. Presumably this meant that he must have been refused previously by the Board of Education which normally dealt with such applications. It would be of interest to know if Ali asked for separate Muslim and Hindu schools, or for Hindu/Muslim schools, or for Muslim schools only. He had encouraged the government to pass a Marriage Ordinance for the Muslims alone when apparently insoluble difficulties arose in framing one to cover both Hindus and Muslims. Ali became the first non-Christian member of the Board of Education from 1938 to 1942, but did not succeed in getting government funds for Indian schools.

The quarrels among different groups of Hindus and among Muslims certainly reached new proportions in the early 1930s. Ali himself, representing the Tackveeyatul Islamic Association, was a great opponent of Haji Rukmudeen of the Anjuman Sunnat-ul-Jammat Association, perhaps the most senior Muslim spiritual leader in the colony; in respect to the Hindus, factionalism between Sanatanists (the Sanatan Dharma Association) on the one hand and Arya Samajists on the other was a fertile source of disunity in the Hindu community. As one scholar has recently argued, Hinduism tended towards multiplicity and diversity which were undervalued by western civilization which preferred unity.[29] For this reason, and for administrative convenience, the government repeatedly tried to "lump all Hindus [or all Indians] into the same entity".[30] The instinctive reaction of senior government officials, none of whom was Indian, was to think of the Indians as an undifferentiated mass of similar people, but to use genuine divisions among them as an excuse for inaction on both the questions of a share of the ecclesiastical grant and a share of government subsidies for education. A Christian government was then basically in no haste to aid non-Christian schools. The Indian leaders who failed to achieve a sufficiently high level of unity must also bear some responsibility for government inaction in aiding Indian denominational schools.

After the Butler riots, the Indians had an opportunity to complain to the Moyne Commission. They felt the Commission had to be told who was responsible for the fact that there were still no subsidies for denominational schools. The Sanatan Dharma Board of Control, representing the Hindu majority, appeared to recognize that Indians had organizational problems of their own making which they had not solved; but it felt that the government had not prepared them, presumably by education, to organize themselves.[31] The Board argued that had the government not helped to organize the Christian groups, presumably by education and appropriate legislation, they too would be disorganized. At the same time, it condemned the government's incorporation of the rival Sanatan Dharma Association in 1932 on the ground that its leadership included Christian Indians (for example, Sarran Teelucksingh). Hence government action could be as undesirable as government inaction.

It remains uncertain how many unaided non-Christian Indian schools were started in the 1920s and 1930s. In 1939 the Sanatan Dharma Board of Control spoke of two dozen non-Christian schools in the colony. This figure almost certainly included Muslim schools; there is an impression that the Muslim minority had started to sponsor schools earlier than the Hindu majority. Some of these schools certainly taught only Indian languages and of course religion; it is doubtful that they were housed in proper school buildings. There had been an Arabic and Urdu school at Princes Town in 1925 started by the Islamic Guardian Association, with the Iman of Princes Town as the teacher. Mohammed Ibrahim, an El Socorro businessman, built a mosque and a school there in 1924, with help from India. From 1927 Haji Gokool sponsored at his own expense a Muslim school at St James (Port of Spain), also with a mosque; and Haji Rukmudeen sponsored a few small schools in St James (Port of Spain). In Princes Town there was also a 1929 report of a Muslim school with pupils between the ages of eight and eighteen years. The arrival of Mehta Jaimini in 1929 led directly to a Vedic school in Marabella teaching Hindi. In 1931 there were two Hindu night schools at Penal on the premises of obliging Indians, two of whom were pundits. Of course, there was the Hindu/Muslim school at Chaguanas, which by 1935 had black children as well, and whose teacher had by then refined its purpose to be the harmonization of Indian culture with western culture.[32] But some of its managers wanted it to be more Indian.

The Hindu/Muslim school at Chaguanas closed rather suddenly in January 1936, apparently without any protest. The exact circumstances of its closure are obscure. In April 1935 Cutteridge asked various Indian groups (Muslim and Hindu) to form one school group; he was going against prevailing religious trends, but possibly the Hindu/Muslim school encouraged him in this line of thought. At a meeting at the Hindu/Muslim school in November 1935 a call was made for an amalgamation of schools, but what this meant is not clear. Was this a call to abolish the school? If Richard Forbes is correct about the predominance of the Arya Samajists at Chaguanas, the Hindu/Muslim school might have been more an example of cooperation between a reforming Hindu sect (the Samajists) and local Muslims than between orthodox Hindus and Muslims.[33] Forbes blames the closure of the school on intense religious rivalries between orthodox Hindus and Samajists and overlapping political struggles between the supporters and opponents of Sarran Teelucksingh. These struggles whittled away the school's community support in Chaguanas.

However justifiable the claim of Hindus and Muslims to their own denominational schools, the outcome was a movement back to the concept and practice of having special or exclusive Indian schools, at least on the level of primary education. If there were doubts about the social consequences of the Canadian

Presbyterian Mission's special Indian schools, whether they encouraged the acceptance of western social values more than Indian racial exclusiveness, the spirit in which the Hindus and Muslims moved for their own schools from the 1920s left little doubt that racial exclusiveness was the deliberate social objective. The aim was to reconstitute Indian ethnic pride through separate schools controlled by non-Christian Indians. Some of the promoters of the movement were also anxious to end miscegenation. A few also showed some concern to elevate the status of Indian women through education, and to terminate Indian child labour on the estates. Arising simultaneously with requests for Indian communal representation in the government, the Hindu and Muslim bids for their own schools recreated and heightened socio-racial challenges to the old ideal of an anglicized Trinidad which nobody had the skill, the experience or the determination to manage successfully. However, the experience of the Hindu/Muslim school at Chaguanas – its admission of black children – was perhaps a lesson that there were limits to the extent to which any one racial group could isolate itself in a small multiracial society. India could not be reconstituted in Trinidad.

The Labour Protest of the Black Teachers 1930-1939

A decisive turning point in the history of Trinidad and Tobago was the labour rebellion of June 1937, otherwise called the Butler riots, which formed part of a series of disturbances in the British Caribbean. This resort to violence in Fyzabad was the outcome of multiple grievances of the working classes which had accumulated over many years: poor public health, deplorable housing, unemployment, low wages, high prices, discrimination on the job, and the absence of recognized machinery for the reconciliation of disputes.[34] The living standard of the working classes was appallingly poor, the major agricultural exports of the colony were depressed and, even in the oil industry, wage rates were low. The violence was preceded by strikes, unrest and hunger marches from 1935.

The primary school teachers could take no part in the protest of the unemployed and the manual workers; such action was unthinkable and would have led to their dismissal. But they were not unaffected by the labour rebellion. As residents in working class districts and, as in many cases, recent escapees from the labouring classes in which some of their relatives and friends were still trapped, the primary school teachers could observe the poverty of the masses daily. Their own pay, housing and general working conditions left much to be desired; they were convinced that they too had oppressive employers, namely the clerical managers and the director of education. Although they had formed a trade union since 1919 to protect their interests, they could not strike or march, and they had to be careful about any form of protest. Nevertheless, it can be shown that concurrent with the rising tide of labour unrest, the teachers' sense of grievances escalated and their willingness to express them grew bolder. On their own level, they took part in the rebellions of employees against employers, of the underprivileged against the privileged, of non-whites against whites.

Cutteridge once remarked that teachers were by profession a set of Oliver Twists; they were always asking for more.[35] What was special about the teachers as a perpetually dissatisfied group of employees was that they were the largest body of articulate educated workers in the pay of the government. By 1937, there were more teachers than civil servants, though only a small minority of teachers were members of the TTTU. From this point of view, the director of education had a more difficult management problem than any other head of department in the civil service, with the exception of the colonial secretary. The dissatisfaction and rising expectations of workers in the early 1930s influenced the teachers, and this fact would have made the administration of the Education Department more problematic in the 1930s, whoever was in charge. But the director from 1934 was Cutteridge, and by then he was already notorious. Enough has been said earlier about Marriott and Cutteridge, especially the headstrong Cutteridge, to make it clear that trouble was on the horizon when he assumed the directorship.

The opposition to Marriott and Cutteridge, especially to Cutteridge, emerged in two waves: the first in the 1920s was dominated by spokesmen from the trade union movement, using the *Labour Leader* as their forum. Drawing part of its ideological force from Garveyism, the protestors' anger was directed against Cutteridge himself and against his *Readers*. The second wave was triggered by the recommendations of the Marriott/Mayhew Report of 1931-1932.[36] The teachers and the TTTU emerged as the major critics of Marriott and Cutteridge while the *Labour Leader* became only a secondary focus of anti-Cutteridge rhetoric. But it is important to understand how the teacher and TTTU opposition unfolded. Before Cutteridge's Code of 1935 it was really individual teachers who criticized the directors through the teachers' press. The 1935 Code marked the point at which the TTTU was galvanized into institutional opposition to Cutteridge and henceforth, into the labour disturbances of 1937, the TTTU turned its face against the director. Yet it is important to observe that the criticisms of the TTTU were not directed so much against Cutteridge personally or against his *Readers* as against his policies in the Education Department, and of course against the pay and working conditions of teachers. The TTTU displayed the decorum appropriate to an association of middle class professionals.

The teachers did not speak with a united voice; there were teachers of government schools and of church schools, and within the latter category there were denominational groups such as the Canadian Presbyterian Mission Teachers' Association and the numerically strong Roman Catholic Teachers' Association. Additionally, from about 1931 the TTTU had developed branch unions or district associations. These different groups of teachers did not always perceive their problems in the same way, nor did they all see the same problems. E. Quinlan, general secretary of the TTTU, wrote in 1936: "There is a strong tendency towards the reorganization of the Union upon the denominational basis." Government school teachers, numerically fewer than those in the denominational schools, generally provided the assertive wing of the TTTU; but the leadership of the union often came from senior headteachers of denominational schools. Port of Spain schools were the centre of teacher dissatisfaction.

The leadership of the TTTU and the editors of the *Teachers Journal* and the *Teachers Herald* often had differing opinions. T.E. Beckles was the teacher whom the Board of Education nominated as a member, and he was sometimes inclined to think of himself as an independent agent rather than the spokesman of any of the teacher groups.[37] In these circumstances he could be found agreeing with government policies which were opposed by TTTU; the *Teachers Journal* reflected views contrary to those of both the TTTU and the teacher member of the Board of Education. The branch unions of the TTTU and the denominational teacher groups were also sources of disunity. It was quite plausible, therefore, for the director to claim on certain issues that he had the agreement of teachers. Many teachers did admire Cutteridge and were disinclined to oppose him. Cutteridge never felt bound to accept representations made by any group of teachers; it was he and not they who determined policies. This approach recurred in 1985 when the minister of education, Overand Padmore, took exactly the same position on policy making. Unlike a factory manager or Padmore, however, Cutteridge had no fear of disruptive industrial action from teachers. The best weapon of teachers against Cutteridge was the sympathetic support of some members of the Legislative Council.

It has been possible to study the section of teacher opinion reflected in the *Teachers Journal* and later in the *Teachers Herald* in the first half of the 1930s. A problem with such a study, though, was the refusal of the great majority of contributors to sign their names. It was known that Marriott and Cutteridge were unfriendly to these publications. Indeed, they would have liked to see them as strictly professional publications used by teachers to educate themselves about new educational methods;[38] instead they were mainly a medium of decorous criticism against the policies of the directors, and the low pay and unsatisfactory status of teachers. The major themes of the *Teachers Journal* in the early 1930s were: the unpalatable dictatorship of Cutteridge, the discriminatory practices of clerical managers, the unfair transfers and demotions of teachers, the unreasonable grading of schools, the miserable salaries and pensions of teachers, and the disparities in pay and privileges between teachers and civil servants.[39] In other words, the teachers' press was primarily concerned with their defence as workers. Professional matters were subsidiary, and it is here that writers tended to sign their names, especially when praising the education authorities.

In view of the blistering attack on Cutteridge's *Readers* by spokesmen of the trade union movement, it is instructive to note that the teachers' press took a different line. There was a measure of praise for them, mixed with a little criticism of their contents.[40] What the *Teachers Journal* deplored most was the manner in which Cutteridge had introduced his *Readers*, forcing them upon the schools without consultation with the teachers, and establishing a nearly complete and profitable monopoly over textbooks.[41] Absent from the teachers' press was any acknowledgement of Cutteridge as a successful administrator of the education system.

In 1939 the Trinidad Labour Party complained before the Moyne Commission about the "supremacy of officialdom", about the heads of departments who turned themselves into 'little Czars'. It was said, that the whole system of "Crown Colony officialdom tends to be a closed one, deaf, reserved, autocratic, independent and sometimes indifferent to local opposition".[42] As the people developed, the stage arrived where Crown Colony departments of government became "a hindrance to social, economic and political development of colonial citizenship; and [a] clash of interests invariably occurs".[43] The Labour Party could easily have been speaking about the Education Department and the primary school teachers.

If the summit of the labour rebellion was in June 1937, the high point of the teachers' protest occurred two and a half years earlier in January 1935. The immediate cause was not increases in the cost of living, but the introduction into the Legislative Council of the new draft Code to govern the primary school system. Unfortunately for Cutteridge, the Code's opponents had been alerted by the earlier release of the Marriott/Mayhew Report of 1931-1932. There had been immediate protest against some of its recommendations, especially the reduction of the number of years which pupils were to spend in primary schools. Both in Trinidad and Tobago, and in other eastern Caribbean islands, some teachers and members of the public interpreted this as an insidious attempt to reduce the amount of education given to children of the masses and to turn their opportunities for secondary education away from the respected grammar school type into something less acceptable and less prestigious.[44] This formed part of the unfavourable reaction to new plans for secondary modern schools.

When Cutteridge became director in 1934, the primary schools and teachers were governed by the Education Ordinance of 1933 and the Education Code of 1921. Attempts to amend the Code in the very early 1930 had been delayed by the appointment of the Marriott/Mayhew Commission; Cutteridge proposed his new Code after it reported taking into consideration some of the Commission's recommendations, and updating the Code of 1921. Cutteridge felt that a lot of time had been wasted: he and Marriott had been thinking about the reforms needed for many years; together they had modernized the Government Training College, the curriculum and textbooks of primary schools and now it was time to complete the programme by a new Education Code. But the new Code suffered from the disadvantage of being part of a series of reforms already under criticism.

Cutteridge was already suspected of hostility to the masses. The Code also came at a time when the habit of bolder speech, as shown in the teachers' press, had taken root; the institutions of the ruling class, in government and industry, and their symbols of authority were under attack in the 1930s. The people and their leaders had outgrown their form of government, and were less inhibited about demonstrating their dissatisfaction. It is within this context that the TTTU itself turned against Cutteridge after the introduction of the 1935 Code. Unlike the previous Cutteridge reforms, the Code involved legislation affecting directly the working conditions of teachers; it dealt with their pay, promotion and conditions of employment. The Code, more than the introduction of *Readers*, was the sort of reform which a teachers' trade union could properly get its teeth into and, like any trade union, the TTTU made its big stand when the interest of its members seemed directly threatened.

Yet the TTTU, partly from strategy, partly from genuine concern for the children of the masses, made the reduction of the number of years in primary schools into the major public issue in its fight with Cutteridge. While Marriott and Mayhew had restricted the primary schools to children between six to twelve years old, they had pleaded for development which might cushion the blow on either side of this age group: infant classes for those below age six, and secondary modern schools for those above age twelve. But Cutteridge proposed the reduction of the period of primary schooling without any assurance that there would be either infant classes or secondary modern schools. The TTTU also put a lot of emphasis on what appeared to be his intention to send College Exhibitioners to intermediate schools instead of the recognized secondary schools like QRC and CIC.[45] These were issues which did not militate against the interests of the teachers as working adults, but they certainly affected the prospects of their children. A most objectionable part of the Code of 1935 was the clause which gave Cutteridge power to demote teachers to lower grade schools, with or without a reduction of salary, and even apparently to deprive them of their teacher qualifications.[46] The prohibition of active participation in politics was another sore point[47] felt to be an invasion of teachers' rights as citizens.

An interesting group which came to life in 1935, possibly as a direct outcome of the struggle with Cutteridge, was the Teachers' Economic and Cultural Association (hereafter TECA). Founded and led by black politically conscious teachers (DeWilton Rogers, John Donaldson, Fitz G. Maynard, and A.A. Alexander), the TECA leadership felt pride in being black and quietly wished to be seen and heard as black achievers. TECA had the dual objective of protecting the economic and professional interests of its teacher members, as well as furthering the cultural and social development of the people of the colony. It sought to carry out the latter objective by organizing literary and dramatic presentations, musical recitals and art shows. These activities reflected the same impulse towards the identification of a West Indian culture which was behind the *Beacon* movement. Most of TECA's impact came during and after World War II, after the heat about the Cutteridge Code had died down. Its leadership obviously had no faith in the TTTU, although they did not break with it formally. The importance of TECA was its effect as a cultural leaven among some of the teachers, including certain female teachers, and its future role as the conduit through which many teachers were led into nationalistic political activity after World War II. In the late 1930s it was impossible for TECA to pose even remotely as a political movement: the government would not have allowed this.[48]

Cutteridge was taken by surprise by the strength of the teachers' opposition, and by the new and troublesome forms it took. In the first two weeks of January 1935 there was extensive coverage of debates in the Legislative Council on the Code in the *Guardian, Port of Spain Gazette* and *The People*. It was not in the tradition of primary school teachers to capture the attention of the press, or to organize petitions after public meetings;[49] it was not their style to come out in large numbers to hear debates in the Legislative Council, in fact filling all the seats.[50] These new responses were made when the Code was being discussed in the Council; and these actions should be understood as the teachers' protest equivalent to the hunger marches and strikes of the manual workers. Tobago teachers organized their own petition against the Code. These petitions and meetings were meant to mobilize public opinion, in the end their strongest weapon. In terms of the actual defence of their interest in the Legislative Council, the teachers had to look to the elected members, who had themselves to take account of public opinion.

Cutteridge was exasperated by the opposition of the teachers. As far as he was concerned he had completed discussions with their leaders; the teacher member of the Board of Education had, he felt, agreed with the Code. Cutteridge reiterated that some of the things the teachers were objecting to had already been agreed to by them in 1930. It was as if they could not change their minds. Cutteridge's problem in 1935 was that he made no allowance for the growing political consciousness of many teachers; as head of department his attitude to them was the same as a decade previously. Dr Arthur McShine, one of the nominated members, compared the code to govern teachers with the regulations drawn up by the Medical Board to govern medical practitioners, an assumption of equality of professional status which would not have been admitted for a minute by Cutteridge. It is only fair to say that the conception of teachers as a body of persons to be ruled sternly by government preceded and survived him; the difference with other directors was that Cutteridge had the temperament *par excellence* to act on the view of teachers as humble servitors of two masters: the clerical managers and the director of education.

In the Council debate Cutteridge was able to clear up some of the misunderstandings of the teachers and Council members sympathetic to them. A compromise was reached on the burning question of the length of schooling in the primary schools: it was changed to encompass the age groups five to fifteen years rather

than six to twelve years. Cutteridge explained that College Exhibitioners were not
to be sent to intermediate schools, and that principals of recognized secondary
schools would not have the power to reject a College Exhibitioner. He explained
that his power of demotion would extend only to the grade of schools to which
the offending teacher was sent; he would not have the power to rescind teacher
qualifications. However, the non-participation of teachers in politics was not
negotiable.[51] McShine distinguished himself in the debate as the champion of the
teachers, a role sometimes assumed by T.M. Kelshall (an honorary member of the
TTTU) in other places. However, in 1935 Kelshall was compromised by having
previously consented to the Code in the Board of Education; C. Henry Pierre had
already agreed to it in Executive Council. M.A. Maillard as well as T.A. Hope, the
latter of whom represented Tobago, voted against it. Sarran Teelucksingh was
absent.

The leaders of the disaffected schoolteachers did not always have reason on
their side; nor was their position without interesting contradictions. It was not
usual for government school teachers to be favourably disposed towards denominational schools and their clerical managers; they also tended to see denominational school teachers as obstacles to the elevation of the profession to the status
of civil servants.[52] Their image of the clerical manager was that of a vindictive
oppressor. In proposals to redistribute power in the dual system, this attitude led
to support for the increase of the power of the government at the expense of the
clerical school managers, especially on the issue of appointment and dismissal.
But the government invariably meant the director, and the director was himself a
most unpalatable dictator. The problem of these disaffected teachers was how to
increase the power of government over clerical managers without increasing the
power of strong willed directors over teachers. Perhaps there was comfort in the
thought that Cutteridge would not be director forever.

The Code was not amended to the satisfaction of Dr McShine and three elected
members of the Legislative Council (Maillard, Hope and Cipriani); nor was the
TTTU satisfied. In Governor Murchison Fletcher who arrived the following year,
and who was still in charge when the fateful Butler riots occurred in June 1937,
the TTTU imagined it saw a friendly person who might listen to its grievances;
but Fletcher was removed as a consequence of his handling of the Butler
disturbances. The British government in September 1937 sent the Forster
Commission to inquire into the circumstances behind the Butler riots; but the
TTTU was not asked to give evidence. In April 1938 the TTTU took its boldest
step: the union sent a petition to the governor in Legislative Council asking for
an inquiry into the administration of primary education.[53] There could be no
mistaking the intention to bring Cutteridge to book; and the governor refused to
allow it. Nor did the TTTU like Captain Daniel, principal of the Government
Training College for a decade (1927-1937); but he was no longer in charge in
1938. Both Captains (Cutteridge and Daniel) were regarded as illiberal adminis-

trators. The violent labour rebellion of June 1937 created unprecedented possibilities for the review of the conduct of the authorities. The opportunity to complain to British appointed inquisitors came in early 1939 when the West India Royal Commission, chaired by Lord Moyne, arrived in the island. An islandwide outpouring of grievances resulted.

Without a direct attack on Cutteridge himself, still the director, the TTTU before the Moyne Commission pointed to him and the Code of 1935 as the embodiment of its troubles. Its wide-ranging list of grievances may be broken down into two categories: those which affected directly the living standard of teachers, and those which sprang from a broad professional concern for education. The most trenchant criticisms were of course reserved for the grievances which affected adversely the working conditions of teachers, although the union modestly outlined their professional concerns first of all. On the question of salaries, the union wanted closer approximation to civil servants' salaries, and as always the drive was for government school teachers at least to be accorded the full status of civil servants, not just their penalties. Teachers were, the TTTU insisted, more highly qualified than the majority of civil servants:

> The Union wishes to press the claims of Teachers employed in Government schools to be recognized as Civil Servants and to be treated as such. In the past their claims had been admitted at least partially, as there were several Government Teachers whose names were included regularly in the Civil List . . .
>
> While for the purposes of discipline Government Teachers are subject to the Civil Service Regulations they are denied the many privileges provided by the same Regulations such as enhanced pension rights, benefits for the widow and orphans, etc., while such privileges are enjoyed by Ward Officers, Railways Station Masters, Sanitary Inspectors and other Government employees, who are in many cases inferior to Teachers in educational qualifications as well as in salary status.
>
> The Union deprecates this discrimination towards members of the profession and would request that justice be done to these deserving servants of the State.[54]

One complaint was that a large percentage of headteachers never reached the maximum of their salary range, viz. $110 per month compared to $160 per month for first-class clerks in the civil service. The union asked for a minimum of $80 per month for headteachers in the rural areas, and $100 per month for those in towns, excluding free housing. The pupil teachers' salaries of $4–$12 per month also needed upward regrading. The union argued that transfers from one school to another, which were frequent and could not be resisted, caused economic hardship as the new assignment might be to a more expensive district. A headteacher transferred from Sangre Grande to Port of Spain had his rent doubled. Transfers in fact were represented as a mechanism of punishment used by both clerical managers and the directors of education rather than a means of promotion, or as a support to the education system. All headteachers and assistant teachers were to be provided with housing or a housing allowance to enable them to live with the dignity which their job required. Existing housing for teachers (only 29.6 percent of headteachers had housing provided) was condemned as a "seemingly wicked and malicious effort on the part of the authorities to suppress the legitimate aspirations of teachers to social advancement and to hold them up perpetually to ridicule and contempt of the public".[55]

Teachers were said to be perpetually in debt, unable to educate their children up to the level expected. That was one reason for the insistence on education benefits for the children of deceased teachers. Teachers needed to be treated, as in the civil service, with high regard for seniority. The union complained that junior men were propelled into headteacherships, even into the hallowed ranks of the inspectorate, over the heads of senior men; that junior teachers, even young persons not yet in teaching, were given preference over seniors in the vital annual competition for scarce places at the Government Training College. Seniority was calculable; merit was disputatious. The union was also opposed to the imposition of extraneous church duties on teachers in denominational schools, in circumstances in which refusal to comply could bring retribution from autocratic clerics. It wished teachers to be treated as possessors of rights: rights as workers to security of employment; rights as citizens to participate in politics.

In the category of grievances of a professional nature, the TTTU mentioned the need to have a proper school medical service, to increase the College Exhibitions and to prevent the intermediate schools with a better class of children and superior teachers from winning a disproportionate share of them. With respect to textbooks, age grouping, and the curriculum of primary schools, the union touched on subjects where Cutteridge was directly involved. The union declared in favour of an admission age as low as three years, and a school-leaving age as high as sixteen years. It gave no reasons, but the subject had been discussed at great length over the previous seven years. While the union acknowledged Cutteridge's textbooks to have some merit, it wanted other books to be used as well: it wanted an end to the near monopoly of Cutteridge's books; it wished teachers to have freedom to choose books for their classes. With respect to the curriculum, the union made the same underlying pleas for freedom for the teachers to be used responsibly. The curriculum was said to be overloaded with subjects; the union wished a return to essentials, namely the three Rs, and the setting of definite standards of attainment in these subjects, at least for the senior pupils. Teachers should be free to add or subtract from the curriculum within the range of subjects prescribed by the director. The union charged that the freedom which Cutteridge wrote into the Code of 1935 was a paper freedom only: teachers knew that they tinkered with his requirements at their peril.

The union also made a telling attack on the dilapidated condition of school buildings, particularly the denominational schools. Sanitary facilities were most unsatisfactory. Here was a type of grievance which was on the border of their professional concern for education and their self-interest in having a pleasant work environment. The learning conditions of pupils were the working conditions of teachers. The poor condition of denominational school buildings, the lack of school furniture and apparatus, were used as a basis for an attack on the dual system. Dual control of schools should end; clerics were said to be mainly interested in teaching religion and teachers in denominational schools were suffering at the hands of clerical managers.

In calling for the end of the dual system, it is not clear whether or not the union meant the abolition of denominational schools. It weakened its own attack by acknowledging that government grants for buildings and furniture were woefully inadequate. On the grievous question of teachers' right to participate in politics, the union complained:

> The Union feels very keenly the infringement of their common rights of citizens as restricted by the Code of 1935. The Regulation which has deprived Teachers of their civil and political freedom is not in accordance with any of the provisions of the Education Ordinance, 1933, which the Code has been designed to implement, and should be regarded as ultra vires in its application.
>
> In the years gone by primary school teachers have been members of Local Boards by election and proved themselves useful and valuable acquisitions to those Institutions. Teachers were also chosen as Jurors by reason of both salary and property qualification. The introduction of the Code has entirely deprived them of these privileges. Teachers are not permitted to take part in political meetings although the local Government is not one of Party Constitution. They are not permitted to nominate any Individual whom they might consider to be a desirable candidate to represent their interests on one or another of the local Civil or rural Bodies or the Legislative Council. Yet they are authorized to teach Civics in schools.[56]

Finally, the TTTU, claiming that as teachers it appreciated the plight of the masses, went beyond its professional platform to endorse the Memorandum of the Trinidad Labour Party and other 'democratic bodies' as long as their proposals did not conflict with its own.

It was not only the TTTU which made representation on education before the Moyne Commission. Several other groups gave their views *en passant*. The most trenchant criticisms came from trade unions which carried their opposition to Cutteridge into the 1930s, often making the same objections as in the 1920s (but without the undertones of Garveyism). This was done particularly in the memorandum of the newspaper the *West Indian Pilot*, which claimed to be the official mouthpiece of the trade union movement.[57] The clearest meeting ground of the TTTU's protest with some of the other submissions relating to education was the desire to have a greater measure of technical/vocational education.

It is also worthwhile to consider the position of Indian teachers in the protest against Cutteridge's Code although there is no evidence that they were a part of it. Indian teachers were almost all Christian Indians working in Canadian Presbyterian Mission schools. They had their own teachers' association which apparently did not support the TTTU against the Code. In fact, the Mission teachers had been slow to associate themselves with the TTTU when it was formed in 1919 and up to 1939 did not provide the TTTU with the leadership commensurate with the number of senior headteachers in the Mission schools. It has been argued earlier that by their participation in the literary and debating society movement, many Indian teachers showed increased political conscious-ness. Some of them sided with the Indian Presbyterian ministers against the white monopoly of power in the Mission, but they did not carry their defiance against Cutteridge. To the extent that opposition to Cutteridge smacked of Garveyism, Indian teachers could not find any emotional ground of sympathy with it.[58] To a lesser extent, the position of the Indian teachers was shared by some black rural teachers in other denominational schools who owed their rise to headteacherships and assistant teacherships to the benevolent actions of particular clerical patrons. Whether or not the rural denominational school teachers, Indian or black, allegedly the most discriminated against, were the least capable of mounting opposition to clerical managers or directors, is a moot point.

In respect to education, the strongest submissions from Indians to the Moyne Commission came from the Sanatan Dharma Board of Control, representing the Hindu majority.[59] This was an attack on the conversion of Hindu children to Christianity in Christian schools as a condition for education and it was a lament over the failure of the government to support the Hindus in their desire to have their own schools. This memorandum helps us to understand why the major concerns of the TTTU were not the major concerns of the Indians. As Hindus outside the influence of the Canadian Presbyterian Mission, most Indians were engaged in a contest at a more fundamental level, at the level of the right to have their own schools aided by the government. It was not at all clear to them that Cutteridge was their main enemy. They saw that main enemy as Christianity, and particularly the Presbyterian Church, also the government in general and the wider community of non-Indians who conspired by silence to ignore the claims of the Hindus and the Muslims for equal treatment in establishing schools. The Christian Indians, which meant overwhelmingly the Presbyterian Indians, in their submission to the Moyne Commission had no complaints against Cutteridge.[60] In other words there was a lack of alignment between the submissions of the TTTU, which was dominated by non-Indians and the Indian submissions, except on the single point of the desirability of more technical/vocational education. One sector of the Indians, the Christian minority, was too satisfied or afraid to protest against the administrators of the education system and the other sector, the non-Christian majority, was too aggrieved with the Christian churches or the government on a matter of principle to criticize the education authorities on details.

The TTTU's protest before the Moyne Commission bore fruit in a number of ways. The Commission's recommendations in favour of greater emphasis on technical/vocational education could hardly be claimed as victories for the TTTU: this was what almost everybody was saying. Perhaps the single most important gain of the TTTU was the recognition of the right of teachers to make public complaints against the administrators of the education system, including the director. The Moyne Report went generally in the direction of acknowledging the right of the ruled to complain against those who ruled. It signalled the end of the era of dictatorial heads of department like Cutteridge, and whether his retirement in 1942 was due or not, it was timely. He had stayed in office long enough to see the approaching modification or reversal of his policies. Acting Director Daniel in 1942 and 1943 said that the curriculum was to be simplified; Cutteridge had added subjects. Daniel said that a beginning was to be made in the distribution of free textbooks; Cutteridge had insisted on selling them. Teachers were to have more freedom in choosing subjects, with the exception of nature study and agriculture which were compulsory in rural schools. The Moyne Commission gave an impetus to plans for the expansion of primary and secondary schools, and the regular increase of the College Exhibitions.[61] Cutteridge was not keen on the expansion of secondary education. Teachers' salaries were revised; Cutteridge thought salaries were sufficient. The Cutteridge era closed in 1942, though his influence remained. The teachers had gained something from the struggle with him, but their gains arose partly from the fact that teachers in other islands had made broadly similar complaints to the Moyne Commission. Some of their problems were West Indian problems.

Amelioration was slow in coming on the vexed question of the participation of teachers in politics. The Franchise Commission of 1943/44 recommended that teachers should be able to participate in politics and become members of road boards and municipal councils. TECA sent a memorandum to the Franchise Committee requesting full civil rights for teachers.[62] Governor Bede Clifford disliked the idea of teachers in politics, fearing their potential to influence opinion.[63] The wind had, however, set in the opposite direction. In 1949 the prohibition was relaxed by an amendment to the Code. The following year TECA spawned a more overtly political offshoot, the People's Education Movement.

Education and Nationalist Strivings in the 1930s

A number of independent black and coloured individuals had strong views about education and its relation to national aspirations in the 1930s. The revolt of the Hindus and Muslims against the Canadian Presbyterian Mission schools and the TTTU's defiance of Captain Cutteridge were examples of non-whites' protest against white 'expatriates' which had the support of institutions, either religious organizations or a trade union. Over time, this opposition was consistent enough to constitute a movement. But additionally, there were disparate statements of certain individuals, expressing their anger, their hopes, their dreams about what education should be or should not be in order to become an instrument consonant with nationalist strivings. Strivings seems an appropriate word; it reflects the powerlessness, the haphazardness, the discontinuity and the incompleteness of these nationalist sentiments.

Two observations should be made at once: the Indians contributed nothing directly to these nationalist strivings since India was their nation; and the blacks and coloureds who had visions of a new political order neglected to consider the role or place of the Indians in it. Secondly, nationalist strivings were not the same as self-government, though the two things were related. Self-government might require simply more education, while nationalist strivings were associated with the advocacy of a different kind of education. Naturally the persons who expressed nationalist sentiments forthrightly were not teachers or employees of the government, but self-employed persons, or persons in private enterprise. Sometimes nothing is known about the writer. One is tempted to use the word 'intellectuals' to describe these people, and to add the adjective 'young'; young intellectuals, fairly independent of government. Without forgetting the posture of the black TECA leadership, it seems reasonable to maintain that only from such a position of independence could one safely criticize education for its failure to contribute to nationalist sentiments.

The establishment of the literary magazines *Trinidad* (1929) and the *Beacon* (1931) is well accepted as the starting point for a new kind of literature in the island. In 1948 one of the important figures of the movement, the novelist Alfred Mendes, described its birth as follows:

> Rather suddenly around 1928 a group of young men and women . . . came together for a single purpose, to argue about the arts and how they affected the islands. A year or so later these same men began to write and paint, and before they realized what was happening a miracle was wrought: they were taking their islands and the people in them, the real people, for grist in their creative mills. [64]

The *Beacon* movement of the early 1930s, multiracial (but not Indian), middle class, anticolonial, shockingly iconoclastic, was largely concerned with the creation of a West Indian literature. As can be seen in C.L.R. James' *Minty Alley*, and Alfred Mendes's *Black Fauns*, a concern for the lives of the black lower classes, the people in the barrack yards of Port of Spain, characterized this new literature. [65] Today it is only with the greatest difficulty that we can appreciate how revolutionary it was to use lower class Trinidadians as the subject of novels or to use dialect in the narrative. It was a form of social protest, and all part of a striving for a suitable cultural identity for blacks and colonials. The *Beacon* movement did not focus on the education system although criticism of it *en passant* was made by some writers. More important was the indirect stimulus of the *Beacon* movement to nationalist strivings in education. If a West Indian literature had to take the culture of the people seriously — even if the Indians were excluded — surely other branches of intellectual activity had to do the same thing. The birth of interest in a genuine

West Indian history was coterminous with the outbreak of creative energies associated with the *Beacon* movement.

If the new West Indian literature had to be written, there was enough history waiting to be discovered; but in the end a new West Indian history would also have to be written. Two sorts of initiatives to produce a West Indian history emerged: one kind was quickly institutionalized in the Trinidad and Tobago Historical Society (founded in mid 1932) and monopolized by respectable professionals, some white amateur historians whose interest centred on the governors and the settlers of the past. Their ideological posture was not nationalistic, but antiquarian and pro-British. The first officers of the Historical Society were Dr Wise, President; Dr Prada, Vice-President; Dr C.Y. Shepherd, secretary/treasurer.[66] The Trinidad and Tobago Historical Society was as colonial as the *Beacon* was anticolonial. In the spirit of the Historical Society was a series of "vignettes of Old Trinidad", appearing in the *Trinidad Guardian* in March 1934 in which slave raiding parties were made to appear like innocent picnics in the forest. The writings of Ernest Digby on the "Great Mutiny" in St Joseph (the Daaga uprising), or on the administration of Governor Woodford and Governor Grant, did not provide any points of departure for concern about nationalism or the education system of the 1930s.[67]

The other drive for a West Indian history was not institutionalized and provided more fruitful ideas. The careers of three young men in the early 1930s provide materials for studying the interplay between education and nationalist sentiment. Eric Williams and C.V. Gocking were at QRC at the same time. Williams won an Island Scholarship in 1931 and went off to Oxford University to study history. He had been good at history at QRC; so too had Gocking who had not won any of the prestigious university scholarships, and had to let down his bucket in Trinidad, first as a clerk at the Cables Office.[68] C.L.R. James was the eldest of the three and had gone through QRC about a decade and a half earlier. His great love at QRC had been English literature; he too was not an Island Scholar.[69] James subsequently taught at QRC itself, at the Government Training College, and at a number of private schools. Teaching was a part-time job; his interests were wider. Instead of studying for an external degree and establishing himself as a teacher at one of the major institutions, James chose the life of a freelance intellectual. He was a link between the *Beacon* movement and the impulse to write and study West Indian history. James wrote a short biography of Michael Maxwell Philip, a coloured lawyer, and a biography of Captain Cipriani; and he left for England in 1932 with Toussaint l'Ouverture of Haiti on his mind.[70]

Eric Williams' decision to study history, despite the advice of his father who wished him to follow so many Island Scholars into law or medicine, turned out to be of great importance for the future of the colony. It remains uncertain how Williams became so interested in history as to choose it as his subject of study at the university level.[71] He too left for England in 1932, and kept in contact with

James, the latter like an elder brother taking an interest in Williams' studies. At home Gocking was one of the founders of the *Royalian*, a QRC literary magazine which reflected something of the spirit of the *Beacon* movement by which it was inspired. The QRC literary society and the *Royalian* differed from the literary and debating societies in that they were more interested in literature than in debates. Gocking wrote about a West Indian literature in the *Royalian* of December 1932, but what he had to say about West Indian history in March 1933 was more relevant to education.

According to Gocking the Trinidad middle class, largely of mixed racial heritage (coloureds), had shown no capacity to combine for group action similar to that of the working classes under Cipriani. He attributed this to colour prejudice among its members and to faulty secondary education. He also acknowledged constraints on action arising from their service function as the employees of private firms and the government. The Hindu and Muslim leaders in the 1920s and 1930s were saying that Indians were in danger of losing their culture, religions and languages. Gocking's position was that the middle class people of African descent had completely lost their ancestral culture and traditions, and imitated those of their European masters, but to no avail as a source of national consciousness or identity. Without their ancestral culture they were atomized into competitive individuals, perhaps cultured, even refined by education, but incapable of group action. He asked of what use to their fellows were such individuals, and his answer was, very little. Secondary education should be made to produce citizens.[72]

In the political awakening of the 1930s, in the development of aspirations for self-government and federation, it was not unusual for middle class intellectuals to attack the West Indian middle class. James did it in his biography of Captain Cipriani; Williams in his *Negro in the Caribbean*. In his article in the *Royalian* Gocking criticized the Trinidad middle class (excluding the Indian middle class) for adopting a European lifestyle which they could ill afford, resulting in small personal savings and their children having to struggle to keep up the standard of living. He felt that the solution to the malaise of the Trinidad, and indeed by extension, West Indian middle class, was partly to be found in new subjects in secondary education.

Gocking recommended reducing the number of subjects then studied in the upper forms of recognized secondary schools to make way for moral philosophy (ethics) and West Indian history. (He himself later sat successfully for ethics and history in the BA external degree of the University of London.) Moral philosophy was the lesser in importance: it was to teach the nature of social obligations. West Indian history was the key: it would teach students that the West Indian peoples were subjected to particular historical conditions which helped to explain their attitudes and the challenges they had to face. History should make them see the relation between their aversion to agriculture and the slave experience; between the slave masters' policy of breaking up tribal alliances and their inability to cooperate; it should inspire them to action. Gocking called for the teaching of English colonial history with special reference to the West Indies in the lower forms, and West Indian history in the higher forms, with the boys taking the university scholarship examination delving into the details of the subject. All college libraries were to have a good West Indian section. Patriotism was to be induced by knowledge of the West Indian past.[73]

Some twenty years passed before the study of West Indian history was taken up seriously at the University College of the West Indies, and that was a prerequisite for its serious pursuit in the secondary schools. Students today might find it difficult to understand the impact which the introduction of West Indian history had upon the students at the University College of the West Indies in the late 1950s and early 1960s. This history was not only a means to self-consciousness and national identity, but a positive aid to social and economic planning. It came into the academic system almost like a social science tool, more revealing, more satisfactory than contemporary economics. Gocking advised the teaching of West Indian history as preparation for self-government. But such a change, not to mention the spirit in which this new history had to be taught to meet his objectives, could hardly predate the assumption of political responsibility by West Indians. British colonial educators would not consciously prepare West Indian leaders in 1933. Marriott and Cutteridge could not be expected to be moved by such ideas. Their declared objective was to train character, by which they meant boys who behaved like English gentlemen. Nothing like West Indian history was planned for the secondary modern schools. History, meaning English history, was to be taught in these schools as a by-product of English literature. Gocking's proposals were almost as hopeless in 1933 as the Garveyites' advocacy of a black-conscious director of education in the late 1920s.[74]

In Haiti the foundations of negritude were being laid in a new literature of protest against the United States occupation. The development of the idea that West Indian history was a social desideratum has a most fascinating chapter which involved the discovery of Toussaint l'Ouverture of Haiti. Somehow, possibly through Garveyite literature or from black North American writers, a few blacks in Trinidad as well as Tobago at the turn of the 1920s into the early 1930s literally discovered Toussaint. An interesting possibility is that of contact between black-conscious individuals in Trinidad and Tobago and Dr Carter Woodson, director of the Association for the Study of Negro Life and History in the USA.[75] Toussaint l'Ouverture fulfilled a psychological need for a black hero of international stature, a towering figure from the past who could be a source of inspiration; a man of action and of ideas. A literary and debating club in Port of Spain took its name from Toussaint l'Ouverture. T. A. Marryshow, the Grenadian trade union leader, came to a Trinidad Working Men's Association rally in Port of Spain in 1933 and made the remark that QRC schoolboys knew nothing about Toussaint, reputedly the greatest black man who ever lived.[76] They studied, he alleged, the

nobodies of English history. The black-conscious editor of the *Tobago Times*
organized an essay competition for Tobago on Toussaint. Indeed, the editor was
an advocate of black history being taught in Tobago's primary schools rather than
the folk tales of Cutteridge's *Readers*.[77] The editor behaved like one of those
unnamed persons from Trinidad or Cuba or the Forum Club of Barbados, who
was believed to be in contact with Woodson on the need for black literature in
the schools of these islands.[78] Whether or not the confluence of the *Tobago Times*,
debates at the Scarborough Ideal Literary and Debating Club, visits and talks by
politically conscious black teachers such as DeWilton Rogers, as well as the black
Tobago based members of TECA, such as John S. Donaldson, heightened black
consciousness in Tobago towards the mid 1930s is a moot point.[79] Its forms of
expression appear to be adequately submerged under more acceptable activity; but
it would be mistaken not to sense new radical thinking in Scarborough in the mid
1930s which informed the protest of some Tobago teachers against the Education
Code of Cutteridge.[80] The Code was recognized as a species of class legislation
which implied legislation against black people.[81]

After the 1880s, the idea that Trinidad had too many doctors and lawyers
surfaced occasionally. This was not the official view of the Board of Education
which controlled the granting of university scholarships (Island Scholarships).
However, the reduction of the scholarships from four to three per annum and
then to two was carried out without a sense that society would suffer in its supply
of lawyers and doctors.[82] In the 1920s discussions about the desirability of
requiring the Island Scholars to study professions preferred by the Board usually
ended up in an admission by its members that the university scholarship was
primarily a personal reward for individual brilliance, and not a means for building
up the human resources most essential for the development of the society. The
winners were not obliged to serve the community which paid for the scholarships;
indeed they were not even required to return to the island after completion of their
studies.[83] The majority did return to work in the island, but differing views could
be taken of the value of the services they rendered. The easiest defence of the
university scholarship system consisted of a recitation of the names of practicing
doctors and lawyers who had qualified by that route; some had made a name for
themselves. This view was concerned only with the availability and quality of their
professional services.

There was a view, however, which gained strength in the 1930s, that the
university scholarship winners should offer political leadership in addition to
professional service. This was the view of some persons who might be said to be
on the 'Left', for example part-Chinese Dr Tito Achong, and Leonard Walcott,
the black editor of *The People*. Achong, a medical practitioner educated in the USA
and an activist in Port of Spain politics, was a fierce critic of higher education in
English.[84] By political leadership such critics did not mean service in the Legislative
Council, even as an elected member. Dr Arthur McShine was the only Island

Scholar in the Council in the 1930s, and he was a nominated member. His politics
was too moderate for the 'Left'. Some of the Island Scholars might have accepted
a nominated seat if asked by the governor, but they would be reluctant to enter
electoral politics. It was leadership of the masses, of the working classes, which
the critics wanted. C. Henry Pierre's determined efforts in the mid 1930s to
increase the university scholarships triggered a press debate on the social usefulness of Island Scholars.[85]

At a dinner given in his honour by the citizens of Port of Spain, L.A.P. O'Reilly,
a distinguished coloured lawyer who was not an Island Scholar, is believed to have
asked what contribution the Island Scholars had made to the solution of social
problems.[86] He meant the answer to be "none". Nevertheless, he was in favour of
increasing the university scholarships. Henry Hudson-Phillips, a black lawyer and
not an Island Scholar, was known in his youthful days as a liberal. He allegedly
said that the professional men had not contributed much to the advancement of
the country,[87] and accused them of "intellectual cowardice".[88] Hudson-Phillips was
opposed to increasing the number of university scholarships; so too were Richard
Brathwaite, a black trade unionist, and Dr Achong.[89] Leonard Walcott, the editor
of *The People* was convinced that more scholarships would only mean more
conservative lawyers and doctors. The coloured Dr Stephen Laurence, an Island
Scholar, and the Indian Anglican clergyman Rev J.D. Ramkessoon, who had
qualified at Codrington College, Barbados, argued in favour of an increase.
H.O.B. Wooding, a black lawyer, also an Island Scholar, argued that the winners
served the community silently and unspectacularly: they gave "friendly advice" and
offered "exemplary conduct".[90] A lame excuse, replied the editor of *The People*.
The Italians had invaded Ethiopia, an issue of world shaking importance, and the
editor of *The People* wanted Wooding to tell him how many Island Scholars have
publicly expressed sympathy for Ethiopia, a thing many Englishmen had done;[91]
how many had contributed to the fund for Ethiopia. M.E. Farquhar, a liberal
coloured Anglican clergyman, who had worked in Africa, remarked critically that
if the Ethiopian fund had been called the 'Scotch or Irish fund', the Island Scholars
would have tumbled over one another to contribute.[92]

The Butler riots confirmed the lack of political leadership from the respectable
professionals. A little known 'uneducated' black preacher-agitator, Uriah Butler,
suddenly took centre stage and moved the politics of the colony a few miles to the
'left'. Butler was not assisted by the black established lawyers. The rise of Butler
led Achong to write in *The People* in January 1938:

> Education and leadership in Trinidad appear to be incompatible things. From the
> coterie of educated natives no leadership has yet sprung and none appears within
> sight. Persons with some sort of education, especially those schooled in the profes-
> sions at the expense of public funds, are dexterous only in angling for subordinate
> jobs, where they are satisfied to live a vegetative life. They show no interest in public
> movements and seem not at all prone to adjusting themselves for disinterested
> service.[93]

The critics of the Island Scholars' lack of political consciousness sometimes connected this shortcoming with their silent conditioning by education in Britain. This was exactly what Charles Warner and Governor Keate had hoped for when they set up the Island Scholarships in the early 1860s. They wished to turn creole boys into English gentlemen. The Board of Education, on which sat some British educated Island Scholars, only slowly accepted the idea that Island Scholars could study at any but British universities. In 1928 the Board was involved in some lively discussions when an Island Scholar, A. Cipriani, expressed a desire to study at the Massachusetts Institute of Technology. Cipriani's case was based on financial considerations, on the opportunities to work and study simultaneously, and on the chance of employment afterwards in the USA.[94] Instead of reprimanding his obvious intention not to return to Trinidad and Tobago, the Board tried to persuade him to attend an English university. Eventually a compromise choice was made: Cipriani was allowed to go to McGill University in Canada.[95]

The great majority of educated persons were absolutely convinced that British universities were the best; and those who were opposed to serious social change might have felt that they were ideologically safer than universities elsewhere. Some of the critics of the Island Scholars thought they saw the baneful social effects of higher education at British universities: mental slavery, for example, the absurd talk of "going home" when going off on a few weeks holiday in England. Even today Trinidadian students (as well as other West Indian students) feel powerful emotional ties to the overseas locations where they experienced the joys and sorrows of university education. When Island Scholars returned with English wives their predisposition to conform to the racially based social structure of the colony was even more marked. In his sociological studies of Trinidad after World War II, Lloyd Brathwaite made the useful point that Trinidadians who studied abroad did so more as scattered individuals than as a group; and hence they tended to nurture loyalties to their foreign universities and institutions. Also they sat mostly professional examinations (law and medicine) which did not involve any research into Trinidad or West Indian society, so they were not equipped to deal with the problems of Trinidad.

It must be remembered, however, that Trinidadians were also going to universities in Canada and the USA. The Indians in particular had established important links to Canada through the Canadian Presbyterian Church. These Indians were conditioned for better or worse by their experiences in North America. But it was the graduates of British universities who were in question. These universities, charged the editor of *The People* in January 1936, had not produced a single coloured West Indian of international reputation nearly a century after emancipation.[96] A petition to the governor in March 1935 against a proposed newspaper Ordinance said that not a single work of merit by a West Indian had emerged from the English system of education in Trinidad and Tobago. By the early 1940s dissatisfaction with the social returns from the university scholarship system might not even have been a particularly radical view. It was expressed in 1944 by the Arya Samajists (Indians), who possibly had in mind black Island Scholars, but it was by then a general reformist complaint. They complained to the Irvine Committee investigating the nature and role of a West Indian university that "on their return our professionals are either drafted into the Government Service, or else they tend towards social isolation and the pursuit of wealth".[97] The criticism of the Island Scholars' lack of political consciousness, the growing expectation of political leadership from them, in the long run helped psychologically to prepare the ground for the providential advent of Dr Eric Williams. His coming was not perhaps prophesied, but it was a kind of fulfillment. Before him another Island Scholar, H.O.B. Wooding, went into politics and at a later stage than 1936 still another, Dr Patrick Solomon – as if to pave the way for the deliverer.[98]

But what of a West Indian university? Should not the critics of British universities be advocates of a West Indian university? They appeared not to be so inclined. The friends of a West Indian university were among the admirers of British universities. In 1927 Captain Cipriani, the leading campaigner for self-government, had introduced a motion into the Legislative Council which expressed the willingness of Trinidad and Tobago to cooperate with other West Indian colonies in establishing a West Indian university. This idea had re-emerged at a West Indian conference in London in 1926 and Cipriani was following it up at the Trinidad level. The debate was a springboard for creole pride in their intellectual abilities, but everybody there knew that the proposal was impractical. Federal sentiments were too feeble; the British government had no money to offer. But no government official wished to incur the odium of outright opposition. Cipriani's motion was quietly passed with an amendment urging caution on the question of finance and quality of teaching.[99] At that time a West Indian university did not seem to have a strong social or political mission. A decade later the political climate had changed. Some of the young intellectuals, including Gocking and DeWilton Rogers, could by then see a West Indian university as an instrument of West Indian self-discovery, as the intellectual base of research into West Indian history.[100]

Although Cipriani was friendly to the establishment of a West Indian university, education in its ideological connection with nationalism was not a major concern for him. His approach to education was more like that of a trade unionist than a reformer. He was in favour of compulsory primary education, a considerable increase in College Exhibitions, the abolition of child labour, competitive examinations to enter the civil service, and generally he was sympathetic to teachers as workers. This focus was the provision of more, rather than a different kind of education, and this too was secondary to his other preoccupations, such as trade union legislation and self-government. Cipriani argued that the colony had already sufficient educated men to warrant the immediate granting of self-government; and no doubt he thought that there was nothing wrong with a British type of education, acquired in the colony or in Britain. He implied as much in a speech before a Labour Conference in England in 1930. He said:

> It is quite true that the natives or inhabitants of the West Indies are, in the majority, coloured people, but there are coloured gentlemen, highly cultured and educated having the same aims and aspirations as the white man, educated in your Public Schools, taking their professions in your Inns of Court, your Universities and Hospitals, and it is this class that is now forced to put up with the big stick autocracy of the official from Africa.[101]

While the young intellectuals talked about the need for West Indian history, Captain Daniel, principal of the Government Training College and assistant director of education, decided to follow the example of his chief, Cutteridge. Cutteridge had given the colony *Readers*, *Arithmetics* and a geography textbook; Daniel set out to fill the gap by providing a West Indian history textbook. His *Histories of the West Indies* (3 vols) appeared in 1936. Inevitably Daniel wrote less about West Indians in the West Indies, and more about Englishmen in the West Indies, including the gentlemen pirates. The *Histories* had much extraneous matter, as Dr Eric Williams realized in 1956.[102] However, to be fair to Daniel, his history books were a vast improvement on what existed previously. For instance, he had a surprisingly objective section on Toussaint l'Ouverture. What Daniel's *Histories* lacked, apart from focus on black or coloured West Indians, was any sense of black pride in the service of a new West Indian social and political order. Gocking's criticism of these *Histories* at a meeting of the QRC Literary Society in May 1937 was that the history of the West Indies must begin in Africa, and must focus on the West Indian peoples.[103] The editor of *The People*, Leonard Walcott, said any history book for West Indian children must go back to the "city states" of Nigeria and the Kingdom of Sudan. It must tell how Africans of every tribe were moulded into "a conglomeration of motley hue and europeanized outlook".[104] It must show the evil of slavery and declare that the world would have been a better place if Africans had been left in Africa. He hailed two volumes (*The Evolution of the Negro*) produced by Norman Cameron of Guyana as evidence that educated West Indians were alive to the need for proper history books. Such books must be written by competent West Indians or sympathetic Europeans. Captain Daniel was neither; and Walcott advised parents not to purchase Daniel's *Histories*.[105]

The Survival of the Dual System 1930-1939

In 1930 the dual system was two generations old, and it looked like a solid and enduring structure. The struggles and tensions continued in the 1930s, but up to 1939 these were not as sharp as the battles between government and the churches during and immediately after World War II. Between 1943 and 1946 the dual system faced its biggest crisis of the first half of the twentieth century when on the advice of Director Robert Patrick, the government sought to introduce legislation to give itself the right to appoint, promote and transfer teachers in denominational primary schools once their religious beliefs and character had been approved by the particular church to which the school belonged.[106] This was successfully resisted by the Christian churches, led by Roman Catholic Archbishop Finbar Ryan. Patrick was transferred to another part of the empire. Nothing as dramatic occurred during the 1930s, but there were minor crises, and above all, the relative strength of the two partners in the dual system, the churches and the government, changed in some subtle ways in favour of the government.

The period of rapid expansion of denominational primary schools which started in the 1870s had continued until the end of World War I. The economic stringency of the 1920s brought an end to this expansion in Trinidad as well as in Tobago. In the 1930s there was also stagnation in the construction of new schools, especially between 1930 and 1937; but in both the 1920s and 1930s schools were repaired, extended and replaced; more school places were created without building absolutely new schools. However, enrolment in Trinidad, but not in Tobago, overtook school places; and it was not until after World War II that an ambitious programme of school building was actually undertaken. One crude measure of judging the importance of each partner in the dual system was the number of schools possessed by each. From this point of view the Christian churches, which had the majority of schools, constituted the more important partner; but things were really not so simple.

At the start of the 1930s government schools, not denominational schools, were still regarded generally as the type of schools whose existence needed to be justified (see Tables 3.1 and 3.2). The dual system and the powerful role of the churches within it received support from the Marriott/Mayhew Commission of 1931/32. But as we have seen, both were criticized by some teachers during the 1930s. Subsequent to the Report of the Moyne Commission it appeared that the colony was on the verge of a new beginning which would involve the reduction of the role of the churches in education. The Moyne Report itself gave critical support to the dual system, and affirmed the social usefulness of the churches in education. The churches were the most widely accepted social institutions, but the Moyne Commission wished to see a reduction in their role in favour of increased activity by colonial governments. On the advice of the Moyne Report considerable sums of British government funds were made available for education, and a team of resident experts under the Colonial Development and Welfare scheme was set up in the West Indies. The education expert of Colonial Development and Welfare, S.A. Hammond, was unfriendly to denominational schools and wished to see stronger controls over the education system by West Indian governments.

In this sense, Colonial Development and Welfare worked in the direction of strengthening the hands of the Trinidad government within the dual system.

To add to the intricacies of the dual system, the Hindus and the Muslims wished to have their own denominational schools. Although this was not allowed until after World War II, the Hindu and Muslim lobbies were a challenge to the dual system from the 1930s on. In retrospect it now seems impossible that Indian denominational schools could have been kept out indefinitely; but the Hindus and Muslims had to await the increasing secularization of the dominant world view in the colony, and the growth of their own political clout in the era of universal adult suffrage and party politics.

Throughout its history the dual system was characterized by tensions and contradictions. The most obvious result of the alarms and uncertainties was that it survived them in the 1930s, as in other eras; indeed it assumed more and more the appearance of a nearly irreversible system, but paradoxically its consolidation was accomplished without its legitimacy being put beyond question. The less obvious development within it was that the balance of power between the two partners kept shifting incrementally in favour of the government, especially in respect to primary education. This did not mean that the Christian churches lacked the influence to oblige the government to back away from certain policies. For instance, in 1930 a proposed new Education Ordinance required denominational secondary schools to account for the expenditure of government grants. The proposal was stoutly resisted by the Roman Catholic Church and, for this reason and others, the Ordinance was shelved.[107] In the same year also, Marriott had to reassure the churches in Tobago that nothing sinister was intended by government in its plans to have a government primary school at Mason Hall.

There were, however, irresistible factors which increased by small installments the government's power over the dual system, even without any growth in the number of government schools. One factor was political, though it operated more powerfully after 1939. The government was slowly assuming a wider responsibility for more aspects of the lives of citizens. Significantly, in the 1930s there was a higher level of government financial input into denominational primary schools; for instance the government offered to pay 50 percent of the cost of new or expanded denominational schools and this gave the government more leverage over the churches. No government in that era would pay out increasing sums of money for education, or any other social service, without wanting increased control over it. Even before the onset of nationalism as the official creed, the equation of more control for more money was a part of the administrative mind of Crown Colony heads of departments and elected members of the Legislative Council. Whether the Christian churches then conceived of increased government aid as in any degree subversive of their authority is another matter: it might have been seen as simply tightening the interdependency of the two partners in the dual system. Greater assistance to denominational primary schools for apparatus and equipment in 1936, and an increased government share of the cost of new denominational primary school buildings in 1948, might even have been seen as a victory for church schools. If so, it was a pyrrhic victory.

But what of secondary education? At the start of World War I there were four recognized government aided secondary schools, one of which was a government college (QRC). The ratio of government to denominational colleges at that time did not seem unreasonable, but from the late 1920s to 1953 the government allowed the churches to open a wider gap in the ratio of denominational to government colleges and in the ratio of students in denominational colleges to those in QRC. It was not until 1953 that a second government secondary school (St George's College, Barataria) was opened, nearly a century after the first (QRC). In the meantime the Christian churches had, almost at ten year intervals between 1924 and 1946, brought small clusters of denominational secondary schools into the dual system, for example Bishop Anstey High School, Naparima Girls' High School, Bishop's High in Tobago (1924/27); St Benedict College, St Joseph High School (1936/37); and Fatima College and Presentation College (1946/47). These new denominational secondary schools were not erected with the financial assistance of the government. No funds for new denominational secondary school buildings were ever advanced until 1956. Government subsidy towards the recurrent cost of denominational secondary schools increased as the schools got larger and more developed, and qualified for increased sums under the system of capitation grants and special grants; but parity in teachers' pay in denominational secondary schools with those teachers at QRC was not achieved until 1955. Hence the financial input of government into the growing number of denominational secondary schools, although increasing, was not of the same order as the input into the denominational primary schools.

The increased power and influence of the government in the dual system at the level of primary education was not paralleled by a similar development at the secondary level. In the later nineteenth century the secondary school sector of the dual system was subjected to fewer administrative changes than the primary school sector; in the twentieth century the secondary sector continued to be the more sacrosanct. As in the later nineteenth century the upper and upper middle class were more sensitive to changes in secondary education since their children would be affected, and the Christian churches could count on solid support from white, black and coloured upper and middle class beneficiaries of their secondary schools. The Roman Catholic Church continued to enjoy tremendous support for its secondary schools from the French creoles.

The critical vigilance of the upper class, the relative weakness of the government's contribution to secondary education both in terms of the number of government colleges and its financial input, combined to stem the growth of government power and influence over the secondary school sector of the dual system. To this we must add the prestige of secondary education, and the commanding intellectual position of the principals of QRC and CIC. It was thought that nobody in the Education Department was more qualified to inspect or supervise these colleges than their principals, and in practice they were run pretty much as autonomous institutions in which the critical areas of staff control and admission of students fell under the full discretion of the principal. This was less true of QRC than of CIC and the other denominational colleges. It must also not be forgotten that the Cambridge external examinations, precisely by putting a considerable part of the curriculum in a straitjacket, exercised a regulatory function over the colleges which was not available in the primary schools. The secondary schools were 'inspected', as it were, by the Cambridge examinations. To a certain extent, it might also be said that the examinations which the government administered were the main controlling mechanism of the government over the denominational teacher training schools, which from the late 1920s lost their importance as bones of controversy in the dual system.

The dual system failed to provide enough school places at the primary or secondary level, but there was not the slightest possibility that either a purely denominational or a purely government system would have produced sufficient school places. From the early 1920s impressive reductions in mortality rates fed an alarming population growth rate, particularly in the under-fifteen age groups. In the 1930s and the 1940s Trinidad and Tobago improved on the enrolment of children between five and fifteen years old, but there was some decline by the middle of the 1950s.

The Absence of a University 1922-1939

At the time the Imperial College of Tropical Agriculture (ICTA) was founded in 1922, Governor John Chancellor expressed the view that it might be the starting point of a West Indian university. The presence of ICTA was generally thought to give Trinidad an advantage in the eastern Caribbean when it came to the location of other regional institutions of higher education. After Codrington College in Barbados was razed by fire in 1925, ICTA was left as the only institution with any pretensions to university standing in the British West Indies. Jamaica had no such institution. The destruction of Codrington College put the question of a West Indian university on the agenda of the West Indies Conference in London in 1926. On Captain Cipriani's initiative, the Legislative Council of Trinidad and Tobago discussed this subject in 1927 and gave cautious approval to further exploration of the question by future West Indies conferences. From about 1926 the British government responded in piecemeal fashion to separate inquiries about the possibility of university education in the colonial empire, including the West Indies. Using hindsight these inquiries seemed premature. In the case of the West

Indies neither the social demand for a university, nor the will of the British government to act positively, had matured. In the case of the British Caribbean, however, the stirrings in the Colonial Office did produce a commissioned report in 1930, by Sir James Currie and R. E. Sedgwick, on the possibility of a West Indian university.[108]

Currie and Sedgwick declared for a centralized university, but could not see their way to siting it in any island but Jamaica which had half the population of the British Caribbean. These planners ignored the apparent advantages which Trinidad and Barbados had respectively in ICTA and Codrington College. ICTA itself (while not a university) had not given rise to demands by any important group in Trinidad for a West Indian university located in Trinidad or elsewhere. In the absence of public support for such an institution in the 1920s and 1930s, the question of a West Indian university was a non-issue in the colony.

When the Irvine Committee toured the West Indies in 1944 to investigate this question, there were clear indications of opposition from some quarters.[109] Opposition might have been even stronger in the 1920s and 1930s. In the May 1927 Council debate, A. V. Stollmeyer, an elected member, reproduced the old argument that the temperate climate of the metropole was more conducive to physical fitness and intellectual accomplishments, and therefore it was better to send West Indian youth to metropolitan universities. More commonly, as can be seen from the evidence presented to the Irvine committee, the objections to a West Indian university sprang from fears that academic standards would be lower than metropolitan levels, or that the cost would be insupportable, or that primary and secondary education would be neglected.[110] It is also vital to understand that in all the British colonies where the university scholarship system had evolved and entrenched itself, it had in fact become a substitute for a West Indian university. Through this system, it was cheaper to select a handful of brilliant youths for professional education in the famous universities of the United Kingdom than to establish a new university. Even after World War II, increasing the number of university scholarships to metropolitan universities was an arguable, if unenlightened, alternative to a West Indian university.

In the case of Trinidad and Tobago, the university scholarship system exercised a tremendous power over the entire education system and the educated classes. Even when a West Indian university was founded it was felt that Island Scholars deserved the privilege of university education in the metropole. Only after World War II when British universities, and also some in Canada, were unable or unwilling to absorb the flow of West Indian students (both independently financed students and government scholarship holders) did the case for a West Indian university take on the greatest urgency.

The scores of holders of Cambridge Higher School Certificates who did not win university scholarships, and who could not afford to pay their own way in metropolitan universities, had to remain at home in disillusionment. The most determined of this group took to studying various subjects by correspondence courses, and it was in this context that the famous system of sitting for the external degrees of the University of London came to life. In the twentieth century the University of London developed as the university of the British empire. London alone among British universities gave external degrees to students who need not fulfill any conditions of residence or attendance at its classes. Its external degrees were technically available in the West Indies from at least the 1880s, by which time they were certainly available in British colonial Africa.[111] Why persons in Trinidad and Tobago did not resort to them before the 1930s is unclear; but it probably was related to the dominance of the Cambridge examination system over the public's imagination, and to the defeat of the proposals in the 1890s to substitute the Matriculation examination of the University of London for the Cambridge examinations in the colony's secondary schools. If the colony did not wish to take the secondary school examination set by the University of London, then how much less its degrees? Even in the 1930s amazingly few people seemed to have known about the facility to take London external degrees. The same atmosphere of secrecy surrounded the availability of certain correspondence courses from abroad. London did not advertise in the local press, and the external degree facility was not mentioned in any official documents from the education authorities before private persons started taking the examinations in noticeable numbers. The government was never the active agent in the emergence of the external degree facility. It was only at the end of the 1940s when self-government became the acknowledged political objective that the stage was set for government sponsorship of university education beyond the university scholarship programme.

In November 1933 the *Teachers Herald* observed that "there are some young men who have matriculated and are taking the intermediate Arts. There will be more BAs than one can count just now". Perhaps the first Trinidadian to get an external degree was the Christian Indian Rawle Ramkessoon, who thereby established himself in the Education Department, and rose from inspector of schools to deputy director of education over a period of some twenty years. J. Hamilton Maurice and C.V. Gocking went the same route from external degrees to positions in the Education Department except that they spent several years teaching in secondary schools before becoming administrators. The 1940s were better years for the acquisition of external degrees than the 1930s (see Tables 3.3 and 3.4). If the numbers sitting the intermediate and final examinations seem pitifully small by today's standard, it should be remembered that only with grit and resolution could candidates hope to succeed when faced with lack of instruction and too few libraries. Trinidad and Tobago actually furnished more candidates for the final examinations between 1935 and 1943 than did Guyana, Barbados or Jamaica.[112] By 1949 of eighty-eight persons with degrees in public schools in Trinidad and Tobago, a total of twenty graduates had external degrees.

Obviously it was better to have an external degree than none in a colony where so few persons had one. Still, the holders of the external degrees of the University of London were regarded as distinctly inferior products compared to graduates who had resided abroad in universities in advanced countries and sat face to face with learned professors. The story of the struggle of holders of external degrees to get jobs in secondary schools or the civil service lies beyond 1939, and cannot be related here. Suffice it to say that up to 1939 the rise of a few persons with external degrees was satisfying to some and threatening to others. In the end, the facility of London external degrees had a considerable impact on higher education and upward social mobility in the West Indies.

The same cloud of suspicion of a locally obtained university degree or university type of qualification hung over the graduates of ICTA. From the start its courses were basically of two kinds: a postgraduate course for graduates from English universities wishing to gain knowledge and experience in tropical agriculture and a course for West Indians wishing a qualification in agriculture which would take them into government agricultural service at the junior level. A subsidiary activity was to offer ad hoc courses to meet local needs. The research portfolio of the Imperial Department of Agriculture was taken over fully by ICTA, and the significance of this development should not be missed. For the first time, an institution of higher learning was implanted in the West Indies with the objectives of doing both teaching and research. These objectives, plus the high qualifications of the staff and the presence of postgraduate students, gave ICTA the appearance of a university level institution from the start (although it did not grant degrees).

ICTA quickly established a reputation for scientific research, largely because it built upon the library, the achievements, and the staff of the Imperial Department of Agriculture. The academic reputation of institutions of higher learning generally rests on their research rather than on their teaching, which is one reason why Codrington College in Barbados could not compete with ICTA as a seat of learning in the West Indies. It is the international reputation of ICTA for scientific research that is most remembered even today, and it is almost sacrilegious to question it.

It might be argued, however, that it was the British government and the special agricultural interests (sugar, cocoa, cotton, etc.) which were most interested in, and benefited most by the research of ICTA. The College had a dual objective: it was to research and to teach, the latter function falling into two broad categories, namely the teaching of postgraduate Englishmen destined for the agricultural service of the empire, and the instruction of West Indian undergraduates for the diploma. The training of the English postgraduates, in so far as it had a research dimension, was deemed part and parcel of the success story of ICTA as a research institute. But what of the West Indians? There were problems which were never solved in the thirty-eight-year existence of ICTA, and these constitute part of the dubious side of ICTA's performance which was seen only in the West Indies and not internationally.[113]

As a specialist college with a strong research focus and a small teaching staff, ICTA could never expand its student population indefinitely. In the first ten years it doubled its student population, but in absolute terms the college still had less than forty students. As a specialist agricultural college professionalizing the study of agriculture, it did not have scope for sustained expansion. Nevertheless it is true that West Indians did not attend it in the numbers expected, and that West Indians with strong academic records in secondary school turned their backs on ICTA. Scholarships were often not taken up. The underutilization of ICTA by West Indians was a chronic problem which persisted beyond its absorption into the University (College) of the West Indies.

The basic failure of ICTA was that it did not offer a degree course; in other words, it failed to be a university. West Indians who sought higher education wanted the prestige of degrees, preferably degrees from metropolitan universities. This was another drawback for ICTA from the point of view of West Indians. It was situated in the West Indies and lacked, even for non-Trinidadians, the glamour and mystique of a truly metropolitan place of learning. Although Trinidadians formed the largest contingent of West Indian students, there were few of them and ICTA was too local to be really attractive to anyone who had the slightest alternative.

There were other problems for West Indians. Agriculture was not a profession comparable to law or medicine. It gave neither independence of action nor satisfactory remuneration. It led typically to a civil service job in the junior ranks of the Department of Agriculture with little prospect of speedy promotion. West Indian students were not owners of, nor heirs to, plantations or large farms; nor could they look forward to satisfactory careers on the plantations or large farms of absentee white owners or companies. This was one reason behind the abolition of the Agricultural Scholarship (one of the university scholarships from 1919 to 1924). The winners, after qualifying abroad, could not find a secure niche in the colony as professionals.[114] There was little prospect of real social mobility for non-whites through training at ICTA, and this upward social mobility was the traditional drive behind higher education. It was not that agriculture was tainted with memories of slavery, though it was never popular; it was a question of restricted job opportunities, poor prospects and the reality of racial discrimination in the civil service or private enterprise.[115]

The Board of Education could not bring itself to oblige winners of the Agricultural Scholarship or the Science Scholarship (which replaced the Agricultural Scholarship from 1925) to attend ICTA. It was a cause for considerable satisfaction when G. Bain, the last winner of the Agricultural Scholarship, decided to go to ICTA instead of Louisiana State University.[116] He lived long enough to regret his choice of ICTA and a career in the civil service. Because the best students from the secondary schools did not turn to ICTA, its West Indian intake was of varied quality and this made it difficult to design courses satisfactory to all. The stronger students felt that they repeated much of the work of the sixth form; and the courses for West Indians got the reputation of being low grade or inadequate. This in turn deterred other students from entering, and so the cycle continued despite occasional assurances from highly placed persons like Dr Leake (one of ICTA's principals) that the diploma course had the status of a university degree.[117]

ICTA was an imperial institution located in the West Indies. Because of its location and service to Trinidad and the West Indies in terms of research, teaching and advice to farmers, some West Indians hoped that it might develop into an institution increasingly adapted to West Indian needs. But it was controlled from England by a governing body which had to respond to the interest of the major financial backers: the British government and certain corporations centred in England, for instance the Empire Cotton Growing Corporation. Part of ICTA's research portfolio had to do with crops which were not of importance to the West Indies, though they made financial contributions and, of course, colonial governments themselves were subject to the British government. The principal and staff were not accountable to any authority in Trinidad or the West Indies, and in Trinidad ICTA was not considered a part of the education system or the civil service. Of course the major export crops of the West Indies did command the attention of ICTA, and benefited from its work, though the same cannot be said with equal confidence about the peasant sector of West Indian agriculture. The imperial focus of the college dominated its regional commitments; and its postgraduate work in training Englishmen for the colonial agricultural service towered over the teaching of West Indians.

Even within Trinidad where ICTA had the greatest opportunity of showing a West Indian face, a social gap opened up between it and the community in which it was located. The college offered 'racial coeducation',[118] but its ethos was distinctly English. The principal and academic staff were recruited from England which was perhaps unavoidable; but so too was the administrative staff. The prestigious section of the student body was the English postgraduate students; English staff, English students and the wives of the English staff reinforced one another and formed a social enclave of English civilization in St Augustine surrounded by black creole and Indian villagers. Structurally, ICTA was a colonial institution, with no openings for non-whites to academic positions. The West Indian students did not set the tone or tempo of life at St Augustine, though they were naturally set above the groundsmen, maids and artisans who kept the physical facilities in good order. It would be too much to believe that racial prejudice and English snobbery did not exist at ICTA as in the social enclaves of the oil industry in southern Trinidad.[119] Racial discrimination, though suspected, was always difficult to prove as Captain Cipriani, the leading radical in Trinidad's politics in the 1920s, was to discover. Professor Harland, a senior academic at ICTA did argue that the black man was genetically inferior to the white man.[120]

Independent of control from within Trinidad, the college appeared to have kept the non-white community at arm's length; ICTA was more or less 'hallowed' ground from its inception to its incorporation into the University (College) of the West Indies. It was the sort of institution which would have attracted suspicion and criticism from those who cherished anticolonial sentiments, from the critics of Crown Colony government, from those resentful (possibly even among the French creoles) of the predominance of English influence in the colony. Unstructured oral evidence suggests that any young non-white creole belles or sons who got an invitation to an ICTA student party had a talking point for the rest of their lives. The college was both welcomed and resented by Trinidadians. Cipriani's attempt to flush out prejudice and discrimination was not sustained partly because the college was in Trinidad, but not of Trinidad; it was within the legitimate scope of criticism and at the same time outside it. It was beyond reform by the Trinidad legislature or by public opinion and, hence, a scandal like the one which arose in 1935 when an English member of the senior academic staff, Professor Harland, was dismissed because he married a local woman of Chinese extraction blew over with remarkably little press commentary.[121] The point is that such goings-on at ICTA were not properly the concerns of the colony any more than social and racial prejudice in the staffing of commercial banks were thought fit subjects for public commentary. When the Irvine Committee visited the West Indies in early 1944 it was troubled by tales of dissatisfaction with ICTA, especially from Jamaica. The difficulty the Irvine Committee had in conceiving ways of integrating ICTA into a University of the West Indies seems to suggest that from a West Indian point of view ICTA was a sort of 'failed success'. It could not be ignored in the plans of the Irvine Committee; and it could not easily be reformed.[122] Such was the Imperial College of Tropical Agriculture.

[4]

Perspectives on Special Topics

Religious Instruction and Education 1834-1939

Considering the long involvement of the Christian churches in the ownership and conduct of schools in Trinidad and Tobago, it is natural that religious instruction played a significant role inside the classrooms and in the debates of education policy makers. The view of all the churches, Christian and non-Christian, has always been that religious instruction must be integrated into the teaching of other subjects, that schools must have a religious atmosphere and that religious instruction must be delivered primarily by classroom teachers whose own lives should exemplify the influence of religion.[1] The Roman Catholic Church went further than other Christian churches in insisting that all its members must send their children to Roman Catholic schools where available. During the time of Archbishop Flood, religious sanctions were applied to negligent parents.[2]

While differing from the churches on the question how religious instruction was to be integrated into the curriculum, government officials responsible for education, from emancipation up to at least the middle of the twentieth century, shared the views of the clerics that religious instruction was an absolute necessity in education. Both clerics and government officials believed that morality and character in children could best be founded on religious instruction, and that the preservation of social order and well-being was dependent on the diffusion of religious morality. As Lord Harris once put it, "without religious principles no society of man can flourish".[3] Clerics and government officials, however, had a long history of differences over the implementation of policy; each side had special interests of great importance to itself, but not necessarily of any priority to the other side.

Religious instruction can be segmented into three broad interrelated areas of activity: the teaching of Bible knowledge which hopefully could aid religious conversion; then character training and morality which were designed to preserve the social order; and finally, congregational activities to ensure denominational loyalties. The churches were interested in all three aspects, but the survival of each particular church as a social force was linked inextricably to the creation of denominational loyalties, producing a faithful membership. Christian conversion and character training were expected to end ideally with fervent membership of particular churches. The church schools were expected to boost church membership through religious instruction. This explains the intense and undeniable competitiveness of churches. Government officials were, on the other hand, mostly interested in character training and morality; in this respect they shared the same aspirations as the majority of parents. The churches' interest in building up denominational loyalties encouraged the view of schools as total institutions where all things should contribute towards the dissemination of religious instruction and the creation of a religious atmosphere. The classroom teachers became the main cogs in this process. For government officials, the fostering of loyalties to the government had always been more important than denominational loyalties;[4] and one way to encourage the former was to ensure schools which were neutral in terms of religion, and presumably attractive to citizens of different religious affiliations. Government schools, therefore, could not be like denominational schools on the score of religious instruction.

There were theoretically two ways in which religious neutrality could be attempted in government schools. All direct religious teaching could be excluded from the curriculum and the teacher forbidden to give any religious instruction;[5] alternatively, religious instruction by various denominations could be offered by visiting clerics or by classroom teachers separating and instructing their coreligionists among the children. An agreed syllabus of religious instruction was never a realistic option in the schools until very recently. One type of religious neutrality, involving Christian literature allegedly approved by all Protestant churches in England, was imported into the colony by the Mico Charity schools (1836-1842), but rejected by Roman Catholics. A pervasive idea in the nineteenth century was that if a school taught religion at all, it could not be neutral in the struggle among the churches because true religious instruction was creedal.[6] A teacher of religion in school was expected to be unfriendly, if not hostile, to churches other than his or her own.

Attempting religious neutrality by allowing all teachers to teach their own faith to coreligionists was hindered by the government's education policy in the mid 1800s which had the usual formula of one teacher to each school. Hence in the absence of an agreed syllabus of religious instruction, only one denominational creed could be taught in each school by its sole teacher. It was only towards the later nineteenth century that government schools began regularly to have two or more teachers but even then, unless carefully organized, all these teachers could be from the same denomination (or conversely, not from the same denomination) as the majority of persons in the district in which the school was located. The government, beginning with Harris, chose the type of neutrality, namely prohibition of direct teaching of religion by teachers, which was most consistent with single-teacher schools.

When the government chose this type of religious neutrality in the mid 1800s there were two other important considerations. First, the government intended its schools to be the only type of public primary schools. It was not thinking of giving financial aid to denominational schools; it was not thinking of a dual system, but of an exclusive system of government schools. It was therefore entitled to believe that its neutral schools would be doubly attractive, first on account of the religious formula, and secondly because of the absence of solid competition. Government schools would be like government hospitals or postoffices which did not discriminate according to religion. The second important consideration was that government at the time had a commanding purpose of using the schools to anglicize the population, to spread the English language and English habits; and the prerequisite for such a policy was that children from all the linguistic and cultural sectors must attend government schools. It made no sense to scare off sectors of the population opposed to the religious instruction of the single teacher, and then anglicize the rest of the pupil population. By providing a viable alternative to government schools, the Christian churches made government schools and government policy appear less logical than they were, while increasing the opportunities for more persons to go to school.

Since all denominational schools had to integrate religious instruction into the curriculum, the main question facing the clerical managers until about 1935 was whether or not they were going to allow rival clerics (or laymen acting on their behalf) to enter their schools to give religious instruction to their coreligionists; or whether or not they would allow the benefit of a conscience clause to children who were not of their own faith, even if no rival clerics or laymen visited the school. There is no adequate record of how the churches answered these questions in practice. Between about 1840 and 1869 it appears that denominational schools normally excluded rival clerics and conscience clauses, the latter of which did not exist officially. With exceptions, this policy of exclusion in denominational schools continued well into the twentieth century. After about 1870 denominational schools receiving government grants were expected to confine deliberate religious teaching and worship to a fixed period, usually before the normal day's work began; but this regulation did not address the question of a conscience clause or access by rival clerics. It appears that small variations from the norm of exclusion took place: visits might be allowed if the school was managed by a Protestant cleric who trusted a particular colleague from a rival Protestant denomination. But there was no mention of Roman Catholic priests or Protestant clerics entering each other's schools. This was unthinkable in the religious fury of the 1880s and 1890s.[7] There were clerics who would claim, as Harvey Morton did for the

Canadian Presbyterian Mission, that no Christian pupil would be forced to take any religious instruction to which their parents objected; but this was a different matter from allowing rival clerics to enter the school. But it should be noted that subsequent to the formation of the Hindu/Muslim school at Chaguanas there was a period when Hindu pundits, if personally approved and if from the neighbourhood of Chaguanas, were allowed to enter the Canadian Presbyterian school at Chaguanas.[8] How long this concession lasted, however, is not clear; nor whether or not it was extended to other Canadian Presbyterian schools. In any case there were too few Christian ministers to make effective any policy of religious instruction through visits to schools by clerics. It was unrealistic to assume that children of a faith different from that of the group owning the school could easily, in a one-room school, be accorded the protection of a conscience clause. Once the government began to subsidize denominational schools in a dual system, it laid down a principle from which it never departed, namely, that no child on grounds of religion (or race or colour) should be excluded from any school. It thus delivered children of different religious creeds to denominational schools, but offered their religious beliefs no legal protection until 1933.

Government schools also had problems. Between 1849 and 1869 a few teachers in government (ward) schools ignored the ban on religious instruction and either gave it illegally in the schools, or acted as catechists for clerics on Sundays, possibly instructing some of the same children who attended their day schools.[9] The rules were more strictly enforced after 1870. The problem for government was how to ensure that children in its own schools did get some religious instruction without getting it from the teachers on or off the school premises. The most consistent government policy for a century (1849-1949) was to invite clerics to enter government schools at specified times any day, or on specific days only, to give instruction to their coreligionists. Governor Lord Harris, for instance, insisted that visiting schools was part of the duties for which government paid the clerics. Another strategy was to name a special day of the week – Wednesday afternoon was chosen by Harris – for children from government schools to be sent to neighbouring churches or chapels for religious instruction.[10] The clerics could come to collect them. Also teachers were encouraged to ask pupils for certificates of attendance at religious instruction in their own churches. But all these devices depended on the cooperation of the clerics which was usually lacking because they had their own schools to look after, or were opposed to government schools. After 1870 teachers in government schools tended not even to encourage children to get religious instruction from their churches. The government strategies were all based on the dubious assumption that religious instruction, even in denominational schools, was given mostly by clerics themselves and not by the teachers. But the clerics knew better. The zealous lay teacher has always been – except in schools taught daily by nuns or priests – the great instrument of religious instruction in schools, naturally under the guidance of clerics.

It is well known that in 1869 Patrick Keenan pronounced religious instruction a failure in government schools. A local Roman Catholic layman, José Manuel Farfan, had made the same judgement in 1868.[11] All the Roman Catholic priests would have said the same thing, and some of the Protestant clergymen as well. But it should be clear that the defect which these persons complained of was an absence of Bible knowledge and catechetical knowledge which constituted only one part of religious instruction. Almost any primary school, apart perhaps from a handful of leading Port of Spain schools, which was tested by an outsider for Bible knowledge or knowledge of catechisms in the nineteenth or early twentieth century would have been found deficient. The deficiency would have been greater in government schools. But knowledge of these subjects was unlikely to be more satisfactory in denominational schools. Neither was reading nor arithmetic, for that matter. In the last resort, Bible or catechetical knowledge was a subject affected unfavourably by all the problems which in other subjects reduced the effectiveness of teaching and learning. It is not at all clear that Farfan, Keenan or the local Roman Catholic priests were saying that pupils in government schools were demonstrably less moral or less well-behaved than children in denominational schools. No such evidence was produced. Since government schools never set out to establish denominational loyalties, it makes no sense to judge them by such a yardstick.

There are three points to make: first, the period from 1865 to 1869 was the only point in the history of education when a deliberate assessment of religious instruction by a school survey was made by any expert, local or foreign; secondly, the assessment was only made in respect to the most measurable, immediately obvious, aspect of religious instruction, namely Bible knowledge and knowledge of catechisms; and thirdly no judgement was pronounced on the important matter of character training and morality, which were the great aim as far as government was concerned. It might not be accurate to assume that if Bible knowledge was deficient, then character training and morality were equally lacking in either government or denominational schools.

From the nineteenth century to the 1930s, both government and denominational primary schools were attended predominantly by infants and young children. Leaving aside a few superior urban schools, an average school had many infants, some young children and a few senior boys and girls, some of whom might be aspiring pupil teachers. Even if we allow for a handful of backward troublemakers in the average schools, we do not have a school population likely to be distinguished by severe misdemeanours. Of course this would not exhaust the range of misbehaviour which would be labelled immoral or lacking in good taste. The point though is that there apparently was no crisis of pupil misbehaviour in primary schools from emancipation up to World War II. If there were serious disciplinary problems, the clerics and government officials suppressed them. This would have been strange for clerics who wished to make the point that religious instruction was needed; but it would not be inconceivable, in view of the silence on the existence of flogging in the schools. It is a mistake to believe that government school teachers, unable to give religious instruction, did not support morality and character training; or that books used in government schools in the nineteenth century, the Irish National School Books, were not filled with Christian based moral precepts.[12] In the nineteenth century and at least until the early 1930s religious instruction in the schools was in fact supported by powerful influences outside the schools: parents, families, and the upper class who themselves took church membership and attendance seriously. Clergymen, priests and nuns were highly respected, and the Christian churches were central to public life. In these circumstances – which were not to last forever – religious instruction in all its aspects constituted a vital input into the schools. The output might be debatable, but not the input.

Curiously, between 1868 and the end of the 1920s the policy makers paid remarkably little attention to the question of religious instruction in the primary schools (in contradistinction to rivalries between government schools and denominational schools). In the reorganization of the dual system in 1890 the government ruled that one hour per day should be set aside for religious instruction. The clerics had used the issue of religious instruction to break into the purely government education system in 1870, and to force the creation of a dual system. They subsequently concentrated on providing religious instruction for their own schools rather than in criticizing government schools for not giving any. The churches preferred to get rid of the government schools rather than to reform them. More denominational schools meant more religious instruction. Strangely this most important subject on the curriculum was not subjected to any public assessment. The inspectors of schools, and later the directors of education, bypassed it on the theory that it did not form a part of the regular curriculum. The Roman Catholic Church did make an extra effort in the 1920s and 1930s to organize special classes in religious instruction, including their own examinations.[13] All the churches had Sunday schools. But the point is that we know very little about the state of religious instruction in denominational schools except that it was going on, and that it had powerful support in the society at large.

A serious challenge to Christian religious instruction surfaced in the twentieth century when Hindu and Muslim leaders demanded protection for Indian children from the christianizing intentions of the Canadian Presbyterian missionaries. Part of the answer to this protest, provided by the Marriott/Mayhew Report, was to have a formal conscience clause built into the education laws. A conscience clause was included in the Education Ordinance of 1933: nothing like it had existed previously in the colony. For the first time parents had the legal right to have their children exempted from religious instruction in any primary school. That such a regulation went into the education laws without any controversy at a time when other aspects of this law were being vigorously challenged is a matter of surprise. A further restriction on the internal management of denominational schools was required to regulate the implementation of such a conscience clause: religious instruction had to be confined to an hour before or after school, as was done in government schools when clerics visited. It should be noted, though, that it was only Bible knowledge, catechisms and worship which were being restricted in this way. Character training and morality, as well as denominational loyalty, could not be so confined. About a decade later Roman Catholic Archbishop Finbar Ryan stated that Roman Catholics never liked having religious instruction confined to periods before or after the day's work, and had only tolerated it.[14] However, it was not until 1949, after an increase in crime among youths, that the government reversed its century-old policy of excluding religious instruction completely from government schools (1849-1890), or from the official curriculum of government and assisted denominational schools (1890-1949).

The exclusion or restriction of religious instruction in government primary schools was generally repeated at the level of the only government secondary school, QRC, and at the Government Training College. No religious instruction was formally given at either. QRC, however, in the late 1920s, had a brief and apparently informal phase of religious instruction in which certain Protestant clerics visited the college. No government schools had boarders[15] since it was widely agreed that no school could take them without provision for their religious instruction, preferably on the same premises. When the government training school at Tranquillity became partly residential in the early twentieth century, the few students were encouraged to repair to their own churches. After the government training school moved to St Vincent Street, the Anglican teacher trainees lived at an Anglican hostel where religious instruction was inescapable. The idea that teachers in training should ideally be in residence sprang from the need to encourage the three aspects of religious instruction in those who were expected to impart them to children: Bible knowledge, denominational loyalty and particularly, character training and morality. The denominational secondary schools and training colleges have always integrated religious instruction into their curriculum with great freedom arising from the total absence of government regulation up to the 1950s. There was no conscience clause. However, in denominational secondary schools, the convention might have been in some cases less intolerant than at first sight; but at the level of the denominational training colleges there was no compromise. At Naparima Training College the trainee teachers had no choice but to conduct the neighbouring Sunday schools of the Canadian Presbyterian Church.[16]

The English Language and Education 1834-1939

After emancipation the early concern of the colonial government to establish a government policy in education sprang from a desire to combat the strong social position of the French creoles and the Roman Catholic Church. Soon after the English captured the island in 1797 there began a movement to anglicize its institutions. Throughout the nineteenth century a French derived Creole (hereafter called Creole) was the most widely spoken language. Until perhaps the late nineteenth century African immigrants and their close relatives spoke African languages and Indians born in India spoke chiefly Hindi and its variants.[17] However, the two major languages of the upper class were English and French; and the struggle to establish the English language as the premier language was first and foremost a struggle against French and Creole. The French creoles were socially the most powerful group before the arrival of the English; the important Spanish families had learnt to speak French and, less often, the French creoles had learnt Spanish. Spanish civil and criminal laws prevailed generally until the 1840s, thus reserving a place of importance for Spanish in the judicial system of the country.[18] French creoles who did not like the spread of the English language or customs found themselves defending the continuation of the French language and Spanish laws in a British colony.

At the insistence of Charles Warner and Governor McLeod, the colonial government declared itself in favour of two basic positions in education which were maintained for about a century: religiously neutral government schools and a non-negotiable monopoly for the English language as the vehicle of teaching in all schools aided by the government. As Governor McLeod wrote to the British government in 1841:

> The difference of language and religion make it more imperative that the system to be adopted should be one under the control of the government, not only with the view to make it accessible to all parties and creeds, but to cause the language spoken to be that of the country to which the colony belongs. [19]

Attempts to encourage Roman Catholic schools to use the English language began in the mid 1830s, but the first schools which unequivocally used it were the government (ward) schools of the period 1849 to 1870.[20] In many cases, the teachers of these schools had themselves to learn it. One of them, J. J. Thomas, wrote a learned treatise on Creole, which he spoke, but he also mastered English.[21] It is important to understand that the battle for the English language was not simply a fight to replace another language: it was *ipso facto* a pro-English culture policy. Warner, McLeod and their opponents understood this clearly. The attempt to give the English language ascendancy was only a part of a wider policy of deliberate anglicization.

As might be expected, there were considerable difficulties in teaching English to children whose home language was something else: Creole (French based or

English based), French, Spanish, Hindi, or possibly an African language. In several localities children came to the government schools not knowing a word of English, but the only language the teachers were allowed to use was English. Alexander Anderson, the English inspector of schools, wrote in 1859 that the French derived Creole was "undoubtedly susceptible of definite grammatical arrangement and expressed with ease and accuracy the ordinary everyday ideas of life".[22] Obviously he regarded it as an inferior language which was defective as a vehicle for serious thought or formal education. Faced with the difficulty of explaining lessons, it cannot be safely assumed that ward school teachers never turned to whatever language might aid comprehension; but such practices were unofficial and an infringement of regulations.

The first person of importance to suggest a different policy was Patrick Keenan in 1869. Keenan refused to see the colony as a community in which English alone should be spoken. He accepted the desirability of making English the official language, the language which all should speak and understand; and he disregarded Creole. French-speaking and Spanish-speaking children should first be taught to read their home language; afterwards they should be taught English. Since Keenan took the same position outside Trinidad in respect to vernacular languages in places controlled by Britain, we might conclude that his position was a pedagogical one and not skillfully manufactured to please the Roman Catholic French creoles. He understood the imperial necessity to make English the official language of the entire British empire.[23]

The largest number of schools in the island in the mid nineteenth century were private (including denominational) schools of various types and levels. They were completely free to teach in whatever languages they desired; if they followed market demands Spanish and French would have been important teaching languages as well as English. With respect to language policy the government's concern was chiefly with the denominational primary schools and the private Roman Catholic secondary schools (then St Joseph's Convent, St George's College and later CIC). These Roman Catholic secondary institutions were undisguisedly French in very important ways, up to the end of the nineteenth century at least: their teaching staff was predominantly French; they were organized on French models for most of the nineteenth century; French was the sole teaching language at St Joseph's Convent, while it shared the classroom with English and Spanish at St George's and CIC.

In 1869 CIC was a trilingual school, with French as the primary language.[24] The most important course was the classical course with a concentration of French-speaking students and staff. Keenan came in 1869 with an impossible reformist formula for CIC: he wished to make the college more English without being less French! He pictured the Roman Catholic staff as caught delicately and unexpectedly in a situation from which they too hoped to escape by the same formula. The sensible direction chosen by CIC, after it became a government aided school sitting the Cambridge external examinations like QRC, was to become less and less French, and more and more English.[25] Fr Anthony De Verteuil has argued convincingly that the key personnel on the staff of CIC who effected the transition to the use of the English language were Irish priests, especially Fr James Browne (1864-1892), Fr Nicholas Brennan (1894-1895) and Fr Carroll (1896-1903).[26]

From 1876 on, every Education Code proclaimed a monopoly for English as a teaching language; the only exception was the use of Hindi in the special Indian schools of the Canadian Presbyterian Mission. The policy of these missionaries was to learn Hindi themselves and to translate hymns into Hindi. Religious reading matter already translated into Hindi was also imported from India for use in churches and schools. Teachers and catechists were encouraged and assisted to become bilingual. Depending on the language skills of the children the teaching was either in Hindi or in English; but the use of Hindi was only a device to attract pupils. Its use on pedagogical grounds, though recognized, apparently won less acknowledgement from the missionaries than its ability to draw into the circle of the Mission pupils who would otherwise have stayed away. The intention was always to teach the English language as soon as possible and to spread English habits. Although Hindi was put on the curriculum of the government training school and made obligatory for teachers of Indian schools, almost all of whom were trained by the Canadian Presbyterian Church, there is reason to doubt that Hindi was regularly taught, if taught at all, at the government training school in the late nineteenth century.

In approving the use of Hindi in these schools the colonial government recognized that the Indians posed a special problem. The obligation of teachers of special Indian schools to know Hindi was not the same as an obligation to teach it. It might be that the reason for officially allowing Hindi in these schools was that the Canadian Presbyterian missionaries wanted the freedom to employ it whenever they deemed fit. Also, for the greater part of the nineteenth century, the colonial government had not yet accepted the idea that Indians would become a permanent addition to the island's population. Hence Hindi was permissible. There came an indeterminable point though, probably towards the very end of the nineteenth century, when the colonial government began to doubt that there was a case for special Indian schools or for the encouragement of Hindi.

Towards the end of his administration as inspector of schools in 1890, Lechmere Guppy claimed that one of his accomplishments was to have secured, through the schools, a greater use of the English language. He had recognized Creole as an obstacle to learning in the schools; his remedy was to discourage teachers from using it and to call the attention of teachers to the need to teach reading and dictation in English.[27] In their examination papers the teachers themselves displayed faults related to the pervasiveness of Creole. In the 1880s and 1890s, whatever progress was made in the spread of English, observers were more aware of the prevalence of Creole than of the new users of English. There is some indication that Creole might have become a focal point for a measure of creole pride against English, the language of the rulers. In the eyes of the black and coloured intelligentsia J. J. Thomas' book, the *Theory and Practice of Creole Grammar*, published in 1869, might have given Creole a measure of dignity which it had previously lacked. The editor of the *San Fernando Gazette* in November 1893 commented:

> The Creole language will continue to be that of the mass of the people for centuries to come. The young people generally speak English, that is to say they can make themselves understood, but the language spoken by them at home is Creole. There is no appearance of any diminution in the general use of the language, and we hope there will never be any.[28]

This was a curiously contradictory statement which acknowledged the spread of English among young people, yet expected that Creole would be spoken for centuries to come. This turned out to be a false prognosis. Yet it could not have been obvious in the early 1890s that a drastic shift in the language situation would have taken place within the next forty years. In 1888 the evidence presented before the Franchise Commission had shown the widespread use of Creole among working class people, apparently strengthening the argument that education had made little progress.[29] It must be remembered that not all users of Creole understood French. The pervasiveness of Creole did not mean the pervasiveness of French, but socially and culturally the two sustained each other. That is, if all the speakers of Creole were removed, the speakers of French would be socially and culturally more isolated, and therefore more open to successful competition from the English language; and if the French creoles stopped using French publicly, the lower class users of Creole would also feel more socially and culturally isolated.

Some events outside education in the 1880s and 1890s had an eventual impact on the balance of languages in the society. The unification of Tobago and Trinidad brought hundreds and later thousands of Tobagonians, who spoke either English or an English derived Creole, into Trinidad in search of employment. It is known that thousands of Barbadians settled in Trinidad in the 1880s and 1890s; they knew no Creole, often to their own undoing.[30] The immigration of Barbadians and other English speaking or English Creole-speaking West Indian migrants into the towns, especially Port of Spain, made a serious contribution to the increased use of the English language.

A development of tremendous importance was the conversion of CIC and St Joseph's Convent into English-speaking schools integrated into the Cambridge external examination system. The increasing ability of CIC to compete successfully with QRC for the university scholarships by the mid 1890s was an indicator of the gradual transformation of the college during the previous twenty years. In the 1890s St Joseph's Convent set about anglicizing its curriculum, a process associated with Mother Milburge Walton, its principal from 1894 to 1919.[31] As in the case of CIC the process was assisted by Irish Sisters of St Joseph of Cluny who were English speakers.[32] French-speaking boys and girls had great difficulty when instructed in English and Fr Lemir, the French principal of CIC between 1892 and 1894, used this to explain why some CIC winners of university scholarships got only third class passes in Cambridge School Certificate. Amazingly, in 1894 Fr Lemir could claim for his college a major role in spreading the English language. In fact, Lemir implied that CIC was a greater contributor to the spread of English than QRC because the latter's students came predominantly from families which already spoke English, while CIC educated the children of the French and Spanish speakers.[33]

The readiness of the Roman Catholic hierarchy of the later nineteenth century, particularly Irish born Archbishop Flood (1887-1907), to cooperate with the official policy of spreading the English language must be taken seriously. According to one historian of the Roman Catholic Church, Flood's total commitment to the use of the English language by all sectors of the Church won him favour from British officials who controlled the government, although not without submerged resistance from some of his French clergy and laymen. The Roman Catholic Church, especially in the later nineteenth century, experienced a double transition which produced tension and disagreement within it: the replacement of French priests and French influence with Irish priests and English influence and, consequently, the substitution of the English language for French.[34]

Since the days of Governor Arthur Gordon the colonial government had abandoned the relentless pursuit of anglicization at the expense of the French creoles and the Roman Catholic Church, which had characterized the leadership of Charles Warner since the late 1830s. But institutionally the tide had already turned in favour of anglicization, thus allowing later governors the luxury of a low profile path to the same goal. The leading French creoles, without any change in their dislike for English officialdom, did not openly resist the spread of the English language in the later nineteenth century. They had gained a greater share of government offices and greater participation in the Legislative Council, plus recognition of the social importance of the Roman Catholic Church and its hierarchy. The imperial necessity to promote English was conceded. A sort of auto-anglicization of educational and religious institutions replaced the government propelled anglicization of the early post-emancipation period.

The acceptance of English as the official language, its use in the schools, the migration of West Indians from other islands into Trinidad – persons who were users of English or of English Creoles – all played some part in the resolution of the language competition to the advantage of English. The contribution of the schools must be taken in combination with certain intergenerational changes.[35] In the early twentieth century the accumulative result of nonreplacement of deceased elderly Creole speakers by young, new speakers became more telling. Older members of French creole families and their domestic servants, a great reservoir of Creole eloquence, died without replacement. In some cases elite bilingual French creoles did not bother to teach their children French.[36] Creole and French withered away together. The younger sons and daughters of elite French creoles had been taught English at CIC, St Joseph's Convent or in schools abroad; migrants into the oil belt carried English to match Hindi or Creole speakers.[37] As for the majority of working class Spanish speakers, from the nineteenth century they had been isolated in the northern cocoa growing valleys. The wealthy Spanish speakers, the Venezuelan refugees or merchants, were without political influence. African languages had all disappeared except for a handful of users who preserved elements particularly in worship and recreation. By the early 1930s persons high in the education hierarchy, for example Director Marriott and C. Bradshaw, a language master at QRC, were predicting the demise of Creole. In 1933 Bradshaw said that in twenty-five years no one in Trinidad would understand a word of Creole. He was nearly right.[38]

A potentially serious challenge to the spread of the English language was the bid of certain Hindus and Muslims from the late 1920s to have their own Hindi and Urdu-speaking schools; but this threat never seriously materialized even after Hindu and Muslim schools became a reality. It remains a matter of uncertainty how much Hindi was taught in these schools from the 1950s. A language census of the country was never made at any time. A recent researcher has estimated that there were less than a thousand Spanish speakers in the late 1960s.[39] What seems clear is that since the 1860s there has been no serious resistance to the use of English as the official language. Not even the proponents of Hindi can be said to have set their face against English. The logic of the ascendancy of English over other languages prevailed in a British colony where all sectors of the people, of whatever race or colour, professed great loyalty to the Crown. By the start of the twentieth century the weight of the British imperial connection for more than a hundred years was the superordinate explanation of the victory of the English language and the prestige of English culture.

The triumph of the English language was something in the nature of a pyrrhic victory. The masses, though weaned from Creole, have never been won for standard English. An English derived Creole has replaced Creole as the language of the majority; but the language situation is even more complex as there are various gradations of the English Creole. It has become quite common today to complain of the poor performance of school children in oral and written English; the problems are deep-seated and longstanding.

Women and Education 1834-1939

We are concerned here with women primarily as schoolgirls and as female teachers. Before the 1870s there is little evidence of gender identification of pupils in the primary schools and, for the most part, when such an identification was made, no special significance was attached to the observation. In the absence of figures, it is not possible to say to what extent, if any, there was an underrepresentation or overrepresentation of either sex. The probable pattern then was that more boys were enrolled in public coeducational primary schools, but it was never suggested by the clerical organizers of schools or by the government in the nineteenth century that either sex was preferable as pupils. The strong religious motivation behind the provision of schooling was not itself gender specific. However, since both in Africa and in England more importance was traditionally attached to the education of boys, it might be assumed that this prejudice in favour of boys as pupils informed the thinking of local educators and parents in Trinidad. It is likely that in the 1830s, as in the 1930s, parents valued the education of boys more than that of girls because of the greater probability of future gain from employment; it is also likely in the 1830s, as in the 1930s and subsequently, that the superior value of young girls as domestic assistants reduced their chances of being sent to school as regularly as their brothers.

The Roman Catholic Church had a traditional preference for single-sex schools even at the primary school level. The West Indies had been notorious for sexual immorality during slavery and the case against coeducational schools, especially those with adolescent girls, seemed too obvious to warrant repeated statements. But the shortage of resources after emancipation made it impossible to establish single-sex schools as the general rule, even for Roman Catholics.[40] In the 1830s there may have been a little known, probably unused, Spanish law against coeducational schools; the Mico Charity leadership certainly seemed worried about it and on one occasion asked Lieutenant Governor Hill to supply details.[41] No further mention was made of it, however.

Far more was written about female teachers than about schoolgirls in the immediate post-emancipation years. Gender differentiation was stronger at the level of teachers than the taught. The presence of girls in the primary schools guaranteed a place for female teachers who were recognized as having a particular role to play, although its nature was seldom explicitly stated; it is assumed that female teachers were seen as protectors of schoolgirls against male teachers or grown boys in coeducational schools. Far more explicit was the role of female teachers in the instruction of infants, and because a high proportion of pupils of both sexes were infants, female teachers were particularly useful. Apart from their usefulness as guardians of girls and surrogate mothers of infants, female teachers had a special value which they retained up to the late 1940s: they were usually paid at a cheaper rate than men even when they had similar or superior qualifications. This was not always true, however, when we consider white expatriate female teachers against non-white teachers; in these instances, racism often wiped out the normal male advantage over females. However, a white female teacher who was a mere assistant to her teacher husband, perhaps in charge of infants, could receive a salary lower than a non-white male headteacher.

It is important to understand that teaching in primary schools, like the preaching of the gospel, first developed essentially as a male occupation. The main successors to the European missionaries or priests who taught the slaves Christianity (or failed to teach them) were black or coloured laymen with a missionary frame of mind, who were in some cases on a career path from teaching to preaching. The proper education of children was sometimes conceived as requiring the administration of corporal punishment, more fittingly delivered by males than females. But there were always contradictions in the social expectations of clerical school managers and government officials which gradually made female teachers as necessary as male teachers; children needed not only flogging, but a measure of maternal guidance: grown boys needed a headmaster who could drive fear into their hearts, but infants needed surrogate mothers. Also, the expansion of education in the post-emancipation era which created new jobs for male teachers was done in a spirit of economy which increased the value of cheaper female assistant teachers. In short, there was a decided place for female teachers, but generally it was a place of strict subordination to men as school managers, headteachers, inspectors of schools and members of the Board of Education. No one would have thought otherwise in the nineteenth century.

It follows that female teachers as well as male teachers needed training. The Mico Charity training school took male and female trainees in the 1830s, and from the start the efforts of the government involved both. Hence the government training school, organized in the 1850s, had two branches, of unequal importance and on separate sites: one for males and the other for females, each with an associated model school. Since females were not expected to outnumber males in the public primary schools, the female training establishment was always smaller. However, it is worth remembering that between the 1850s and the 1870s the number of trainees of both sexes rarely rose above twelve.

When the government adopted a secular system of government schools, the denominational primary schools outside this system did not look to the government training school for their trained teachers. Nor did the churches have any teacher training facilities of their own at that time. The point is that the graduates of the government training school were expected to find employment in government schools. Their slow growth, turning soon into stagnation, posed a particular hardship for female teacher trainees. They had little or no prospect of jobs in government schools. A chance development in 1860 was seen as the possible dawn of a new day for female teachers: because the ward of St Ann was poor it could only afford a female teacher, and so a young woman left the training school to become the first 'headmistress' of a government school.[42] This encouraging start was not to continue. A more promising opening was the abandonment of the formula of one teacher to each school, in favour of two or three teachers depending on the number of pupils. This policy meant jobs for female assistant teachers and this was their primary role up to World War II.

We know nothing in terms of gender differentiation about the unpaid monitors and the lowly paid pupil teachers, whose rise from the 1830s resulted from new opportunities in teaching for young, poorly qualified persons, themselves under instruction in the schools. Monitors and pupil teachers might be male or female; since most of them did not pass into the ranks of the adult teachers, still less the trained adult teachers, it might be a mistake to assume that the predominance of males among the adult teachers was replicated among the monitors and pupil teachers. There could have been more females.

The ideal of the single-sex school has always been more powerfully expressed in Trinidad at the level of secondary institutions. The Roman Catholics began with St Joseph's Convent in Port of Spain for fee-paying girls, and soon followed with St George's College for fee-paying boys, later replaced by CIC also exclusively for boys. It was not until the establishment of Bishop's High School in Tobago in 1925 that the colony got its first coeducational secondary school; but that was in Tobago which was not quite like Trinidad. However, it should be noted that the private secondary schools from the early twentieth century broke with the tradition of single-sex secondary schools, though they sometimes appeared to enrol more girls than boys.

For the entire nineteenth century and beyond, St Joseph's Convent was the premier girls' school in the island. Next in reputation was the Girls' Model School. Although it was the largest primary school in the 1860s, this model school was not, strictly speaking, an 'Intermediate school', only a superior primary school. It was a school for middle class girls; St Joseph's Convent was for upper class girls, mostly of French creole extraction. But what were women to be educated to do? Thousands of females were employed as labourers in and outside agriculture, but schooling ignored this reality except in so far as religious instruction prepared people to accept a life of hard work. The most respectable public career for women in the nineteenth century was teaching, and we have already suggested that this was not very promising. Apart from white expatriate female teachers, it appears that teaching was for spinsters. It is easy to forget that the nuns of St Joseph's Convent were the best qualified female teachers; in fact they belonged to an Order (St Joseph de Cluny) which specialized in teaching. Nevertheless, nuns had to be nuns first and teachers afterwards and only a few chosen local girls could hope to get into teaching by this route. The ideal career for women was the unpaid private career of mother and wife. To be a virtuous, skillful mother and wife was the highest ideal of womanhood.

The nuns at St Joseph's Convent believed that they had perfected the means of coming close to their ideal of womanhood. In 1936 a Roman Catholic priest, a former principal of CIC, wrote of St Joseph's Convent:

> ... though absolutely speaking the intellect takes precedence of the will, in our actual world it is the will, properly directed, which makes the true man or woman; hence, the radical importance of will training, of character-formation. We should endeavour to fashion not merely savants, but saints ... [43]

The leadership at St Joseph's Convent between 1836 and the 1870s would easily have accepted this objective. The aim to produce good wives and mothers, fit companions for respectable men of the upper class, was reflected in its curriculum in the 1860s. This included "reading, writing, arithmetic, history and geography, the English and French languages, composition, the rules of good taste, and polite literature, music, needlework, embroidery, etc."[44] French was the academic strongpoint of the school for nearly a century; to produce saintly girls compulsory religious instruction and exercises were abundant; discipline was strict; morality was emphasized at every turn. No illegitimate girls could enter the school. Men, even close relatives, were kept at a distance or under strict surveillance once inside the school gate.[45] In fact, only parents could see their daughters without the presence of a nun. A handful of worthy candidates were allowed to take the veil, although the girls (all boarders) were in some respects made to behave as if they were all intending to be nuns.[46]

The insensitivity to gender identification which characterized the education authorities in the first forty years after emancipation continued into the later nineteenth and early twentieth centuries. After the inauguration of the dual system all government schools with girls were required to have a female assistant teacher; needlework – the first kind of 'women's work' introduced into the schools – was added to the curriculum, and taken by almost all the girls, though it was not compulsory. Inspector Guppy backed the development of infant teaching methods in the schools. The presence of girls, infants and needlework, ensured the place of female teachers in the schools. Although the proportion of female teachers increased dramatically both in the schools and in the government training school in the 1880s and 1890s, female teachers were not yet in a majority except in the category of assistant teachers.[47] In the government training school the proportion of females rose and in 1879, apparently for the first time, more females than males took the Teachers' Certificate Examination.[48] This superiority was only slight, but it continued up to at least 1917.

The pattern was for females to be assistant teachers and a male the headteacher; the few female teachers who were headteachers (32 out of 237 in 1902 or 13.5%), or more commonly heads of infant departments, tended to be better qualified than male headteachers. A woman had few chances of becoming headteacher or head of department if she did not have the Teachers' Certificate. On the whole, the churches were slow to promote females. The Canadian Presbyterian Church, in particular, did not offer a headteacher's position to a woman until the 1960s. As usual, and as in England, women were less well paid than men; but the salary gap was narrower among the assistant teachers than among the headteachers. The firmer position of females in government schools was due to rules about needlework which did not apply to denominational schools. More female assistant teachers did appear in denominational schools in the later nineteenth century, and this was reflected in the formation of two new training schools for them: the Roman Catholic Female Training School in Port of Spain, and later the female teacher training department of Naparima Training College.

The smaller number of girls in the primary schools did not cause any alarm among government officials except in schools for Indians. It was only in Roman Catholic schools that girls were more numerous than boys, and this strange situation was probably due to the fact that these schools were in Port of Spain, San Fernando or rural towns. They were essentially urban or semi-urban schools. Port of Spain was where female education most prospered. Ambitious black and coloured middle class parents – as well as the respectable working class – sent their girls to school in Port of Spain. The Girl Model School was perennially well attended, and from the early twentieth century it attracted willing recruits to its unofficial secondary education programme in its so-called Higher Class. The relative unwillingness of Indian parents to send their daughters to school was noted and regretted by educators, but no corrective action was undertaken by the government. This was seen as the business mainly of the Canadian Presbyterian missionaries.

Despite the underrepresentation of Indian girls in primary schools, this was not the level at which the conviction grew that female education posed a problem. It was first conceived as a problem of female secondary education, and it remained so up to at least the early 1960s. The Canadian Presbyterian missionaries, and less so the inspector of schools and some concerned Indian parents, expressed dissatisfaction with the low attendance of Indian girls in the primary schools. The wives of the missionaries took remedial action in special homes for some Indian girls.[49] The Indian population was regarded as a culturally intractable minority by the dominant English and French creoles, by government officials, and by the black and coloured middle class who shared the cultural perspectives of the dominant whites.[50] Their attitudes were informed by considerations both of class and race: if they cared little for Indians, they probably cared only slightly more for working class children. Still, in the later 1800s and early 1900s a few less illiberal persons from among these groups began to perceive that there was a secondary school deficit for girls.

Religious rivalries helped to sharpen the perception of a shortage of secondary schools for girls in the 1890s and onwards. The only secondary school for girls – other than strictly private efforts by individual teachers – was St Joseph's Convent. Hence Protestant parents lacked a reputable secondary school for their daughters. An Englishwoman, Miss Buncle who conducted a private school for girls in Port of Spain, stirred ripples by boldly applying in 1895 for affiliation to QRC. In other words, she wished for government recognition, aid and permission to send up girls for Cambridge examinations, and presumably, university scholarships. The Roman Catholic supporters of CIC were flabbergasted.[51] The male education administrators were also astonished; the College Council, which dealt with matters concerning government aided secondary schools, turned down the proposal; so too the Legislative Council. The Roman Catholic editor of the *Catholic News* opined that scholarships to girls would be of "no real advantage in life and of no use for the good of the colony".[52] The new editor of the *San Fernando Gazette* looked at Buncle's application from another angle: she kept a racially exclusive school and was therefore not entitled to assistance from the taxpayers. Nor could the editor, like other leading males, see any serious role in the economy or society for women, beyond that of "good wives and excellent mothers".[53]

The question of affiliation for this secondary school also involved thorny issues of religious rivalry. It attracted Protestant girls. It was obvious that the still unaided St Joseph's Convent would have to be taken into account in any upgrading of the provision for female secondary education. George Goodville was a Scottish member of the Legislative Council, a fierce defender of government schools, who tried vainly to persuade the government to subsidize female secondary schools, either those existing or new ones to be formed.[54] The government's answer was that it was already spending too much money on secondary education for boys. It looked to private citizens to endow female secondary schools, or at least to parents to pay for their daughters' education.

In 1911 the headmistress of the Girls' Model School, Miss Bushe, without prior permission from the Board of Education, organized what come to be known as the Higher Class at the school. It consisted of older girls attempting the Cambridge Preliminary and Junior Cambridge examinations. The experiment proved very successful. Numbers grew; certificates were won. This section of the school at first was self-supporting; by 1920 it had to be transferred to larger accommodation in the old Prince's Building in the 'Little Savannah'. The formula was that the government paid the salaries of four female teachers (as primary school teachers), with all the fees from the Higher Class which exceeded the extra costs going into the Treasury: the government had thus begun indirectly to subsidize female secondary education. Partly for this reason, St Joseph's Convent decided to seek government financial assistance.[55]

It is quite clear that support for secondary education of girls grew significantly in the early decades of the twentieth century. The same thing could be said of education in England; it was not unusual for metropolitan directions in education to be reflected in the thinking of local educators. Trinidad and Tobago's dynamic was an inflation in educational requirements for certain jobs. Also the black and coloured middle class groups created partly by the educational opportunities for men in the later nineteenth century were part of the pool of anxious fathers wishing education of a secondary type for both sons and daughters. Middle class migrants of all colours from the smaller islands in the later nineteenth century would be in the same position, as well as English creole families who did not have funds to send their daughters to Barbados or England. By the end of the nineteenth century there were Indian families sufficiently established to pay for their daughters' higher education, although in the mid-1920s Naparima Girls' High School was still hobbled by some Indian parents' refusals to keep girls in school beyond the middle forms.[56]

It was not the Roman Catholics (who already had St Joseph's Convent) who responded to the new situation: it was the Church of England clergy, and other Protestant churches, such as the Canadian Presbyterian Church. After the battle with the Roman Catholic clergy to establish QRC as a viable government institution, it was unlikely that the government would attempt to establish a female counterpart. Secondary education for girls had to be carried forward by the Protestant churches. If the leaders of the Canadian Presbyterian Church and the Church of England had been asked why they spearheaded female secondary education in the early decades of the twentieth century, they would not have confessed any desire to promote careers for women; they did not want to increase the number of secretaries or nurses, or even teachers, though of course, these careers did benefit. There were no manpower training motives in their promotion of female secondary education. The rationale, as in the nineteenth century, was to produce good wives and mothers and, of course, to increase the support for their particular church among the influential classes. The promoters of female secondary education acknowledged that there was a social demand for it; if the Protestants had not satisfied it, some of their daughters would have been obliged to seek entry into Roman Catholic St Joseph's Convent or to continue the trek to Barbados.

Women played a greater part than is at first apparent in the new concern for female education: Miss Buncle wanted to send up her girls for the prestigious Cambridge external examinations; Miss Bushe developed the Higher Class at Tranquillity; and a recent historian of the Presbyterian Church has noted that the extraordinary concern for Indian female education, both primary and secondary, at the start of the twentieth century was really the work (as in the later nineteenth century) of Canadian female teachers, not the male missionaries.[57] The remarkable educational leadership of the Church of England's Bishop Anstey might seem to negate this thesis, but even in his case there were female supporters in the background: Mrs Stollmeyer who ran fund-raising campaigns; Audrey Jeffers who offered to supervise female boarders; also wives of certain Port of Spain Protestant businessmen. The social subordination of women prevented any of these ladies from emerging into positions of independent leadership in these enterprises on behalf of female schools. The actions of these female supporters of girls' education should be taken as indications of a growing consciousness of the importance of women.[58]

The three new institutions which carried forward female secondary education in the early twentieth century were Naparima Girls' High School, Bishop Anstey High School and Bishop's High School in Tobago. By 1939 these three colleges had about three hundred girls without any falling off in attendance at St Joseph's

Convent. It is unfortunate that we have no detailed breakdown of the social and economic background of these girls; nor do we know much about the proportions of black, coloured or white children in attendance. Broadly, they were from the middle and upper classes; possibly there were more coloured than white girls in these new institutions; black girls, we might safely guess, would have been in the minority, except at Bishop's High School in Tobago. These colleges were racially mixed, though few, if any, Indians might have been at the two Bishops' schools. In respect of Naparima Girls' High School, there were some unusual considerations not to be missed. This college, so overwhelmingly associated with Indian girls, had a longer gestation period before government recognition and aid than either of the others. A notable aspect of its prerecognition history between 1912 and 1925 was that Indian girls constituted a decided minority. In 1920 there were only three Indian girls of a total of sixty girls. Secondary education of girls was a very radical concept for Indian parents, even those born in Trinidad. This college did not have from the start the same highly Indian imprint as Naparima College for boys.[59]

It is not unusual for parents to have different motives from the clerical promoters of schools. If advancing women's careers was not the clerics' objective, it should not be assumed that parents had no such ambitions. There were, in the 1920s and 1930s, relatively new areas of work for women and the development of these fields is still largely unresearched.[60] Firstly, there was the increasing feminization of commercial studies, possibly spurred on by the adoption of the typewriter as an office machine. It is easy now to forget that commercial studies were once the domain of males. Then there was nursing as a career for women. New openings occurred in the 1930s, even for a few Indian girls.[61] Elected members of the Legislative Council in the late 1920s and 1930s thought there were non-white nurses in need of protection, especially from expatriate female head nurses.[62] New opportunities as secretaries and nurses partly explained the social demand for secondary education of girls.

The opening of new secondary schools for girls enabled the education administrators to begin to offer a few scholarships to bright girls from primary schools. Female winners of scholarships came on centre stage in the second half of the 1920s. In 1926 two girls created history as the first winners of prestigious College Exhibitions in competition with boys; and in 1929 a girl topped this examination for the first time. By the end of the 1920s girls were not only winning, but forming regularly 50 percent of the candidates for the College Exhibitions. It was impossible for female exhibitioners to go on to win university scholarships as the girls' colleges did not prepare students for the Oxford and Cambridge Higher Schools examinations on which these scholarships were based. Indeed, even as old a college as St Joseph's Convent made a weak start with this examination only in the early 1930s.

One graduate of St Joseph's Convent who did not stay there long enough to try for the Cambridge Higher School Certificate was Mona Rigsby. Born in 1918 the daughter of a solicitor and conveyancer, Mona Rigsby passed Cambridge School Certificate at fifteen years of age, and the London University Matriculation Examination in 1935, at age seventeen. She was sent to England to study law where she graduated in 1939, and returned to Trinidad to have the honour of being the youngest female lawyer in the colony.[63] She was black. She was not the first female lawyer, however, as Gladys Ramsaran, an Indian, appears to have been the first in 1931.[64]

It is unfortunate that the lack of gender identification in the statistics for the total teaching force of the primary schools or for pupil teachers and monitors does not allow us to analyse properly the progress of women as teachers. In the training colleges in the early and mid 1920s, the difference between the number of male and female trainee teachers was not great, but it widened in favour of males in the later 1920s through to the 1930s. Except for 1927 the males, however, were never as many as twice the number of females, even when the unofficial students were included (see Table 4.1). The academic performance of students in the training colleges and in the Teachers' Certificate Examinations varied, but without evidence that either sex consistently did better than the other. Despite the strong presence of females in the classroom, teaching was still a male dominated occupation at most levels excluding private schools and girls' secondary schools. In the 1920s when a handful of non-white male headteachers were being advanced (temporarily) to the rank of assistant inspectors, nothing similar happened to the non-white female teachers. In fact, only one female teacher ever acted as assistant inspector in the 1920s: she was Miss Hilda Bushe, the white headteacher of the Girls' Model School. Nor were there any females on the Board of Education until 1930 when Mrs Masson, who was not a teacher, was given a seat.[65] These two women were the first females in the top hierarchy of education.

It is fairly well known that World War II provided female teachers with new opportunities to tighten their hold on the profession. The need for more teachers resulted from rapid population increases, arising partly from immigration from the smaller eastern Caribbean islands. Primary school enrolment grew rapidly during and after the war; the government was taking the objective of universal compulsory primary education more seriously than it had before. Many of the new teachers were women. Even some married females who had been forced to retire because of the rules were recalled temporarily to fill difficult rural slots. Female teachers were then nearly 50 percent of the total teaching force of the primary schools: in 1945 there were 1,435 males and 1,329 women; and in 1949 there were 1,574 male and 1,489 female teachers. This high proportion of female teachers was maintained until the late 1950s when the number of females exceeded males for the first time, and stayed ahead.[66] The oil boom of the 1970s provided men with more remunerative employment outside the schoolroom and consolidated the ascendancy of female primary school teachers.

World War II also stimulated new thinking about the role of women in society, and certain constitutional changes towards the end of the war increased the influence of elected politicians who tended to be more sympathetic than Crown Colony government officials to the cause of women. Two grievances in particular needed to be redressed: equal pay for women and the right of married women to stay in the teaching service without loss of status or pay. Lower pay for women dated from at least the immediate post-emancipation era. In the upward regrading of primary school teachers after World War I, Dr George Masson, a coloured member of the Board of Education, and Emanuel Lazare, a black unofficial member of the Legislative Council, made unsuccessful pleas for equal pay for female teachers.[67] The Board of Education was also in favour of equal pay for women, but the Legislative Council was not so disposed.

The expulsion of married women from the teaching service was decreed by the Education Code of 1921, but the practice might have existed previously. It certainly was done in England. In the infamous Code of 1935 drafted by Cutteridge the rule against married teachers was restated. The male dominated *Teachers Journal* never fought this injustice. The same can be said about the issue of equal pay. Another great injustice was the loss of pension rights and gratuity by female teachers forced out of the service on marriage. The only argument explicitly used by the director of education for this treatment of married women teachers was that the same thing was done in England.[68] However, two female assistant teachers giving evidence before the Education Commission of 1914/1916 hinted that children asked embarrassing questions when married teachers became pregnant. They added, with some resentment, that in cases where female teachers were married to headteachers the latter might indulgently allow them to leave school early to look after domestic matters![69]

Some of the elected and nominated members of the Legislative Council in 1936 (Kelshall, McShine, O'Reilly) were sympathetic to the plight of female teachers, especially on the point of loss of pension. This last issue was the first to be remedied; then unequal pay was ended and finally expulsion of married female teachers. Women became enfranchised in 1946, and this spurred on politicians such as Roy Joseph and Albert Gomes to make the defence of teachers, male and female, a part of their political platform. Some female teachers associated with the People's Education Movement even agitated quietly on their own behalf, especially for equal pay.[70]

The regular dispatch of females abroad for university education began, it appears, in the later 1930s, and it was not brought to an end by World War II. The Canadian Presbyterians' connections with Canada, which had worked so well for Indian males from the early twentieth century, began to work for females in the 1940s. A handful of Indian women acquired Canadian university degrees, and returned to assume teaching posts at Naparima Girls' High School. Indian women going abroad to study also showed a strong inclination to study medicine, sometimes in England. On the other hand, nursing (which in the 1940s and perhaps until the 1970s provided the biggest block of female students abroad) was not a favourite area of study for Indian females. It became very popular with black girls. In 1948 about 32 percent of Trinidadian students in the United Kingdom were females, and they were studying mostly nursing and medicine.[71] Among female students in Canada, the arts seemed most popular. These studies, plus those at home, indicate what were the major areas of employment for educated females: health care professions; child related professions like teaching, and secretarial services. Recent research by Rhoda Reddock has documented a history of struggle by women (but not Indian women) in Trinidad – mostly of cooperative struggle alongside men – against oppression. Very little of the struggle was explicitly against the oppression of women per se, and hence discrimination against women in education was not generally a strong focus of attention for women with feminist consciousness. An exception appears to have been the middle class movement called the Coterie of Social Workers, led by Audrey Jeffers.[72]

Private Schools and Education 1834-1939

No history of education in Trinidad and Tobago can be complete without adequate consideration of private schools. A private school might be defined as a day school which was neither a government school nor a school aided regularly by government. Usually a private school was owned by an individual proprietor and operated as a business for profit; but notable exceptions were denominational schools, especially Roman Catholic schools under the control of Teaching Orders which were private, but not profit oriented. A very useful initial distinction in discussing private schools, then, is that between an individually owned profit oriented day school and a corporately owned nonprofit school, typically operated by a church. Distinctions can also be made in terms of the level of the school: whether it was for infants, primary (or 'preparatory'), intermediate or secondary students.

Before emancipation there were only two 'government' schools in Trinidad, the two Cabildo schools founded in the time of Governor Woodford. All other schools were private, and were seldom operated by churches. Only a handful of Roman Catholic priests were resident, and very few clerics of other denominations. There is no clear evidence of anything like a proper secondary school run by an individual between 1797 and 1834, although there should have been individuals capable of teaching secondary level courses.[73] The free coloured community wished to start a college, but were prevented by Governor Woodford for whom such a plan was starkly subversive of the social order.[74]

We are left to wonder how hundreds of male residents attained literacy. Granted that the society was characterized by a high proportion of immigrants of all colours who imported their literacy or illiteracy, there must have been a few private schools in Port of Spain, perhaps on the verandahs or ground floor of residences, where the children of upper class French creoles, the British merchants or planters, or wealthy free coloureds acquired more than a basic education. The wealthy whites or free coloureds would aim to send their sons – the capable ones at least – to France, England or Ireland for education.[75] A long sea voyage, however, would hardly be attempted too early in the life of a child; hence some local schools could find a market among the children of the rich, although each tutor might have only a few children. A good example of this type of education can be derived from the career of Jean Baptiste Philip. His family was wealthy, his father was a free coloured planter; he and later a younger brother were sent abroad for secondary and university education.[76] Obviously there must have been some kind of local schooling, and it could hardly have come from their parents since their father had little education and their mother was illiterate. One source of schooling in the rural areas, which probably went unrecorded in many cases, occurred in the nineteenth and early twentieth centuries when a capable planter's wife offered free instruction to the young children of neighbours and friends as a way of passing her leisure hours.

Governor Woodford, in the name of social security, also set up a Board of Education on which sat leading Roman Catholic clerics to monitor the establishment of all schools. This could only mean private schools. It was not that he meant to offer them financial assistance; it was simply a matter of watching to ensure that such schools did not violate the social principles of the subordination of all non-whites to whites, and of slaves to masters. Primary school level education of blacks, whether free or slaves, was highly unusual. Woodford and the Roman Catholic priests also monitored the character of would-be teachers of private schools. It was not surprising, therefore, that neither the governor nor the clerics thought that Francis DeRidder, the coloured rebel Roman Catholic priest, had the moral right to run a school for coloureds. He got away with it for some time because he could pretend that it was a congregation of worshippers under his spiritual leadership.[77] A layperson could not have kept a private school in defiance of the authorities. Another indication of the existence of private schools operated by individuals came shortly after emancipation. When asked to give a report of how many schools the Roman Catholic Church had, the church hierarchy included private, individually owned schools operated by Roman Catholic laypersons as Roman Catholic schools, simply because their operators were Roman Catholic, or because priests gave their blessing or their religious ministrations to the venture.[78]

In the pre-emancipation period private schools had to be small if they were not to be socially subversive. Emancipation expanded the market for education by adding thousands of ex-slaves to the list of potential students, and by gradually infusing the British and colonial governments with a higher sense of responsibility for the spread of literacy. It marked the beginning of a gradual reversal of the pre-emancipation situation in which private schools were in the mainstream of provision, and public schools, like the Cabildo schools, were extraordinary. The lack of proper statistics about private schools in the nineteenth and twentieth centuries, makes it difficult to chart the course of this reversal; there are, however, positive indicators that the ascendancy of private schools for infants and very young pupils waned first, probably by the middle of the nineteenth century when the dual system added new public primary schools (both denominational and government) at a great speed. By 1890, for example, it would be safe to say that there were more public primary schools and more children in such schools than in private primary schools. In 1890, however, there were only two public secondary schools, CIC and QRC; St Joseph's Convent at that time was a private school. It is quite likely that private schools which aspired to secondary school status were then more numerous and had more children than the public secondary schools. Not until the first quarter of the twentieth century did the public secondary schools place themselves in a position to rival the increasing private secondary schools in terms of student population. As we shall see, the private secondary schools occupied a powerful second place, one of increasing importance by the middle of the twentieth century.

During the first forty years after emancipation, the status of certain primary schools changed from private to public, and from public to private. Take, for instance, a Roman Catholic school in the late 1830s which had not been built with funds from the British government, but which got a small irregular grant from the colonial government. Such a school was still a private nonprofit school; for the aid was not enough, nor was it a part of a systematic provision, to warrant its assignment to the public category. In fact, between 1834 and 1840 no primary school received systematic financial aid from the colonial government; yet some of them, for instance the Church Missionary Society's schools and the Church of England's schools, had been built with funds directly from the British government and had small amounts of money for teachers' salaries from the same source.[79] Curiously, such schools were more like public schools in their interface with the British government, and more like private schools than public schools in their relations with the Trinidad government. However, since the Trinidad government was the direct agent of the British government under the system of Crown Colony government, all schools built by the British government's subsidy or in receipt of funds from such a source for teachers' salaries were morally public schools although there were no rules of laws which made them so. A complication occurred, however, when the Trinidad government under Harris refused to aid any denominational schools (after the British government had brought its aid to an end). Under the government school system all the denominational schools became private schools, if they were not already such. The government schools were the only public primary schools, plus of course the schools conducted by the municipal authorities of Port of Spain and San Fernando. While the system of government schools lasted, there were two types of private primary schools: the individually owned profit oriented schools which were private because their owners wished them to be so; and the church owned nonprofit schools, some of which had once been public at least morally, which had been rendered private against their will. When the dual system was adopted, these latter schools gradually reemerged as public schools, thus beginning a decisive movement in favour of public over private schools at the primary school level.

Before the foundation of QCS in 1859 there were no public secondary schools. St Joseph's Convent and St George's College were private schools run by nuns and priests, of the nonprofit variety. Secondary level education was particularly compatible with the private school idea because it was widely believed that those who wished a superior education for their children should pay for it. Secondary education was by tradition costly. A corporation such as a church was in a better position than an individual to organize an expensive secondary school. The individual entrepreneur in secondary education could survive best if he avoided the overheads of buildings or rents, and operated from his own residence, sometimes teaching students individually. The activities of such persons have gone largely unrecorded: a Church of England clergyman who had a degree from Oxford or Cambridge was a prime candidate for this type of teaching even on a part-time basis. Laymen with similar university qualifications and good character were in very short supply. The Church of England scooped up a certain Mr Pix in 1854 to head a private secondary school for Protestant boys but failed to gather enough students to pay him:[80] Pix resigned for greener pastures taking his own students with him. Even as headmaster of this short-lived school, Pix had been allowed the right to have a few private students; this was not an unusual formula for a struggling Protestant private secondary school in other islands in the nineteenth century.

Schools endowed by wealthy individuals were entirely unknown in Trinidad and Tobago, unlike Barbados or Jamaica where certain planters in the eighteenth century left funds for the education of poor white boys. The decision to be made by the Trinidad colonial government by the mid nineteenth century was not how it could reform and revitalize badly managed endowed schools, but how to start its own secondary school from public funds. A specific set of circumstances led to the single intrusion of the government (QRC) into the field of secondary education for nearly a century. A more fruitful role for the colonial government was found from the 1870s in assisting private secondary schools, first of all CIC, to become public secondary schools through the exchange of public funds for public responsibility as defined by the government. Government assistance was not supposed to be given to a private school until it had shown its viability, and given proof of attainment. CIC and St Joseph's Convent became public schools only after lengthy periods, (including the St George's College preparation for CIC); but Naparima College passed from private to public status in only five years, and in the 1920s a new set of schools (Bishop Anstey High School, for example) were to accomplish the transition in even shorter time. It is important to remember that up to the mid twentieth century almost every public denominational secondary school spent a number of years as a private institution. This had to be so since the government did not give assistance with secondary school buildings until the 1950s; it only assisted with maintenance grants which, by regulation, should be given only after the school had shown its worth.

A very important phase in the history of secondary schools occurred in the first two decades of the twentieth century. The nineteenth century private secondary school, operated by individuals for profit, involved a very limited number of students who were usually taught by one teacher. It also characteristically aspired after social exclusiveness, and could often achieve this because of its small size. The average teacher of such a school was not likely to have been the descendant of ex-slaves; he or she might be from a section of the older free coloured families, possibly of French creole extraction. However, access to QRC and CIC in the later nineteenth century produced, by the 1900s, black and coloured graduates who began to invest in private secondary schools as a form of business. They aimed for a 'mass' market. Particularly in Port of Spain there were hundreds of frustrated parents who wished some secondary education for their children, but could not afford the fees at a public school. Possibly some could not gain entry to public secondary schools on social grounds. It was these circumstances, of an oversupply of secondary school aspirants and a handful of Cambridge School Certificate holders who dared to be different, which gave rise to something new: the nonexclusive, profit making, single-owner, private secondary school. In 1907 Pamphylian High School was started by Patrick Alexis; in 1907 the Iere Central High School was founded by J.D. Regis;[81] in 1910 it was the turn of David Bichlow, a former CIC student, to establish the Sangre Grande High School with Fr Dominic. Contemporaneously, certain private commercial schools also came into existence, for example those run by Mr Constaste and Mr Bartholomew. Since these commercial schools also taught French and Spanish, they aspired to secondary school status.

Within a few years these new private secondary schools had increased their intake beyond the size of any single-owner private secondary school of the nineteenth century. For instance, by 1915 Iere Central High School had 90 students; Cummings School of Commerce taught 130. The size of these schools enabled a lowering of fees; in the case of Iere Central School fees ranged from $1 to $2 per month; and at Cummings School of Commerce, where older students studied, they varied from a low of 60 cents to $5 per month. The fees at the public secondary schools at that time were about $15 per month, with a special reduction if more than one family member were at the school. Hence the new type of secondary private schools offered a cheaper education; but it was a lower level of education than was offered at the public schools. The usual formula for these new schools was to teach all the primary school subjects plus Latin, French and sometimes Spanish. The object of a school like Pamphylian High School or Iere Central High School differed from that of the commercial schools. The latter were preparing students for entry into the job market. The schools named above openly admitted that their primary aim was to prepare boys for entry into QRC and CIC.[82] These schools were coeducational, but St Joseph's Convent, more socially selective than either QRC or CIC, and not yet linked to the primary schools by way of the College Exhibition examination, was too prestigious for Regis and Alexis to penetrate with their girls. St Joseph's Convent was also outside the competition for the university scholarships.

Whatever their difficulties, and there were several, the social importance of these new schools was to spread educational opportunities at a secondary or quasi-secondary level to hundreds who could not otherwise have afforded it. In so doing these schools helped to create educational inflation in the 1920s and 1930s. They also became a slender source of employment for Cambridge Certificate holders who were waiting to find their future careers. With the advent of these schools, secondary education sprang out of control of the education authorities; if they had wished to limit numbers, they could no longer do it. At first however these private secondary schools were not seen as multipliers of Cambridge School Certificates; indeed they were perceived at first in the way some perceived themselves, namely, as self-constituted adjuncts to QRC and especially CIC. The schools' role as 'feeder' to CIC was enhanced by the manner in which its principal sought to promote their development. The fact of the matter was that the two school owners, Alexis and Regis, were Roman Catholics, and the principal of CIC saw how these schools could be utilized in the struggle with QRC for bright boys with the potential to win the university scholarships.

A key attraction of these new private secondary schools was the exhibitions or free places they offered. Following the model of CIC they held their own exhibition examination, and in time Pamphylian High School offered four. Patrick Alexis outclassed his rivals in public relations skills, and Pamphylian High School became the best known of these schools for about twenty-five years (1905-1930). Just as CIC followed the careers of their Island Scholars abroad, so Alexis watched the triumphs of the boys who had passed through his school to CIC or QRC. Their triumphs were brazenly credited to Pamphylian in public press advertisements. The connection with CIC was strengthened when Pamphylian and other private schools under Roman Catholic principals were allowed to compete for the CIC exhibitions. Through representation from the Roman Catholic hierarchy to the education authorities, an extra College Exhibition was provided from about 1918, exclusively for candidates from private schools. The winners went either to QRC or CIC. This special Exhibition increased the prestige of these schools and attracted students; it was easier to win this particular Exhibition than any other since the number of boys competing was much smaller than that from the public primary schools. Should no boy from these private schools reach the required minimum standard, the Exhibition would not be awarded.

While the major objective of these private schools was to prepare students for entry into QRC or CIC they did make attempts to pass boys and girls in the Junior Cambridge examinations and, less so, in the Cambridge School Certificate examination. Like Miss Bushe with the Higher Class at Tranquillity, the principals of these schools found out that students taught by teachers without university degrees could succeed in the Cambridge examinations. This was something of a social discovery. The Cambridge certificates could be acquired without what might be called a regular secondary school programme. It was secondary education without the frills. Although the failure rate of private secondary school candidates was extremely high, the lesson was learnt that some academic success was possible without expensive buildings, good furniture or teachers with university degrees, and without nuns and priests (see Tables 4.2 and 4.3). This lesson was not lost on a second generation of private mass oriented secondary schools from the late 1930s. These abandoned the role of feeder schools for QRC and CIC and made the Cambridge examinations their *raison d'être*.

However, Pamphylian High School, Iere Central High School and Sangre Grande High School did not outlive the 1930s to join the next generation of private schools.[83] Exactly when or why they succumbed is a mystery, but it is doubtful that it was due to lack of students. Like any small business, a private school could close suddenly because of any misfortune to its owner. The high point of the history of this first generation of mass oriented private secondary schools was reached when Pamphylian High School applied for affiliation to QRC in early 1929. In other words, Alexis wished to have his school recognized and aided by the government on the usual conditions applying to the recognized public colleges. He was refused.[84] In 1930 he had the question raised in the Legislative Council by Captain Cipriani; this bid failed. Some people, including the pro-labour editor of the *Labour Leader*, were quick to diagnose colour and racial prejudice: a black man with a school of mostly black youths had not been taken into the dual system by the white education administrators.[85] In view of the bias of the colonial system against blacks and lower class people, prejudice was doubtless a factor; but how decisive it was is clouded, as usual, by certain legitimate considerations.

At the time Pamphylian High School applied for affiliation to QRC it was actually passing students at both Junior Cambridge and School Certificate levels, but more at the Junior Cambridge level. From this point of view it was, in 1929, a better applicant for aid than Bishop Anstey High School or Bishop's High School in Tobago at the time of their successful application. Pamphylian High School had the confidence to launch a building fund in 1929 with a target of $16,000. But Bishop Anstey High School and Bishop's High School in Tobago most likely had better accommodation than Pamphylian at the time they were affiliated. Additionally, they were church schools for which an argument for affiliation could be made in a plausible form: for instance, the special need to educate Indian girls in the case of Naparima Girls' High School, or Anglican girls (Bishop Anstey High School), or Tobagonians (Bishop's High School). The equivalent argument for Pamphylian could only be the need to educate the blacks of Port of Spain: but urban blacks were not yet considered a special interest group for secondary education. The editor of the *Port of Spain Gazette* was right to note that the refusal was a blow to the aspirations of parents of lesser means, and of a lower social rank than the parents of the boys who went to QRC and CIC.[86] According to Marriott, Pamphylian High School was not a necessary school.

Surprisingly, one important argument against Alexis did not surface publicly: his school was a profit-making enterprise, not owned by a responsible corporation like a church. Was Alexis willing to convert it into a nonprofit school, with himself not as owner, but as a salaried employee (possibly still as principal) under a board of trustees? It is not clear; but unless he had such a plan in mind it was unrealistic to expect a government subsidy for his business. In giving evidence before the Education Commission in 1915, Pamphylian High School, Iere Central High School and three commercial schools had expressed a desire for aid without any mention of plans to alter their character as private profit-making institutions.[87]

After the governorship of Woodford (1813-1828) no government permission was needed to commence any type of private schools. In the early 1920s, however, the need for some kind of regulation of private schools had begun to exercise the mind of the education authorities. A wide variety of private schools existed in the 1920s, some of which we hear of only very indirectly. There were impecunious widows and ambitious ladies who kept private and exceedingly exclusive schools for young boys and girls. There was no check at all on their qualifications or the residences which housed their schools. It is alleged that in the latter 1920s and early 1930s a new crop of private primary schools came into existence out of dissatisfaction with the textbooks which Cutteridge had written and imposed on the schools.[88] These schools apparently made not the slightest pretense at being anything but primary. If we assume that these new private primary schools were owned and taught by blacks or coloureds, it would mean that private initiatives by black and coloured teacher-entrepreneurs had reached new heights at both primary and secondary levels. If we recall the contemporary role of certain headteachers and assistant teachers in preparing pupils for the College Exhibitions, often for a fee, then the widespread use of schools as a form of small business by the descendants of ex-slaves and others can be appreciated. The early years of the twentieth century constituted the first period in which the descendants of the ex-slaves created their own schools. They did it, however, on the models pioneered by the whites.

The official excuse for the regulation of private schools was related to two broad movements of the 1920s: compulsory primary education and medical inspection of primary school children. If pupils were going to be compelled to attend schools, said Director McKay in 1922, then the schools must provide a better environment than their homes; hence the need to look more carefully at school buildings, floor space allotted to each child, the condition of latrines, and the supply of drinking water. Also the defaulters from compulsory education could not be detected if no account of attendance at private schools was taken. Similarly, medical inspection of schools, begun in the late 1920s, encouraged the education authorities to want to know about sanitation in all schools. These considerations led to the passing of a Private School Ordinance in 1935; it had been preceded by a Compulsory Education Ordinance of 1921, applying to areas of Port of Spain and St James which was not really implemented until 1935. The Private School Ordinance, however, seemed like mild medicine; it did not say anything about what should be taught or who should teach it beyond a basic requirement that no teacher should have a criminal record or be grossly immoral. What the legislation sought was statistical information and a basic minimum standard of buildings and sanitary conditions. Government inspectors could visit the private schools, but no permission was required before private schools could be founded. The immediate effect was to close only a few schools.[89] Still, the law can be seen as an expression of the desire of the professional directors of education for increased power over the entire education system. Nobody seemed to have argued in the press that the closure of such schools was a denial of education to deserving students. Nevertheless, in the long run government tended to leave private schools unregulated.

In 1936 the first comprehensive return of private schools showed a total of eighty-nine schools of which forty-four were in Port of Spain, eleven in San Fernando, and twenty-nine in rural Trinidad, with five in Tobago. In attendance were 2,677 students.[90] Unfortunately there is no way to distinguish between the purely private primary schools and the others. For instance, those in Tobago were primary schools run by the Seventh-Day Adventists. There was a nearly total lack of official information on private schools of all types during World War II and immediately after it; but when official attention was turned on them in the late 1940s they occupied a most remarkable position within the secondary school sector. The construction of United States military bases in Trinidad during the early 1940s led to the increased circulation of money. It might be assumed that private secondary schools would find an expanding market in these circumstances. However, such a movement is not readily detected in the statistics for 1949. In this year there were twenty-one registered private secondary schools with 2,866 students on roll.[91] This was about half as many as the total enrolled in the ten public secondary schools. Osmond High School, with an enrolment of 994 students, was second in size only to CIC; Progressive Educational Institute (461 on roll) was about as large as Bishop Anstey High School or Naparima Girls' High School. Of seventeen private secondary schools in what was called Category B (schools where students had to sit a preliminary test before being allowed to sit the Cambridge School Certificate Examination), only Ideal High School and Haig Girls' School had names which went back to the 1920s. The schools in Category B were by and large the second generation of mass oriented, privately owned secondary schools. They now had a few teachers with external university degrees from the University of London, as well as quite a few of their own superior graduates.

Education, The Creative Arts and Libraries 1834-1939

Although the creative arts here will be taken to include drawing, crafts, singing, music, drama and dancing, there is no record of dancing in the primary or secondary schools before World War II, except for 1933 at St Joseph's Convent when the junior girls staged nursery rhymes with songs and dance. It might very well be that there were other similar occasions at this school, especially at prize-givings. But dancing was the most rarely practised of the creative arts now under discussion. A possible explanation is that vigorous body movements were perceived as being too sensuous, or potentially seductive, to be allowed a regular place in a scheme of education which was religiously motivated or sponsored by the churches. Ballet appeared to have existed outside the schools and was not for non-whites.

Of the other creative arts, singing was undoubtedly the first to achieve a regular place in the primary schools. Class singing has always been the most popular form of music in these schools. Still, if we leave aside the 'singing' of arithmetical tables, singing was not a part of the curriculum in the immediate post-emancipation period. The earliest report of singing as a separate school subject was in 1858 at the Girls' Model School in Port of Spain. It was also reported at the Boys' Model School in 1861[92.] In fact, it seems that Inspector Anderson promoted singing in government schools in the 1860s. The majority of government schools eventually did singing, though not all pupils were involved. The Girls' Model School was said to have the best singing groups, a possible explanation being that all the classes sang and singing was by note.

In the 1870s there were two significant developments in singing. The more important of the two was the introduction of music as an official subject in the Teachers' Certificate Examination. Henceforth, trained teachers at the government training school and uncertified classroom teachers sitting the Teachers' Certificate Examination could take music, there being two parts to the examination: musical theory and musical practice. The practical part, however, did not involve the playing of any instruments. The other development was a campaign mounted by Inspector Guppy, apparently at the instigation of the governor in 1878, to improve singing in the schools. Guppy concluded that this was not possible without a shift from singing by ear to singing from musical notes. As in every new thrust in the schools, nothing could be achieved without the cooperation and involvement of some teachers. Fortunately, the recently appointed principal of the government training school, J.H. Collens, was found to have some knowledge of music; also one of the trainee teachers, Mr Lennard, had some skills. The latter was employed after graduation as a peripatetic music teacher, his range of visits apparently not going beyond ten schools in Port of Spain where all improvements began.[93] His special mission was to extend the practice of singing by note from the Model schools into the primary schools. Here we observe the start of the dilemma of the creative arts: they tended to be the business of a specialist, not the business of the classroom teachers. As scarce accomplishments, the greatest difficulty was encountered in introducing them as a regular part of the curriculum. Guppy and Collens used the pupils at the Boys' Model School (where there was a drum and fife band) in an experimental concert at the Prince's Building, attended by the governor; and the plan was to stage an annual concert using the school choirs which Lennard was to assist in developing. Had the planners persisted, it could have been the start of a music festival of a sort; but they did not. On leaving office in 1890, Guppy did not claim improved singing as one of his achievements.

Inspector Guppy spoke about the desirability of musical instruments in every school, but the government made no grants for these; and managers of primary schools introduced instruments at a snail's pace and in such a haphazard manner as to produce little or no impact on the education system. In 1876 six of the forty-eight government primary schools had managed to acquire harmoniums and either this or the piano was the usual musical instrument. No African or Indian musical instrument was considered appropriate. Another weakness of the scheme was the lack of trained music teachers who could teach singing properly or play an instrument. Singing and music were outside the system of payment by results in the nineteenth century: there was no financial incentive for headteachers or assistant teachers to undertake it, and little opportunity in the rural schools, which had no 'speech days', to display it. There was, however a syllabus for singing, with prescribed textbooks. In 1900 some schools, including schools in Port of Spain, were encouraged by inspectors to stop singing by note in favour of the 'sol-fa system'; but after only two years, singing by note was included in the system of payment by results.[94] From the 1890s, one interesting development helped to rescue singing from dullness: the adoption of drill for recreation and discipline. Singing became associated with drill and since drill was a subject in which children usually satisfied the inspector, reports on 'singing and drill' were better than reports on singing alone.

Singing and music were nonexistent at QRC. They had a place at St Joseph's Convent from the nineteenth century. CIC had the first school band in the island, though there was no mention of singing. It seems that both at the level of primary and secondary school, singing was mostly an activity for girls. Music teaching in public schools was one of the subjects which started as a male area of interest and evolved gradually as a female speciality; but the timing of the shift is not clear. St George's College, CIC, and Naparima College were not as renowned for singing as St Joseph's Convent was; music examinations were a feature at St Joseph's Convent long before the school entered for Cambridge examinations; and the speech days were occasions for displays of the girls' musical talents. In the primary schools run by the Sisters of St Joseph, singing was also good in the late nineteenth century. A useful generalization would be that Roman Catholic secondary schools were more interested and skilled in music and singing than other schools, their taking in boarders being one reason as well as their more relaxed pace of academic instruction; and that girls' schools, Roman Catholic or Protestant, primary or secondary, were more interested in these subjects than boys' schools.

Though they tended to ape the older schools, the newer secondary schools from the mid 1920s did not always seek to follow these others strictly in activities outside the Cambridge examination system. Bishop Anstey High School, for instance, did not try to imitate the musical achievements of St Joseph's Convent, but struck out more in the direction of organized inter-house games and charitable work.[95] The principals of Bishop's High School in Tobago and of Naparima Girls' High School tried to add some special activities which would distinguish their schools in the late 1920s and 1930s. The same might be said of the next generation of secondary schools in the 1940s. Up to a point these schools were unable to appropriate, without embarrassment, the traditions of CIC and St Joseph's Convent, the two schools which enjoyed the most loyal parental and old students' support, and lived off the affective and financial support of the French creoles.

The persistent, but not unrelieved, tone of dissatisfaction taken by the inspectors with singing and music in the government training school and the primary schools (there was no inspection of these subjects in the secondary schools) might appear odd to anyone acquainted with the reputation of Trinidadians as 'natural' musicians. Acting Inspector Ralph Gomes made a remark which helps to reconcile these two positions. He wrote: "The West Indian is a born musician, and can reproduce a tune on first hearing; but does not take so readily to the scientific appreciation of the art."[96] By West Indians here Gomes did not mean Indians, not even Indians born in Trinidad. A remarkable stereotype of the Indians by the white or near white inspectors of schools was that they were not a 'musical' people. There was complete disregard for, or ignorance of, Indian singing and music outside the schools. There might also have been a cultural block, a sheer inability to appreciate Indian musical modes or songs in Hindi which J.H. Collens, principal of the government training school had in 1888 characterized as "melan-choly, lugubrious and depressing".[97] It followed that special efforts seemed necessary to improve singing and music in the Canadian Presbyterian schools. The results of these efforts are not known.

Drawing in the primary schools eventually graduated into art for the more talented pupils, but not before World War II. The earliest mention of drawing was in the Girls' Model School in 1870 where a qualified master was said to be giving lessons. Subsequently, however, there was no mention of drawing in any public school at any level until 1916. Because of the erratic and inconsistent nature of 'cultural' subjects in schools, there might have been instances of drawing which escaped the attention of the education authorities. It was not an examination subject. Freehand drawing as a primary school subject improved with the arrival of Cutteridge in 1921. He said drawing was of great importance in England; in the teachers' colleges there, it was compulsory. Cutteridge himself had some skill in drawing and, through the government training school and in-service courses, he set out to make it a regular school subject. A modern Trinidadian art scholar notes that Cutteridge, though influenced by the Progressive movement, did not appear to favour freedom in drawing. He also attempted by reproductions of paintings by European masters in his *Readers* to stimulate teachers to introduce art appreciation.[98] After he left the government training school, other specialist teachers of drawing, Thomas Spencer and then Ernest Davies, were appointed in the 1920s. The key to the spread of drawing in the primary schools was its fate in the government training school. Students came forward to take it as an optional subject, doing little preparatory work, depending on their natural skills. This attitude was usually condemned, but in the end the inspectors had to acknowledge that the trainee students had a point: it was one of those subjects in which one could score high marks without much preparation if one had the talent.

Schools reflected the dominant formalistic conceptions of drawing, obstructing the transition from drawing to art. According to Isaiah Boodhoo, the principle was for the teacher to draw an object on the chalkboard and then the pupils would draw from the teacher's drawing, never from the object itself.[99] This mechanical conception of drawing prevailed more or less down to the mid twentieth century, with a few enlightened teachers occasionally introducing the object to be drawn. Whatever the object, the teachers and pupils were vigorously encouraged by inspectors to reproduce it exactly as it was, and not what it should be like. No portraits were allowed which inhibited non-whites from conceiving themselves as objects of art. Drawing was said to develop the hand and eye, not the imagination or self-expression or race pride. The only school where art in the sense of painting was done in the early twentieth century was St Joseph's Convent, though we should be cautious in thinking that freedom of subject matter or style was allowed.[100]

It is quite possible that a fair amount of art as an elite pastime was done outside the schools. As in the case of creative literature and drama, the 1930s were a turning point in art. It was then that a few painters outside the schools, from a sense of pride and rebellion, began to see their mission as one of bringing art 'to the people'.[101] The objection might be raised that Michel Cazabon, Trinidad's most famous nineteenth century painter, painted the local scenery successfully; but his was an individual achievement, not the start of a cultural movement.[102] This feeling of pride was the cultural springboard for indigenous paintings; but it took another decade at least before drawing in the schools, under the influence of M.P. Alladin, formerly director of culture, began to free itself from the shackles of mechanical reproduction. It thus became more like art as it is understood today.

Singing got into the syllabus of the primary schools from the 1860s; music, in contradistinction from singing, in the later nineteenth century; drawing in the 1920s. The 1930s was the first decade of drama. But it should be understood that, from the start, drama was more at home in the secondary schools than in the primary schools. An important explanation was that drama developed in the service of the Cambridge external examinations; the dramatic societies at St Joseph's Convent and CIC, for example, fed on Shakespeare's plays, with (in the case of St Joseph's Convent) the occasional religious drama thrown in. It would be a mistake to think that QRC, Bishop Anstey High School, Bishop's High School in Tobago, or Naparima Girls' High School never staged plays in the 1930s, or at least excerpts from plays. But they did this from organizational bases other than dramatic clubs, which they apparently lacked at that time. At the Government Training College there apparently was no organized drama teaching, but this did not prevent individual trainees from developing their talents as playwrights and producers. A notable example was L.A. Roberts who taught in primary schools both in Port of Spain and in Tobago in the 1930s, where he wrote and staged local plays acted by his pupils. Of all the art forms discussed, it appears possible that a West Indian context first appeared in art and drama.

Today art and crafts in schools have been awkwardly tied together administratively and conceptually; but this has been a recent development. The alliance is between two subjects of unequal prestige; if drawing turned into art for many, the path of crafts has been from handwork to handicraft and then to crafts; and as the business of primary schools, crafts were never prestigious. Of all the creative arts discussed, crafts were the only one to find a normal place in the work of classroom teachers in primary schools. It might be said to have commenced with sewing by girls in the later nineteenth century, but since sewing was done by girls only, it remained a thing apart from crafts. Crafts were boosted at the same time as drawing by Cutteridge's personal interest. In the 1920s crafts took the form mostly of work with straw and paper and, like drawing, they were dominated by considerations of accuracy above creative self-expression. Once crafts went into the primary schools, they became institutionalized, largely because they were not conceived as the activity of specialist teachers, but of ordinary classroom teachers. The larger participation of many schools in them than in any of the other creative subjects was the base for annual Handicraft Exhibitions from the 1920s to the 1950s. Because they were not a specialist activity, because the secondary schools neglected them, because of the materials they used, crafts remained pejoratively associated with manual work; the superior prestige of art was reflected later in the tendency to put, at the level of the Ministry of Education, art educators in charge of crafts, the latter, like agriculture within the technical/vocational complex, being slow to produce acknowledged leaders.

The Trinidad Public Library was inaugurated in 1851, and although it was not until the 1940s that it first began to respond formally and directly to the educational needs of children, it was not irrelevant to the development of an educated middle class. The first impact of the library on the schools was indirectly through its usefulness to the small core of studious black and coloured teachers in Port of Spain in the later nineteenth century who taught themselves various subjects beyond the level of their formal schooling. These persons were part of what the librarian in 1890 called the "young men of a most deserving class who come to the rooms upstairs for the purpose of studying and to consult works of reference".[103] Persons studying locally for any examination not covered by the schools, such as the solicitors' examination, fell into this category. The public library therefore was, like QRC and CIC, part of the expanding educational facilities of the later nineteenth century. It seems inconceivable that leading intellectuals of all colours such as Charles Warner, J.J. Thomas, Maxwell Philip, or Sylvester Devenish did not make use of its lending facilities.

The fragmentary nature of the library's history has so far inhibited attempts to understand it sociologically. As an institution having its origins in the Port of Spain Borough Council it might be useful to regard it as a creole creation, despite Lord Harris's prudent swiftness in putting the stamp of English officialdom upon it by an Ordinance. In its fledgling years Chief Justice George Knox gave it 59 volumes; Alexander Fitzjames, the first coloured lawyer, donated 105 volumes of the *Journal of the House of Commons*; Thomas Hinde, a coloured spokesman of Port of Spain bequeathed his entire library to the public library.[104] This attribution of a creole character to it does not mean that Englishmen were unconnected with its management, but that the creole intelligentsia of Port of Spain, white and non-white, soon felt committed to its defence. This spirit of creole pride, married to a municipal sense of jurisdiction over and against the encroachments of the central government, appears to have been the key to its survival as an autonomous institution well into the twentieth century, even after a rival central library system was started.

Like all post-primary educational institutions, a dominant theme in the history of the Trinidad Public Library was the widening of access to its benefits; this took the management of the library in two directions, one of which was permanently successful. The subscription to the library was lowered from $9.60 per annum (1851) to $4.80 per annum (1859), and then to $2.88 per annum (1890), with the addition of two cents a day to use the reading room from 1886. However, it was a long time before the library became completely free in 1951.[105] The other direction was the opening of small branches in a few other parts of the island, including San Fernando; but this was not successful in the long run, one reason being the strong municipal sense (or Port of Spain loyalty) of some members of its management team; eventually branches were confined to greater Port of Spain. Profiting from the experience of the Trinidad Public Library and the generosity of the Carnegie Corporation, the Carnegie Free Library, when it was founded in San Fernando in 1919, eschewed subscriptions and islandwide ambitions and settled down quickly to the role of a city library.

Libraries within primary schools are essentially very recent creations, particularly since the oil boom of the second half of the 1970s. Lord Harris, in proposing his education scheme of 1851, mentioned the desirability of a library in each primary school, but this objective was forgotten for more than a century. None of the three basic requirements for a school library – space, books and a librarian – could be afforded; this remains the position in most primary schools at present. At the same time, poorly housed libraries sprang into existence in the leading secondary schools, and from at least the early twentieth century at Tranquillity Boys' and Girls' Schools, apparently as part of the preparation for external examinations. No government grants were given for these libraries; laboratories were assisted by government before school libraries. Hence the three basic patterns which presently characterize school libraries became evident quite early: inadequate provision in the assisted secondary schools was vastly superior to anything in the primary schools; the provision of library facilities in secondary schools was geared towards students preparing for examinations, in other words towards the older students; and very little, if any, in government grants went towards school libraries of any sort.

There is absolutely no mention of primary school libraries in the reports of inspectors of schools and directors of education in the nineteenth and early twentieth centuries. Nor was there any government policy on the subject at that time. Even in the secondary schools, libraries were not part of their image which they projected to the public. Principals would report on sports or drama, on literary societies, but not on libraries, or the need to bring them into existence. The first government document on education to outline a government policy on school libraries, or to accept government responsibility for this branch of education, was the Draft Fifteen-Year Education Plan (1968-1983).

The Management of Education 1834-1939

Management of education in Trinidad and Tobago was divided between the managers of the education system at the centre, in other words the chief government education administrators, and the local managers of the schools, if not on the spot, at least physically nearer to them than the government administrators. Local managers appeared before government administrators because schools existed before the government decided to establish a board of education and an inspectorate of schools in 1846. In several West Indian islands, as in England itself, a Board of Education and an inspector of schools signalled the advent of systematic government intervention in education, and in most cases these institutions were administratively the beginning of education departments and, ultimately, ministries of education. The Education Department came formally into existence in Trinidad and Tobago from about 1918, and the Ministry of Education from about 1950. As an index of the rate of growth of the bureaucracy at the centre it might be pointed out that for the first thirty years (1846-1876) there was only one inspector; between 1918 and 1921 there were a director of education and five assistant inspectors; and in 1937 the total was seven assistant inspectors. The number of primary schools and enrolment grew from a handful of schools and a few hundred children in 1849 to 80 schools and 6,501 pupils in 1876, and 293 schools with 72,776 pupils in 1937. It is doubtful whether the government ever had enough administrators.

Leaving aside private schools run as a form of business, the clerics emerged quite early, because of the religious purpose of schools, as the typical managers of schools; notable exceptions were the two Cabildo schools managed by laymen in the Cabildo of Port of Spain. Until about 1875 the Borough Council of Port of Spain, and from the 1850s to 1875 the Borough Council of San Fernando as well, paid for and managed their own schools. From the 1820s to the 1840s Port of Spain councillors were the only laymen managing public schools; in the late 1840s they were joined by the wardens as local managers of the government schools, and in the 1850s by the Councillors of the San Fernando Borough Council. Bearing in mind that denominational schools between 1849 and 1869 were private schools (because they were not getting government aid or recognition), then this was in fact a period when all public primary schools (borough council and government schools) were managed by laymen, and had originated from the initiative of lay persons. In the late nineteenth century the laymen's role in the management of schools decreased, and continued to be substantially smaller than that of the clerics in the twentieth century.

It is difficult to offer a decided opinion about the quality of education management. The management of primary schools, whether by individuals at first or by Boards of Management from the 1930s, was sadly in the backwater of discussion of education; teachers never complained publicly about local managers in the nineteenth century, and had to be careful even in the first half of the twentieth century; in fact the directors, especially Cutteridge, were criticized more openly by teachers and the TTTU than were local managers of schools. Another reason for this difficulty in determining the quality of local management is that local managers of primary schools and the top government administrators shared a conspiracy of silence about each other's performance. Parents did not become a factor in the public assessment of local managers until the 1960s, except occasionally on the question of religious proselytization. Hence very little public discussion of the performance of local managers arose. Indeed the managers of the education system, whether at the centre or at the district level, were there to assess the performance of pupils and teachers, not to have their work judged by others. This was one reason why Cutteridge was so annoyed with his critics. It might therefore have been a shock to both Inspector Anderson and the gentlemen on the Board of Education, as well as to the warden managers of government (ward) schools, to hear adverse comments from Keenan, the only expatriate expert who ever made the management of schools the central focus of a report and recommendations.

It must be said at once that the management of Roman Catholic secondary schools was special in that these schools were owned and managed by Teaching Orders. Until recently all principals of such schools belonged to an Order. From the foundation of St Joseph's Convent to the present time, these Orders have preserved a deserved reputation as the very best managers of schools, particularly of secondary schools. They assumed financial responsibility for their secondary schools and, by putting some of their own resources into them, have always succeeded, at least until the advent of the new government schools of the 1970s, in having the best maintained secondary school buildings. By the protracted tenures of principals, by having members of the controlling Orders resident on or near the school premises, the Teaching Orders secured for their secondary schools advantages not usually available to other schools. Their devotion to their schools has become legendary in the country, and a good deal of this reputation as managers rubbed off – not always justifiably – on secular Roman Catholic priests who managed primary schools. It was probably only in recent times that the management of primary schools became a burden which many Roman Catholic priests – as well as some Church of England clergymen – would rather not have on their shoulders.[106]

Keenan hinted that Inspector Anderson spent insufficient time inspecting the schools. The Board of Education which Harris had intended should meet once a month seldom met in the late 1850s and 1860s, thus leaving the management of the schools to the inspector. His job was well paid and fairly comfortable; once in it, inspectors stayed – Anderson for approximately twenty-two years, and Guppy another twenty-two years. The wardens as government officers, connected with the planter class, had no experience and little taste for the management of schools; still they were the only managers the government could find for government schools. Keenan actually made the point that there was no provision in law to appoint wardens as managers of these schools; that they were just asked to act as managers.

The wardens were not eager promoters of schools or keen local inspectors; the deplorable condition of ward school buildings, and the weak academic performance of pupils, were attributed by Keenan partly to their negligence. Keenan's grand position was that clerics made the best managers, and that denominational schools integrating religious instruction were more desirable than secular government schools.[107] It might be presumed, therefore, that the existing denominational schools under clerical management had an overall superiority over the government schools, but this was not the case. It was not that Keenan was incorrect in his opinion that clerics made the best managers; the history of education in the colony tends to support this statement. Clerical management alone, however, was not enough to overcome other obstacles such as shortage of funds, teacher deficiencies or public indifference. Despite Keenan's bias towards denominational schools, what really surfaces powerfully today from his report is not the contrast between government and denominational schools, but the desperately inadequate kind of education given in all primary schools, whoever managed them.

Before and after Keenan's visit the assessment of the management of primary schools presents great difficulties. It is unfortunate that the minutes of the Board of Education – which in practice was the supreme educational authority over primary schools from the mid 1840s to 1918 – have not been found; nor have the many letters which clerical managers wrote to the inspectors, directors, or Board. One suspects that it was never easy to get constructive action from the centre in response to a request for aid; most likely replies were slow. The experience of Inspector Anderson in travelling to rural schools attests to genuine difficulties of communication and the high cost of travel. A school in Cedros or La Brea could not expect to be visited more than once per year when there was only one inspector for the entire island. Schools along the corridor from Port of Spain to Arima could expect to see him twice or three times a year.

As the number of schools and pupils grew in the later nineteenth century without any increase in the number of inspectors, and as the system of payment by results demanded an examination at each school, not simply an inspection, the burden of work for Inspector Guppy became too much. Each school ideally wished to be examined during the same period of the year, the second quarter, when the weather was dry and attendance tended to be at its best. Obviously one inspector could not accomplish this, and something of an alternating system of claims to optimal examination time had to be informally introduced. The problems of managing the Tobago schools centrally from Port of Spain were presumably mitigated by a resident inspectorate from the 1930s. The difficulty of visiting rural schools was also experienced by some local managers, not all of whom lived on the spot. Both wardens and clerics had other business to accomplish in the course of which they had to travel in directions away from the rural schools they managed. The small evidence we have indicates mostly that rural schools were not watched over meticulously by wardens or clerical managers.

One of the most essential functions of a school manager was to attend to finances. In the case of clerical managers of denominational schools, raising the proportion of funds not covered by government grants was a major responsibility. After 1875 the managers had the additional burden of collecting school fees and initiating legal proceedings against defaulting parents. Responsibility for the upkeep of furniture and buildings was also theirs, as well as supervision of the staff, and the granting of leave. Some of these duties ruled out headteachers from being considered as managers, but there was a sense, especially in the prolonged absence of the authorized managers, local or central, in which every headteacher carried out day-to-day managerial functions over his or her school.

As the system of wardens lost its vitality in the twentieth century, many government schools appeared to be without local managers, except for the inspector in charge of the region. The fact that managerial functions were assumed by headteachers was not recognized by the white local managers or the education authorities (although the management function of secondary school principals was welcomed); this situation arose partly because primary school headteachers (except for a few expatriates at the model schools) were non-whites. It was part of the colonial mentality and practice not to think of non-whites as managers even when books on school management were introduced in the later nineteenth century in the government training school. In every Education Code in the late nineteenth century and first half of the twentieth century, it was stated explicitly that teachers could not be managers.

As the average primary school got larger, the role of the headteachers as informal managers became so important that they gave less and less of their time to teaching, and more and more to the management of children and staff, and to dealing with parents. A school of 250 children obviously needed more management than one of 30 or 70 children. It would have been a matter of surprise if mature headteachers, with long service records, had not acquired more expertise in the management of their schools than some local managers, especially wardens or busy clerics. The government never overcame the shortage of persons willing and qualified to act as local managers of government schools. Ironically, the Education Codes in the later nineteenth and early twentieth centuries asked for two local managers or more when already it was difficult to find one. As rural schools multiplied, a warden came to have four or more schools under his jurisdiction; his predecessors had not done well in the mid nineteenth century when they had one to manage. Laymen who were sufficiently educated and interested in education often chose to give their services to a church rather than to the government schools. The inspectorate became larger, especially after World War II, and more often resident in its local district, and assumed some of the functions of local managers of government schools. Eventually the point was reached, at different times, at which some government schools had more to do with inspectors and the Education Department than with local managers. Headteachers came to deal directly with the Ministry of Education, something unheard of in the nineteenth or early twentieth centuries.

A development of long-term significance was the legal inauguration of denominational boards of management from 1925. These dealt with primary schools only. This improvement, not seen as such initially by the Christian churches, was brought about by the professional directors, partly in their own interest, and partly on the insistence of the teachers, who felt safer from arbitrary action from a board than from individual clerical managers.[108] Ultimately, Hindu and Muslim promoters of schools had to adopt, however slowly or painfully, this mode of operation in order to access government funds. The boards of management evolved into useful administrative devices, improving communication between government and the churches. The selection of members of these Boards was left entirely to the church authorities although the government always reserved the right to remove local managers. There is no record of any individual manager who was removed on request of the government, or by direct action of the government. If the government could have organized boards of management for its own schools, they would have benefited.

From the 1880s Trinidad was divided into two school districts for the purpose of inspection: a northern and a southern district. When a central district was added in the 1890s, Tobago was part of it. The inclusion of Tobago in the central district arose from the purely fortuitous circumstance of Charles Hobson, the first Trinidad inspector sent to report on the Tobago schools at the time of amalgamation, being in charge of the central district. By the early twentieth century Tobago was included in a district consisting of itself and the Trinidad north coast; by the mid 1920s Tobago was a part of the northern district where it stayed until World War II. It then became a separate district in a much expanded system of eleven school districts. The development of school districts should not be confused with decentralization of the management of schools. The inspectors were increasingly tied residentially to districts – and some had clerks – but they had no separate budgets, and no power to pursue any separate directions in education. In 1959 the Maurice Commission recommended what appears to be a larger measure of decentralization:[109] distinct education districts, with separate education departments and separate advisory councils. Decentralization, however, was completely opposed to the trend of PNM policies and was not implemented.[110]

The slow inclusion of non-whites in the lower echelons of the education administration in Port of Spain is part of the story, repeated over and over again in each department of government, of the painful upward crawl of the descendants of the ex-slaves and ex-indentured Indians into the civil service. A landmark was the employment of Nelson Comma, headteacher of Mouton Hall Methodist School in Port of Spain, as assistant inspector in 1923, replacing Sydney Smith, another non-white, who had enjoyed the job temporarily after he had retired from teaching.[111] Thereafter the technique in the later 1920s and 1930s was to bring in, as temporary vacancies occurred, successful headteachers, (for example, E.B. Grovesnor, Charles Gayadeen, V.R. Vidale, A.J. Mohammed) to act as junior inspectors under the guidance of the directors, the assistant director, the principal of the Government Training College, and the two senior inspectors – all of whom were whites or near whites. Their good work indicated that there was substantial talent among the long-serving senior headteachers all across the country. It would be wrong to represent these men as superefficient, but they knew more about the teaching and management of primary schools than the white or near white inspectors, for instance J.E. Clarke, George Von Weiller, Charles Hobson, William Robinson, William Kenny or even J.E. Stoer.[112] Marriott and Cutteridge looked for headteachers who accepted their ideas. An unusual appointment to the rank of junior Inspector was that of Rawle Ramkessoon in 1931. His advantage was having a university degree; his disadvantage was not having been a headteacher; but by further studies Ramkessoon made good his lack of experience in teaching, and rose to be the highest paid and most senior Trinidadian in the Education Department on the eve of World War II. After World War II the number of Indian inspectors was rather surprising in view of the Indians' later start in education. Part of the explanation was the tendency for Indians to be appointed headteachers in Canadian Presbyterian Mission schools earlier in their careers than in the case of blacks in other schools, and hence they had an advantage in seniority. It could not be said, as it could in other sectors of the civil service, that Indians were underrepresented in the Education Department before or after 1939.

Society, Education and Educational Expansion 1834-1939 – a Summary

Before and after Slavery

The abolition of slavery marked the real beginning not only of popular education, but of public education in Trinidad and Tobago. The only public schools which existed before emancipation were two Cabildo (municipal) schools in Port of Spain. Trinidad, unlike Barbados or Jamaica, had no pre-emancipation endowed or charity schools founded by rich planters for poor white boys. The island had been an underdeveloped plantation society of new immigrants and conflicting nationalities, without an eighteenth century or pre-emancipation nineteenth century golden age of economic prosperity which could have unloosed the philanthropy of successful planters and merchants.

Without endowed or charity schools for poor white boys, there was no history of free coloured youths before emancipation struggling to gain access, as at Wolmers in Jamaica, to all-white public schools. The free coloureds themselves, numerically significant and not without families with large landed property, did not establish any public schools, although there were small private schools for those who had the funds and the interest. One attempt to have a well-endowed public school for free coloured children was thwarted by Governor Woodford. Nor were there any significant attempts, in the absence of enterprising evangelical Protestant missionaries, to teach literacy to small groups of urban slaves as sometimes happened in other British Caribbean islands as emancipation neared. In short, emancipation overtook Trinidad before it had achieved enough economic maturity and social confidence in its future as a New World creole society; hence it had not generated endowed public schools for different classes and colours. At the time of emancipation, the impulse to provide primary schools for the masses came overwhelmingly from outside, from England; and in explaining the origins of St Joseph's Convent, the first proper secondary school, it might also be maintained that the push came mostly from outside, in fact from Martinique and France.[113]

Trinidad had been a Spanish colony for centuries, but when the English captured it in 1797, more Frenchmen than Spaniards were settled there. The French creoles were the backbone of the planter class and the aristocratic core of the elite whites. The English rulers were determined to stamp an English character upon the polyglot, multiracial society of the island. Education was eventually one of their chosen instruments to anglicize Trinidad.[114] After emancipation, education was developed on the British model; there was no indigenous, traditional education, as in Africa, to pose resistance to the British model. For most of the nineteenth century the Roman Catholic secondary schools of the French creoles (St Joseph's Convent, St George's College, and the College of the Immaculate Conception) borrowed from the practice of French metropolitan schools; but these colleges did not for long resist the influences of the British model replicated, as usual, in a watered down colonial form.

As in England, the Christian churches took the lead in pioneering inexpensive elementary schools, also known as primary schools, meant to effect conversion, to improve Christian moral standards, and to cement denominational loyalties as well as to provide literacy. The intention was not to promote upward social mobility since the colony needed a plantation labour force. These primary schools were meant for the black and coloured lower class, and from the later nineteenth century for the children of the thousands of Indian indentured immigrants who came to Trinidad between 1845 and 1917 to work on the sugar and cocoa estates.[115] Unprepared to, or incapable of, pioneering their own schools (partly from a sense of powerlessness to shape their own future), the black, coloured and Indian labouring classes had to accept the schools and curriculum provided for them by their betters.[116] These schools ignored the popular culture of the people for whom they were intended, the schools for the blacks and coloureds moreso perhaps than the Canadian Presbyterian Mission schools for Indians. On the other hand, the assumption that any and every aspect of popular African or Afro-Trinidadian culture would be welcomed was unjustified as Captain Cutteridge, deputy director of education, discovered in the 1920s when he published his *West Indian Readers*.[117]

Secondary Schools and High Prestige

A separate provision of a few secondary schools developed in the nineteenth century. Although these were meant primarily for the white upper class, in the absence of an impassable colour barrier in schools privileged coloureds of means and a sprinkling of blacks (mostly on scholarships) were able to attend. These secondary schools corresponded to the public schools of England and they all charged fees. The fact that the first such college (St Joseph's Convent) was for girls was a quirk of fortune as secondary education was most explicable as a provision for boys who alone could have responsible public positions and professional careers. The domestication of upper and upper middle class women left them with only the careers of wives and mothers during the nineteenth century. But a broadening of career opportunities for educated middle class women came in the 1920s and 1930s. New secondary schools for girls such as Bishop Anstey High School and Naparima Girls' High School, increased the scope for female secondary education from the 1920s.

In a plantation society based essentially on race, social mobility was always difficult, and secondary education reflected starkly the societal divisions. The main characteristics of this secondary education, whether for girls or boys, were that it was separate from primary school education and meant for a different social group, indeed largely for students of a different race and colour than those in the primary schools. For this reason their curriculum had to be like the public schools of either England or France. Progressively, however, more and more non-whites entered public secondary schools in the 1920s and 1930s, two decades in which the nineteenth century social order was further shaken severely. Bishop's High School, started in Tobago in 1925, was almost entirely for blacks. This astounding variant in Tobago still could not have happened in Trinidad in the 1920s. Nor could a black man have been principal of a public secondary school in Trinidad in 1925 as Rawle Jordan, a black Barbadian, was of Bishop's High School in Tobago. Despite this variation, it is still important to keep in mind that secondary education there, as in Trinidad, was controlled by white persons.

Secondary education at its best was also classical education, narrowly modelled on the grammar schools of England and to a certain extent France, but of a high quality by contemporary standards. The establishment of Queen's Collegiate School in 1859 (later to be Queen's Royal College) as a colonial replica of the best English grammar schools strengthened the influence of the English model on secondary education, and all the newer public secondary schools from the 1920s thought of Queen's Royal College, and sometimes of the College of the Immaculate

Conception, as their model.[118] As in the British schools, there was, from the 1870s, a narrow and insecure bridge from the primary schools to the secondary schools, over which successive handfuls of brilliant boys, most of them black and coloured, passed as free-place scholars into secondary schools. The latter commanded far greater prestige than the teacher training schools which had developed to provide instructors for the primary schools.

Since there was no local university, the three public secondary schools, CIC, QRC and Naparima College enjoyed the highest respect. Even the advent of the first institute of specialized technical training in 1922, namely, the Imperial College of Tropical Agriculture, did not immediately detract from their educational ascendancy. ICTA was essentially a school for the British empire and not for Trinidad and Tobago.[119] As in the English model, it was a long struggle to establish the validity of any but a classical education as genuine secondary education; or to convert the public to the idea that it was a stage, not a type of education. This latter view was the unheeded message of white experts and professional directors of education from the days of Marriott and Cutteridge. Director Marriott's attempts to discourage reliance on Cambridge secondary school certificates and to promote the idea of the untried and untested secondary modern school were met with parental suspicion and indifference.[120]

The steam-driven sugar mills, the new railways and expanding urban life of the post-emancipation years required a fair number of skilled workmen. Many came from the neighbouring British islands. Apprenticeship to trades outside the family probably had a stigma attached to it as a result of the legacy of slavery and the reality of Indian indentureship. Until the early twentieth century there was no organized system of training tradesmen, though from the 1850s a small beginning was made through legislation by which boys and girls, often orphans, delinquents or Indians, could be apprenticed to master tradesmen. This was done as much as a measure of social control as to promote skills training. Skills passed often from father to son, or through private apprenticeship arrangements. Technical/vocational education was slow to develop, and had to do so in the shadow of a bookish curriculum both at the secondary and primary levels.

Despite the introduction first of school gardens, of crafts, then of domestic science and woodwork classes into primary schools from the early twentieth century, the most serious institutional expression of technical/vocational education, the Board of Industrial Training (BIT), was characteristically separate from, and inferior to, secondary education. The Board of Industrial Training provided for trades training outside the ordinary schools, and none of the plans from the 1930s to the 1950s to join farms to primary or secondary schools materialized. The Junior Technical School in San Fernando, established in 1943, was the first of its kind, and it evolved separately from the ordinary schools for the decade of its existence. It was only under the government of Dr Eric Williams from 1956 that serious attempts were first made, not altogether successfully, to integrate technical/vocational education into the mainstream of secondary education.

It was inevitable that examinations would play a most important role in the selection system since demand for secondary education was consistently greater than the supply. The two leading examinations sat locally were the College Exhibition examination and the university scholarship (Island Scholarship) examination. The College Exhibition caused the greatest anxiety to parents; it selected annually a few brilliant boys for free secondary education. The competitors for the university scholarships were fewer than for the College Exhibitions. The university scholarship examination was a notable event in Port of Spain. Competitive examinations for scarce university education left few pleasant alternatives to the losers who had to fall back, at least temporarily, into the ranks of disappointed youths. Fortunately, from the 1930s the facility to take external degrees of the University of London enabled determined handfuls of these persons to refloat their ambitions.

The fiercely contested examinations for free secondary and free university education brought considerable social and economic returns to those who succeeded, and hence they became powerful channels of upward social mobility for a few black and coloured youths.[121] Up to 1939 Indians and Tobagonians were not substantial beneficiaries. Few had access to the better urban or suburban schools. The College Exhibition and the university scholarship examinations, together with the Cambridge secondary school examinations, aroused much public interest in the performance of schools, and created a climate in which scholastic achievement was lionized by most sections of the society.

The Enterprise of the Clerics

In the English model of education, the private enterprise of churches played a most important part in the provision of primary and secondary schools; and so it was in Trinidad and Tobago. The tradition of minimum government interference, especially in secondary education, passed to Trinidad and Tobago, and to owner-operators (the churches) of denominational secondary schools; this custom remained intact down to the 1950s. Nevertheless, this should not blind us to the gradual growth of government interest in, and control over, schools in return for grants. Primary education fell quickly into the sphere of government but secondary schools were more resistant. At certain critical stages, the desire of government to control aspects of education became so pronounced as to lead to serious conflicts with the churches, especially the Roman Catholic Church. The potential of government schools to work as an integrative force in a racially heterogeneous and religiously divided society was quickly grasped, and there were two outstanding thrusts by government to implement policies based on such a perception. One was made in the nineteenth century by Charles Warner, attorney general between

1839 and 1869, a great anglophile. The other followed about a century later when Dr Eric Williams, prime minister from 1956 to 1981, looked at the education system from the same vantage point. Warner desired to give government schools an overwhelming role in education in order to integrate the society on the basis of English culture;[122] Williams wished to do the same on the basis of a vague, superordinate Trinidadian national culture still in the making. Williams and Warner both espoused government schools and denounced denominational schools as obstacles to integration. The opposition of the Roman Catholic Church served to restrict and frustrate seriously the efforts of both Warner and Williams.

Before and after emancipation, the Roman Catholic Church as the church of the majority of Christians in Trinidad, including the French creoles, a powerful white group, had a tremendous amount of social influence. The less powerful Church of England was still a force to be reckoned with because of support from the governors and senior English civil servants. Other Christian churches, such as the Moravians and the Methodists, had small but faithful followers. From the later nineteenth century the rise of the Canadian Presbyterian Church, with several thousands of Indian supporters and converts, and, indeed, the increasing salience of other religions such as Hinduism and Islam, all signalled the deep roots which religious organizations had in Trinidadian society. The neo-African or Afro-Christian churches, like the Orisha religion or the Shouter Baptists, were submerged or proscribed remnants which had no schools and apparently did not desire to run schools.[123] Their labouring class members sought solace through religion, not power through schools. Since most of the churches had schools or wanted to have schools, the stage was set from the immediate post-emancipation period for repeated battles between the churches and government for control and influence over schools and children.

Frenchmen, Englishmen and Indians

From the late 1830s the development of education in Trinidad was characterized by fairly constant tension and sporadic struggles between government and the churches, and between one church and another. The right to have denominational schools became an article of religious faith. In particular the Roman Catholic social doctrine of the preeminence of the family in the provision of education, though more usually stated during the nineteenth century as the primacy of the church, provided a firm philosophical base from which to fight off the centralizing efforts of Protestant oriented or secular governments. The Roman Catholic Church, as the church of the powerful French creole sector of the local upper class, always led the movements to restrict the expansion of government control of education. Protestant Englishmen's dominance over the machinery of government for much of the nineteenth century made matters worse since the clash of government and the Roman Catholic Church thereby assumed the character of a rivalry of nationalities between English colonists and English officials on the one hand, and French creole planters, businessmen and professionals on the other. In resisting the expansion of the government's role in education, especially between the 1840s and 1860s, the Roman Catholic leaders and their French creole allies were setting limits to the imposition of English culture on a cosmopolitan society. But in the later nineteenth century when compensated with greater social consideration, with the legal entrenchment of the dual system of education and with limited political patronage, the Roman Catholic Church and the French creoles came to agree with the English that English culture should be the superordinate European culture. They all reckoned without the large-scale settlement of Indian indentured workers who retained high levels of Indian culture and thus reconstituted the cultural pluralism of the society on a new and more resistant foundation.

The dual system which allowed both churches and government to establish schools on recognized principles of participation was adopted first in 1870, although adumbrated from the time of Governor Woodford. It provided the fundamental framework within which education up to the secondary level was offered. Paradoxically, the consolidation of the dual system was achieved without the dissolution of doubts about its legitimacy. Apart from the experimental period of government (ward) schools between 1849 and 1869, it was generally assumed by the government – up to the time of Eric Williams – that denominational schools were essential. However, the churches never commanded financial resources to equal those of the government, although they always claimed greater prudence in spending government funds, often perceived to be nothing but the taxes of church members. Increasing government expenditure on schools became an irreversible trend which gradually strengthened the authority of the government, although on a per capita or even per school basis the grants were not impressive as aids towards maintenance and repairs. The government's power and influence were pushed gently by the directors of education and grew noticeably from the 1920s. As long as the government did not assert a philosophy of education contrary to the churches', as long as increased government control appeared more bureaucratic than ideological, and as long as vital aspects of the denominational identity of schools (such as real control of teachers, of the curriculum or of the admission of students) were not challenged, the constant tension between government and churches was contained at tolerable levels of disagreement. Tobago was untroubled by conflicts between government and the churches until 1930, and even then not severely.

The supreme creative function of the conflict between government and the churches, and moreso among the churches, was to expand the provision of education at both primary and secondary school levels. The churches today find their history of mutual rivalries embarrassing to acknowledge; hence they are more apt to emphasize that they were the first to start schools rather than to proclaim that it was their fierce, unholy competition which provided the chief mechanism for the expansion of the education system. It might even be maintained that, for most of the nineteenth century, the supply of primary school places by the churches and by the government, more than the demand from the ex-slave and Indian population, explained the growth of the primary school system. In the nineteenth century the rewards for staying in primary school were not so great as to sustain high enrolments.[124] In the early twentieth century, the demand for primary education in urban areas became strong enough to surpass its provision by competitive suppliers, and hence urban schools were chronically overcrowded from the 1920s. Outside the urban areas, the unfriendly rivalry of churches was still highly responsible for the expansion of educational facilities, even in the mid twentieth century, from which time several motivating factors entered parental calculation, and made parental ambition, together with government's political response to it, the wheels which moved the education system forward.

Investment in Schools – Whose Responsibility?

The forces making for increased enrolment in, and expansion of, the primary school sector had to strain against restrictive ideas of race, colour and class. In a society which was structured essentially on race and colour, a persistent upper class attitude to the lower classes (mostly Indians and blacks, and, to a much lesser extent, coloureds) was that they should not be 'pauperized' by indulgent government provision of free social services, including education. Government officials and the upper class disliked what they thought were the exaggerated expectations of the lower classes that government should do a great deal for them; these upper class people felt it was a mistaken policy for government to subsidize social welfare.[125] These ideas were strongest between the later nineteenth century and World War I, a period of severe economic hardship for the sugar industry.

Strange to say, similar ideas are now resurfacing at the end of the twentieth century, in less vicious forms, in some Commonwealth Caribbean countries as governments seek to reduce expenditure on the social services. But then, as now, there were contradictions and countercurrents, and the government itself pursued a mixed policy of *laissez-faire* and subsidized social welfare. Government expenditure on education and public health did in fact expand. *Laissez-faire* ideas served not to bar the growth of subsidized social services, but to hamper it. Whatever was done for the welfare of the lower classes was done as cheaply as possible. Education for them was not to be overambitious; something was done, but not too much. These attitudes conformed to the essentially conservative function assigned to popular education. The purpose was to spread Christianity, literacy and, as always in education, social discipline preferably without social change. The maintenance of the colonial social structure and the labour requirements of the sugar plantations and sugar companies were compatible with an oversupply of illiterate or barely literate youths. Hence the persistence and even open defence of child labour into the 1930s. The provision of schools fortunately enjoyed a certain autonomy from the plantation system; hence excessively conservative opinions such as those of E.A. Robinson, director of Woodford Lodge Estates Company, in favour of child labour rather than schooling, did not block the increase of school places.[126] The main mechanism of growth of the education system after emancipation, namely the competitive energies of the churches within a regulatory framework provided by Crown Colony government, was not entirely stifled by planters and merchants.

The improvement in secondary school enrolment in the years between 1834 and 1902 was extremely sluggish. This was basically because the pool of students was limited by the fees charged, and by the society's narrow perception of the groups which qualified for secondary education. The French creole community commanded a larger portion of the potential fee-paying students, and this partly accounted for CIC outdistancing QRC in enrolment. For the most part, QRC and CIC had different but restricted constituencies and the competition between them was more for government grants than for the same students, except for potential university scholarship winners. St Joseph's Convent had no competition at all for nearly a century, from 1836 to 1925. The returns on parental investment from the education of girls at St Joseph's Convent were mostly nonfinancial; attendance could increase the respectability and marriageability of daughters. Boys acquired higher status from secondary education; finding a useful place in life was not always easy. In the absence of the army as a career (or even the church), a post in the civil service was 'the Promised Land'. Beyond this, brilliant or wealthy boys found their way to British and American universities to become professionals. The possibility of winning university scholarships (Island Scholarships) elicited strong parental support for QRC and CIC.

Queen's Royal College and the College of the Immaculate Conception

The expansion of secondary school facilities beyond the outstanding original triad of St Joseph's Convent, CIC and QRC owed a great deal to demand from urban middle class families of lesser means than those who habitually patronized these three prestigious colleges. The signs of this demand could be seen in the mid nineteenth century in the upgrading of the curriculum of the two leading Port of Spain primary schools (called the Girls' Model School and the Boys' Model School). The demand was also visible by the second decade of the twentieth century in the emergence of a new generation of denominational secondary schools such as Bishop Anstey High School and Bishop's High School in Tobago. Moreover, unaided by government, a development of tremendous importance in secondary education occurred: this was the mushrooming of mass oriented private secondary schools. These schools, which soon began to register successes in the Junior

Cambridge Examination, took control of the output of graduates of secondary schools partly out of the hands of government and the churches, and were the means whereby several underprivileged youths painstakingly made a name for themselves.

The conflict between state and government in education, between the supporters of denominational schools and the advocates of government schools, expressed itself most dramatically through QRC and CIC. These were the two most famous colleges in the island and in fairly close physical proximity in the same town. For at least a generation in the later nineteenth century, the leaders yearned to destroy each other's college. In no other West Indian island was there anything like this furious intercollegiate madness. The academic competition between them was not without positive results, and eventually antagonism was transmuted into a more mature mutual toleration, ensuring for the religiously divided cosmopolitan society the alternative colleges which its Roman Catholic and Protestant middle and upper classes desired. The esteem accorded these colleges was the highest awarded locally to schools, and for nearly a century the male population could be divided gloriously between those who went to QRC or CIC on the one hand and the rest who did not, on the other. For nearly a century it was impossible to win a university scholarship unless one attended CIC or QRC; and their principals were the most widely respected educators even after the arrival of the professional directors. Any assessment today of the relative merits of CIC and QRC is bound to meet with partisan disbelief by old boys of one or the other; but judged by the criteria which they cherished most, namely the university scholarships, the medals, and the House Scholarships, QRC was on top in the period from 1870 to 1939, with CIC having to come from behind in the later nineteenth century, and outperforming QRC in selected years (see Tables 4.4 and 4.5).

Canadian Aid in Education

No fact is as well known in the history of education in Trinidad as the sterling contribution of the Canadian Presbyterian Church to the education of the Indians. They came, they saw and, working partly through the culture of the Indians, they took on, nearly singlehandedly, the education of a race of underprivileged workers neglected on the estates and in the villages. The Canadian Presbyterian Mission put the education of the Indians in Trinidad ahead of that of Indians in Guyana, the only other British Caribbean country with a comparable number of Indians. To the extent that by 1939 Indians had been brought within the mainstream of the society by education, that superb achievement was almost entirely to the credit of the Canadian Presbyterians. In the process of providing a separate education for thousands of Indians, the race consciousness and exclusivism of the Indians, already deep-rooted, were encouraged. The resulting societal divisions, however, were not accompanied by a high level of racial violence between Indians and blacks.

The outcome of the work of the Canadian missionaries, then, was both integrative and disintegrative. But it was their integrative function which was more socially significant because integration might not have happened otherwise. Although their work won them enduring loyalty from scores of Indian families, many Indian leaders from the late 1920s and the 1930s became determined to establish Hindu and Muslim schools as a means of preserving Indian religions and culture against the christianizing and westernizing influences of the churches. This put a stop to the growth of the Presbyterian Church, but not before their schools had provided the means for upward social mobility for hundreds of Indians – subject to the restrictive ethics of lingering India – derived notions of caste. Mission education worked best when allied with high caste, ascriptive values. Other Indians made it from indentureship to the middle class over the same period by the patient route of business success.[127]

Up the down Escalator

Between 1834 and 1939 secondary education provided a vital lever of upward social mobility for black, coloured and Indian persons. As the editor of the *Catholic News* insightfully wrote in 1920:

> Every lad who goes through College and enjoys the blessings of Secondary Education rises in the social scale, and drags up with him the circle of his family and relations together with a wider range of friends and acquaintances. A greater sense of responsibility pervades the lot: the children of the next generation are better tended, efforts are made for their better education and altogether valuable assets are added to the State.[128]

It has been well said by Lloyd Best, one of the leading black intellectuals of Trinidad and Tobago, that the business of black people has been in the field of education. This is not to deny the achievements of other racial groups in the classroom. The point is that, short of fortunate marriages, the educational route seemed the only way up for blacks in particular. In fact, scholastic and occupational success enabled men to marry upwards, often to women higher on the colour scale, even to white women.[129] On the whole, black people did not have the capital, the patronage, the experience or the confidence to develop and successfully preserve careers as businessmen.[130] Their neglect of family capitalism, and dislike of agriculture, generally inhibited capital accumulation for entry into business. The blacks were neither satisfied with nor committed to a predominantly economic role in the society as were the Chinese, Portuguese or Levantines.[131] Some exceptions existed, but education as the way up from manual labour, around business and into salaried white-collar occupations or remunerative professions, was a compelling attraction. This preference for education as the path to social and economic advancement necessitated individual scholastic achievement by members of families, and since this generally was less reliable than intergenerational business success by minority groups, there were many academic failures or dropouts in the family histories of the educated black middle class.

It has been shown that nineteenth century Trinidad had a rather large coloured middle class, many of whom were wealthy.[132] Within one generation after emancipation a new group, of less than a hundred primary school teachers, joined the lower middle class on the basis of achievement in primary and teacher training schools. By the end of the nineteenth century there were not only more teachers including Indians, but black and coloured solicitors, lawyers, medical practitioners, journalists and pharmacists. In the early twentieth century there was a small but important educated middle class. The blacks and the coloureds who won university scholarships, and who were able to establish themselves as respectable professionals, were an inspiration to the rest of the non-white people. Their schoolboy scholastic reputations followed them to their graves in a society which never forgot intellectual accomplishment. The Island Scholars, though sometimes in and out of politics, did not provide the political leadership for the non-white community which many had expected, especially in the troubled 1930s.[133] They preferred to advance their own careers and standard of living. However, they did form part of a professional elite which could be used by the British authorities to assist with the administration of social services; their opinions were especially sought after in education. Their social importance must not be underrated simply because they left political leadership of the masses to the less schooled trade union activists.

It is not now possible to establish with a high degree of accuracy the extent of the social mobility experienced by individuals and groups in the century after emancipation. There were no revolutionary changes in the British West Indies in this century. For students and academics of the last thirty years (1960s to the 1990s) inclined to use the socialist revolution, sometimes the Cuban revolution in particular, or generally the abolition of inequality, as the sole or most important test of change, the century after emancipation in Trinidad and Tobago must seem a disaster. The existence of oppressive social, political and economic structures was, after all, the basic cause of the reformist uprisings of the working class in the 1930s. But the continued dominance of a white minority did not preclude perceptible social change, and scholars should be wary of writing as though nothing worthwhile happened between 1838 and 1937.[134] How, then, is the balance to be struck between the apparently unchanged predicament of the oppressed Indian and black working class over the century after emancipation, and the thousands of blacks, coloureds and Indians who, because of education or success in business, had higher occupational status and higher standards of living than their forefathers in the immediate post-emancipation period?

The researcher who has given the greatest attention to the question of social mobility in Trinidad from the nineteenth century into the early twentieth century did so as long ago as 1954. In his insightful sociological study of social stratification in Trinidad, Lloyd Braithwaite concluded that there was social mobility, but not enough to disturb the structure of Trinidad society as it was at emancipation.[135] If, as is often assumed, Trinidadian society was changing faster immediately after World War II than in the 1920s or 1930s, Braithwaite's conclusion would be even more applicable to the 1920s or 1930s than the early 1950s. He saw very little mobility from the lower class to the middle class, and when it did occur, he interpreted it more as a function of light skin colour, especially for females, than of educational achievement. Braithwaite apparently saw social mobility among the black and coloured people (excluding Indians) as upward mobility within their existing social class than as movement from one class to another. Race and colour for him seemed to have erected a caste-like society with little mobility across caste/class lines. While acknowledging that educational prowess and success facilitated upward mobility of black and coloured professionals, Braithwaite perceived this as occupational mobility within the middle class rather than social mobility into the upper class which was closed because its members were white. Race, colour and marriage appeared to be more determinant of social mobility (or the lack of it) than education. It does not appear then that Braithwaite was denying the enlargement of the middle class through education; and it might well be that historical analysis over time is more apt to reveal the growth and functioning of such an enlarged educated middle class than static fixed-frame sociological analysis. Braithwaite appeared to have underestimated the cumulative force of education as a lever of change over the century.

The upward mobility of thousands of blacks, coloureds and Indians through education during the century after emancipation meant that Trinidad's society did not remain static. This was more obvious in 1939 than in 1909, and more apparent in 1909 than in 1879. The society was increasingly more stratified according to economic classes, though the racial and cultural divide between the Indians and the rest of the non-white community remained in place as well as a measure of caste distinctions among the Indians. Correspondingly, the spread of education moved the society away from the paramountcy of what Braithwaite calls particularistic-ascriptive values characteristic of slave societies towards the greater, but imperfect, acceptance of universalistic-achievement values in a less unequal, but still racist society. This was a modernizing function of education; it had the effect of modifying the plural society.

Although blacks and coloureds to 1939 achieved more upward social mobility through education than Indians, and therefore came to share more common values with the whites (English and French creoles) sooner than Indians, the fact must not be missed that a minority of Indians, through the schools of the Canadian Presbyterian Church, participated in this incomplete ongoing process of creolization. These Christian Indians appeared to have placed more value on the Euro-creole Christian aspects of the shared values than on the Afro-creole elements, but they were probably the parents or grandparents of the Christian

Indians whom Yogendra Malik in the mid 1960s (or Selwyn Ryan in the mid 1980s) found to be least opposed to mixing with blacks and to the principle of interracial marriages.[136]

The Power of the Metropole

Trinidad was a Crown Colony in which there were no elected representatives of the people until 1925. The British government had ultimate power, but in the field of education, if not in others, it left the local governor and Legislative Council to do pretty much as they pleased – provided they could secure the agreement of significant local groups, like the churches. Before World War I generally, the secretary of state for the colonies had no established way of formulating policies for education in the colonies.

Joseph Chamberlain, a strong secretary of state for the colonies, between 1895 and 1903 imposed his own ideas of imperial development on the British Caribbean. Among other things, he wished to promote agricultural education in the colonies. The momentum from his policy rippled throughout the British Caribbean for at least the first two decades of the twentieth century, and in this sense the British government provided the imperial stimulus behind the considerable expansion of interest and practice of agriculture in schools in the British Caribbean from the early twentieth century. But agricultural education was a special case. One could still maintain that education generally was in the backwater of business between the British and the colonial governments; British officials in the colony were left to follow English models which were the only ones they really knew.

Throughout the entire century after emancipation, the English model of education exercised a more profound influence on education in Trinidad than the British government itself. The education system of the island was shaped by the colonial government without much direct supervision from London. By the 1930s a higher level of British government interest in education in Africa spilled over into the British government's relationships with the West Indies, creating the context in which the decision gestated in 1931 to dispatch the Marriott/Mayhew Commission to the West Indies. Whether or not the Marriott/Mayhew Report of 1931/1932 represented the official policy of the British government is a moot point. Official British government policy in education was enunciated in respect to Africa rather than the West Indies.

It was not until the labour movement had consolidated itself after World War I that representatives of the workers, some of whom were Marcus Garvey sympathizers, began to challenge the education policies of the colonial government. By this time the movement for self-government was on the boil, and Crown Colony government was on the defensive. The teachers, too, began to give unsolicited advice. From that point onwards, education policy had to run the scrutiny of teachers, and of self-appointed and elected leaders of the people, who brought to their criticism some perspectives different from the clerical obsession with the churches' rights to receive funds for education. The first call for education to contribute to the dignity of black people which came from the labour movement, inspired the outcry against the Cutteridge reading books for schools.[137]

Curriculum Reform under Suspicion

Curriculum reform in Trinidad and Tobago was met with suspicion, leading to ineffective implementation or postponement of solid ideas into the distant future. In accordance with the English model, in which technical/vocational education of school-age children had never been in popular demand, the curriculum of primary and secondary schools of the nineteenth and early twentieth centuries was bookish and literary, with only slight concessions to practical work and that mostly at the primary school level.[138] Efforts to introduce practical and vocational subjects into the curriculum went through three broad overlapping phases in the very late nineteenth century and the early twentieth century, preceded by a less well-defined post-emancipation effort. Although there were feeble calls in the immediate post-emancipation period for 'industrial' education, meaning agricultural work more than trades, to be made a part of the primary school curriculum, with the intention of preparing the ex-slaves' children to become wage labourers on the sugar estates, these came to nothing. Here the intention was both 'vocational' and pre-vocational: some unskilled work was to be done by the children, but also it was intended to build what was called 'habits of industry', in other words to prepare children psychologically for work, for the benefit of the planters and upper class. The need to implement such socially problematic reforms was apparently reduced by the coming of Indian indentured workers. At any rate, the suspicion of a return to slavery was too strong for such proposals to succeed.

The first phase of serious curriculum reform in the direction of practical and vocational subjects came towards the end of the nineteenth century. It was a time of crisis in the sugar industry and, in addition, there were many signs of rural unemployment. It was somehow thought that agricultural education might be a means of escape for the depressed sugar industry; hence the renewed call for the introduction of the subject, this time backed more seriously by the British government, did result in the imposition of school gardens on most primary schools. These were adjudged to have been failures by World War I partly because the upper class expected too much from these endeavours without having improved the income and life styles of peasants and small farmers. At the same time that school gardens were introduced, QRC and CIC made marginal and unsuccessful attempts to introduce agricultural chemistry without laboratory space.

Contemporaneously with the introduction of school gardens came the beginnings of trades training by the BIT, and this was the second phase. It arose from the greater complexity and variety of technology in the island, from the untrained state of most of the tradesmen and from the demand of the upper class for better workmanship. Trades training was also gaining ground in North America as the best form of education for the urban working class. But it is to be noted that this trades training and its associated apprenticeship programmes was a part-time evening programme, completely separated from the ordinary schools. It was meant to be vocational. Until 1939 when this trades training programme moved to southern Trinidad, it had substantially excluded Indians. The third phase in the introduction of practical subjects came in the 1920s. It led to the gentle introduction of crafts (or handicrafts, sometimes called handwork) in primary schools. Surprisingly, the intention was declared by the directors to be educational, not vocational; the children themselves, rather than the employers or planters were seen as the potential beneficiaries, and the practical work to be done was not in agriculture. A wide variety of materials were brought into the classroom allegedly to train the mind by developing the dexterity of the hands. Curiously, this method was not used to develop the brains of the upper class children in the island.

Crafts did not drive out the discredited school gardens; rather it was superimposed on them. School gardens and crafts, especially the former, created suspicion in the minds of some parents; but no curriculum reform caused as much controversy as the reading books of Cutteridge who, in the 1920s, had introduced a certain amount of African or Afro-Trinidadian materials in them, and had moved swiftly from conception to implementation. All these innovations – school gardens, crafts and *West Indian Reader* – met with slow and limited success, despite pedagogical arguments in their favour.

The Wisdom of Stupidness

Whether in the direction of a localization of reading materials or the introduction of crafts, the success of the curriculum changes in primary schools depended on the quality of the teachers. It would be erroneous not to recognize that on the whole the primary schools of Trinidad and Tobago were better in 1939 than in 1839; it is a mistake to speak of a century of stagnation.[139] In 1966, comparative education expert C.E. Beeby wrote a seminal book in which he developed a model of the stages through which primary schools in developing countries must pass in the life history of a system of popular education.[140] He wrote of a dame school stage in which the teachers were poorly educated and either untrained or barely trained. Teaching would be mechanical and confined to little more than the three Rs. A second stage, called the stage of formalism, is characterized by teachers better trained, but still poorly educated. Here the syllabus is rigid, textbooks narrow, examinations strict, and the inspections rigorous. There is a great deal of emphasis on book knowledge, without appeal to the children's imagination. The third stage is transitional on the way to the fourth and last stage (stage of meaning). This marks modern education in developed countries. In the third stage, teachers are better educated and better trained than in the second stage because they have some secondary education and have been to a properly organized teacher training college. In this third stage the teachers begin to have a wider conception of education, and they begin to have the skills to take their pupils along with them. There would still be official textbooks, but also supplementary reading materials. Education would be more meaningful without being quite modern.

However severely criticized, especially on the question whether the stages were distinct or overlapping, the Beeby model (revised by Beeby himself in 1980) has the merit of insisting that the trained teacher is the key to change in the quality of education.[141] If we look at the history of teacher preparation in Trinidad, it does seem that there were phases in the primary school system which roughly resembled what Beeby had in mind. For instance, during most of the years between 1834 and 1870, primary schools displayed mechanical learning, and the teachers were poorly educated and in several cases untrained. What Beeby calls the stage of formalism bears a resemblance to the system of payment by results between the 1870s and 1921. In this period, the schools did become more formalized, more tightly organized with regular inspections and examinations. The teachers were better trained, as certificates were required from all teachers. It was the aim of Director Marriott and Director Cutteridge to take the schools out of this stage into what Beeby calls the stage of transition; but by 1939 most of the primary schools had not reached anything like stage four. Marriott and Cutteridge did raise the standard of teacher education by recruiting some graduates of secondary schools, and they improved the quality of many teachers by organizing a proper Government Training College whose graduates were put at the top of the teaching service as trained certified teachers. Cutteridge thought that his curriculum revolution gave education meaning.

While it might be readily believed that all the schools by the 1890s had been upgraded from stage one to stage two, it is debatable how far by 1939 Marriott and Cutteridge had managed to transform the primary school system. Cutteridge himself believed that he had succeeded, but his critics made unfavourable judgements of the schools of his day. To the extent that Marriott and Cutteridge did improve the quality of the teachers, it is reasonable to believe that the schools had been improved in their time. But by how much? This question of the quality of the primary school of the 1920s and 1930s is still of great relevance today as hundreds of older Trinidadians and Tobagonians are products of the Cutteridge schools. The Mighty Sparrow (Trinidad's leading calypsonian for many years) might in 1963 make fun of Cutteridge's school books (the *Readers*) and of primary school education in his calypso "Dan is the Man in the Van"; he might imagine that bright pupils ran the risk of learning a lot of "stupidness" from these *Readers*,[142] but the schools then (from the 1920s to the 1940s) were better than the post-emancipation schools.

Comparative Perspectives

There are two regions of the world from which a study of education in Trinidad and Tobago could benefit by way of comparison. Leaving aside the metropole which provided the education models, it would be worthwhile to compare the development of education in Trinidad and Tobago with that in other English-speaking Caribbean territories, and in West African states, especially those which were formerly British colonies. There are difficulties, however: in respect to West Africa, the vastly larger size of the countries and the school population compared to that of Trinidad and Tobago discourage comparisons. The Commonwealth Caribbean countries which have been the subject of most research are the larger units: Jamaica, Barbados and Guyana. We might justifiably be disappointed by the habit of metropolitan scholars and international agencies of lumping the English-speaking Caribbean with Latin America, but making references only to the Spanish Antilles or to Haiti in their studies. As for scholarly work dealing with the Third World, one might easily conclude that the English-speaking Caribbean is not part of it. The pitfalls of international comparative studies in education are many. It is extremely difficult to discover figures which can be confidently used as the base for comparisons. What follows – and it has been confined to the English-speaking Caribbean – is a mixture of inadequate comparisons of statistical indicators plus generalized informed opinions.

The person who first had the opportunity of comparing education in the English-speaking islands was Charles Latrobe, the British government appointed inspector who reported on the use made of the Negro Education Grant. Latrobe travelled throughout the islands and Guyana in 1838 and 1839 and he presented separate reports on the major territories. There was not much to compare in the very infancy of popular education.[143] Not until the Marriott/Mayhew tour of Trinidad and several of the eastern Caribbean islands in 1931/32, that is nearly a century later, did another education expert travel through the chain of islands specifically to report on education.

Marriott and Mayhew made several remarks of a comparative nature. Within Trinidad and Tobago, the only official who was likely to make public comparisons between education there and other West Indian territories was the inspector (or the director); but nothing like this happened until the later nineteenth century when the inspectors of the eastern Caribbean islands found themselves operating a similar system of payment by results. This method of paying teachers' salaries was designed to keep expenditure in check; it encouraged calculations of expenditure per pupil. The inspector for the Leeward Islands about 1877 set out expenditure per pupil in various English-speaking islands. Inspector Guppy of Trinidad declined to compare Trinidad with other islands in 1878, but a decade later he reproduced a chart of the cost per pupil in different islands. This document was originally compiled by the inspector in Jamaica in 1883. Apparently the latter felt pleased by the fact that the chart showed Jamaica with by far the lowest annual cost per pupil (20 cents); with Barbados and Trinidad at 40 cents; and Guyana at 60 cents.[144] Inspector Guppy deplored the idea of low cost as an objective of government policy in education; still it seems clear that the only attraction of comparisons among the West Indian islands from the late nineteenth century to 1939 (the Marriott/Mayhew Report excepted) was to monitor the relative cost of primary education. It was imagined that low cost in education was a measure of efficiency; but the low cost was more valued than the supposed efficiency.

The Education Commission of 1914/16 decided that the best way to test whether Trinidad's expenditure on education was excessive in proportion to its revenues was to compare its expenditure with Guyana's, a colony thought to be similar in many respects. The result varied according to the indicator used; but the Commission concluded that education was far more costly in Trinidad and Tobago than in Guyana[145] since the annual per pupil cost to government was $9.56 in Trinidad and Tobago and $8.38 in Guyana. But there was no difference between the percentage of government revenues spent on primary education in the two colonies. In 1916 as well as in 1934 government appointed committees thought that teachers in Trinidad and Tobago were better paid than their counterparts in Guyana, Barbados and Jamaica. No account was taken of the relative cost of living in the different islands.

It is noticeable that the quality of education did not enter into the calculations of the Education Commission of 1914/16 or the Education Committee of 1934. Nor did the authorities in Trinidad and Tobago seem to have any figures about secondary education in the other territories. The system of education in other English-speaking colonies was not made a point of comparison. Nevertheless, the evolution of these systems had been basically along the same lines as in Trinidad and Tobago; they had their origins in missionary efforts to provide schools followed by government participation as arbiter and provider of grants to approved schools. Apart from differences in the pace of developments, however, Trinidad was distinguished by its special experiment with an exclusive system of government secular schools in the nineteenth century, and by an extraordinarily bitter rivalry, apparently beyond the limits of the rivalries in other islands, between the government and the Roman Catholic Church. The pressures and claims of the Roman Catholic Church and the heterogeneous nature of Trinidad's population gave a greater urgency than in most other islands to a controlling governmental agency at the centre of the education system. Hence the Moyne Commission in

1939 rightly sensed that government regulation of church schools had been carried furthest in Trinidad and Tobago.

The conviction of the Trinidad upper class that their island had more resources, and was potentially richer than any other English-speaking island, goes back at least to the immediate post-emancipation period: it was based then on the alleged fertility of the soil, the abundance of unappropriated land and, to a lesser extent, on the commercial location of the island in relation to South America. The expansion of the frontier of internal settlement throughout the nineteenth century, the economic resilience brought about by the cocoa industry towards its end, the island's position as an important shipping place, these factors confirmed the long-held view of Trinidad as the leader, at least of the eastern Caribbean; and this happened even before the oil industry had arisen. There was one cardinal development in education in the 1920s which added considerably to Trinidad and Tobago's claim to leadership in the English-speaking Caribbean: the siting of the Imperial College of Tropical Agriculture in the colony. Henceforth, the gregariousness of institutions of higher education made Trinidad a serious contender for the site of every regional institution of higher learning. The presence of ICTA strengthened the colony's claims as the logical site of a proposed central teacher training college with students from the eastern Caribbean. From the mid 1920s to the mid 1950s students did travel from the other islands to the Government Training College, although the planned central teacher training college failed to materialize.

The only time the question of quality ever entered the comparisons between education in Trinidad and Tobago and the other islands was in the Marriott/Mayhew Report of 1931/32. It was quite clear then that, with the exception of Barbados, no island in the eastern Caribbean had any schools or educational features which were thought superior to those which existed in Trinidad and Tobago. Barbados and Trinidad and Tobago in some respects were in a class by themselves above the other eastern Caribbean islands. Barbados was thought to have performed better than Trinidad and Tobago with respect to expenditure on education, resulting in its having the best school buildings and equipment.[146] In 1937 S. A. Hammond produced figures which showed that Barbados spent a higher percentage of its budget on education than Trinidad and Tobago, though the latter spent more money on a per pupil basis (see Table 4.6). The acme of Barbados' achievement, however, was its secondary schools where boys and girls reached remarkably high standards in the classics. Although Barbados had a superior position in the provision of secondary education, it was behind Trinidad and Tobago in teacher training facilities, and in the quality of its management team (see Table 4.7). Marriott and Cutteridge as directors in Trinidad and Tobago were unsurpassed in the contemporary English-speaking Caribbean. Barbados in fact only got its first director in 1943. In justifying proposals to place the central teacher training college in Trinidad, Marriott and Mayhew wrote:

The standard of primary school teaching in Trinidad is considerably higher than any of the other islands. Thanks largely to a highly qualified Training College staff, the right atmosphere and traditions have already been established. For manual training, domestic science, and infant teaching an expert staff is already provided. In co-operation with a strong Agricultural Department a scheme of effective training in nature study and garden work is being elaborated. Use can be made of its experimental stations, and teachers under training will have opportunities of seeing demonstration work in fruit, cocoa, and coffee as well as sugar cane. There is also animal husbandry work to be studied, and the work of the Imperial College of Agriculture to be observed, in itself a stimulating example of what science can do for agricultural development. Much of the Canadian Mission work, and more particularly their recent development of domestic science, will suggest to outside teachers valuable ideas of village community work. In the admirable school medical service that is being carefully built up by the Medical Department they will find a much needed stimulus. On the industrial side they have the oil fields and other important undertakings to observe, and in the work of the Board of Industrial Training they will find the beginnings of the application of education to industry . . . There are not wanting schools in which outside teachers can observe the application of methods acquired during training.[147]

Additionally the salaries of primary school teachers had, it was claimed by the Marriott/Mayhew Report, been put on a satisfactory footing, and "its [Trinidad and Tobago's] secondary schools, within the restricted sphere of the Cambridge certificate examinations, have reached a fair level of attainment and by their discipline and school life are exercising a real influence".[148] A weak spot in the Trinidad educational framework was the Indian population which was described by the Marriott/Mayhew Report as "educationally backward" in relation to other sections of the population. Despite the inadequacies of the provision for the Indian population, Trinidad and Tobago and Barbados preserved their position of leadership in education in the eastern Caribbean from the 1930s into the 1940s and up to their emergence as independent nations.

Epilogue

The Next Forty-Two Years (1939-1981)

The development of education over these forty-two years will form the subject of a separate study; here it is hoped to provide no more than a foundation for those readers who are anxious to relate the subject of this book to contemporary education policies. The forty-two years between 1939 and 1981 fall conveniently into three stages: the years of World War II (1939-1945); the decade after World War II (1945-1955); and the long regime of Dr Eric Williams and the People's National Movement (PNM) from 1956 to 1981. It is traditional to stress that no primary schools were built during World War II. A more accurate statement would be that the primary schools built were almost exclusively replacements for old schools demolished or extensions of old schools, in many cases resulting in more school places. Only one absolutely new primary school was built during the war. The schools therefore became more overcrowded. The problem was not strictly a shortage of funds as the government had not spent much of the loan of $240,000 for building new schools, effected before the war; also wartime prosperity arising from the construction of United States naval bases gave the government sizeable surplus revenues from 1941 to 1943, with reduced surpluses in 1944 and 1945.[1] The major constraints were the difficulties the churches had in finding their portions of funds for new school buildings and, of course, the shortage of imported building materials in wartime.

Leaving aside problems arising from overcrowding, both the primary and secondary schools seemed little affected by World War II, unlike ICTA which depended completely on England for postgraduate students and staff. Enrolment in secondary schools, including Bishop's High School in Tobago, reached unprecedented heights, giving rise to the view that wartime prosperity enabled more parents to pay for secondary education. More and more candidates sat and passed the precious Cambridge external examinations. The schools participated in the Grow More Food campaign and their internal organizational life might even have benefited from the increased incidence of Girl Guides and Boy Scouts at a time when it was a sign of loyalty to be in uniform. Nor did the war bring to a halt the outflow of students to study abroad, especially in Canada; and the British government made it possible to take the bar examinations locally without having to risk a sea voyage to England. Candidates continued to take various levels of examinations to qualify for external degrees from the University of London. In short, educational opportunities continued to grow during World War II.

As is well known the preliminary report of the Moyne Commission made recommendations which constituted a landmark in the development of British colonialism in the West Indies. The key concept endorsed was the idea of social development; if, as has been shown, the Commission did not originate this idea, it gave it powerful endorsement. During the war British officials in Trinidad and Tobago knew that because of the labour disturbances, because of the war and the consequential reshaping of British colonial policy, vast changes were to come when peace returned.[2] Trinidad and Tobago was to undertake social, political and even economic development, and education was to be brought into the service of these objectives. It was the first time that education was openly given such a large secular role in the shaping of West Indian society. If the masses were to be given more political power, they had to be educated; if the West Indian middle class was to be given jobs in the upper levels of the civil service as a preparation for self-government, there had to be more scholarships to secondary schools and universities. If the education system was to facilitate social reforms – the most important kind of development in the mind of the British government – it had to be reshaped. It was the function of British education experts, led by Hammond, the Colonial Development and Welfare adviser on education, to provide a new blueprint which the British government could finance. The British government did make available a large amount of money. Hammond began to write some astonishing reports, unlike anything produced by the inspectors and directors in the islands. The Irvine Committee also visited the West Indies and made recommendations for a West Indian university. Implementation of several new beginnings awaited the end of the war.

After World War II the main controllers of primary and secondary education in Trinidad and Tobago – the colonial government, the churches, and the new politicians – chose to expand the education system on its existing base rather than to reorganize it drastically as Colonial Development and Welfare advised. Colonial Development and Welfare wanted to convert the education system into a means to adult education and rural community development in which the primary schools would be very much in contact with the life of the peasants and small farmers. The slogan was 'Education for better living'.[3] This was not to be education for upward social mobility. Secondary education was to be subordinated to primary education, and the model of the secondary modern school was preferred over the grammar school. Colonial Development and Welfare was convinced not only that the structure of West Indian education was too British oriented, but that without structural adjustment the colonies did not have the financial resources to expand it independently of British government support.

Constitutional reforms from 1946 meant that the elected members of the Legislative Council were returned on a system of universal adult suffrage. They could now claim unambiguously to be representatives of the masses. This detracted from the power and influence of the church leaders and the director of education as formulators of education policy, and brought the Legislative Council, from which the director was now excluded, onto centre stage in the making of education policy. These changes – and not only in education – were formalized by the appointment in 1950 of five ministers of government, one of whom was minister of education.

The new politicians – those elected by adult suffrage – responded to popular demand for more primary and secondary education by making the building of schools the supreme issue in the education system. Hence, between 1950 and 1955 the minister of education, Roy Joseph, built his career on the provision of more new primary places than in any previous five year period. Another development of tremendous importance was the admission of Hindu and Muslim denominational schools into the dual system. The Hindus found an aggressive leader in Bhadase Maraj who used their political clout to force a change of policy on the government. Another sign of the times was discussions about the possibility of introducing free secondary education.[4] The people wanted not secondary modern schools, but schools like QRC, CIC and St Joseph's Convent. The churches obliged. By the time Dr Eric Williams came to power in 1956, the education system had been expanded, but on its pre-1939 base.

The long regime of Williams and the PNM was preceded by a period of some twenty-three years in which providence seemed to have prepared him for the role of nationalist leader and father of the nation. Sent away in 1932 to study history at Oxford as an Island Scholar, Williams distinguished himself as an undergraduate and won awards to do historical research into West Indian history leading to the prestigious PhD of the same university. He resided in the USA from 1938 to 1948 and his research and experience there led him to become a West Indian nationalist. During and after World War II, when decolonization was a burning issue, he emerged from his academic post at Howard University as a spokesman for the Caribbean. Having consolidated his academic reputation by early scholarly publications (one of which, *Capitalism and Slavery*, brought him international recognition), he gained employment with the newly created Caribbean Commission and was stationed as an international civil servant in Trinidad and Tobago from 1948 to 1955. Eventually the contradictions between his nationalist posture and political interest on the one hand, and the conservatism of his employers on the other, broke down, and Williams was dismissed, an outcome which cleared the way finally for a full-time political career.[5]

A key theme in the education policy of Williams, and the PNM government which he headed from 1956 to 1981, was the attempt to build a nationalist education system responsive to the will of the sovereign government, and not to that of the churches. In an ethnically and politically divided society it was unthinkable that a nationalist government could overlook the transforming potential of education. Williams and the PNM hoped to use the education system to bring about social integration and economic development, the former chiefly by bringing youths of different races and classes into the same schools and the latter by downplaying the colonial grammar school type of secondary education, to the benefit of technical/vocational education and training befitting a country bent on industrialization. The consequential centralization and consolidation of government power over education was just one point of a multifaceted process of nation building common to several Third World countries in the postwar era.

Williams himself was anticlerical and opposed to denominational schools which he stigmatized as a "breeding ground of disunity".[6] His regime reorganized the dual system since, among other reasons, he was convinced that the churches had traditionally been supporters of the white colonial ruling class. His government reversed decisively the long established tradition, both in primary and secondary education, for the churches to build more schools and provide more new school places than the government. The most staggering results were achieved at the level of the secondary schools. Starting from a paltry total of three government secondary schools in 1957 (QRC, St George's College, and the San Fernando Technical Institute), the PNM government raised the number to twenty-one by 1967, only two fewer than the denominational colleges. After 1967, the government consolidated its ascendancy in secondary education with the new junior secondary and senior secondary schools, each costing far more than the churches could afford. By 1963 the reversal of the position of the government vis-à-vis the churches in relation to new schools was even more pronounced in the field of teacher training. Starting with one Government Training College in 1957, the government by 1963 had three such institutions, producing many more graduates than the denominational teacher training colleges. Directly and indirectly the government discouraged the building of denominational schools and colleges of all types.

Williams and his PNM government struggled to gain greater control over the education system through legislation. Since the authority of the government before 1950 was already ample in relation to denominational primary schools, the government's upgrading of its authority here was not as sensational as in the area of secondary schools. By the Education Act of 1966 denominational secondary schools were brought under the 'inspection' of government. The control of denominational school teachers was a flashpoint in the dual system. At the time the PNM came to office, the government had no control over the appointment of these teachers beyond checking the suitability of their academic qualifications. They now were put by the Education Act on the same footing as teachers in government primary schools; that is, the government was the final authority in their appointment, transfer, promotion and dismissal. It was a major victory for government control. The government also successfully asserted a right to control the admission policy of the denominational secondary schools.

The acquisition of new powers by the government was not accomplished without public agitation, more intense in 1965 than in any previous controversy over education. It was a struggle in which each side declared conflicting ideologies fundamentally incompatible. The leaders of the churches' case – the Roman Catholic Church – claimed that the family and not the government had the responsibility to provide education;[7] the other side asserted the right of the constitutionally elected government to control education in the national interest.

In bringing pressure on its denominational partners in the dual system, the government practised the fine art of taking one step backwards and two steps forward. For instance, two steps forward were taken after the brash Maurice Committee Report of 1959 provided the government with the basis for the government proposal of July 1960.[8] It looked then as if the denominational character of the church schools was about to be utterly eroded; then with the 1961 election in mind, the government took one step backwards by the *Concordat* of December 1960. The churches were confirmed in their ownership of their schools; negotiations were to precede changes. Then between 1962 and 1966 another two steps forward were taken in the furious year of 1965. A Draft Education Act and accompanying Education Code were put before the public, sparking off a great controversy. When the dust settled after the passing of the Education Act of 1966 there was still a dual system, but the relative power of the government and churches had shifted further in favour of the government. Then came the government junior secondary and senior secondary schools of the 1970s. To the question whether a dual system exists today a possible answer is that an incomplete national system and a constricted overlapping dual system exist side by side.

From the point of view of education, the long regime of the PNM can be subdivided into three periods. From 1956 to 1962 one might conclude that expansion of the stock of schools, especially government schools, took place rather than the promised reorientation of the education system. In this phase came the much vaunted beginning of free secondary education, and the deliberate spread of government secondary schools to rural areas, including Tobago. More university scholarships were provided in these six years than in the previous twenty-five, and the traditional Island Scholarships lost their special significance as a means of getting a profession. A high point of this period was the inauguration of the one-year Emergency Teachers' College in Port of Spain, and the beginnings of plans for a large government teachers' college at Mausica. The one major exception to emphasis on expansion over reflection and reorientation was the setting up and reporting of the Maurice Committee, the first blueprint for change in education by local non-white experts.

The next discernible period was between 1963 and 1972. It was characterized by plans to reorient the education system before further expansion was undertaken. It was the most difficult period for the government because emphasis on plans meant delays and promises of a new future while existing problems piled up. The country had become independent in August 1962, and it was time to rethink the education system. The major achievement of these years was the beginning of educational planning marked by the publication of the Draft Fifteen-Year Education Plan 1968-1983. This plan defined the nature of the two-cycle secondary education system of junior secondary schools (age group 11 to 14 years) and senior secondary schools (age group 14 to 18 years). The senior secondary schools were to provide a broad range of academic courses and practical training in agricultural, technical and commercial courses with the option to specialize in one aspect of the curriculum. Technical schools were then conceived as a separate provision. The publication of the Education Plan coincided with the peaking of the Black Power movement between 1968 and 1970. Increasing unemployment and unemployability of youths, plus disillusionment with independence at a time when the youths of the developed world were staging marches for idealistic causes, lay behind the Black Power movement. This movement spurred a further rethinking of the curriculum of secondary schools, some of which had participated in the upheaval; and it also led to more programmes for trades training.

Although planning rather than implementation was so conspicuous during the 1960s, it is worthy of note that a branch of the University of the West Indies was established in Trinidad and Tobago in 1961, first through the integration of ICTA into the university as its Faculty of Agriculture, and then with a Faculty of Engineering (1962), followed by a College of Arts and Sciences. Rapid expansion of student intake, and the commencement of the Faculty of Social Sciences, gave Trinidad and Tobago the capacity to produce enough graduates to staff its expanding secondary schools.[9] Since the government paid the fees of its nationals on the St Augustine campus, the nation could boast that it had free education (for those who qualified) from primary schools to university.

Between 1973 and 1981 the PNM government sought to carry forward reorientation and expansion simultaneously. The showpiece of the expansion was a spectacular array of new junior secondary and senior secondary schools which set a new standard for school building and school equipment in the nation. The dramatic increases in the price of oil from late 1973 provided the government of oil rich Trinidad with unprecedentedly large revenue surpluses, and the lack of money ceased to be a problem in education policy from 1974 to about 1981. School attendance was made more attractive by large government subsidies towards school uniforms, school bus service, school meals and the school medical service. The availability of large-scale capital funds and energy resources led to a decision to enter heavy industry which in turn increased the urgency to produce skilled workers. The curriculum change which most mirrored this decision was the shift in government policy away from separate technical schools to the integration of specialized craft training in some of the senior secondary schools. This became probably the most fateful reorientation of the curriculum of schools in the late 1970s. When Williams died in March 1981, Trinidad and Tobago had the most impressive education structure in the Commonwealth Caribbean. But all was not well.

Appendixes

Appendix I

List of Island Scholars 1863-1903

Year	Name	Class	College
1863	J.R. Cadiz	Class II	QRC
1864	H.C. Bowen	Class I	QRC
1865	J.R. Fabien	Class I	QRC
1866	J.N. Rat	Class I	QRC
	J.K. Wright	Class I	QRC
1867	No nominations		
1868	W. Eccles	Class II	QRC
1869	R.G. Bushe	Class I	QRC
	G.M. Knox	Class I	QRC
1870	A.W. Wright	Class II	QRC
	J.J. Cornilliac	S	CIC
	L.J. Fabien	S	QRC
	G.L. Latour	S	QRC
1871	R. Eccles	Class II	QRC
1872	A.A. Boucaud	Class II	QRC
1873	No nominations		
1874	No nominations		
1875	J.A.R. Stollmeyer	———	QRC
1876	W.E. Cleaver	Class I	QRC
	G.S. Dorville	Class II	QRC
	R.S.A. Warner	Class III	QRC
1877	H.A. Alcazar	Class I	CIC
	A.R. Gray	Class I	QRC
	R.W.C. Norman	Class II	QRC
1878	A.E. Hendrickson	Class III	CIC
1879	W.J. Locke	Class I	QRC
	C.R. Alston	Class III	QRC
	L.A. Wharton	Class III	CIC
1880	J. Cornilliac	Class III	CIC
1881	C.A. Locke	Class II	QRC
	E.G. Blanc	Class III	QRC
	A.N. Darwent	Class III	QRC
1882	A.A. Bruére	Class II	CIC
	C.B. Reid	Class III	QRC
	G.G. Savary	Class III	CIC
1883	S.M. Laurence	Class II	QRC
	E. Prada	Class III	CIC
	C. Williams	Class III	QRC
	C.F. O'Connor	Class III	CIC
1884	R.A. Falconer	Class I	QRC
	J.R. Dickson	Class III	QRC

[293]

List of Island Scholars 1863-1903 (continued)

Year	Name	Class	College
1885	C.P. David	Class II	QRC
	G.L. Fitzjerald	Class III	QRC
	H.P. Ganteaume	Class III	CIC
1886	H.E.A. Horsford	Class III	QRC
	W.B. Wilson .	Class III	CIC
	R. Scheult	Class III	CIC
1887	C.A. Farrell	Class II	QRC
	A.S. Morton	Class II	QRC
	W.F. Kirton	Class III	QRC
	L.A.A. Solomon	Class III	CIC
1888	C.G. Archibald	Class III	QRC
	W.B. Fraser	Class III	QRC
	P.E.H. Giuseppi	Class III	CIC
	J.H. Seon	Class III	CIC
1889	J.F. Gibbon	Class III	QRC
	J. MacFarlane	Class III	QRC
	C.F. Lassalle	Class II	CIC
1890	H.H. Morton	Class II	QRC
	W. Brown	Class II	QRC
	F.M. Simmonds	Class II	QRC
1891	H.H. Boissiere	Class I	QRC
	A.A. Robinson	Class III	QRC
	A.S. Allum	Class I	CIC
	G.A. Vincent	Class II	CIC
1892	W.C. Morton	Class I	QRC
	F.A. Boissiere	Class II	CIC
	J. Alcindor	Class II	CIC
1893	P.G. Ganteaume	Class II	CIC
	P.C. Compariole	Class III	CIC
	H. St Clair	Class II	CIC
1894	D.B. Hughes	Class I	QRC
	E.H. Gibbon	Class II	QRC
	A.L. Nestor	Class III	CIC
	H. Bishop	Class III	CIC
1895	W.H. Meyer	Class I	QRC
	P. Telles	Class II	CIC
	J.D. Hobson	Class II	QRC
	G. Perreira	Class II	CIC
1896	W.C.D. Innis	Class I	QRC
	B.P. Ghose	Class II	CIC
	A.H. McShine	Class II	QRC
	R.E. Phipps	Class II	QRC
1897	C.S. René	Class I	CIC
	L.A.H. Lack	Class I	QRC
	C. Dumanoire	Class II	CIC
	E.A. Turpin	Class II	QRC

List of Island Scholars 1863-1903 (continued)

Year	Name	Class	College
1898	J.M.P. Grell	Class I	QRC
	K.V.A. Inniss	Class I	QRC
	C.S. Doorly	Class I	QRC
	J.M. Flament	Class II	CIC
1899	A.A. Ollivierre	Class I	QRC
	R.A.G. Fitzwilliam	Class I	CIC
	P.L. Giuseppi	Class I	CIC
	F.L. Guppy	Class I	CIC
1900	E.J. DeVerteuil	Class I	CIC
	C.J. Milne	Class I	QRC
	J.A. Burke	Class I	CIC
	J.A. Kernathan	Class I	CIC
1901	E.M. Figari	Class I	CIC
	H. Cross	Class I	CIC
	W. Savary	Class II	CIC
	F.E.M. Hosein	Class I	QRC
1902	C.L. Laurent	Class I	QRC
	C. Eckel	Class I	QRC
	T.F. Tomlinson	Class I	QRC
	R.C. Wuppermann	S	CIC
1903	J.A. Tomlinson	Class I	QRC
	J.H. Carter	Class I	QRC
	J.E.T. Oxley	S	CIC
	A.E. Milne	Class II	QRC

Source: C.P. 76 of 1904 Annual Report of the Principal of QRC for 1903/1904 (W. Burslem)

Notes: 1. S = over the age of 19 years.
2. Burslem remarked that this list was not compiled purely from official sources, implying that there were gaps in the official records.

Appendix II

Growth of the College Exhibitions 1872-1937

Year[1]	No. of Exhibitions granted	No. of entrants[2]	Boys/girls entrants	Comments
1872	3	12	-	3 schools participated
1873	3	16	-	-
1874	6	13	-	-
1875	4	15	-	-
1876	2	36	-	9 schools participated
1877	2	29	-	-
1878	1	7	-	Standard of entry raised to Standard V of primary schools. Also age limit reduced from 14 to 12 years
1880	2	14	-	-
1888	-	-	-	In 1888 there were 9 Exhibitioners in QRC- evidence that the system continued between 1881 and 1890
1890	-	-	-	Exhibitions abolished by Education Ordinance of 1890, but it appers that at least one was granted (see Brereton, *Race Relations*, 198)
1891	-	-	-	None granted
1892	-	-	-	Exhibitions restored. Decided to grant 8 annually, but this soon reduced to 4 per annum. CIC allowed to take winners
1893	8	-	-	-
1905	4	-	-	18 Exhibitioners were at QRC; 6 at CIC
1910	4	-	-	Naparima College qualified to admit Exhibitioners
1912/13	4	108	-	-
1913	4	141	-	-
1914/15	4	116	-	-
1916	4	110	-	No examinations held this year, but candidates sat with 1917 group. This incidental doubling apparently suggested the level of increase Hancock desired
1917[3]	8	91 (plus others)	-	Standard raised and number doubled
1918	8	77	-	-
1920	8	114	-	23 Exhibitioners at QRC; 19 at CIC

Growth of the College Exhibitions 1872-1937 (continued)

Year	No. of Exhibitions granted	No. of entrants	Boys/girls (entrants)	Comments
1922	8	90	.	Apparently examinations changed in direction of an intelligence test. One additional Exhibition made available to candidates from private schools, but not won this year
1923[4]	8+1	84	9 girls	34 schools participated
1924	8+1	120	17 girls	48 schools participated
1925	8+1	180	51 girls	60 schools participated
1926	8	181	44 girls	2 girls among winners for first time
1927	8+1	186	38 girls	60 schools participated
1928	8+1	180	42 girls	53 schools participated. Revival of rule that each candidate must have passed Standard VI of primary school.
1929	8	157	40 girls	58 schools participated. A girl topped list of winners for the first time. All winners came from primary schools.
1930	8+1	168	46 girls	.
1931	8+1	195	62 girls	A girl topped list of winners.
1932	8+1	241	73 girls	A girl topped list of winners.
1933	8	304		
1934	8+1	269	.	Policy changes: decided to increase Exhibitions to 10 in 1935, 12 in 1936 14 in 1937 and 16 in 1938.
1935	10	220	.	4 girls among winners.
1937	14	260	.	From 1936 all candidates had to pass a preliminary test set by the director.

Source: Reports of Inspectors of Schools (or Directors of Education) 1872-1937

Notes:
1. No information has been found for the years omitted.
2. Before 1923 all candidates were boys.
3. For the doubling of Exhibitions in 1917 another explanation offered was that since the colleges were changing the start of their academic year from January to July from 1917, it would have been unfair to the 1916 group of candidates if the number was not doubled in 1917.
4. From 1923 an additional Exhibition was made available to private schools. Plus one (eg. 8+1) in the Table means that a private school candidate won the additional Exhibition that year. Occasionally an extra Exhibition was granted (for example 1923) because of tied marks.

Appendix III

Winners of the Silver Medal of the Agricultural Society for agriculture in primary schools 1920-1937 (including Tobago except for 1920)

Year	No. of competing schools	Winners	Comments
1920	.	Iere Govt	.
1921	.	Ecclesville CM	.
1922	.		No competition
1923	63	Ecclesville CM	Tabaquite CM came second
1924	106	Lochmaben RC	Ecclesville CM came second
1925	109	San Juan CM	Palmyra CM came second
1926	95 (but 19 withdrew)	Arouca Boys RC	San Juan Govt came second
1927	71	Torrib Trace CM	Harbargain Govt. came second
1928	87	Tacarigua CM	Jordan Hill CM came second
1929	.	Freeport CM	Jordan Hill CM came second
1930	84	Arouca CE	Jordan Hill CM came second
1931	98	Jordan Hill CM	Arouca CE came second
1932	181	Jordan Hill CM	Arouca CE came second
1933	145	Jordan Hill CM	Arouca CE came second
1934	155	Arouca CE	
1936	151	Caroni CM	
1937	165	Tacarigua CM	

Source: Reports of Directors of Education 1920-1937

Notes:
1. The Medal was inaugurated in 1902.
2. In 1920 Tobago had its own competition won by Scarborough CE
3. By 1934 a new medal was donated as Jordan Hill CM was allowed to keep the original one.

Appendix IV

Junior Cambridge Examination results 1930-1936[1]

Year	School	No. of candidates	No. successful in hons	(Percent)	No. successful (merely satisfied)	(Percent)	No. who failed	(Percent)
1930	Nap. College	15	1	(6.7%)	7	(46.7%)	7	(46.7%)
	St Joseph's Convent	53	8	(15.1%)	34	(64.2%)	11	(20.8%)
	Bishop Anstey	22	4	(18.2%)	11	(50.0%)	7	(31.8%)
	Nap. Girls' HS	6	Nil	·	6	(100.0%)	Nil	·
	Bishop's (Tobago)	11	Nil	·	8	(72.8%)	3	(27.2%)
1931	Nap. College	19	2	(10.6%)	12	(63.2%)	5	(26.2%)
	St Joseph's Convent	37	6	(16.2%)	24	(64.8%)	7	(19.0%)
	Bishop Anstey	25	4	(16.0%)	20	(80.0%)	1	(4.0%)
	Nap. Girls' HS	7	1	(14.3%)	6	(85.7%)	Nil	·
	Bishop's (Tobago)	9	Nil		9	(100.0%)	Nil	
1932	Nap. College	29	Nil	·	25	(86.2%)	4	(13.8%)
	St Joseph's Convent	38	7	(18.5%)	23	(60.4%)	8	(21.0%)
	Bishop Anstey	25	7	(28.0%)	15	(60.0%)	3	(12.0%)
	Nap. Girls' HS	7	Nil		7	(100.0%)	Nil	·
	Bishop's (Tobago)	9	Nil		5	(55.6%)	4	(44.4%)
1933	Nap. College	27	3	(11.1%)	17	(63.0%)	7	(25.9%)
	St Joseph's Convent	45	13	(28.9%)	29	(64.4%)	3	(6.7%)
	Bishop Anstey	22	5	(22.7%)	16	(72.7%)	1	(4.6%)
	Nap. Girls' HS	13	Nil		10	(77.0%)	3	(23.0%)
	Bishop's (Tobago)	11	Nil		6	(54.6%)	5	(45.4%)
1934	Nap. College	31	No honours reported		14	(45.1%)	17	(54.9%)
	St Joseph's Convent	54		·	40	(74.0%)	14	(26.0%)
	Bishop Anstey	23	·	·	19	(82.6%)	4	(17.4%)
	Nap. Girls' HS	11	·	·	9	(81.8%)	2	(18.2%)
	Bishop's (Tobago)	12		·	5	(41.7%)	7	(58.3%)

Junior Cambridge Examination results 1930-1936 (continued)

Year	School	No. of candidates	No. successful in hons	(Percent)	No. successful (merely satisfied)	(Percent)	No. who failed	(Percent)
1935[2]	Nap. College	33	No honours reported	-	26	(78.8%)	7	(21.2%)
	St Joseph's Convent	62		-	46	(74.2%)	16	(25.8%)
	Bishop Anstey	24		-	23	(95.9%)	1	(4.1%)
	Nap. Girls' HS	12		-	11	(91.7%)	1	(8.3%)
	Bishop's (Tobago)	8		-	6	(75.0%)	2	(25.0%)
1936	Nap. College	29	No honours reported	-	11	(38.0%)	18	(62.0%)
	St Joseph's Convent	58		-	37	(63.8%)	21	(36.2%)
	Bishop Anstey	27		-	21	(77.8%)	6	(22.2%)
	Nap. Girls' HS	10		-	7	(70.0%)	3	(30.0%)
	Bishop's (Tobago)	10		-	4	(40.0%)	6	(60.0%)
	St Benedict	6		-	6	(100.0%)	Nil	-
	St Joseph HS	11		-	6	(54.6%)	5	(45.4%)

Source: Reports of Directors of Education 1930-1936

Notes: 1. The Junior Cambridge Examination for government supported schools was discontinued from 1936.
2. From 1935 successful candidates were 'passed' or failed, with honours abolished.

Appendix V

Cambridge School Certificate Examination results 1930-1937

Year	School	No. of candidates	No. successful in hons	(Percent)	No. successful (merely satisfied)	(Percent)	No. who failed	(Percent)
1930	Nap. College	9	1	(11.2%)	4	(44.8%)	4	(44.3%)
	St Joseph's Convent	16	1	(6.3%)	14	(87.5%)	1	(6.2%)
	Bishop Anstey	9	Nil	-	7	(77.8%)	2	(22.2%)
	Nap. Girls' HS	3	Nil	-	1	(33.3%)	2	(66.6%)
	Bishop's (Tobago)	3	Nil	-	1	(33.3%)	2	(66.6%)
1931	Nap. College	9	Nil	-	6	(66.6%)	3	(33.3%)
	St Joseph's Convent	20	6	(30.0%)	8	(40.0%)	6	(30.0%)
	Bishop Anstey	9	2	(22.3%)	2	(22.3%)	5	(55.4%)
	Nap. Girls' HS	2	Nil	-	2	(100.0%)	Nil	-
	Bishop's (Tobago)	6	Nil	-	1	(16.7%)	5	(83.3%)
1932	Nap. College	17	1	(5.9%)	9	(53.0%)	7	(41.1%)
	St Joseph's Convent	17	Nil	-	11	(64.7%)	6	(35.3%)
	Bishop Anstey	16	2	(12.4%)	7	(43.8%)	7	(43.8%)
	Nap. Girls' HS	1	Nil	-	1	(100.0%)	Nil	-
	Bishop's (Tobago)	4	Nil	-	3	(75.0%)	1	(25.0%)
1933	Nap. College	25	2	(8.0%)	17	(68.0%)	6	(24.0%)
	St Joseph's Convent	17	7	(41.2%)	9	(52.9%)	1	(5.9%)
	Bishop Anstey	13	4	(30.8%)	8	(61.5%)	1	(7.7%)
	Nap. Girls' HS	3	Nil	-	Nil	-	3	(100.0%)
	Bishop's (Tobago)	4	Nil	-	1	(25.0%)	3	(75.0%)
1934	Nap. College	23	No honours reported		13	(56.5%)	3	(75.0%)
	St Joseph's Convent	23			17	(73.9%)	10	(43.5%)
	Bishop Anstey	18			11	(61.1%)	6	(26.1%)
	Nap. Girls' HS	8			5	(62.5%)	7	(38.9%)
	Bishop's (Tobago)	7			1	(14.3%)	3	(37.5%)
							6	(85.7%)

Cambridge Examination results 1930-1937 (continued)

Year	School	No. of candidates	No. successful in hons	(Percent)	No. successful (merely satisfied)	(Percent)	No. who failed	(Percent)
1935	Nap. College	21	No honours reported	'	15	(71.4%)	6	(28.6%)
	St Joseph's Convent	25		'	19	(76.0%)	6	(24.0%)
	Bishop Anstey	15	'	'	8	(53.3%)	7	(46.7%)
	Nap. Girls' HS	7	'	'	3	(42.8%)	4	(57.2%)
	Bishop's (Tobago)	6		'	1	(16.7%)	5	(83.3%)
1936	Nap. College	25	No honours reported	'	11	(44.0%)	14	(56.0%)
	St Joseph's Convent	32		'	21	(65.6%)	11	(34.4%)
	Bishop Anstey	16	'	'	9	(56.2%)	7	(43.8%)
	Nap. Girls' HS	10	'	'	6	(60.0%)	4	(40.0%)
	Bishop's (Tobago)	8	'	'	5	(62.5%)	3	(37.5%)
	St Benedict	5	'	'	4	(80.0%)	1	(20.0%)
	St Joseph Girls' HS	6	'	'	5	(83.3%)	1	(16.7%)
1937	Nap. College	25	No honours reported	'	9	(36.0%)	16	(64.0%)
	St Joseph's Convent	38		'	22	(57.9%)	16	(42.1%)
	Bishop Anstey	11	'	'	8	(72.7%)	3	(27.3%)
	Nap. Girls' HS	6	'	'	4	(66.7%)	2	(33.3%)
	Bishop's (Tobago)	9	'	'	4	(44.4%)	5	(55.6%)
	St Benedict	2	'	'	2	(100.0%)	Nil	'
	St Joseph HS	7	'	'	6	(85.7%)	1	(14.3%)

Source: Reports of Directors of Education 1930-1937

Note: From 1934 the system of honours was discarded in favour of grades not included in this Table.

Appendix VI

The Higher Class at Tranquillity[1] 1911-1920

Year	No. of new admissions	Total enrolment	Cambridge Preliminary Exams[2]		Junior Cambridge Exams		Senior Cambridge Exams		Fees (TT$)	Expenditure
			No. sitting	No. passing	No. sitting	No. passing	No. sitting	No. passing		
1911	22	-	-	-	-	-	-	-	-	-
1912	-	40	-	8	-	-	-	-	-	-
1913	-	-	-	7	-	-	-	-	-	-
1914	-	-	-	4	-	5	-	-	-	-
1915	-	-	-	4	-	6	-	6	$1,267	$1,435
1916[3]	-	51	14	9	-	5	-	2	$1,478	$1,708
1917	-	52	10	7	8	5	4	2	$1,636	-
1918	32	57	-	-	6	-	5	-	-	-
1919	-	-	-	-	-	-	-	-	-	-
1920	-	48	14	6	10	8	5	3	$1,569	$2,644

Source: Reports of Inspectors of Schools 1911-1920

Notes:
1. The School started in 1911 and ended in 1922. In 1916 it moved from the Model school to the Prince's Building in Port of Spain itself.
2. Cambridge Preliminary means Junior Cambridge Preliminary.
3. In 1916 it was said that 73 students were on the books; 51 on the roll.

Appendix VII

Number of elementary schools 1834-1937

Year	Total no. of schools	No. of government schools	No. of church schools	Enrolment	Average attendance	Estimated no. of children of school age
1834	36	2†	34	'	'	'
1847	53	Nil	53	2,416	1,682	'
1870	62	31	31*	7,400*	'	'
1886	126	57	69	14,527	9,933	22,500‡
1902	237	51	186	33,872	19,562	'
1918	293	52	241	45,501	26,786	'
1937	292	45	247	72,776	50,799	'

Source: Reports of Inspectors of Schools and Directors of Education 1870-1937

† indicates 2 Cabildo schools (town council schools)
‡ in 4-14 age group
* estimated

Notes:
1. All figures before 1902 exclude Tobago. Indian schools included after 1886.
2. In 1834 some of the church schools were more private schools with strong connection to churches than church schools properly speaking.

Appendix VIII

Number of public secondary schools 1836-1939

Year	No. of church schools	No. of govt schools	Enrolment
1836	1	Nil	20*
1850	2	Nil	80*
1871	2	1	224
1886	2	1	385*
1902	3	1	575*
1918	3	1	879
1939	8	1	2,259

Source: Reports of Inspectors of Schools or Directors of Education 1870-1939);
Catholic News 5 July 1901, editorial

* estimated

Notes:
1. From 1902 figures include Naparima College.
2. The 1836 estimate refers to St Joseph's Convent; in 1839 it had 50 students.
3. This Table excludes private secondary schools of laymen, but includes St Joseph's Convent and St George's College, schools which were really private in the nineteenth century but had a public character.

Appendix IX

List of Tables

1.1 The ward schools 1858-1870

1.2 Government and denominational schools 1876-1887 (see p. 32 this volume)

1.3 Distribution of College Exhibition winners among schools 1872-1878

1.4 Occupational choices and fate of 65 Island Scholars 1876-1896

1.5 Senior Cambridge Examinations results 1895-1914

2.1 Number and percentage of pupils in Standards I-VII (excluding Tobago)

2.2 Number of pupils in first three and first four Standards (excluding Tobago)

2.3 Percentage passes in core subjects (including Tobago)

2.4 Enrolment at teacher training schools 1898-1913

2.5 Enrolment in government supported secondary schools 1893-1918

2.6 Enrolment and government subsidy to QRC and CIC 1871-1916

2.7 Ownership of primary schools (including Tobago) 1920-1929

2.8 Government expenditure on government and denominational primary schools 1920-1929

2.9 Government and church expenditure on Tobago primary schools 1891-1933

2.10 Government expenditure on teacher training 1922-1937

2.11 Estimated enrolment of teacher training colleges 1931-1937

2.12 Number of students in teacher training colleges 1931-1937

2.13 Number and classification of teachers in Trinidad and Tobago 1920-1937

2.14 Junior Cambridge Examination results: private schools and private candidates 1920-1929

2.15 Cambridge School Certificate results: private schools and private candidates 1920-1929

2.16 Junior Cambridge Examinations: performance of all candidates 1920-1929

2.17 Cambridge School Certificate Examinations: performance of all candidates 1920-1929

2.18 Oxford and Cambridge Higher School Certificate Examinations: performance of all candidates 1920-1929

2.19 Enrolment and attendance in primary schools in Trinidad (Tobago excluded) 1927-1937

2.20 Attendance at primary schools in Trinidad and Tobago 1930-1937

2.21 Number of students enrolled in government supported secondary schools 1930-1938

2.22 Oxford and Cambridge Higher School Examination results 1930-1937

2.23 QRC and CIC: Junior Cambridge Examination results 1930-1936

2.24 QRC and CIC: Cambridge School Certificate Examination results 1930-1937

2.25 Distribution of registered apprentices of the Board of Industrial Training

2.26 Occupations of 864 primary school pupils who successfully completed Standard VII of primary school in 1938

2.27 List of primary school teachers acting as inspector of schools or appointed inspector 1922-1937

2.28 Number of College Exhibition winners (by school) 1901-1937

3.1 Ownership of primary schools in Trinidad (excluding Tobago) 1930-1937

3.2 Ownership of primary schools in Tobago 1930-1937

3.3 Number of persons sitting and passing intermediate examination of the University of London

3.4 Number of persons sitting and passing final examination for external degrees of the University of London

4.1 Number of male and female students in the teacher training colleges 1925-1937

4.2 Cambridge School Certificate Examinations results: private schools and private candidates 1930-1937

4.3 Junior Cambridge Examinations results: private schools and private candidates 1930-1936

4.4 Number of Island Scholarships won by CIC and QRC

4.5 Number of Jerningham Gold and Silver Medals won by CIC and QRC 1897-1937

4.6 Comparative expenditure on education in the West Indies in 1937

4.7 Secondary education per 1000 persons in the West Indies in 1942

Table 1.1

The ward schools 1858-1870

Year	No. of schools	No. of rolls	Average daily attendance	(% of no. on rolls)	Number in the Alphabet	(% of no. on rolls)	No. in 1st Book	(% of no. on rolls)	No. in 2nd Book and sequel	(% of no. on rolls)
1858	26	1684	985	(58.5)	204	'	642**	'	'	'
1859	27	1664*	827	(49.7)	329	'	469	'	502	'
1860	30	1819	972	(53.4)	344	'	620	'	533	'
1861	31	2072	939	(45.3)	432	'	707	'	434	'
1862	30	2113	1054	(49.9)	451	(21.3)	662	(31.3)	564	(26.7)
1863	30	2064	1069	(51.8)	416	(20.2)	669	(32.4)	562	(27.2)
1864	30	1823	958	(52.6)	341	(18.7)	535	(29.3)	558	(30.6)
1866	32	1877	1007	(53.6)	335	'	602	'	529	'
1867	31	1873	1007	(53.8)	347	(18.5)	583	(31.1)	516	(27.6)
1868	30	2241†	1076	(48.0)	'	'	'	'	'	'
1869	31	3139‡	1186	(37.8)	'	'	'	'	'	'
1870	31	3750‡	1336	(35.6)	'	'	'	'	'	'

Source: Reports of the Inspector of Schools 1858-1870

* Figure for the last quarter of the year
** And also sequel to 2nd book
† The highest number on rolls
‡ The total number who attended in 1869 and 1870

Note: 1. The totals in these years are not stated since they do not agree with the numbers stated to be on the rolls. For this same reason the percentage of pupils reading in each book has not been calculated.

Table 1.3

Distribution of College Exhibition winners among schools 1872-1878

Schools	No. of Exhibitions	Comments
Boys' Model School	11	This school was attached to the government training school at Woodbrook and was the forerunner of Tranquillity Boys' School
Park Street RC	5	Also called St Thomas, then the leading RC school
Laventille Govt	1	
San Fernando Borough Council	1	
Mission Village Govt	1	Situated in the Naparimas
Diego Martin Govt	1	
St Joseph's Govt	1	Situated in the Naparimas
Total	21	

Source: CP 44 of 1877 Report of Inspector of Schools for 1877/78

Table 1.4

Occupational choices and fate of 65 Island Scholars 1876-1896

Occupation	Number	Comments
Medical practitioners	17	8 worked in Trinidad; 2 in Tobago; 3 in private practice in Trinidad; and 3 in private practice elsewhere
Medical students	20	
Barristers	11	9 practising in Trinidad; 2 practising elsewhere
Law students	3	
Surveyors	2	Practising in Trinidad
Civil servants	1	In India
Teachers	1	In England
Ministers of the Gospel	3	All Presbyterian Ministers in Canada
Studying for Ministry of the Gospel	1	Presbyterian
Died while studying	2	
Fell ill	1	Returned to Trinidad
Failed to become professionals	2	Apparently failed examinations or dropped out
Still to leave Trinidad	1	
Total	65	

Source: CO 295/381, Jerningham to British government 29 Sept, 1897, encl., Letter from Burslem, principal of QRC.

Note: 24 of the 65 (36.9%) were working in Trinidad in 1897.

Table 1.5

Senior Cambridge Examinations results 1895-1914

Year	School	No. of candidates	No. successful in honours	(Percent)	No. successful (merely satisfied)	(Percent)	No. of failures	(Percent)
1895	QRC	15	7	(46.7)	5	(33.3)	3	(20.0)
	CIC	11	3	(27.3)	1	(9.1)	7	(63.6)
1896	QRC	14	5	(35.7)	5	(35.7)	4	(28.6)
	CIC	13	3	(23.1)	5	(38.5)	5	(38.5)
1897	QRC	.	6	.	6	.	.	.
	CIC	.	4	.	6	.	.	.
1899	QRC	13	4	(30.8)	6	(46.2)	3	(23.1)
	CIC	17	6	(35.3)	7	(41.2)	4	(23.5)
1900	QRC	11	4	(36.4)	6	(54.5)	1	(9.1)
	CIC	15	6	(40.0)	6	(40.0)	3	(20.0)
1903	QRC	21	.	.	.	.	.	.
	CIC	16	.	.	.	.	.	.
1907	QRC	22	9	(40.9)	8	(36.4)	5	(22.7)
	CIC	17	7	(41.2)	5	(29.4)	5	(29.4)
1909	QRC	23	9	(39.1)	12	(52.2)	2	(8.7)
	CIC	18	4	(22.2)	10	(55.6)	4	(22.2)
1912	Nap. College	4	1	(25.0)	3	(75.0)	Nil	.
	QRC	27	14	(51.9)	10	(37.0)	3	(11.1)
	CIC	38	17	(44.7)	15	(39.5)	6	(15.8)
1913	Nap. College	.	Nil	.	.	.	.	.
	St Joseph's Convent	4	.	.	3	(75.0)	1	(25.0)
	QRC	28	12	(42.9)	8	(28.6)	8	(28.6)
	CIC	29	9	(31.0)	13	(44.8)	7	(24.1)
1914	Nap. College	1	Nil	.	1	(100.0)	Nil	.
	St Joseph's Convent	4	.	.	4	(100.0)	Nil	.
	QRC	31	16	.	4	.	.	.
	CIC	.	.	.	.	.	.	.

Source: *Catholic News* 6 April 1898; POSG 17 June 1915; CP 130 of 1896; CP 51 of 1897; CP 90 of 1900; CP 82 of 1900; CP 76 of 1908; CP 69 of 1910; CP 118 of 1914
Reports of Principal of QRC

Table 2.1

Number and percentage of pupils in Standards I-VII (excluding Tobago)

Government Schools Year	I	II	III	IV	V	VI	VII	Total
1901/2	840 (34.7%)	604 (24.9%)	431 (17.8%)	235 (9.7%)	180 (7.4%)	87 (3.5%)	40 (1.6%)	2,417
1911/12	1,053 (33.7%)	580 (18.5%)	538 (17.2%)	371 (11.8%)	250 (8.0%)	207 (6.6%)	121 (3.8%)	3,122

Denominational Schools Year	I	II	III	IV	V	VI	VII	Total
1901/2	1,899 (35.2%)	1,416 (26.2%)	1,047 (19.4%)	577 (10.7%)	300 (5.5%)	129 (2.3%)	23 (0.4%)	5,391
1911/12	3,265 (34.9%)	1,815 (19.4%)	1,699 (18.1%)	1,063 (11.3%)	815 (8.7%)	374 (4.0%)	307 (3.2%)	9,338

Source: CP 37 of 1903; CP 53 of 1913, Reports of Inspectors of Schools

Note: This Table excludes infants. Standard = Grade

Table 2.2

Number of pupils in first three and first four Standards (excluding Tobago)

Government Schools

Year	No. in Standards 1-III		No. in Standards 1-IV		Total pupils
1901-1902	1,875	(77.5%)	2,110	(87.0%)	2,417
1911-1912	2,173	(69.6%)	2,544	(81.4%)	3,122

Church Schools

Year	No. in Standards 1-III		No. in Standards 1-IV		Total pupils
1901-1902	4,362	(80.9%)	4,939	(91.6%)	5,391
1911-1912	6,779	(72.5%)	7,842	(83.9%)	9,338

Source: CP 37 of 1903; CP 53 of 1913, Reports of Inspectors of Schools

Note: This table excludes infants. Standards = Grades

Table 2.3

Percentage passes in core subjects (including Tobago)

Year	Reading		Writing		Arithmetic		English		Geography	
	Examined	Passed (%)	Examined	Passed (%)	Examined	Passed (%)	Examined	Passed (%)	Examined	Passed (%)
1901-2	9,893	(97.0)	9,848	(96.2)	9,829	(86.5)	2,241	(92.9)	2,241	(89.1)
1904-5	11,670	(97.9)	12,206	(98.2)	11,689	(87.1)	2,919	(97.7)	2,919	(95.6)

Source: CP 37 of 1903 and CP 94 of 1905, Reports of Inspectors of Schools

Table 2.4

Enrolment at teacher training schools 1898-1913

Year	Govt (Male)	Govt (Female)	RC (Male)	RC (Female)	Naparima Training College	Total
1898	9	14	7	-	8	38
1908/9	-	-	-	-	-	42
1909/10	10 (4 NR)	11 (7 NR)	8 (2 NR)	7 (1 NR)	9 (4 NR)	45
1910/11	-	-	-	-	-	47
1911/12	9 (3 NR)	11 (7 NR)	8 (2 NR)	7 (1 NR)	11 (5 NR)	46
1911/13	11* (4 NR)	12 (8 NR)	8 (2 NR)	7 (1 NR)	14 (8 NR)	52

Source: CP 16 of 1911; CP 53 of 1913; CP 77 of 1913; Reports of Inspectors of Schools

NR = non-resident
*including 1 from Grenada

Table 2.5

Enrolment in government supported secondary schools 1893-1918

Year	QRC	CIC	Naparima College	St Joseph's Convent
1893	79	174	-	-
1895	79	170	-	-
1897	95	195	-	-
1899	89	210	-	-
1901	-	-	-	-
1903	109	220	46	-
1905	158*	230	36	-
1907	200	230	50	-
1909	196	-	-	-
1911	-	-	-	-
1913	209	275	72	204†
1916	135	267	87	210
1918	171	374	80	254

Source: Reports of Inspectors of Schools 1893-1918; Blue Books 1893-1918

* another figure found is 197

† in addition St Joseph's Convent (a girls' school) in 1913 had 67 boys and in 1916 and 1918, 60 and 61 boys respectively

Table 2.6

Enrolment and government subsidy to QRC and CIC 1871-1916

Year	Enrolment (QRC)	Enrolment (CIC)	Govt subsidy (QRC) (TT$)	Govt subsidy (CIC) (TT$)
1871	75	67	-	$4,800
1875	60	114	-	$4,800
1880	80	142	-	$4,800
1885	79	170	-	$4,800
1890	70	170	-	$4,800
1895	79	170	$9,662*	$6,000
1900	88	213	-	$6,000
1905	158**	230	$20,496	$6,000
1910	231	237	$20,486	$7,200
1916	135	267	$24,734	$7,200

Source: Figures with respect to enrolment from 1871 to 1900 taken from *Catholic News* 5 July 1901, Roman Catholic Memorial to British government; figures for 1905, 1910 and 1916 come from the Blue Books for these years.

* This was the figure for 1894
** Another figure found for this year is 197

Notes:
1. The politics of school statistics (enrolment) of QRC and CIC was extremely contentious in the later nineteenth century, and the figures given above would not necessarily have been acceptable to all contenders.
2. Disputes abound about the way government subsidy to QRC should be calculated. For instance the rent for QRC premises (before 1902) and repairs after 1902 were not shown on the education budget, but under Public Works. See *Catholic News* 25 July 1901 for estimates.
3. The government subsidy to CIC remained the same for about 25 years because it was based on a convention and not on enrolment or number of students passing the Cambridge examinations.
4. This Table excludes the cost of the university scholarships; also the government bore the entire cost of QRC minus the fees, but the precise figures are not known except as stated in the Table.

Table 2.7

Ownership of primary schools (including Tobago) 1920-1929

	1920	1921	1922	1923	1924	1925	1926	1927	1928	1929
Govt	50	49	49	49	48	48	48	47	45	44
RC	95	94	95	95	95	95	95	94	95	96
CE	56	56	56	56	56	55	55	55	55	55
CM	68	69	69	69	69	68	68	68	68	69
Methodist	12	12	12	12	12	12	12	12	12	12
Moravian	11	11	11	11	11	11	11	11	11	11
Baptist	1	1	1	1	1	1	1	1	1	1
	293	292	293	293	292	290	290	288	287	288

Source: Reports of Directors of Education 1920-1929

RC = Roman Catholic
CE = Church of England
CM = Canadian Mission (Presbyterian)
Govt = Government

Table 2.8

Government expenditure on government and denominational primary schools
1920-1929 (TT$ thousands)

Year	Government schools	(%)	Denominational schools	(%)	Total govt expenditure
1920	$87.6	(22.4)	$303.5	(77.5)	$391.2
1921	85.7	(21.5)	311.3	(78.4)	397.1
1922	116.3	(20.6)	446.8	(79.3)	563.2
1923	104.8	(20.1)	416.4	(79.8)	521.3
1924	89.9	(20.6)	345.3	(79.3)	435.2
1925	92.5	(20.6)	356.4	(79.3)	448.9
1926	99.3	(20.9)	375.4	(79.1)	474.7
1927	94.7	(19.6)	387.9	(80.4)	482.7
1928	126.2	(23.6)	407.4	(76.4)	533.7
1929	115.8	(21.4)	424.4	(78.6)	540.2

Source: Reports of Directors of Education 1920-1929

Notes: 1. Total govt expenditure excludes expenditure on administration, but includes upkeep of govt schools.
2. Expenditure on government schools excludes fees from Tranquillity Boys' and Girls' Schools in Port of Spain.

Table 2.9

Government and church expenditure on Tobago primary schools 1891-1933 (TT$)

Year	No. of schools	Govt expenditure	Church expenditure	Total expenditure
1891	23	$2,299	$825	$3,124
1904	30	11,606	2,548	14,154
1909	-	-	-	-
1913	36	20,726	993	21,719
1918	36	23,971	5,520	29,491
1923	36	45,244	4,281	49,525
1928	36	48,062	3,787	51,849
1933	36	57,475	6,912	64,387

Source: Blue Books 1891-1933

Note: The term used in the Blue Books for church expenditure is 'Voluntary contributions'
It excludes the cost of buildings.

Table 2.10

Government expenditure on teacher training 1922-1937 (TT$ thousands)

Year	Total govt expenditure on primary schools	Exp. on govt training schools	stated as % of total exp. on primaary schools	Exp. on denominational training schools stated as	stated as % of total exp. on primaary schools
1922	$593.8	$10.6	(1.8)	$5.3	(0.9)
1925	477.1	9.4	(2.0)	4.4	(0.9)
1928	565.7	10.4	(1.8)	12.9	(2.2)
1931	614.3	17.5	(2.8)	14.5	(2.3)
1934	667.6	24.0	(3.6)	12.5	(1.9)
1937	778.5	24.2	(3.0)	12.1	(1.5)

Source: Reports of Directors of Education 1922-1937.

Total government expenditure includes cost of administration, upkeep of government
schools, grants for new school buildings and teachers' salaries.

Table 2.11

Estimated enrolment of teacher training colleges 1931-1937

Year	Govt Training College	RC Men's Training College	Women's Training College	Naparima Training College	Total
1931	33	11	11	21	76
1932	34	12	11	24	81
1935	80	-	18†††	25*	123
1936	88†	-	16†††	30**	134
1937	94††	-	15††††	24***	133

Source: Reports of Directors of Education 1931-1937

† 38 unofficial students included
†† 41 unofficial students included
††† 5 unofficial students included
†††† 4 unofficial students included
* 10 unofficial students included
** 15 unofficial students included
*** 9 unofficial students included

Notes: 1. As this Table is estimated from the pass list of the colleges the totals do not coincide exactly with the totals in Table 2.12
2. From 1935 the students at the RC Men's Training College were amalgamated with those at the Govt Training College.
3. An unofficial student paid tuition fees.

Table 2.12

Number of students in teacher training colleges 1931-1937

Year	Males	Females	Total	Comments
1931	45	33	78	This total includes 7 unofficial students
1932	48	32	80	Includes 10 unofficial students
1933	50	37	87	Includes 16 unofficial students
1934	54	46	100	Includes 30 unofficial students and 1 special student from Grenada
1935	66	56	122	Includes 48 unofficial students
1936	.	.	132	Includes 7 students from other islands; also includes 58 unofficial students
1937	76	57	133	Includes 8 students from other islands; also includes 54 unofficial students

Source: Reports of Directors of Education 1931-1937

Notes:
1. The Colleges included in this Table are: Government Training College; The Roman Catholic Men's Training College; The Roman Catholic Women's Training College; Naparima Training College.
2. Some students did a three-year course; others a two-year course; a few a special one-year course (for Class II teachers).
3. An unofficial student paid for tuition; most of these students were at the Government Training College.

Table 2.13

Number and classification of teachers in Trinidad and Tobago 1920-1937

Year	Head-teachers	Assistant teachers	Pupil teachers	Needlework teachers	Others	Total
1920	293	336	619 (45.2%)	119		1,367
1923	293	412	796 (48.7%)	133		1,634
1925	290	452	781 (48.8%)	77		1,600
1927	-	-	726	-	-	-
1929	-	-	609	-	-	-
1931	-	-	771	-	-	-
1933	290	829	1,087 (47.5%)	82	-	2,288
1935	292	840	806 (38.9%)	60	71	2,069
1937	-	-	729	-	-	-

Source: Reports of Directors of Education 1920-1937

Notes:
1. The pupil teacher category includes monitors.
2. The total numbers of teachers in 1933 and 1937 exceed the totals given by the director because the monitors have been added.
3. In 1933 and 1935 qualified teachers working as pupil teachers have been classed under assistant teachers.
4. The 'others' in 1935 were called complementary teachers and special subject teachers.

Table 2.14

Junior Cambridge Examination results: private schools and private candidates 1920-1929

Year	Schools/ Candidates	No. sitting	Successful candidates	(%)	Failed candidates	(%)
1920	Private schools	44	19	(43.2)	25	(56.8)
	Private candidates	.	.	.	.	.
1921	Private schools	.	.	.	.	.
	Private candidates	.	.	.	.	.
1922	Private schools	.	.	.	.	.
	Private candidates	.	.	.	.	.
1923	Private schools	63	25	(39.7)	38	(60.3)
	Private candidates	6	0	6	(100.0%)	.
1924	Private schools	50	17	(34.0)	33	(66.0)
	Private candidates	8	3	(37.5)	5	(62.5)
1925	Private schools	61	19	(31.1)	42	(68.9)
	Private candidates	4	1	(25.0)	3	(75.0)
1926	Private schools	66	25	(37.9)	41	(62.1)
	Private candidates	12	5	(41.7)	7	(58.3)
1927	Private schools	55	17	(30.9)	38	(69.1)
	Private candidates	13	5	(38.5)	8	(61.5)
1928	Private schools	83	36	(43.4)	47	(56.6)
	Private candidates	13	3	(23.1)	10	(76.9)
1929	Private schools	75	32	(42.7)	43	(57.3)
	Private candidates	31	7	(22.6)	24	(77.4)

Source: Reports of Directors of Education 1921-1929

Note: A few students (7) passed honours during this period. In 1923 mostly girls were successful; in 1927 only girls were successful.

Table 2.15

Cambridge School Certificate results: private schools and private candidates 1920-1929

Year	Schools/ Candidates	No. sitting	Successful candidates	(%)	Failed candidates	(%)
1920	Private schools					
	Private candidates	6	.	.	.	.
1921	Private schools	.	.	.	.	.
	Private candidates	.	.	.	.	.
1922	Private schools	.	.	.	.	.
	Private candidates	.	.	.	.	.
1923	Private schools	7	1	(14.3)	6	(85.7)
	Private candidates	6	2	(33.3)	4	(66.6)
1924	Private schools	14	3	(21.4)	11	(78.6)
	Private candidates	5	1	(20.0)	4	(80.0)
1925	Private schools	23	9	(39.1)	14	(60.9)
	Private candidates	9	3	(33.3)	6	(66.7)
1926	Private schools	14	6	(42.9)	8	(57.1)
	Private candidates	8	3	(37.5)	5	(62.5)
1927	Private schools	18	9	(50.0)	9	(50.0)
	Private candidates	3	.	.	.	.
1928	Private schools	11	5	(45.5)	6	(54.5)
	Private candidates	10	2	(20.0)	8	(80.0)
1929	Private schools	25	9	(36.0)	16	(64.0)
	Private candidates	8	3	(37.5)	5	(62.0)

Source: Reports of Directors of Education 1920-1929

Note: In 1925, five private schools sent candidates.

Table 2.16

Junior Cambridge Examinations: performance of all candidates 1920-1929
(including private candidates)

Year	No. of candidates	No. successful in hons.	(%)	No. successful (merely satisfied)	(%)	No. of failures	(%)
1920	113	11	(9.7)	54	(47.8)	48	(42.5)
1921	112	21	(18.8)	64	(57.1)	27	(24.1)
1922	100	15	(15.0)	48	(48.0)	37	(37.0)
1923	194	15	(7.8)	86	(44.3)	93	(47.9)
1924	192	29	(15.1)	97	(50.5)	66	(34.4)
1925	215	32	(14.9)	95	(44.2)	88	(40.9)
1926	208	27	(13.0)	108	(51.9)	73	(35.1)
1927	215	33	(15.4)	108	(50.2)	74	(34.4)
1928	258	27	(10.5)	137	(53.1)	94	(36.4)
1929	278	34	(12.2)	146	(52.5)	98	(35.3)

Source: Reports of Directors of Education 1920-1929

Table 2.17

Cambridge School Certificate Examinations: performance of all candidates 1920-1929
(including private candidates)

Year	No. of candidates	No. successful candidates	(%)	No. of failures	(%)
1920	29	13	(44.8)	16	(55.2)
1921	27	14	(51.8)	13	(48.2)
1922	-	-	-	-	-
1923	84	51	(60.7)	33	(39.3)
1924	95	56	(59.0)	39	(41.0)
1925	113	65	(57.6)	48	(42.4)
1926	107	59	(55.1)	48	(44.9)
1927	105	66	(62.8)	39	(37.2)
1928	117	72	(61.5)	45	(38.5)
1929	140	84	(60.0)	56	(40.0)

Source: Reports of Directors of Education 1920-1929

Note: This Table includes private schools/private candidates.

Table 2.18

Oxford and Cambridge Higher School Certificate Examinations: performance of all
candidates 1920-1929 (including private candiates)

Year	No. of candidates	No. successful	(%)	No. of failures	(%)
1920	27	15	(55.5)	12	(44.5)
1921	30	14	(46.7)	16	(53.3)
1922	26	14	(53.8)	12	(46.2)
1923	23	.	.	.	.
1924	30	.	.	.	.
1925	30	20	(66.6)	10	(33.3)
1926	35	27	(77.1)	8	(22.9)
1927	34	27	(79.4)	7	(20.6)
1928	33	23	(69.7)	10	(30.3)
1929	30	22	(73.3)	8	(26.7)

Source: Reports of Directors of Education 1920-1929

Table 2.19

Enrolment and attendance in primary schools in Trinidad (Tobago excluded) 1927-1937

Year	No. of schools	Enrolment	Average attendance	Average attendance %
1927	252	55,237	34,192	61.9
1930	251	57,890	36,932	63.8
1931	254	59,589	38,793	65.1
1932	254	61,506	42,562	69.2
1933	254	64,276	41,205	64.1
1934	254	66,434	41,993	63.2
1935	256	64,670	43,028	66.5
1936	.	65,913	43,858	66.5
1937	257	66,524	46,137	69.3

Source: Reports of Directors of Education 1930-1937

Note: Average attendance means average daily attendance of those enrolled.

Table 2.20

Attendance at primary schools in Trinidad and Tobago 1930-1937

Year	Average attendance in Tobago (%)	Average attendance in Trinidad (%)
1930	66.2	63.8
1931	66.1	65.1
1932	73.5	69.2
1933	68.0	64.1
1934	68.7	63.2
1935	71.3	66.5
1936	70.4	66.5
1937	74.5	69.3

Source: Reports of Directors of Education 1930-1937

Note: Average attendance means average daily attendance of those enrolled.

Table 2.21

Number of students enrolled in government supported secondary schools 1930-1938

Schools	1930	1931	1932	1933	1934	1935	1936	1937	1938
QRC	287	296	265	260	255	269	289	293	335
CIC	462	535	530	510	441	447	457	512	623
St Joseph's Convent	496	444	410	415	351	363	354	354	309
Naparima College	172	185	193	197	202	221	230	227	219
Bishop Anstey	135	142	149	160	157	155	166	178	209
Nap. Girls' HS	138	168	126	163	172	181	194	224	231
Bishop's (Tobago)	69	71	64	48	53	55	56	64	82
St Benedict	·	·	·	·	·	·	113	149	130
St Joseph HS	·	·	·	·	·	·	146	136	121
Total	1759	1841	1737	1753	1631	1691	2005	2137	2259

Source: Reports of Directors of Education 1930-1938

Notes:
1. The figures are usually those at the end of term III.
2. The figures for 1938 are taken from the Blue Book 1938.
3. The figure for Nap. Girls' HS in 1932 is purely for the high school and excludes 23 students in the elementary section of the school. It is likely that the figures for other years included children from the elementary section of the school.
4. St Benedict and St Joseph HS started in 1936.
5. It is possible that the fall in numbers at St Joseph's Convent (a girls' school) from the figures in 1930 and 1931 represents the exclusion of young boys from the statistics.

Table 2.22

**Oxford and Cambridge Higher School Examination results 1930-1937
(excluding private schools and private candidates)**

Year	School	No. of candidates	No. successful	(%)
1930	QRC	15	11	(73.3)
	CIC	16	11	(68.7)
1931	QRC	17	10	(58.8)
	CIC	19	14	(73.7)
1932	QRC	15	10	(66.7)
	CIC	14	9	(64.3)
	St Joseph's Convent	3	3	(100.0)
1933	QRC	11	5	(45.4)
	CIC	15	9	(60.0)
1934	QRC	14	10	(71.4)
	CIC	12	11	(91.7)
	St Joseph's Convent	4	2	(50.0)
1935	QRC	18	14	(77.8)
	CIC	15	9	(60.0)
	Naparima College	5	0	(0.0)
1936	QRC	16	11	(68.7)
	CIC	17	15	(88.2)
	Naparima College	3	1	(33.3)
1937	QRC	17	12	(70.6)
	CIC	14	11	(78.6)
	Naparima College	2	2	(100.0)
	St Joseph's Convent	1	1	(100.0)

Source: Reports of Directors of Education 1930-1937

Table 2.23

QRC and CIC: Junior Cambridge Examination results 1930-1936

Year	School	No. of candidates	No. successful in honours	(Percent)	No. successful (merely satisfied)	(Percent)	No. of failures	(Percent)
1930	QRC	34	12	(35.3)	17	(50.0)	5	(14.7)
	CIC	63	10	(15.9)	33	(52.4)	20	(31.7)
1931	QRC	46	9	(19.6)	31	(67.6)	6	(13.0)
	CIC	71	13	(18.3)	26	(36.6)	32	(45.1)
1932	QRC	40	8	(20.0)	22	(55.0)	10	(25.0)
	CIC	86	17	(19.8)	26	(30.2)	43	(50.0)
1933	QRC	34	10	(29.4)	16	(47.0)	8	(23.6)
	CIC	82	21	(25.6)	43	(52.4)	18	(22.0)
1934	QRC	36	No honours	'	28	(77.8)	8	(22.2)
	CIC	71	reported	'	45	(63.4)	26	(36.6)
1935	QRC	37	No honours	'	31	(73.8)	6	(16.2)
	CIC	72	reported	'	50	(69.5)	22	(30.5)
1936	QRC	33	No honours	'	27	(81.9)	6	(18.1)
	CIC	90	reported	'	56	(62.3)	34	(37.7)

Source: Reports of Directors of Education 1930-1936

Note: Absent or withdrawn candidates not counted as failures. This examination was abolished for government supported schools in 1936.

Table 2.24

QRC and CIC: Cambridge School Certificate Examination results 1930-1937

Year	School	No. of candidates	No. successful in honours	(Percent)	No. successful (merely satisfied)	(Percent)	No. of failures	(Percent)
1930	QRC	31	9	(29.1)	12	(38.7)	10	(32.2)
	CIC	52	6	(11.6)	15	(28.9)	31	(59.5)
1931	QRC	33	9	(27.3)	13	(39.4)	11	(33.3)
	CIC	50	2	(4.0)	28	(56.0)	20	(40.0)
1932	QRC	44	6	(13.6)	14	(31.8)	24	(54.6)
	CIC	51	4	(7.9)	26	(50.9)	21	(41.2)
1933	QRC	49	7	(14.3)	25	(51.0)	17	(34.7)
	CIC	45	5	(11.1)	29	(64.5)	11	(24.4)
1934	QRC	41	No honours	.	27	(65.8)	14	(34.2)
	CIC	68	reported	.	37	(54.4)	31	(45.6)
1935	QRC	48	No honours	.	32	(66.7)	16	(33.3)
	CIC	55	reported	.	37	(67.3)	18	(32.7)
1936	QRC	45	No honours	.	24	(53.3)	21	(46.7)
	CIC	56	reported	.	34	(60.7)	22	(39.3)
1937	QRC	52	.	.	36	(69.2)	16	(30.8)
	CIC	77	.	.	41	(53.2)	36	(46.8)

Source: Reports of Directors of Education 1930-1937

Note: Absent or withdrawn candidates not counted as failures.

Table 2.25

Distribution of registered apprentices of the Board of Industrial Training

Trade	Number of apprentices					
	1910	1917	1918	1924	1929	1937
Blacksmith/Welder	Nil	-	-	1*	2*	3
Boilermaker	Nil	-	-	Nil	3	3
Bookbinder	8	-	-	9	16	7
Boot/Shoemaker	Nil	-	-	Nil	11	4
Cabinetmaker	5	-	-	Nil	10	38
Carpenter	12	-	-	3	10	4
Compositor	Nil	-	-	3	24	20
Fitter	26	-	-	21	25	11
Motor Mechanic	Nil	-	-	Nil	Nil	20
Painter/Decorator	Nil	-	-	Nil	Nil	2
Photoengraver	Nil	-	-	Nil	Nil	1
Pressman	Nil	-	-	3	9	5
Printer	8	-	-	Nil	Nil	7
Tailor	4	-	-	3	14	43
Turner	2	-	-	3	9	21
Upholsterer	Nil	-	-	Nil	1	3
Watchmaker	Nil	-	-	Nil	Nil	1
Moulder	2	-	-	1	3	Nil
Pattenmaker	1	-	-	Nil	2	Nil
Fitter & Turner	Nil	-	-	Nil	4	Nil
Saddler	Nil	-	-	1	Nil	Nil
	68	150	122	48	143	193

Source: Minutes of BIT 25 Feb. 1924; CP 89 of 1910; CP 31 of 1920; CP 31 of 1938; CP 6 of 1930

* blacksmiths

Table 2.26

Occupations of 864 primary school pupils who successfully completed Standard VII
of primary school in 1938

	Entire colony				Port of Spain only			
	Boys	Girls	Total	(%)	Boys	Girls	Total	(%)
No. completing Standard VII successfully	507	357	864	-	140	142	282	-
White-collar Occupations								
To higher education	114	96	210	-	38	38	76	-
To pupil teaching	68	41	109	-	9	9	18	-
To clerical work	22	10	32	-	11	7	18	-
To work in stores	21	7	28	-	19	5	24	-
Total white-collar occupations	225	154	379	(43.8)	77	59	136	(47.3)
Blue-collar Occupations (Tradesmen)								
Engineering	16	-	16	-	5	-	5	-
Motor mechanics	27	-	27	-	12	-	12	-
Tailors	10	-	10	-	7	-	7	-
Bootmakers	13	-	13	-	1	-	1	-
Printers	10	-	10	-	6	-	6	-
Bookbinders	8	-	8	-	8	-	8	-
Carpenters	31	-	31	-	9	-	9	-
Cabinetmakers	20	-	20	-	9	-	9	-
Painters	3	-	3	-	1	-	1	-
Dressmakers	-	106	106	-	-	46	46	-
Total blue-collar occupations	138	106	244	-	58	46	104	-
Other Trades	18	-	18	-	5	-	5	-
Domestic Service	-	22	22	-	-	14	14	-
Agriculture	95	-	95	-	-	-	-	-
Unaccounted for	31	75	106	-	-	23	23	-
Grand Total	507	357	864	-	140	142	282	-

Source: CP 16 of 1940, Report of Special Committee on Vocational Education 1939

Note: Higher education probably meant commercial schools or some form of secondary education, for example recognized secondary schools or private secondary schools.

Table 2.27

List of primary school teachers acting as inspector of schools or appointed inspector 1922-1937

Year	Name of teacher	School	Acting position
1922	Miss Hilda Bushe	'Higher Class' Tranquillity	Temporary Assistant Inspector
1923	Nelson Comma (replacing Sydney Smith)	Mouton Hall Wesleyan	Appointed Assistant Inspector
1924	D.E. Poyer	Chaguanas Govt	Acting Assistant Inspector
	Mrs A. Ferreira (acting for Miss Hilda Bushe)	Eastern Girls Govt	Acting Assistant Inspector
1925	A.M. Mills	Tunapuna Govt	Acting Assistant Inspector
1926	Robert James	Arima Govt	Acting Assistant Inspector
1929	V.R. Vidale	Wesleyan Boys	Acting Assistant Inspector
1930	Alexander Brown	Nelson Street Boys RC	Acting Assistant Inspector
	Nelson Comma Assistant Inspector		Acting Junior Inspector (Southern Division)
1931	E.B. Grovesnor Assistant Inspector		Assistant Inspector (Tobago)
	Rawle Ramkessoon BA		Assistant Inspector
1932	Nelson Comma Assistant Inspector		Acting Junior Inspector
	C. Gayadeen	Caroni CM	Acting Assistant Inspector
	H. McAlister	Cedros Govt	Acting Assistant Inspector
1933	V.R. Vidale		Acting Assistant Inspector
1935	C. Gayadeen (LCP; MRST)	Caroni CM	Appointed Assistant Inspector E.B. Grovesnor (retired)
1937	Rawle Ramkessoon BA		Acting Senior Inspector
	A.J. Mohammed		Acting Assistant Inspector

Source: Reports of Directors of Education 1922-1937

Notes:
1. For a list in 1936, including Miss D. Brodie, see *A Teacher's Annual*, 1936.
2. Wesleyan = Methodist
3. Gayadeen same as Guyadeen elsewhere in text

Table 2.28

Number of College Exhibition winners (by school) 1901-1937

Schools	Years 1901/1917	Years†† 1918/1934	Years 1935/1937
Arima Girls' Govt	-	2	1
Arima Govt	Nil	3	Nil
Arima RC	2	Nil	Nil
Arouca Boys' RC	1	2	Nil
Belmont Boys' RC	3	9	3
Belmont Wesleyan	Nil	2	Nil
Couva CE	Nil	2	Nil
Cunapo Govt	1	Nil	Nil
Eastern Boys' Govt	Nil	2	1
Eastern Girls' School	-	1	Nil
Elswick CM	1	Nil	Nil
Gaines Normal AME	-	1	Nil
Gloster Lodge Moravian	Nil	1	Nil
Guaico CM	Nil	Nil	1
Mouton Hall Wesleyan	9	2	Nil
Mucurapo RC	Nil	1	Nil
Nelson Street Boys' RC	4	5	7
Nelson Street Girls' RC	-	2	1
Park Street RC (St Thomas)	1	2	1
Princes Town Wesleyan	Nil	1	Nil
Richmond Street CE	2	6	1
Sacred Heart RC	-	2†††	Nil
San Fernando Boys' Govt	2	Nil	Nil
San Fernando Boys' RC	Nil	4	1
San Fernando CM	Nil	2	Nil
San Fernando Girls' RC	-	Nil	1
San Fernando Wesleyan	Nil	1	Nil
Sangre Grande Govt	Nil	2	1
St Ann Road Govt	2	Nil	Nil
St Joseph Boys' RC	Nil	3	Nil
St Joseph Girls' RC	-	2	Nil
St Joseph Govt	Nil	2	Nil
Tacarigua CE	Nil	Nil	1
Tranquillity Boys'	7	20	9
Tranquillity Girls' Intermediate	-	9	6
Tunapuna Boys' RC	1	4	1
Tunapuna CE	Nil	1	Nil

Source: Reports of Inspectors of Schools (or Directors of Education) 1901-1937; POSG 8 Dec. 1915.

CE = Church of England; RC = Roman Catholic; CM = Canadian Mission (Presbyterian);
Govt = Government; AME = American Methodist Episcopalian.

†† excludes 1922, 1923 and 1924.

††† Some difficulties of interpretation exist. Up to 1918 or thereabouts the school was listed as Sacred Heart; afterwards apparently as Sacred Heart Girls; but since this school won an Exhibition in 1921 when no Exhibition for girls existed, it might have been a coeducational school.

Notes: 1. Girls were allowed to compete for the first time in 1926.
2. In the Table a dash means that there was no winner in a situation where there could not have been a winner, for example in a girls' school before 1926; Nil on the other hand means that there was no winner in a situation where there could have been a winner.
3. Between 1901/1917 a total of 4 Exhibitions per year was given; between 1918/1929 a total of 8 Exhibitions per year was available; in 1935, 1936 and 1937, a total of 10, 12 and 14 Exhibitions respectively were given.
4. The Table excludes one Exhibition per year for a student from a private school.

Table 3.1

Ownership of primary schools in Trinidad (excluding Tobago) 1930-1937

School Proprietor	1930	1931	1932	1933	1934	1935	1936	1937
Govt	43	44	43	43	43	45	-	45
RC	92	93	93	93	93	93	-	93
CE	40	40	41	41	41	41	-	43
CM	69	69	69	69	69	69	-	68
Methodist	4	4	4	4	4	4	-	4
Moravian	2	2	2	2	2	2	-	2
Baptist	1	1	1	1	1	1	-	1
AME	-	1	1	1	1	1	-	1
Total	251	254	254	254	254	256	-	257

Source: Reports of Directors of Education 1930-1937

CE = Church of England; RC = Roman Catholic; CM = Canadian Mission (Presbyterian);
Govt = Government; AME = American Methodist Episcopalian.

Table 3.2

Ownership of primary schools in Tobago 1930-1937

School Proprietor	1930	1931	1932	1933	1934	1935	1936	1937
Govt	Nil	Nil	Nil	Nil	Nil	Nil	Nil	Nil
RC	4	4	4	4	4	4	4	4
CE	15	15	15	15	15	15	15	15
Methodist	8	8	8	8	8	8	8	8
Moravian	9	9	9	9	9	9	9	9
Total	36	36	36	36	36	36	36	36

Source: Reports of Directors of Education 1930-1937

CE = Church of England; RC = Roman Catholic; Govt = Government

Table 3.3

Number of persons sitting and passing intermediate examinations of the University of London

Year	Arts		Economics		Commerce		Science		Law	
1939	9	(1)	1	(1)	-	-	2	(2)	1	(1)
1940	12	(9)	4	(3)	1	(1)	1	(1)	4	(1)
1941	10	(5)	6	(6)	2	(1)	-	-	1	(1)
1942				SCRIPTS	ALL	LOST				
1943	6	-	3	-	-	-	1	1	-	-
1944	16	-	6	-	-	-	3	2	-	-

Source: Commission on Higher Education (Asquith Commission) Memoranda and Notes of Evidence 1944, Memorandum from the Civil Service Association of Trinidad and Tobago, 2 March 1944

NB: Figures in brackets are for those who passed.
     Dash means no students sat or passed.

Table 3.4

Number of persons sitting and passing final examinations for external degrees of the University of London

Year	BA (General)		BA (Hons.)		BSc (Econ)		B Comm		LLB		DPA
1939	3	(1)	-	-	1	(1)	-	-	-	-	-
1940	3	(2)	-	-	-	-	-	-	-	-	-
1941	-	-	2	(2)	-	-	1	(1)	-	-	-
1942				SCRIPTS	ALL	LOST					
1943	3	(1)	1	(1)	2	-	1	-	1	(1)	1
1944	8	-	1	-	-	-	1	1	-	-	1

Source: Same as in Table 3.3

NB: Figures in brackets are for those who passed.
     Dash means no students sat or passed.

Table 4.1

Number of male and female students in the teacher training colleges 1925-1937 (excluding 'unofficial students')

Year	Males	Females	Total
1925	10	13	23
1927	20	14	34
1929	39	26	65
1931	45	33	78
1933	43	28	71
1935	42	29	71
1937	76	57	133

Source: Blue Books 1925-1937

Note: These figures exclude unofficial students most of whom were probably males. 'Unofficial' students paid tuition fees. The exclusion of 'unofficial students' means that the Table has lower values than Table 2.11 (see section on Govt Training College, Table 2.11).

Table 4.2

Cambridge School Certificate Examinations results: private schools and private candidates 1930-1937

Year	School	No. of candidates	No. successful in honours	(Percent)	No. successful (merely satisfied)	(Percent)	No. of failures	(Percent)
1930	Private schools (6)	22	Nil	-	7	(31.9)	15	(68.1)
	Private study	17	Nil	-	4	(23.6)	13	(76.4)
1931	Private schools (6)	25	2	(8.0)	10	(40.0)	13	(52.0)
	Private study	21	Nil	-	10	(47.7)	11	(52.3)
1932	Private schools (10)	39	2	(5.1)	15	(38.5)	22	(56.4)
	Private study	17	Nil	-	2	(11.8)	15	(88.2)
1933	Private schools (11)	47	Nil	-	27	(57.4)	20	(42.6)
	Private study	22	Nil	-	7	(31.8)	15	(68.2)
1934	Private schools (16)	58	No honours		18	(31.0)	40	(69.0)
	Private study	33	reported		5	(15.2)	28	(84.8)
1935	Private schools (16)	78	No honours		52	(66.7)	26	(33.3)
	Private study	31	reported		7	(22.6)	24	(77.4)
1936	Private schools (15)	71	No honours		26	(36.6)	45	(63.4)
	Private study	48	reported		12	(25.0)	36	(75.0)
1937	Private schools (12)	82	No honours		31	(37.8)	51	(62.2)
	Private study	49	reported		10	(20.4)	39	(79.6)

Source: Reports of Directors of Education 1930-37

N.B. The figure in brackets immediately after 'Private schools' indicates the number of private schools.

Table 4.3

Junior Cambridge Examinations results: private schools and private candidates 1930-1936

Year	School	No. of candidates	No. successful in honours	(Percent)	No. successful (merely satisfied)	(Percent)	No. of failures	(Percent)
1930	Private schools (9)	81	3	(3.7)	38	(47.0)	40	(49.4)
	Private study	29	Nil	-	9	(31.1)	20	(68.9)
1931	Private schools (7)	77	Nil	-	26	(33.8)	51	(66.2)
	Private study	34	Nil	-	5	(14.7)	29	(85.3)
1932	Private schools (10)	151	1	(0.7)	50	(33.2)	100	(66.1)
	Private study	26	Nil	-	7	(27.0)	19	(73.0)
1933	Private schools (25)	149	2	(1.4)	83	(55.7)	64	(42.9)
	Private study	74	Nil	-	18	(24.3)	56	(75.7)
1934	Private schools (34)	175	No honours reported	-	62	(35.4)	113	(64.6)
	Private study	42		-	10	(23.8)	32	(76.2)
1935	Private schools (29)	163	No honours reported	-	71	(43.6)	92	(56.4)
	Private study	47		-	16	(34.1)	31	(65.9)
1936	Private schools (23)	170	No honours reported	-	68	(40.0)	102	(60.0)
	Private study	61		-	8	(13.2)	53	(86.8)

Source: Reports of Directors of Education 1930-36

N.B. The figure in brackets immediately after 'Private schools' indicates the number of private schools.

Appendixes

Table 4.4

Number of Island Scholarships won by CIC and QRC

	1870/1893	1894/1917	1918/1939	Total
QRC	37	45	22	104
CIC	23	34	28	85
Total	60	79	50	189

Source: CP 76 of 1904, Annual Report of the Principal of QRC 1903/1904; also Reports of Inspectors of Schools and Directors of Education 1870-1939

Note: The scheme of Island Scholarships started in 1863, but CIC did not enter the competition until 1870. Between 1863 and 1869 QRC students received 9 Island Scholarships.

Table 4.5

Number of Jerningham Gold and Silver Medals won by CIC and QRC 1897-1937

	Gold Medals 1897/1919	Silver Medals 1897/1919
QRC	12	18
CIC	11	5

	Gold Medals 1920/1937	Silver Medals 1920/1937
QRC	12	5
CIC	6	12

Source: Reports of Inspectors of Schools and Directors of Education 1897-1937; also Centenary Record of Holy Ghost Fathers, Appendix C.

Note: The Silver Medal was granted to the leading candidate in the Junior Cambridge examination up to 1936, and thereafter on the Cambridge School Certificate. It was therefore unrelated to the Island Scholarships. The Gold Medal went to the Island Scholar with the highest number of marks.

Table 4.6

Comparative expenditure on education in the West Indies in 1937

Colonies	Expenditure on education (TT$)	Expenditure on education as % of total government expenditure	Expenditure on education per head of population (TT$)
Trinidad & Tobago	$894,475	9.4%	$1.97
Barbados	304,515	12.3	1.61
Guyana	456,969	8.5	1.38
Jamaica	1,168,342	11.6	1.02
Antigua	28,379	7.3	0.83
St Kitts/Nevis/Anguilla	43,554	9.4	1.16
Montserrat	13,308	9.1	0.97
Dominica	35,652	11.3	0.76
St Lucia	33,167	7.4	0.50
St Vincent	57,872	13.8	1.02
Grenada	77,426	10.7	0.90

Source: Adapted from S.A. Hammond, 'The cost of education', *Development and Welfare in the West Indies*, Bulletin no. 5 (1945) : 25

Table 4.7

Secondary education per 1,000 persons in the West Indies in 1942

Colonies	No. of secondary school students between 12-18 years old	No. of secondary school students per 1,000 of population
Trinidad & Tobago	2,436	4.7
Barbados	1,547	7.7
Guyana	511	1.4
Jamaica	2,648	2.1
Antigua	152	3.7
St Kitts/Nevis	101	2.8
Montserrat	38	2.6
Dominica	90	1.7
St Lucia	139	1.9
St Vincent	212	3.8
Grenada	319	3.5

Source: S.A. Hammond, 'The cost of education'. *Development and Welfare in the West Indies*, Bulletin no. 5 (1945): 18. The Table excludes students in private secondary schools.

Notes

Chapter One

1. S. Gordon, *A Century of West Indian Education* (London, 1963), 19-42; C. Campbell, "Towards an imperial policy for the education of negroes in the West Indies after Emancipation", *Jamaican Historical Review* 7, nos. 1 and 2 (1967): 68-102.

2. C. Campbell, "The development of education in Trinidad 1834-1870" (PhD diss., UWI, 1973), chaps. 2 and 3.

3. A. De Verteuil, *Sir Louis De Verteuil: His Life and Times, Trinidad 1800-1900* (Port of Spain, 1973), chap. 7; J. Harricharan, *The Catholic Church in Trinidad 1498-1852* (Port of Spain, 1981), chap. 6.

4. J. Millette, *The Genesis of Crown Colony Government* (Port of Spain, 1970), chap. 1; L. Newson, *Aboriginal and Spanish Colonial Trinidad: A Study in Culture Contact* (London, 1976), 184-226.

5. J. Millette, *Crown Colony Government*, chaps. 3-4; C. Campbell, "The transition from Spanish law to English law in Trinidad before and after Emancipation", in *Some Papers on Social, Political, and Economic Adjustments to the Ending of Slavery in the Caribbean* (ACH, 1975), 25-52.

6. For the social life of Dr St Luce Phillip, a prominent coloured, in upper class circles after emancipation, see *Diary of Amelia Gumbs Catherine Gomez, née Sanderson and Widow of the Honourable R. O. Smith from 30th April 1841 to the 19th May 1843*.

7. L. Braithwaite, "Social stratification in Trinidad: a preliminary analysis", *Social and Economic Studies* 2, nos. 2 and 3 (1953): 38-60. See Figure 4, p. 47.

8. For peons, see D. Whiteman, "The immigration of peons to Trinidad and their contribution to the development of the cocoa industry 1811-1891" (MA thesis, UWI, 1990).

9. This Charity was originally founded by a bequest of £1,000 (sterling) by Lady Mico in 1670 for the redemption of Christian slaves held in captivity by the Moors. It was never used for this purpose, and by the beginning of the 19th century the accumulated interest had swelled the fund to over £100,000 (sterling). It was then agreed that the income from this fund should be used for the education of children in the former slave colonies; see F. Klineberg "The Lady Mico Charity Schools in the British West Indies 1835-1842", *Journal of Negro History* 24 (July 1939): 295-97.

10. C. Campbell, "The development of education", 134-40.

11. C. Campbell, "Charles Warner and the development of education in Trinidad 1838-1870", *Journal of Caribbean History* 10 and 11 (1978): 59-64 (hereafter cited as *JCH*).

12. C. Campbell, "The development of education", 194-98.

13. For copies of these Ordinances, see *Port of Spain Gazette*, 19 March 1847 (hereafter cited as *POSG*).

14. C. Campbell, "Thomas Hinde of Trinidad 1838-1848", *JCH* 21, no. 2 (1988): 95-116; also C. Campbell, "The development of education", 171-73.

15. CO 295/162, Harris to Grey, 19 June 1848, no. 71.

16. C. Campbell "The development of education", 171-73.

17. Ibid., 168-70.

18. Ibid., 174-78.

19. C. Campbell, "Charles Warner".

20. D. Wood, *Trinidad in Transition* (Oxford, 1968), 221-23.

21. *POSG*, 4 April 1851; Legislative Council, 2 April 1851, Message from Harris.

22. C. Campbell, "The development of education", 180-84.

23. Patrick Keenan, chief inspector of schools in Ireland, was employed by the British government to investigate the system of education in the island. His report is by far the best known by students of education in Trinidad; see P. Keenan, *Report upon the State of Education in the Island of Trinidad* (Dublin, 1869), 11.

24. CO 295/171, Harris to Grey, 17 Oct. 1850, confidential, enclosure: P. N. Aumaitre to Harris, 9 Feb. 1850.

25. C. Campbell, "The development of education", 194-98; J. Harricharan, *The Catholic Church*, 129-30.

26. One unfriendly warden specifically named was Jules Leotaud of St Ann's ward; see *Sentinel*, 12 July 1860, letter from 'The One who bides his Time'. Three wardens were mentioned as exceptions: Leonard Rostant, F. C. Bowen, and Robert Guppy; see *Sentinel*, 8 Sept. 1859, letter from 'An Educationist'.

27. C. Campbell, "The development of education", 198-202.

28. Ibid., 207-209.

29. CO 300/60, Return of local revenues 1850-1870; also for ward expenditure on schools from 1864 to 1865, see D. Hart, *Trinidad and the Other West Indian Islands and Colonies* (Port of Spain, 1866), 29-45.

30. The government assumed responsibility for these schools in return for a portion of the Borough Council's revenues, see *POSG*, 31 Aug. 1875, Meeting of Board of Education (hereafter cited as BOE) and Meeting of Borough Council. In 1888 it was reported that the Borough Council of Port of Spain gave $2,400 p.a. towards two government schools in the town (Eastern Government School and Western Government School); but it is not clear if this was over and above the municipal revenues given to the Executive for education; see J. H. Collens, *Guide to Trinidad* (1888), 249.

31. *Centenary Record of the Sisters of St Joseph of Cluny, 1836-1936* (Trinidad, 1936), 31-37; see also J.M. Feheney, "Catholic education in Trinidad in the 19th century", (MA thesis, UWI, 1975), 350.

32. Gabrielle Mason, "The Sisters of St Joseph of Cluny 1836-1936", (Caribbean Study paper, UWI, Trinidad, 1977).

33. J.M. Feheney has made the point that when St Joseph's Convent opened it was a day school, but it subsequently (apparently soon) became a boarding school. His point is that as a boarding school it had more reasons to be exclusive; see J.M. Feheney, "Catholic education", 350.

34. The secondary schools at St Joseph, San Fernando (boarding) and Arima continued as private schools well into the 20th century, and largely escaped media attention. It might be of some significance that three Roman Catholic clerics who have written on St Joseph's Convent (Sr Gabrielle Mason) and on CIC (Fr Feheney, and Fr A. De Verteuil) have all suggested that the controlling Teaching Order might have acted with less social exclusiveness had it not been for their local French creole supporters; see G. Mason, "The Sisters"; J.M. Feheney, "Catholic education", 346; and A. De Verteuil, *Sylvester Devenish and the Irish in 19th Century Trinidad* (Port of Spain, 1986), 86.

35. J.M. Feheney, "Catholic education", 331-48.

36. Ibid., 337-38.

37. C. Campbell, "Charles Warner", 64.

38. D. Wood, *Trinidad in Transition*, 199-206.

39. CO 295/196, Keate to Labrouchere, 6 Sept. 1857, enclosure: printed speech of Warner to Legislative Council, 2 Sept. 1857.

40. Ibid.

41. Ibid.

42. Ibid.

43. CO 295/195, Keate to Labrouchere, 7 Aug. 1857, no. 75, enclosure: Message to Council.

44. Free places for sons of deceased civil servants continued (perhaps with an interruption) up to 1939; see Angela Hamel-Smith, "A history of education 1900-1938" (MPhil thesis, UWI, 1983), 138. A discussion in the BOE in 1922 suggests that either this privilege had been abolished between 1909 and 1922 or that unwittingly it had no legal basis between these years; see Weekly Guardian (hereafter cited as WG), 4 March 1922, Meeting of BOE.

45. CO 295/196, Keate to Labrouchere, 6 Sept. 1857, enclosure: printed speech of Warner.

46. Ibid.

47. Ibid.

48. C. Campbell, "The etablishment of Queen's Collegiate School in Trinidad 1857-1867", Caribbean Journal of Education 2, no. 2 (1975): 75-78.

49. C. Campbell, "The development of education", 351-53.

50. C. Campbell, "The establishment of Queen's Collegiate School", 79.

51. Ibid., 80-83.

52. POSG, 26 March 1862, Report of Principal Deighton.

53. POSG, 15 April 1863, Editorial.

54. See Appendix 1.

55. POSG, 15 April 1863, Editorial.

56. C. Campbell, "Charles Warner", 73-74.

57. J.M. Feheney, "Catholic education", 348. There is a discrepancy between the accounts of two Roman Catholic priest-historians. Feheney indicates that the legitimacy requirement was instituted at CIC between 1863 and perhaps 1870; Fr Athony De Verteuil appears to locate it sometime after 1892 (for a few years). See A. De Verteuil, Sylvester Devenish, 86.

58. For protest of some Roman Catholics, see Star of the West (hereafter cited as SW), 17 Feb. 1870, Editorial; SW, 16 June 1870, letter from Fr Corbet.

59. A. Fremantle, The Papal Encyclicals in their Historical Context (London, 1963), 129-56.

60. C. Campbell, "The development of education".

61. D. Leotaud and C. Leotaud (eds) Memoirs of an Honourable Gentleman (Port of Spain, 1988), 24. This is a short biography of Charles Leotaud (a member of a leading French creole family).

62. C. Campbell, "The development of education", 400-408.

63. D. Wood, Trinidad in Transition, 265-66; also J.K. Chapman, The Career of Arthur Hamilton Gordon 1829-1912 (Toronto, 1964), 50-51.

64. P. Knaplund, Gladstone and Britain's Imperial Policy (1927; reprint, London 1966), 50-51.

65. D. Wood, Trinidad in Transition, 292-93; J.K. Chapman, Arthur Hamilton Gordon, 50-56.

66. M. Cruickshank, Church and State in English Education (London, 1963), 14-37.

67. This alternative law of 1875 meant that the Ordinance of 1870 was still in force, a situation not always understood. For a good explanation of the juxtaposition of the Education Ordinances of 1870 and 1875, see San Fernando Gazette (hereafter cited as SFG), 13 July 1889.

68. Catholic News (hereafter cited as CN), 17 Feb. 1899, Lenten pastoral of Archbishop Flood.

69. SFG, 18 May 1889, Editorial; CO 295/324, Fowler to Knutsford, 16 Aug. 1889, enclosure: Petition of Protestants.

70. POSG, 4 Sept. 1889; 11 Sept. 1889; 14 Sept. 1889; 19 Sept. 1889, Meeting of BOE; SFG, 22 June 1889, Editorial; SFG, 14 Sept. 1889, Editorial.

71. Despite my best efforts, I have never seen the Lumb Commission Report itself. The Report was missing from the Colonial Office files in the Public Records Office by 1970. The section of the PSOG of 1889 with it has crumbled.

72. J. H. Collens, Guide to Trinidad, 244. For a summary of Ordinance 17 of 1890, see SFG, 10 May 1890.

73. Up to 1914 a distinction was made between Canadian Mission schools,

(CM) and Canadian Mission Indian schools (CMI). These latter were the 'special' schools; see *POSG*, 22 Oct. 1914, Evidence of Rev Harry Morton before the Education Commission 1914/16. It is not clear when the Mission dropped the words 'special' and 'Indian' from the names of its schools.

74. *POSG*, 27 Feb. 1895, Debates in the Legislative Council. In the debate on increased government grant to CIC there was a deadlock of six Protestant votes against six Roman Catholic votes which Governor Napier Broome broke in favour of CIC.

75. *POSG* for 1889, for example 23 Jan. 1889, Editorial; 13 Feb. 1889, Editorial; 23 March 1889, letter from 'F.A.G.R.'; also see *CN* for 1893, for example 27 Jan. 1893, and 9 March 1893.

76. *CN*, 23 May 1901, Editorial; 31 May 1901, Editorial; also *POSG*, 16 July 1901, letter from 'Lucidus'.

77. See Table 4.4.

78. For a defence of Guppy's administration, see the book by his daughter: Yseult Bridges, *Child of the Tropics. Victorian Memoirs*, edited and compiled by Nicholas Guppy (London 1980), 168-69.

79. *New Era*, 10 Jan. 1870 (hereafter cited as *NE)*, letter from 'Cassius'; *NE*, 23 May 1870, Address to A. B. Knox and his reply; also *SFG*, 3 June 1889, letter from 'A West Indian'.

80. Quoted in B. Samaroo, "The Presbyterian Canadian Mission as an agent of integration in Trinidad during the 19th and early 20th centuries", *Caribbean Studies* 14, no. 4 (1975): 53.

81. Articles in the *SFG* in 1870, 1889 and particularly in 1890 reflect these views. The editor Samuel Carter, a coloured man, was consistently anti-Roman Catholic priests; see *SFG*, 3 June 1889, letter from 'A West Indian'; 8 June 1889, letter from Emilie Marese Paul; 14 Sept. 1889, Editorial. For the political posture of this newspaper, see Brereton, *Race Relations in Colonial Trinidad* (Cambridge, 1979), 96. Some persons appreciated the international dimensions of the struggle between the Roman Catholic Church

and governments, and felt that what was happening in Trinidad was an extension of it, see *SFG*, 1 Feb. 1890, letter from T. R. Eriche; also *SFG*, 15 Feb. 1890, letter from 'Alpha'.

82. *SFG*, 19 July 1890, Editorial; *POSG*, 22 June 1901, Petition to British government (including signatures of Edgar Maresse Smith and Emanuel Lazare).

83. *SFG*, 19 July 1889, Editorial, CO 295/324, Fowler to Knutsford, 16 Aug. 1889, enclosure: Petition of Protestants; also *Mirror*, 14 Aug. 1901, letter from 'Lux'.

84. *POSG*, 27 Feb. 1895, Speech of T. Fenwick in BOE.

85. *CN*, 28 June 1901, Editorial: *POSG*, 13 July 1895, Editorial; CP 121 of 1899, Letter of Bishop of Trinidad to Governor, Sept. 1899.

86. CP 161 of 1900, Chamberlain to Acting Governor, 21 Aug. 1900.

87. CO 295/324, Fowler to Knutsford, 16 Aug. 1889, enclosure: Petition of Protestants.

88. *Trinidad Royal Gazette*, 1872 (hereafter cited as TRG), Report of Inspector of Schools for 1871; CP 34 of 1875, in *TRG*, 1875, 280.

89. H. Johnson, "Crown Colony government in Trinidad 1870-1897" (PhD diss., Oxford University, 1969), 164-66, 381.

90. *TRG*, 6 Oct. 1875, Speech of Governor Irvine to Legislative Council, 1 Oct. 1875.

91. CP 35 of 1892, Report of Inspector Bushe in *TRG*, 4 May 1892.

92. *CN*, 15 Feb. 1901, Memorial of managers of Catholic assisted schools to British government, 25 Sept. 1899.

93. CP 121 of 1899, Letter from Bishop of Trinidad, Sept. 1899.

94. Ibid.

95. *Special Reports on Educational Subjects XII. Educational Systems of the Chief Crown Colonies and Possessions of the British Empire, including Reports on the Training of Native Races* Part I. (London, 1908), Appendix D.

96. *Reports on Educational Subjects*, enclosure: Napier Broome to Colonial Office, 6 Oct. 1895.

97. CP 121 of 1899, Letter of Bishop of Trinidad to Governor, Sept. 1899; CN, 8 Sept. 1899, letter from G. Vincent Sutherland.

98. TRG, 2 March 1892, Meeting of BOE 19 Feb. 1892; also TRG, 6 April 1892, Meeting of Legislative Council; 4 April 1892.

99. CP 161 of 1900, Jerningham to Chamberlain, 13 March 1900, enclosure: Report of a Special Committee on Education.

100. P. Keenan, *The State of Education*, 47-48.

101. C. Campbell, "The development of education", 229-30.

102. G. Mount, *Presbyterian Missions*, 298-304.

103. The same point can be made about the Indians in Guyana; see Z. Dunne, "The Canadian Mission to the Guyanese Presbyterian Church", in *Indenture and Exile*, edited by Frank Birbalsingh (Toronto, 1989), 218-24.

104. G. Mount, *Presbyterian Missions*, 218-24.

105. Ibid., 233-37.

106. I. Hamid, *A History of the Presbyterian Church in Trinidad 1868-1968: the Struggle of a Church in Colonial Captivity* (Port of Spain, 1980), 236-37.

107. TRG, 7 April 1875, list of schools under Rev Morton and Rev Grant and supported by proprietors.

108. TRG, 7 April, Report of annual statistics of immigration for 1873-1874. This shows 3,822 black men; 1,815 black women; 770 boys and girls (excluding infants) working on sugar estates.

109. CO 295/334, Napier Broome to Knutsford, 2 Dec. 1895.

110. D. Moore, "The origins and development of racial ideology in Trinidad" (PhD diss., Queen's University, Canada, 1980), 293-94.

111. For one proponent of these views here rejected, see Moore, "Racial ideology".

112. C. Campbell, "The development of education", 231-32.

113. CP 49 of 1876, Report of Inspector of Schools for 1876, Appendix D. Re-

turn of East Indian schools for 1875. The fullest treatment of this question of black children in special Indian schools is in Moore, "Racial ideology"; see for example Table 6-3, 290; also POSG, 10 Sept. 1914, Evidence of Von Weiller.

114. Moore does not know how this exclusion was done. It could have been by positive instruction from missionaries or by attrition. See Moore, "Racial ideology", 290-91.

115. POSG, 22 Nov. 1916, letter from W. I. Green.

116. Y. Malik, *East Indians in Trinidad: a Study in Minority Politics* (London, 1971), 10.

117. For another scholar's difficulties in drawing up the Canadian Presbyterian Church's balance sheet of integrative and non-integrative contribution, see I. Hamid, *History of the Presbyterian Church*, 258; for B. Samaroo's conclusions, see his "Presbyterian Canadian Mission", 53-55.

118. *Reports on Educational Subjects*, Appendix C. This figure (427 children) meant that 12.8 percent of Indians enrolled in primary schools were in government schools. (Total enrolment in 1898 was 427 in government schools and 2,891 in Canadian Presbyterian Mission Schools.) Angela Hamel-Smith was the first researcher to emphasize the significant proportion of Indian children in government schools; see Hamel-Smith, "Education in Trinidad", 105-106.

119. POSG, 15 May 1895, Evidence of C. W. Mitchell before the Education Commission.

120. The main source of information on the Mico Charity in Trinidad is the Anti-Slavery Papers E1/4 and E1/13, 1836-1842, Rhodes House Library, Oxford, England.

121. C. Campbell, "The development of education", 77-78.

122. For instance, T. R. Eriche, when he left it in 1862, had to open a private school; see SFG, 10 May 1870, letter from Eriche.

123. C. Campbell, "The development of education", 249-52.

124. For instance, an old boy tradition (followed later by a model school ex-pupil association) developed around Woodbrook Model School ('dear old Woodbrook') from the 1870s, whereas the government training school had no such overt expressions of pride; see NE, 6 Aug. 1877, Ad-dress by L. B. Tronchin on retirement.

125. P. Keenan, *State of Education*, 29-31.

126. It is widely believed that the govern-ment training school was abolished, and that training in a college was reintroduced in the 1890s; see for example, *Report on Teacher Education and Training for the Primary Level* (Trinidad and Tobago, 1980), Appendix 1, 6-8.

127. P. Keenan, *State of Education*, 31-32.

128. According to one source, Keenan was in favour of teacher training schools in Ireland by 1859, but felt that Trini-dad did not have enough students for this to work; see J. M. Feheney, "Catholic education", 476.

129. C. Campbell, "The development of education", 486; NE, 18 April 1870, letter from 'Atticus'; NE, 14 Nov. 1870, Editorial.

130. Henry Sylvester Williams, the future Pan-Africanist, took up residence in this school in 1884 as a youth of 15 years; see O. Mathurin, *Henry Sylvester Williams and the Origins of the Pan-African Movement 1869-1911* (Westport, 1976), 19-20.

131. These institutions were called by vari-ous names soon after their founda-tion. For example, the training school for females was also called the Kent Street Roman Catholic Training School or the Pembroke Street Train-ing School for Female Teachers; the training school for males was called the Nelson Street Roman Catholic Training School or the Cathedral Training School for Males; see CN, 21 May 1869; 9 May 1902; 8 May 1903. For teacher training arrange-ments by the Canadian Presbyterian Mission, see T. Turner, "The work of the Presbyterian Church of Canada in the field of secular education in Trini-dad 1868-1953" (MEd thesis, Univer-sity of New Brunswick, 1966), 62-63.

132. A. De Verteuil, *Eight East Indian Immi-grants* (Port of Spain, 1989), 55-59.

133. CP 40 of 1897, Annual Report of the Inspector of Schools for 1896.

134. C. Campbell, "The rise of a free col-oured plantocracy in Trinidad, 1783-1813", *Boletin de Estudios Latinoameri-canos y del Caribe* 29 (1980): 33-53.

135. B. Brereton, *Race Relations*, chap. 5.

136. The fullest treatment of race conscious-ness and the black and coloured mid-dle class of the later 19th century can be found in B. Brereton, *Race Rela-tions*, chap. 5; also B. Brereton, "J. J. Thomas, an estimate", JCH 9 (May 1977): 22-42.

137. POSG, 11 April 1860, Report of Inspector Anderson for 1859; also CO 299/10, Report of Inspector Anderson for 1858.

138. NE, 6 Aug. 1877, Address of L. B. Tronchin.

139. See for example the organization of a 'Higher Class' at the Port of Spain Borough Council School in 1849, including for a fee of $2 per month "Latin, Geometry, Mensuration, book-keeping, use of globes, elements of physical sciences". See Minutes of the Port of Spain Borough Council 1849, Appendix to Minutes, 28.

140. P. Keenan, *State of Education*, 30-31.

141. B. Brereton, "J. J. Thomas", also C. Campbell, "John Jacob Thomas of Trinidad: the early career of a black teacher and scholar 1855-1870", *African Studies Association of the West Indies Bulletin* VIII (1976): 4-17.

142. C. Campbell, "The development of education", 297-98.

143. POSG, 2 April 1862, Report on the subject of education for 1861.

144. Ibid.

145. Ibid.

146. J.M. Feheney, "Catholic education", 33-34.

147. C. Campbell, "The development of education", 303-305.

148. Usually not all four were awarded, see C. Campbell, "The College Exhibition in Trinidad and Tobago 1872-1938", *History Teachers' Journal* 2 (March 1983): 44-46. The history of these Exhibitions between 1872 and 1890 abounds with uncertainties over details, arising from differences in the interpretation of the rules, and the slight information provided in the Reports of the inspectors of schools. For instance, how consistently and for how long was there a distinction between winners from rural primary schools and urban (Port of Spain and San Fernando) schools? Did the rules allow only government primary schools to compete? If so, how did St Thomas Roman Catholic School win Exhibitions? For how long was the distinction maintained between Exhibitions given by QRC's principals and those chosen by the BOE?

149. J. J. Thomas, *Froudacity, West Indian Fables Explained* (1889; reprint, London, 1969), 86.

150. *POSG,* 6 March 1915, Editorial.

151. B. Brereton, *Race Relations,* 82.

152. However, a remark by Burslem, the principal, that A. A. Olivierre was (in 1899) the first "Board of Education Exhibitioner" to win a university scholarship is hard to reconcile with this sentence. Perhaps Burslem meant in his time as principal, or more likely there were different types of exhibitioners at QRC; see CP 82 of 1900, Report of principal of QRC for 1889.

153. J. H. Collens, *Guide to Trinidad* 246, also B. Brereton, *Race Relations,* 198.

154. C. Campbell, "The College Exhibition", 44-46.

155. *POSG,* 3 Feb. 1894, Editorial. In 1893 the cost of the College Exhibitions to the government was a mere $600 per annum of a total expenditure on education of $154,392; see *POSG,* 25 Sept. 1895, Meeting of BOE.

156. *CN,* 26 July 1901, Editorial.

157. The original discussions in 1893 have not been seen; see *New Dawn* 1, no. 12 (Nov. 1941): 4.

158. *St Mary's College of the Immaculate Conception, Port of Spain: Its First Fifty Years, 1863-1913,* 27. An illustration of the illiberal administration of the College Exhibition occurred in 1903 (or for 1903) when three of the four winners were disqualified because they were over the required age. No substitutions were made; see *Mirror,* 20 Jan. 1902. In 1936 the editor of the *Teacher's Annual* attempted to list all the scholarships available to secondary schools apart from the government's College Exhibition. His list was as follows: CIC and St Joseph's Convent gave four each from Roman Catholic primary schools; Naparima College gave four from Canadian Mission schools and Naparima Girls' High School offered two for Indian girls; St Benedict's College offered four for Roman Catholic schools in southern Trinidad; there was a Green Pastures Butter exhibition presumably provided by a commercial company; Pamphylian High School (a private school) offered four. The Young Ladies Debating Association of San Fernando offered one; Pamphylian High School also gave one scholarship to its students for attendance at CIC or QRC; there were also two special Exhibitions to mark the Wilberforce Centenary, but the source of these funds is not clear. There were Exhibitions to Bishop's High School in Tobago, but the editor had no precise information; see *A Teacher's Annual* 1936.

159. C. Campbell, "The College Exhibition".

160. D. Trotman, *Crime in Trinidad: Conflict and Control in a Plantation Society 1838-1900* (Knoxville, 1986), 97.

161. *WG,* 21 Feb. 1925.

162. H. Johnson, "Crown Colony government", 85.

163. *Trinidad Guardian,* 13 March 1927 (hereafter cited as *TG*).

164. *NE,* 22 Jan. 1872, Editorial.

165. D. Trotman, *Crime in Trinidad.*

166. See Appendix I. Another count put the first class Island Scholars between 1876 and 1893 at 5 percent; see *CN,*

16 March 1894, College Council 7 March 1894.

167. TG, 7 Oct. 1922, Meeting of BOE, speech of Mr Low, principal of QRC.

168. For example, Henry Sylvester Williams and Eusebio Valerio. See J. R. Hooker, *Henry Sylvester Williams* (London, 1975); E. A. Valerio, *Seiges and Fortunes of a Trinidadian* (Port of Spain, 1919).

169. SFG, 22 June 1889, letter from Emilie Marese Paul; also B. Brereton, *Race Relations*, 88.

170. For his career, see POSG, 3 Jan. 1929.

171. *Labour Leader*, 17 Feb. 1923 (hereafter cited as LL), Career of H. A. Nurse (father of Malcolm Nurse or George Padmore). For a description of Nurse's reading habits; see C.L.R. James, *Spheres of Existence: Selected Writings* (London, 1980), 240-41.

Chapter Two

1. R. Beachy, *The British West Indian Sugar Industry in the Late 19th Century* (Oxford, 1957), chap. 7.

2. For a full account of events from the 1880s leading to the start of the Imperial Department of Agriculture and Morris' involvement; see *West Indian Bulletin* (hereafter cited as WIB) XVIII (1921), article by Dr Watts.

3. S. Gordon, *West Indian Education*, 140-42.

4. WIB III (1902): 110, Report of Inspector Bushe.

5. CP 37 of 1903, Report of Inspector of Schools for 1901/2. For a rather surprising rejection of agricultural education, see Report of L.P. Pierre, Warden of Blanchesseuse, in CP 6 of 1903, Report of the Committee on technical education.

6. B. Samaroo, "Education as socialization: form and content in the syllabus in the Canadian Mission Presbyterian schools in Trinidad from the late 19th century" (paper presented at the 15th conference of the ACH, UWI, Mona, 1983), 14.

7. POSG, 15 Oct. 1914, and 22 Oct. 1914, Evidence of Nurse before the Education Commission 1914/16. The government made no grants to denominational schools to buy tools for school gardens.

8. *Proceedings of the Agricultural Society* (hereafter cited as PAS) II, (1896/97), Meeting of 8 June 1897, Report of Prof. Carmody; PAS III, (1898/99), Meeting of 11 Jan. 1898, Report of a committee to consider the question of agricultural education; PAS XIII, (1913): 56-61, Report of a government appointed committee; also Report of a Select Committee of the Agricultural Society.

9. For instance, note the ease with which P. E. T. O'Connor in about 1919/20, as an Irish creole youth of about 20 or 21 years old, acquired a temporary post as overseer at Woodford Lodge estate from his uncle, although he knew nothing about sugar or labour management. See P. E. T. O'Connor, *Some Trinidad Yesterdays* (Port of Spain, 1978), 78-79.

10. PAS XII, (1912), Meeting of 12 April 1912, paper by Dr Fredholm.

11. PAS XIII (1913), Speeches at meeting of Agricultural Society, 7 Feb. 1913.

12. WIB VI (1906): 213, Report of Carmody.

13. Education Commission 1916, Original Documents, 2, Statement by Burslem, 18 Feb. 1913.

14. PAS II (1896/97), Submission of Carmody, 8 June 1897.

15. N. Lamont, *Problems of the Antilles* (Glasgow, 1912), 3-30.

16. PAS XIII (1913), Speech of Lamont, 7 Feb. 1913.

17. Dr Watts hinted at this; see WIB XIV (1914), article on agricultural education.

18. For imperial propaganda favourable to the establishment of ICTA; see T. August, *The Selling of the Empire. British and French Imperialist Propaganda 1890-1940* (Westport, 1985), chap. 1. Also R. Porter, *The Lion's Share: a Short History of British Imperialism* (London, 1975), 237-79.

19. For the interest of Milner and Amery in colonial agriculture; see L. S. Amery, *My Political Life*, 2 (London, 1953), 338-42.

20. For planter understanding of the international dimension of the college, see PAS XIII (1913), Speech on 7 Feb. 1913.

21. PAS XII (1922), Report of Dr Watts, 8 June 1922.

22. Possibly eleven from the West Indies and four from England, see PAS XXIV (1924), Report of laying of foundation stone of new building, 14 Jan. 1924.

23. PAS XXIII (1923), Meeting on 9 Aug. 1923.

24. The rate for a 'pass' in school garden (maximum) was 96 cents for each pupil in average attendance during the year; see WIB III (1902), Report by Bushe.

25. There was no examination in agriculture; see POSG, 13 Aug. 1914, Evidence of Hancock before Education Commission of 1914/16.

26. WIB XIV (1914): 171.

27. E. Williams, *History of the People of Trinidad and Tobago* (London, 1964), 214, 225.

28. PAS XX (1920): 64, enclosure: British Government to Chancellor, 27 Jan. 1920; PAS XX (1920), paper by G. Moody Stuart, 26 March 1920.

29. WG, 7 June 1924, Meeting of BOE.

30. CP 37 of 1903, Annual Report of inspector of schools for 1901/02.

31. POSG, 11 May 1895, Evidence of Charles Soodeen before the Education Commission; also POSG, 15 May 1895, Evidence of Miss Blackadder and C. W. Mitchell.

32. Snippets of information about the system of payment by results can be gleaned from the evidence presented to the Education Commission of 1914/16 by the inspectors. For example; see POSG, 23 July 1914, 30 July 1914, 13 Aug. 1914, and 27 Aug. 1914.

33. The 'pass' mark in arithmetic was 25 out of 100, and in rural schools easier arithmetical questions were asked than in urban schools, see POSG, 8 Oct. 1914, Evidence of W. Kenny.

34. See, for example, POSG, 30 Aug. 1916, Meeting of BOE; also POSG,1 Nov. 1916, Meeting of BOE for bitter rivalry between Roman Catholics and Canadian Presbyterians in Caparo.

35. CP 168 of 1916, Report of the Education Commission appointed by Sir G. R. LeHunte on 16 June 1914 (Port of Spain, 1916), 7.

36. Up to this point (1916), it does not appear that the teacher training schools had separate diploma examinations; see POSG, 5 Aug. 1916, Editorial.

37. For a rather complacent description of the government male training school at Tranquillity, see POSG, 21 Jan. 1915, Evidence of C. L. Boland.

38. POSG, 1 Oct. 1914, Evidence of W. Kenny.

39. POSG, 13 Feb. 1889, Editorial; CN, 13 Jan. 1893, copy of Napier Broome to British government, 4 Aug. 1892; CN, 27 Jan. 1893, Editorial; CN, 9 March, 1893, Editorial.
In 1937/38 the question of switching from the Cambridge examinations to London Matriculation Examination was again discussed at the BOE, but this time the principal of CIC among others, was opposed to it; see *The People*, 31 Dec. 1937, Editorial; also *The People*, 3 Sept. 1938, Editorial; *The People*, 9 July 1938.

40. CN, 23 Feb. 1893, Report of College Council 18 Feb. 1893, Letter from Miles to British government 29 July 1892.

41. Education Commission 1916, Original Documents, 2, Statement by Burslem, 18 Feb. 1915.

42. S. Ryan, *Good Innings 1901-1990: the Life and Times of Ray Edwin Diffenthaller* (Port of Spain, 1990), 2-5.

43. In the continual disputes between supporters of government schools and friends of denominational schools, the *Catholic News* and the *Port of Spain Gazette* (after 1914) took the side of the Roman Catholics and the *Mirror* the side of government

schools. See for example *POSG*, 22 and 26 July 1914, Editorial.

44. *NE*, 15 Aug. 1870, letter from 'Several'; also *NE*,15 Nov. 1870, letter from 'ABC'.

45. Of eleven inspectors between 1890 and 1914 only two had any experience in teaching secondary schools; see POSG, 27 Aug. 1914, Evidence of E. G. Penaloza.

46. *WG*, 16 Dec. 1922, Speech of Fr Lacy at CIC prize-giving.

47. QRC's science teacher (part-time) was said to have seen service in World War I, and it was only in 1923 that science teaching became organized; see *WG*, 31 March 1923, Speech of principal at QRC prize-giving. QRC did not send up candidates for the Agricultural Scholarship between 1919 and 1924; see *WG*, 7 June 1924, Meeting of BOE, Speech of Mr Low.

48. The syllabus for both the Agricultural Scholarship and later the Science Scholarship was narrower than that for the Modern Studies Scholarship, and candidates could win with fewer marks. See *WG*, 11 Dec. 1926, Meeting of BOE, Speech of Dr Laurence; also *WG*, 7 June 1924, Meeting of BOE, Speech of Mr Low.

49. *WG*, 7 June 1934, Meeting of BOE; *WG*, 5 July 1924, CIC prize-giving, Speech of Fr English; *WG*, 26 Feb. 1927, Meeting of BOE; *WG*, 5 March, 1927, letter from Dr S. Laurence.

50. For some opposition to the dropping of Greek at QRC, see *LL*, 21 Aug. 1926.

51. C. Campbell, "Education and black consciousness: the amazing Captain J. O. Cutteridge in Trinidad and Tobago 1921-1942", *JCH* 18 (1984): 35-66.

52. Clear statements of the philosophy of the directors were made at the West Indian Education Conference of 1921; see CP 94 of 1922, West Indian Education conference, Hancock on "Present aims, methods and instruction", 5-6; Cutteridge on "The making of the teacher", 14-15, and "The value of handwork", 24-25.

53. Another aspect of the new view of children was concern to promote their health, hence medical inspection of schools came into focus; but this has been ignored in this book. See *WG*, 18 Aug. 1923, Teachers' Conference, speech of Director Mackay.

54. *Teachers Herald*, Sept. 1935.

55. R. Selleck, *English Primary Education and the Progressives 1914-1939* (London, 1972), chap. 2. An interesting social aspect of the Marriott/Cutteridge partnership was that at least in 1923 Marriott lived as Cutteridge's house guest. See *LL*, 15 Sept. 1923.

56. *POSG (Weekly)*, 29 July 1929, Annual Handicraft Exhibition, Speech of Cutteridge.

57. *East Indian Patriot*, March 1924 (hereafter cited as *EIP*). Guyadeen (also known as Gayadeen) had an ACP and he acquired the LCP in 1923, the first primary school teacher to do so; see *East Indian Weekly*, 12 March 1932 (hereafter cited as *EIW*). Guyadeen was a strong supporter of Cutteridge's teaching methods and Cutteridge thought highly of him. See *Trinidad Presbyterian* 27, no. 2 (Feb.1930). An Indian ex-teacher later claimed that Guyadeen inspired Cutteridge's books (presumably the *Readers*); see S. Doodnath, *A Short History of the Early Presbyterian Church and the Indian Immigrants in Trinidad 1845-1945* (Port of Spain, 1983), 92-93.

58. T. Martin, "Marcus Garvey and Trinidad", in *Garvey, Africa, Europe and the Americas*, edited by R. Lewis and M. Warner-Lewis (Kingston, 1986), 52-88.

59. *LL*, 6 Oct. 1928, letter from 'Couvan Toiler'. Since the *Readers* did not have stories about Brer Anancy, 'Nancy stories' could possibly mean 'nonsense story'; see E. Genevese, *The World the Slaves Made* (1976), 436.

60. *LL*, 15 Sept. 1928, Letter from 'Atticus'.

61. *LL*, 30 Oct. 1929, letter from Samuel Smith.

62. C. Campbell, "Education and black consciousness", 45.

63. Ibid., 47.

64. *LL*, 7 Nov. 1931, letter from 'Spectator'.

65. An outstanding theme in the poetry was the inculcation of "a love for the virtues of poetry and empire"; see G. Rohlehr, "Sparrow as poet", in *David Frost Introduces Trinidad and Tobago*, edited by M. Anthony and A. Carr (London, 1975), 95. However, these aspects of Cutteridge's books were so traditional that they escaped commentary.

66. *POSG (Weekly)*, 5 Oct. 1931, questionnaire of Marriott.

67. *POSG (Weekly)*, 8 Feb. 1932, Speech of Cutteridge at San Juan government school; also *POSG (Weekly)*, 28 March 1932, Speech of Cutteridge at St Therese Roman Catholic School. For a hostile reply to Cutteridge; see *POSG*, 11 April 1932, letter from J. Arthur Procope.

68. *EIW*, 26 March 1932, Speech of Cutteridge at San Fernando Canadian Presbyterian Mission School.

69. *LL*, 31 Oct. 1931, Editorial; also *LL*, 4 Nov. 1931, letter from 'Spectator'; also *LL*, 12 Dec. 1931, letter from 'A Parent'. In November 1931 a debate for the Clarke Trophy at the Royal Victoria Institute had a moot involving the *West Indian Readers*. The team defending the *Readers* won, one argument used being the result of the questionnaire. See *LL*, 7 Nov. 1931, letter from 'Spectator'.

70. *POSG*, 15 Aug. 1922, Address to Teachers' Conference.

71. *The People*, 18 March 1939, letter from 'West Indian'.

72. *Teachers Herald*, Nov. 1931. DeWilton Rogers read a paper at the Teachers' Conference in 1931 in favour of the introduction of 'Negro culture' into the schools. See *Teachers Herald*, Nov. 1931.

73. Unfortunately I have failed, after diligent inquiry, to locate the Minutes of the Board of Education, a very important source. It was seen in the early 1970s by a senior official at the Ministry of Education, but not since then. My knowledge of the operations of the Board comes mostly from the newspapers, especially the *Trinidad Guardian*.

74. CP 8 of 1919, Correspondence with Secretary of State relating to the educational system; see Protest of the Roman Catholic archbishop, 18 April 1918.

75. CP 168 of 1916, Report of the Educational Commission, Minority Report of Fr Crehan.

76. CN, 14 May 1921; CN, 12 Dec. 1925, Editorial.

77. For one such issue; see WG, 21 March 1925, Meeting of BOE.

78. WG, 3 Oct. 1925, Report of the BOE; WG, 3 Oct. 1925, article on editorial page. Captain Cipriani in 1932 also questioned Cutteridge's qualifications to act as director; see *POSG (Weekly)*, 18 April 1932, Editorial.

79. CN, 4 Oct. 1930, Report of the BOE.

80. WG, 21 March 1925, Report of the BOE, Protest of Dean Holt.

81. For example CN, 7 June 1924, Editorial; WG, 1 Aug. 1925, article on editorial page; WG, 7 Dec. 1925, article on editorial page; WG, 31 Oct. 1925, article on editorial page. The *POSG* and the *Catholic News* were in favour of denominational schools while the *Trinidad Guardian* preferred government schools.

82. CN, 26 Aug. 1922, Report of conference of visiting and local teachers.

83. WG, 5 July 1924, Petition of Trinidad and Tobago Teachers' Union to British government.

84. WG, 5 Sept. 1925, Report of BOE.

85. CN, 8 Nov. 1930, letter from Archbishop Dowling.

86. *A Brief Account of Education in the Anglican Schools in Trinidad and Tobago from 1918 to 1930* (Port of Spain, 1931), 5.

87. CN, 15 Nov. 1930 and 22 Nov. 1930, Editorial.

88. WG, 19 Sept. 1930; WG, 24 Nov. 1930, Legislative Council Debates.

89. *Education in the Anglican Schools*, 5.

90. CO 318/400, M. Robertson to Colonial Office (Darnley), 24 June 1930, enclosure: Preliminary note on the need for a Commission to investigate

educational problems in certain parts of the West Indies (by Arthur Mayhew).

91. *WG*, 29 Dec. 1930, Legislative Council Debates; *LL*, 10 Oct. 1931, Editorial.

92. *Tobago Gazette*, 23 Dec. 1892, Report of a Committee appointed by the Financial Board.

93. Report on the Elementary Schools of Tobago, 5 July 1892; Report of the Tobago schools, 10 Sept. 1895; Report on the Elementary Schools of Tobago 1896, (found in Tobago Archives, Tobago).

94. *Teachers Journal*, July 1931, Tobago Notes; *Teachers Journal*, Sept. 1931. For conditions favouring the growth of a peasantry, see Susan Craig, *Smiles and Blood: the Ruling Class Responds to the Workers' Rebellion in Trinidad and Tobago* (London, 1988), 6-11.

95. *Teachers Journal*, Sept. 1931.

96. *The Diocese of Trinidad and Tobago 1872-1972* (San Fernando, n.d.), 34.

97. Tobago Census 1881. This shows twelve persons born in India.

98. Did a boy living in Tobago win a College Exhibition sometime between 1918 and 1923? In March 1923 there was a report of a case in court in Tobago in which a teacher sued a parent for non-payment of fees for private lessons given to his son. It was said that the boy got an Exhibition, but there were no further details. See *WG*, 24 March 1923, Tobago court case.

99. Minutes of the Board of Industrial Training (hereafter cited as BIT), 21 Feb. 1912.

100. Minutes of BIT, 6 Oct. 1909; also 6 April 1910.

101. B. Samaroo, "Constitutional and political development in Trinidad 1898-1925" (PhD diss., University of London, 1969), 192.

102. Debates in the Legislative Council, 21 Oct. 1927, Speech of attorney general.

103. *POSG (Weekly)*, 10 March 1930, Meeting of BOE.

104. *POSG (Weekly)*, 14 July 1930.

105. *WG*, 19 July 1930, Speech of Biggart in Tobago.

106. Debates in the Legislative Council, 14 Nov. 1930.

107. *WG*, 23 Aug. 1930; 6 Oct. 1930. In 1930 the Methodists were celebrating a century of work in Tobago.

108. *WG*, 17 Nov. 1930.

109. For a strong vindication of neglected denominational schools in Tobago, see *WG*, 2 Aug. 1930, letter from 'A Tobago teacher'.

110. *WG*, 30 Aug. 1930, Report of the Board of Education.

111. *Tobago Times*, 17 Aug. 1935.

112. *Tobago Times*, 18 Nov. 1933.

113. *WG*, 28 Dec. 1931. This school under Edwards won two Tobago Exhibitions to Bishop's High School between 1931 and 1933; see *Teachers Herald*, Oct. 1933.

114. *WG*, 15 Sept. 1930, letter from Bishop Anstey. At Chacon Street Anglican School Smith taught Nelson Comma who in turn was the teacher of H. O. B. Wooding. See *WG*, 8 Sept. 1923. Smith might have written an arithmetic book for schools, see *LL*, 28 Feb. 1931, letter from 'Fairplay'.

115. *The Diocese of Trinidad and Tobago*, 34.

116. *WG*, 28 Dec. 1929, Speech by Bishop Anstey.

117. *A Brief Account in the Anglican Schools*, 21.

118. Ibid., 19-23. The POSG (a pro-Roman Catholic newspaper) was opposed to it and the *Trinidad Guardian* was in favour of it.

119. *Education in the Anglican Schools*, 23-24; *WG*, 23 Oct. 1926, and 13 Nov. 1926, Meetings of the BOE.

120. *WG*, 5 Jan. 1929, Speech of Principal Jordan at prize-giving.

121. *Tobago Times*, 25 May 1935.

122. I. Caesar, *Vignettes of Tobago*, (Trinidad, 1984), 15, quoting from the *Trinidad Guardian*, 5 Aug. 1973.

123. *WG*, 5 Jan. 1929, Speech of Principal Jordan at prize-giving.

124. *Tobago Times*, 3 March 1934; 6 Oct. 1934, letter from 'Tobagonian'.

125. *WG*, 17 Dec. 1927, Legislative Council Debates, 9 Dec. 1927.

126. CP 94 of 1922, Education Conference of Representatives of the Lesser Antilles and British Guiana, Trinidad, 2 April 1921, 18-21.

127. WG, 5 Sept. 1925, Report of the BOE.

128. For a brief biography of Joseph; see TG, 18 Feb. 1963.

129. WG, 26 Dec. 1925, Report of the BOE. There were seven female bursars in December, 1927.

130. WG, 5 Sept. 1925, Report of the BOE; also WG, 21 Nov. 1925.

131. WG, 29 May 1926, Report of the BOE.

132. WG, 5 Sept. 1925, Report of the BOE; WG, 5 Sept. 1925, letter from Fr English.

133. WG, 7 Aug. 1926, commentary on Education Report for 1925.

134. WG, 7 Aug. 1926, Report of BOE.

135. *Teachers Herald*, April 1935, article entitled "First-class teachers and the training college".

136. WG, 4 June 1927, Report of BOE; WG, 17 Dec. 1927, Legislative Council Debates, 9 Dec. 1927.

137. WG, 17 Dec. 1927, Legislative Council Debates.

138. LL, 12 Jan. 1929, letter from 'Atticus'; LL, 15 Dec. 1929, letter from 'Atticus'.

139. *Teachers Journal*, Dec. 1931.

140. WG, 29 Sept. 1928, Report of the BOE.

141. CO 295/196, Keate to Labrouchere, 6 Sept. 1857, enclosure: printed speech of Warner to Legislative Council, 2 Sept. 1857.

142. *Teachers Journal*, Dec. 1931; also *Teachers Herald*, Jan. 1934, Editorial.

143. CP, 94 of 1922, Education Conference, Part 1, 14-18.

144. POSG, 19 June 1933, Speech of Daniel at prize-giving. The College got its first student with Cambridge Higher School Certificate in 1932; see POSG *(Weekly)*, 30 Jan. 1933, Report of BOE. For a stern critique of the organization of the College, see the *Teachers Herald*, Feb. 1936. The author of this article claimed that the College was chaotic and ineffective.

145. *The People*, 10 Feb. 1934, letter from 'Pedagogue'; also *Teachers Herald*, Nov. 1934, article by 'Onlooker'.

146. *Teachers Journal*, Aug. 1931.

147. For an informative report on pupil teachers, see WG, 27 Dec. 1924, Report of Director Mackay.

148. WG, 19 Nov. 1928, Report of BOE. The director of education had nothing to do with monitors.

149. The rules governing pupil teachers and monitors were often breached since too many of them existed for the government to supervise effectively. For example, pupil teachers who failed their examinations could be re-employed as monitors by headteachers, and allowed to do the same work. See WG, 11 Dec. 1926, Meeting of BOE, Speech of director.

150. POSG *(Weekly)*, 30 Jan. 1933, Meeting of BOE.

151. CP 78 of 1934, Report of a Committee to consider to what extent the general progress of Educational expansion recommended by the Education Commission can be undertaken.

152. A. M. Huberman, *Understanding Change in Education: an Introduction* (Paris, 1973).

153. CO 950/786, Memorandum of the TTTU to the Moyne Commission, 1938; also *Teachers Herald*, May 1935.

154. *Teachers Herald*, Jan. 1934, Editorial.

155. *Teachers Herald*, May 1935; also *The People*, 24 April 1937, Editorial.

156. *Teachers Herald*, Jan. 1934, Editorial.

157. *Teachers Herald*, Dec. 1931. For the career of Alexander Brown, see LL, 21 April 1932, and POSG *(Weekly)*, 18 April 1932.

158. POSG *(Weekly)*, 9 May 1932, extract from *Teachers Journal*.

159. It appears that Naparima College did not have preparatory classes until 1931; see WG, 17 Aug. 1931 expansion of Naparima College.

160. Between 1921 and 1925 Naparima Girls' High School was an intermediate school; see WG, 13 March 1926, Prize-giving speech of Miss Young.

161. POSG *(Weekly)*, 5 Oct. 1931, Questionnaire of Marriott.

162. *Report of the Consultative Committee on the Education of the Adolescent* (Board of Education, London, 1938) – otherwise known as the Hadow Report, 1926.

163. POSG *(Weekly)*, 5 Oct. 1931, Questionnaire of Marriott.

164. *POSG (Weekly)*, 21 March 1932, Speech of Marriott at CIC prize-giving.

165. These were Richmond Street and Belmont Road Church of England schools; see *POSG*, 26 May 1930, and I. Rouse, "Labours of the Anglican breed", *Trinidad and Tobago Education Forum* 1, no. 3 (1980): 17-19. E. B. Grovesnor is said by Rouse to have pioneered woodwork in primary schools at Richmond Street Church of England School when he was headteacher.

166. *POSG*, 29 July 1929, Speech of Cutteridge at Handicraft Exhibition.

167. *PAS*, XXVIII (1928), Meeting held 12 July 1928.

168. *POSG (Weekly)*, 29 July 1929, Exhibition speech by Cutteridge.

169. *WG*, 20 Nov. 1926, letter from 'A Lover of Classics'. For a defense of Latin at Naparima Girls' High School, see *POSG (Weekly)*, 28 March 1932, Editorial.

170. Between 1929 and 1931 a total of 155 persons were placed on the waiting list, and up to 1931 only 37 were placed; see Legislative Council Debates, 24 April, 1931, Speech of colonial secretary.

171. *POSG (Weekly)*, 21 March 1932, Speech of Hollis at CIC, prize-giving.

172. *POSG (Weekly)*, 8 Feb. 1932, Speech of Cutteridge at Jordan Hill School.

173. *WG*, 17 Nov. 1928, Speech of Fr English at BOE.

174. *WG*, 12 March 1927, Speech of Marriott at prize-giving of Southern High Schools.

175. *POSG*, 9 Dec. 1929, Speech of Bishop Anstey.

176. *POSG (Weekly)*, 22 June 1931, Speech of Marriott before Trinidad Literary Club Council; also *POSG (Weekly)*, 25 April 1932, Speech Day at Naparima College, Speech of Marriott.

177. *POSG (Weekly)*, 25 April 1932, Speech of Kelshall at Naparima College. Kelshall was also an elected member of the Legislative Council.

178. *POSG (Weekly)*, 22 June 1931, Speech of Marriott.

179. *LL*, 7 March 1925, Debates in the Legislative Council, question by Cipriani; also *LL*, 24 March 1925, Editorial; and *LL*, 28 March 1925, Legislative Council, reply to question by Cipriani.

180. Report of a Commission appointed to consider problems of secondary and primary education in Trinidad, Barbados, Leeward Islands and Windward Islands, 1931/32 (HMSO, 1933) – (otherwise known at the Marriott/Mayhew Report.)

181. *Teachers Herald*, Dec. 1940, Editorial.

182. E. Furlonge, "The development of secondary education in Trinidad and Tobago" (PhD diss., University of Sheffield, 1968), 354.

183. *Trinidad Presbyterian* 29, no. 3 (March 1936); also *POSG* 21 Feb. 1931, Speech of Cipriani at Iere Central High School.

184. Education Commission, 1916, Original Documents, 2.

185. For movement in levels of oil production and prices in the 1930s; see V. Mulchangsingh, "The origins, growth and development of the oil industry in Trinidad 1857-1965" (PhD diss., Queen's University, Ireland, 1967), 62-87.

186. Debates in the Legislative Council, 15 Feb. 1935, Speech of Governor Hollis.

187. CP 78 of 1934, Report of a Committee to consider the general programme of education.

188. Debates in the Legislative Council, 21 Feb. 1936, Speech of Governor Hollis; also Debates in the Legislative Council, 19 Feb. 1937, Speech of Governor Fletcher.

189. Debates in the Legislative Council, 21 Feb. 1936, Speech of Governor Fletcher.

190. Debates in the Legislative Council, 29 May 1936, Speech of Pierre.

191. Debates in the Legislative Council, 29 May 1936, Speech of Daniel.

192. Ibid., Speech of O'Reilly.

193. CP 49 of 1937, Report of a Committee on Island Scholarships.

194. *The People*, 27 March 1937. Editorial, and Meeting of BOE.

195. A. Hamel-Smith, "Education in Trinidad", 176, quoting a report of a committee on technical education.
196. CP 66 of 1908, Report of BIT.
197. Minutes of BIT, June 1909, Uncatalogued Documents, RVI.
198. Minutes of BIT, 7 June 1911, Uncatalogued Documents, RVI.
199. POSG, 16 June 1916, Film show at RVI. Its educational programme was alleged to have been inspired by the London Polytechnical Institute, See Y. Bridges, *Child of the Tropics*, 17; *Mirror*, 11 Feb. 1916, Editorial complained that it had departed from the founders' intentions by having a tennis court and billiards room. Apparently the building only became impressive from 1901 when the Memorial Wing was built; see *Victoria Institute Industrial Trinidad 1903*, (found at New York Public Library). There are discrepancies about the starting date of this institution. For example, Prof Carmody said in 1916 that the RVI started in 1887; see POSG, 16 June 1916.
200. Ordinance 4 of 1931, Ordinance to vest in the Board of Industrial Training the property of the Royal Victoria Institute and to amend the Industrial Training Ordinance.
201. Minutes of the BIT, 21 Oct. 1918 (found at National Training Board).
202. WG, 26 Jan. 1929.
203. CP 66 of 1908, Report of the BIT for 1908; Minutes of the BIT 4 Aug. 1909; see also J. D. Tyson, Memorandum of Evidence for the Royal Commission to the West Indies (New Delhi, 1939), 48.
204. Uncatalogued Documents, RVI, Evidence of BIT to the Moyne Commission, 16 March 1939.
205. CP 16 of 1940, Report of the Special Committee on Vocational Education, 20 Feb. 1939.
206. WG, 25 May 1931, Report of the BIT.
207. Uncatalogued Documents RVI, Cutteridge to BIT, Oct/Nov. 1938.
208. The firms were A. B. H. Rose Ltd (cabinet making and upholstering); A. H. Heath (tailoring); Borneo's Shoe Syndicate; Horsford Printing Works; Yuille's Printery; and the Government Printing Office; see Uncatalogued Documents RVI.
209. CP 16 of 1940, Report of the Special Committee on Vocational Education.
210. There is a suggestion that the arrangements for P. E. T. O'Connor to study engineering at the University of Birmingham (1920-1923), were facilitated by John Cadman, said to be an oil consultant and professor of mining at the above university; see P. E. T. O'Connor, *Trinidad Yesterdays*, 78-80. O'Connor (an Irish creole intimately connected to the French creoles) was the first Trinidadian to be employed in the oil industry as a university graduate.
211. WG, 7 April 1928.
212. WG, 13 Nov. 1926, opening of Queen Victoria Memorial Wing.
213. Debates in the Legislative Council, 18 March 1938, Speech of Rienzi.
214. Winston Mahabir (future People's National Movement Minister of Health) went from Naparima College to QRC in the 1930s; see *Trinidad Chronicle*, 24 Oct. 1956.
215. *East Indian Patriot* (hereafter cited as *EIP*), Sept. 1924. This newspaper carried a few rags-to-riches stories of Indian merchants and other Indians (including headteachers) building 'palatial' residences; see *EIP*, Oct. 1921; July 1924.
216. *EIP*, Oct. 1921; Nov. 1921.
217. WG, 21 March 1925, Meeting of the BOE. It is to be noted that in the 1920s Island Scholars studying medicine had to get financial assistance from parents as the total emoluments of the scholarship (c.TT$3,360) were inadequate; see for example WG, 28 Dec. 1929, Meeting of BOE. About the time of World War I, it cost about $960 p.a. to support a student for an Arts degree (presumably the same for Law) at Cambridge or Oxford Universities; see POSG, 13 April 1955, letter from H. Hudson Philips.
218. *EIP*, Oct. 1921.
219. Ibid., Oct. 1924.

220. Ibid., Nov. 1924. W. Griffith, headteacher of Calvary Roman Catholic school and an immigrant from Barbados, sent his son to Scotland to study medicine. So too did Alexander Brown, editor of the *Teachers Journal*; see *Teachers Journal*, July 1931.

221. *EIP*, Nov. 1921; April 1925.

222. Kazim Bacchus, "The education of the East Indians in Guyana", in *Indenture and Exile*, edited by F. Birbalsingh (Toronto, 1989), 157-60.

223. WG, 7 Aug. 1920.

224. *EIP*, Nov. 1924 Hosein was chairman of a meeting of "select Indians to establish a Colonial Indian Club" in Port of Spain.

225. *EIW*, 20 Oct. 1928, Address by Hosein to East Indian Literary and Debating Association; also see B. Samaroo, "Presbyterian Canadian Mission".

226. Debates in the Legislative Council, 4 April 1931, speech of Teelucksingh.

227. Ibid.; also *POSG (Weekly)*, 5 Oct. 1931.

228. *Teachers Herald*, Jan. 1935, Editorial.

229. *Trinidad Year Book*, 1919.

230. LL, 6 June 1931.

231. WG, 4 Feb. 1922, submission of TTTU to Major Wood; also WG, 5 July 1924, Petition of TTTU to British government.

232. WG, 5 July 1924, Petition of TTTU to British government.

233. WG, 20 Sept. 1922, letter from J. Hamilton Maurice.

234. *EIP*, Sept. 1921; March 1923; Sept. 1923; Sept. 1924; July 1925. Friendly societies are excluded from the analysis. The literary and debating societies did more debating than literary production, and must not be allowed to steal the credit of the *Beacon* movement as the original matrix of creative writing, Following in the wake of the *Beacon* movement, a few teachers began to write poetry in the *Teachers Journal*, said to have been the longest surviving periodical in the island.

235. *EIP*, Jan. 1924.

236. *Teachers Herald*, Feb. 1936.

237. *EIP*, April 1924. The Legislative Council voted a special grant of $480 to him for services to education. In 1932 DeSuze was made a MBE (Member of the Order of the British Empire); see *POSG (Weekly)*, 2 May 1932.

238. POSG, 5 Nov. 1914, Evidence of DeSuze before Education Commission of 1914/16 .

239. After the salary regrading of 1920, headteachers had a maximum (fixed) salary of $960 p.a.; an assistant inspector earned between $1,200 and $1,440 p.a. with travelling allowance; see WG, 4 Feb. 1922, submission of TTTU to Major Wood; also WG, 8 Sept. 1923. For more on salaries of teachers in the early 20th century; see Hamel-Smith, "A history of education", 233-39.

240. WG, 8 Sept. 1923.

241. LL, 9 Jan. 1932, article on sanitary inspectors.

242. *Teachers Herald*, Nov. 1938.

243. *The People*, 27 March 1937.

244. This school was also said to have been founded by Fr Dominic to "cater for the dozen or so sons and daughters of the principal shopkeepers of the village who could presumably pay the small fee for the 'higher education' of their children". It was located in a "corner of the primary school building" of the Roman Catholic church. See P. E. T. O'Connor, *Trinidad Yesterdays*, 62-63. It might be that Bichlow was the principal and the Roman Catholic Church the proprietor.

245. The fee at the Higher Class at Tranquillity in 1920 was $32 p.a.; see WG, 17 Sept. 1921, Meeting of BOE.

246. Olga Comma-Maynard, *Brierend Pattern: the Story of Audrey Jeffers (OBE) and the Coterie of Social Workers* (Port of Spain, 1971), 1. For good examination results of what must have been the first batch of candidates for the Cambridge examinations, see POSG, 21 April 1915.

247. *The People*, 9 Feb. 1936.

248. The ending of the Higher Class appears to have been more complex than this explanation, but the details

are not clear; see *WG*, 24 March 1923, Tranquillity Girls' Intermediate school prize-giving.

249. *Centenary Record of the Holy Ghost Fathers*, Appendix C.

250. *POSG (Weekly)*, 3 April 1933, QRC prize-giving speech of Mr Cambridge.

251. See Appendix II.

252. *WG*, 7 Aug. 1929, Meeting of BOE.

253. *POSG (Weekly)*, 2 Nov. 1931, Meeting of BOE.

Chapter Three

1. G. Tikasingh, "Towards a formulation of the Indian view of history: the representation of Indian opinion in Trinidad 1900-1921", in *East Indians in the Caribbean*, edited by B. Brereton and W. Dookeran (New York, 1982), 12.

2. K. Laurence, "Indians as permanent settlers in Trinidad before 1900", in *Calcutta to Caroni: the East Indians in Trinidad*, edited by J. LaGuerre (Port of Spain, 1985), 95-116.

3. C. Campbell, *Cedulants and Capitulants: the Politics of the Free Coloureds in the Slave Society of Trinidad 1783-1838* (Port of Spain, 1992).

4. C. Campbell, "The rebel priest: Francis DeRidder and the fight for free coloured rights in Trinidad 1825-1829", *JCH* 15 (1981): 20-40.

5. I. Hamid, *History of the Presbyterian Church*, 252-55.

6. Ibid., 256-63; also *EIW*, 31 Oct. 1931, letter from 'Patience'.

7. One source claimed that it was only after the Indian ministers demanded more power in the Mission that funds from Canada declined, thus causing the Canadian ministers to require financial contributions from teachers, see; *EIW*, 31 Oct. 1931, letter from 'Patience'.

8. In 1931 the Canadian Presbyterian Mission demoted and transferred the headteacher of its school at Hermitage because he assisted with the cutting of his sugar cane on a Sunday (Sabbath-breaking). See *POSG (Weekly)*, 18 May 1931.

9. *CN*, 24 April 1937, Editorial.

10. See, for example, a Presbyterian Teachers' Association resolution in 1930 that devotion to religious work should be the prime qualification for promotion; see B. Samaroo, "Education as socialization", 15.

11. CO 950/951, Memorandum of the Trinidad and Tobago Teachers' Union to the Moyne Commission, 19 Jan. 1939.

12. *LL*, 13 March 1926, Meeting of Hindu and Muslims at Penal.

13. *EIW*, 8 Sept. 1928; 11 Aug. 1928; 5 Jan. 1929; 25 May 1929; 8 June 1929; 29 July 1929.

14. *EIW*, 19 Oct. 1929. The most extensive treatment of the Hindu/Muslim school can be found in R. Forbes, "Arya Samaj in Trinidad: an historical study of Hindu organizational process in acculturative conditions" (PhD diss., University of Miami, 1984), 64-75.

15. *EIW*, 26 Oct. 1929.

16. Ibid.

17. *EIW*, 26 Nov. 1929, letter from Sudamaji.

18. *EIW*, 23 Nov. 1929, Editorial.

19. *EIW*, 23 Nov. 1929.

20. *EIW*, 16 Nov. 1929, letter from Ralph Benjamin.

21. *EIW*, 21 Dec. 1929, article by S. Naipaul.

22. In this study the term Hindi will be retained although recent research indicates that what most Indians spoke as Hindi was a version of it, namely Bhojpuri; see Peggy Mohan, "A language implodes: the death of Trinidad Bhojpuri" (Paper presented at the third conference on East Indians in the Caribbean, Trinidad, 1984.)

23. Rev C. D. Lalla was alleged to have exploited his knowledge of English to keep himself in the leadership of the Indian National Congress for several years; see *EIW*, 19 Dec. 1931, Editorial.

24. *CN*, May 1931, Editorial.

25. Education in the West Indies: Report of a Commission appointed to consider problems of Secondary and Primary Education in Trinidad, Barbados, the Leeward Islands and the Windward Islands, (Sept. 1932). This is a smaller report than the better known Marriott/Mayhew Report of 1931/32, and it deals specifically with Trinidad. (Found in the Library of the House of Representatives, Red House, Port of Spain.)

26. Ibid.

27. Ibid.

28. Debates in the Legislative Council, 16 Feb. 1932; 17 Feb. 1933; 16 Feb. 1934; 16 Feb. 1935; 21 Feb. 1936, Speech of Governor Hollis.

29. R. Forbes, "Hindu organizational process in acculturative conditions: significance of the Arya Samaj experience in Trinidad" (Paper presented at the Third Conference on East Indians in the Caribbean, Trinidad, 1984), 9-11.

30. CO 950/951, Memorandum of the Sanatan Dharma Board of Control to the Moyne Commission, 1939.

31. Ibid.

32. WG, 3 Jan. 1935.

33. R. Forbes has commented on the role of the Arya Samaj in the Hindu/Muslim school at Chaguanas. (The Arya Samaj was a Hindu reformist movement introduced into Trinidad in the 1930s.) Forbes's thesis is that some of the Indians who started the school later became Samajists, and that its closure was also due partly to the internal squabbles between the Samajists and Sanatanists at Chaguanas. See R. Forbes, "Arya Samaj as catalyst: the impact of a modern Hindu reform movement on the Indian community of Trinidad between 1917 and 1939" (Paper presented at the Second Conference on East Indians in the Caribbean, Trinidad 1979) 23, 29.

34. B. Brereton, *A History of Modern Trinidad* (Kingston, 1981), 179-80.

35. Debates in the Legislative Council, 11 Jan. 1935, Speech of Cutteridge.

36. *A Teacher's Annual*, 1936; also WG, 7 June 1932, Meeting of TTTU.

37. T. E. Beckles, President of the TTTU between 1931 and 1935, and the teacher member of the BOE, was thought too conciliatory by the editor of the *Teachers Herald* (who had been earlier editor of the *Teachers Journal*); see The *Teachers Herald*, Oct. 1935, Editorial.

38. CN, 2 Nov. 1929, Address of Cutteridge to teachers at Tranquillity Boys' School.

39. *Teachers Journal*, July 1931, Editorial; *Teachers Journal*, Aug. 1931; also Sept. 1931, article by 'Trinculo'; also Nov. 1931, letter from 'Sidelight'; also Feb. 1932, article by 'M.A.J.'; also April 1932, Editorial; *Teachers Herald*, Dec. 1933; *Teachers Herald*, June 1933, Editorial.

40. *Teachers Journal*, Aug. 1931, letter from R. C. Thomas; *Teachers Journal*, Dec. 1931, Editorial. A harsher judgement can be found in *Teachers Herald*, July 1935, Editorial.

41. *Teachers Journal*, Dec. 1931, Editorial.

42. CO 950/951 Memorandum of Trinidad Labour Party to Moyne Commission.

43. Ibid.

44. West Indian Royal Commission Report (Moyne Report), (HMSO, 1945), 113-17.

45. Marriott/Mayhew Report, chaps 5, 10. It is to be noted that they were thinking of fees for infant classes, and also for the senior course in the secondary modern schools. Intermediate schools were primary schools with higher forms doing secondary school-work and taking Cambridge external examinations. For a list of such schools in 1936; see *A Teacher's Annual*, 1936.

46. Debates in the Legislative Council, 14 Dec. 1934, Speech of McShine.

47. Article 72 of the Code of 1935 reads: "No teacher shall engage in any business or occupation that interferes with his duty as a Teacher, nor shall he serve as a member of a Local Road Board or a Municipal Council. Without the express permission of the governor, a teacher may not act as the editor of any newspaper nor take part di-

rectly or indirectly in the management hereof, nor contribute anonymously thereto; nor publish in any manner anything which may be properly regarded as of a political or administrative nature. He may however publish signed articles upon subjects of general interest". See *Ordinances and Regulations* (Education Department), printed by A. L. Rhodes (Trinidad and Tobago 1936).

48. D. Rogers, *The Rise of the People's National Movement. In the Beginning,*(Port of Spain, n.d.), 1-8; also S. Ryan, *Race and Nationalism in Trinidad and Tobago: a Study of Decolonization in a Multiracial Society* (1972; reprint, Jamaica, 1974), 106-107.

49. *The People*, 12 Jan. 1935, petition of Tobago teachers signed by 1,100 "taxpayers, parents and guardians"; Debates in the Legislative Council, 11 Jan. 1935, Speech of Hope; also *POSG*, 3, 5, 6, 9, 10 and 11 Jan. 1935.

50. *Teachers Herald*, Jan. 1935.

51. Debates in the Legislative Council, 14 Dec. 1934, Speech of Cutteridge.

52. *Teachers Journal*, Feb. 1932, article on "Security of tenure" by 'MAJ'.

53. CO 950/786, Memorandum of the TTTU to the Moyne Commission.

54. Ibid., 13.

55. Ibid., 10

56. Ibid., 13. An interesting grievance which the male dominated TTTU did not mention was discrimination against married female teachers, see R. Reddock, "Women, labour and struggle in 20th century Trinidad and Tobago 1898-1960" (PhD diss., University of Amsterdam, 1984), 403-406.

57. CO 950/953, Memorandum of the *West Indian Pilot* to Moyne Commission, sgd. T. Romney, editor.

58. T. Martin, *The Pan-African Connection: From Slavery to Garvey and Beyond* (London, 1983), chap. 5.

59. CO 950/951, Memorandum of the Sanatan Dharma Board of Control to the Moyne Commission.

60. CO 950/951, Memorandum of the Presbyterian Church in Trinidad to the Moyne Commission.

61. The government was already committed to this before 1937, but larger increases followed the Moyne Report, see Debates in the Legislative Council, 14 Dec. 1934, speech of Cutteridge.

62. CP 35 of 1944, Report of Franchise Committee 1933, Appendix IX, Submission of Teachers' Economic and Cultural Association.

63. CO 295/630, Clifford to Oliver Stanley, 12 Dec. 1943.

64. *Clarion*, 20 March 1948.

65. R. Sander, "The Trinidad awakening: West Indian literature of the 1930s" (PhD diss., University of Texas, Austin, 1979).

66. Dr Wise was the Surgeon General Dr Shepherd taught at ICTA, and Dr Prada was a medical practitioner. Shepherd wrote a seminal piece on the cocoa industry, but the point here relates to social attitudes; see C. Y. Shepherd, *The Cocoa Industry in Trinidad* (Port of Spain, 1932).

67. *WG*, 26 Sept. 1932 and 17 Oct. 1932, articles by E. Digby. The latter was a Canadian resident in Trinidad. See also K. S. Wise, *Historical Sketches of Trinidad and Tobago*, Vol. 2 (Port of Spain, 1936).

68. Interview with Gocking, 19 Aug. 1981. This was not a government post.

69. For details of James' life, see the autobiographical work, C. L. R. James, *Beyond a Boundary* (London, 1963).

70. J. LaGuerre, "The social and political thought of Aimé Césaire and C. L. R. James: some comparisons", in *Dual Legacy in the Contemporary Caribbean: Continuing Aspects of British and French Dominion*, edited by P. Sutton (London, 1986), 263-64.

71. Williams' autobiography explains the choice of teaching, not the choice of history; see Eric Williams, *Inward Hunger: the Education of a Prime Minister* (London, 1969), 35-39.

72. *The Royalian* vol. 1 (March 1933).

73. Ibid.

74. *LL*, 16 March 1929, letter from 'Plain Talk'.

75. *LL*, 25 April 1931, and 5 Sept. 1931.

76. *The People*, 23 Sept. 1933.

77. *Tobago Times*, 2 Jan. 1935; 14 Dec. 1935.

78. *LL*, 25 April 1931; 5 Sept. 1931.

79. *Tobago Times*, 25 Aug. 1934.

80. *The People*, 12 Jan. 1935, Petition of Tobago section of primary school teachers.

81. *Tobago Times*, 22 Dec. 1934, Editorial.

82. *Centenary Record of Holy Ghost Fathers*, Appendix C. The reductions in 1902 and 1919 were not done primarily in the name of economy. In 1902 the value of the reduced scholarships was the same as of four scholarships between 1870 and 1902; but in 1919 the value of the two scholarships was about $1,920 less than of three scholarships; see ibid.

83. For an unfriendly and unofficial estimate of the number of Island Scholars after 1918 who returned to the island, see *The People*, 2 May 1936, Editorial.

84. *LL*, 2 March 1929, letter from Achong.

85. *The People*, 6 June 1936. *The People* was opposed to it, and the *Guardian* in favour; see *The People*, 11 July 1936, Editorial.

86. *The People*, 2 May 1936, Editorial.

87. *The People*, 11 Jan. 1936, Editorial.

88. Ibid.

89. *The People*, 27 June 1936.

90. *The People*, 18 Jan. 1936, Editorial.

91. Ibid.

92. Ibid.

93. *The People*, 22 Jan. 1938.

94. *WG*, 14 April 1928, Report of BOE.

95. *WG*, 24 March 1928; 14 April 1928, Report of BOE. Some years previously the board had allowed an Island Scholar to study sugar technology at the Louisiana State University, since no university in England had such a course.

96. L. Braithwaite, "The problems of cultural integration in Trinidad", *Social and Economic Studies* 3, no. 1 (1954): 83-96; also *The People*, 11 Jan. 1936, Editorial.

97. Commission on Higher Education in the Colonies (Asquith Commission), Memorandum and Notes of Evidence 1944, Notes from Arya Pratinidhi Sabha (UWI Files, Mona).

98. S. Ryan, *Race and Nationalism*, chaps. 3-4.

99. Debates in the Legislative Council, 13 March 1927, Speech of Cipriani.

100. *The People*, 16 July 1938; 27 July 1938.

101. C. L. R. James, *Life of Captain Cipriani: an Account of British Government in the West Indies* (Lancashire, 1932), 104; also *WG*, 24 Nov. 1930, Memorandum on education submitted by Captain Cipriani on behalf of the Trinidad Workingmen's Association. Even Cipriani's call for a farm school was not connected to a nationalist perspective. For child labour; see *WG*, 16 April 1927, Legislative Council Debates.

102. E. Williams, "The need for instructional materials related to the Caribbean environment", in *Education in the Caribbean* (Port of Spain, 1956), 3-11.

103. Interview with Gocking, 19 Aug. 1981. When interviewed by the QRC principal in 1939 for a job, Gocking was asked if he was a communist.

104. *The People*, 29 May 1937, Editorial.

105. *The People*, 24 April 1937, Editorial.

106. S. A. Hammond, *Education in St Vincent* (St Vincent, 1943), 23-24. Some of the correspondence in this struggle can be found in CO 318/467 file in the Documentation Centre, Institute of Social and Economic Research, UWI, Mona.

107. *WG*, 29 Sept. 1930, New Draft of Education Bill; also *WG*, Nov. 1930, Legislative Council Debates.

108. C. Campbell, "The university of our dreams: centralization versus decentralization in the planning of the University of the West Indies 1943-1944", *Jamaican Historical Review* 15 (1988): 17-32.

109. J. Raymond Priestly, *West India Journal*, vol. 2. [Diary], 9 May 1944, UWI.

110. Report of the West Indies Committee (Irvine Committee) of the Commission on Higher Education in the Colonies (1945), 12-15.

111. M. Omolewa, "The promotion of London University Examinations in Nigeria 1807-1951", *The International Journal of African Historical Studies* 13, no. 4 (1980): 651-71.

112. Report of the West Indies Committee (Irvine Committee), Appendix 4B.

113. C. Campbell, "The dual mandate of the Imperial College of Tropical Agriculture 1922-1960", *Jamaican Historical Review* 16 (1988): 1-16.

114. WG, 7 June 1924, Meeting of BOE.

115. *New Dawn* 1, no. 2 (1940), "editorial notes".

116. WG, 25 July 1925, Meeting of the BOE.

117. WG, 25 Sept. 1926.

118. PAS XII, (1912), Meeting of 12 April 1912, Paper by Dr Fredholm.

119. L. Braithwaite, "Social stratification in Trinidad", 94. For glimpses of the social life of the oilfield settlements; see P. E. T. O'Connor, *Trinidad Yesterdays*, chap. 12.

120. WG, 12 April 1930, Legislative Council Debate, Speech of Cipriani; also R. Sander, "Trinidad awakening", 58, 68-69.

121. *The People*, 30 July 1938, Editorial; also C. Campbell, "The dual mandate". Prof Harland successfully sued in England the Cotton Growing Corporation (his true employer) for wrongful dismissal.

122. C. Campbell, "The university of our dreams".

Chapter Four

1. A good source for Roman Catholic statements on the role of religion in education are the Lenten Pastorals of the archbishops from Gonin onwards. For example, see POSG, 16 March 1869, Lenten Pastoral of the late Archbishop Gonin.

2. CN, 17 Feb. 1899, Lenten Pastoral of Archbishop Flood.

3. POSG, 2 Feb. 1847, Legislative Council, 1 Feb. 1847.

4. CO 295/134, McLeod to Russell, 13 Oct. 1841, no. 92; also C. Campbell, "The development of education", 481.

5. This was the model used by the ward schools; see C. Campbell, "The development of education", 179-80.

6. Ibid., 77-78; 135-39.

7. POSG, 30 July 1895, Editorial.

8. One such pundit, Ramnarine Permanand, had attended a Canadian Presbyterian Mission school and Naparima College; see WG, 27 July 1931. For a slightly more indulgent picture of Canadian Presbyterian Mission religious policy on schools, see *East Meets West in Trinidad* (Canadian Mission Council, 1934), 59.

9. P. Keenan, *The State of Education*, 39-40.

10. C. Campbell, "The development of education", 177-78; 181-83.

11. Ibid., 416-30.

12. For an analysis of the Irish National School Books, see D. H. Akenson, *The Irish Education Experiment: the National System of Education in the 19th Century* (London, 1970), 235-40.

13. CN, 6 May 1916; also CN, 29 Jan. 1921, letter from 'A Catholic Reader'; also CN, 5 April 1930.

14. CO 318/467, Archbishop of Port of Spain to Secretary of State for the Colonies, 20 Aug. 1944. (Found at ISER Documentation Centre, UWI, Mona.)

15. QRC actually took few a boarders during the time of Principal Burslem, but his successors did not continue the practice; see LL, 15 Sept. 1923.

16. WG, 4 Feb. 1928, Speech Day at Southern High Schools, Speech of J. S. Sammy.

17. M. Warner, "Africans in 19th century Trinidad", *African Studies Association of the West Indies Bulletin*, no. 5 (1972): 27-59 and no. 6 (1973): 13-37; also Peggy Mohan, "A language implodes".

18. C. Campbell, "The transition from Spanish law", 25-52.

19. CO 295/134, McLeod to Russell, 13 Oct. 1841, no. 92.

20. TRG 1869, 21 April 1869, Report of the Inspector of Schools for 1868.

21. C. Campbell, "John Jacob Thomas"; also B. Brereton, "J. J. Thomas: An Estimate".

22. C. Campbell, "John Jacob Thomas", 12.

23. P. Keenan, *Report upon the Education System of Malta* (Dublin, 1879).

24. P. Keenan, *Report upon the State of Education*, 62-71.

25. CN, 16 March 1894, Meeting of College Council, 7 March 1894, Speech of Fr Lemir.

26. A. De Verteuil, *Sylvester Devenish and the Irish*, 38-42.

27. CP 44 of 1878, Report on public instruction 1877-1878.

28. SFG, Nov. 1893, J. H. Collens, principal of the government training school and of Tranquillity Boys' School described Creole in 1888 as "a compound of bad French and English, with some Spanish thrown [in]"; and he confessed that J. J. Thomas, "a native of considerable ability", had elevated it to the dignity of a language; see Collens, A *Guide to Trinidad*, 48.

29. B. Brereton, *Race Relations*, 163-66.

30. H. Johnson, "Barbadian immigrants in Trinidad 1870-1897", *Caribbean Studies*, 13, no. 3 (1973): 5-30.

31. A. De Verteuil, *Sylvester Devenish and the Irish*, 49; also *Centenary Record of the Sisters of St Joseph*, 52.

32. A. De Verteuil, *Sylvester Devenish and the Irish*, 47-50.

33. CN, 16 March 1894, Meeting of College Council, 7 March 1894, Speech of Fr Lemir.

34. De Verteuil, *Sylvester Devenish and the Irish*, 38-47; 51-58.

35. POSG, 17 Sept. 1914, Evidence of Von Weiller before Education Commission of 1914/16.

36. P. E. T. O'Connor, *Trinidad Yesterdays*, 61.

37. One of the earliest studies on forces working to spread the English language was done by Daphne Cuffy; see

D. Cuffy, "Problems in the teaching of English in the island of Trinidad from 1797 to the present day" (MA thesis, University of London, 1963).

38. *WG*, 6 June 1933, article on "Patois".

39. K. Laurence, "The survival of Spanish in Trinidad: an historical *aperçu*", *Nieuwe West-Indische Gids* 54 (1980): 213-28.

40. For a later reassertion of the Roman Catholic ideal of single-sex schools, see CN, 2 Oct. 1903, Minutes of BOE.

41. Anti-Slavery Papers E1/4, 1836-1842, Bilby to Lt Governor Hill, 21 Sept. 1837.

42. C. Campbell, "The development of education", 268-69.

43. Foreword by Dr Meenan to *Centenary Record of the Sisters of St Joseph of Cluny 1836-1936*.

44. *Centenary Record of the Sisters of St Joseph*, 119-20, quoting *Star of the West*, 29 May 1862.

45. Ibid.

46. A. De Verteuil, *Sylvester Devenish and the Irish*, 58.

47. The question of the relative number of male and female teachers in Caribbean education systems has become a focal point of the gender debate since the pioneering theorizing of Errol Miller in Jamaica. See E. Miller, *Marginalization of the Black Male: Insights from the Development of the Teaching Profession* (Jamaica, 1986). The calculation in Trinidad can be complicated by adding or excluding pupil teachers. In 1893 there were 162 male and 135 female teachers in Trinidad (excluding pupil teachers who numbered 300). See CP 52 of 1893, Report of the Inspector of Schools for 1892. Usually the gender of pupil teachers was not given in school statistics. The question of the ratio of male to female teachers can also be complicated by taking the total number of teachers in an island rather than the total in the public education system. See for instance Hamel-Smith, "A history of education", 210.

48. CP 70 of 1898, Report of Inspector of Schools for 1897.

49. Hamel-Smith, "Primary education and the East Indian woman in Trinidad 1900-1956" (third conference on East Indians in the Caribbean, UWI, Trinidad, 1984). For a more recent survey of the predicament of Indian girls; see Shameen Ali, "A social history of East Indian woman in Trinidad since 1870" (MPhil thesis, UWI, 1993), chap. 3.

50. B. Brereton, *A History of Modern Trinidad*, 110-12; also K. Singh, *Bloodstained Tombs: the Muharram Massacre 1884* (London, 1988), chap. 1.

51. CN, 27 March 1896, Editorial.

52. Ibid.

53. SFG, 12 Dec. 1895, Editorial. Apparently Mrs Bundle tried again – unsuccessfully – in 1908; see CN, 13 June 1908. In 1910, a Mrs Miller, headmistress of a private school (Trinidad High School for Girls) deferred an application to the College Council for affiliation of her school to QRC, See CN, 23 July 1910.

54. Debates in the Legislative Council, 21 March 1904 and 1 Oct. 1904, Speech of Goodville.

55. CN, 23 July 1910, Meeting of the College Council. There is some confusion about the financial arrangements for the Higher Class, as one report was that Miss Bushe would get TT$40 (fees of first the 20 students) and any fees above this would go into the Treasury (after purchase of apparatus). See CN, 1 April 1911, Meeting of the BOE.

56. WG, 3 March 1926, prize-giving at Naparima College and Naparima Girls' High School.

57. Hamid, *History of the Presbyterian Church*, 210-20. After 25 years as a teacher and social worker in the Canadian Presbyterian Mission, a white Canadian teacher, Miss Blackadder, felt that she had suffered discrimination on the grounds of her sex by her male missionary colleagues; see I. Hamid, ibid., 216.

58. The four female assistant teachers who volunteered to give evidence before the Education Commission of 1914/16 (the only females to do so) showed an awareness of the importance of female teachers although the two who were actually called by the Commissioners did not aggressively ask for equal rights for female teachers; see POSG, 20 Nov. 1914, Evidence of Miss Sarjeant and Miss Albert.

59. For the history of Naparima Girls' High School, see Agnes Rampersad, *A History of Naparima Girls' High School 1912-1967*; also *Naparima Girls' High School Golden Jubilee 1912-1962* (pamphlet).

60. Hancock, acting inspector of schools, spoke of a "growing demand for female typists" in 1918; see CP 88 of 1918, Report of the Inspector of Schools for 1917; also R. Reddock, "Women, labour and struggle", 291; see also interesting remarks on the career of Miss Pujadas in POSG *(Weekly)*, 23 May 1932.

61. POSG *(Weekly)*, 5 Oct. 1931, Report on Southern Certified Nurses' Association formed in 1930.

62. Debates in the Legislative Council, 23 Feb. 1934, Speech of M. A. Maillard; 15 Dec. 1936, Speech of Colonial Secretary in reply to Captain Cipriani; 21 April 1939, Speech of Maillard.

63. *The People*, 29 July 1939. A certain Iris de Freitas, BA was reported in 1929 to be the first female lawyer, but she does not appear to have been born in Trinidad; see LL, 14 Sept. 1929.

64. EIW, 19 Dec. 1931. No further details of Mrs Ramsaran have been found. It is also not clear if she was born in Trinidad.

65. For a critique of her appointment, see LL, 8 Feb. 1930. Mrs Masson was the wife of a coloured medical practitioner (Dr George Masson) and might herself have been coloured.

66. Administration Report of the Education Department for 1953 (Government Printing Office, Port of Spain, 1955), 5; also Administration Report of the Education Department, Annual Summary for 1957 (Government Printing Office, Port of Spain, 1963),

55. The lead of female teachers, however, was not great in the late 1950s, and would be even less if the pupil teachers are excluded.

67. WG, 28 Feb. 1920, and WG, 2 July 1920, Legislative Council debates.

68. A. Hamel-Smith, "A history of education", 214.

69. POSG, Nov. 1914, Evidence of Miss Sarjeant and Miss Albert before the Education Commission; also R. Reddock, "Women, labour and struggle", 404; for more details on the question of lower pay for female teachers and other forms of discrimination against them, see Hamel-Smith, "A history of education", 210-16.

70. D. Rogers, *The Rise of the People's National Movement*, 8. For attitudes of female teachers towards the issue of equal pay, see Evidence of Sarjeant and Albert before the Education Commission in POSG, 20 Nov. 1914; also *Teachers Journal*, July 1934, article by Virginia Bayack; also Hamel-Smith, "A history of education", 213-14.

71. Annual Report of the Director of Education for 1948 (Government Printery, 1949), Appendix VI.

72. R. Reddock, "Women, labour and struggle", 326-38.

73. There is mention of a college for Irish boys (possibly in Port of Spain) in 1800, but nothing extensive has been written about it; see A. De Verteuil, *Sylvester Devenish and the Irish*, 5.

74. C. Campbell, *Cedulants and Capitulants*, 332-33.

75. The most elaborate description of the metropolitan education of one such person can be found in A. De Verteuil, *Sylvester Devenish and the Irish*, 95-110.

76. C. Campbell, "Jean Baptiste Philippe: man from the Naparimas", Foreword in [J.B.Philippe] *Free Mulatto* (1823; reprint Paria Publishing Company, Port of Spain,1987), xi-xxix.

77. C. Campbell, "The rebel priest".

78. J. M. Feheney, *Catholic Education in Trinidad*, 189-90.

79. C. Campbell, "The development of education", chap. 3.

80. Ibid., 323-26.

81. POSG 16 Aug. 1914, prize-giving ceremony.

82. *Evening Star*, 13 Nov. 1926, advertisement of Pamphylian High School; also WG, 24 Aug. 1931.

83. A reference to Pamphylian School was found in 1950, but nothing in the 1940s; see *Trinidad Presbyterian*, Aug. 1950.

84. POSG, 16 Jan. 1929, Meeting of BOE; also POSG, 27 March 1929, Meeting of BOE.

85. LL, 4 Feb. 1930; 1 March 1930; 20 June 1931; 11 July 1931.

86. POSG, 31 March 1921, Editorial.

87. POSG, 15 March, 1915, Evidence of J. D. Regis and J. R. Cummings before Education Commission.

88. LL, 30 May 1931, letter from 'Philip'; POSG *(Weekly)* 22 Aug. 1932, letter from 'Parent'.

89. According to Director Cutteridge 132 private schools applied for registration and up to the time of going to press with the Education Report for 1935, a total of 72 were registered.The impression he gives is that he expected the great majority to be eventually registered, and only a few closed; see CP 22 of 1936, Administration Report of the Director of Education for 1935, 13-14.

90. CP 69 of 1937, Administrative Report of the Director of Education for 1936, 25.

91. The figures for 1936 included an indeterminate number of private primary schools while the figures for 1949 excluded them; see CP 22 of 1936, Administrative Report of the Director of Education for 1936.

92. CO 299/12, Report of the Subject of Education for 1861.

93. CP 54 of 1879, Report on Public Instruction 1878-1879.

94. CP 73 of 1901, Annual Report of the Inspector of Schools for 1900, 13; also Annual Report on primary education for 1902-1903, 7. It is possible that the Inspector's account of the sequence and relationship between singing by note and singing by other systems is confused.

95. CP 72 of 1934, Administrative Report of the Director of Education for 1933, 28.

96. CP 78 of 1917, Report of the Inspector of Schools for 1916.

97. J. H. Collens, *Guide to Trinidad*, 50.

98. I. Boodhoo,"A curriculum model in art education for the primary schools of Trinidad and Tobago" (PhD diss., University of Indiana, 1974), 66-70.

99. Ibid.

100. CN, 21 April 1928, Art exhibitions at St Joseph's Convent.

101. H. Guggenheim, "Social and political change in the art world of Trinidad during the period of transition from colony to new nation" (PhD diss., New York University, 1968), 36-40.

102. G. MacLean, *An Illustrated Biography of Trinidad's Nineteenth Century Painter, Michel Jean Cazabon* (Port of Spain, 1986).

103. "Trinidad Public Library: one hundred years of service" (no author, no date, being 6 typed pages of History of the Library). This was seen there in 1986. Some of the Library's early history is recounted in E. H. Morton, *Development of Library Service* (UNESCO, Dec. 1972), 102-104.

104. *Proceedings of the Scientific Association of Trinidad* (founded in 1863), vol. 1, 1860-1869, Address by Lechmere Guppy, 13 Oct. 1869.

105. "Trinidad Public Library: one hundred years".

106. *Anglican Review*, Dec. 1968, letter from the Rev M. Rose; also see *Conference on the Church [Roman Catholic] and Education* (Port of Spain, Oct. 1973), 11-13.

107. P. Keenan, *The State of Education*, 42.

108. WG, 4 Feb. 1922, submission of Teachers' Union to Major Wood; also WG, 5 July 1924, Petition of TTTU to British government.

109. The Committee on General Education (Maurice Report), 1959, 9-13.

110. Decentralization has never really emerged as a substantial issue in education. In 1982 a new Minister of Education (Mr Padmore) brushed it aside with the rejoinder that it was not clear what its supporters wanted to have decentralized; see Debates of the Senate of the Republic of Trinidad and Tobago, 8 Jan. 1982, Speech of Padmore.

111. WG, 8 Sept. 1923; see also Table 2.27

112. Mr Clarke was a near-white creole; see photograph in POSG, 26 May 1948. He was described to me by a Trinidadian writer, his contemporary, as a "coloured man, not very dark". Penalosa and Stoer were the only ones among the old guard of assistant inspectors who had any previous experience in teaching.

113. *Centenary Record of the Sisters of St Joseph*, 31-37.

114. C. Campbell, "The transition from Spanish law", 25-52.

115. K. O. Laurence, *A Question of Labour: Indentured Immigration into Trinidad and British Guiana 1875-1917* (Kingston, 1994).

116. The Shouter Baptists had no schools; and the mission stations sponsored by the Baptist Missionary Society from 1843 to about 1892 had very few schools. See Eudora Thomas, *A History of the Shouter Baptists in Trinidad and Tobago* (Ithaca, 1987). Also J. Hacksaw, *The Baptist Denomination* (1992), 54-58.

117. C. Campbell, "Education and black consciousness", 35-66.

118. C. Campbell, "The establishment of Queen's Collegiate School", 71-86.

119. C. Campbell, "The dual mandate", 1-16.

120. C. Campbell, "New perspectives on secondary education in Trinidad and Tobago 1926-1935", in *Education in Caribbean Historical Perspectives*, edited by Ruby King (UWI, 1988), 145-62.

121. C. Campbell, "The College Exhibition", 42-53.

122. C. Campbell, "Charles Warner", 54-81.

123. See James Houk, "The Orisha religion in Trinidad: a study of culture process and transformation" (PhD diss., Tulane University, 1992).

124. This paragraph has benefited from the seminal analysis of M. Archer, *The Sociology of Educational Expan-*

sion: *Take-Off, Growth and Inflation in Educational Systems* (London, 1982).

125. H. Johnson, "Crown Colony government in Trinidad", 365; 403-405.

126. C. L. R. James, *Life of Captain Cipriani*, 45; also A. Hamel-Smith, "Education and the East Indians in Trinidad 1900-1938" (Postgraduate seminar paper, UWI, St Augustine, 1979), 17-23.

127. See D. Ramsaran, *Breaking the Bonds of Indentureship: Indo-Trinidadians in Business* (ISER, 1993).

128. CN, 7 Aug. 1920, Editorial.

129. L. Braithwaite, "Social stratification in Trinidad", 97-98.

130. For recent attempts to explain the relative success of Blacks and Indians in business; see S. Ryan and L. A. Barclay, *Sharks and Sardines: Blacks in Business in Trinidad and Tobago* (Port of Spain, 1992); also D. Ramsaran, *Breaking the Bonds*.

131. See T. Millett, *The Chinese in Trinidad* (Port of Spain, 1993), 37-59.

132. C. Campbell, *Cedulants and Capitulants*, chap. 1.

133. For the career of one such scholar; see S. Ryan, *The Pursuit of Honour: the Life and Times of H. O. B. Wooding* (Port of Spain, 1990).

134. A leading scholar who supports changes in the post- emancipation period is Bridget Brereton. See "Social organization and class, racial and cultural conflicts in 19th century Trinidad", in *Trinidad Ethnicity*, edited by K. Yelvington (London, 1993), 33-35. The social scientists are less likely to perceive any important change; see R. Henry, "Notes on the evolution of inequality in Trinidad and Tobago", in *Trinidad Ethnicity*, 64.

135. L. Braithwaite, "Social stratification", 46-48, 57, 122-26.

136. Y. Malik, *East Indians in Trinidad: A Study of Minority Politics* (Oxford, 1971), 17-18; S. Ryan ed, *Trinidad and Tobago: the Independence Experience 1962-1987* (Port of Spain, 1988), 217.

137. C. Campbell, "Education and black consciousness".

138. V. Judges, "Recent trends in English education", *International Review of Education* 1 (1955): 264-65.

139. R. H. E. Braithwaite, *Moral and Social Education* (Port of Spain, 1991), 10-21.

140. C. E. Beeby, *The Quality of Education in Developing Countries* (Cambridge, Mass., 1966).

141. G. Guthrie, "Stages of educational development? Beeby revisited", *International Review of Education* 26, no. 4 (1980): 411-35; also C. E. Beeby, "The thesis of the stages fourteen years later", *International Review of Education* 26, no. 4 (1980): 451-72.

142. For the words of this memorable calypso; see S. Brown, M. Morris, G. Rohlehr, eds, *Voiceprint: an Anthology of Oral and Related Poetry from the Caribbean* (London, 1988), 129-30.

143. Latrobe wrote three reports, namely P. Latrobe, *Report on Negro Education in Jamaica 1837*; *Report on Negro Education in British Guiana and Trinidad 1838*; *Report on Negro Education in the Windward and Leeward Islands, 1838*.

144. CP 78 of 1887, Report on Public Instruction, 1885-1887.

145. CP 168 of 1916, Report of the Education Commission, 8-14.

146. The Marriott/Mayhew Report, 17.

147. Ibid., 26.

148. Ibid., 17.

Epilogue

1. See F. Baptiste, *War, Cooperation, and Conflict: the European Possessions in the Caribbean 1939-1949* (Westport, 1988), chap. 9.

2. H. Johnson, "The West Indies and the conversion of the British official classes to the development idea", *Journal of Commonwealth and Comparative Politics* 15, no. 1 (March 1977): 55-83; D. J. Morgan, *The Origins of British Aid Policy 1924-1945*, vol. 1 (London, 1980) 23-79.

3. S. H. Hammond, *The Cost of Education* (1943); S. H. Hammond, *Education in St Vincent* (1943); S. H. Ham-

mond, *Education in Grenada* (1945); S. H. Hammond, *The Development of Secondary Education in Grenada* (1945); S. H. Hammond, *Memorandum on Education in St Vincent (1943)*; S. H. Hammond, *Education in Dominica* (1944); S. H. Hammond, *Education in Jamaica* (1941).

4. Debates in the Legislative Council, 14 and 21 Jan. 1949, Speech of Albert Gomes.

5. E. Williams, *Inward Hunger*, 118-60.

6. TG, 18 May 1955.

7. (Archbishop Finbar Ryan), *The Catholic Church and the Draft Education Act 1965* (n.d., pamphlet), 3-9.

8. Cabinet Proposals on Education (Government Printing Office, Port of Spain, 1960, pamphlet, 27 pages).

9. C. Campbell, "The St Augustine campus of UWI: success and excess" *Jamaican Historical Review* 16 (1988): 54-63.

Select Bibliography

A. PRIMARY SOURCES

Official Documents: Great Britain

Colonial Office Correspondence:

CO 295 Dispatches of Governors to the Colonial Office 1834-1939

CO 318/400, Preliminary note on the need for a commissioner or commission to investigate educational problems in certain parts of the West Indies

CO 950/933, Evidence of the Joint Deputation of the British West Indies and British Guiana Teachers' Association and the Trinidad and Tobago Union before the Moyne Commission 1939

CO 950/933, Evidence of Captain Cutteridge before the Moyne Commission 1939

CO 950/933, Evidence of S. A. Hammond before the Moyne Commission 1939

CO 950/953, Memorandum of the *West Indian Pilot* to Moyne Commission 1939

CO 950/786, Memorandum of the Trinidad and Tobago Teachers' Union to the Moyne Commission 1939

CO 950/951, Memorandum of Trinidad Labour Party to the Moyne Commission 1939

CO 950/951, Memorandum of the Sanatan Dharma Board of Control to the Moyne Commission 1939

West India Royal Commission Report (Moyne Report) 1945

Semi-Official Documents: Great Britain

Anti-Slavery Papers E1/13, 1836-1842 (Rhodes House Library, Oxford)

Official Documents: Trinidad and Tobago

Trinidad Royal Gazette 1857-1859; 1870-1939

Tobago Gazette 1881 (Tobago Archives)

Census of the Colony of Trinidad 1891 (compiled by H. J. Clark, Government Statistician)

Tobago Census 1892 (Tobago Archives)

Census of Trinidad and Tobago 1911

Uncatalogued Documents, Royal Victoria Institute: Minutes of the Board of Industrial Training 1919-1939

Debates in the Legislative Council of Trinidad and Tobago 1915-1939

Council Papers of the Legislative Council of Trinidad and Tobago 1882-1939

Minutes of the Board of Industrial Training 1908-1975 (National Training Board, Ministry of Education)

Ordinances and Regulations (Education Department), printed by A. L. Rhodes, Government printer, Trinidad and Tobago, 1936

Reports of the Inspector of Schools/Director of Education 1856-1939

Report of Mr L .B. Tronchin, Acting Superintendent of the Normal School, POSG, 30 Oct. 1861

Report of the Principal of the Queen's Collegiate School for the quarter ending 1 March, 1862, POSG, 26 March 1862

Report of the Queen's Collegiate School for the year ending 1862, POSG, 15 April 1863

CP 19 of 1876, Rules for the government of the Model Schools

CP 48 of 1876, Rules and regulations for the government of primary schools under the Education Ordinance 1870

CP 69 of 1891, Rules under the Elementary Education Ordinance 1890

CP 168 of 1893, Correspondence concerning education

CP 202 of 1893, Letter from Archbishop Vincent supporting CIC petition for additional funds

CP 121 of 1899, Elementary Education (Letter from the Bishop of Trinidad)

CP 82 of 1900, Report of Principal of QRC for 1899

CP 90 of 1900, Report of Principal of QRC for 1900

CP 161 of 1900, Minute (no. 47 of 1900) by Actg Governor laying correspondence with the Secretary of State

CP 85 of 1901, Report of Burslem on the appointment of two additional masters

CP 7 of 1902, Dispatch from the Secretary of State on the subject of primary education in Trinidad

CP 97 of 1902, Code of Rules under the Elementary Education Ordinances 1890-1902

CP 76 of 1904, Annual Report of the Principal of QRC for 1903-1904

CP 55 of 1907, Report of the Principal of QRC for 1906-1907

CP 76 of 1908, Annual Report of Principal of QRC for 1907-1908

CP 66 of 1908, Report of the Board of Industrial Training 1908

CP 99 of 1909, Report of the Board of Industrial Training 1909

CP 89 of 1910, Report of the Board of Industrial Training 1909-1910

CP 12 of 1913, Report of Board of Industrial Training 1911-1912

CP 118 of 1914, Report of the Principal of QRC for 1913-1914

CP 138 of 1912, Report of the Board of Industrial Training 1912-1913

CP 17 of 1918, Report of Principal of QRC for 1917

CP 30 of 1919, Report of Principal of QRC for 1918

CP 31 of 1938, Report of the Board of Industrial Training for 1937

Reports on Education

Peter Latrobe, Report on Negro Education in Jamaica 1837

Peter Latrobe, Report on Negro Education in British Guiana and Trinidad 1838

Peter Latrobe, Report on Negro Education in the Windward and Leeward Islands 1838

Patrick Keenan, Report upon the State of Education in the Island of Trinidad (printed by Alexander Thom, Dublin 1869)

Report on the Elementary Schools of Tobago 15 July 1892 by Hobson (Tobago Archives)

Report on the Tobago Schools 10 Sept. 1895 by W. H. Robinson (Tobago Archives)

CO 295/373, Meetings of the Education Commission on free and compulsory education in primary schools, from the *Daily News* of 10 and 11 May 1895, and POSG 11 May 1895

CP 82 of 1896, Minute no. 32 from the governor with reference to the Report of the Commission on free and compulsory education in primary schools

CP 152 of 1896, Minute no. 65 from the governor laying a report by the inspector of schools dealing with the recommendations of the Commission on free and compulsory education in primary schools

Report on the Elementary Schools of Tobago 1896 by Charles Hobson (Tobago Archives)

Petition of J. D. Williams on behalf of other teachers (Tobago) to Board of Education 1 Aug. 1896 (Tobago Archives)

Petition of eleven teachers (Tobago) to Board of Education 6 Nov. 1896 (Tobago Archives)

Report of the Schools Inquiry Committee 26 June 1897 (Tobago Archives)

Report of the Commission appointed to enquire into the question of free and compulsory education in the primary schools of the colony. See Appendix D, Special reports on educational subjects vol. XII, Educational Systems of the Chief Crown Colonies and Possessions of the British Empire, including reports of the training of native races, Part 1 (Dawson of Pall Mall, London 1908)

CP 168 of 1916, Report of the Education Commission appointed by Sir G. R. LeHunte on 16 June 1914 (Government Printing Office, Port of Spain, 1916)

CP 67 of 1921, and CP 94 of 1922, Educational Conference of representatives of the Lesser Antilles and British Guiana and Trinidad, 2 April 1921, Part I and Part II

Report of a committee appointed to consider problems of secondary and primary education in Trinidad, Barbados, Leeward Islands and Windward Islands 1931-1932 (HMS, 1933) (otherwise known as the Marriott/Mayhew Report)

Education Commission 1916 Original Documents vol.2 (being that part of the Marriott/Mayhew Report specifically dealing with problems of Trinidad; found at the Library of the House of Representatives, Port of Spain, Trinidad)

"A Brief Account of Education in the Anglican Schools in Trinidad and Tobago from 1918 to 1930" (Franklin's Electric Printery, Port of Spain, 1931)

F. C. Marriott, "Education in Trinidad and Tobago", in *Year Book of Education*, London (Evans, 1932)

CP 78 of 1934, Report of a Committee to consider to what extent the general programme of education recommended by the Education Commission can be undertaken

CP 16 of 1940, Report of the Special Committee on Vocational Education 20 Feb. 1939

Report of the West Indies Committee of the Commission on Higher Education in the Colonies (1945) (otherwise known as the Irvine Report)

Newspapers/Bulletins/Journals

Clarion

Catholic News

Evening Star

East Indian Patriot

East Indian Weekly

Labour Leader

Port of Spain Gazette

Port of Spain Gazette (Weekly)

Public Opinion

Star of the West

Trinidad Guardian

Weekly Guardian

New Era

Mirror

Proceedings of the Trinidad Agricultural Society 1896-1928

Teachers Journal

Teachers Herald

The Trinidad Presbyterian 1904-1939

The People   The Royalian
San Fernando Gazette   A Teacher's Annual 1936
Sentinel   Trinidad Year Book 1919
Tobago Times   West Indian Bulletin 1902-1921
The Echo of Trinidad
(For abbreviations of some of these sources, see List of Abbreviations)

B. SECONDARY SOURCES

Books

Akenson, D. H. 1970. *The Irish Education Experiment: The National System of Education in the 19th Century*. London: Routledge and Kegan Paul.

Anthony, M. 1986. *Heroes of the People of Trinidad and Tobago*. Port of Spain: Circle Press.

Anthony, M., and A. Carr, eds. 1975. *David Frost Introduces Trinidad and Tobago*. London: André Deutsch.

Archer, M. 1982. *The Sociology of Educational Expansion: Take-Off, Growth and Inflation in Educational Systems*. London: Sage Publications.

August, T. 1985. *The Selling of the Empire: British and French Imperialist Propaganda 1890-1940*. Westport: Greenwood Press.

Beachy, R. W. 1957. *The British West Indies Sugar Industry in the Late 19th Century*. Oxford: Blackwell.

Beeby, C. E. 1966. *The Quality of Education in Developing Countries*. Cambridge, Mass.: Harvard University Press.

Brandow, M. 1983. *The History of our Church Women: Trinidad 1868-1983*. Manitoba: Friesen Printers.

Braithwaite, R. 1991. *Moral and Social Education*. Trinidad: University of the West Indies, School of Continuing Studies.

Brereton, B. 1979. *Race Relations in Colonial Trinidad*. Cambridge: Cambridge University Press.

———. 1981. *A History of Modern Trinidad*. Kingston: Heinemann.

Brereton, B., and W. Dookeran, eds. 1982. *East Indians in the Caribbean: Colonialism and the Struggle for Identity*. New York: Kraus International Publications.

Bridges, Yseult. 1980. *Child of the Tropics. Victorian Memories*. Compiled and edited by Nicholas Guppy. London: Collins Harvill Press.

Caesar, I. 1984. *Vignettes of Tobago*. Trinidad.

Campbell, C. 1992. *Cedulants and Capitulants: the Politics of the Coloured Opposition in the Slave Society of Trinidad 1783-1838*. Port of Spain: Paria Publishing Co. Ltd.

1963. *Centenary Record of the Holy Ghost Fathers in Trinidad and of St Mary's College 1863-1963*. Port of Spain: Yuille's Printers.

(n.d.) *Centenary Record of the Sisters of St Joseph of Cluny 1836-1936*. Port of Spain: Yuille's Printers.

Chapman, D. 1964. *The Career of Arthur Hamilton Gordon 1829-1912*. Toronto: University of Toronto Press.

Collens, J. H. 1888. *A Guide to Trinidad*. n.p.

Collens, J. H., ed. 1912. *Handbook of Trinidad and Tobago for the Use of Settlers*. n.p.

Craig, S. 1988. *Smiles and Blood: The Ruling Class Responds to the Workers' Rebellion in Trinidad and Tobago*. London: New Beacon Books.

Cruickshank, M. 1963. *Church and State in English Education*. London: Macmillan.

De Verteuil, A. 1973. *Sir Louis De Verteuil: His Life and Times, Trinidad 1800-1900*. Port of Spain: Columbus Publishers.

——. 1986. *Sylvester Devenish and the Irish in 19th Century Trinidad*. Port of Spain: Paria Publishing Co.

——. 1989. *Eight East Indian Immigrants*. Port of Spain: Paria Publishing Co.

De Verteuil, L. A. A. 1884. *Trinidad: Its Geography, Natural Resources, Administration, Present Condition and Prospects*. London: Ward and Lock.

(n.d.) *The Diocese of Trinidad and Tobago 1872-1972*. San Fernando: Rahaman Printery.

Doodnath, S. 1983. *A Short History of the Early Presbyterian Church and the Indian Immigrants in Trinidad 1845-1945*. Port of Spain: n. p.

Freemantle, A. 1963. *The Papal Encyclicals in their Historical Context*. London: n. p.

Gordon, S. 1963. *A Century of West Indian Education*. London: Longmans.

Grant, K. 1923. *My Missionary Memoirs*. Halifax: Imperial Publishing Co.

Hamid, I. 1980. *A History of the Presbyterian Church in Trinidad 1868-1968: the Struggle of a Church in Colonial Captivity*. Port of Spain.

Hammond, S. A. 1943. *Education in St Vincent*. Kingstown, St Vincent: Government Printer.

Hart, D. 1866. *Trinidad and the Other West Indian Islands and Colonies*. Port of Spain: Chronicle Publishing Office.

Harricharan, J. 1981. *The Catholic Church in Trinidad 1498-1852*. Port of Spain: Inprint Caribbean Ltd.

Hennessy, A., ed. 1992. *Intellectuals in the Twentieth Century Caribbean*. Vol. 1. London: Macmillan.

Hill, S. 1988. *To Live Twice Over, To Live Forever: Memoirs of Sir Lindsay Grant*. Port of Spain: Schill Publishers.

Hooker, J. 1975. *Henry Sylvester Williams*. London: Rex Collins.

Huberman, A. M. 1973. *Understanding Change in Education: an Introduction*. Paris: UNESCO.

James, C. L. R. 1932. *Life of Captain Cipriani: an Account of British Government in the West Indies*. Nelson, Lanchashire: Coulton and Co.

Kirpalani, M. 1945. *Indian Centenary Review: 100 Years of Progress 1845-1945*. Port of Spain: n. p.

Klass, M. 1961. *East Indians in Trinidad: a Study of Cultural Persistence*. New York: Columbia University Press.

Knaplund, P. 1966. *Gladstone and Britain's Imperial Policy*. 1927. Reprint, London: Frank Cass.

Lamont, N. 1912. *Problems of the Antilles*. Glasgow: John Smith and Sons.

LaGuerre, J., ed. 1985. *Calcutta to Caroni: The East Indians of Trinidad*. 1974. Reprint, Port of Spain: University of the West Indies, Extra-Mural Studies.

Leotaud, D. and C. Leotaud, eds. 1988. *Memoirs of an Honourable Gentleman*. Port of Spain: Andres Printery.

Lewis, R., and M. Warner-Lewis, eds. 1986. *Garvey, Africa, Europe, the Americas*. Kingston, Jamaica: Institute of Social and Economic Research.

Look Lai, W. 1993. *Indentured Labour, Caribbean Sugar: Chinese and Indian Migrants to the British West Indies 1838-1918*. Baltimore: Johns Hopkins University Press.

MacLean, G. 1986. *An Illustrated Biography of Trinidad's Nineteenth Century Painter, Michel Jean Cazabon*. Port of Spain: Acquerella Galleries.

Mahase, A. 1992. *My Mother's Daughter: the Autobiography of Anna Mahase Snr 1899-1978*. Claxton Bay, Trinidad: Royards Publishing Co.

Malik, Y. 1971. *East Indians in Trinidad. A Study in Minority Politics*. London: Oxford University Press.

Martin, T. 1983. *The Pan-African Connection: from Slavery to Garvey and Beyond*. Cambridge, Mass: Schenkmann Publishing Co.

Mathurin, O. 1976. *Henry Sylvester Williams and the Origins of the Pan-African Movement, 1869-1911*. Westport: Greenwood Press.

Mayhew, A. 1938. *Education in the Colonial Empire*. London: Longmans, Green and Co.

Massiah, J., ed. 1982, *Women and Education*. Vol. V. Barbados: Institute of Social and Economic Studies.

Millette, J. 1970. *The Genesis of Crown Colony Government*. Port of Spain: Moko Enterprises Ltd.

Morton, S., ed. 1916. *John Morton of Trinidad*. Toronto: Westminster Co.

Mount, G. 1983. *Presbyterian Missions to Trinidad and Puerto Rico*. Nova Scotia: Lancelot Press.

(1962) *Naparima Girls' High School: Golden Jubilee 1912-1962*. Port of Spain: n. p.

Niddrie, D. 1961. *Land Use and Population in Tobago: an Environmental Study*. Bude, Cornwall: Geographical Publications Ltd.

Newson, L. 1976. *Aboriginal and Spanish Colonial Trinidad: a Study in Culture Contact*. London: Academic Press.

O' Connor, P. E. T. 1978. *Some Trinidad Yesterdays*. Port of Spain: Inprint Caribbean Ltd.

(1986) *One Hundred and Fifty Years of Witness and Worship: The Sisters of St Joseph of Cluny in the Caribbean 1836-1986*. Port of Spain: n. p.

Oxaal, I . 1982. *Black Intellectuals and the Dilemmas of Race and Class in Trinidad*. Cambridge, Mass: Schenkmann Publishing Co.

(1970) *QRC 100, Being a Record of the Queen's Royal College 1870-1970*. Port of Spain: n. p.

Rampersad, A. *A History of Naparima Girls' High School 1912-1967*. Port of Spain: n. p.

Ramsaran, D. 1993. *Breaking the Bonds of Indentureship: Indo-Trinidadians in Business*. UWI, St Augustine: Institute of Social and Economic Research.

Rogers, D. N.d. *The Rise of the People's National Movement. In the Beginning: an Excursus and a Biography*. Port of Spain: Ideal Printery.

Ryan, S. 1974. *Race and Nationalism in Trinidad and Tobago: A Study of Decolonization in a Multiracial Society*. 1972. Reprint, Kingston, Jamaica: Institute of Social and Economic Research.

——. 1990. *Good Innings 1901-1990: the Life and Times of Ray Dieffenthaller*. Port of Spain: Paria Publishing Co.

Ryan, S., and L. A. Barclay. 1992. *Sharks and Sardines: Blacks in Business in Trinidad and Tobago*. UWI, St Augustine: Institute of Social and Economic Research.

Samaroo, B., and D. Dabydeen, eds. 1987. *India in the Caribbean*. London: Hansib Publishing Co.

(1913) *St Mary's College of the Immaculate Conception, Port of Spain: Its First Fifty Years 1863-1913*. Port of Spain: n. p.

Selleck, R. 1972. *English Primary Education and the Progressives 1914-1939*. London: Routledge and Kegan Paul.

Shepherd, C. Y. 1932. *The Cocoa Industry in Trinidad*. Port of Spain: n. p.

Singh, K. 1988. *Bloodstained Tombs: The Muharram Massacre 1884*. London: Macmillan Caribbean.

———. 1994. *Race and Class Struggles in a Colonial State: Trinidad 1917-1945.* Kingston, Jamaica: The Press University of the West Indies.

Sutton, P. 1986. *Dual Legacy in the Contemporary Caribbean: Continuing Aspects of British and French Dominion.* London: Frank Cass.

Thomas, J. J. 1969. *Froudacity. West Indian Fables Explained.* 1889. Reprint, London: New Beacon Books.

Trotman, D. 1986. *Crime in Trinidad: Conflict and Control in a Plantation Society 1838-1900.* Knoxville: University of Tennessee Press.

Tyson, J. D. 1939. *Memorandum of Evidence for the Royal Commission to the West Indies.* New Delhi: Government of India Press.

Vertovec, S. 1992. *Hindu Trinidad: Religion, Ethnicity and Socioeconomic Change.* London: Macmillan.

Williams, E. 1964. *History of the People of Trinidad and Tobago.* London: André Deutsch.

———. 1969. *Inward Hunger: the Education of a Prime Minister.* London: André Deutsch.

Wood, D. 1968. *Trinidad in Transition: the Years after Slavery.* Oxford: Oxford University Press.

Yelvington, K., ed. 1993. *Trinidad Ethnicity.* London: Macmillan.

Articles

Braithwaite, L. 1953. "Social stratification in Trinidad". *Social and Economic Studies* 2, nos. 2 and 3.

———. 1954. "The problem of cultural integration in Trinidad". *Social and Economic Studies* 3, no. 1

———. 1958. "Higher education in the West Indies". *Social and Economic Studies* 7, no. 1.

Brereton, B. 1977. "J. J. Thomas: an estimate". *Journal of Caribbean History* 9 (May).

Campbell, C. 1967. "Towards an imperial policy for the education of Negroes in the West Indies after Emancipation". *Jamaican Historical Review* 7, nos. 1 and 2.

Campbell, C. 1978. "Charles Warner and the development of education in Trinidad 1834-1870". *Journal of Caribbean History* 10 and 11.

———. 1975. "The establishment of Queen's Collegiate School in Trinidad 1857-1867". *Caribbean Journal of Education* 2, no. 2.

———. 1976. "John Jacob Thomas of Trinidad: the early career of a black teacher and scholar 1855-1870". *African Studies Association of the West Indies Bulletin* 8.

———. 1980. "The rise of a free coloured plantocracy in Trinidad 1783-1813". *Boletin de Estudios Latinoamericanos y del Caribe*, no. 29.

———. 1984. "Education and black consciousness: the amazing Captain Cutteridge in Trinidad and Tobago, 1921-1942". *Journal of Caribbean History* 18.

———. 1988. "The university of our dreams: centralization versus decentralization in the planning of the university of the West Indies 1943-1944". *Jamaican Historical Review* 16.

———. 1988. "The dual mandate of the Imperial College of Tropical Agriculure 1922-1960". *Jamaican Historical Review* 16.

———. 1988. "The St Augustine Campus of UWI: success and excess". *Jamaican Historical Review* 16.

Guthrie, G. 1980. "Stages of educational development? Beeby revisited". *International Review of Education* 26.

James, C. L. R. 1931. "Michel Maxwell Philip 1829-1886: sometime solicitor general of Trinidad. An impression". *Beacon*.

Johnson, H. 1973. "Barbadian immigrants in Trinidad, 1870-1897". *Caribbean Studies* 13, no. 3.

———. 1977. "The West Indies and the conversion of the British official classes to the development idea". *Journal of Commonwealth and Comparative Politics* 15, no. 1 (March).

Judges, V. 1955. "Recent trends in English education". *International Review of Education* 1.

Klineberg, F. 1939. "The Lady Mico Charity schools in the British West Indies 1825-1842". *Journal of Negro History* 24.

Laurence, K. 1980. "The survival of Spanish in Trinidad: an historical *aperçu*". *Nieuwe West-Indische Gids* 54.

Omolewa, M. 1980. "The promotion of London University Examinations in Nigeria 1857-1951". *The International Journal of African Historical Studies* 13, no. 4.

Rouse, I. B. 1980. "Labours of the Anglican breed". *Trinidad and Tobago Education Forum* 1, no. 3.

Samaroo, B. 1975. "The Presbyterian Canadian Mission as an agent of integration in Trinidad during the 19th and early 20th centuries". *Caribbean Studies* 14, no. 4.

Trinidad Public Library. N.d., "one hundred years of service" (6 typed pages at the Public Library).

Warner, M. 1972-1973. "Africans in 19th century Trinidad". *African Studies Association of the West Indies Bulletin*, nos. 5 and 6.

Williams, E. 1956. "The need for instructional materials related to the Caribbean environment", in *Education in the Caribbean*. Kent House, Trinidad: Caribbean Commission Central Secretariat.

Unpublished theses and papers

Ali, A. 1975. "The development of higher education in Trinidad and Tobago 1498-1965". PhD diss., University of Ottawa.

Ali, S. 1993. "A social history of East Indian women in Trinidad since 1870". MPhil. thesis, University of the West Indies.

Baghan, C. 1963. "A critical study of the development of education in Trinidad". MA thesis, University of London.

Boodhoo, I. 1974. "A curriculum model in art education for the primary schools of Trinidad and Tobago". PhD diss., University of Indiana.

Campbell, C. 1973. "The development of education in Trinidad 1834-1870". PhD diss., University of the West Indies.

Cuffy, D. 1963. "Problems in the teaching of English in the island of Trinidad from 1797 to the present day". MA thesis, University of London.

Dyal, G. 1976. "A historical study of the Arya Samaj movement in Trinidad". Caribbean Study paper, University of the West Indies, St Augustine.

Feheney, J. M. 1975. "Catholic education in Trinidad in the 19th century". MA thesis, University of the West Indies.

Fergus, C. 1986. "Education in the movement for self-government in Trinidad 1931-1956". MA thesis, University of the West Indies.

Forbes, R. 1979. "Arya Samaj as catalyst: the impact of a modern Hindu reform movement on the Indian community of Trinidad between 1917 and 1939". Paper presented at the second conference on East Indians in the Caribbean, University of the West Indies, St Augustine.

——. 1984. "Hindu organisational process in acculturative conditions: significance of the Arya Samaj experiences in Trinidad". Paper presented at the third conference on East Indians in the Caribbean, University of the West Indies, St Augustine.

——. 1984. "Arya Samaj in Trinidad: an historical study of Hindu organizational process in acculturative conditions". PhD diss., University of Miami.

Furlonge, A. 1968. "The development of secondary education in Trinidad and Tobago". PhD diss., University of Sheffield.

Hamel-Smith, A. 1979. "Education and the East Indians in Trinidad 1900-1938". Postgraduate seminar paper, University of the West Indies, St Augustine.

——. 1983. "A history of education in Trinidad, 1900-1938". MPhil thesis, University of the West Indies.

——. 1984. "Primary education and the East Indian woman in Trinidad 1900-1956". Paper presented at the third conference on East Indians in the Caribbean, University of the West Indies, St Augustine.

Guggenheim, H. 1968. "Social and political change in the art world of Trinidad during the period of transition from colony to new nation". PhD diss., New York University.

Johnson, H. 1969. "Crown Colony government in Trinidad". PhD diss., Oxford University.

Mason, G. 1977. "The Sisters of St Joseph of Cluny 1836-1936". Caribbean Study paper, University of the West Indies, St Augustine.

Mohammed, A. 1991. "The history of Point Fortin, 1900-1930s". MA thesis, University of the West Indies.

Mohan, P. 1984. "A language implodes: the death of Trinidad Bhojpuri". Paper presented at the third conference on East Indians in the Caribbean, University of the West Indies, St Augustine.

Moore, D. 1980. "The origins and development of racial ideology in Trinidad". PhD diss., Queen's University, Canada.

Mulchangsingh, V.1967. "The origins, growth and development of the oil industry in Trinidad 1857-1965". PhD diss., Queen's University, Ireland.

Pemberton, R. 1984. "Towards a re-evaluation of the contribution of the West Indian peasantry: a case study of Tobago 1900-1949". MA thesis, University of the West Indies.

Reddock, R. 1984. "Women, labour, and struggle in 20th century Trinidad and Tobago 1898-1960". PhD diss., University of Amsterdam.

Samaroo, B. 1969. "Constitutional and political development of Trinidad 1898-1925". PhD diss., University of London.

——. 1983. "Education as socialization: form and content in the syllabus in the Canadian Mission Presbyterian schools in Trinidad from the late 19th century". Paper presented at the fifteenth conference of the Association of Caribbean Historians, University of the West Indies, Mona.

Sander, R. 1979. "The Trinidad awakening: West Indian literature of the 1930s". PhD diss., University of Texas.

Sitahal, H. 1967. "The mission of the church in Trinidad: an examination of the church's work and influence among the descendants of the East Indians". MTh thesis, McGill University.

Turner, T. 1966. "The work of the Presbyterian Church of Canada in the field of secular education in Trinidad, 1868-1953". MEd thesis, University of New Brunswick.

Whiteman, D. 1990."The immigration of peons to Trinidad and their contribution to the development of the cocoa industry 1811-1891". MA thesis, University of the West Indies.

Index

Abolition: and day schools for black and coloured children, 1

Absentee owners: influence of, in British government circles, 84

Acham, Bernard See Chen, Eugene

Achong, Tito: on university scholarships, 207, 208

Adult suffrage: constitutional reform and, 288-289

African languages: disappearance of, 234

Age grouping: in schools, 151-152

Agostini, Edgar, 76

Agricultural college: committee on tropical, 84; Imperial Department of Agriculture as, 85; support for idea of imperial, 83-84; World War I and lobby for specialist, 84

Agricultural credit bank: establishment of, 148

Agricultural education: Canadian Presbyterian Mission and introduction of, 80; introduction of, at postprimary level, 81; need for, as expressed by West Indian Royal Commission, 78; origin of, in schools, 78; in primary schools, 79, 80; social considerations regarding, at postprimary level, 81

Agricultural inspectors: criticism of, 86

Agricultural research: need for institution for, 82

Agricultural Scholarship: abolition of, 87, 219; conversion of, to Science Scholarship, 96; creation of, 83

Agricultural shows: and official expectations from agricultural training, 86

Agricultural Society of Trinidad: establishment of, 78; and support for specialist agricultural college, 83

Agriculture: as compulsory subject in Teachers' Certificate Examination, 80; criticism of teaching of, in primary schools, 85; in curriculum of Bishop's High School, Tobago, 119; debate on specialist college of, 83; jobs relating to, for non-whites, 81

Agriculturists: demand for trained, 81

Alcazar, Henry, 76

Alcock, Susan Mrs: and Girls' Model School, 59, 60

Alexis, Patrick, 236, 249, 250, 251

Ali, Moulvi Ameer: on Board of Education, 189

Alladin, M.P.: and drawing in schools, 258

Alleyne, Gabriel: as winner of trade bursary, 114

Anderson, Alexander: as inspector of schools, 12, 13; on role of education for black children, 69

Anglicization: role of English language in, 229; of schools, 38; of Trinidad, 2, 56, 267

Anjuman Sunnat-ul-Jammat Association: formation of, 181, 183

Anstey, Bishop, 241; on Boards of Management for schools, 110; role of, in establishing Bishop's High School (Tobago), 118-119

Apprenticeship: legal recognition of girls under, 162; reaction to use of word, 161

Art: at St Joseph's Convent, 257; West Indian context in, 258

Articled clerkship: development of system of, 73

Aumaitre, P.N.: on the Harris education plan, 11

Ayra Samajists, 189

Bacchus, Kazim: on Indian interpretation of schooling, 167

Bain, G., 219

Barbados: and leadership in education up to 1940s, 286; as proposed site for training college, 123

Batson, Valeria, 177

Beacon: and nationalist strivings in education, 203-204; role of, in Trinidad literary life, 203

Beckles, T.E.: on Board of Education, 193

Beeby, C.E.: on primary schools in developing countries, 281-282

Beet sugar: as competition for cane sugar, 78

Bell-Smythe, John, 71

Bertín, Abbé, 15-16

Best, Lloyd: on blacks and education, 276

Biggart, James: in debate on denominational training schools, 126; role of, in establishing Bishop's High School, Tobago, 118-119; as Tobago's elected representative, 114-115

Bilby, Thomas: and Mico Charity, 57, 58

Bishop Anstey High School, 214; and education of girls, 241; and grammar school education model, 136-137; teaching of botany at, 96

Bishop, Howard: and criticism of Cutteridge's textbooks, 99

Bishop's High School, Tobago, 115, 118-119, 214; blacks in, 268; and education of girls, 241; as first coeducational secondary school, 119; and grammar school education model, 136-137; opposition to establishment of, 119; role of, in society, 120

Black consciousness: emergence of, 171; in Tobago, 207, 268

Black Power movement: and effect on school curriculum, 292

Blacks: postprimary education of, 66; stereotyping of, in Cutteridge's readers, 100; in trades training, 163

Board of Education: call for Indian representative on, 184, 189; classroom teacher representation on, 169; conflict between Department of Education and, 106; establishment of, 261; functioning of, 12, 246; and licensing of teachers, 31; proposal for, 9; role of, after 1918, 104 -105; of Tobago, 112; views on integration of Indian children, 55

Board of Industrial Training (BIT), 156-159; award of trade bursaries, 114, 162; classes offered by, 159-160; and continuation classes, 163-164; extension of classes to Tobago, 114; joint board of management for RVI and, 161; link between City and Guilds Institute and, 160; and management of the Institute of the Blind, 161; operation of, 1906-1939, 158-159; programme of, in South Trinidad, 160; responsibility of, 157; and technical/vocational education, 114

Boards of Management: functioning of, 265; incorporation of, into dual system, 109; legal inauguration of, 265; response of churches to, 110

Bowen, H.: as university scholarship winner, 26

Boys: in public coeducational primary schools, 235; secondary education of, 135

Boys' Model School, 59; singing as a subject at, 254; success of former pupils of, 67

Braithwaite, Lloyd: on Imperial College of Agriculture, 84; on overseas studies by Trinidadians, 209; on social mobility in Trinidad, 277-278; on social structure of Trinidad, 3

Braithwaite, Richard: on university scholarships, 208

Brereton, Bridget: on black and coloured middle class in nineteenth century, 65, 76

Brown, Alexander: on government training school graduates, 134-135

Brown, Vincent, 72

Buncle, Miss: and application for affiliation to QRC, 239-240

Bunsee, David, 166

Bursar system, 62, 109; abolition of, 125; debate on, in Legislative Council, 126; development of, 121; problems relating to, 123-127; social significance of, for blacks and coloureds, 126-127

Bursars: resentment of, by teachers, 126; selection of, 123

Burslem, William: at QRC, 93

Bushe Hilda: as assistant inspector of schools, 243; and organization of Higher Class for girls, 174-175, 240

Bushe, R. Gervase, 26-27; as inspector of schools, 37, 94; on introduction of agriculture in schools, 79

Butler riots: effect of, on primary school teachers, 191-192; Forster Commission on, 197; reasons for, 191

Butler, Uriah: and political leadership, 208

Cabildo: management of schools of, 261; schools of, in Port of Spain, 3, 245

Cadet system: introduction of, 82

Cadiz, J.: as university scholarship winner, 26, 27

Caird, Henry, 24

Calvert, Edward: as headmaster of Queen's Collegiate School, 24

Cambridge examinations: attack on, by Marriott and Cutteridge, 140; discontinuation of, for lower forms, 142; and domination of education in Trinidad and Tobago, 176; as measure of students' performance, 143; preparation for, at Queen's Collegiate School, 26

Cambridge School Certificate: exclusion of girls from, 74-75; private candidates for, 137; significance of, in nineteenth century, 74

Cameron, Norman, 211

Campbell, A. Wilson, 128

Canadian Presbyterian Mission: in agriculture teaching in schools, 80; and Christianizing of Indians, 48; degree of success of, at conversion of Indians, 51; distinction between Mission schools and Mission Indian Schools, 342n73; and education of Indians, 48-52; in emergence of middle class Indians, 166; and establishment of Naparima College for boys, 50; and establishment of Naparima Training College, 34, 50; and establishment of theological college, 50; evidence of, before Marriott/Mayhew Commission, 187-188; role of, in Trinidad education, 275-276; and segregated approach to Indian education, 52-54; social consequences of special Indian schools of, 190-191; and success of school gardens, 86; and tertiary education for women, 244-245; and tertiary training for Indians, 76, 209; and training of Indian ministers, 181; and training of Indian teachers, 64, 181; use of estate school technique by, 49; value of schools of, to Indians, 184-185; and Westernization of Indians, 54-55

Caparo Mission School, 54

Carmody, Professor: on introduction of agriculture in schools, 79

Carnegie Free Library: founding of, 260

Caroni: and association with Indians, 183

Carpentry: in curriculum at Bishop's High School, Tobago, 119-120

Catholic Social Guild, 110

Cazabon, Michel, 258

Chaguanas: establishment of Hindu/Muslim primary school at, 181,183-184, 188, 190; pundits at Mission school at, 225

Chamberlain, Joseph: and concern for imperial agricultural resources, 79; and imperial development, 78

Chen, Eugene: career of, 73, 154

Child labour, 191

Child marriage: among Indians, 88

Child welfare: notion of government responsibility for, 150

Children: changing attitudes to, 97

Church *See* Canadian Presbyterian Mission; Church of England; Methodist Church; Roman Catholic Church; Seventh-Day Adventists

Church of England: and establishment of male hostel, 126; and opening of primary schools, 3; and response to demand for girls' secondary school, 241; response of, to Harris' education plan, 11; rivalry between Roman Catholic church and, 2, 29-30; and schools for Indians, 48; in Trinidad, 1

Church of England Grammar School: collapse of, 19; establishment of, 14-15

Church Missionary Society: and opening of primary schools, 3

Churches: competition among, 223; conflict between government and, 272-273; and controversy over denominational hostels, 122; and dependence on government for school financing, 40; and opening of new secondary schools, 214; and opposition to government schools, 32; rivalry among, 2, 32; role of, in education, 5-6, 107-108, 267, 270-271; and school building costs, 149; and teacher training, 34

Cipriani, Capt Arthur: approach of, to education, 210-211; biography of, 204; on competitive civil service examinations, 144; in debate on denominational training schools, 126; on establishment of West Indian university, 210, 215

City and Guilds Institute of London: link between BIT and, 160

Civil service: Cipriani on competitive examinations for, 144; competitive examinations for entry into, 74; as desired placing for nonprofessionals, 144; and employment of scholarship candidates, 156; lack of Indians in, 168; penetration of, by non-whites, 72-73; suspension of competitive exams for entry into, 74

Class: consciousness of, as reflected in schools, 69; determinants of, in pre-emancipation period, 65; and reaction of ex-slaves to education opportunities, 69-70; tension in urban schools, 69

Clerical managers: and criticisms of government schools, 45-46; powers of, 36

Clifford, Bede (Governor): on teachers in politics, 202

Codrington College, 215, 216

College Council: and control of secondary schools, 36, 104

College Exhibitions, 345n148; addition to, for private school candidates, 250-251; administration of, 345n158; development of system of, 72; difficulty of passing, 176; discontinued, 71; girls and, 242; and Indians, 92; as means of penetration of secondary schools, 70; request for, for Tobago, 115; TTTU and calls for improvement in distribution of, 199

College of the Immaculate Conception (CIC): and academic competition with QRC, 275; advantages of, 28; conversion of, into English-speaking school, 232-233; establishment of, 15, 27-28; and exclusion of illegitimate children, 28; fight for government support of, 28; and organization of exhibitions, 72; prestige of, 274-275; proposed reform programme for, 93; rising level of achievement at, 175; and science teaching, 96; as trilingual school, 230;

Collens, J.H., 33; as inspector of schools, 94-95

Colonial Development and Welfare: establishment of scheme for, 212-213, 288; on government control of education system, 212

Colour: consciousness of, as reflected in schools, 69; and reaction of ex-slaves to education opportunities, 69-70

Coloureds: acceptance of, at Queen's Collegiate School, 23-24; in trades training, 163

Comma, Nelson: as school inspector, 172-173, 265

Competition: as characteristic of the dual system, 29; among churches, 223; in education, analysed, 74; between government and denominational schools, 32; for teaching jobs, 63

Compulsory attendance. *See* School attendance

Compulsory education ordinance, 253

Constitutional reform: and adult suffrage, 288-289

Coterie of Social Workers, 245

Crafts: in primary schools, 258; teaching of, in Tobago schools, 117; utilization of Indian skills in, at Naparima Training College, 129; value of, in education, 98-99

Creative arts: scope defined, 254

Creole (language): Alexander Anderson on French, 230; demise of, 233-234; description of, 360n28; role of Thomas' treatise on, 232; treatise on, by J.J. Thomas, 229

Creoles: French, influence of, on St Mary's College, 28; French, and integration into officialdom, 233; French, and support for Roman Catholic schools, 17; government efforts to combat social position of French, 229; and Island Scholarships, 27

Crown Colony government: criticism of, by Trinidad Labour Party, 194; and recognition of religious leaders, 186; resentment of, 134

Cultural resistance: by blacks, 3

Culture: move towards identification of West Indian, 195; role of the *Beacon* in development of West Indian, 203-204

Curriculum: need for reform at QRC and CIC, 93-94; of primary schools, 89; restructuring of, in primary schools, 78, 97; status of, in Tobago, 115; suspicion of reform in, 280-281

Cutteridge, Capt J.: and attack on Cambridge examinations, 140; and belief in liberal education, 127; cultural bias of textbooks by, 100-101; and defence of his teaching methods, 101; as

director of education, 98, 145; and innovations
in primary education, 98-99; and interest in craft,
258; and introduction of new primary textbooks,
98; and new perspectives in education, 137-139;
opposition to policies of, by teachers, 192-194;
opposition to, by trade unions, 200; policy of,
on education expenditure, 145; response of, to
debate on 1935 Code, 196-197; retirement of,
202; and trades training, 164; and transformation of primary school system, 282; views of
teachers on *Readers* of, 101-102

Dancing: in schools, 254
Daniel, Capt William, 128, 197; and *Histories of
the West Indies*, 211; on number of univer-
sity scholarships, 154-155; race prejudice of, 155;
and simplification of primary curriculum, 202
Darling, John, 49
Darlington, Levi A.: career of, 173
David, C.P.: as scholarship winner, 71
De Verteuil, Louis: and efforts to abolish Model
schools, 45; and establishment of St Mary's
College, 27; on introduction of agriculture in
schools, 79; on St George's College, 18
Deighton, Horace: as headmaster of Queen's
Collegiate School, 24
Denominationalists: arguments of, 38-39
Deonarine, Krishna: career of, 170-171 see also
Rienzi, A.C.
Department of Agriculture: establishment of, 78
Department of Education: conflict between Board
of Education and, 106; establishment of, 261;
Indians in, 266; recommendation of, 95; role of,
105; and Tobago, 105
Desouze, Joseph A., 172
Digby, Ernest, 204
Director of education: consequence of appointing
professionals as, 107; institution of post of, 98;
professional status of, 107
Dixon, John, 12, 59
Domestic science: in curriculum at Bishop's High
School, 119-120; in primary school curriculum,
146
Donaldson, John S., 195, 207
Drama: at Government Training College, 258; in
secondary schools, 258
Drawing: at Girls' Model School, 257; mechanical conception of, up to mid twentieth century,
257; in primary schools, 257; West Indian
context in, 258
Dual system: adjustments to, 29, 31-32, 33, 34;
admission of Hindu and Muslim schools into,
289; call by teachers for end to, 200; competition
and, 29; control of, 104, 109, 213; control of
primary and secondary education under, 36, 213,
272; crisis in, 212; in England, 31; financial
crisis of, 47; financing of, 41; and government
expenditure on education, 41; inclusion of
non-Christian denominational schools in, 147;

incorporation of Board of Management into, 109
110; influence of Roman Catholic Church on,
29; integration of Indian schools into, 34; nonex-
istence of, in Tobago, 114; opening of denominational secondary, 214; opposition to, by Protestants, 30; rationale for, 29; in secondary schools,
35-36, 119; status of, 91; support of, by
Marriott/Mayhew Commission, 212; support of,
by Moyne Commission, 212

East End Foundry, 160
East Indian National Association: founding of, 180
East Indian National Congress: founding of, 180
Economic development: and government policy,
148
Education Act (1966), 290-291
Education: comparisons relating to, 283-284;
competition in, analysed, 74; contribution of, to
nationalist strivings, 203, 204; as a development
cost, 149; effect of changes in system on primary
schools, 133; expenditure on, in 1930s, 148;
expenditure surveyed, 41-45; impact of new
teachings on primary, 97-98; of Indian girls, 88;
influence of government on, 4; influence of the
metropole on, 279-280; as instrument of anglicization in postemancipation period, 2, 3; leadership
of Trinidad and Barbados in, 286; liberalism in,
31; management of, 260-261; need for management of system, 94; new perspectives in,
137-139; non-whites in administration of, 265;
plan for Tobago, 116; proposals to cut expenditure on, 45-46; quality of, 284; rate of growth of
bureaucracy, 261; reaction of ex-slaves to opportunities for, 69-70; reflection of racial divisions in
system of, 171; relative cost of primary, 284;
resistance of whites to, for non-whites, 69; role of
church in, 5-6, 107-108; role of government in,
107-108; scope of practical, 139; of slaves, 1; and
social mobility, 22, 103
Education, agricultural See Agricultural education
Education Code (of 1929): demand for
observance of conscience clause under, 184
Education Code (of 1935), 145, 194-195;
criticisms of, 198, 199, 200; debates on, in
Legislative Council, 196-197; protest by Tobago
teachers against, 207; for Tobago, 112; and
working conditions of teachers, 195
Education Commission (1914-1916): on agricultural science in secondary schools, 96; on agricultural teaching in primary schools, 85; on amalgamation of schools, 91; on appointment of assistant inspectors, 95; on bonus payments, 86; on
teacher education standard, 92; on teachers'
colleges, 121
Education, compulsory: proposal to introduce, 46
Education League: formation of, 30
Education Ordinance (1870): and dual system,
29; and relation to secondary education, 35
Education Ordinance (1933): conscience clause
in, 227

Education plan: formulation of, 147-148
Education Plan, Draft Fifteen-Year, 260; publication of, 292
Education policy: of British government, 4; criticism of, by Legislative Council members, 153; criticism of, by working class spokesmen, 142; government attempts to enforce, 6; need for, 2; role of Charles Warner in making, 9
Education, primary: control of, under dual system, 36; principle of free, introduced, 10
Education rate: abolition of, 41; imposition of, 41
Education scheme: debate on, 10; problems in implementation of, 11-12; as proposed by Lord Harris, 9-10; responses to, 10-11
Education, secondary: control of, under dual system, 36; grammar school model of, 135; overseas, 75; and social mobility of blacks, 276-279; view of Gocking on role of, 205
Education subsidy: in British Caribbean, 1; reduction of, 4
Education tax: suggestion of, 45
Education Trust: suggestion of, 45
Education Week: in Tobago, 117
Elliot, Charles (Governor): attitude of, to ward school system, 13
Employers: and rejection of idea of trades school, 164-165
English, Fr: as principal of CIC, 96
English language: attempts to encourage use of, in Roman Catholic Schools, 229; challenge to, from Indians, 234; lack of, as hindrance to Indians, 92; legislation proclaiming, as teaching language, 231; as requirement for teaching in Indian schools, 34; role of, in anglicization policy, 229; struggle to establish, as main language, 229; use of, in government schools, 6; in ward schools, 229
English Party, 2, 5
Estate schools: biracial operation of some, 51; black children in, 53-54; financial support for, by planters, 49; use of technique of, by Canadian Presbyterian Mission, 49
Evolution of the Negro (Norman Cameron), 211
Examinations: competitive, for civil service entry, 74; educational value of, 140, 143; preparation for, at Queen's Collegiate School, 25-26; for pupil teachers, 63; role of, in selection system, 270; as route to upward mobility for non-whites, 141 *see also* Cambridge examinations
Exhibitions: offered by private secondary schools, 250 *see also* College Exhibitions; Handicraft Exhibitions
Export earnings: decrease in, and effect on education expenditure, 44
External degrees: as means of tertiary education, 217-218

Fatima College, 214
Federation: notion of, by British government, 123

Feheney, Fr Matthew, 17
Fitzpatrick, George, 168
Floating Dock, 160
Folk tales: in Cutteridge's reading books, 99-100
Forbes, Richard, 190
Forster Commission of Inquiry: on implementation of secondary modern schools, 164; and inquiry into Butler riots, 197
Fowler, Henry, 32-33
Franchise Commission (1943/44): recommendation of, regarding teachers in politics, 202
Fraser, Constance: as vice principal of Government Training College, 129
Fredholm, A., 83
Free coloureds: and establishment of public schools, 266-267; rebellion of, in early nineteenth century, 180
Free places: introduction of, 70
French: influence of, on Trinidadian lifestyle, 2
French creoles *See* Creoles

Garveyites: and criticism of Cutteridge's textbooks, 99-101; on termination of bursar system, 126, 127
Gender identification: lack of, in official records, 234-235
German: teaching of, at Queen's Collegiate School, 25
Girls: and College Exhibition, 242; eligibility of, for Handicraft Exhibition, 162; and exclusion from Cambridge School Certificate examination, 74-75; Higher Class for, at Girls' Model School, 174-175, 240; Indian, in primary schools, 239; Indian, in nurses' training, 168; recognition of, as legal apprentices, 162; in Roman Catholic schools, 239; schooling of Indian, 87; secondary schooling for, 175, 240; and university scholarships, 242
Girls' Model School: attendance at, 239; establishment of, 59, 60; Higher Class at, 174-175, 240; singing as a subject at, 254
Gladstone, William, 30
Gocking, C.V., 204; and criticism of *Histories of the West Indies*, 211; on Trinidad middle class, 205; views of, on role of West Indian history, 205-206
Gokool, Haji, 190
Gomes, Ralph: on West Indians and music, 256
Goodville, George: and support for subsidized female secondary schools, 240
Gordon, Arthur (Governor): and dual education system, 29, 30-31; and restructuring of primary and secondary school policies, 28
Government policy: as regards child welfare, 150; on exclusion of children from school, 225; regarding expenditure on schools, 108-109; on separate Indian schools, 55
Government Railways, 160

Government revenue: reorganization of sources of, 8

Government Training College: admission policy of, 130-131; attendance figures for, 129; as coeducational institution, 129; criticisms of, 133-135; improved status of, in 1930s, 128-129; internal organization of, 130; new curriculum for, 124; reform of, 121, 122; removal of, 129; specialist instructors at, 128; widening of curriculum at, 128

Government training school: Keenan on, 60; as lever of upward mobility, 67; male and female branches of, 236; as partly residential institution, 62; and postprimary education of blacks, 66; quality of training at, 59, 60; and recruitment of pupil teachers, 62; relocation of, 62

Grant, Bernice, 177

Grosvenor, E.B.: as inspector of schools, Tobago, 117

Guppy, Lechmere: criticism of, 94; and criticisms of the dual system, 37; as inspector of schools, 13; on use of English in schools, 231

Guy, Marjorie, 177

Guyadeen, Cyril, 99, 172

Hamid, Idris, 51

Hancock, H.: as director of education, 98

Handicraft Exhibitions, 117,177-178; abolition of, for girls, 162; eligibility of girls for, 162; as lever of social advancement, 178

Handwork *See* Crafts

Harland, Professor: on inferiority of blacks, 221

Harris, Lord (Governor): and anglicization policy, 6; education scheme of, presented to Legislative Council, 9-10; and establishment of ward schools, 6, 8, 9; and notion of civic consciousness, 7-8; and religious teaching in government schools, 8; and reorganization of government revenue sources, 8; and vision of open education system, 9

Hart, J.: on introduction of agriculture in schools, 79

Higher Class: organization of, at Girls' Model School, 174-175, 240

Hindi: calls for introduction of, in schools, 184, 185; in curriculum of government training school, 231; remarks on teaching of, by Canadian Presbyterian Mission, 187; as requirement for teaching in Indian schools, 34, 231; Teachers' Certificate examination paper in, 64

Hinduism: intensification of, 180

Histories of the West Indies: criticisms of, 211

History, West Indian: efforts to produce, 204-206; teaching of, at University of the West Indies, 206

Hollis, Governor: and call for back-to-the-land movement, 141; and criticism of Tobago education, 115-116

Holy Ghost Fathers, 15; arrival of, in Trinidad, 27

Hope, T.A.: on Education Code of 1935, 197

Hosein, F.E.M.: on Legislative Council, 186; as university scholarship winner, 168

Hostels: controversy over, 122; conversion of denominational training schools to, 121

House Scholarships, 176

Hudson-Phillips, Henry: on university scholarships, 208

Ibrahim, Mohammed, 190

Iere Central High School: founding of, 249

Illegitimacy: rules against, at St Mary's College (CIC), 28

Imperial College of Tropical Agriculture (ICTA): establishment of, 84-85; as first intercolonial enterprise in education, 85; imperial focus of, 220; problems of, 218-221; integration of, into a university of the West Indies, 221; integration of, into the University of the West Indies, 292; reputation of, for scientific research, 218; significance of, to Trinidad, 285; social gap between community and, 220; suspicion of graduates of, 218; tax to finance, 85; training at, and prospects for social mobility, 219

Imperial Department of Agriculture: consequences of establishment of, 79; dismantling of, 83; establishment of, 78; and postprimary agricultural training scheme, 82; support for, from Trinidad officials, 79

Incorporated Law Society of London: use of examinations of, 73

Indenture: reaction to use of word, 161

Indenture system: support for, by Rev John Morton, 49

Indian community: consolidation of position of, 179, 180; rebellion of, against Canadian Presbyterian Mission, 180

Indian Educational Association: formation of, 188

Indian Marriage Ordinance, 186

Indian ministers: treatment of, by Canadian Presbyterian Mission, 182-183

Indian nationalism: emergence of, 171

Indians: absence of, from trades training, 163; and acceptance of conversion, 51; awakening of race consciousness among, 181; child labour among, 191; child marriage among, 88; contribution of, to nationalist strivings, 203; disagreements among associations representing, 189; dissatisfaction of teacher/catechists with mission, 182; economic interpretation of schooling, 167-168; education of, 47-48; in Education Department, 266; girls in nurses training, 168; girls in primary schools, 239; incorporation of religious associations among, 181; and land ownership, 76; and literary and debating associations, 170-171; in Marriott/Mayhew Report, 286; in medical profession, 167; and overseas study, 209; perception of, by whites, as regards music, 256; perceptions of, of government officials, 189; and population increase, 42, 47; rate of natural increase of, 179; religious consciousness among,

181; resistance of some leaders to missionaries, 56; revolt of, in sphere of education, 181; rise of, to middle class, 76, 166-167; schooling of, 87; social consequences of special schools for, 190-191; status of women, 191; tertiary training for, 76; training of, as teachers, 64; treatment of in Cutteridge's textbooks, 102; value of mission schools to, 184-185; in ward schools, 47-48; Westernization of, through Canadian Presbyterian Mission, 54-55

Innis, L.O., 37-38

Inspector of schools: Alexander Anderson as, 12; dilemma of, 37; establishment of post of, 261; Indians as, 266; proposal for appointment of, 9; role of, 94-95

Institute for the Blind: under management of BIT, 161

Intelligentsia: formation of, in Trinidad, 77

Irish National School books, 14

Irvine Commission: on West Indian university, 210, 216

Irvine, Henry (Governor): and adjustments to dual system, 31-32, 33, 34; views of, on free schooling for the masses, 41

Islam: intensification of, 180

Islamic Guardian Association: founding of, 180, 190

Island Scholars, 26, 27, 75, 176; and civil service employment, 156; and engineering, 166

Jaimini, Mehta, 190

James, C.L.R., 203; contribution of, to study of West Indian history, 204

Jeffers, Audrey, 241; and Coterie of Social Workers, 245

Jordan, Rawle, 120

Joseph, Harry, 126, 127

Juvenile reformatories: government aid to, 34

Kabir Panth Association: formation of, 181

Keate, Robert (Governor): attitude of, to ward school system, 13; and establishment of Queen's Collegiate School, 19, 22-23; on St George's College, 17

Keenan, Patrick, 340n23; on government training school, 60; on introduction of teachers' certificate, 61; on language policy for Trinidad, 230; on management of schools, 262; proposals regarding pupil teachers, 61; on religious instruction in schools, 226; on St Joseph's Convent, 17; on school management by clerics, 263; and support for denominational schools, 30; views on Harris' education scheme, 10; on ward schools, 14

Kelshall, T.M.: on Education Code of 1935, 197

Lalla, Rev C.D.: on Legislative Council, 186; as moderator of Canadian Presbyterian Church, 183

Lamont, Norman: and campaign for agricultural college, 83; and support for imperial agricultural college, 83-84

Land ownership: and social mobility of Indians, 76

Lange, Eugene, 71

Language: as barrier to integration for black and Indian children, 51; demand for teaching of Hindu and Urdu in schools, 185; events affecting balance of, in late nineteenth century, 232; government concern for, in denominational primary schools, 230; Keenan policy for Trinidad, 230 see also English language; Hindi; Urdu; French; Spanish

Latrobe, Charles: and comparison of education in English-speaking Caribbean, 283

Laurence, Stephen: as scholarship winner, 71, 76; on university scholarships, 208

Law: and opportunities for advancement for non-whites, 73

Lazare, Emanuel See Lazare, Mzumbo

Lazare, Mzumbo: career of, 76

Legislation: concerning education, 110

Legislative Council: criticism of education policy in, 153; and debate on bursar system, 126; debate on 1935 Code, 196-197; and education policy making, 289; effect of introduction of elected representatives, 114-115; and support of need for superior government college, 35; and support for teachers, 193

Leotaud, Charles, 30

Liberalism: in education, 31

Libraries, lending: in primary schools, 260; proposed, 10

Literary and debating associations: history of, 170; and Indian community, 170-171; role of, in political consciousness raising, 170; role of teachers in, 170

Loan financing: recommendation to institute, for educational expansion, 149

London University Matriculation Examination, 93

Losh, John, 5

l'Ouverture, Toussaint, 204; significance of 'discovery' of, to West Indian history, 206

Lumb Commission: and favouring of denominational schools, 33

Mackay, George: death of, 107; as director of education, 98

MacLeod, Rev J.W.: and training of Indian teachers, 64

Mathura, C.B.: and support for missions, 185

Maingot, F.J., 73

Mandingos: and cultural resistance, 3

Marese-Smith, E., 73

Maraj, Bhadase, 289

Marriott, Frederick: and abolition of bursar system, 125; and attack on Cambridge examinations, 140; and criticism of Tobagonians, 116, 117; and new perspectives in education, 137-139;

and notion of flexibility of secondary schools, 97; on role of church and government in education, 107-108; position of, on non-Christian denominational schools, 186; views of, on teacher training, 125-126

Marriott/Mayhew Report: acceptance of, by Trinidad government, 145; on education in Trinidad and eastern Caribbean, 144, 283; evidence of Canadian Presbyterian Mission before, 187-188; on expansion in education, 146-147; Indian delegation to, 186-187; on Indians, 286; reactions to, 145; and recommendation of secondary modern school, 144; recommendations of, on non-Christian denominational schools, 188; and transformation of primary school system, 282

Marryshow, T.A.: on Toussaint l'Ouverture, 206

Mason Hall, Tobago: government primary school at, 117

Mason, Sister Gabrielle: on social exclusiveness of Roman Catholic schools, 16

Maurice Report (1959), 128-129

Mausica Teachers' College, 127

Mayhew, Arthur: and investigation of education in Eastern Caribbean, 111; and recommendation of new type of school, 144

Maynard, Fitz G., 195

McLeod, Governor: and support for nondenominational schools, 5

McShine, Arthur: in debate on denominational training schools, 126; in debate on 1935 Code, 196, 197; as scholarship winner, 71, 207

McShine, Umilta, 175

Medical profession: as favoured by Indians, 167

Men: as headteachers, 238; non-white professionals, in late nineteenth century, 75; social mobility of black, 67

Mendes, Alfred, 203

Methodists: and opening of primary schools, 3

Mico Charity, 339n9; in Antigua, 57; collapse of, 4, 56; and education in Trinidad, 4, 236; in Jamaica, 57; operation of, in Trinidad, 57-58; opposition of established churches to training school of, 57; and postprimary education of blacks, 66; and promotion of religious neutrality, 223; rejection of, by ward schools, 6; white expatriate teachers in system of, 58

Middle class: composition of, in pre-emancipation period, 65; growth of Indian, 166-167; non-whites in, by end of nineteenth century, 75; rise of Indians to, 76; role of Trinidad Public Library in development of, 259; teachers in, from late nineteenth century, 168-170; views of Gocking regarding, 205

Mighty Sparrow: on primary education in Trinidad, 282-283

Migration: effect of, on language in Trinidad, 232

Miles, William: at QRC, 93; views of, on free place winners, 71

Milner, Lord: and support for notion of imperial college of agriculture, 84

Mitchell, Lionel: and adoption of Cutteridge's methods in Tobago, 117

Model school: efforts to abolish, 45; establishment of, at Woodbrook Estate, 12

Morris, Daniel, 79

Morton, Rev Harvey, 182

Morton, Rev John: and Canadian Presbyterian Mission, 48; and perception of racial affinity between Indians and Aryans, 52; and support for indenture system, 49

Moyne Commission: and proposals for trade and farm schools, 164; recommendations of, 201, 202, 288; TTTU and representation before, 198-200

Municipal councils: non-formation of, 11-12

Municipal Ordinance (1847), 7

Music: at QRC, 256; in Teachers' Certificate Examination, 254; teaching of, in public schools, 256; and West Indians, 256

Naparima Girls' High School, 214; in education of girls, 241; and grammar school education model, 136-137; Indian girls as minority at, 1912-1925, 242

Naparima Training College: establishment of, 34; and social mobility of Indians, 166; and utilization of traditional Indian skills, 129

Needlework: in curriculum of government schools, 238; teaching of, to girls, 85

Negro Education Grant: use of, in Trinidad, 4, 283-284

Normal school: proposed, 10

Nuns: French, in Roman Catholic Schools, 15; and ideal of womanhood, 237-238

Nurse, Hubert Alphonso, 77; on resistance to school gardens, 80

Occupations: of women, 237, 242

O'Connor, P.E.T., 353n210

Old Boy tradition, 344n124

Oil industry: apprenticeship training in, 165-166; effect of, on education system, 165-166, 292; employment possibilities in, 165; in Trinidad economy, 148

Ordinance 17 (1890): and benefits to denominational schools, 33

O'Reilly, L.A.P.: in debate on denominational training schools, 126; on university scholarships, 155, 208

Padmore, Elsie: as Handicraft Exhibition winner, 178

Padmore, Overand, 193

Pamphylian High School, 251; founding of, 249; and offer of exhibitions, 250

Parents' Union: on university scholarships, 153

Paul, Emilie Marese, 75

Payment by results system, 32, 46, 74, 283-284; criticism of, 86; and government promise of fee payment, 33; problems of, 89-90; reduction of bonuses under, 33; weaknesses in, 94

People's Education Movement: formation of, 202

Philip, Jean Baptiste, 246

Philip, Michael Maxwell, 17; biography of, 204

Pierre, C. Henry: in debate on denominational training schools, 126; on Education Code of 1935, 197; social advance of, 172; on university scholarships, 153-154, 208

Pix, Rev George, 18

Plantation system: establishment of new, in late nineteenth century, 74

Planters: and financial support for estate schools, 49; response of, to education scheme, 10-11; and support for special Indian schools, 53

Political consciousness: of postwar Trinidad, 142

Population growth: reasons for, 42

Port of Spain: establishment of secondary schools in, 14-15; and management of schools, 261

Port of Spain Borough Council: and closure of ward schools, 13; Higher Class at school of, 344n139; and impact on social mobility of blacks and coloureds, 67; and Trinidad Public Library, 259

Presentation College, 214

Press: coloureds and, in late nineteenth century, 66

Princes Town, 190

Private School Ordinance (1935), 253

Proctor, Samuel, 59

Professionals: increase in black and coloured, in early twentieth century, 171-172

Prussia: as mid nineteenth century superpower, 25

Pundits: independence of, 186; at Mission school at Chaguanas, 225

Pupil teacher system: criticism of, 63; examinations for, 63; gender differentiation in, 237; link between government training school and, 62; pass rate for examinations under, 131; proportion of teachers in school under, 91; recommendations by Keenan regarding, 61; rules regarding pay of, 62; use of, in rural areas, 132; working of, 62-63

Qualifications: increased demand for, 136; inflation in, for jobs, 240; inflation in, for primary school teaching, 136

Queen's Collegiate Grammar School: acceptance of coloured boys at, 23-24; advantages of, 28; criticism of, by Roman Catholic Church, 27; curriculum of, 20, 24-25; effect of establishment of, on ward school system, 22; establishment of, 15, 19, 24; impact of scholarship preparation on curriculum at, 25-26; as modelled on English grammar schools, 15, 268; and participation in Cambridge examinations, 26; renamed Queen's Royal College, 28; role of, in education anglicization policy, 19-21; secular principles of, 15; as social barrier against blacks and coloureds, 21-23; 69

Queen's Park Savannah, 159

Queen's Royal College (QRC): and academic competition with CIC, 275; criticism of focus of, 136; exclusion of religious instruction at, 228; prestige of, 274-275; proposed new building for, 35-36; proposed reform programme for, 93; Queen's Collegiate School as, 28; race discrimination at, 71; rising level of achievement at, 175; science teaching at, 96; singing and music at, 256

Race: awakening of consciousness of, among Indians, 181; contradictions of, in criticisms of Cutteridge, 103

Race discrimination: against graduates of the Royal Victoria Institute, 141; at ICTA, 221; against non-white teachers, 133; in legal profession, 73; at QRC, 71

Racial segregation: education system as reflection of, 171; as feature of Trinidad population, 171; reasons for, by Canadian Presbyterian mission, 52-54

Ragbir, Charles, 182

Ragbir, Frank, 167

Ramkessoon, J.D.: on university scholarships, 208

Ramkessoon, Rawle, 266; and external degree, 217; as inspector of schools, Tobago, 117

Ramsaran, Gladys: as first female lawyer, 243

Rates: proposed, for financing education, 10

Reading: student performance in, 102-103

Reddock, Rhoda: on women's struggle in Trinidad, 245

Reid, Kenneth, 119

Religious instruction: activities related to, 222-223, 227; conscience clause relating to, in Education Ordinance of 1933, 227-228; debate on exclusion of, in schools, 10; exclusion of, from curriculum, 4; exclusion of, in government secondary school, 228; Hindu and Muslim protests relating to, in schools, 227; as integrated into school curriculum, 224; reversal of government policy on, in 1949, 228; school survey to assess, 226; in schools, 222; in ward schools, 225

Religious neutrality: attempts to promote, 223-224

Rienzi, A.C.: 184; on promotion of engineering studies, 166 *see also* Deonarine, Krishna

Rigsby, Mona, 243

Roberts, L.A.: as playwright, 258

Robinson, William (Governor): and adjustments to the dual system, 33

Rogers, DeWilton: 195, 207; as advocate of black culture in schools, 103

Roman Catholic Church: and classes for religious instruction, 227; and criticism of Queen's Collegiate School, 27; and disagreement over bursar system, 124; distrust of, by Trinidad government, 2; and education in the eastern Caribbean, 1; and establishment of secondary schools, 14-15; and establishment of teacher training schools, 64; girls in, 239; government efforts to combat social position of, 229; and influence on dual system, 29; lack of financial support for schools of, 5; and management of secondary schools, 262; and opening of primary schools, 3; and preference for single-sex schools, 235; response of, to Harris' education plan, 11; rivalry between Church of England and, 2, 29-30; and sanctions to ensure non-secularization, 38, 222; social exclusiveness of secondary schools of, 16; and strategy to counter secularization, 28, 29; support of French creoles for schools of, 17; and willingness to use English as official language, 233

Roman Catholic Female Training School, 129

Roman Catholic Male Training School, 129

Roodal, Timothy, 184; on Legislative Council, 186

Royal Victoria Institute (RVI), 156, 159; graduates of, 141; joint board of management for BIT and, 161

Royalian: founding of, 205

Rukmudeen, Haji, 189, 190

St Augustine Government Farm, 85

St Benedict College, 214

St George's College: establishment of, 14, 17-18; Keate and Warner on, 17

St George's College (Barataria): opening of, 214

St Joseph's Convent: aim of curriculum of, 238; art at, 257; conversion of, into English-speaking school, 232-233; establishment of, 14; 15-17; girls' boarding school, 16-17; multiple school technique of, 16; science teaching at, 96-97

St Joseph's High School, 214

St Mary's College *See* CIC

St Thomas Roman Catholic School, 31

Sammy, J.S.: at Naparima Training College, 129

San Fernando Borough Council: and management of schools, 261

San Fernando Junior Technical College: establishment of, 166

Sanatan Dharma Association of Trinidad: 189; incorporation of, 181

Sanatan Dharma Board of Control, 189; before Moyne Commission, regarding Indian education, 201; incorporation of, 181

Sangre Grande High School: founding of, 249

Sanitary inspectors, 173

Sankerali, E.T., 167

Scarborough, 114

Scarborough Anglican School, 117

Scarborough Ideal Literary and Debating Club, 207

Scholarships: female candidates for, 176; need to increase number of, 92; impact of, on Queen's Collegiate School curriculum, 25-26; to secondary schools in 1936, listed, 345n158; from Tobago primary schools, 120 *see also* Agriculture Scholarship; College Exhibitions; House Scholar-

ships; Island Scholars; Science Scholarship; University scholarship

School age population: size of, 87-88

School attendance: commission to investigate compulsory, 42; level of, among non-whites, 87; in the 1930s, 151

School bus service: introduction of, 150

School districts: implementation of system of, 265

School fees: abolition of, 34, 41-42, 46; collection of, 43, 264; commission to investigate, 42; in primary schools, 41

School gardens: agricultural society on reorganization of, 139-140; criticism of standard of, 85-86; initial resistance to, in Trinidad, 80, 81; spread of, throughout the British Caribbean, 80, 81; success of, of Canadian Presbyterian mission, 86; in Tobago, 112

School managers: clerics as, 261; councillors as, 261; wardens as, 261

School medical service, 150, 199

School places: inadequacy of, 87-88

Schools: amalgamation of, 108-109, 116; building of, through Negro Education Grant, 4; building programme in 1930s, 149; criteria used for inspecting, 151; expenditure on, 273-274; expenditure on, in Tobago, 113; as form of business, 252-253; government versus denominational in Tobago, 116; increase in number of, under dual system, 63; for Indians, in early twentieth century, 190; inspection of, in Tobago, 112; introduction of age grouping in, 151-152; issue of control of, 1-2; management of, in Tobago, 263; as mechanisms for social mobility, 65; need to regulate private, in 1920s, 252, 253; number of private, in 1936, 253; official policy regarding expenditure on, 108-109; private, sources of, 246; ratio of government to denominational, 33-34; rivalry and conflict among, 37; situation of, in Tobago, 112-114

Schools, commercial, 249

Schools, day: for black and coloured children, 1

Schools, denominational: arguments against, 5; benefits to, of Ordinance 17 (1890), 33; competition between government and, 32; conditions in, 14; establishment of Hindu/Muslim, at Chaguanas, 181, 183-184, 188, 190; and exclusion of rival clerics, 224-225; Gordon's plan for, 31; government funding of, 34; opening of, 3; ratio of government schools to, 33-34; request for government aid for, 189

Schools, government: arguments against, 39; competition between denominational and, 32; criticisms of, by clerical managers, 45-46; financing of, 6; opening of secondary, 214; as preferred by Indian leaders, 40; as purveyors of English cultural values, 38; ratio of denominational schools to, 33-34; religious instruction in curriculum of, 224

Schools, Indian: attendance of non-Indian children at, 51; establishment of Hindu/Muslim, at Chaguanas, 181, 183-184, 188, 190; government policy on separate, 55; integration of, into dual system, 34-35, 213; integrative function of, 54-55; official recognition of, 34; social consequences of, 54

Schools, nondenominational: support for policy of, 5

Schools, primary: boys in coeducational public, 235; building of, 1939-1981, 287; educational achievement in, 90; educational achievement in urban, 90; expansion of denominational, 212; introduction of code to govern, in Legislative Council, 194; gap between, of Trinidad and Tobago, 115; libraries in, 260; management of, 261-262; singing in, 254; suggestion of amalgamation of, in Tobago, 116; teaching of agriculture in, 79, 80, 85

Schools, secondary: academic performance of, in 1930s, 152-153; demand for, 137; emergence of private, for blacks and coloureds, 137,174; enrolment in, after 1939, 287; establishment of, for boys, 18; establishment of, in Port of Spain, 14-15; establishment of, in Tobago, 118; grammar school type curriculum of, 268; lack of government control over, 214-215; prestige of older, 269; as public, 248-249; shortage of, 239; social exclusiveness of Roman Catholic, 16; social importance of new, 250; standard of education at private, 250; start of private, in early twentieth century, 249

Schools, secondary modern: erection of, in 1960s, 146; introduction of idea of, 138-141, 144-145; as model for educational development, 288

Schools, teacher training See Government Training College; Government training school; Naparima Training College; Teacher training

Schools, technical/vocational: introduction of idea of, 138-141

Schools, ward See Ward schools

Science Scholarship: introduction of, 87, 96

Science teaching: introduction of, in secondary education system, 95-97

Sealey, Ben, 117

Secular schools See Ward schools

Secularists: arguments of, 38-39

Sellier, J.D., 73

Seventh-Day Adventists: and private primary schools in Tobago, 253

Singing: under payment by results system, 255; in primary schools, 254, 255; at QRC, 256; syllabus for, 255

Sisters of St Joseph de Cluny, 15-16

Smith, Charles, 117

Smith, Patrick: on Harris' education scheme, 11

Smith, Sydney: as assistant inspector of schools, 265

Social development: and government policy, 148

Social mobility: education and, 22, 65; education and black, 276-279; of Indians, 166-167

Social structure: of Trinidad, 3

Solicitors: restrictions imposed, for admission as, 73

Solomon, Dr Patrick, 210

Soodeen, Charles, 64

Soodeen, Clarence, 167

Spaccapietra, Archbishop, 17-18; and criticism of Queen's Collegiate School, 27

Spanish: influence of, on Trinidadian lifestyle, 2; isolation of speakers of, 234

Stollmeyer, A., 83; in debate on denominational training schools, 126

Student enrolment: at denominational secondary schools, 92-93

Sugar: prosperity from, for Trinidad, in World War I, 84

Sugars, Mr: at Boys' Model School, 59

Tacarigua Orphans Home, 48

Tackveeyatul Islamic Association of Trinidad: incorporation of, 181, 183

Taxes See Rates

Teacher training: as based on secondary education, 102; controversy over system of, 121-122; delays in building of central college, 150; downgrading of denominational schools for, 122; under dual system, 91; establishment of denominational schools for, 64; establishment of school for, 12, 56, 59; government aid for denominational schools, 34; government dominance of, 56-57; for Indians, 64; proposal for central college, 123, 147; reform of, 121; religious instruction at denominational colleges for, 228

Teachers: and assertion of rights to shape education policy, 169; as assistant school inspectors, 172; as base of intelligentsia, 77; cause of protest by, 194; certification of, 37, 61; control of, 109; control of, by clerical managers, 36; and criticism of Marriott and Cutteridge, 192-194; demand for head teachers, 63-64; demand for qualifications as, 131; Indian, on Code of 1935, 200-201; married women as, 244; in middle class, from late nineteenth century, 168-170; new demands on, in primary schools, 132; number of, trained annually, 129; oversupply of trained male, 60; in primary schools, as vanguard of new middle class, 65; and prohibition from political involvement, 197, 200, 202, 357n47; proportion of female to male, 243-244; as public opinion makers, from 1920s, 169-170; quality of certification of, 65; quality of trainees, in late nineteenth century, 58; rate of pay of female, 235; recommended training of, in agriculture, 79; and resentment of bursars, 126; response of, to Education Code debate, 1935, 196-197; role of Director of Education in appointment and dismissal of, 110; role of female, 235, 236;

salaries of primary school, 286; support of
Legislative Council for, 193; training of female,
121; views of, on Cutteridge's *Readers*, 101-102;
white expatriate, in Mico Charity system, 58;
women among, 169; World War II and opportunities for female, 243

Teachers' Certificate Examination: agriculture as
compulsory subject in, 80; as centre of teacher
training programme, 62; Hindi paper included
in, 64; music in, 254; pass rate of, 131; suggestion of, by Keenan, 62

Teachers' Economic and Cultural Association:
objectives of, 195

Teachers Herald: as organ of teachers' views,
193-194

Teachers Journal: as organ of teachers' views,
193-194; views of, on Cutteridge's *Readers*, 194

Teachers' salaries, 286; part payment of, by
government, for denominational primary schools,
33

Teaching: as male occupation, 236

Teelucksingh, Sarran, 168, 186; in debate on
denominational training schools, 126; on
Legislative Council, 186

Textbooks: call by TTTU for additional, in
school system, 199; criticism of Cutteridge's,
99-100; cultural orientation of reading books,
103; introduction of new, by Cutteridge, 99-101

Thomas, J.J., 59, 95; as example of social
mobility through education, 68, 74; role of his
Theory and Practice of Creole Grammar, 232;
treatise on creole grammar by, 229

Thornhill, Samuel, 127

Tikasingh, Gerad, 179

Tobago: adoption of Cutteridge's teaching
methods in, 117; black consciousness in, 207;
Board of Education of, 112; curriculum of, 115;
and Department of Education, 105; and
Education Code, 112; education plan for, 116;
establishment of secondary school in, 118;
Exhibition system in, 120; incorporation of, 34;
management of schools in, 263; private primary
schools in, 253; and request for College Exhibitions, 115; in school district system, 265; school
expenditure in, 113; school gardens in, 112;
schools of, as beneficiary of union with Trinidad,
113; state of education in, in 1889, 111; tension
between Trinidad and, 113; union between
Trinidad and, 111

Tobago Teachers' Union, 116

Tobago Times: and essay competition on
l'Ouverture, 207

Trade bursaries: awarded by BIT, 162; award of,
114; termination of, 162

Trade unions: and opposition to Cutteridge, 200

Trades training: as dominated by black and
coloured youth, 163

Tradesmen: and need for certification, 114;
recognition of need for skilled, 157

Tranquillity Estate: government training school
at, 62

Tranquillity Boys' School: BIT classes at, 161

Tranquillity Girls' School: end of independent
position of, 129; Higher Class at, 174-175

Trinidad (magazine): role of, in Trinidad literary
life, 203

Trinidad: anglicization of, 2, 56, 267; as site for
central training college, 123, 146; social structure
of, 3; sociocultural characteristics of, nineteenth
century, 3; tension between Tobago and, 113

Trinidad Labour Party: and criticism of Crown
Colony government, 194

Trinidad Public Library: access to, 259-260; and
Port of Spain Borough Council, 259; role of, in
development of middle class, 259

Trinidad and Tobago: and leadership in education up to 1940s, 286

Trinidad and Tobago Friendly Society's Union:
on university scholarships, 153

Trinidad and Tobago Historical Society: posture
of, 204

Trinidad and Tobago Teachers' Union (TTTU):
criticism of Marriott and Cutteridge, 192-194,
195; and endorsement of Trinidad Labour Party,
200; formation of, 109, 169; presentation of
grievances and demands before Moyne Commission, 198-200; on reduction of school years, 195;
on termination of bursar system, 126; and
working conditions of teachers, 195

Tronchin, Louis, 59; on Boys' Model School, 67

University: discussions on West Indian, 215-216;
as instrument of West Indian self-discovery, 210;
Irvine Committee on West Indian, 210;
opposition to idea of, 216; report on West
Indian, in 1930, 216; scholarships as substitute
for West Indian, 216

University of London: value of external degrees
of, 217

University scholarships, 71, 291; debates on, 153-
156; establishment of committee to examine,
155-156; and girls, 242; reduction in number of,
207; role of, in society, 207-208; significance of,
in Trinidad and Tobago, 216-217; social returns
from, 209-210; subject regrouping of, 95-96; as
substitute for West Indian university, 216

University of the West Indies: establishment of
branch of, in Trinidad, 292; and teaching of
West Indian history, 206

Urdu: calls for introduction of, in schools, 184, 185

Walcott, Leonard: on university scholarships, 207

Ward schools: achievement of, 14; aim of, 6;
attitude of Governors Elliot and Keate to, 13;
closure of, by Port of Spain Borough Council,
13; curriculum of, 14; drawbacks of system of,
13-14; effect of the Queen's Collegiate School on,
22; English language in, 229; establishment of,
by Lord Harris, 6, 8; exclusion of religious

teaching in, 4, 225; functioning of, 12-14; scheme for, as presented to Legislative Council, 9

Ward unions: introduction of, 13

Wardens: powers of, 36; as school managers, 262-263, 264

Wardens Ordinance (1847), 7, 12

Warner, Charles, 12; on English language as vehicle of teaching, 229; and establishment of the Queen's Collegiate School, 19-20, 22-23; role of, in education policy making, 9; on St George's College, 17; and support for nondenominational schools, 5, 9

Warner, R.S.A. Aucher: career of, 75

Watts, Dr Francis: as principal of Imperial College of Agriculture, 85

West Indian Agricultural College *See* Imperial College of Tropical Agriculture

West Indian education conference: in Port of Spain, 123

West Indian History *See* History, West Indian

West Indian Pilot, 200

West Indian Royal Commission (Norman Commission) (1897): and recommendations regarding agriculture, 78-79

West India Royal Commission, 1939 *See* Moyne Commission

West Indies Conference: West Indian university on agenda of, 215

Whites: and academic honours, 75; resistance of, to education of non-whites, 69, 141

Williams, Eric, 146,159, 204, 210; career of, 289; contribution of, to study of West Indian history, 204-205; death of, 292; education policy of, 289-290

Williams, Henry Sylvester, 344n130

Women: education of, 135-136; enfranchisement of, 244; equal pay for, 244; as headteachers, 238; jobs for, as assistant teachers, 236; non-white professionals in late nineteenth century, 75; occupations of, 237, 242; overseas university education for, 244-245; right of married, to teach, 244; role of, in female education, 241; role of, in society since World War II, 244; as teachers, 169, 235-236

Woodbrook Estate: model school at, 12, 59; teacher training school at, 56, 59

Woodford, Governor: and efforts to anglicize Trinidad, 2

Wooding, H.O.B., 173, 210; on university scholarships, 208

Woodson, Carter, 206

World War I: effect of, on world sugar market, 84; as favourable to pro-specialist agricultural college lobby, 84

World War II: effect of, on schools, 287; and opportunities for female teachers, 243; and role of women in society, 244

www.ingramcontent.com/pod-product-compliance
Lightning Source LLC
Chambersburg PA
CBHW020237290326
41929CB00044B/86